DEACONS AND DEACONESSES
THROUGH THE CENTURIES

Deacons and Deaconesses Through the Centuries

REVISED EDITION

Jeannine E. Olson

CONCORDIA PUBLISHING HOUSE · SAINT LOUIS

To my mother, Evelyn Ellingson Fahsl

1 2 3 4 5 6 7 8 9 10   14 13 12 11 10 09 08 07 06 05

CONTENTS

ABBREVIATIONS

AEG	Archives D'État de Genève
AELC	Association of Evangelical Lutheran Churches
ALC	American Lutheran Church
CDC	Concordia Deaconess Conference
CO	*Ionnis Calvini Opera Quae Supersunt Omnia*
COCU	Consultation on Church Union
CUIC	Churches Uniting in Christ (the renamed Consultation on Church Union)
DACE	Diaconal Association of the Church of England
DCE	Director of Christian Education
DCO	Director of Christian Outreach
DELTO	Distance Education Leading toward Ordination
DOTAC	Diakonia of the Americas and the Caribbean
DPM	Director of Parish Music
ELCA	Evangelical Lutheran Church in America
ELCIC	Evangelical Lutheran Church in Canada
LCA	Lutheran Church in America
LCMS	The Lutheran Church—Missouri Synod
LDA	Lutheran Deaconess Association
LW	Luther's Works (American Edition)
NAAD	North American Association for the Diaconate
Not.	Notary
PG	Patrologia graeca
S.P.G.	Society for the Propagation of the Gospel
UMC	United Methodist Church
WA	Weimar Ausgabe (the German edition of Luther's Works)
WABr	*Briefwechsel* (the German edition of Luther's letters)
YMCA	Young Men's Christian Association
YWCA	Young Women's Christian Association

PREFACE
TO THE REVISED EDITION

The first edition of *Deacons and Deaconesses through the Centuries* brought many rewards. A year after Concordia Publishing House published it, the book received a commendation from the Concordia Historical Institute for "a very scholarly yet very readable history of deacons and deaconesses, including their role in American denominationalism. The value of this work is further enhanced by excellent notations, bibliography and index." Since that first edition, I have been asked to write the articles on the diaconate for the *Oxford Encyclopedia of the Reformation* and the article on "deaconess, deacon" for the new *Encyclopedia of Protestantism*.[1]

The diaconate has evolved considerably in the dozen years since the first edition of this book. Dialogues between church bodies have identified differences and similarities in the roles of deacons, deaconesses, and diaconal ministers. Deacons and diaconal ministers themselves have become better organized at national and international levels. The Lima Document of the World Council of Churches—*Baptism, Eucharist and Ministry*—has had a continued influence. Individual churches have changed their positions. In the United States, the Evangelical Lutheran Church in America, a denomination that formerly did not have rostered diaconal ministers at the national level, has instituted them alongside rostered deaconesses. The United Methodists, a denomination that had diaconal ministers, now ordains deacons. The United Methodists also have eliminated transitional or sequential deacons, and other denominations, such as the Episcopalians, have discussed the possibility thereof.

At the same time the literature about deacons and deaconesses has been significantly enlarged. German-speaking people, with their rich archives of the deaconess movement of the nineteenth and twentieth centuries, have published sophisticated scholarly works, including a history of deaconesses in the evangelical church in Austria and monographs on the role of deaconesses in protecting the handicapped during World War II. International agreements and dialogues, such as the Porvoo agreement, have produced well-structured comparative studies of the diaconate by representatives of the Churches of England, Norway, Sweden, and the Evangelical Church of Finland, which formed the Anglo-Nordic Diaconal Research Project. There are also many works that take a definite position on the diaconate, usually positive, or are of a polemical nature. There have been publications that are more immediate in nature and geared toward the interests of a particular denomination. Not all of these authors are historians nor do all possess the language skills that make it possible to be international in scope and to place the movement within the broadest historical context.

Even with all that is written about the diaconate, some deacons receive less attention than others. The literature tends to concentrate on the ordained deacon or on the full-time or would-be full-time deacon. Deacons elected in congregations at the local level, as some denominations do, tend to receive less coverage and little acclaim. The deaconess movement that dates to Fliedner and the nineteenth century has been given inadequate coverage for its grand contribution to society, to the women themselves, and to the women's movement. This book includes these neglected deacons and deaconesses, who are so important to Lutheran churches, especially.

I wish to thank Concordia Publishing House for making it possible to produce this revised edition of the history of deacons and deaconesses. When I discovered that the first edition of this book was being used at universities and seminaries and in the educational programs of deacons and deaconesses, I resolved to expand the bibliography and to be as precise as possible in my information to make it useful as a reference tool for those who are examining a particular era or denomination, as well as for those who are seeking a comparative study. Thus where a denomination does diaconal work through people who do not carry the title of "deacon" or "deaconess," I give the broadest possible scope, for example, including lay ministers and associates in ministry in my sections on church office. I also have added material that has been published within the last twelve years to every chapter of the book but most voluminously to chapter 9 on contemporary trends, which contains the latest information. This book is comprehensive denominationally and geographically.

This revised edition, like the first edition, was produced with the generous contributions of many people. Professors Nancy Weatherwax, Susan Graham, Mary Ann Donovan, and Rebecca Lyman helped with the chapters on the ancient world, especially with updating the bibliography. For the modern world, Wilbert Rosin pointed the way in the LCMS. Samuel H. Nafzger, executive director of The Lutheran Church—Missouri Synod Commission on Theology and Church Relations, provided information on church office, as did Mary Diederich, supervisor for Rosters and Statistics, and John O'Hara, Research Services. Roger Altenberger, director of the Deaf Institute of Theology in St. Louis, Missouri, sent literature on deaf ministry in the LCMS. Alberto L. García, professor of theology and director of the Lay Minister Program and of the Theological Education by Extension program, Concordia University Wisconsin, and John W. Oberdeck, assistant director, gave comprehensive detail on their programs and more. Deaconesses Theresa List and Joyce Obermann described the new graduate programs for deaconesses in formation at Concordia Seminary in St. Louis, Missouri, and Concordia Theological Seminary in Fort Wayne, Indiana. Deaconess Kristin Wassilak, director of the Concordia Deaconess Program, provided up-to-date and historical data on the deaconess program at Concordia University, River Forest, Illinois. Deaconess Louise Williams, president of World Diakonia and executive director of the Lutheran Deaconess Association, and Deaconess Diane Marten, director of Education and Formation of the Lutheran Deaconess Association, gave detailed information on the Lutheran Deaconess Association based in Valparaiso, Indiana. Deaconess Elizabeth Steele, chairperson of the Board of Directors of the Deaconess Community of the Evangelical Church in America, brought information up-to-date on the ELCA deaconess community, whereas Carol Schickel, director for Candidacy, ELCA Division for Ministry, and Richard Bruesehoff, director for Leadership Support in the ELCA, gave the most recent information on diaconal ministers and associates in ministry in the denomination. Deacon William T. Ditewig, executive director of the Committee on the Permanent Diaconate of the National Conference of Catholic Bishops, spent extensive time in telephone interviews and went over the section on permanent deacons in the Roman Catholic Church in detail. Deaconess Betty Purkey, executive secretary of the Deaconess Program Office of the General Board of Global Ministries of the United Methodist Church, and Deacon Joaquín García, assistant general secretary for the Section of Deacon and Diaconal Ministers, Division of Ordained Ministry, General Board of Higher Education and Ministry of the United Methodist Church, supplied me with the rich literature on modern deaconesses, deacons, and diaconal ministers in the United Methodist Church, which has documented itself so well. Mark Tammen, director of Constitutional Services for the Presbyterian Church

(U.S.A.), filled me in on changes and attempts at change with regard to Presbyterian deacons and Christian educators in the last dozen years.

The people whom I have quoted have had an opportunity to read over and to correct what I have written about them and their programs. In addition, Sister Teresa of the Community of St. Andrew, long-time editor of the international *Diakonia News: Newsletter of Foundation Diakonia World Federation of Diaconal Associations and Diaconal Communities*, went over the last chapter on the modern world and the earlier sections on Anglicans. Dr. Gardiner Shattuck Jr., historian and coauthor of the history of Episcopalians,[2] also reviewed the last chapter and the earlier section on Episcopalian deaconesses. Archdeacon Ormonde Plater and Deacon Edwin Hallenbeck met with me at the Episcopal Convention in Minneapolis, provided information, and also examined the section on Episcopalians. Without these people, this book could not be what it is.

Besides the enhanced opportunity that bibliographic searches via the Internet provide, I have had the opportunity to expand the number of libraries that I used in person. Special thanks to the University of Minnesota and to Luther Seminary in St. Paul, Minnesota, which has rich resources on Scandinavian, German, and American deacons.

Once again the American Academy of Religion, the Research Committee of Rhode Island College, and the National Endowment for the Humanities provided financial support for this project, the latter through a summer seminar on the English Reformation and an institute on early-modern women writers.

The first edition of this book enriched my life in a personal way through the contacts I made. Through the many telephone calls and interviews with church executives and those responsible for diaconal programs, I made new acquaintances and enriched my own knowledge considerably. Some of the deaconesses mentioned in the preface to the first edition of this book have passed on or retired, but shortly after the first edition came out, Sister Teresa of the Community of St. Andrew, sought me out. Through her, I had the opportunity to make more contacts and to stay with the original deaconess community of the Church of England at St. Andrew's House while I did research in England.

Since the publication of the first edition, Lewis W. Spitz, my doctoral advisor at Stanford University and the person who encouraged me to write this book, has passed on (1999). His widow, Edna Spitz, survives him and continues to offer sound advice and friendship. It might be fitting to dedicate this edition of *Deacons and Deaconesses through the Centuries* to them again or to the deacons and deaconesses who are the subject of the book, but it is not on their dining room table that I wrote this edition. I wrote it largely in St. Paul, Minnesota, at the home of Evelyn Ellingson Fahsl, my mother, who did without my companionship for hours of many days and months while I concentrated on this work. It is to her that I dedicate this book, who with my father, Aloysius Fahsl (died 1984), made it all possible, allowing me to forge ahead on my own and providing me with intellect, encouragement, and a superb education.

PREFACE TO THE FIRST EDITION

A book of this scope could not have been written without the cooperation of scholars who generously read portions of the manuscript and offered bibliographic references in their specialties. From the Graduate Theological Union in Berkeley, I consulted Professors Massey H. Shepherd Jr. (died 1990) and Rebecca Lyman of the Church Divinity School of the Pacific; William Short, O.F.M., of the Franciscan School of Theology; Hilary Martin, O.P., of the Dominican School of Philosophy and Theology; Michael Aune and Martha Stortz of Pacific Lutheran Theological Seminary; John Baldovin, S.J., and Mary Ann Donovan, S.C., of the Jesuit School of Theology in Berkeley. I am beholden to Professors Elsie McKee of Princeton Theological Seminary, Hans Hillerbrand of Duke University, Robert Rosin of Concordia Seminary (St. Louis), and Catherine Prelinger of Yale University (died 1991).

In so many ways, the people with whom one works daily support a colleague who is writing a book. I want to thank especially my chairperson, Professor George Kellner, and my deans, Professors Richard Weiner and James McCroskery, for convenient course schedules and for their patience.

As an historian, one deals primarily with the dead, whose input is limited to the traces they have left behind. The contemporary aspects of this book brought me into contact with those who are making history today, a refreshing change, but one fraught with its own complexities. This book could not be current without the input of Paul Nelson, director of the ELCA Study of Ministry; Samuel M. Taub, executive director of the Secretariat for the Permanent Diaconate of the National Conference of Catholic Bishops; Paul Van Buren of the Division of Diaconal Ministry of the United Methodist Church, Ridgway Shinn of the Commission for the Study of Ministry, and Betty Letzig, executive secretary of the Deaconess Program Office of the General Board of Global Ministries of the United Methodist Church; Gardiner Shattuck Jr. and Ormonde Plater of the Episcopal Church; Edwin Hallenbeck, president of the North American Association for the Diaconate; John Burgess and Aurelia Fule of the Presbyterian Church (U.S.A.); Kerstin Otterstein of Wesselburen in Schleswig-Holstein; Deaconesses Kristin Wassilak, director of the Concordia Deaconess Program, and Nancy Nemoyer, past director; Deaconess Louise Williams, executive director of the Lutheran Deaconess Association; and Sisters Nora Frost, directing deaconess, and Collette Brice, director of Education and Interpretation of the Deaconess Community of the ELCA. These people had an opportunity to review for accuracy what I have said about them and the programs they represent.

I received supporting grants from the American Academy of Religion and Rhode Island College during the writing of this book and benefited from National Endowment for the Humanities seminars on Religious Reform and Social Change. Interpretations of the Reformation (1992) and "The Woman Question, 1750–1880" (1990). I also attended National Endowment for the Humanities institutes on Dante's *Divine Comedy* (1989) and on French Archival Sciences (1991) at the Newberry Library in Chicago. I used the resources of that library for this book, as well as those of Stanford, Duke, and Brown Universities; the University of Chicago; Union Theological Seminary in Richmond; the Graduate Theological Union in Berkeley; Concordia Seminary in St. Louis; and the Concordia Historical Institute in St. Louis.

To make this book as accessible as possible to the entire readership, quotations are in English and, where possible, I cite English translations of foreign language works.

When I began this book, I was familiar with deacons through the research for my last book, *Calvin and Social Welfare: Deacons and the Bourse Française*, but the history of deaconesses was a path to be explored. They had touched my life at various points: A Lutheran deaconess midwife attended me when I gave birth to my son in Garoua Boulai, Cameroon; my daughter was born in Deaconess Hospital in Minneapolis, Minnesota; and when she was 13, a Swiss deaconess, Elizabeth Bodemann, watched over her, enabling her to finish the school year in Geneva when I had to return to the United States to pursue my doctoral research in 1979. This book provides background to their story.

To no one does this book and its author owe more than to Lewis W. and Edna Marie Spitz, who contributed greatly to bringing it to fruition. Professor Spitz, my doctoral advisor at Stanford University, formed me as a scholar and as a teacher. It is to him and to Edna that I dedicate this book, in gratitude for a multitude of favors.

NOTES

1.   New York: Routledge, 2004.
2.   Hein and Shattuck, *Episcopalians*.

INTRODUCTION

Since its founding, the church has had a concern for the disadvantaged and those in need. Early Christians cared for widows and orphans, fed the hungry, and housed the homeless. One of the earliest accounts of the church describes the apostles selecting seven men from the Christian community to manage the daily distribution to the widows (Acts 6:1–6). Among those selected was Stephen, the first Christian martyr.

The church created the office of deacon because of an ongoing need to administer charity. In a sense the history of the diaconate can be viewed as the history of social welfare in the church. By the time of the writing of the first letter to Timothy, deacons are so familiar as to merit description of their ideal attributes (1 Timothy 3:8–13). As time passed the office continued to be responsible for the poor but was modified by growing hierarchical structures. During the medieval period, the diaconate became a stepping-stone to the priesthood.

Protestant reformers of the sixteenth century desired to return to the sources, and some wanted to reconstruct the office as they thought it had been in the early church. Where Protestants restored the diaconate, they opened it to laypeople who were responsible for charity. As governments became more willing to take over the burden of social welfare, deacons continued to serve through visitation and the lending of a helping hand. The office took on new meaning in Germany in the nineteenth century when groups of deacons and deaconesses formed that were dedicated to social welfare, nursing, parish work, and inner-mission in the cities. This became the full-time occupation of these men and women for all or part of their lives. The movement spread to other parts of Europe and to the New World, and it continues today.

Overall, the office of deacon has evidenced considerable flexibility over the centuries, responding to the times and to general conceptions at any given time of what a deacon should be. The role and functions of deacons were conceived in the early church and continue to the present. Many Protestant congregations today retain the office, selecting deacons from their own membership, yet practices vary widely from one congregation to another. Some congregations have a comprehensive diaconal structure that attempts to cover need both within the community and outside of it. Others have no deacons at all or deacons with minimal activity.

At the denominational level differences are even more marked. Lutherans and Protestants of the Reformed tradition followed the examples of the sixteenth-century Protestant Reformation, whereas Catholics, Episcopalians, and Methodists retained the medieval model of the diaconate as a step toward the "higher" ordained ministry. Within the last several decades, the permanent, perpetual, or vocational deacon has become prominent in the Catholic and Episcopal Churches. The Episcopal Church considered eliminating the sequential diaconate, which leads to the priesthood, at its 2003 convention. United Methodists have already eliminated the sequential diaconate and now ordain deacons who consider their work a vocation and do not intend to "go on" to become pastors or elders in the Methodist Church. The modern Roman Catholic Church allows married men to be ordained deacons. Married deacons cannot be ordained priests, but the office of deacon has shown promise of supplementing the role of priests in charitable and educational endeavors. The duties of the deacon are too limited to relieve the pressure of the diminishing pool of candidates for the celibate priesthood, however, because only priests can celebrate the Mass. Especially among Protestants engaged in ecumenical dialogue, the question of whether deacons should be ordained is asked. Because of these concerns, there is a growing body of literature on deacons from Catholic, Protestant, and academic presses, a body of materials that began at least with the Second Vatican Council in Rome (1962–1965).[1]

Over the centuries, deacons disappeared from the church at certain times and in particular places, but the functions that deacons performed remained. For at least some of the reformers of the Protestant Reformation, spirit was more important than structure, and roles changed as the church made its way in the world. The disappearance of deacons in parts of the institutional church has provoked modern Christians to speculate as to whether the office should be restored where it does not exist and what the role of modern deacons should be.

Discussion of the diaconate today can benefit from a deeper understanding of the history of deacons. The approach of this book is different from that of other works on this subject because, though brief, it attempts to be comprehensive. The deacon over the centuries has had many roles and functions that have varied with time and place. These can be considered under two broad categories: liturgy and charity. Deacons also have engaged in teaching, preaching, and administrative tasks. There is more information readily available in the sources on the liturgical roles of deacons than on their charitable functions. Thus some of the literature on deacons tends to concentrate on their role in liturgy. Yet the role of deacons in gathering resources and dispensing charity was as important as their function in worship, at least to the poor. Although not neglecting the liturgical roles of deacons, this study will attempt to redress the imbalance as far as the sources allow, covering charity, philanthropy, and the deacons' role as teachers.

Any consideration of fund-raising and dispensing charity in the church goes beyond deacons because others have administered social welfare. For example, in the medieval period, religious orders provided for the poor, and today's management of church homes for the mentally challenged or for the elderly often bypasses deacons. Without departing entirely from the office of deacon, this book covers charitable functions that deacons once had. It considers the social welfare stance of the church in any given epoch, on the premise that the functions of deacons were at least as important as the office. The book covers, then, both deacons and *diakonia*. It traces the trail not only of people with the title of deacon or deaconess but also of service activities related to Christian churches or done by Christians. Likewise, it covers offices that have evolved from the diaconate or are related to it, such as subdeacons, acolytes, and widows.

Research into the deaconess movement revealed that these women had been neglected in modern historical surveys, histories of the church, and even histories of denominations in which the movement has been strong.[2] There were thousands of deaconesses in the nineteenth and twentieth centuries. In some countries they had an important role in social welfare, teaching, parish work, the inner-city work of the church, and the development of professional nursing. One cannot study the diaconate without studying deaconesses. Without neglecting more traditional coverage, this book rectifies that information gap to supply as comprehensive a survey of the diaconate as space allows.

For modern Christians the diaconate at its origins is of particular interest as a model that some want to imitate and from which few desire to depart radically. Some modern Christians view the evolution of the diaconate within the growing hierarchical structures of the centuries that followed as a natural phenomenon. Others, especially Protestants, view this evolution with suspicion and are relieved that the Reformation era attempted to return the diaconate to its earlier roots.

This book begins with deacons at their origins and proceeds in chronological order. The first chapter is devoted to the deacon and deaconess in Scripture and the early church up to Constantine. Chapter 2 covers the evolution of the diaconate from the fourth century through medieval times. Chapter 3 considers the readjustments that the Protestant Reformation made to the diaconate. Chapter 4 covers the development of the diaconate of the Reformation era in the seventeenth to the nineteenth centuries. Chapters 5 and 6 concentrate on new forms of deacons and deaconesses springing from the Inner Mission movement of the nineteenth century. Chapters 7 and 8 continue the story of the diaconate in the twentieth century, and chapter 9 covers the contemporary scene.

NOTES

1. Rahner and Vorgrimler, *Diaconia in Christo über die Erneuerung des Diakonates*; Krimm, *Das diakonische Amt der Kirche*; a standard Episcopalian study is that of Barnett, *The Diaconate* (rev. ed.); of the Catholic contributions, a Jesuit has written an often quoted yet brief, clear, and scholarly book that provides good coverage of women: Echlin, *Deacon in the Church*; the Catholic University Press has published a collection of essays: Halton and Williman, *Diakonia*; Elsie McKee, a Presbyterian scholar at Princeton Theological Seminary, offers an exegetical study of the diaconate that includes the early church: *Calvin on the Diaconate*; Jaap Van Klinken, general chairman of the Diaconal Office of the Reformed Churches in the Netherlands, has written *Diakonia, Mutual Helping*. German works include: Krimm, *Quellen zur Geschichte der Diakonie*, 2 vols. An example of scholarship on social welfare and deacons based on pioneering archival research is that of Jeannine Olson, *Calvin and Social Welfare*.

2. See, for example, Aland, *History of Christianity*, vol. 2: *From the Reformation to the Present*, which is translated from the German *Geschichte der Christenheit*, vol. 2: *Von der Reformation bis in die Gegenwart*.

CHAPTER ONE

DEACONS AND DEACONESSES
IN THE BIBLE
AND THE EARLY CHURCH
THE FIRST TO THE FOURTH CENTURIES

The history of deacons goes back to the beginnings of the church, and the Scriptures provide early information. An analysis of the diaconate in the New Testament begins with the Greek words for deacons and their work: the verb *diakoneo* and its cognate nouns *diakonos* and *diakonia*.[1] Herodotus (ca. 485–425 B.C.) is the first prose writer to use words of this group, and he used them in the sense of attending on a royal person or a royal household. *Diakonein* meant "to serve," but not, in Herodotus, in the limited sense of waiting on tables, as has sometimes been alleged.[2] When ancient Greeks used the word, they were not trying to convey "loving and caring service." An historian of the diaconate, John Collins, suggests that neither did the New Testament nor other early Christian documents; instead, these notions were added later to the original meaning of the Greek word.[3] The meaning of the words should not be construed narrowly because their semantic range is wider than generally appreciated.[4]

In the New Testament, *diakonein* is used to describe Jesus' own way of service in Matthew 20:28; Mark 10:45; and Luke 22:27: "The Son of man came not to be served but to serve"; "I am among you as one who serves." *Diakonein* is also translated as *to minister, to provide for*, or *to help* someone. Mary Magdalene, Mary the mother of James and Joseph, and the mother of the sons of Zebedee ministered to Jesus (Matthew 27:55–56; Mark 15:40–41). Mary Magdalene; Joanna, the wife of Herod's steward; Susanna;

and others provided for Jesus and the apostles out of their means (Luke 8:1–3). In the New Testament, the verb *diakoneo* generally has been translated into English using words of the *ministry* group, though in recent Bibles one may often find words of the *service* group.[5]

The noun *diakonos*, or deacon (*diakonoi* in the plural), meaning servant, appears thirty times in the New Testament as, for example, in Mark 9:35: "And he sat down and called the twelve; and he said to them, 'If any one would be first, he must be last of all and servant of all.' " *Diakonos* is also translated "minister," as when Paul refers to himself in Ephesians 3:7: "Of this gospel I was made a minister according to the gift of God's grace which was given me by the working of his power."

Just as *diakonos* refers to ministers or servants, the noun *diakonia* means ministry or service. The author of the Book of Acts uses *diakonia* in Acts 1 for Peter's reference to the work of the Twelve as they prepare to replace Judas. Paul speaks of "varieties of service" in 1 Corinthians 12:5. There is the "ministry of the word" in Acts 6:4 and "of reconciliation" in 2 Corinthians 5:18. One book on deacons is called *Service in Christ*.[6] This present book will cover the office of deacon, related offices that sprang from it, and the *diakonia* of the church, especially in eras when it was separate from the office of deacon.

In summary, *diakonos*, *diakoneo*, and *diakonia* appear to have been used in a general way to refer to ministers, servants, ministry, and service in the church before *diakonos* was used to designate the office of deacon. In light of the initial broad use of *diakonos*, *diakoneo*, and *diakonia* to refer to Jesus, his followers, and their work, one might conceive of a diaconate of all believers similar to Martin Luther's priesthood of all believers because all church members are called to serve and to minister apart from a particular office of deacon or pastor. Nevertheless, an office of deacon came into being just as did offices of presbyter (elder, later priest) and bishop. There were practical reasons for these offices developing within the church as it matured. It is to that evolution that we now turn.

In the beginning, the early Christians had little reason for elaborate structure and offices because, after Jesus left, they were waiting for his imminent return. In the interim, the Jewish Christians continued to use religious institutions that were present already, the temple and synagogues in particular.[7] It was out of their common life together that the need for designated responsibilities arose because, as Acts 2:44–45 records: "[A]ll who believed were together and had all things in common; and they sold their possessions and goods and distributed them to all, as any had need." The division and distribution of goods led to conflict and discipline in the early church. According to the account in Acts 5:1–11, Ananias and Sapphira appear to have died precipitously because of their dishonesty in declaring to the apostles that they had delivered to them the whole of the proceeds of a piece of property of which they had kept a part.

> [T]he Hellenists [Greek-speaking Jews] murmured against the Hebrews [Aramaic-speaking Jews] because their widows were neglected in the daily distribution. And the twelve summoned the body of the disciples and said, "It is not right that we should give up preaching the word of God to serve tables. Therefore, brethren, pick out . . . seven men of good repute whom we may appoint to this duty. . . . These they set before the apostles, and they prayed and laid their hands upon them. (Acts 6:1–3, 6)

Nowhere does the New Testament name as deacons these seven men who were chosen to serve tables or administer charity, but toward the end of the second century, in the treatise *Against Heresies* (ca. A.D. 185), Irenaeus of Lyons (ca. A.D. 135–200), an early church father and apologist for Christian beliefs, praised "Stephen, who was chosen the first deacon by the apostles, and who, of all men, was the first to follow the footsteps of the martyrdom of the Lord, being the first that was slain for confessing Christ . . . ."[8] Thus Irenaeus articulated a tradition in the church that Stephen and the six others were the first deacons. This tradition has lived into the present, but with dissenting opinions.

Not everyone agreed with Irenaeus that the seven were the first deacons, including the early church father John Chrysostom, the great preacher who became bishop of Constantinople in A.D. 398.[9] Many twentieth-century scholars, such as John Collins, also differ with Irenaeus.[10] Some disagree with Irenaeus either because of a more fluid view of ministry in the early church or because of personal conceptions of the ideal deacon.[11] Modern denials center around the fact that the seven were not called deacons in Scripture and that their activities were broad, including preaching and baptizing, functions that some modern scholars consider inappropriate to deacons as the office was later conceptualized. Before Stephen was stoned, he was accused before the Sanhedrin of never ceasing "to speak words against this holy place and the law" (Acts 6:13). The author of Acts then depicts Stephen as delivering what could be called a sermon, which is the entire seventh chapter of Acts. Another one of the seven men selected by the apostles, Philip, called the evangelist, proclaimed Christ and performed miracles in Samaria. He also converted and baptized the Ethiopian eunuch.[12]

Whether the seven in Acts 6 were called deacons or not, the dominant tradition in the church after Irenaeus considered them so. Aside from that tradition, a view of deacons from a functional perspective places the charitable responsibilities of the seven within the realm of the activities of the diaconate. Moreover, the later history of the church during the Protestant Reformation reveals that some people assumed the responsibilities of deacons before the church gave them that title.

New Testament texts other than Acts 6 reveal the presence of deacons in the church less ambiguously by using the term directly. The first reference to deacons as officeholders is in the salutation of Paul in the first verse of Philippians, which was written sometime between A.D. 53 and 58: "to all the saints in Christ Jesus who are at Philippi, with the bishops and deacons."[13] Nothing is said in this letter of the duties of the deacons, but their presence fortifies a thesis that deacons and bishops arose in Gentile churches such as that of Philippi in contrast to Jewish-Christian communities, which produced elders or presbyters on the model of the synagogue.[14] Other scholars, however, suggest that all three offices—bishop, elder, and deacon—came from similar offices in synagogues that were carried over into Christian communities as Jewish Christians gradually separated from the synagogues in which they first worshiped.[15]

The office of presbyter or elder is a clear possibility of a carryover from the synagogue because elders had the same title in synagogues.[16] The origin of the Christian bishop is less clear. The office could have been a carryover from the community chief of the synagogue (the *archisynagôgos*), or he could have emerged from among the elders as a presiding elder.[17]

A related question is who these first bishops were. This is a special concern for those churches that hold to the succession of bishops from the original apostles. Roman Catholic scholars acknowledge difficulties with that concept as it has traditionally been taught. Raymond Brown points out that the New Testament does not show the twelve apostles laying hands on bishops as successors, which calls into question the passing of powers through ordination.[18] James Burtchaell asserts that the first bishops were likely to have been men other than the apostles of Jesus, certainly not Peter, though possibly James the brother of Jesus fits better into this role because though he was not an apostle, he headed the Christian community in Jerusalem.[19]

Just as the elder and bishop might have carried over from the synagogue so, too, could the Christian deacon have been a carryover from the assistants or Levites in the Jewish temple.[20] These assistants were used in the synagogues too. This "assistant" had evolved into an all-purpose employee, the *hazan*, "a combination choir director, sacristan, master of ceremonies, janitor, Hebrew teacher, hostel manager, bailiff, caterer, plumber, clerk, scribe, welfare officer, penal officer, and gravedigger."[21] The Christian deacon is sometimes referred to as a Levite.

In Romans 16:1–2, Paul wrote of "our sister Phoebe, a deaconess [*diakonos*] of the church at Cenchreae . . . she has been a helper of many and of myself as well."[22] Of the three church offices—deacon, presbyter, bishop—some authors believe the office of deacon could have been open to women. Other scholars argue that women were not allowed in church office and when Paul "was writing to the Romans, *diakonia* had not yet given rise to a title of office; it was still a generic term designating the service that any activist might offer."[23] Putting it more positively, Bonnie Thurston suggests that in the early stages of the church, ministry was an "attitude of service before it was an office. . . . Ministry was charismatic and not institutional."[24] Early churchmen such as Origen and John Chrysostom, however, considered Phoebe a deacon, just as John Chrysostom considered the women mentioned in 1 Timothy 3:11 to be deacons.[25] Robert Jewett suggests that Phoebe was also a leader of her congregation in Cenchreae, the port city of Corinth; the courier carrying Paul's letter to the Romans; and perhaps the patroness of the projected mission of Paul to Spain referred to in Romans 15:24 and 28.[26] Roman Garrison calls Phoebe a "servant-benefactor," a part of an early tradition in the church that the wealthy were "uniquely equipped to be 'deacons' in their ministry to the poor." He asserts that "Phoebe regarded her affluence as an incentive, even a qualification, for becoming a deacon of the congregation at Cenchreae."[27] More provocatively, Elisabeth Schüssler Fiorenza asserts that *diakonoi* such as Phoebe "served in the 'official' capacity of missionary preachers and teachers."[28] Whether or not Phoebe formally held church office, to assert that no women were appointed presbyters or deacons is to ignore later injunctions against women presiding over the Eucharist that seem to imply that they were doing just that.[29]

Whether they held church offices in the formal sense or not, charismatic roles were allowed women in the early church, and some scholars feel that in the first century these roles might have been more influential than those of the elected officers when they did appear. Woman prophesied (the daughters of Philip in Acts 21:9). They hosted house churches in their homes and taught, though without the title of teacher. A number of affluent upper-class women became Christians and were of influence.[30]

Paul's first letter to Timothy described the attributes desirable in deacons:

Deacons likewise must be serious, not double-tongued, not addicted to much wine, not greedy for gain; they must hold the mystery of the faith with a clear conscience. And let them also be tested first; then if they prove themselves blameless let them serve as deacons. The women likewise must be serious, no slanderers, but temperate, faithful in all things. Let deacons be the husband of one wife, and let them manage their children and their households well; for those who serve well as deacons gain a good standing for themselves and also great confidence in the faith which is in Christ Jesus. (3:8–13)

Throughout the centuries, exegetical issues in this text centered on the women. The majority of scholars consider the women in v. 11 to be deacons.[31] Others viewed v. 11 as an interpolation in the text or as a reference to women in general or to the wives of deacons. *Diakonissa*, later a feminine form of deacon, could refer to the wife of a deacon,[32] but *diakonissa* does not appear in the New Testament and does not enter the early church literature until perhaps the fourth century.[33]

The statement that deacons should be the husband of one wife led some to interpret the text as proscribing remarriage, even in the case of the death of a spouse, as would Tertullian, a church leader of North Africa who died in approximately A.D. 225. Although many modern commentators prefer to argue that the proscription against more than one wife in Timothy bars polygamy or serial marriage after separation from a living wife, this injunction has had modern ramifications in the Catholic permanent diaconate because if a married deacon's wife dies, he is not to remarry.

The first letter to Timothy opens yet another window to the organization of the church. In 1 Timothy 3:1–13 and 5:17–22, Paul mentions bishops (*episkopoi*), elders, (*presbyteroi*), and deacons—three offices in the church.[34] Some authorities see earlier Jewish and Hellenistic organizations merging into the threefold offices listed in 1 Timothy, but others argue that there were only two offices at this time, deacon and bishop-elder. They base this position on the grounds that in 1 Timothy bishop and elder are two titles for the one office of *episkopos-presbyteros*.[35] Still other interpreters consider presbyter to be a status title used for mature Christians, and they treat bishop and deacon as functional titles.[36]

A possible additional office was that of the widows discussed in 1 Timothy 5:3–16:[37]

Honor widows who are real widows. If a widow has children or grandchildren, let them first learn their religious duty to their own family and make some return to their parents; for this is acceptable in the sight of God. She who is a real widow, and is left all alone, has set her hope on

God and continues in supplications and prayers night and day; whereas she who is self-indulgent is dead even while she lives. Command this, so that they may be without reproach. If any one does not provide for his relatives, and especially for his own family, he has disowned the faith and is worse than an unbeliever.

Let a widow be enrolled if she is not less than sixty years of age, having been the wife of one husband; and she must be well attested for her good deeds, as one who has brought up children, shown hospitality, washed the feet of the saints, relieved the afflicted, and devoted herself to doing good in every way. But refuse to enroll younger widows; for when they grow wanton against Christ they desire to marry, and so they incur condemnation for having violated their first pledge. Besides that, they learn to be idlers, gadding about from house to house, and not only idlers but gossips and busybodies, saying what they should not. So I would have younger widows marry, bear children, rule their households, and give the enemy no occasion to revile us. For some have already strayed after Satan. If any believing woman has relatives who are widows, let her assist them; let the church not be burdened, so that it may assist those who are real widows.

Some scholars feel that the mention of widows elsewhere in the New Testament reinforces an implication in 1 Timothy of the existence of a circle of widows as a religious order. For example, some scholars understand Tabitha (Dorcas) in Acts 9:36–43 to be a widow of independent means who befriended a group or society of widows who were supported by the early Christian community.[38] It is possible that membership in this circle of widows became so popular that limitations were imposed, as in 1 Timothy 5:3–16, on the basis of age, need, children, and the number of times a woman had been married.[39] Other scholars consider Tabitha and her good works as the prototype of the future deaconess.[40]

Although 1 Timothy says little about what the widows were doing, aside from being constant in prayer, some exegetes of the Protestant Reformation, such as Philipp Melanchthon, elaborated on their activities in social welfare. Others, such as John Calvin, connected these widows with the deaconess of Romans 16:1–2 and bemoaned the fact that there was no longer a formal office of widow.[41] Despite the fact that they were to have been married, the early church came to associate the office of widow with dedicated virgins or, later, with nuns.

There is relatively little in the New Testament itself about deacons and widows, perhaps because then, as now, there is a tendency to neglect to write about what is a familiar part of daily life.[42] What texts there are reveal an evolution in these roles that is collaborated by other writings of the era of the early church. These sources include letters, church orders, liturgies, treatises, sermons, acts of the martyrs, and eventually decrees of church councils and histories of the church. The rest of this chapter will consider these sources from the first to the fourth centuries with some attempt to be geographically specific about practices that grew up in various parts of the Roman Empire. The primary concern of this discussion will be to establish the various precedents for church office that the early church provided, for example, deaconesses were to be found primarily in the eastern part of the Roman Empire and acolytes in the West, but both created precedent for later ages of the church.

The period from the first century to the fourth is sometimes called the golden age of the diaconate because of the important role deacons had in the church at this time. Some authors would extend that golden age until at least A.D. 600. For the sake of clarity of exposition, it is convenient to take the fourth century as a demarcation because the legalization of Christianity within the Roman Empire in A.D. 313 under Constantine (A.D. 306–337) resulted in changes in the church that had important ramifications for the diaconate.

Consider deacons in the centuries immediately prior to the legalization of Christianity. What were their functions? How did their role evolve? One practical way of answering these questions in these early centuries before Constantine is to look at the texts of the era as historians do. Beginning with the late first century after the ascension of Christ, documents of the church other than those that were to become part of the New Testament mention deacons. At first there were relatively few documents that pertained, and these were cited repeatedly through the centuries. For purposes of consideration, they can be blocked into periods into which the early church is traditionally divided: the Age of the Apostolic Fathers or the subapostolic era (from the late first century to the mid-second) and the period that follows from the apologists of the second and third centuries to Constantine.

THE AGE OF THE APOSTOLIC FATHERS

One early document that mentions deacons is *1 Clement*, a letter written sometime between A.D. 95 and A.D. 97 from the church of Rome to the church at Corinth,[43] which was in revolt against its presbyters. Clement was a bishop or presbyter of the church at Rome. He mentioned deacons but did not describe what they did. The letter appealed to the Corinthians to be obedient to their presbyters, using the words *presbyter* and *bishop* interchangeably. Some interpreters would argue that *1 Clement* makes an early case for apostolic succession of bishops from the apostles because the letter stated that "the apostles . . . appointed their first converts . . . to be the bishops and deacons of future believers."[44] They and their successors who ministered well were not to be deposed.[45]

Another early document, *The Teaching of the Twelve Apostles, Commonly Called the Didache*, compares the ministry of deacons and of bishops to that of prophets and teachers. The *Didache* is a compilation from before A.D. 150 of two works, the second of which is a church order, perhaps from late first-century Syria.[46] Some scholars feel that it reflects an era of transition from charismatic leaders, the traveling prophets, and teachers to one in which officers of the church were attached to one place.[47] The *Didache's* joint comparison of bishops and deacons to prophets and teachers has led some commentators to conclude that deacons as well as bishops preached and taught.[48] The same passage gives insight into the ideal traits of those who hold these officers and suggests that these men merit respect:

> You must, then, elect for yourselves bishops and deacons who are a credit to the Lord, men who are gentle, generous, faithful, and well tried. For their ministry to you is identical with that of the prophets and teachers. You must not, therefore, despise them, for along with the prophets and teachers they enjoy a place of honor among you.[49]

A letter written sometime in A.D. 111–113 by the Roman administrator Pliny the Younger of Bithynia, which was along the Black Sea, to the emperor Trajan appears to testify to women deacons or deaconesses. In an attempt to find out more about the Christians, Pliny tortured "two maidservants who were called deaconesses [Latin: *ministrae*]."[50] Some authors consider this indicative of the importance of women, in this case slaves who were deaconesses, evangelizing in pagan households in these early centuries of the church.[51] Not every scholar would translate *ministrae* as "deaconesses," but among those who do are scholars who allow the possibility of an early, perhaps ongoing, separate office of deaconess in parts of the eastern Roman Empire.[52]

Seven letters collected by Polycarp, bishop of Smyrna and eventual martyr, from Ignatius, bishop of Antioch, mention deacons. Ignatius wrote to Polycarp and six churches on a trip to Rome, where he was condemned to fight with wild beasts, perhaps during the reign of Trajan (A.D. 98–117).[53] Like Clement, Ignatius's concern was for obedience to church officers and for the unity of the churches, perhaps to combat heresy and schism. Unlike Clement, who equated bishop and presbyter, Ignatius

referred to three separate offices of bishop, presbyter, and deacon, signaling the beginning of what was called the monepiscopate with the bishop at
the head of a council of presbyters, and perhaps deacons, that governed the
local church. The authority of these officers in Ignatius originated not
from their direct succession from the apostles but from an analogy with
God and the apostles in which the deacons represented Jesus Christ:

> . . . everyone must show the deacons respect. They represent Jesus
> Christ, just as the bishop has the role of the Father, and the presbyters
> are like God's council and an apostolic band. You cannot have a church
> without these.[54]

Again Ignatius wrote:

> I urge you to aim to do everything in godly agreement. Let the bishop
> preside in God's place, and the presbyters take the place of the apostolic
> council, and let the deacons (my special favorites) be entrusted with the
> ministry of Jesus Christ who was with the Father from eternity and
> appeared at the end [of the world].[55]

On the face of it, it would appear that within a short time of a dozen
years or less there was a shift from Clement's use of the words *bishop* and
presbyter interchangeably to Ignatius's separation of bishop from presbyter,
but perhaps this only reflected a difference in usage between Rome and
Antioch. Many scholars recognize marked diversity in early Christianity.[56]
Also some authorities have questioned the dating and authenticity of the
letters of Ignatius. One such theory suggests earlier dates for their writing,
perhaps A.D. 80–100,[57] and another theory promotes later dates, perhaps
A.D. 160–170.[58] Such interpretations have implications for the dating of the
development of the monepiscopate.

Ignatius called deacons his fellow servants or slaves, causing some commentators to consider the author of some of the letters of Ignatius to be a
deacon.[59] He asked the Ephesians to let him keep one of their deacons with
him and used Burrhus, the deacon, as an aid, companion, and conveyer of
messages.[60] These letters revealed that deacons may have had a role in the
liturgy or in charity because they "do not serve mere food and drink, but
minister to God's church. They must therefore avoid leaving themselves
open to criticism, as they would shun fire."[61] Although servants of the
church, deacons deserved respect and obedience:

> You should all follow the bishop as Jesus Christ did the Father. Follow,
> too, the presbytery as you would the apostles; and respect the deacons
> as you would God's law.[62]

I give my life as a sacrifice (poor as it is) for those who are obedient to the bishop, the presbyters, and the deacons.[63]

Ignatius mentioned the widows and greeted the virgins enrolled with the widows, referring, perhaps, to unmarried women associated with the widows. These unmarried women came to be known as consecrated virgins because of their commitment to celibacy.[64]

Polycarp, like Ignatius, gave insights into the roles of widows and deacons. He called widows "God's altar" in a letter to the Philippians (ca. A.D. 130). They "should be discreet in their faith pledged to the Lord, praying unceasingly on behalf of all, refraining from all slander, gossip, false witness, love of money, in act, from evil of any kind, knowing that they are God's altar."[65] Polycarp also reiterated some of the themes of the letters of Ignatius, such as obedience: "Be obedient to the presbyters and deacons as unto God and Christ."[66] This phrase has been interpreted by some to indicate that deacons were a part of the ruling council of the church at Philippi.[67] The deacons also were to be above criticism and models for the young:

Likewise the deacons should be blameless before his righteousness, as servants of God and Christ and not of men; not slanderers, or double-tongued, not lovers of money, temperate in all matters, compassionate, careful, living according to the truth of the Lord, who became a "servant of all."[68]

Although praising the deacons, Polycarp appeared to give presbyters a part of the traditional diaconal role in charity and care of the sick:

Also the presbyters must be compassionate, merciful to all, turning back those who have gone astray, looking after the sick, not neglecting widow or orphan or one that is poor . . . refraining from all anger, partiality, unjust judgment, keeping far from all love of money . . .[69]

Another probable early second-century document, the *Shepherd of Hermas* (Rome, before ca. A.D. 175 but as early as A.D. 70 or A.D. 80),[70] considered deacons—alongside apostles, bishops, and teachers—as fair white stones in a building that is the church.[71] Yet some of the deacons had been dishonest. Some had stolen the livelihood of widows and orphans and were, in effect, blemished stones in the edifice of the church.[72] Financial integrity among deacons, and the lack of it, was a theme that would be repeated in the writings of the early church.

In the mid-second century, the Age of the Apostolic Fathers merged into that of the great apologists of the Christian faith who wrote to combat heresy and Gnosticism. Their treatises revealed more about the function of the deacon. Justin Martyr, in his *First Apology* (ca. A.D. 153–155), described the role of deacons in the Eucharist as that of distributing the bread and wine to those present and absent:

> When the president has given thanks and the whole congregation has assented, those whom we call deacons give to each of those present a portion of the consecrated bread and wine and water, and they take it to the absent.[73]

In the centuries after Justin, the role of the deacon varied from his description from less participation in the Eucharist to more participation. For example, by the third and fourth centuries, the deacons were limited in some regions to offering only the cup to the communicants. The bishop or presbyter distributed the bread. Deacons assisted the bishop or presbyter by caring for the altar and its utensils and bringing the oblations of the people, including the bread and wine for the Eucharist, to the altar to be consecrated. Writing between A.D. 215 and A.D. 217, Hippolytus of Rome, author of the *Apostolic Tradition*, took from the deacon the administration of the cup at the Paschal Communion, if there were sufficient presbyters to do it.[74] However, the *Apostolic Tradition* may not reflect accurately the practice of the Church of Rome. The conflict of Hippolytus, a presbyter, with Callistus, an archdeacon, may account for the subordination of deacons to presbyters in this church order.[75]

The *Apostolic Tradition* made a distinction between those offices that required ordination and those that were filled by appointment. Ordination required the laying on of hands by the bishop and prayer over the candidate. Appointment was a matter of being selected and recognized. For example, a bishop handed a book to one who was appointed a reader. For Hippolytus, the only offices that required ordination were those of bishop, presbyter, and deacon. Widows were appointed. Virgins were simply recognized for a choice they had made for themselves. The insistence of Hippolytus that widows should not be ordained might have indicated that they were being ordained in the Roman church, and he wanted it to stop. Hippolytus knew of no women deacons or an office of deaconess in Rome.[76]

In contrast to these limitations on the role of the deacon in the Eucharist, in other regions deacons conducted the Eucharist alone. Tertullian allowed that laics could celebrate the Eucharist and baptize in cases of necessity.[77] In times of rapid growth, such as the third century, the use of deacons to administer the sacraments seems to have become a convenient expedient.[78]

In the absence of sufficient presbyters, bishops seem to have appointed deacons as overseers of individual churches. These men, with apparent permission of their bishops, celebrated the Eucharist and baptized, at least until councils of the church disallowed them the right to celebrate the Eucharist. The council of the church at Arles in A.D. 314 observed that the deacons were "offering [the Eucharist] in many cases."[79] The council ordered this to cease. A few years later in A.D. 325 the Council of Nicaea declared that deacons could not distribute Communion to bishops or presbyters.[80] Presbyters were becoming senior to deacons in a growing hierarchy of church office, but deacons apparently continued to oversee individual churches and to baptize throughout the fourth century.[81]

The documents of the years between the Apostolic Fathers and Constantine reveal that the deacons had other liturgical roles. They took an active part in worship and may have preached. They prepared candidates for Baptism and participated in the Sacrament of Baptism itself. They heard the confessions of dying Christians who had received letters from the martyrs of the mid-third century North African persecution.[82] According to one interpreter of Tertullian, the deacons, along with widows, assisted in the marriage liturgy.[83]

During the worship service, deacons linked the bishop or presbyter and the people. They gave instructions and exhorted those at variance with one another to reconcile. They were doorkeepers. Deacons arranged the placement of the congregation and kept order, preventing whispering, sleeping, and disruption. They made sure the elderly had places to sit. They were "holy criers" for the church.[84] The *Didascalia Apostolorum* (ca. A.D. 220–250), a Syrian church order, directed the bishops to let the deacon say with a loud voice, "Is there perhaps anyone who keeps some grudge against his fellow?" Thus if there were any who had a lawsuit or quarrel with another, the bishops could make peace between them and the oblations and prayers would be acceptable.[85]

The question of whether or not deacons preached in the early church is controversial. Some authors would claim that they did, regularly, as a part of their office. Others would deny that they preached or admit only a few isolated instances of deacons preaching.[86] The case for deacons preaching is strong in the very early church, if one considers as deacons Stephen the Martyr and Philip the Evangelist from the New Testament. Some would argue, however, that Philip became a presbyter or priest. Later it seems likely that deacons preached to those congregations over which they were the local overseer. There are records of specific deacons, mentioned by name, preaching.[87] This limits the controversy over such activity to determining how widespread it was. The issue of preaching by deacons is complicated further by the difficulty of differentiating teaching from preaching. That deacons taught is generally accepted. That they regularly gave sermons during worship is not. By the high Middle Ages, preaching is extended to the diaconal office not as an exception but as a function that belonged to deacons.[88]

There was a great need for teaching in the early church to instruct the new converts. In Acts 8:26–39, Philip instructed the Ethiopian eunuch before baptizing him. What began in an informal way in the very early church became more structured over time. Hippolytus of Rome directed the deacons and presbyters to assemble daily at a place appointed by the bishop to teach those in church and to pray. The deacons, especially, were to be regular in attendance.[89] By the beginning of the third century, adult candidates for Baptism spent as long as three years in the catechumenate receiving instruction before Baptism.[90] Deacons or others who were designated as catechists taught these candidates. Eventually, catechetical schools developed that became veritable centers of sacred learning in this era long before the rise of universities in the Middle Ages. Perhaps the most famous of these was the school at Alexandria that was headed by Origen (born A.D. 182–185 and died A.D. 251 or A.D. 254).[91]

Deacons not only instructed catechumens but also participated in the Sacrament of Baptism itself. Adult baptism prevailed in these early centuries when there were more converts to Christianity than people born into the faith, but children, even infants, were not excluded. Although Tertullian rejected infant baptism, Cyprian, Hippolytus, and John Chrysostom approved it, and Origen asserted that the baptism of infants came down from the apostles.[92]

Baptism was a moving ceremony as described by Hippolytus in the *Apostolic Tradition* and by the anonymous author of the *Didascalia*.[93] Baptismal candidates would disrobe with deacons standing by, holding the oils used for anointing. After the candidates had renounced the devil and all his works, the presbyter would anoint them with the oil of exorcism. (Some say that a deacon or deaconess performed the anointing.)[94] A deacon would enter the water with the candidates. The candidates would respond to the three baptismal interrogatories concerning their faith, and the presbyter would immerse or wash each candidate three times. The presbyter would anoint the newly baptized with the oil of thanksgiving as they came out of the water. Dry and clothed, the newly baptized were brought to the assembled congregation, where the bishop would lay a hand on each, pray, and anoint each on the forehead, making the sign of the cross.

The *Didascalia* contains the first outline of the specific office of deaconess. This church order reflects the situation in the churches of Syria and Palestine during the third century.[95] In geographic areas of the church where there were deaconesses, such as in Syria and Palestine, they would anoint the bodies of the female baptismal candidates and accompany them into the water. Another woman might fill in for the deaconess in Baptism. The deaconesses were charged with instructing women. Sometimes deacons baptized, with the authorization of a bishop. Other people could baptize, too, if necessary, but at this time in the early church, it was not thought appropriate for women to baptize.

Closely linked to the liturgical roles of the deacons was their work in charity, as reflected in the close link between worship and service in the early church. The Eucharist was itself a bridge between liturgy and charity. The offerings of the people that were not eaten at the common meal were given to the poor. Justin Martyr describes this in his account of the Divine Service:

> Those who prosper, and who so wish, contribute, each one as much as he chooses to. What is collected is deposited with the president, and he takes care of orphans and widows, and those who are in want on account of sickness or any other cause, and those who are in bonds, and the strangers who are sojourners among [us], and, briefly, he is the protector of all those in need.[96]

When the common meal was eaten apart from the Eucharist, both continued to have a charitable component. This meal, called the *agape* or love feast, resembled somewhat the modern potluck church dinner as a function of the community to build goodwill, but its purpose was also poor relief. Igino Giordani discusses these meals in the chapter entitled "Solidarity" in his book *The Social Message of the Early Church Fathers*.[97] He calls the *agape* meals "a concrete expression of social affection" characterized by their name, "love."[98] In these meals one person often donated the meal. The *agape* meal had a strong liturgical component. The bishop was in charge, but in his absence a presbyter or deacon could preside over the prayers and the formal blessing, breaking, and sharing of the bread.[99] The meal was followed by Scripture reading and hymn singing. The deacon or the donor distributed the surplus. Individual Christians would pay for *agape* meals on the occasion of a funeral or the anniversary of the death of a loved one, much like Roman commemorative meals of the time, which were sometimes held in banquet halls built at the tomb of the deceased. Like some of these Roman banquets, widows and the poor were invited to the Christian *agape* meal.[100]

Besides paying for an *agape* meal and bringing offerings to the Eucharist, the early church encouraged individual Christians to give alms directly to the poor. In the *Shepherd of Hermas*, Hermas is told to fast on bread and water and give the cost of a full meal to a widow, orphan, or poor person. Fasting and almsgiving were linked in the early church.[101]

Tertullian indicated that early Christians gave voluntarily on a regular basis:

> Even if there is a chest of a sort, it is not made up of money paid in entrance-fees, as if religion were a matter of contract. Every man once a month brings some modest coin—or whenever he wishes, and only if he does wish, and if he can; for nobody is compelled; it is a voluntary offering. You might call them the trust funds of piety. For they are not spent upon banquets nor drinking-parties nor thankless eating-houses; but to feed the poor and to bury them, for boys and girls who lack property and parents, and then for slaves grown old and ship-wrecked mariners; and any who may be in mines, islands or prisons, provided that it is for the sake of God's school, become the pensioners of their confession.[102]

The wealthy were to be good stewards of their possessions. Cyprian castigated the rich who contributed nothing at the Eucharist, partaking of the oblations brought by the poor. The rich did not have to give up all their possessions, however, unless they were obsessed with them.[103] Clement, a teacher of Alexandria (?–ca. A.D. 215), addressed the question in *The Rich Man's Salvation*:

> Can you also rise superior to your riches? Say so, and Christ does not draw you away from the possession of them; the Lord does not grudge. But do you see yourself being worsted and overthrown by them? Leave them, cast them off, hate them, say goodbye to them, flee from them.[104]

Christians took care of their sick. This became noticeable to the non-Christian world in times of disaster, such as the outbreak of the plague at Carthage in A.D. 252. Christians tended the sick and dying, while others fled possible contagion.[105] Such charity extended beyond the immediate Christian community to those who were not in the church. The extent to which this was so has been debated, but it was remarked upon. A century after the events in Carthage, the emperor Julian (A.D. 361–363), in an attempt to revive the ancient religion of Rome, called on its priests to imitate the charitable practices of the "impious Galilaeans."[106]

It was not only the goodwill of the Christian community that surpassed the actions of those around them, it was also that many of their charitable efforts were organized. Important in this charitable organizational structure were the deacons. Like other Christians, deacons individually visited the sick and those in prison or in the mines. Some deacons and priests practiced medicine, especially in the eastern end of the Roman Empire, because many ancient physicians were Greek. Then Lukas Chrysoberges (1157–1170), a patriarch of the twelfth century, forbade clerics to join a physicians guild. Regardless of other functions, deacons were charged with ongoing responsibility for the poor beyond the private almsgiving of individual Christians. Thus they collected and distributed gifts of the faithful. Deacons, together with the bishop, provided an organizational framework for charity to ensure maximum coverage.[107] Ultimately deacons also became involved in property management to deal with the accumulation of legacies. This task grew as congregations moved out of private homes into church buildings and, in the third century, acquired cemeteries for their dead.[108]

Long before this happened, the bishops had become responsible for charity in the church, and deacons had become their assistants. In this role, deacons reported illnesses, problems, and matters requiring discipline to the bishop, thus becoming his eyes and ears in the early church. Lay Christians often spoke to the bishop through the deacon. Deacons also conveyed messages from the bishop to the congregation or to individuals and distributed necessities, thus becoming the bishop's right hand and heart. Deacons administered discipline for the bishop, took responsibility for the excommunicated, represented the bishop at councils of the church, voted as a proxy for him, became his assistant, and often succeeded him as bishop. When Bishop Cyprian of Carthage was in hiding during the persecutions (A.D. 250–251) of Emperor Decius (A.D. 249–251), he turned to his presbyters and deacons for the administration of the church, writing to them: "I beg you, by your faith and your religion, to discharge there both your own office and mine . . ."[109] According to Cyprian (*Epistle* 18.1) and several ecclesiastical synods, deacons were empowered to reconcile sinners at the point of death with the church.[110] The deacon was often compared to the Levite of the Old Testament, and the deacon's relationship to the bishop was symbolized by the fact that the bishop alone imposed hands on the deacon when he was ordained, whereas other presbyters also imposed hands on presbyters.[111] In times of persecution, deacons sometimes accompanied their bishops to a martyr's death, as did the deacons attached to Cyprian, who died September 14, 258, at Carthage under the Emperor Valerian. In the same year the bishop of Rome and four of his deacons had been arrested while officiating at services held in the catacombs; they were martyred on August 6. Four days later their colleague, the famous deacon Lawrence, was also martyred, but despite torture, he is credited with protecting the wealth of the church.[112] In this relationship of bishop and deacon, some deacons were given more responsibilities by their bishops than others. They were, like Lawrence at Rome, a senior or principal deacon. Some of them began to be called archdeacons in the third century.[113]

By the middle of the third century, the liturgical and teaching responsibilities of the deacons plus their charitable tasks outstripped the number of deacons in some churches. The threefold pattern of bishops, presbyters, and deacons found in the letters of Ignatius was expanded. In a much quoted letter of A.D. 250 or A.D. 252, Cornelius, bishop of Rome, described the church there as having one bishop, "forty-six presbyters, seven deacons, seven sub-deacons, forty-two acolytes, fifty-two exorcists, readers and doorkeepers, above fifteen hundred widows and persons in distress, all of whom are supported by the grace and loving kindness of the Master."[114] In this list, presbyters outnumbered deacons, perhaps because it had become traditional to limit the number of deacons in Rome to the seven mentioned in Acts 6. Cornelius's predecessor had divided the church in Rome into seven regions. In each region there was one deacon and one subdeacon to assist him.

Hippolytus had mentioned subdeacons as early as A.D. 215–217. In commenting on their installation in office, Hippolytus stated that "[h]ands shall not be laid upon a subdeacon, but he shall be named that he may serve the deacon."[115] As this quotation indicates, subdeacons were assistants to the deacons in their liturgical and charitable work. They informed the bishop of who was sick. They carried letters. They prepared the sacred vessels before Communion. They also served as doorkeepers at the women's door, but they had no place in the sanctuary. Subdeacons could not touch the vessels at the Communion table, administer the chalice, or wear a stole, at least not in the fourth century.[116]

The forty-two acolytes had responsibilities to assist the deacons and subdeacons, carrying letters, distributing alms, and ministering in prison. Eventually it became their responsibility to light the candles in church. Long before there were acolytes, candles or oil lamps had been lit for the evening services. Only some of the churches of the Roman Empire had acolytes.

The exorcists were responsible for the demoniacs (the demon-possessed or mentally ill) for whom the church provided. Exorcists prayed for them, cared for them, and exorcised them.

The office of reader or lector developed out of an earlier tradition in the synagogues of calling on those who were able to read the Scriptures aloud during services. The church historian Adolf von Harnack felt that the readers might also have preached on the texts they read. The office was of transitory importance in the church because in the fourth century the deacons took over the reading of the Gospel, and in A.D. 813 the Council of Rheims declared that the Epistle was to be read by a subdeacon.[117]

The doorkeepers inherited their task from deacons, subdeacons, and deaconesses. A deacon guarded the men's door during the Eucharist, while subdeacons or deaconesses guarded the women's door. The office of doorkeeper pointed to another purpose for the five minor offices on Cornelius's list. Besides being of assistance to the deacons, the minor offices provided a supervised apprenticeship for aspirants to the superior offices.[118]

The widows whom Cornelius numbered among the fifteen hundred supported by the church might have been members of a circle or order of widows. They were like some of the clergy because they lived from the offerings of the faithful. The *Didascalia* stated that they should have half as much silver as each of the deacons or presbyters.[119] In the *Didascalia* a woman could be enrolled as a widow at the age of 50 rather than 60, perhaps because of Roman marriage law, which freed widows of that age from the requirement of remarriage within a year of their husband's death.[120]

In the third century, the order of widows had a prominent place, perhaps their highest point.[121] Widows both received charity and gave charitable service. They were like some of the clergy because they lived from the offerings of the faithful. They appear to be an official part of the growing church hierarchy and are listed with the clergy, but as far as the *Didascalia* (which reflected church practices in Syria and Palestine) was concerned, widows were not to be ordained nor were they to teach, accept donations, baptize, or even to fast with, pray over, or lay hands on anyone without the command of a deacon or bishop. Again, the fact that an issue was made of these practices might have been because some widows were doing these things. The emphasis for widows was on the virtue of silence, stability, and obedience, characteristics that many of these mature women might not have had.[122]

By the time of the consolidation of these roles, women had long served the church in formal and informal ways. As mentioned above, the Gospels include accounts of women who ministered to Jesus, and the Epistles mention widows and wives of deacons or female deacons (Matthew 27:55–56; Mark 15:40–41; Luke 8:1–3; 1 Timothy 3:11; 1 Timothy 5:3–16; Romans 16:1–2). Other documents of the early church mentioned widows, virgins, and, less frequently, deaconesses. Many of these references are brief and assume a contemporary knowledge of the roles of these women that the modern reader does not have. This has led to controversy over their roles between those who feel these women had a formal active position in the early church and those who understand their role as informal and less prominent.

Some modern scholars view widows in the early church as groups of women who sought equality, independence, and a consecrated Christian life. They assert that some communities of widows came to include not only true widows and virgins but also women who had separated from their husbands because of a desire for sexual continence. One scholar credits a community of such widows with the authorship of the Apocryphal Acts of the Apostles, a collection of stories featuring the apostles that was written around A.D. 160–225 and that gave a central role to women.[123]

Some scholars state that as early as 1 Timothy 5:3–16 the use of the word *widow* included virgins.[124] Tertullian objected to combining the two groups. He protested the placement of a woman of less than 20 years of age in the order of widows:

> I know plainly, that in a certain place a virgin of less than twenty years of age has been placed in the order of *widows*! Whereas if the bishop had been bound to accord her any relief, he might, of course, have done it in some other way without detriment to the respect due to discipline; that such a miracle, not to say monster, should not be pointed at in the church, a *virgin-widow*! . . . in that seat . . . to which (besides the "sixty years") not merely "single-husbanded" (*women*), that is, *married women*, are at length elected, but "mothers" to boot, yes, and "educators of children"; in order, forsooth, that their experimental training in all the affections may, on the one hand, have rendered them capable of readily aiding all others with counsel and comfort, and that, on the other, they may none the less have travelled down the whole course of probation whereby a *female* can be tested. . . . Nothing in the way of public honour is permitted to a *virgin*.[125]

This particular virgin did not even wear the customary veil of consecrated virgins.

In other respects, the schismatic group of Montanist Christians, to which Tertullian belonged in his later years (ca. A.D. 206–213), was friendly toward women and may have allowed female officeholders to an extent that was not acceptable among other Christians.[126] Some authors claim literary evidence of female bishops among the Montanists, for example, and assert that women fared better "in Christian communities in which the Spirit was more important than theological and social norms that . . . attempted to restrict them."[127]

These quotations from the early church only hinted at what the widows were doing, but they and 1 Timothy 5:9–16 imply that these women were engaged in prayer and perhaps in visitation of some sort. During periods of persecution, widows ministered to the martyrs in prison and took up collections for them.[128] Because of possible impropriety and temptation to remarry, there was concern about the minimum age of widows—age 60 in 1 Timothy 5:9 but age 50 in the *Didascalia*.[129] Individual bishops displayed flexibility in appointing younger women to this order, but whatever their age, a lapse of time after the death of the spouse was prudent to ensure that a woman intended to remain single. How were these requirements reconciled with the need of recently bereaved women for charity? Some of the widows were sheltered by the bishops according to the *Shepherd of Hermas*.[130] Also a double tier seems to have developed between those widows on welfare and those who were part of an order of widows. Some scholars would date the beginnings of a differentiation as early as Tabitha (Dorcas), who is mentioned in Acts 9:36–43.[131] In the passage quoted above, Tertullian wrote of an "order of widows" and of a special seat for them. The *Didascalia* described the women of the order of widows in Syria accepting gifts of wool to make garments for the poor. Under the orders of the bishop, they also laid hands on the sick, prayed over them, ate and drank or fasted with them, but they were not to teach.[132]

There is another office for women that Cornelius did not mention, perhaps because it was not prevalent in the Western Roman Empire in the first three centuries after Christ. This is the office of deaconess. Scholars who feel that deaconesses originated in the third century suggest that they might have come out of the order of widows, just as other minor offices developed about the same time from the diaconate in response to the needs of growing churches.[133]

The first document that specifically mentions deaconesses, in the sense of an office, is the *Didascalia*, which dates from the first half of the third century. The *Didascalia* reflects the practices of the region of Syria, not of the entire church. The author gives deacons and deaconesses a place of prominence, asking the bishop to take to himself as helpers these "workers for justice":[134] "But the deacon stands in the place of Christ, and you should love him. The deaconess, however, shall be honored by you in place of the Holy Spirit."[135]

The institution of the office of deaconess in the eastern part of the Roman Empire appears to have been based on the need to serve women and to maintain modesty, as well as, perhaps, a desire to situate women within an organized hierarchy and regulate their activities. Deaconesses visited women who were ill and bathed them as deacons did for men. Deaconesses went to Christian women in pagan homes to which men could not be sent. They anointed the naked bodies of women as part of the baptismal rite and instructed them afterward, a role forbidden to the widows in the *Didascalia*, who were not supposed to teach. A man was to recite the invocation in the water, but the deaconess instructed and educated the baptized women.[136] If there was no deaconess available, some manuscripts of the *Didascalia* allowed another woman to anoint, but if only men were present, only the women's heads were to be anointed.[137] Some authors, such as Francis Cardman, view the emerging role of the deaconess as more limited than that of the widow, and the eclipse of the "charismatic" role of the widow by the deaconess as a marginalization of women.[138]

The *Didascalia of the Apostles*, as its full name would imply, claimed early origins for the office of deaconess by calling Mary Magdalene a deaconess, but scholars who credit the third century with the beginnings of the office argue that deaconesses were of recent origin when the *Didascalia* was written, and deaconesses in the *Didascalia* were appointed, not ordained.[139] These commentators reject earlier evidence for deaconesses in the eastern Roman Empire, such as that found in Pliny's letter of A.D. 111–113. An intermediate position is that of scholars who acknowledge female deacons or deaconesses from the time of Phoebe and the apostles but look to the third century for the establishment of an ecclesiastical order of deacons.[140]

Another possibility for the history of deaconesses that is based on the nature of institutions and the textual evidence is that during the very early years of the church, when the boundaries between church office and the congregation were less well defined, women moved more easily into an office or role that could be designated as that of a deacon or deaconess. That flexibility gradually disappeared with the general recognition of three liturgical offices of bishop, presbyter, and deacon in the church and the development of the monepiscopate.[141] In the eastern Roman Empire, women as deacons lived on in memory or fact, depending on the region. The deaconess as a formal office surfaced as a solution to the problems of modesty in Christian Baptism and during visits of women in the home. The desire of the church to bring its women under the control of the establishment also may have been a motivating factor.[142] These problems were resolved differently in the Western Roman Empire, where there was a less marked separation of men and women, in part by the use of widows. Because functions of the widows and deaconesses were similar, some nineteenth-century historians dealt with deaconesses by treating them as one with widows.[143] After the rediscovery of the *Didascalia* in 1854, a clearer differentiation was possible.

The first three centuries of the church were a golden age for deacons. Toward the end of that era, there were premonitions of a change. In the course of the third century, the church began "to see the diaconate as a lower rung in a ladder of preferment . . . a transitional step to the priesthood."[144] Already the church had moved from the monepiscopate, with bishops making decisions in a council of elders that sometimes included deacons, to the monarchical episcopate, with bishops ruling more directly on their own. A symbol of that transition was the movement from the selection of deacons by the body of the disciples, as in Acts 6:2–6, to their selection by the bishop, as in the *Didascalia*.[145] An intermediate position seemed to have been the selection of deacons with public scrutiny, as Cyprian preferred.[146] The fourth century, with the end of persecution and the legalization of Christianity in the Roman Empire, would be an era of radical transitions in the church and its diaconate.

NOTES

1. For the meaning and use of these words, see Arndt and Gingrich, *Greek-English Lexicon*, 183; Lawrence R. Hennessey, "*Diakonia* and *Diakonoi* in the Pre-Nicene Church," in Halton and Williman, *Diakonia*, 60–68; C. E. B. Cranfield, "Diakonia in the New Testament," in McCord and Parker, *Service in Christ*, 37–38.

2. See Collins, *Diakonia*. Herodotus, who was born at Halicarnassus in Asia Minor but emigrated to Athens, was known as the "Father of History."

3. Collins, *Deacons and the Church*, 13.

4. Bash, "Deacons and Diaconal Ministry," 41.

5. Collins, *Diakonia*, 3.

6. McCord and Parker, *Service in Christ*.

7. Burtchaell, *From Synagogue to Church*, 339.

8. *Against Heresies* 3.12.10, in Alexander Roberts and James Donaldson, eds., *The Ante-Nicene Fathers: Translations of the Writings of the Fathers Down to A.D. 325*, vol. 1: *The Apostolic Fathers with Justin Martyr and Irenaeus*, ed. A. Cleveland Coxe (n.p.: Christian Literature Publishing, 1885; repr., New York: Charles Scribner's Sons, 1903), 434.

9. In *Homily 14* on Acts 5:34ff., Chrysostom asked rhetorically what sort of office the seven received: "Was it that of Deacons? And yet this is not the case in the Churches. But is it to the Presbyters that the management belongs? And yet at present there was no Bishop, but the Apostles only. Whence I think it clearly and manifestly follows, that neither Deacons nor Presbyters is their designation" (Schaff, *Select Library of the Nicene and Post-Nicene Fathers*, 11:90–91).

10. Collins, *Deacons and the Church*, 49.

11. Cooke, *Ministry to Word and Sacraments*, 347; Dunn, *Unity and Diversity*, 107, 112–14; Mitchell, *Mission and Ministry*, 6:108.

12. Acts 8:4–13, 26–40. On the issue of deacons preaching see, for example, Barnett, *The Diaconate* (1981), 191–92.

13. The words translated as *bishops* and *deacons* in Philippians 1:1 could also be translated as *overseers* and *servants*.

14. Hennessey, *"Diakonia,"* 73. Some proponents of a more fluid view of ministry in the early church would postpone the development of the offices of bishop and deacon in Philippi and elsewhere to the post-Pauline era or to the second century; see Dunn, *Unity and Diversity,* 113.

15. Burtchaell, *From Synagogue to Church,* 339.

16. Burtchaell, *From Synagogue to Church,* 228–40.

17. Burtchaell, *From Synagogue to Church,* 240–44.

18. Brown, *Priest and Bishop,* 55.

19. Burtchaell, *From Synagogue to Church,* 342.

20. Burtchaell, *From Synagogue to Church,* 246–48.

21. Burtchaell, *From Synagogue to Church,* 246–49.

22. The RSV translates *diakonos* in Romans 16:1 as "deaconess." Many scholars feel that "deacon" would be a better translation because the technical term *diakonissa* was not generally used until the fourth century. Before that the feminine article was sometimes used with *diakonos* to connote a female. Some prefer to translate *diakonos* in Romans 16:1 as "servant." Others give Phoebe the title of deacon or deaconess but feel that it is too early to understand it as connoting a formal office. See Martimort, *Deaconesses,* 19–20; G. W. H. Lampe, *"Diakonia* in the Early Church," in McCord and Parker, *Service in Christ,* 62.

23. Burtchaell, *From Synagogue to Church,* 328.

24. Thurston, *Women in the New Testament,* 53–54.

25. Kyriaki Karidoyanes FitzGerald, "The Characteristics and Nature of the Order of Deaconess," in Hopko, *Women and the Priesthood,* 77–78.

26. Robert Jewett, "Paul, Phoebe, and the Spanish Mission," in Neusner et al., *Social World of Formative Christianity and Judaism,* 142–43, 147–53.

27. Roman Garrison, "Phoebe, the Servant-Benefactor and Gospel Traditions," in Wilson and Desjardins, *Text and Artifact,* 67.

28. Fiorenza, *In Memory of Her,* 171.

29. See, for example, a papal letter of 11 March 494, Gelasius I, *Epistle,* 14.26: "We have heard to our annoyance that divine affairs have come to such a low state that women are encouraged to officiate at the sacred altars, and to take part in all matters imputed to the offices of the male sex, to which they do not belong." English translation in Rossi, "Priesthood, Precedent, and Prejudice," 81.

30. Burtchaell, *From Synagogue to Church,* 327.

31. *New Catholic Encyclopedia,* 2d ed., s.v. "Deaconess"; and Stiefel, "Women Deacons in 1 Timothy," 442–57.

32. Davies, "Deacons, Deaconesses and the Minor Orders," 1–2.

33. *New Catholic Encyclopedia,* 2d ed., s.v. "Deaconess"; Stiefel, "Women Deacons in 1 Timothy," 447.

34. Dunn, *Unity and Diversity,* 352; Hennessey, *"Diakonia,"* 73.

35. Mitchell, *Mission and Ministry,* 153.

36. Douglas Powell, "Ordo Presbyterii," *Journal of Theological Studies,* n.s. 26 (October 1975): 311, 321–22.

37. See McKee, *Calvin on the Diaconate,* 205–23, for an exegetical history of the texts relating to deaconesses and widows: Romans 1–2; 1 Timothy 3:11; 5:3–10.

38. McKenna, *Women of the Church,* 42; Thurston, *Widows,* 31–35.

39. Bassler, "Widows' Tale," 36–40.

40. Witherington, *Women in the Earliest Churches*, 150–51.

41. Calvin, *Institutes of the Christian Religion*, 2:1061. For a discussion of the office of widow and Calvin's views in an historical and exegetical context, see McKee, *Calvin and the Diaconate*, 205–23.

42. For women in the New Testament and early church, see, for example, the essays in Dautzenberg, Merklein, and Müller, *Die Frau im Urchristentum*.

43. Holmes, *Apostolic Fathers*, 23.

44. *1 Clement* 42, in Richardson, *Early Christian Fathers*, 62. This volume includes English translations of other Apostolic Fathers.

45. *1 Clement* 44, in Richardson, *Early Christian Fathers*, 63–64.

46. The proposed dates for the *Didache* vary from before A.D. 50 to the third century or later. Michael Holmes suggests the *Didache* "may have been put into its present form as late as 150, though a date considerably closer to the end of the first century seems more probable" (Holmes, *Apostolic Fathers*, 247).

47. For more on the transition from charismatic to noncharismatic ministries, see the chapter by that name in Schweizer, *Church Order in the New Testament*, 181–87; and Dunn, *Unity and Diversity*, 121–22.

48. Echlin, *Deacon in the Church*, 17.

49. *Didache* 15.1–2, in Richardson, *Early Christian Fathers*, 178.

50. Pliny, *Epistle* X, 96.8, in Stevenson, *New Eusebius*, 14.

51. MacDonald, *Early Christian Women*, 52–53, 235–36.

52. Lampe, "*Diakonia*," 62.

53. Richardson, *Early Christian Fathers*, 74–75; Holmes, *Apostolic Fathers*, 131. William Schoedel states: "There is no reason to doubt that he died a martyr's death in Rome as he had expected, but we have no certain knowledge of that event" (*Ignatius of Antioch*, 11). Glanville Downey suggests that Ignatius was arrested and condemned in A.D. 115; see *History of Antioch*, 292–93.

54. *Trallians* 3.1–2, in Richardson, *Early Christian Fathers*, 99.

55. *Magnesians* 6.1, in Richardson, *Early Christian Fathers*, 95.

56. Dunn, *Unity and Diversity*, 372.

57. Also according to J. Rius-Camps, Ignatius may neither have died from persecution nor have known Polycarp; see *Four Authentic Letters of Ignatius*, 138, 143–44, 146.

58. Joly, *Le Dossier d'Ignace d'Antioche*, 100–101, 121–27.

59. *Smyrnaeans* 12.2, in Richardson, *Early Christian Fathers*, 116. See Rius-Camps, "Bishop or Deacon?" in *Four Authentic Letters of Ignatius*, 34–38.

60. *Ephesians* 2.1 and *Smyrnaeans* 12.1, in Richardson, *Early Christian Fathers*, 88, 116.

61. *Trallians* 2.3, in Richardson, *Early Christian Fathers*, 99.

62. *Smyrnaeans* 8.1, in Richardson, *Early Christian Fathers*, 115.

63. *Ignatius* 6.1, in Richardson, *Early Christian Fathers*, 119.

64. "Greetings to the families of my brothers, along with their wives and children, and to the virgins enrolled with the widows" (*Smyrnaeans* 13.1, in Richardson, *Early Christian Fathers*, 116).

65. *Polycarp* 4.3, in Richardson, *Early Christian Fathers*, 133.

66. *Polycarp* 5.3, in Richardson, *Early Christian Fathers*, 133.

67. Barnett, *The Diaconate* (1981), 51.

68. *Polycarp* 5.2, in Richardson, *Early Christian Fathers*, 133.

69. *Polycarp* 6.1, in Richardson, *Early Christian Fathers*, 133–34.

70. Holmes, *Apostolic Fathers*, 330.

71. " 'Now let me tell you about the stones that go into the building. The square, white stones that fit accurately in their joinings, these are the apostles, bishops, teachers, and deacons who walk in accordance with God's reverence by administering with purity and sanctity the office of bishops, of teachers, and deacons for God's elect. Now, they have always been in mutual agreement; they are at peace with one another and listen to one another. For this reason in the tower-building their joinings fit accurately' " (Third Vision 5.1, in *The Shepherd of Hermas*, trans. Joseph M. F. Marique, in *Fathers of the Church*, trans. Glimm et al., 1:245). See also Frend, *Early Church*, 40; Echlin, *Deacon in the Church*, 17–18; and Goodspeed and Grant, *History of Early Christian Literature*, 31.

72. "The stones with spots are the deacons who administered their office wickedly and robbed widows and orphans of livelihood; who make profit for themselves out of the ministry they received to administer. If they persist in the same [evil] desire, they die and there is no hope of life in them, but, if they turn from their ways and fulfill their ministry with probity, they can live" (Parable 9.26.2, in *The Shepherd of Hermas*, trans. Joseph M. F. Marique, in *Fathers of the Church*, trans. Glimm et al., 1:341).

73. Justin, *1 Apology* 65, in Richardson, *Early Christian Fathers*, 286.

74. "[The Paschal Mass] . . . And the presbyters, but if there are not enough [of them] the deacons also, shall hold the cups . . ." (*Apostolic Tradition*, 23, in Dix, *Treatise on the Apostolic Tradition*, 40–41). For an analysis of the role of the diaconate in the *Apostolic Tradition* and derived documents, see Otterbein, *Diaconate according to the Apostolic Tradition*.

75. Francine Cardman, "Women, Ministry, and Church Order in Early Christianity," in Kraemer and D'Angelo, *Women and Christian Origins*, 306.

76. Cardman, "Women, Ministry, and Church Order," 306–7.

77. "Are not even we laics priests? . . . Accordingly, where there is no joint session of the ecclesiastical Order, you offer [the Eucharist], and baptize, and are priest . . . Therefore, if you have the right of a priest in your own person, in cases of necessity, it behooves you to have likewise the discipline of a priest whenever it may be necessary to have the right of a priest" (*On Exhortation to Chastity* 7.8–9, 11, in *The Ante-Nicene Fathers: Translations of the Writings of the Fathers Down to A.D. 325*, vol. 4: *Fathers of the Third Century: Tertullian, Part Fourth; Minucius Felix; Commodian; Origen, Parts First and Second*, ed. A. Cleveland Coxe [n.p.: Christian Literature Publishing, 1885; repr. New York: Charles Scribner's Sons, 1905], 54).

78. Barnett, *The Diaconate* (1981), 63.

79. "The Decisions of the Council of Arles," Canon 16, in Stevenson, *New Eusebius*, 324.

80. "The Canons of Nicaea, 325," Canon 18, in Stevenson, *New Eusebius*, 363.

81. This is the opinion of Barnett based on Jerome and Cyril of Jerusalem; see *The Diaconate* (1981), 75.

82. Cyprian, *Epistle* 18.1, in Stevenson, *New Eusebius*, 234.

83. Echlin makes this interpretation in *Deacon in the Church*, 31, based on this text from Tertullian: ". . . with what face do you request (the solemnizing of) a matrimony which is unlawful to those of whom you request it; of a monogamist bishop, of presbyters and deacons bound by the same solemn engagement, of widows whose Order you have in your own person refused?" (*On Monogamy* 11, in *Ante-Nicene Fathers*, 4:67).

84. Bingham, *Antiquities of the Ancient Church*, 1:89.

85. Vööbus, *Didascalia Apostolorum in Syriac*, 1:59. "Is there any man that keepeth aught against his fellow?" (R. Hugh Connolly, trans., *Didascalia Apostolorum: The Syriac Ver-*

sion 2.54 [Oxford: Clarendon, 1929], 117, quoted in Barnett, *The Diaconate* [1981], 69). Otterbein dated the *Didascalia* about A.D. 220; see *Diaconate according to the Apostolic Tradition*, 19.

86. Barnett, *The Diaconate* (1981), 47, 78–80.

87. Barnett, *The Diaconate* (1981), 79–80.

88. Cooke, *Ministry to Word and Sacraments*, 278.

89. "And let the deacons and presbyters assemble daily at the place which the bishop shall appoint for them. And let not the deacons especially neglect to assemble every day unless sickness prevents them. And when all have assembled they shall instruct those who are in the assembly. And having also prayed, let each one go about his own business" (*Apostolic Tradition* 33.1–2, in Dix, *Apostolic Tradition*, 60).

90. González, *Story of Christianity*, 1:96.

91. Goodspeed and Grant, *History of Early Christian Literature*, 134–35; Bingham, *Antiquities of the Ancient Church*, 1:94, 121; Chadwick, *Early Church*, 100.

92. Finn, *Early Christian Baptism*, 15; Finn, *Liturgy of Baptism*, 25–26.

93. *Apostolic Tradition* 21, in Dix, *Apostolic Tradition*, 33–38; and *Didascalia Apostolorum*, in Martimort, *Deaconesses*, 38.

94. Cooke, *Ministry to Word and Sacraments*, 263.

95. Cardman, "Women, Ministry, and Church Order," 308.

96. Justin, *1 Apology*, 67, in Richardson, *Early Christian Fathers*, 287.

97. Giordani, *Social Message of the Early Church Fathers*, 298–320.

98. Giordani, *Social Message of the Early Church Fathers*, 309.

99. Otterbein, *Diaconate according to the Apostolic Tradition*, 61.

100. Lampe, "*Diakonia*," 55; Hennessey, "*Diakonia*," 75–76.

101. "This is the way to keep the fast you intend to observe: Before anything else, abstain from every wicked word and every evil desire, and clear your heart of all the vanities of this world. If you observe this, your fast will be perfect. Act as follows: After having done what is prescribed, on the day of your fast do not taste anything except bread and water. Compute the total expense for the food you would have eaten on the day on which you intended to keep a fast and give it to a widow, an orphan, or someone in need. In this way you will become humble in soul, so that the beneficiary of your humility may fill his soul and pray to the Lord for you" (Parable 5.3.5–7, in *The Shepherd of Hermas*, trans. Marique, 294–95).

102. *Apology* 39.5–6, in Stevenson, *New Eusebius*, 174–75.

103. "You are wealthy and rich, and do you think that you celebrate the Lord's Supper, not at all considering the offering, who come to the Lord's Supper without a sacrifice, and yet take part of the sacrifice which the poor man has offered?" (Cyprian, *Treatise* 8.15, "On Works and Alms," in Alexander Roberts and James Donaldson, eds., *The Ante-Nicene Fathers: Translations of the Writings of the Fathers Down to A.D. 325*, vol. 5: *Fathers of the Third Century: Hippolytus, Cyprian, Caius, Novatian, Appendix*, ed. A. Cleveland Coxe [n.p.: Christian Literature, 1886; repr. New York: Charles Scribner's & Sons, 1903], 480).

104. *The Rich Man's Salvation* 24.1, in Stevenson, *New Eusebius*, 202.

105. Dionysius of Alexandria as quoted in Stark, *Rise of Christianity*, 83.

106. Lampe, "*Diakonia*," 50.

107. Miller, *Birth of the Hospital*, 57–58.

108. The Roman church appears to have acquired cemeteries beginning in the time of Bishop Zephyrinus (A.D. 198 or A.D. 199–217); see González, *Story of Christianity*, 1:95.

109. Cyprian, *Epistle* 4.1.2, "To the Presbyters and Deacons," in *Ante-Nicene Fathers*, 5:282.

110. *New Catholic Encyclopedia*, 2d ed., s.v. "Deacon."

111. Hippolytus, *Apostolic Tradition* 9.1, in Dix, *Apostolic Tradition*, 15; Bingham, *Antiquities of the Ancient Church*, 1:86.

112. Echlin, *Deacon in the Church*, 41.

113. Bingham, *Antiquities of the Ancient Church*, 1:98.

114. Eusebius, *Church History*, VI, 43.11–12, in Stevenson, *New Eusebius*, 264–65.

115. Hippolytus, *Apostolic Tradition* 14, in Dix, *Apostolic Tradition*, 22.

116. Davies, "Deacons, Deaconesses and the Minor Orders," 6–7.

117. Davies, "Deacons, Deaconesses and the Minor Orders," 10–13.

118. Bingham, *Antiquities of the Ancient Church*, 1:107.

119. "But however much is given to one of the widows, let the double be given to each of the deacons in honor of Christ, (but) twice double to the leader for the glory of the Almighty. But if anyone wished to honor the presbyters also, let him give him a double, as to the deacons" (*Didascalia Apostolorum* 9, in Vööbus, *Didascalia Apostolorum*, 101). The gift to the presbyter in this quotation was a matter of choice, perhaps indicating that deacons acquired full-time support from the church before presbyters.

120. Cardman, "Women, Ministry, and Church Order," 309.

121. McKenna, *Women of the Church*, 51.

122. Thurston, *Widows*, 94, 96, 104; Cardman, "Women, Ministry, and Church Order," 310–11.

123. Davies, *Revolt of the Widows*, 50, 63–64, 100; for excerpts and a description of the Apocryphal Acts, see Elizabeth A. Clark, "Women Endangered, the Apocryphal Acts and Martyrdom," in *Women in the Early Church*, 77–96; François Bovon, Ann Graham Brock, and Christopher R. Matthews, eds., *The Apocryphal Acts of the Apostles* (Cambridge: Harvard University Press, 1999).

124. Bassler, "Widows' Tale," 35; McKenna, *Women of the Church*, 36–37, 41.

125. "On the Veiling of Widows" 9, in *Ante-Nicene Fathers*, 4:33 (*original emphasis*).

126. Witherington, *Women in the Earliest Churches*, 197.

127. Eisen, *Women Officeholders*, 207–8.

128. Bingham relies on Lucian and Libanius for this information; see *Antiquities of the Ancient Church*, 1:102–3. See also Lucian, *On the Death of Peregrinus* 12, in Stevenson, *New Eusebius*, 135.

129. *Didascalia Apostolorum* 14, in Vööbus, *Didascalia Apostolorum*, 63.

130. "Bishops friendly to strangers . . . receive the servants of God into their homes gladly, without sham. They have given shelter constantly by their own ministrations to the indigent and widows, and their conduct has always been pure. Therefore, they will be given shelter by the Lord forever" (Parable 9.27.2–3, in *The Shepherd of Hermas*, trans. Marique, 342).

131. Thurston, *Widows*, 31–35.

132. *Didascalia Apostolorum* 16, in Vööbus, *Didascalia Apostolorum*, 62–63; Echlin, *Deacon in the Church*, 52; Davies, "Deacons, Deaconesses and the Minor Orders," 5.

133. Davies, "Deacons, Deaconesses and the Minor Orders," 4–5; McKenna takes a modified stand by stating that "partial ground for the establishment of the diaconate, were a special category of widows" (*Women of the Church*, 41).

134. *Didascalia Apostolorum*, in Martimort, *Deaconesses*, 38.

135. *Didascalia Apostolorum* 9, in Vööbus, *Didascalia Apostolorum*, 100.

136. *Didascalia Apostolorum*, in Martimort, *Deaconesses*, 38.

137. Different manuscripts of the *Didascalia* have different instructions on whether a woman other than a deaconess could anoint in Baptism. The oldest text allowed a woman other than a deaconess to anoint: "When women go down into the water, it is required that those who go down into the water shall be anointed by a deaconess with the oil of anointing. And where there is no woman present, and especially no deaconesses, it is necessary for him who baptized to anoint her who is baptized" (*Didascalia Apostolorum* 16, in Vööbus, *Didascalia Apostolorum*, 59–60). A revision allowed only a deaconess to anoint: "When women go down to the water it is necessary that they be anointed by a deaconess and it is not lawful that the anointing oil should be given to a woman to touch but rather (only) to the deaconess" (*Didascalia Apostolorum*, in Martimort, *Deaconesses*, 38).
138. Cardman, "Women, Ministry, and Church Order," 314.
139. Cardman, "Women, Ministry, and Church Order," 314, 318; Davies, "Deacons, Deaconesses and the Minor Orders," 4.
140. "The deaconesses, though they existed from Apostolic times, became an order only in the third century. Before that time their ministry had been strictly a private and unofficial one" (McKenna, *Women of the Church*, 64).
141. Thurston, *Widows*, 19.
142. McKenna, *Women of the Church*, 66.
143. Bingham, *Antiquities of the Ancient Church*, 1:99–104.
144. Hennessey, "*Diakonia*," 83.
145. *Didascalia Apostolorum*, in Martimort, *Deaconesses*, 38.
146. "Which very thing, too, we observe to come from divine authority, that the priest should be chosen in the presence of the people under the eyes of all, and should be approved worthy and suitable by public judgment and testimony . . . God commands a priest to be appointed in the presence of all the assembly; that is, He instructs and shows that the ordination of priests ought not to be solemnized except with the knowledge of the people standing near, that in the presence of the people either the crimes of the wicked may be disclosed, or the merits of the good may be declared, and the ordination, which shall have been examined by the suffrage and judgment of all, may be just and legitimate. . . . Neither do we observe that this was regarded by the apostles only in the ordinations of bishops and priests, but also in those of deacons . . ." (Cyprian, *Epistle* 67.4, in *Ante-Nicene Fathers*, 5:370–71).

CHAPTER TWO

F ROM C ONSTANTINE TO L UTHER

THE FOURTH TO THE FIFTEENTH CENTURIES

In the early fourth century, the church experienced a great Roman persecution (A.D. 303–312) before the emperors Constantine (A.D. 306–337) and Licinius announced official toleration of the Christian faith in A.D. 313.[1] The fourth century marked a decisive change in the conditions that surrounded the church, its growth, and its relationship to the state. As Constantine's political fortunes rose and he became sole emperor, he became the church's benefactor and protector. Although he was not baptized until near his death (A.D. 337), he financed church buildings, sponsored the great ecumenical council at Nicaea in A.D. 325, and allowed the church to inherit property (A.D. 321).[2] In A.D. 380–382, the Emperor Theodosius, through decrees and church councils, required that people of the empire practice orthodox Christianity.[3] In less than eighty years, Christianity went from a persecuted minority to the official religion of the Roman Empire.

With the advent of toleration in A.D. 313, the church experienced changes that affected the role of the clergy and the administration of social welfare. The size of the church grew. Worship moved from house churches to large basilicas that were elaborately decorated and endowed with gold and silver.[4] Worship leaders adopted distinctive liturgical dress. Church office became a full-time occupation for many bishops, presbyters, and deacons, who became dependent upon ecclesiastical revenues for support. The empire helped by exempting clergy from certain taxes and from secular office, but the empire also sought to prevent wealthy people from escaping taxes and civic responsibilities through ordination. In their new relationship with the church, the emperors relied upon the bishops. Bishops could judge civil suits if both parties agreed, and the bishop's role as advocate of the poor increased. The property of widows and orphans was often entrusted to the church for management.[5]

The enlarged church of the fourth century would have needed many more bishops if they were to have retained their traditional role of personally presiding over the Eucharist. The alternative was for bishops to delegate responsibilities. In the third century, under pressure of persecution, Cyprian already had given over some of his tasks as bishop to his presbyters and deacons; so, too, had other bishops so the demands of a growing church could be met. For example, Cyprian was willing to permit deacons "to effect the reconciliation of penitents" if no presbyter was available.[6] Bishops continued to delegate responsibilities in the fourth century, but they retained responsibility for ordination, though presbyters presided over the Eucharist in their absence.[7] The presbyters came to be thought of as possessing certain liturgical functions denied to both deacons and laypeople. This was increasingly thought of as the presbyter's right, not merely as a concession from the bishop.[8] The Council of Arles (A.D. 314) noted that deacons were presiding over the Eucharist in many places and ordered the practice to cease.[9] The Council of Nicaea even barred deacons from giving Communion to presbyters or bishops.[10] Presbyters came to be regarded as the normal heads of congregations. It appears that only sometime later did presbyters begin commonly to be called "priests."[11]

Despite the increasing role of presbyters, deacons remained important in the church. They shared with bishops the responsibility of managing the extensive properties that the local church inherited, now that the empire recognized the church as a legal entity capable of owning property (A.D. 321).[12] Deacons also had responsibility, under the bishop, for gifts to the church. These consisted of (1) oblations brought to the altar at the Lord's Supper; (2) money and goods for the poor; (3) provisions from the Roman state; (4) the property of Roman temples; and (5) special collections. Of these, the councils of the fourth century limited oblations at the altar to bread and, on certain days, milk, honey, and oil for use in worship. Other natural products were brought to the bishop's house or to a place of reception on the east end of the church.[13] Christians contributed property and money, sometimes generously, as did Ambrose, who sold his gold and silver for the church when he became bishop of Milan (A.D. 373–397).[14] Some Christians, like Cyprian, sold possessions on the occasion of their conversion and gave the proceeds to the church.[15] Soon after Constantine recognized the Christian church, he awarded provisions "to virgins and widows, and to those who were consecrated to the divine service."[16] When ordinary revenues did not suffice, the church would sometimes make special collections, as Cyprian had done at Carthage for the prisoners of war in Numidia.[17]

A fourth- or fifth-century manual of church life, the *Apostolic Constitutions* (ca. A.D. 380), encouraged Christians to sell their livelihood to redeem prisoners, and if they had nothing to give, they were to fast for one day and set apart the money they would have spent for food.[18] This was the voice from the age of the martyrs, but one that would come to life again with the barbarian invasions of the Roman Empire. Not only individuals ransomed prisoners but also the church, which could sell its treasures to accomplish this.[19]

The ability to inherit property made it possible for the church to gather an endowment. By the time of Pope Gregory the Great (born ca. A.D. 540, pope A.D. 590–604), this included far-flung properties in Gaul and elsewhere in the Roman Empire. At Rome, deacons administered great estates, and their financial responsibilities no doubt enhanced their considerable prominence in the city.

If the church's resources were greater, so also were the demands upon them because the Roman Empire now vested considerable responsibility for the poor in the church. For example, the church was given the oversight of prison conditions and the care of widows, orphans, and abandoned children.[20] The church encouraged Christians to adopt these children, especially the orphans of martyrs.[21] The bishop of Hippo, Augustine (A.D. 354–430), corresponded about arrangements for the marriage of orphans entrusted to the church. Poor fugitives were maintained at the church's expense.[22] The church was an advocate for people with the government and paid the debts of individuals or sometimes lent them money to pay their taxes.[23] The state recognized the right of sanctuary for thirty days for those who took refuge in a church, except for murderers, adulterers, "carriers-off of virgins," and public debtors.[24]

The matricula, or roll, of those given financial support numbered in the thousands at some churches. In Antioch alone, John Chrysostom (baptized ca. A.D. 370, died A.D. 407) attests to 3,000 widows and virgins, plus prisoners, the ill, strangers, lepers, daily suppliants, and those to whom the church gave food and clothing.[25] Out of a city and a church that Chrysostom estimated to have 100,000 people, 10,000 were well-to-do and 10,000 were quite poor.[26] Augustine indicated he had to turn away the greater part of those who haunted him daily for assistance. In these responsibilities, deacons, deaconesses, and widows were the assistants of the bishops. The widows, especially, were often entrusted with the care of orphans.[27]

WIDOWS AND DEACONESSES

All these offices were in transition in the centuries after Constantine but the offices of the widows and deaconesses perhaps most of all. In the fourth century, with the legalization and expansion of Christianity, conceivably there were more adult baptisms, but by the fifth and sixth centuries, the decline in the number of adult baptisms in favor of the baptism of children diminished the need for widows or deaconesses to anoint the nude women in the baptismal ceremony. The changed relationship with the government after Christianity became the state religion made it less likely that women would be chosen for church leadership roles that involved additional financial, legal, and administrative responsibilities. The growth of communities of women provided an alternate outlet for female leadership. All this affected women's roles in the church.[28]

The office of widow was particularly vulnerable. Within the imperial church of the fourth and fifth centuries, the widows appear to have lost responsibilities to the deaconesses, especially in the eastern part of the Roman Empire, but the details of how and when this happened are unclear, and initially widows may have retained their importance.[29] A term came into use to distinguish "official widows" from other widows. The official widows were called *presbytides* or *presbytidas* ("elder women" or "female presidents"). In the *Testamentum Domini nostri Jesu Christi* (*Testament of Our Lord Jesus Christ*), a document of the church that gave widows a prominent role, these special widows had a privileged place in church next to the presbyters on the bishop's left.[30] The Council of Laodicea (after A.D. 341 but before A.D. 381), however, forbade the appointment of *presbytides*.[31] This could perhaps have been because they had overstepped what was perceived as their authority.[32]

Other documents from the period are contradictory about the status of widows. This may be a product of the interchangeable use of the words *deaconess* and *widow* in this era, varying practices in different geographic regions, and the biases of those who compiled and edited the sources. It is revealing to examine the role of the deaconesses and widows in these various documents.

For example, the *Testament of Our Lord Jesus Christ* favored widows. This great ecclesiastical order of the post-Constantine era purported to be a last will or testament that Jesus gave his apostles in the forty days after the resurrection.[33] Scholars date the document from as early as A.D. 350 to at least as late as the second half of the fifth century.[34] This ecclesiastical order, like others, attempted to harmonize the *Apostolic Tradition* of Hippolytus of Rome and the *Didascalia*, while including other things.[35] In the *Testament of Our Lord*, widows had an educational and disciplinary role among the women, made home visits, and may have supervised deaconesses. The widows lived together with the virgins and led them in prayer.[36] Scholars have interpreted the installation of widows in the *Testament of Our Lord* as an ordination.[37]

> From the time that she is ordained, she should pray without intermission and be perfect in everything . . . possessing nothing in this world . . . continuing night and day with the altar services . . . If she has one or two or three companions united in spirit in my Name, I will be among them. . . . Let her exhort the disobedient women, teach the ignorant ones, convert the guilty ones and teach them to be chaste. And she should supervise the deaconesses.[38] She should make sure those who enter the church know how to behave, and those who remain outside she shall encourage. To those who will hear she patiently offers counsel regarding what things are good. The disobedient, after three admonitions, she shall not address. She shall foster the women who wish to live in virginity or purity. Modestly and peaceably she shall correct those who show opposition. With all she shall be peaceable. She should privately rebuke those who speak vainly and too much, but if they will not listen she should adjoin to them a woman advanced in age or bring the matter to the ears of the bishop. In church she should be silent, she should be assiduous in prayer, she should visit the sick, she should help them and bring one or two deacons with her to all of them on the Lord's day. If she possess anything, she shall distribute it among the poor and faithful. But if she does not possess anything she shall be aided by the Church.[39]

Most documents of the fourth and fifth centuries placed widows in a less prominent role than the *Testament of Our Lord*, rendering their position within the church difficult to explain. Some scholars circumvent this problem by dating the composition of the *Testament of Our Lord* at approximately A.D. 350, which is earlier than these other documents. Thus they view it as a description of a transitional state for widows, who were in reality becoming mere welfare recipients and losing status in the church to deaconesses and virgins.[40] One solution to the varied interpretations of the roles of widows, deaconesses, and virgins in late antiquity is that of Susanna Elm, who suggests that the "office" of widow merged with the functions of the deaconess, producing, in effect, the "widow-deaconess." Ultimately, "deaconess" became a catchall designation that included virgins. "Virgin-widow-deaconesses" could be leaders of ascetic communities.[41]

A GROWING CHURCH HIERARCHY

In the growing hierarchy of church office, subcategories continued to develop within the diaconate, presbyterate, and episcopacy. As there were archdeacons among the deacons of a given region, there were archpresbyters among the presbyters. By the time of the Council of Chalcedon in A.D. 451, the most important cities boasted patriarchs: Rome, Alexandria, Constantinople, Antioch, and Jerusalem. The bishop and patriarch of Rome made claims to authority over other bishops that would gain him ascendancy in the church as pope in the western Roman Empire. Church organization came to reflect territorial and administrative divisions of the empire, such as the diocese, a term that today still designates the territory for which a bishop is responsible.[42]

At the same time, because the liturgy was becoming more elaborate and congregations were becoming larger, the work of deacons in worship increased. Deacons took over the reading of the Gospel from the readers in some churches and chanted parts of the liturgy.[43] The *Apostolic Constitutions* (ca. A.D. 380), a compilation that drew in part on the *Apostolic Tradition* of the third century, elaborated on the role of deacons in worship. Deacons called for silence at Scripture readings; announced the stages of the service; directed everyone to kneel;[44] dismissed the hearers after the sermon and the penitents, catechumens, and energumens after they had been prayed over and before the Eucharist;[45] announced the kiss of peace with the rubric "Salute ye one another with the holy kiss";[46] brought the gifts to the bishop at the altar; stood beside the altar with fans to keep insects from the cups;[47] partook of Communion after the bishop and presbyters but before the subdeacons, readers, singers, ascetics, deaconesses, virgins, widows, children, and the rest of the people, in that order;[48] gave the cup, saying, "The blood of Christ, the cup of life";[49] and proclaimed the biddings or intercessions for prayer in the litanies, replacing the more primitive silent prayers. The deacon addressed the congregation with the rubric "Let us pray," followed by petitions, which were interspersed with prayers addressed to God by the celebrant and congregation.[50] Jerome (A.D. 345 or A.D. 347–419 or A.D. 420) recorded that the deacon publicly recited in church the names of those who had made donations.[51] At Rome, deacons sang the Gradual between the Epistle and Gospel.[52] Deacons also dismissed the congregation with the rubric "Depart in peace."[53]

The *Apostolic Constitutions* denied deacons the right to administer a Baptism, whereas Tertullian earlier had allowed presbyters and deacons to baptize with the authorization of the bishop, and laymen (but not lay-women) could baptize in cases of genuine necessity.[54] The *Apostolic Constitutions* said of the candidates: "Dip them in the water; and let a deacon receive the man, and a deaconess the woman, so that the conferring of this inviolable seal may take place with a becoming decency."[55] There was no reference to deaconesses instructing women after Baptism in contrast to other early documents.[56] In the baptismal rite in the *Testament of Our Lord*, the widows performed the tasks assigned to deaconesses in other church orders, such as anointing the female candidates. In addition, they covered the baptismal candidates with a veil, apparently to conceal their nudity.

> The women must be anointed by the widows who have precedence while the priest recites the prayers over them. Similarly, the widows will cover them with a veil while the bishop reads out what they must confess and what they must deny.[57]

Women ministered to other women, especially in the home. According to the *Testament of Our Lord*, deaconesses were to bring Communion to sick women.[58] The *Apostolic Constitutions* acknowledged the ministry of deaconesses in pagan households where it would have been difficult to send men.[59]

The *Apostolic Constitutions* emphasized the role of deaconesses as door-keepers: "Let the porters stand at the entries of the men, and observe them. Let the deaconesses also stand at those of the women, like shipmen. For the same description and pattern was both in the tabernacle of the testimony and in the temple of God."[60] The ordination prayer for deaconesses in Book 8 of the *Apostolic Constitutions* echoed the same role for the deaconess:

> O Eternal God, the Father of our Lord Jesus Christ, the creator of man and of woman, who didst replenish with the Spirit Miriam, and Deborah, and Anna, and Huldah; who didst not disdain that Thy only begotten Son should be born of a woman; who also in the tabernacle of the testimony, and in the temple, didst ordain women to be keepers of Thy holy gates,—do Thou now also look down upon this Thy servant, who is to be ordained to the office of a deaconess, and grant her Thy Holy Spirit, and "cleanse her from all filthiness of flesh and spirit," that she may worthily discharge the work which is committed to her to Thy glory, and the praise of Thy Christ, with whom glory and adoration be to Thee and the Holy Spirit for ever. Amen.[61]

These doorkeeper-deaconesses were ushers, keeping order, screening strangers, finding places for women, and removing the younger attendees to find space for those who were older.[62] In Book 8 of the *Apostolic Constitutions*, the subdeacons rather than the deaconesses attended the women's doors.[63]

As for deacons, the ability to sing became a positive attribute and perhaps a criterion for selection. Pope Gregory the Great forbade deacons to sing in the liturgy:

> A very reprehensible custom has arisen whereby certain cantors are chosen for the ministry of the altar and are constituted in the order of deacons for the modulation of their voice . . . . In this See ministers of the altar are not to sing, and during mass let them only read the gospel. Psalms and other readings should be recited by subdeacons or, if necessary, by those in minor orders.[64]

Despite Gregory's dictum, deacons were still chanting in church centuries later. By no later than the early sixth century, deacons blessed the paschal candle at the Easter Vigil.[65]

Besides their liturgical roles, the *Apostolic Constitutions* reveal the presence of deacons on panels with other clerics to adjudicate quarrels among Christians.[66] Deacons served as bishops' representatives to church councils and meetings. Deacons and deaconesses also continued their former functions in charity, the instruction of catechumens, and service as messengers and intermediaries between the bishop and the people.[67] The *Apostolic Constitutions* says of the women: "Let not any woman address herself to the deacon or bishop without the deaconess."[68]

Because of these duties, the church of late antiquity compared deacons to angelic orders and clothed them in white albs or tunics for their liturgical participation.[69] *The Testament of Our Lord* described the role of the deacon of late antiquity well:

> Let him be the counsellor of the whole clergy, and the mystery of the Church; who ministereth to the sick, who ministereth to the strangers, who helpeth the widows, who is the father of the orphans, who goeth about all the houses of those that are in need, lest any be in affliction or sickness or misery. Let him go about in the houses of the catechumens, so that he may confirm those who are doubting and teach those who are unlearned.

> Let him clothe those men who have departed, adorning (them); burying the strangers; guiding those who pass from their dwelling, or go into captivity. For the help of those who are in need let him notify the

Church; let him not trouble the bishop; but only on the first day of the week let him make mention about everything, so that he may know.[70]

According to the *Didascalia*, the bishop appointed a deacon, male or female.

Wherefore, O bishop, appoint thee workers of righteousness as helpers who may cooperate with thee unto salvation. Those that please thee out of all the people thou shalt choose and appoint as deacons; a man for the performance of the most things that are required, but a woman for the ministry of women.[71]

A bishop was also to ordain a deacon or a deaconess, though John Cassian (d. A.D. 450) reported an instance of a presbyter ordaining a deacon.[72] There were exceptions to the requirement to submit to the rite of ordination, a rite that involved the laying on of hands and prayer over the candidate for office: Confessors who had confessed their faith during times of persecution and survived were exempted from ordination in some church orders of the era, especially if they had suffered. This was true if the confessors were to be deacons or presbyters.[73]

One also could be degraded from office. Deacons were to be degraded for refusing to minister, praying with a degraded cleric, insulting a ruler or cleric unjustly, striking someone, indulging in dice or drinking, permitting heretics to perform sacred ceremonies, serving in the army, praying with Jews or celebrating Jewish festivals with them, not fasting, and for usury, fornication, adultery, perjury, or theft.[74] On the other hand, a deacon was not to abstain from drinking entirely, especially on feast days.[75] Deacons were to be excommunicated for refusing to explain their failures to take Communion; praying with someone who was excommunicated or with heretics; eating in a tavern when not on a trip; denying the name of Christ; or mocking a deaf, blind, or maimed person.[76] Being a slave or possessed by a devil could impede one from becoming a cleric until one was freed.[77]

The *Apostolic Constitutions* gave deaconesses and virgins precedence over widows. The minimum age for the enrolled widows was raised to 60 as in 1 Timothy.[78] Deaconesses administered charity to the widows, who were admonished not to complain at their share.[79] Deaconesses were considered clergy, subordinate to the deacons but "ordained" to their office by the laying on of hands and prayer by the bishop, though some commentators have noted that the prayer for the ordination of a deaconess asks that she be cleansed from "all filthiness of flesh and spirit," unlike the prayer for the ordination of deacons or others.[80]

The first six books of the *Apostolic Constitutions* contain an edited version of the *Didascalia*. The text in the original *Didascalia* that exhorted widows to obey bishops and deacons expanded in the *Apostolic Constitutions* to ask the widows also to obey presbyters and "deaconesses, with piety, reverence and fear," and if they did not, they were to be punished with fasting.[81] With the important role of the deaconess in the *Apostolic Constitutions*, it is no wonder that Susanna Elm says that, when the *Apostolic Constitutions* were compiled in the late fourth century, a "new function for women had emerged."[82]

The *Apostolic Constitutions* esteemed virginity over widowhood as indicated in the statement: "Let the deaconess be a pure virgin; or, at the least, a widow who has been but once married, faithful, and well esteemed."[83] When receiving Communion, deaconesses and virgins preceded widows, who came just before the children.[84] The *Apostolic Constitutions* added derogatory comments about widows concerning strife and envy among them: They gossip and gad about, seeking additional income over above what the church has allotted them.[85] Finally, the *Apostolic Constitutions* stated that "a widow is not ordained"; rather, widows of good reputation were "chosen into the order of widows."[86] Some of the responsibilities that the *Apostolic Constitutions* did not give to the widows went to the deaconesses, but the *Apostolic Constitutions* also made deaconesses dependent on deacons in a growing hierarchy of church office. The edited version of the *Didascalia* in the *Apostolic Constitutions* added passages that refer to the deaconess as subordinate to the deacon: Let the deaconess "not do or say anything without the deacon."[87]

The ordination of deaconesses, subdeacons, and lectors with the laying on of hands and the invocation of the Holy Spirit in the *Apostolic Constitutions* was a departure from the earlier *Apostolic Tradition* of Hippolytus, which denied ordination to widows, subdeacons, and lectors and did not mention deaconesses. Some scholars question the ordination in the *Apostolic Constitutions* and the validity of the document as a reflection of practice in the early church.[88] The Council of Chalcedon (A.D. 451) set a minimum age of 40 for the laying on of hands and forbade a deaconess to marry afterward.[89] There are epitaphs for deaconesses on tombs from this era.[90]

There is a difference of opinion over whether deaconesses were fully and properly ordained and, if so, to what.[91] Scholarship has moved in the direction of acknowledging the ordination of deaconesses. For example, the article on deaconesses in the 2003 *New Catholic Encyclopedia* remarks that the Council of Nicaea spoke of the ordination of deaconesses and that a

FROM CONSTANTINE TO LUTHER__61

1995 ad hoc committee of the Canon Law Society of America concluded that "women in times past were ordained deacons and [that] it would be possible for the Church to determine to do so again."[92] This is in contrast to a more negative attitude toward women in a diaconal role in the original *Catholic Encyclopedia* of 1913.[93]

The western part of the Roman Empire was generally less favorable toward deaconesses than the East, and there seems to have been fewer deaconesses in the West. The Councils of Orange (A.D. 441) and of Orleans (ca. A.D. 533) forbade the ordination of deaconesses:

> In no way whatsoever should deaconesses ever be ordained. If there already are deaconesses, they should bow their heads beneath the blessing which is given to all the people.[94]

> No longer shall the blessing of women deaconesses be given because of the weakness of the sex.[95]

Deaconesses were better received when they became part of the monastic establishment, perhaps because they were easier to supervise.

According to the *Apostolic Constitutions*, at the celebration of Communion, deaconesses followed the bishop, presbyters, deacons, subdeacons, readers, singers, and ascetics.[96] Deacons could excommunicate subdeacons, lectors, singers, and deaconesses, but these latter could not excommunicate anyone else "for they are the ministers to the deacons."[97] Surplus offerings at the time of the Eucharist were to go "to a bishop, four parts; to a presbyter, three parts, to a deacon, two parts; and to the rest of the sub-deacons, or readers, or singers, or deaconesses, one part."[98]

Overall in late antiquity, the church seems to have restricted the roles for women as compared to earlier centuries and subordinated women's offices to the male deacon. In the early days of the Christian movement, the church appeared to allow women more responsibility than later when the establishment became more formal. The roles and status of Christian women seem to have thrived better in the less hierarchical church of the centuries of persecution than in the church of the post-Constantinian era. It is true that, over time, the deaconesses fared better than the widows, who became subordinate to them, but the deaconesses themselves remained limited in what they could do within the church and in public life. Some women, powerful in their own right, avoided ordination because of the constraints the office of deaconess would place upon them. For example, when Emperor Theodosius II (A.D. 401–450) refused to dismiss his older sister, Pulcheria Augusta (A.D. 399–453), from her governing role, his wife convinced him that because Pulcheria had adopted a celibate ascetic life she should be made a deaconess, which effectively removed her from public life. The bishop of Constantinople warned the capable Pulcheria of the plot so she could avoid ordination as a deaconess.[99] Pulcheria had helped educate Theodosius II, acted as his regent, and is said to have given of her own funds to establish churches, monasteries, and shelters for the homeless.[100]

The office of deaconess, nevertheless, attracted some outstanding and wealthy individuals in the fourth through sixth centuries, most famous of whom is perhaps Olympias, friend of John Chrysostom.[101] She was born in Constantinople in the A.D. 360s and was educated in the Scriptures. Married in her teens or early 20s and widowed within two years, she refused remarriage and devoted her life and her wealth to the church. She was ordained a deaconess when she was about 30 years of age, Susanna Elm maintains, "in defiance of both ecclesiastical and, indeed, imperial regulation" as a special recognition for services rendered.[102] Olympias supported churches with gifts of land and money, cared for the sick, and corresponded with Chrysostom while he was in exile.[103]

Deaconesses also had wealthy supporters, including Melania the Younger, who was born into a wealthy family in A.D. 383 in Rome. Upon the death of her two children she went to Africa, then to Jerusalem, where she founded a hospice for pilgrims and monastic communities. One of the communities was for virgins, many of whom were deaconesses.[104] Susanna Elm allows a considerable role to these and the other female ascetics who were too wealthy to be ignored. They possessed "vast financial resources and high-ranking connections," personal relationships with leading bishops, "and immense influence."[105]

In the fourth century some additional minor offices took on some diaconal duties. For example, alongside the growing role of deacons in liturgical music, there were cantors or singers to lead the people in singing. The ancient tradition was for the congregation to sing together. The custom arose in some churches for the singer to sing half a verse of a psalm or hymn and the people to respond with the latter part. The decrees of the Council of Laodicea forbade any except the canonical singers to sing in church.[106]

The cantor was but one of a number of offices that developed within the larger churches of late antiquity. From responsibilities that deacons still held in smaller churches, other offices evolved in larger churches. For example, diaconal care of the sick and dying developed in the fourth and fifth centuries into an order of men called *parabolani* who attended the sick in some larger eastern churches, such as that of Alexandria.[107] They served in hospitals that the church established after its legalization under Constantine, but they also took on less charitable roles and were active as partisans in theological disturbances in the mid-fifth century.[108]

These institutions may have arisen out of the early tradition of the bishop putting up Christian travelers in his home.[109] But such guests had different needs. Some needed a place to stay; some required medical care; others were disabled and needed long-term sustenance and care. This tradition of hospitality might have led to the establishment of separate guest-houses as the number of guests outgrew the bishop's accommodations, those of the members of his congregation, and the local inns.[110] An example of such an establishment was the hospice for the poor founded by Basil (born ca. A.D. 330; died A.D. 377, 378, or 379),[111] bishop of Caesarea, which is in modern-day Turkey. Basil built a hospice for the poor on his family's estate that contained apartments for himself and for his guests, as well as for travelers and for the poor. Here, physicians, nurses, and servants cared for the sick. The able poor worked in trades.[112]

In larger churches after Constantine, separate institutes specialized in the care of the sick, the elderly, the poor, the disabled, lepers, pilgrims, abandoned children, orphans, recovering prostitutes, widows, and virgins. Private individuals and the state, especially in the person of the Roman emperor, endowed such institutions. Wealthy patrons offered bedside care. In the fourth century, even Empress Flaccilla, wife of Theodosius I, went into the hospitals, waited on the poor, and gave them food like a maid.[113] Fabiola (d. A.D. 399), a friend of Jerome, worked in the hospital she founded. Jerome said of her, "She was the first person to found a hospital."[114] Despite examples to the contrary, it was uncommon for upper-class women to provide direct bedside care. It was more common for them to donate funds or to endow charitable institutions.[115] The deaconess Olympias, as mentioned, distributed her immense wealth, built hospitals, and gathered women to serve therein. Donation of property was common when one entered a convent.[116]

Beginning with Constantine, the government at first seemed to help maintain the hospitals. Constantine allocated a share of the tax revenues to charitable institutions of the church, but eventually charitable institutions would come entirely under the management of the church.[117] All the benevolent institutions of a diocese and the clergy therein fell under the auspices of the bishop.[118] As Origen stated: "The church was the inn to which the Good Samaritan, Christ, could bring the needy of the world for help."[119]

As the resources of the church increased, control of charity and financial resources by the bishops could be difficult to maintain. Canons 7 and

8 of the Synod at Gangra, which was held in the middle of the fourth century, indicate difficulties in the centralization of charity and finances:

> If any one appropriates to himself the tithes of fruit (oblations) belonging to the Church, or distributes them outside the Church, that is, to those who are not ministers of the Church, without the consent of the bishop, or without being authorized by him, and will not act according to his will, let him be anathema.

> If any one gives or receives such offerings without the consent of the bishop, or one appointed by him for the administration of charities, the giver as well as the receiver shall be anathematized.[120]

The famines of the Roman Empire were now also the concern of the bishops on a larger scale. This was reflected in sermons. At the time of the severe Cappadocian famine of A.D. 368, Basil of Caesarea admonished Christians in graphic terms in a sermon titled "In Time of Famine and Drought" to repent and to feed the starving in their midst.[121] Basil was not an isolated individual. He was a member of a wealthy family known for its charitable acts, a family that included Gregory of Nyssa, Basil's brother, and their older sister, Macrina (A.D. 330–379), who supported churches with gifts of land and money, cared for the sick, and established a monastic community in her own household that included women she had found starving along the roads.[122]

A Roman law of A.D. 361 referred to the recent institution of copiates, or *fossarii*, to bury the dead.[123] The internment of the dead, especially the poor who had no one to bury them, was also the responsibility of all Christians and became one of the recognized acts of charity in the Middle Ages. Another important role in late antiquity was that of the *defensor*, the defender of the church and the poor. Sometimes defensors were members of the clergy, but by the fifth century they could be advocates at law. The Council of Chalcedon (A.D. 451) empowered them to admonish idle monks and clerks, and Emperor Justinian (A.D. 527–565) gave defensors, along with the *oeconomi*, a supervisory role over the copiates.[124]

Oeconomi were stewards of the church who, in some dioceses, were chosen by common consent from among the clergy to manage the revenues under the auspices of the bishop. This was also a function of archdeacons. *Oeconomi* provided a precautionary audit and safeguard of church property.[125] They also took care of the revenues of a church upon the death of its bishop.[126] The insertion of stewards and others between the bishop and the deacons in the service of the poor may have contributed to the decline of the diaconate. Gerhard Uhlhorn observed that the loss of responsibility to the bishop for the revenues of the church meant there was a gradual decay of the diaconate after the latter half of the fifth century.[127]

For centuries, the church had used notaries as record keepers of important events, such as the acts of the martyrs. This order grew with the need for synodical minutes, transcriptions of sermons, and legal documents; thus deacons and presbyters were sometimes notaries. Another unique order was that of interpreters, who served congregations whose members spoke several languages.[128] Many of these orders were compatible with others, and an individual did not lose an order when gaining a higher one. Therefore, deacons could also serve as notaries, stewards, defensors, catechists, or exorcists.[129]

These orders performed important functions for the church, but only sometimes were they a step toward "higher" office. Some orders, such as that of *parabolani* and copiates, remained specific to one region of the church. Other orders, such as notaries and stewards, were not peculiar to the church. A few endured throughout the decades as minor orders in the church. They eventually became stepping-stones to the priesthood and a form of apprenticeship for those from whom the church would select its higher clergy.

Apprenticeship in minor orders was facilitated by some bishops who established the custom of living together with their clergy, for example, Augustine of Hippo (A.D. 354–430). The younger members of the community, those beginning service to the church, were able to learn firsthand from the older. About the end of the fifth century, it became the custom in Spain for parents to dedicate young children to the church and to give them to the bishop to raise.[130] This became a normal channel of entry into religious life with the rise of monasteries that received child oblates.

The nature of each minor order varied with time and place. For example, the Council of Laodicea's list of those ecclesiastical orders whose members ought not enter a tavern included subdeacons, readers, singers, exorcists, and doorkeepers.[131] Acolytes were important in the West, especially in Rome, as indicated by their appearance in the mid-third century list of Cornelius, bishop of Rome. A standard early medieval authority, Isidore of Seville (ca. A.D. 560–636), includes acolytes and uses the word *psalmist* for singer or cantor.[132] Singers were absent from many lists, but one can argue that they and the readers were related because there is evidence that some readers sang. Beginning in the seventh century, the *schola cantorum* at Rome consisted mainly of lectors until children took over as singers.[133] With the passing of some of the practices of the early church, the doorkeepers lost their function in worship. The Council of Toledo in A.D. 597 assigned them the task of cleaning and lighting church buildings.[134]

A different list of minor orders was that through which Photius passed. He became patriarch of Constantinople in A.D. 858 after on successive days being made a monk, a reader, a subdeacon, a deacon, a presbyter, and finally the patriarch.[135] Although Photius was certain evidence of a candidate for high office going through several orders on successive days, this may have occurred as early as Ambrose, who was baptized on November 30, 374, *after* he had been elected bishop of Milan.[136] Acclaimed bishop by the people, some later scholars state that Ambrose passed "through the various ecclesiastical grades in eight days."[137] This is generally denied by liturgical scholars today because ecclesiastical grades were not clearly fixed during Ambrose's lifetime.

Whether or not Ambrose passed through eight successive orders in as many days or not, there is evidence that by the fourth century the church considered such progression desirable. As early as A.D. 251–253, Cyprian wrote of Pope Cornelius that

> he was not one who on a sudden attained to the episcopate; but, promoted through all the ecclesiastical offices, and having often deserved well of the Lord in divine administrations, he ascended by all the grades of religious service to the lofty summit of the Priesthood.[138]

Progression through the orders provided experience before assuming high office. The Council of Nicaea legislated against recent converts with little instruction being advanced to the presbyterate or the episcopate.[139] Nevertheless, there were numerous examples in late antiquity of promotions of new Christians to the priesthood or episcopacy. This may have been difficult to avoid because some scions of Christian families, such as Ambrose, waited to be baptized until they had completed their careers in the Roman government, where their responsibilities might require them to do something they considered incompatible with Christianity, such as sentencing someone to death. A delayed Baptism also made it possible for these individuals to be well-educated in the faith, and men who delayed their Baptism were attractive to the church to fill responsible positions because of their experience in state office.

Thomas Finn asserts that almost all the leaders of the fourth-century church were baptized as adults, though they had been raised in Christian homes. A public penitential system for grave post-baptismal sin and only one chance for reconciliation also might have discouraged catechumens from Baptism, perhaps because they felt they could not lead the kind of life that Baptism required. Whatever their reasons, catechumens kept putting off the decision to be baptized. Some, like Constantine, waited until their deathbeds, a practice that John Chrysostom decried. He felt the meaning of Baptism was lost to a person in the throes of death.[140]

Even after the tradition was established that a priest passed through the minor orders, the office of presbyter was frequently skipped by deacons who became bishops. Centuries later, some bishops continued to come directly from the diaconate, such as Hildebrand, who was archdeacon and still in the diaconal office when chosen bishop of Rome (Pope Gregory VII, r. 1073–1085).[141] There also were deacons who never became priests, such as Alcuin (ca. A.D. 735–804), the learned British advisor to Emperor Charlemagne.[142] Also under the direction of Charlemagne was Paul the Deacon, who compiled the "official" homiliary, or collection of sermons, of the Carolingian revival. This book contained homilies from the Venerable Bede of England and Gregory the Great, among others.[143] There was at least one cleric of the ninth century who is known historically by the title of deacon, though he became bishop of Nicaea: Ignatios the Deacon of the Great Church of Constantinople.[144] A century earlier, it was a deacon of that church who wrote one of the most important sources on Byzantine iconoclasm: *Life of Stephen the Younger*.[145] The most famous librarian of the Benedictine monastery at Monte Cassino in Italy in the twelfth century was Peter the Deacon.[146] Although there were deacons in important roles, a hierarchy of clerical office was growing in which deacons ranked below bishops and presbyters.

Ultimately, an orderly progression in office, the ecclesiastical *cursus honorum*, triumphed in the West. Some scholars would say this happened as early as the fourth or fifth century.[147] Many would date it later, especially because the order of the offices varied for a long time, even in the same author, for example, Isidore of Seville.[148] Barbarian invasions of the fifth century had destroyed the imperial schools, and bishops needed to recruit their clergy as boys, some as young as 7 years old, who lived with them and were educated by them.[149] An episcopal family, or *familia*, was composed of large numbers of clergy in minor orders and a smaller number of subdeacons, deacons, and presbyters. In a small diocese, the episcopal family could be the entire clergy of the bishop's see, serving his cathedral and outlying chapels. As a boy grew up, he would move up through the grades of clergy, spending ten years or more in the diaconate. The classical eight grades came to be doorkeeper, lector, exorcist, acolyte, subdeacon, deacon, presbyter, and bishop.[150] Of course, not everyone became a bishop, and not all deacons became presbyters.

Deacons

The development of a fixed progression through the minor orders to the priesthood or episcopacy worked to the detriment of the deacon, who was lower than the priest. The diaconate gradually became a rung on the ladder toward the priesthood. Once that happened, there were few reasons for a cleric to remain a lifelong deacon unless he wanted to retain his position as an archdeacon. Pope Gregory supported the efforts of an archdeacon of Salona to avoid being "forced by his bishop to be advanced against his will, in a way contrary to custom, to a higher order," namely, the priesthood.[151] Much later, in the thirteenth century, it was perhaps out of humility that Francis of Assisi never became a priest. Some scholars presume that he was a deacon from a reference to him as a Levite made by his earliest biographer, Thomas of Celano.[152] There is no mention of the ordination of Francis as a deacon, however. In his last testament, Francis said of priests:

> The Lord gave me and still gives me such faith in priests who live according to the manner of the holy Roman Church because of their order, that if they were to persecute me, I would [still] have recourse to them. And if I possessed as much wisdom as Solomon had and I came upon pitiable priests of this world, I would not preach contrary to their will in the parishes in which they live. And I desire to fear, love, and honor them and all others as my masters. And I do not wish to consider sin in them because I discern the Son of God in them and they are my masters.[153]

Centuries before Francis, John Chrysostom, in his eleventh homily on 1 Timothy, assumed a progression beyond the diaconate:

> "They that use the office of a Deacon well, purchase to themselves a good degree," that is advancement, "and much boldness in the faith of Jesus Christ"; as if he would say, that those who have been found vigilant in the lower degree will soon ascend to the higher.[154]

Esteeming deacons lower than presbyters was reinforced by ordination prayers for deacons such as that in the *Apostolic Constitutions*: "O God Almighty . . . Do Thou render him worthy to discharge acceptably the ministration of a deacon, steadily, unblamably, and without reproof, that thereby he may attain an higher degree."[155] The *Statuta Ecclesiae Antiquae*, a collection of church rules from approximately A.D. 480, stated that "the deacon should acknowledge himself minister of the presbyter as well as the bishop."[156]

As assistants to bishops, deacons remained prominent in worship and social welfare in the fourth and fifth centuries, though in many ways deacons were losing power to presbyters at this time, even losing some of their responsibilities in poor relief. In larger churches of the eastern Roman Empire, such as that of Constantinople, deacons grew in numbers, but in churches modeled on Rome, which limited the number of deacons to seven, their influence was increased because there were fewer deacons than presbyters. That this caused some friction is evident from the canons of the councils of the church and from letters of church leaders of late antiquity, such as Jerome. The Council of Nicaea decreed that deacons "keep within their proper bounds, knowing that they are the ministers of the bishop and inferior to the presbyters."[157] The council further forbade deacons from sitting with presbyters. Jerome called it madness to place deacons before presbyters and criticized Rome for allowing deacons to recommend presbyters for ordination.[158] Jerome said of a presbyter that "although he may be less highly paid than a deacon, he is superior to him in virtue of his priesthood."[159]

There was cause for complaints against the presumptions of deacons. At Rome a deacon who was disappointed in not being elected bishop of Rome fomented a schism:

> A certain Ursinus, a deacon of that church, had been nominated among others when the election of a bishop took place: as Damasus was preferred, this Ursinus, unable to bear the disappointment of his hopes, held schismatic assemblies apart from the church, and even induced certain bishops of little distinction to ordain him in secret.[160]

Deacons became noted teachers and partisans on both sides of theological issues, the most enduring of which was the fourth-century debate over the relationship of God the Father (God the Creator) to God the Son. A key figure in this debate was the archdeacon Athanasius (A.D. 300–373). He and his party affirmed that God the Son and God the Father had existed through all eternity. The Arians, on the other hand, held that God the Son was *not* coeternal with God the Father. The position of Athanasius was recognized as orthodox and is represented in the Nicene Creed, which Christian churches recognize today, but the conflict between the two parties raged throughout the fourth century and affected all levels of the church.

The Arian Controversy is pertinent to social welfare in the church because of the competition it unleashed between the two parties in the dispute. The controversy between the Arians and the orthodox was not merely a matter of theological conviction. Social welfare was important to both sides in the quarrel because the provision of charity and medical care could attract adherents. In *The Birth of the Hospital in the Byzantine Empire*,

Timothy Miller asserts that the "Arian dispute played a central role in stimulating the foundation of philanthropic institutions."[161] He asserts that before the fourth century there were no public institutions offering medical care to the sick, and by the end of the fourth century, there were such institutions in the eastern end of the Roman Empire, which would later be known as the Byzantine Empire, especially after the fall of Rome and of the western Roman Empire in the fifth century. For example, in A.D. 357, an Arian was appointed bishop of Alexandria, the capital of Egypt. He constructed hospitals for the poor and organized a free burial service.[162]

It is difficult to prove that the actions of the Arian bishop were motivated by the desire to win adherents to his position because he did not say so. However, in the sixth century, the Monophysites were more explicit in acknowledging that conspicuous philanthropic projects were used to gain adherents. Monophysites hold that Christ has one nature, not two, a position in contradiction to the Council of Chalcedon (A.D. 451), which affirmed that Christ had two natures, human and divine. When the Monophysites organized a church separate from the orthodox church in the eastern end of the Roman Empire, their patriarch, Paul of Antioch, established institutions called *diakoniai* to help the poor and sick in Constantinople and other cities.[163]

Among the most famous of the deacons involved in the fourth-century Arian Controversy was Aetius (or Aetios) of Antioch. Aetius has been considered the father of Neo-Arianism. He was an adolescent at the time of the Council of Nicaea (A.D. 325); therefore, he was not a member of the first generation of Arians. Born in approximately A.D. 313, Aetius initially worked as a goldsmith like his father. He also acquired a medical and theological education before being selected as a deacon by his former mentor and then bishop of Antioch, Leontius.[164] Around A.D. 346–347, Aetius became a celebrated teacher in Antioch, and he also apparently offered free medical care to the poor.[165] However, he appears to have been forced to give up diaconal duties in Antioch because of his theological beliefs.[166] From approximately A.D. 348 to A.D. 351, Aetius taught in Alexandria, Egypt, a center of learning, and in approximately A.D. 352, he became the personal teacher of Gallus Caesar, the ruler of the eastern Roman Empire, who was enthralled with Aetius.[167] Influence over the politically powerful, such as Gallus Caesar, prolonged the life of Arianism in the church. Some of the students of Aetius became influential bishops, but he was later exiled and deposed from the diaconate by the Council of Constantinople in January 360.[168] Upon his appointment to a bishopric in A.D. 360, Eumonius, a student of Aetius who shared the role of spokesperson for Neo-Arianism, agitated to rescue Aetius, but Eumonius himself was later exiled.[169]

According to church orders of late antiquity and the early Middle Ages, which varied over time and space, deacons were ordained at 25 years of age and presbyters at 30 years of age. This age difference may have made it seem natural to think of deacons as junior.[170] As it became the custom for presbyters to spend years in the diaconate, it was logistically impossible to limit the number of deacons in major cities to seven and still train enough priests. Yet the fifth-century *Testament of Our Lord* stated that there should be seven deacons: "In the church let there be twelve presbyters, seven deacons, fourteen subdeacons, thirteen widows who sit in front . . . ."[171] Nevertheless, one author estimates that by A.D. 520 Rome had a hundred deacons. This number represented the deacons of the seven regions of the city, as well as deacons associated with the stational churches and the tombs of the martyrs.[172] On March 16, 535, Emperor Justinian announced his intention to cut back, for economic reasons, the number of clerics in the great church at Constantinople to no more than sixty priests, one hundred male deacons, forty female deacons, ninety subdeacons, one hundred and ten lectors, and twenty-five cantors.[173]

The archdeacon continued to be influential as the bishop's chief assistant at the altar and in administration, taking over some of the weightier responsibilities of ordinary deacons. In turn, stewards, the *oecomoni*, had taken on some financial responsibilities so ordinary deacons were being moved out of property management and social welfare administration. The movement of deacons out of charity had progressed so far that by A.D. 692 the Council in Trullo commented that Stephen and the six others who served the poor widows in Acts 6 were unlike seventh-century deacons "who served at the Mysteries."[174]

Archdeacons sometimes represented the bishop in the governmental affairs of the church and had jurisdiction that did not reflect their order but exceeded it. They had the power to appoint presbyters and others and were in excellent position to become bishops. For example, Athanasius was an archdeacon at the Council of Nicaea (A.D. 325). Five months later, the bishop of Alexandria died and Athanasius became bishop.[175] Archdeacons had jurisdiction over other deacons and the minor orders in the West, though not in the East, and they assisted in the ordinations of candidates for minor orders.[176] Pope Leo I (A.D. 440–461) appeared to consider archdeacons superior to presbyters, as evidenced by his letter to Anatolius of Constantinople reprimanding him "for degrading his archdeacon Aetius by making him a presbyter."[177]

Celibacy

In the fourth century, the church moved, step by step, in the direction of requesting celibacy of its clergy, a practice it had long required of its widows. The first step was to ask men to abstain from sex because of their responsibilities at the altar, even if they were married. The Council of Elvira (ca. A.D. 305), a city near Granada, Spain, ordered bishops, presbyters, and deacons to forego conjugal relations:

> Bishops, presbyters and deacons—indeed, all clerics who have place in the ministry [of the altar]—shall abstain from their wives and shall not beget children—this is a total prohibition: whoever does so, let him forfeit his rank among the clergy.[178]

The Council in Ancyra (A.D. 314) allowed deacons to marry only if they informed their bishop before ordination:

> As many as are being ordained deacons if at the time of ordination they have made a declaration and stated that they must marry and cannot remain celibate, such persons, should they marry thereafter can remain in their office, as the bishop had granted them the right to marry at their ordination. But if any held their peace and accepted celibacy at their ordination, and afterwards marry, such persons shall cease from their ministry.[179]

In fairness to women, however, the *Canons of the Apostles* forbade bishops, priests, and deacons who were already married from casting off a wife "under pretense of piety." If they did so, they were to be excommunicated; if they persisted, they were to be degraded.[180] If their wives died, however, clergy were to remain single. The church of late antiquity tried to regulate the kind of woman that a cleric could marry. In the *Apostolic Constitutions* a man who had married an actress, widow, slave, prostitute, niece, divorced woman, or sister of a former wife was not to become a deacon, priest, or bishop.[181]

As the church moved toward tighter rules for its clergy, it appeared at first to be more concerned with sexual continence in those who served at the altar than with whether or not they were married. Pope Leo I (A.D. 440–461) allowed married men to live with their wives after ordination but without having sexual intercourse.[182] He extended to subdeacons this obligation of continence.[183] This arrangement did not work for many clerical couples, and they continued to have children. Later, the church in the western Roman Empire expected couples to separate at the husband's ordination. Their wives, known as *presbyterissae* (*presbyterae*) or *diaconissae* (*dia-*

conae), received a special blessing, wore distinctive garb, and were not to remarry.[184]

The church in the eastern Roman Empire took a different course. Although it prohibited marriage after ordination, it allowed priests, deacons, and subdeacons who already were married to remain with their wives and to continue normal sexual relations.[185] Only bishops were obliged to separate from their wives. The emerging Orthodox church of the East chose bishops from among celibate monks.

As for celibate women, from early on there had been young women who chose to become dedicated virgins. Initially they remained in their own homes and with their own families; later, they lived communally. As we have seen, Tertullian (died ca. A.D. 225) had complained about a virgin of less than 20 years of age being included among the widows.[186] Eventually, expectations of celibacy were extended to include deaconesses. By the sixth century, Justinian's *Novellas* stated that "deaconesses who violate their vow of chastity are to lose their ecclesiastical ministry and are to spend the remainder of their lives in a monastery."[187] Feelings that menstruating women were unclean may have made people uncomfortable with women coming close to the altar.[188]

James Barnett has argued that including deacons in the increasing restraints on clerical sexuality in the western Roman Empire encouraged them to become priests because remaining as a deacon did not gain them the right to a wife.[189] Whatever the rules, many clergy continued to live with women. In the eleventh century, Pope Gregory VII attempted to enforce celibacy, but it was not until the Second Lateran Council (1139) that marriages of subdeacons, deacons, and priests were declared invalid. Despite this rule, many parish priests still lived with women and had families up until the time of the Protestant Reformation. The bishops at the Council of Trent (1545–1563) reinforced clerical celibacy, but they recognized that it was not a positive divine law. It could be changed. Long before Trent, an institution had developed and matured that was more successful at enforcing celibacy. This was monasticism.

MONASTICISM

Monasticism developed within the expanding church of the third and fourth centuries. People withdrew from society for many reasons, including escape from a failing society in the third century.[190] Some Christians left organized churches and moved to the desert for prayer and meditation. They became hermits or ascetics, especially in Egypt and Syria. The most famous of these was Anthony (A.D. 251–356), the renowned ascetic and "Desert Father" about whom Athanasius (A.D. 300–373) wrote a biography. There also were "desert mothers," women who moved to the desert and led lives similar to the men. Some ascetics valued stability and lived in one place; others wandered about, sometimes on pilgrimage[191] and sometimes as a way of life.[192] Anthony attracted laypeople-disciples, as did other ascetics. Some of these disciples came together and lived a common life.

With toleration of Christianity in the fourth century, the threat of martyrdom declined. Christians no longer risked life and property for their beliefs. As danger decreased, insincere members crept into the church. Some Christians, especially dedicated virgins, continued to practice asceticism in their homes and families as they had done previously in an attempt to live a better Christian life. Other virgins lived together communally. Still other dedicated virgins cohabited with male members of the clergy in pseudo-marriages without having sex, or so it is presumed. The women in these pseudo-marriages took care of the household. The men provided financial support. The church did not approve of this cohabitation, but it had a great deal of practical appeal to women without money and clerics without wives or housekeepers.[193] There were virgins of both Arian and orthodox persuasion.[194]

Some ascetics moved to the desert or attempted to separate themselves in other ways, which was not easy to do in late antiquity. Like the oracles of the ancient world, "holy men" were sought after for advice, consolation, justice, and help. An extreme example was Simeon the Stylite, who was born in the late fourth century in Syria, where the climate made it possible to live outdoors. After Simeon was converted, he attempted a communal life of austerity and prayer, but he spent the last years of his life alone and approximately 60 feet off the ground, standing on a 6-foot-square platform on top of a pillar. There he alternately stood and prostrated himself until his death in A.D. 459. Still Simeon was not completely alone. Both the prosperous and the needy flocked to his pillar, seeking advice and help. Simeon inspired those who were able to aid their neighbors, thus he enabled social welfare and Christian charity.[195] On at least one occasion, he enlisted the help of a deacon.[196]

Well before Simeon ascended his pillar, a movement toward communal monasticism had begun. Pachomius, a soldier (A.D. 292–346), had been impressed by the kindness of Christians toward soldiers in Thebes. After discharge, Pachomius was baptized and began to share his food with the poor and with strangers. Acquiring a following, Pachomius encouraged communal religious life because the solitary way could make the commandment to active charity difficult. He founded ascetic communities for men and, when his sister, Maria, approached him, for women as well. Upon his death, Pachomius left behind nine monasteries and several thousand adherents.[197] A generation later, Basil, bishop of Caesarea, (A.D. 370–379), established monastic rules for the eastern Roman Empire that encouraged service to the community, including the foundation and staffing of schools and hospitals by monks.[198]

From the East, monasticism spread to the western Roman Empire. Leaders of the church such as Augustine gathered around themselves communities of celibates and encouraged widows such as Proba and her daughter-in-law, Juliana, in prayer and asceticism.[199] Some widows lived in community; some lived in communities with virgins. Other widows lived at home.[200] In Rome, wealthy widows Albina, Marcellina, and Paula (d. A.D. 404) formed a community of women close to Jerome. Leaving behind her young son, Toxatius, Paula and her daughter, Eustochium, followed Jerome to Palestine (A.D. 386), where they founded a monastic community at Bethlehem.[201]

Monastic communities were active in social welfare, providing hospitality, feeding the hungry, and nursing the sick. Already in the fourth century, Basil's community fulfilled such functions in the eastern Roman Empire. In the western Roman Empire, the rule of Benedict (ca. A.D. 480–550), of the monastery of Monte Cassino in the south of Italy, eventually dominated for both men and women, though monks appear initially to have been greater in number.

In the fourth century, the Order of Virgins grew. Bishops formally consecrated professed virgins, who wore special clothing. By the time of the *Apostolic Constitutions*, virgins superseded widows. A cross between the two, by modern standards, was the wealthy monastic founder Macrina (A.D. 327–379), whose intended spouse had died when she was 12 years old. She considered it to be a marriage and refused other suitors.[202] Gradually what was left of the Order of Widows was absorbed into the monastic movement.[203]

In general, in the eastern part of the Roman Empire, deaconesses rather than widows eventually formed the core of communities of celibate women and often headed them. A modern female deacon-scholar, Sister Teresa (Joan White) of the London community of female deacons[204] (originally deaconesses) of St. Andrew, identified the Widow Publia of the mid-fourth century as the first recorded example of a female deacon heading a community of celibate women. According to Sister Teresa, the Widow Publia housed young women who had vowed virginity, as mentioned by

Theodoret, and continually sang praises to God. In effect, Publia was a female deacon or deaconess in charge of consecrated virgins, which Sister Teresa calls the first stage of the development of the Deacon Abbess because Publia's role as deacon was more important than her role as abbess: She was a deacon first and an abbess second. In effect, Publia was a Deacon (Abbess).[205]

The second stage in this development was that of the hyphenated Deacon-Abbess, whose status as an abbess over a group of women was almost as significant as her status as a female deacon. Some of these communities of women grew out of households. Although some deaconesses still lived at home, others were beginning to live in community, sometimes because they had no families and sometimes because their families were not receptive to their religious convictions or role.[206] As household groupings of consecrated virgins came together or expanded into monasteries of a more organized nature, it came to be taken for granted that they would be headed by female deacons. Sister Teresa places Macrina in this evolution, though scholars question whether Macrina was a deaconess.[207] Whether Macrina was a deaconess or not, her brother, Gregory, bishop of Nyssa, records that a deaconess named Lampadion, who was in charge of a group of women, informed him of his sister's decisions about her burial. Thus Lampadion reveals that there were groupings of women headed by deaconesses at the time of Macrina.[208] A more certain example of a Deacon-Abbess is John Chrysostom's acquaintance Olympias, who, by the time Chrysostom became bishop of Constantinople in A.D. 398, already had founded a convent next to the city's cathedral. The convent, called the *Olympiados*, was for female deacons and virgins. As many as 250 women lived there.[209]

The third stage in the development of the Deacon Abbess occurred when the abbess had to be a female deacon.[210] By the middle of the ninth century, it was expected that an abbess must first be ordained a deacon.[211] The *Pontificale Romano-Germanicum* of the tenth century includes rites for the ordination of deaconesses.[212]

The fourth and final stage of the evolution of the Deacon Abbess was when the abbess was elected from among her sister nuns because of her qualities of leadership and after the election was ordained a deacon. There was no emphasis on her diaconate, however. That role had been eclipsed. She was, in effect, an Abbess-(Deacon).[213]

Although Sister Teresa's stages in the evolution of the female deacon as abbess overlap and vary in diverse parts of the Roman Empire, the point is that the female deacon rose to prominence within monastic communities and, over time, was eclipsed. Gradually, the Order of Deaconesses was absorbed into the monastic movement in both the East and West. As this happened, abbesses sometimes retained liturgical roles in their communities that would not ordinarily have been theirs, such as reading the Epistle and Gospel, wearing the diaconal stole, taking the Eucharist to sick women, and perhaps anointing the sick.[214] In a letter of 1210 to the Bishop of Burgos and the Abbot of Morimundo, Pope Innocent III called it "incongruous and absurd, that abbesses bless their own nuns, hear their confessions of sins, and reading the Gospel presume to preach publicly." He ordered this prevented, "lest this be done by others."[215] Some later authors also considered these activities to be an abuse of the role of the abbess.[216]

WELFARE AND EDUCATION
AFTER THE FALL OF ROME

With the barbarian invasions of the fifth century and the fall of Rome in the West (A.D. 476), many government services collapsed or fell into the hands of the bishop of Rome, who at times negotiated with the barbarians himself for lack of an effective state. The popes were left with responsibility for Roman social welfare and education, and some of them rose magnificently to the task. Gregory the Great, the genius administrator, managed the possessions of the church as the patrimony of the poor in a time when there was no government in the West capable of meeting the needs of the people as effectively. On his way to the papacy, Gregory was trained as one of the seven deacons of Rome, each of whom was charged with administering a region of the city. He felt so responsible for the welfare of those in the city that he considered himself the murderer of a man who had died of starvation in Rome.[217]

In outlying parts of the Roman Empire, bureaucracy collapsed with the invasions and the dissolution of the empire. In many areas, it would be centuries before social services and education reemerged with the building of monasteries and the establishment of parishes. After the collapse of Roman institutions, monastic schools and libraries became primary centers of learning in Europe. Those monasteries located in the country could be the only recourse for a weary traveler who needed a night's lodging. Those monasteries situated in urban areas served the press of people at their door. By the late Merovingian period in the West, bishops were involved in the development of social institutions; indeed, they were governing some cities.[218] Beginning at least in the seventh century, social welfare centers in Rome known as deaconries distributed food and cared for the poor. There is mention of deaconries in Ravenna and Naples in the letters of Pope

Gregory the Great.[219] Their name reflected their diaconal service functions, not necessarily their staff, which in Rome consisted of monks. The deaconries probably were initially subject to monasteries. The popes supported them, and eventually the ecclesiastical administrative machinery absorbed them. The deaconries took over the administration of the church's charities, but direct contact with the poor at the deaconries was retained for a while by the monks, presumably from nearby monasteries.[220] Authorities vary in the extent to which they credit the deaconries with involvement with the poor and for how long this activity endured.[221]

Monks were performing some of the social welfare functions that deacons once had held. This trend would continue with the foundation of monastic orders and communities of men and women in the Middle Ages. Already in the first half of the seventh century, the *Maison Dieu*, or "House of God," of Paris, the precursor to the hospital or *Hôtel Dieu*, began as a refuge and nursing home. A community of religious women was in charge. From the hospital attendants in the Middle Ages emerged the orders that ministered to the sick and the poor. On Maundy Thursdays two hundred years later, the priests of Notre Dame began a custom of washing the feet of the poor, but the welfare institutions of Paris were not necessarily replicated everywhere.[222] For example, in England it would be difficult to prove the existence of freestanding independent hospitals until after the Norman conquest of 1066. Although the Romans had brought military hospitals to England as early as A.D. 83–86, they did not survive the end of Roman rule.[223]

A window of light in education and letters during the Carolingian Renaissance of Charlemagne (king of the Franks with his brother A.D. 768, alone A.D. 771, Holy Roman emperor A.D. 800–814) closed with the Viking invasions of the ninth and tenth centuries. Europe retreated into feudalism and self-contained manors. The absence of government services was such that the building of a bridge was an act of Christian charity undertaken by individuals, monasteries, or, later, people working together in brotherhoods.[224]

THE MEDIEVAL PERIOD

Hospitals such as the *Hôtel Dieu* sprang up in many European cities as the continent emerged from the devastation of the waves of barbarian, Viking, and Magyar invasions that preoccupied Europe from the late Roman Empire to the tenth century. Beginning in 1096, the Crusades were an impetus to the foundation of hospitals through increased contact with the Byzantine East and with the Islamic world.[225]

Medieval hospitals provided for both the religious and the physical needs of the poor. They fed the poor and provided medical and nursing care to address the physical needs, and the hospitals provided priests, the Mass, confession, last rites for the dying, and Christian burial to meet the spiritual needs.[226] In western Europe, however, hospitals provided less access to physicians than those of the Byzantine Empire. According to Michel Mollat, "the hospitals provided more shelter than treatment," and even that shelter was limited.[227] Conditions in the 400-bed *Hôtel Dieu* of Paris were inadequate in the late Middle Ages and early modern period: several patients to a bed, outbreaks of scurvy because of insufficient fruits and vegetables, and at least one instance of patients freezing their noses because of inadequate heating.[228] By 1328, the population of Paris was estimated at more than two hundred thousand with approximately sixty hospitals to serve the residents.[229]

There were a variety of benefactors for these institutions, especially with the surge in hospital foundations in the twelfth and thirteenth centuries established by kings, feudal lords, bishops, guilds, merchants, and municipalities.[230] Pope Innocent III (1198–1216) took seriously his episcopal responsibilities for the poor.[231] He ordered a 300-bed hospital built in Rome that could feed a thousand poor daily. The recently founded religious of the Holy Spirit took charge. In time its members toured the city weekly to bring in the sick. The hospital maintained rooms for nobles and for women in childbirth, though those who were able generally preferred to give birth or die at home. The members also fed the needy whom they did not house, as did other hospitals of the era.[232]

In the Middle Ages and early modern times, many hospitals were all-purpose welfare institutions, closer to the original sense of "hospice." They housed indiscriminately in the same building the disabled, the aged, orphans, the sick, and travelers. Hospitals offered little, if any, contact with physicians or may have restricted the care of physicians to a select few, such as the staff and wealthier patients.[233] Some hospitals refused the sick or those with particular illnesses or conditions, such as pregnant women, epileptics, people with contagious diseases, or the mentally ill. An exception to this practice was the hospital of St. Mary of Bethlehem in London, more popularly known as Bedlam, which in 1377 began to specialize in providing care for the insane.[234] To that end, St. Mary's acquired manacles, chains, locks, and stocks to restrain those with mental illnesses.[235] Also some hospitals specialized in contagious diseases such as leprosy (technically Hansen's disease) or the plague. Some plague victims were housed in hospitals for lepers, both being a group that medieval society wanted to exclude.[236] Some institutions specialized in a particular group of people, such as the blind or women rescued from prostitution or members of a particular guild. The blind received specialized hospitals in the thirteenth and fourteenth centuries.[237] Brian Pullan maintains that beginning in the thirteenth century in western Europe hospitals existed that were concerned at least partially with foundlings (abandoned children of unknown parentage).[238] Aristocrats used hospitals as retirement homes for their servants.

In 1096 the Crusades to recover the Holy Land from the Muslims began, and within the next hundred years, orders of knights were created that pledged to protect pilgrims. Of these, the Knights of St. John were named after the Hospital of St. John the Baptist in Jerusalem, which was built in 1063 as a hospice for pilgrims. This hospital was staffed with two doctors and two surgeons, more physicians than European hospitals of the period. In 1310 the center of the Knights of St. John shifted to Rhodes before moving again in 1530 to Malta.[239] The Hospitallers, as the knights were called, also founded hospitals in Europe or took over the supervision of hospitals that already had been organized. They made popular the statement: "Our lords, the poor, our lords, the sick."[240] The London headquarters of the Knights of St. John was attacked during the Peasant's Revolt of 1381 when the prior of the order, Robert of Hales, who was also treasurer of England, was held responsible for the hated poll tax that had set off the revolt. The Knights of St. John continue work with the world's poor to the present day.[241] More specialized than the Hospitallers, the Knights of St. Lazarus worked with lepers.

With the advent of peace in the eleventh century, the revival of trade, and a money economy, towns grew again. During the latter half of the twelfth century, England witnessed a crescendo in the foundation of hospitals, so by the year 1200, England had approximately 252 hospitals. In 1530, on the eve of the English Reformation, England had more than twice as many hospitals, approximately 585, though some of these were small.[242] Before the need for sophisticated modern medical equipment, hospitals sometimes proliferated rather than grew in size.

In Europe, medieval hospitals were considered religious institutions, which was reflected in the name *Maison Dieu* ("House of God"). Similar to the monastic model, hospitals had "rules" that governed the organization and daily life of staff and patients. A popular "rule" adopted by hospitals was that of St. Augustine because it was flexible enough to allow staff to do tasks in the outside world.[243] To enter a hospital was to submit to limitations.

Residents were housed in dormitories. In some hospitals, staff and patients wore distinctive dress. Worship was central to hospital life, and patients and staff were expected to participate. Hospitals had chapels, some of which even functioned as parish churches in medieval times.[244] So close was hospital life to monastic life that it is no wonder that "lay" staff evolved into religious orders over time.

Some hospital foundations fed or housed students, and some were converted into schools.[245] Educational institutions revived in the medieval period, and new forms of schools evolved beyond the monastic model. For example, cathedral schools rose to prominence. Pope Alexander III (1159–1191) promulgated a canon in the Third Lateran Council of 1179 providing a teacher for every cathedral:

> Since the Church of God, like a devoted mother, is bound to provide lest the poor who cannot be helped by the labors of their parents should lose the opportunity of studying and profiting thereby, a suitable benefice is to be provided in each cathedral church for a master who shall give free instruction to the clerics of the church and to poor scholars.[246]

In the Fourth Lateran Council of 1212, Pope Innocent III (1198–1216) extended the provision of a master providing free instruction to poor students to every church that could afford one.[247] In the late twelfth and thirteenth centuries, universities developed.

The trade with the Middle East encouraged by the Crusades enhanced the growth of European cities. They were poorly served by rural monasteries such as those of the Cistercians, a reforming offshoot of the Benedictine Order. Benedict himself had insisted that strangers and the poor be received in his monastery as if they were Christ, and monasteries had built charity into monastic life, for example, by collecting the share of a fasting monk's food for the poor.[248] Monasteries also had almoners in charge of collecting and distributing alms, clothing, and gifts to the poor.[249] Some monks visited the sick and poor in their homes, such as the monks of Cluny, France, a monastery founded in the tenth century.[250] Brenda Bolton claims, however, that by the twelfth century the practice of the contemplative life had taken precedence for many in monastic orders, and the care of the poor had far too often degenerated into symbolic acts.[251] Some monasteries maintained houses outside their gates for the poor, the sick, and lepers, but others limited their charity to a few symbolic gifts at specific times in the liturgical year, such as during Holy Week. Other historians of poverty, such as Michel Mollat, would emphasize the thirteenth century as the one in which there was a noticeable decline in monastic charity: "The leading abbeys devoted no more than two to five per cent [*sic*] of their income to distributions and hospitality."[252]

By the thirteenth century, others were available to help the poor. Princes had their almoners who were in charge of handing out royal alms. The princely almoners have been considered among the first "secular" charitable institutions, though even these almoners were typically clerics.[253] The church continued to be active in charity on some level. The wave of new monasteries in isolated locations, especially the Carthusian and Cistercian monasteries, had subsided, and a new form of religious life was emerging in the cities: friars dedicated to preaching, teaching, and serving the poor in urban areas. The friars were mendicants who were poor and willing to beg to survive. Many of them were followers of Dominic (born between 1171 and 1173 and died in 1221) and Francis (1181 or 1182 to 1226). Both male and female followers of these men continue into modern times as Dominicans, Franciscans, and Poor Clares. The medieval church considered the voluntary poverty and begging of the Dominicans and Franciscans to be acts of merit. Laymen and laywomen joined the third orders attached to these groups of friars. At the other end of the spectrum of wealth in the church, the pope, residing in Avignon in the fourteenth century, created a department for paupers in the papal Curia.[254]

Laypeople also participated in helping the poor through "poor tables," or charity funds, at the parish level. In the Holy Roman Empire and in the Low Countries (modern Belgium and the Netherlands), the expression referred to an actual table near the door of the church that was used to make distributions.[255] Laypeople also participated with clergy in confraternities: quasi-religious, quasi-social societies often dedicated to patron saints. On the patron saint's special day, the confraternity would sponsor religious processions and celebrations. Members of the confraternity looked to one another for mutual help, especially in times of illness or death. Confraternities also supported larger charitable projects beyond their own membership, such as the founding and staffing of hospitals, the provision of bread for the poor, and even the building of bridges, but hospitals also were sometimes responsible for maintaining bridges.[256]

Some confraternities were local, specializing in the welfare needs of a specific region or in some aspect of those needs, such as the endowment of dowries for poor women of the area or the redemption of prostitutes. Other confraternities were more comprehensive in their care of the poor or spread into many cities or regions, performing similar services wherever they established themselves. For example, the *Misericordia* of Florence, of uncertain thirteenth- or fourteenth-century origins, aided the sick who had been deserted by their relatives and buried the dead. By popular demand, the *Misericordia* reorganized in 1475 when a deserted corpse lay in the street for some time. They are still active in Italian cities, providing emergency and ambulance service.[257]

Although there had been confraternities in Europe before the mendicant orders, Franciscan and Dominican friars promoted them and often were members and chaplains. The fourteenth and fifteenth centuries witnessed tremendous growth in the confraternity movement. As confraternities grew, they became specialized. Some confraternities even organized exclusively for the young, that is, for young men generally between 13 and 24 years of age. Such youth confraternities originated in early fifteenth-century Florence as a youth movement.[258] Likewise, Franciscans were active in Italy in the promotion of a new type of credit institution for the poor, the *Monti di Pietà*. Funded essentially by the wealthy faithful, these institutions were designed to give the poor a way to borrow cheaply to tide themselves over during periods of famine and unemployment.[259] In 1221 Franciscans also were the first to found an affiliate, or "third order," specifically for the laity who could not join the order. This was "a means of spiritual perfection," as one recent author put it.[260] Augustinians followed with a third order in 1400, Dominicans in 1406, Servites in 1424, and Carmelites in 1425. The mendicant orders exerted influence over the laity through their tertiaries, as third orders were called, as they did through confraternities. Different orders promoted different forms of devotion. The Dominicans promoted the rosary, for example.[261]

Medieval theology addressed charity. Medieval Christians were enjoined to give from their surplus, which was defined as anything that was not a necessity.[262] The medieval church taught that a Christian who ignored a poor person refused Christ. Peter Damian reminded the people of the eleventh century that "a Christian has no right to eat that which he has denied Christ."[263] The enumeration of the works of mercy in the twelfth or thirteenth centuries guided the medieval Christian to

> visit the sick, refresh the thirsty, feed the hungry, redeem the prisoner, clothe the naked, take the stranger in, bury the dead, counsel the perplexed, correct the sinner, comfort . . . [the] sad, forgive the offender, bear with . . . [the] burdensome, and pray for all.[264]

The order of charity was to be "first ourselves, then our parents, then our relatives, then the neighbors, then the strangers, and finally, the enemies."[265]

Many acts of charity continued regularly throughout the year, but others, even bread handouts, increased at special times in the church calendar, such as during Holy Week. This tendency to focus charity on religious days, together with a proliferation of uncoordinated small charitable institutions of marginal size, led later critics to consider medieval poor relief to be haphazard, disorganized, and based on the whims of individual donors. A preference for private almsgiving reinforced this caricature of medieval charity as indiscriminate. In the Middle Ages, charity was highly personal, often a handout to a beggar in the street. Individual donors hoped to see the face of Christ in the poor. This may have encouraged them to give directly to the needy rather than to channel donations through institutions or third parties. Even funds dispensed by rulers were considered the personal alms of the king, not the charity of the state.[266] Princes had their own almoners.

Two factors worked to prevent haphazard distribution of charity within a system of individualized donations in the medieval period: canon law and secular government. Neither of these developed fully until the barbarian and Viking threats subsided.

Canon Law and Parish Poor Relief

Medieval law concerning poverty was a branch of canon, or church, law, which until the twelfth century was an accumulation of opinions of church fathers such as Augustine and Jerome, canons of general and local councils, and papal decrees. About 1140, Gratian, a monk of Bologna, systematized these in the *Decretum*. Periodically thereafter, popes promulgated additional volumes, codifying their new decrees and the decisions of later general councils of the church. These, together with Gratian's work, composed the medieval body of canon law.[267]

Because poor law was a part of church law, church courts governed issues surrounding charity. The church made a special effort to protect the poor by eliminating their court fees and providing them with legal counsel and representation. At this time priests normally were allowed to plead before the law courts only if defending a poor man or if they, themselves, were too poor to hire representation.[268]

Much of the law relating to poor relief was collected in the *Decretum* and dated from the fourth through sixth centuries. Thus it is not surprising that it laid the responsibility for the poor on the bishop just as the early church had in a classical division of church revenue into four parts: (1) one part for himself, (2) one part for his clergy, (3) one for church building and repair, and (4) one for the poor. These four parts were not necessarily equal.[269]

The concentration of revenues in the bishop, described in the *Decretum*, reflected late antiquity but was out of step with the organization of dioceses in the high Middle Ages. In the fourth through sixth centuries, a bishop cared for all the poor of the diocese. After that, the custom grew of dividing each diocese into smaller units or parishes.[270] A parish consisted of a region with a church and the people who attended it. Each parish was a separate economic unit, and the parish priest was responsible for its revenues.[271] These revenues were threefold: income from land with which the church had been endowed; offerings or customary gifts for baptisms, marriages, or funerals; and the tithe, which was a tax on each parishioner's produce and had been mandatory since the sixth century.[272] Such revenues did not come to the bishop. The responsibility for the poor within each parish fell on the parish and its priest. Already in A.D. 567, the Synod of Tours had made each parish responsible for its own poor.[273] If each parish had had enough money, this system of poor relief should have covered the needs of the poor within Christendom better than indiscriminate handouts to beggars.

But parishes did not have enough money for all their social welfare needs. In addition, the parish lost local revenue to outsiders with the growth of the proprietary church controlled at the local level by nonclergy. A tradition of appropriations of parochial revenues developed in the early feudal era. A layperson or monastery absorbed a parish's income and appointed a representative or vicar to serve as parish priest on a partial income. By presenting their clerks to ecclesiastical benefices such as these, kings and popes provided for the salaries of the clergy who worked in their chanceries. Local revenues were used later as "scholarships" to support students. The reformers John Wycliffe (1325?–1384) and John Calvin (1509–1564) both benefited from this type of financial support. Calvin resigned his benefices in 1534 when he became part of the Protestant Reformation, but Wycliffe lived at Oxford most of his life, drawing the income of two English churches that he rarely visited.[274]

Appropriations of parochial revenues were open to abuse. Even if used well, they could leave the priest at the local level impoverished and unable to provide either for himself or for the neighborhood poor because money diverted from local parishes through appropriations was unlikely to return to the needy it left behind. As for the use of this money, some of the monasteries that received diverted parochial funds were impoverished, but many of the laypeople were not. Moreover, though some monasteries may have used part of the money for the poor, studies of income and expenditures of English monasteries in the late Middle Ages and sixteenth century estimate that only 3 to 5 percent of revenue was spent on alms and hospitality.[275] This did not include the most common form of monastic poor relief, which was the distribution of leftover food. The 3 percent figure comes from a study of monasteries under Henry VIII (1535) in preparation for their dissolution (1536–1540). Only those revenues the monasteries were obliged to spend on charity because of the terms of a bequest were included in the 3 percent, not money they actually spent beyond that amount.[276] Nevertheless, the poor appeared to be the losers when parochial revenues were appropriated to a monastery, unless one considers the poor monks as worthy recipients of welfare.

Perhaps one fourth of the parishes of England had revenue appropriated from them by the end of the thirteenth century.[277] Fortunately for the poor, the church was attempting to stem the abuse of appropriations. In a step described as the "Magna Carta of the parish priest," the Fourth Lateran Council of 1215 provided that every parish with an absent priest should have a resident vicar who was to be endowed with an adequate portion of the parochial revenues.[278] The vicar's income was to be large enough to make it possible for him to render hospitality, which in medieval terminology included poor relief. This did not mean that poor priests necessarily lived entirely on their own stipends. Canon law allowed them to work at an occupation. In England, many farmed. Despite attempts by the church to halt the abuse of appropriations, so many exceptions were made that absentee pluralists (those who held more than one church office) increased in the fifteenth century.[279]

In 1313, Pope Clement V addressed the need for hospital reform, pointing out that the administrators of hospitals often were neglecting the poor and using hospital profits for themselves. He declared that offices in hospitals could not be conferred on secular clergy as benefices unless prescribed in the foundation ordinances.[280] Thus a layperson could be in charge of a hospital, and its revenues could not be diverted from the original charitable purposes to become an absentee cleric's income. However, in the late Middle Ages, the larger hospitals increasingly obtained exemption from the control of bishops, who could audit them, and diverted revenue from the foundation into comfortable incomes for the administrators.[281] Pope Clement's decree anticipated calls for hospital reform in the fourteenth and fifteenth centuries in England. The Lollard followers of John Wycliffe began a crescendo of agitation for hospital reform in the 1390s, and the English House of Commons passed a reform-ing statute in 1414.[282]

Despite abuses in the system of medieval poor relief, it appeared to work reasonably well at the local level at least until the fourteenth century. Parochial poor relief was helped by the fact that parishioners were expected to make donations beyond their tithes, as they did for church repairs. The endowment of a fund for the parish poor administered by the priest was a popular option. That the fate of the parish poor was watched over is evi-dent in the licenses granted to clerics to absent themselves from their parish for study at a university on the condition that specific sums would be paid for the poor during the absence.[283]

THE SECULAR GOVERNMENT IN WELFARE AND EDUCATION

As the church attempted to make social welfare comprehensive within Christendom, secular government moved to ensure a more equitable dis-tribution of poor relief as well. This was true after governments revived from the difficulties of the Viking and Magyar invasions of the eighth through the tenth centuries. Within several centuries, some governments had an interest in social welfare and education at the local level. City schools arose among the older cathedral and monastery schools. Social welfare branched out beyond individual donors and the church.

As states and cities grew in the late Middle Ages and the Renaissance, they sometimes attempted to organize or limit the activities of the church in the areas of poor relief and education. Governments set up new institu-tions alongside the old or attempted to coordinate the multifaceted insti-tutions that were in existence. Secular governments began to try to provide for everyone within their jurisdiction. Magistrates wanted comprehensive systems that squelched dissatisfaction, prevented hunger riots, and met the needs of as many people as possible.

Although the church still had the official role in social welfare in the late medieval and Renaissance periods, secular institutions and governments were making their presence known at a time when the church's own hold on poor relief was slipping. Communes, confraternities, and guilds were drawing control of charitable foundations away from church bodies. In Florence in 1419, the commune and the silk guild collaborated to construct the Hospital of the Innocents, an orphanage and foundling home designed by the renowned architect Filippo Brunelleschi. This institution is still in use today.[284] Many private donors favored lay trustees or boards of trustees that were partially lay and partially clerical to control their bequests.

The fourteenth and fifteenth centuries brought especially trying circumstances. The bubonic plague struck Europe in 1348–1349 when the population already had been weakened by crop failure and famine. The initial waves of the plague killed as many as a quarter to a half of the people in some regions, and Europe did not return to pre-plague population levels until the sixteenth century. Hospital income declined, as did the number of people seeking services. In England perhaps 20 percent of hospital foundations disappeared in the latter half of the fourteenth century. The remaining hospitals retained clergy to serve the institution and to say Masses for dead benefactors. Thus the percentage of hospital income spent on the clergy rose even as the percentage spent on the sick and poor declined.[285] A smaller population meant more land for some people, higher wages, and greater job mobility, but it also meant dissatisfaction with conditions that did not seem to be improving fast enough, to say nothing of the shock of the loss of so many family members at once. Many people set out to seek their fortune and new relationships, looking for better jobs and greater opportunities, which often failed to materialize. Sometimes people had to leave their homes because land they had been farming was enclosed for pasture. Many who set out on the road to riches ended as vagrants or thieves.[286]

The social welfare of the late Middle Ages was not constructed to cope with vagrancy. A parish's responsibility for its own poor presumed that the poor stayed put. Hospitals in urban centers were geared to handle the indigenous poor, not to care for every beggar who wandered through the city gate. In the religious world of the late Middle Ages, pilgrims were welcome to stay the night, as long as they moved on the next day on their pilgrimage toward a specific holy destination. Vagrants were not welcome, nor were foreign beggars or any poor person who could not support himself or herself.

The problem of vagrancy required a solution at a higher level than the local parish or diocese, but the church at its highest levels was beset with distractions: the Avignon papacy (1309–1377), when the pope moved from Rome to the Rhone River with the encouragement of the king of France, was followed by the Great Schism of the church when there were two and three popes at the same time (1378–1417). Then beginning in the mid-fifteenth century, in all but art and letters, the Renaissance popes lacked the leadership and moral character of the papacy of the high Middle Ages. At the local level there was a shortage of priests after the Black Death. Many men who previously would never have been given authority were assigned to parishes. Ecclesiastical poor law became less effective from the mid-fourteenth century on, and complaints about the neglect of parochial poor relief increased by the end of that century.[287]

In the fourteenth and fifteenth centuries, governments had their own problems in dealing with the problems of welfare. The states of Europe were beset with peasant rebellion and war. Resentment ran deep between the rich and the poor amid the death pangs of a dying manorialism and the last vestiges of feudalism. The hearts and minds of generations of French and English rulers were preoccupied with the claims and counterclaims of the Hundred Years War (1337–1453). The Holy Roman Empire was decentralized. Spain had not yet completed reunion. Only Italy was beginning to experience a Renaissance of art and letters. For example, Northern Italy introduced some interesting innovations in social welfare, such as low-interest lending funds to help small businesses and craftspeople and to dower young girls: the *Montes pietatis* that the Franciscans promoted.[288]

Despite the difficulties of the times, government, by its nature, had features that were helpful in meeting welfare and educational needs, such as the ability to tax and to make laws. The state was a potential conduit for social welfare. Governments could create new institutions and better organize the welfare and educational systems that already were in place. During the late Middle Ages and Renaissance, governments moved toward centralizing, rationalizing, and laicizing (that is, getting more laypeople involved) social welfare systems, but that story is continued in the next chapter on the sixteenth-century Reformation.

THE DIACONATE IN THE MIDDLE AGES

The overall social welfare picture in the late Middle Ages was multifaceted, and both the church and state were active. Within the church, monasticism and the new forms of religious community life of the high Middle Ages had taken over much of the work that deacons had performed in antiquity in the areas of education and poor relief. In turn, laypeople, through confraternities and city councils, were taking the place of clerics in charitable activities.[289]

The diaconate had become a stepping-stone to the priesthood, and the deacon was subordinate to the priest. Deaconesses had disappeared by the twelfth or thirteenth centuries in Europe and by the eleventh century in the eastern Mediterranean.[290] Deacons primarily had liturgical roles. The blessing of a deaconess may have been revived in some convents in the fourteenth and fifteenth centuries to enable them "to play a role in the celebration of the divine office."[291]

As the diaconal role in social welfare and property administration declined and as deacons became subordinate to priests, ecclesiastical writers made the other functions of deacons seem indispensable, especially in the liturgy. According to Peter Lombard, by the twelfth century, deacons read the Epistle as well as the Gospel reading. They carried the cross and read the names of new catechumens.[292] Deacons also accompanied priests into women's religious communities and the homes of infirm women who could not confess their sins in church.[293]

At the same time, the medieval theologians restricted the sacramental role of the deacon. In the twelfth century deacons were admonished to administer Communion to the sick only in grave necessity.[294] According to Thomas Aquinas (1224 or 1225–1274), a deacon was to baptize only in urgent necessity because a deacon does not "by reason of his own office . . . confer the sacrament of baptism. Rather in the conferral of this and other sacraments he assists and ministers to those in higher orders."[295] Deacons were not to administer Extreme Unction at all because it was not a necessary sacrament.[296] They were not to hear confessions and pronounce absolution, though in emergencies even confession to a layperson remained popular in the fourteenth century, though it was not sacramental.[297] Although the sacramental role of deacons was limited in the high Middle Ages, formally, they now could preach.[298]

Archdeacons retained important responsibilities in the financial, judicial, and charitable work of the church because of the jurisdiction given to them. Medieval archdeacons were legal representatives of the bishops. By the Carolingian period, the archdeacon had priests and archpriests subject to him. In the larger diocese north of the Alps, one bishop plus one archdeacon was no longer enough. One solution was to appoint an additional bishop to administer part of the diocese, called a *chorepiscopus*, a rural bishop. This was done in the West often between the mid-eighth and mid-ninth centuries, but the council of Paris of A.D. 849 passed a canon to suppress such appointments, though the practice continued until the late twelfth century. As the office of *chorepiscopus* lapsed, it appears that there was a multiplication of archdeacons and a division of a diocese into archdeaconries.[299]

By the ninth century, some archdeacons were priests. In the West by the twelfth century, archdeacons were generally priests, but they have never been priests in the East.[300] Some archdeacons were neither priest nor deacon, for example, Thomas à Becket (1118?–1170), archdeacon of Canterbury and chancellor to Henry II. Thomas was ordained a priest the day before he was consecrated a bishop (1162).[301] Archdeacons accompanied their bishops for parish visitations and eventually made visitations alone, in effect giving them jurisdiction over parish priests.[302]

Around 1100 in Rome, the deaconries and the seven diaconal regions of the city combined, resulting in cardinal deacons. They were in charge of the administrative regions of the diocese.[303] Besides these cardinal deacons, some of the clergy of the diocese of Rome were cardinals: some of the staff of the bishop of Rome (the pope), priests who were pastors of the papal or "titular" churches, and the pope's episcopal assistants or so-called "suburbicarian" bishops. The Roman Synod of 1059 under Pope Nicholas II (1058–1061) placed the election of the pope in the hands of the cardinals, who have continued to elect popes to the present day.[304]

SUMMARY

Deacons evolved considerably since New Testament times, a time when they were key figures in charitable work. They began in the first century with little, if any, obvious place in the liturgy and a large role in providing for the poor. Gradually, as assistants to the bishops, deacons and the widows assumed some importance in the liturgy alongside their role in social welfare. By the third century, deacons, deaconesses, and widows had a function in the Rite of Baptism. Both deacons and deaconesses taught. Some deacons celebrated the Eucharist. It is controversial whether it was appropriate for deacons to preach.[305] In the fourth and fifth centuries, deacons became subordinate to presbyters, deaconesses to deacons, and widows to deaconesses. Deacons retained a role in social welfare and property management at least into the fourth and fifth centuries. They lost this role by the time of the Council in Trullo (A.D. 692). Eventually the deaconesses and widows were absorbed into the monastic movement, and the male diaconate became a stepping-stone to the priesthood. As deacons lost their social welfare functions, the church increasingly emphasized their liturgical roles.

Archdeacons retained some of the charitable and administrative responsibilities of the diaconate. By the twelfth century, most archdeacons in the West were priests. The priesthood thus absorbed the archdiaconate and with it the important financial activities that had been the responsibility of deacons.

By the fifteenth century, deacons had moved into a role that was almost exclusively liturgical. The diaconate prepared men for the priesthood. For most clergymen, it was an apprenticeship through which one passed on the way to higher office. The reformers of the sixteenth century would find the diaconate ripe for reform on the model of the early church.

NOTES

1. Diocletian (A.D. 284–305) had divided the empire into eastern and western halves, allocating responsibilities to two emperors with the titles of "Augustus" and their successors as two "Caesars." Galerius issued an edict of toleration toward Christians on April 30, 311, to which Maximin Augustus agreed at first, but his adherence was insincere, allowing persecution. Persecution was most severe in the east; see Lactantius, *On the Deaths of Persecutors* 34, in Stevenson, *New Eusebius*, 296. Constantine Augustus and Licinius Augustus met in Milan in A.D. 313 and agreed on religious toleration and restoration of church property that had been taken during the persecution; see Lactantius, *On the Deaths of Persecutors* 48.2–12, in Stevenson, *New Eusebius*, 300–302.

2. Mollat, *Poor of the Middle Ages*, 19.

3. Frend, *Early Church*, 175–77.

4. Smaller Christian community centers also continued to be used for worship until, in time, some of them were transformed into basilicas. See Baldovin, *Urban Character of Christian Worship*, 111–12.

5. Uhlhorn, *Christian Charity*, 385.

6. Cyprian, *Epistle* 18.1, in Bradshaw, *Liturgical Presidency*, 27.

7. See, for example, a letter of St. Jerome: "For with the exception of ordaining, what does a bishop do which a presbyter does not?" (Jerome, *Epistle* 146.1.6, in Stevenson, *New Eusebius*, 378).

8. Bradshaw, *Liturgical Presidency*, 27.

9. "The Canons of Arles," in Stevenson, *New Eusebius*, 324.

10. "It has come to the knowledge of the holy Synod that in certain places and cities, the deacons give the Eucharist to the presbyters, whereas neither canon nor custom allows that they who have no authority to offer should give the Body of Christ to those who do offer. It has also been made known that now some of the deacons receive the Eucharist even before the bishops. Let all such practices be done away, and let the deacons keep within their proper bounds, knowing that they are the ministers of the bishop and inferior to the presbyters. Let them, therefore, receive the Eucharist, according to their order, after the presbyters, either the bishop or presbyter administering it to them. Further, the deacons are not to be allowed to sit among the presbyters" ("The Canons of Nicea," Canon 18, in Stevenson, *New Eusebius*, 363).

11. Bradshaw, *Liturgical Presidency*, 27.

12. Gillet, "Deacons in the Orthodox East," 416.

13. Uhlhorn, *Christian Charity*, 145, 256.

14. Ambrose did reserve a portion of his wealth for his sister Marcellina; see Uhlhorn, *Christian Charity*, 264. Some scholars feel that the church began to possess an increasing accumulation of goods donated for charity already in the third century, as evidenced in part by Constantine's decree in A.D. 313 that ordered restoration to the church of property taken from it; see Cooke, *Ministry to Word and Sacraments*, 353–54.

15. Uhlhorn, *Christian Charity*, 154.

16. "He measured the amount of their annual allowance more by the impulse of his own generosity than by their need" (*The Ecclesiastical History of Theodoret* 1.10, in *Nicene and Post-Nicene Fathers*, 2d ser., vol. 3: *Theodoret, Jerome, Gennadius, Rufinus: Historical Writings, etc.* [N.Y.: Christian Literature Co., 1892], 48).

17. Uhlhorn, *Christian Charity*, 153–54.

18. The *Apostolic Constitutions* claim to be church regulations from the apostles via Clement of Rome, but nearly all scholars agree it was compiled ca. A.D. 380 in Syria by an Arian or Arianizer. It instructs, exhorts, and gives examples of the Christian life. The most voluminous of all ancient collections of canons, the *Apostolic Constitutions* include the *Didascalia*, the *Didache*, the *Apostolic Tradition* of Hippolytus, several series of canons (including the 85 so-called apostolic canons), and, in Book 8, one of the oldest examples of Christian liturgy. The compiler modified the texts of the older documents, probably to reflect practices contemporary with his own time, making it useful for noting changes in practice. See "The *Apostolic Constitutions*: Meeting Place of Diverse Traditions," in Martimort, *Deaconesses*, 59–75; Fiensy, *Prayers Alleged to Be Jewish*, 19. Mary McKenna is among those who ascribe the *Apostolic Constitutions* to the fifth century; see *Women of the Church*, 65. The *Apostolic Constitutions*, referring to prisoners for the sake of religion, states of the free Christian: "If any one has not, let him fast a day, and set apart that, and order it for the saints. . . . If he can possibly sell all his livelihood, and redeem them out of prison, he will be blessed, and a friend of Christ" (*Constitutions of the Holy Apostles* 5.1, in Alexander Roberts and James Donaldson, eds., *The Ante-Nicene Fathers*, vol. 7: *Fathers of the Third and Fourth Centuries: Lactantius, Venantius, Asterius, Victorinus, Dionysius, Apostolic Teaching and Constitutions, Homily, and Liturgies*, ed. A. Cleveland Coxe [n.p.: Christian Literature Publishing, 1885; repr. Grand Rapids: Eerdmans, n.d.], 437).

19. Uhlhorn, *Christian Charity*, 391.

20. Uhlhorn, *Christian Charity*, 185, 199, 365. An imperial decree of A.D. 400 delegated to bishops the duty of determining whether prisoners were humanely treated and detained lawfully; see *Cod. Theod.* 9.3, *de custod. reor.* 1.7, in Uhlhorn, *Christian Charity*, 387. By the end of the sixth century, the bishop was to appoint someone to care for prisoners, and the church was to feed them; see Uhlhorn, *Christian Charity*, 388.

21. "When any Christian becomes an orphan, whether it be a young man or a maid, it is good that some one of the brethren who is without a child should take the young man, and esteem him in the place of a son; and he that has a son about the same age, and that is marriageable, should marry the maid to him: for they which do so perform a great work, and become fathers to the orphans, and shall receive the reward of this charity from the Lord God. . . . Have a greater care of the orphans, that nothing may be wanting to them; and that as to the maiden, till she arrives at the age of marriage, and ye give her in marriage to a brother: to the young man assistance, that he may learn a trade, and may be maintained by the advantage arising from it; that so, when he is dexterous in the management of it, he may thereby be enabled to buy himself the tools of his trade, that so he may no longer burden any of the brethren, or their sincere love to him, but may support himself: for certainly he is a happy man who is able to support himself, and does not take up the place of the orphan, the stranger, and the widow" (*Constitutions of the Apostles* 4.1–2, in *Ante-Nicene Fathers*, 7:433).

22. Uhlhorn, *Christian Charity*, 366, 385.

23. Examples of such actions include Basil, Augustine, and Pope Gregory the Great. See Uhlhorn, *Christian Charity*, 367, 380–84.

24. Uhlhorn, *Christian Charity*, 365–66.

25. *Homily on Matthew* 67, as cited in Uhlhorn, *Christian Charity*, 248–49.

26. *Homily on Matthew* 66.3, in Uhlhorn, *Christian Charity*, 250.

27. Uhlhorn, *Christian Charity*, 167, 277.

28. For support for a prominent role for women in the early church, see Ide, *Woman as Priest, Bishop and Laity in the Early Catholic Church*; Gryson, *Le ministère des femmes dans l'Église ancienne*; Bangerter, *Frauen im Aufbruch*; Stark, *Rise of Christianity*, 107–11; Elm, *"Virgins of God."*

29. Elm, *"Virgins of God,"* 169–74.

30. "[The bishop] offers within the veil together with the priests, the deacons, the canonical widows, the subdeacons, the deaconesses, the readers and those having charisms. First the bishop takes his place in the middle, right after him the presbyters on the one side and on the other, and after the presbyters who are on the bishop's left, the widows follow, after the presbyters on the right, the deacons stand, and after them the lectors and subdeacons, and after the subdeacons, the deaconesses" (*Testament of Our Lord* 1.23, in McKenna, *Women of the Church*, 61). There is an alternate translation in Cooper and Maclean, *Testament of Our Lord*, 70.

31. "Presbytides, as they are called, or female presidents, are not to be appointed in the Church" (*The Canons of the Synod Held in the City of Laodicea, in Phrygia Pacatiana, in Which Many Blessed Fathers from Divers Provinces of Asia Were Gathered Together*, Canon 11, in *Nicene and Post-Nicene Fathers*, 2d ser., vol. 14: *The Seven Ecumenical Councils of the Undivided Church: Their Canons and Dogmatic Decrees, Together with the Canons of All the Local Synods Which Have Received Ecumenical Acceptance*, ed. Henry Percival [New York: Charles Scribner's Sons, 1900], 129). Hefele translates Canon 11 as: "The appointment of the so-called female elders or presidents shall not take place in the church" (*History of the Councils of the Church*, 2:305); see also McKenna, *Women of the Church*, 119–21. The western part of the Roman Empire where widows were strong "did not agree in making this change" (Uhlhorn, *Christian Charity*, 173).

32. Hefele, *History of the Councils of the Church*, 2:305.

33. Otterbein, *Diaconate according to the Apostolic Tradition*, 10.

34. For the earlier date, see, for example, Thurston, *Widows*, 114. For the later date, see Otterbein, *Diaconate according to the Apostolic Tradition*, 14; Martimort, *Deaconesses*, 47; Elm, *"Virgins of God,"* 175. McKenna says it was written ca. A.D. 475; see *Women of the Church*, 53.

35. The *Testamentum Domini* might have come from eastern Syria. There are Syriac, Arabic, and Ethiopic versions, but, as with the *Didascalia*, it may have been written originally in Greek; see Martimort, *Deaconesses*, 46–47. McKenna suggests Egyptian origin; see *Women of the Church*, 53, 62.

36. "When she gives thanks or renders praise, it will be better if she has some like-spirited virgin friends with her to answer: Amen" (*Testament of Our Lord* 1.42, in McKenna, *Women of the Church*, 58; Cooper and Maclean, *Testament of Our Lord*, 109).

37. "You shall ordain a widow in this way: While she herself is praying on the steps of the altar with eyes downcast, the bishop says in a subdued voice, but so that the priests can hear . . . [the] Prayer for Establishing Widows Having Precedence in the Seating" (*The Testament of Our Lord* 1.41, in McKenna, *Women of the Church*, 56–57). For a translation that avoids the word *ordained*, see "Let the appointment be thus. . . ." in Cooper and Maclean, *Testament of Our Lord*, 108. Not all commentators would allow that widows were truly ordained, in part because there was no laying on of hands: "It is thus an error to speak of the ordination of widows" (Martimort, *Deaconesses*, 51).

38. There is disagreement over this sentence between those who translate the Syriac verb as "to superintend" or "to supervise" the deaconesses and those who translate it as "to follow in [their] footsteps." See *Testament of Our Lord* 1.40, in McKenna, *Women of the Church*, 55; Martimort, *Deaconesses*, 48n. Cooper and Maclean translate the sentence: "Let her prove the deaconess" (*Testament of Our Lord*, 106).

39. *Testament of Our Lord* 1.40, in McKenna, *Women of the Church*, 55; Cooper and Maclean, *Testament of Our Lord*, 106.

40. Thurston, *Widows*, 114.

41. Elm, *"Virgins of God,"* 175–77, 182.

42. Barnett, *The Diaconate* (1981), 200.

43. The *Apostolic Constitutions* state that either a deacon or a presbyter can read the Gospel and provide for the reader as follows: "Let the reader stand upon some high place: let him read the books of Moses, of Joshua the Son of Nun, of the Judges, and of the Kings and of the Chronicles, and those written after the return from the captivity; and besides these, the books of Job and of Solomon, and of the sixteen prophets. But when there have been two lessons severally read, let some other person sing the hymns of David, and let the people join at the conclusions of the verses. Afterwards let our Acts be read, and the Epistles of Paul our fellow-worker, which he sent to the churches under the conduct of the Holy Spirit; and afterwards let a deacon or a presbyter read the Gospels . . . while the Gospel is read, let all the presbyters and deacons, and all the people, stand up in great silence; for it is written: 'Be silent, and hear, O Israel [Deuteronomy 27:9].' And again: 'But do thou stand there, and hear [Deuteronomy 5:31]' " (*Constitutions of the Apostles* 2.57, in *Ante-Nicene Fathers*, 7:421).

44. *Constitutions of the Apostles* 8.9, in *Ante-Nicene Fathers*, 7:485.

45. For the prayers over the catechumens, energumens, and penitents, see *Constitutions of the Apostles* 8.6–7, 9, in *Ante-Nicene Fathers*, 7:483–85.

46. "And let the clergy salute the bishop, the men of the laity salute the men, the women the women" (*Constitutions of the Apostles* 8.2, in *Ante-Nicene Fathers*, 7:486).

47. *Constitutions of the Apostles* 8.2, in *Ante-Nicene Fathers*, 7:486.

48. *Constitutions of the Apostles* 8.2, in *Ante-Nicene Fathers*, 7:490.

49. *Constitutions of the Apostles* 8.2, in *Ante-Nicene Fathers*, 7:491.

50. Taft, *Beyond East and West*, 155–56; see the bidding prayers in the *Apostolic Constitutions*, 8.6–8, 10, 13–14, 41, in *Ante-Nicene Fathers*, 7:483–85, 490–91, 497.

51. "And the deacon in church recites the names of those who offer" ("publiceque diaconus in ecclesia recitet offerentium nomina") (Jerome on Ezekiel 18, in Bingham, *Antiquities of the Ancient Church*, 1:87n).

52. Echlin, *Deacon in the Church*, 68.

53. *Constitutions of the Apostles* 8.13, in *Ante-Nicene Fathers*, 7:491.

54. *Apostolic Constitutions* 3.11, 20; 8.28, 46, and Tertullian, *De Baptismo* 17, in Bradshaw, *Liturgical Presidency*, 26–27.

55. Compare to the *Didascalia*: "And when she who is being baptized has come up from the water, let the deaconess receive her, and teach and instruct her how the seal of baptism ought to be (kept) unbroken in purity and holiness" (*The Catholic Didascalia That Is Teaching of the Twelve Holy Apostles and Disciples of Our Saviour* 3.12.5, in R. Hugh Connolly, trans., *Didascalia Apostolorum: The Syriac Version Translated and Accompanied by the Verona Latin Fragments* [Oxford: Clarendon, 1929], 147; *Constitutions of the Apostles* 3.16, in *Ante-Nicene Fathers*, 7:431).

56. "Those chosen for the ministry of the baptism of women should be so instructed for this office that they can teach uneducated women with apt and sound words how they should answer the baptismal question at the time of their baptism, and how they should live once they are baptized" (*Statuta ecclesiae antiqua*, Canon 12, in McKenna, *Women of the Church*, 69–70).

57. *Testament of Our Lord*, Bk. 2, 8.12, in Martimort, *Deaconesses*, 47–48; Cooper and Maclean, *Testament of Our Lord*, 127.

58. *Testament of Our Lord* 2:20, in Cooper and Maclean, *Testament of Our Lord*, 135.

59. See the discussion of the role of deaconesses based on the *Constitutions of the Apostles* 3.15, in MacDonald, *Early Christian Women*, 52–53, 218.

60. *Constitutions of the Apostles* 2.57, in *Ante-Nicene Fathers*, 7:421. At this time, men and women worshiped on separate sides of the church.

61. *Constitutions of the Apostles* 8.20, in *Ante-Nicene Fathers*, 7:492. There is a reference to

women ministering at the doors of the Tent of Meeting in Exodus 38:26. Nowhere in the Bible does it indicate women were guardians of the temple doors; see Martimort, *Deaconesses*, 70.

62. *Constitutions of the Apostles* 2.58, in *Ante-Nicene Fathers*, 7:422.

63. *Constitutions of the Apostles* 8.11, in *Ante-Nicene Fathers*, 7:486.

64. Echlin, *Deacon in the Church*, 68, 79.

65. Echlin, *Deacon in the Church*, 79, 92. A work of Ennodius, bishop of Pavia (A.D. 514–521), includes two blessings for the paschal candle; see Ennodius, *Opuscula miscella* 9 and 10, "Benedictio Cerei," in *Corpus Scriptorum Ecclesiasticorum Latinorum*, vol. 6: *Magni Felicis Ennodii Opera Omnia*, ed. Wilhelm Hartel (Vindobonae: Apud C. Geroldi Filium Bibliopolam Academiae, 1882), 415–22, in Barnett, *The Diaconate* (1981), 78.

66. "Let your judicatures be held on the second day of the week, that if any controversy arise about your sentence, having an interval till the Sabbath, you may be able to set the controversy right, and to reduce those to peace who have the contests one with another against the Lord's day. Let also the deacons and presbyters be present at your judicatures, to judge without acceptance of persons, as men of God, with righteousness" (*Constitutions of the Apostles* 2.47, in *Ante-Nicene Fathers*, 7:417).

67. McKenna, *Women of the Church*, 69–70; Pseudo-Dionysius (ca. A.D. 450), *Ecclesiastica Hierarchia*, PG 3:524, 508, 544, in Echlin, *Deacon in the Church*, 75–76.

68. *Constitutions of the Apostles* 2.26, in *Ante-Nicene Fathers*, 7:410.

69. Liturgical vestments were developing at this time from late Roman dress. For diaconal vestments (alb, girdle, amice, stole, dalmatic, surplice), see Barnett, *The Diaconate* (1981), 200–205; Echlin, *Deacon in the Church*, 76.

70. *Testament of Our Lord*, 1.34, in Cooper and Maclean, *Testament of Our Lord*, 98.

71. *Didascalia* 3, 12, as quoted in Otterbein, *Diaconate according to the Apostolic Tradition*, 26.

72. John Cassian, *Collations*, cited in Echlin, *Deacon in the Church*, 76.

73. Otterbein, *Diaconate according to the Apostolic Tradition*, 42–49.

74. *The Ecclesiastical Canons of the Same Holy Apostles*, 7, 12, 25, 28, 37, 42, 44, 45, 65, 69, 70, 83, 84, in *Ante-Nicene Fathers*, 7:500–505.

75. *Canons of the Same Holy Apostles*, 53, in *Ante-Nicene Fathers*, 7:503.

76. *Canons of the Same Holy Apostles*, 9, 11, 45, 54, 57, 62, in *Ante-Nicene Fathers*, 7:500–504.

77. *Canons of the Same Holy Apostles*, 79, 82, in *Ante-Nicene Fathers*, 7:504–5.

78. Francine Cardman, "Women, Ministry, and Church Order in Early Christianity," in Kraemer and D'Angelo, *Women and Christian Origins*, 315.

79. "But those widows which will not live according to the command of God, are solicitous and inquisitive what deaconess it is that gives the charity, and what widows receive it. And when she has learned those things, she murmurs at the deaconess who distributed the charity, saying, Dost not thou see that I am in more distress, and want of thy charity? Why, therefore, hast thou preferred her before me? She says these things foolishly, not understanding that this does not depend on the will of man, but the appointment of God. . . . She ought to understand who it is that made this constitution, and to hold her peace, and not to murmur at the deaconess who distributed the charity, but to enter into her own house, and to cast herself prostrate on her face to make supplication to God that her sin may be forgiven her" (*Constitutions of the Apostles* 3.14, in *Ante-Nicene Fathers*, 7:430).

80. Cardman, "Women, Ministry, and Church Order," 317. The ordination prayer is as follows: "O Eternal God, the Father of our Lord Jesus Christ, the Creator of man and

of woman, who didst replenish with the Spirit Miriam, and Deborah, and Anna, and Huldah; who didst not disdain that Thy only begotten Son should be born of a woman; who also in the tabernacle of the testimony, and in the temple, didst ordain women to be keepers of Thy holy gates—do Thou now also look down upon this Thy servant, who is to be ordained to the office of a deaconess, and grant her Thy Holy Spirit, and 'cleanse her from all filthiness of flesh and spirit,' that she may worthily discharge the work which is committed to her to Thy glory, and the praise of Thy Christ, with whom glory and adoration be to Thee and the Holy Spirit for ever. Amen" (*Constitutions of the Apostles* 8.20, in *Ante-Nicene Fathers*, 7:492). Compare to the prayer for the ordination of a deacon: "O God Almighty, the true and faithful God, who art rich unto all that call upon Thee in truth, who art fearful in counsels, and wise in understanding, who art powerful and great, hear our prayer, O Lord, and let Thine ears receive our supplication, and 'cause the light of Thy countenance to shine upon this Thy servant,' who is to be ordained for Thee to the office of a deacon; and replenish him with Thy Holy Spirit, and with power, as Thou didst replenish Stephen, who was Thy martyr, and follower of the sufferings of Thy Christ. Do Thou render him worthy to discharge acceptably the ministration of a deacon, steadily, unblamably, and without reproof, that thereby he may attain an higher degree, through the mediation of Thy only begotten Son, with whom glory, honour, and worship be to Thee and the Holy Spirit for ever. Amen" (*Constitutions of the Apostles* 8.18, in *Ante-Nicene Fathers* 7:492).

81. "Widows ought then to be modest, and obedient to the bishops and the deacons, and to reverence and respect and fear the bishop as God" (*Didascalia* 3.8, in Connolly, *Didascalia Apostolorum*, 138). "The widows therefore ought to be grave, obedient to their bishops, and their presbyters, and their deacons, and besides these to the deaconesses, with piety, reverence, and fear; not usurping authority, nor desiring to do anything beyond the constitution without the consent of the deacon" (*Constitutions of the Apostles* 3.7, in *Ante-Nicene Fathers*, 7:429).

82. Elm, *"Virgins of God,"* 171.

83. *Constitutions of the Apostles* 6.17, in *Ante-Nicene Fathers*, 7:457.

84. *Constitutions of the Apostles* 8.13, in *Ante-Nicene Fathers*, 7:490.

85. Compare *Didascalia* 3.5–8, 10, in Connolly, *Didascalia Apostolorum*, 132–45, to *Constitutions of the Apostles* 3.7, 12, 14, in *Ante-Nicene Fathers*, 7:428, 430.

86. *Constitutions of the Apostles* 8.25, in *Ante-Nicene Fathers*, 7:493.

87. *Constitutions of the Apostles* 2.26, in *Ante-Nicene Fathers*, 7:410.

88. *Constitutions of the Apostles* 8:19–22, in *Ante-Nicene Fathers*, 7:492–93. For the debate over ordination in the *Apostolic Constitutions* and the validity of this document as a reflection of practice in the early church, see Roger Gryson's response to A. G. Martimort in "L'ordination des diaconesses d'après les 'Constitution Apostoliques,' " 41–45.

89. "A woman shall not receive the laying on of hands as a deaconess under forty years of age, and then only after searching examination. And if, after she has had hands laid on her and has continued for a time to minister, she shall despise the grace of God and give herself in marriage, she shall be anathematized and the man united to her" (*The XXX Canons of the Holy and Fourth Synods of Chalcedon*, Canon 15, in *Nicene and Post-Nicene Fathers*, 14:279).

90. The epitaph of the Deaconess Athanasia from fifth-century Delphi: "The most pious deaconess Athanasia having lived a blameless life modestly having been ordained a deaconess by the most holy bishop, Pantamianos, made this monument, in which lie her remains" (Guarducci 4:345, in Kraemer, *Maenads, Martyrs, Matrons, Monastics*, 223).

91. Martimort insists that deaconesses were not deacons in the eyes of the church; see *Deaconesses*, 243–47. On the other hand, Echlin argues that Chalcedon (A.D. 451) legis-

lated for deaconesses in terms so similar to those for clerics that "it is difficult to maintain that women were not ordained to a female diaconate" (*Deacon in the Church*, 73). McKenna says that whether deaconesses received a major order and the Sacrament of Holy Orders and an indelible character is unresolved; see *Women of the Church*, 78. For a study of medieval arguments against the ordination of women, see Martin, "Ordination of Women," *Escritos del Vedat* 16 (1986): 115–77, and *Escritos del Vedat* 18 (1988): 87–143.

92. *New Catholic Encyclopedia*, 2d ed., s.v. "Deaconess."

93. Herbert Thurston, in an article in *The Catholic Encyclopedia*, asserted that "the Church as a whole repudiated the idea that women could in any sense be recipients of the Sacrament of Order" (*Catholic Encyclopedia*, s.v. "Deaconesses").

94. *Council of Orange*, Canon 25, in Martimort, *Deaconesses*, 193.

95. *Council of Orleans II*, in McKenna, *Women of the Church*, 131.

96. *Constitutions of the Apostles* 8.13, in *Ante-Nicene Fathers*, 7:490.

97. *Constitutions of the Apostles* 8.28, in *Ante-Nicene Fathers*, 7:494.

98. *Constitutions of the Apostles* 8.31, in *Ante-Nicene Fathers*, 7:494.

99. Holum, *Theodosian Empresses*, 192.

100. Alice-Mary Talbot, "Byzantine Women, Saints' Lives, and Social Welfare," in Hanawalt and Lindberg, *Through the Eye of a Needle*, 107.

101. Elm, *"Virgins of God,"* 178–81.

102. Elm, *"Virgins of God,"* 179, 182.

103. Palladius, *Palladius*, 137, 212–13.

104. McKenna, *Women of the Church*, 84–91. For Melania the Younger and her mother, Melania the Elder, see "Piety, Propaganda, and Politics in the Life of Melania the Younger," in Clark, *Ascetic Piety and Women's Faith*, 61–94. See also Palladius, *Palladius*, 123–25, 134–36, 205–6, 210–11; Elm, *"Virgins of God,"* 274, 277–79, 319, 326.

105. Elm, *"Virgins of God,"* 182–83.

106. "No others shall sing in the Church, save only the canonical singers, who go up into the ambo and sing from a book" (*Canons of Laodicea*, Canon 15, in *Nicene and Post-Nicene Fathers*, 14:132).

107. Bingham, *Antiquities of the Ancient Church*, 1:118–19.

108. Chastel, *Charity of the Primitive Churches*, 233–34.

109. Uhlhorn, *Christian Charity*, 325–26.

110. Uhlhorn, *Christian Charity*, 324; Cooke, *Ministry to Word and Sacraments*, 355.

111. For the debate concerning the date of Basil's death, see "Appendix III: The Date of Basil's Death and of the *Hexaemeron*," in Rousseau, *Basil of Caesarea*, 360–63.

112. Holman, *Hungry Are Dying*, 74.

113. Talbot, "Byzantine Women," 108.

114. Jerome, *To Oceanus*, Letter 77, in *Nicene and Post-Nicene Fathers*, 2d ser., vol. 6: *St. Jerome: Letters and Select Works* (New York: Christian Literature Co., 1893), 160.

115. Talbot, "Byzantine Women," 114–15.

116. Talbot, "Byzantine Women," 109, 115; Martimort, *Deaconesses*, 136; McKenna, *Women of the Church*, 86.

117. Miller, *Birth of the Hospital*, 8; Uhlhorn, *Christian Charity*, 331–32.

118. Uhlhorn, *Christian Charity*, 332. "Let the clergy of the poor-houses, monasteries, and martyries remain under the authority of the bishops in every city according to the tradition of the holy Fathers; and let no one arrogantly cast off the rule of his own bishop; and if any shall contravene this canon in any way whatever, and will not be

subject to their own bishop, if they be clergy, let them be subjected to canonical cen-
sure, and if they be monks or laymen, let them be excommunicated" (*Canons of Chalcedon*, Canon 8, in *Nicene and Post-Nicene Fathers*, 14:273).

119. Origen, sermon on Luke 34, cited by Cooke, *Ministry to Word and Sacraments*, 357.

120. See the discussion of the Synod at Gangra in Hefele, *History of the Councils of the
Church*, 2:325, 330.

121. For an English translation, see "In Time of Famine and Drought," in Holman, *Hungry Are Dying*, 183–92.

122. Holman, *Hungry Are Dying*, 76.

123. *The Theodosian Code*, xvi.2.15, as cited in Davies, "Deacons, Deaconesses and the
Minor Orders," 14; Bingham, *Antiquities of the Ancient Church*, 1:117–18.

124. "It has come to the hearing of the holy Synod that certain clergymen and monks, having no authority from their own bishop, and sometimes, indeed, while under sentence
of excommunication by him, betake themselves to the imperial Constantinople, and
remain there for a long time, raising disturbances and troubling the ecclesiastical state,
and turning men's houses upside down. Therefore the holy Synod has determined that
such persons be first notified by the Advocate of the most holy Church of Constantinople to depart from the imperial city; and if they shall shamelessly continue in the
same practices, that they shall be expelled by the same Advocate even against their
will, and return to their own places" (*Canons of Chalcedon*, Canon 23, in *Nicene and
Post-Nicene Fathers*, 14:283–84; Bingham, *Antiquities of the Ancient Church*, 1:122–23).

125. Canon 26 of the Council of Chalcedon describes the steward's function and relationship to the bishop: "Forasmuch as we have heard that in certain churches the bishops
managed the church-business [sic] without stewards, it has seemed good that every
church having a bishop shall have also a steward from among its own clergy, who shall
manage the church business under the sanction of his own bishop; that so the administration of the church may not be without a witness; and that thus the goods of the
church may not be squandered, nor reproach be brought upon the priesthood; and if
he [i.e., the Bishop] will not do this, he shall be subjected to the divine canons"
(*Canons of Chalcedon*, Canon 26, in *Nicene and Post-Nicene Fathers*, 14:285; Bingham,
Antiquities of the Ancient Church, 1:125–26).

126. This was apparently to safeguard the income of the church. "Forasmuch as certain of
the metropolitans, as we have heard, neglect the flocks committed to them and delay
the ordinations of bishops, the holy Synod has decided that the ordinations of bishops
shall take place within three months, unless an inevitable necessity should some time
require the term of delay to be prolonged. And if he shall not do this, he shall be liable
to ecclesiastical penalties, and the income of the widowed church shall be kept safe by
the steward of the same Church" (*Canons of Chalcedon*, Canon 25, in *Nicene and Post-
Nicene Fathers*, 14:285).

127. Uhlhorn, *Christian Charity*, 267.

128. Bingham, *Antiquities of the Ancient Church*, 1:127–28.

129. Eusebius mentions an individual named Romanus who was both deacon and exorcist; see
Martyrs of Palestine 2.1, in Davies, "Deacons, Deaconesses and the Minor Orders," 10.

130. Bingham, *Antiquities of the Ancient Church*, 1:107.

131. "No one of the priesthood, from presbyters to deacons, and so on in the ecclesiastical
order to subdeacons, readers, singers, exorcists, door-keepers, or any of the class of
the Ascetics, ought to enter a tavern" (*Canons of Laodicea*, Canon 24, in *Nicene and Post-
Nicene Fathers*, 14:144). For an alternate translation, see Hefele, *History of the Councils
of the Church*, 2:314: "No clerics from the presbyters to the deacons, and so on in
ecclesiastical order, down to the ministers (sub-deacons), readers, cantors, exorcists,
doorkeepers, or any of the ascetic class, shall enter a public-house "

132. *De ecclesiastics officiis*, L. II, cc. 10–15, cited in Roger Reynolds, "A Florilegium on the Ecclesiastical Grades in CLM 19414: Testimony to Ninth-Century Clerical Instruction," *Harvard Theological Review* 63 (1970): 238.

133. Davies, "Deacons," 14.

134. Davies, "Deacons, Deaconesses and the Minor Orders" 14.

135. Barnett, *The Diaconate* (1981), 111.

136. Finn, *From Death to Rebirth*, 214–15.

137. Frend, *Early Church*, 179.

138. Cyprian, *Epistle* 51.8, in Alexander Roberts and James Donaldson, eds., *The Ante-Nicene Fathers: Translations of the Writings of the Fathers Down to A.D. 325*, vol. 5: *Fathers of the Third Century: Hippolytus, Cyprian, Caius, Novatian, Appendix*, ed. A. Cleveland Coxe (n.p.: Christian Literature, 1886; repr. New York: Charles Scribner's & Sons, 1903), 329.

139. "Persons who have lately come over to the faith from a heathen life, and have been taught for a short time, have been presently brought to the spiritual laver, and at the same time that they have been baptized, have been promoted to the episcopate or presbyterate—it appears right to determine that nothing of the sort shall be done for the future; for some time is necessary for the state of a catechumen, and a fuller probation after baptism; for the Apostolic decree is clear, which says, *Not a novice, lest being lifted up with pride he fall into a snare and the judgement of the devil*" ("Canons of Nicaea," Canon 2, in Stevenson, *New Eusebius*, 359 [*Stevenson's emphasis*]).

140. Finn, *From Death to Rebirth*, 193.

141. At this time, the archdeacon of Rome apparently was still a deacon rather than a presbyter; see Barnett, *The Diaconate* (1981), 82.

142. Alcuin, of Northumbria, England, served Charlemagne from A.D. 782 until his death on May 19, 804; see *New Catholic Encyclopedia*, s.v. "Alcuin." Charlemagne was king of the Franks from A.D. 768–814 and emperor of the Holy Roman Empire from A.D. 800–814.

143. Hill, *Bede and the Benedictine Reform*, 7.

144. Ignatius the Deacon, *Correspondence of Ignatios the Deacon*, 5.

145. Stephen the Deacon, *La Vie d'Étienne le Jeune par Étienne le Diacre*.

146. Bloch, *Atina Dossier of Peter the Deacon*, 9.

147. Bligh, "Deacons in the Latin West," 421–22.

148. *De ecclesiastics officiis*, L. II, cc. 10–15; *Etymologies*, L. Vii, c. xii, 3–32, in Reynolds, "Ecclesiastical Grades," 238.

149. Deanesly, "Archdeacons of Canterbury," 1–2.

150. Reynolds, "Ecclesiastical Grades," 242.

151. "Try by exhortation to induce Natalis, our brother and fellow-bishop [*sic*], who has been admonished by so many letters, to restore the above-mentioned Honoratus to his place immediately" (Letter 20 to Antoninus, Subdeacon, in *The Book of Pastoral Rule, and Selected Epistles, of Gregory the Great, Bishop of Rome*, trans. James Barmby, in *Nicene and Post-Nicene Fathers*, 2d ser., vol. 12: *Leo the Great; Gregory the Great* [New York: Christian Literature Co., 1895], 105. The works of Leo [12:1–205], which come first, and of Gregory are paginated separately.)

152. Thomas de Celano, *Vita Prima S. Francisci Assisiensis et Eiusdem Legenda ad Usum Chori* (Florence: Collegii S. Bonaventurae Ad Claras Aquas [Quaracchi], 1926), 90–91.

153. "The Testament," in Armstrong and Brady, *Francis and Clare*, 154. For an older translation, see the will of St. Francis in Sabatier, *Life of St. Francis of Assisi*, 337–38. For a Latin text, see "Testamentum," in Esser, *Opuscula Sancti Patris Francisci Assisiensis*, 20ff.

154. *Nicene and Post-Nicene Fathers*, vol. 13: *Saint Chrysostom: Homilies on Galatians, Ephesians, Philippians, Colossians, Thessalonians, Timothy, Titus, and Philemon* (New York: Charles Scribner's Sons, 1905), 441–42.

155. *Constitutions of the Apostles* 8.18, in *Ante-Nicene Fathers*, 7:492.

156. Charles Munier, ed., *Statuta Ecclesiae Antiquae* (Paris: n.p., 1950), 89–90, cited in Echlin, *Deacon in the Church*, 78.

157. "Canons of Nicaea," Canon 18, in Stevenson, *New Eusebius*, 363.

158. "I am told that someone has been mad enough to put deacons before presbyters . . . . How comes it then that at Rome a presbyter is ordained on the recommendation of a deacon?" (Jerome, "To Evangelus," *Letter* 146.1–2, in Greenslade, *Early Latin Theology*, 386).

159. Jerome, "To Evangelus," *Letter* 146.2, in Greenslade, *Early Latin Theology*, 389.

160. *The Ecclesiastical History of Socrates* 4.29, in *Nicene and Post-Nicene Fathers of the Christian Church*, 2d ser., vol. 2: *Socrates, Sozomenus: Church Histories* (Grand Rapids: Eerdmans, 1997), 113.

161. Miller, *Birth of the Hospital*, 74.

162. Miller, *Birth of the Hospital*, 76.

163. Miller, *Birth of the Hospital*, 74, 76. Monophysites believed in "one nature" in Christ rather than two—human and divine. Today's Monophysite churches are centralized in what had been the eastern end of the Roman Empire and beyond, including Armenia, Syria, Egypt, and Ethiopia.

164. Kopecek, *History of Neo-Arianism*, 2:61.

165. Miller, *Birth of the Hospital*, 77.

166. Kopecek, *History of Neo-Arianism*, 2:100–102, 111.

167. Kopecek, *History of Neo-Arianism*, 2:105, 111–12, 114.

168. Kopecek, *History of Neo-Arianism*, 2:114, 353–59.

169. Miller, *Birth of the Hospital*, 77; Kopecek, *History of Neo-Arianism*, 1:1; 2:299–350, 359.

170. "No one shall be ordained presbyter under the age of thirty years: even if the person concerned is completely worthy, he must wait. For the Lord Jesus Christ in his thirtieth year was baptized, and began to teach" ("Canons of Neocaesarea," Canon 11, in Stevenson, *New Eusebius*, 313). "Let the canon of our holy God-fearing Fathers be confirmed in this particular also; that a presbyter be not ordained before he is thirty years of age, even if he be a very worthy man, but let him be kept back. For our Lord Jesus Christ was baptized and began to teach when he was thirty. In like manner let no deacon be ordained before he is twenty-five, nor a deaconess before she is forty" (*The Canons of the Council in Trullo; Often Called the Quinisext Council, A.D. 692*, Canon 14, in *Nicene and Post-Nicene Fathers*, 14:372). See also Bingham, *Antiquities of the Ancient Church*, 1:94; Echlin, *Deacon in the Church*, 80.

171. James Cooper, ed., *Testament of Our Lord*, Ante-Nicene Christian Library (Edinburgh: n.p., 1902), 97–99, quoted in Echlin, *Deacon in the Church*, 77.

172. Bligh, "Deacons in the Latin West," 423.

173. Number 3 of Justinian's *Novellae*, 5th ed., ed. R. Schoell and G. Kroll, in *Corpus iuris civilis*, 3 (Berlin: Weidmann, 1928), 18–22, cited in Martimort, *Deaconesses*, 109.

174. *Canons of Trullo*, Canon 16, in *Nicene and Post-Nicene Fathers*, 14:373.

175. Athanasius was called "principal deacon"; see Theodoret, *Ecclesiastical History of Theodoret* 1.25, in *Nicene and Post-Nicene Fathers*, 3:60–61.

176. Bingham, *Antiquities of the Ancient Church*, 1:96–97; Barnett, *The Diaconate* (1981), 199.

177. St. Leo the Great, *Letters*, Fathers of the Church (New York: n.p., 1957), 248, quoted in Echlin, *Deacon in the Church*, 74.

178. "Canons of the Council of Elvira," Canon 33, in Stevenson, *New Eusebius*, 307.

179. "Canons of Ancyra," Canon 10, in Stevenson, *New Eusebius*, 312.

180. *Canons of the Apostles*, Canon 6, in Alexander Roberts and James Donaldson, eds., *The Ante-Nicene Fathers*, vol. 7: *Fathers of the Third and Fourth Centuries: Lactantius, Venantius, Asterius, Victorinus, Dionysius, Apostolic Teaching and Constitutions, Homily, and Liturgies*, ed. A. Cleveland Coxe [n.p.: Christian Literature Publishing, 1885; repr. Grand Rapids: Eerdmans, n.d.], 500; *New Catholic Encyclopedia*, s.v. "Celibacy, History of."

181. "He who has taken a widow, or a divorced woman, or an harlot, or a servant, or one belonging to the theatre, cannot be either a bishop, priest, or deacon, or indeed any one of the sacerdotal catalogue" (*Canons of the Apostles*, Canons 18 and 19, in *Ante-Nicene Fathers*, 7:501.7).

182. Schillebeeckx, *Celibacy*, 40.

183. Day, *Subdiaconate*, 22–23.

184. *New Catholic Encyclopedia*, s.v. "Celibacy."

185. These customs were solidified at the Synod in Trullo in A.D. 692. See "Canons of Trullo," Canons 3–6, in *Nicene and Post-Nicene Fathers*, 14:362–68; Schillebeeckx, *Celibacy*, 36.

186. Tertullian, *On the Veiling of Widows* 33.7, in *The Ante-Nicene Fathers: Translations of the Writings of the Fathers Down to A.D. 325*, vol. 4: *Fathers of the Third Century: Tertullian, Part Fourth; Minucius Felix; Commodian; Origen, Parts First and Second*, ed. A. Cleveland Coxe (n.p.: Christian Literature Publishing, 1885; repr. New York: Charles Scribner's Sons, 1905), 33.

187. Justinian, *Novella* 123, c. 30, in H. J. Schroeder, ed., *Disciplinary Decrees of the General Councils* (St. Louis: n.p., 1937), 108, quoted in McKenna, *Women of the Church*, 80.

188. Uhlhorn, *Christian Charity*, 413n.

189. Barnett, *The Diaconate* (1981), 113, 115.

190. Brown, *Body and Society*.

191. For important sites in the lives of martyrs as pilgrimage sites, see Davis, *Cult of Saint Thecla*, 113–48.

192. Elm, *"Virgins of God,"* 257–72, 275, 279–81.

193. Elm, *"Virgins of God,"* 47–51.

194. Elm, *"Virgins of God,"* 353.

195. Doran, *Lives of Simeon Stylites*, 16–20, 22–23, 27–29, 159, 196, 222.

196. Doran, *Lives of Simeon Stylites*, 168.

197. Elm, *"Virgins of God,"* 284–96.

198. Frend, *Early Church*, 190–95.

199. McKenna, *Women of the Church*, 123.

200. "Ascetic Renunciation and Feminine Advancement: A Paradox of Late Ancient Christianity," in Clark, *Ascetic Piety and Women's Faith*, 175–208.

201. For the importance of women to Jerome, see Clark, *Jerome, Chrysostom, and Friends*.

202. Gregory, Bishop of Nyssa, *Life of Saint Macrina*, 12, 29–30; see also the discussion of Macrina in Elm, *"Virgins of God,"* 39–47.

203. McKenna, *Women of the Church*, 100, 102.

204. The title "female deacon," which Sister Teresa prefers, is used in this text as synonymous with "deaconess" because Sister Teresa uses the nomenclature of the modern Church of England in which "deacon" refers either to men or women.

205. White, "Development and Eclipse of the Deacon Abbess," 111–12.

206. White, "Development and Eclipse of the Deacon Abbess," 111–14.

207. White, "Development and Eclipse of the Deacon Abbess," 112.

208. Gregory, *Life of Saint Macrina*, 16, 52–53.

209. White, "Development and Eclipse of the Deacon Abbess," 113–14.

210. Suzanne Fonay Wemple, "Women from the Fifth to the Tenth Century," in Klapisch-Zuber, *History of Women in the West*, vol. 2: *Silences of the Middle Ages*, 195.

211. White, "Development and Eclipse of the Deacon Abbess," 115.

212. *New Catholic Encyclopedia*, 2d ed., s.v. "Deaconess."

213. White, "Development and Eclipse of the Deacon Abbess," 115–16.

214. *New Catholic Encyclopedia*, 2d ed., s.v. "Deaconess."

215. Innocent III, as quoted in Gary Macy, "The Ordination of Women in the Early Middle Ages," in Cooke and Macy, *History of Women and Ordination*, vol. 1: *The Ordination of Women in a Medieval Context*, 11, 27–28n73.

216. *Catholic Encyclopedia*, s.v. "Deaconesses," 652.

217. Uhlhorn, *Christian Charity*, 266.

218. Cooke, *Ministry to Word and Sacraments*, 353, 359n34.

219. G. Barrois, "On Mediaeval Charities," in McCord and Parker, *Service in Christ*, 65.

220. Ferrari, *Early Roman Monasteries*, 354–61.

221. For a conservative estimate of their involvement with the poor, see Collins, *Diakonia*, 67.

222. Barrois, "Mediaeval Charities," 67.

223. Orme and Webster, *English Hospital*, 15, 20.

224. Brotherhoods financed, built, and maintained bridges over the Rhone River in France at Avignon, Lyons, and Pont-Saint-Esprit; see Boyer, "Bridgebuilding Brotherhoods," 635–50. See also Uhlhorn, *Christian Charity*, 357.

225. Miller, *Birth of the Hospital*, 4, 7.

226. Barrois, "Mediaeval Charities," 67–68.

227. Mollat, *Poor of the Middle Ages*, 151.

228. Miller, *Birth of the Hospital*, 6; Mollat, *Poor of the Middle Ages*, 149.

229. Mollat, *Poor of the Middle Ages*, 147.

230. Tierney, *Medieval Poor Law*, 85.

231. Brenda M. Bolton, "Hearts Not Purses? Pope Innocent III's Attitude to Social Welfare," in Hanawalt and Lindberg, *Through the Eye of a Needle*, 123.

232. Barrois, "Mediaeval Charities," 67.

233. Orme and Webster, *English Hospital*, 81.

234. Orme and Webster, *English Hospital*, 58, 119.

235. Orme and Webster, *English Hospital*, 119.

236. Orme and Webster, *English Hospital*, 23, 27.

237. Mollat, *Poor of the Middle Ages*, 152.

238. Pullan, *Orphans and Foundlings*, 16.

239. Miller, *Birth of the Hospital*, 6; Barrois, "Mediaeval Charities," 67.

240. Mollat, *Poor of the Middle Ages*, 146.

241. Miller, *Birth of the Hospital*, 72, 103.

242. Miller, *Birth of the Hospital*, 11, 37.

243. Miller, *Birth of the Hospital*, 70.

244. Miller, *Birth of the Hospital*, 49–55, 69, 121, 125.

245. Miller, *Birth of the Hospital*, 144, 146.

246. X. 5.5.1., in Schroeder, *Disciplinary Decrees*, 229, 556, as cited in Tierney, *Medieval Poor Law*, 19.

247. X. 5.5.1., in Schroeder, *Disciplinary Decrees*, 229, 556, as cited in Tierney, *Medieval Poor Law*, 19–20.

248. Mollat, *Poor of the Middle Ages*, 49.

249. Mollat, *Poor of the Middle Ages*, 49, 87.

250. Mollat, *Poor of the Middle Ages*, 88.

251. Bolton, "Hearts Not Purses?" 132–33.

252. Mollat, *Poor of the Middle Ages*, 135.

253. Mollat, *Poor of the Middle Ages*, 139.

254. Mollat, *Poor of the Middle Ages*, 136.

255. Mollat, *Poor of the Middle Ages*, 139.

256. Boyer, "Bridgebuilding Brotherhoods," 635–50; Orme and Webster, *English Hospital*, 67; Olson, *Calvin and Social Welfare*, 115.

257. Barrois, "Mediaeval Charities," 69–70.

258. Konrad Eisenbichler, "Italian Youth Confraternities in an Age of Reform," in Donnelly and Maher, *Confraternities and Catholic Reform*, 28–29.

259. Rotzetter, Van Dijk, and Matura, *Un chemin d'évangile*, 240–41; Pullan, "Catholics and the Poor," 23–24.

260. Michael W. Maher, "How the Jesuits Used Their Congregations to Promote Frequent Communion," in Donnelly and Maher, *Confraternities and Catholic Reform*, 76.

261. Maher, "How the Jesuits Used Their Congregations," in Donnelly and Maher, *Confraternities and Catholic Reform*, 76–77.

262. Aquinas, *Summa Theologiae*, 2a, 2ae, ques. 32, art. 6, in Barrois, "Mediaeval Charities," 77. This idea is found in Augustine: "All that God has given us beyond what is necessary, He has not properly speaking given to us, He has but entrusted it to us, that it may by our means come into the hands of the poor" (S. 219; in Psalm 147; S. 249, in Uhlhorn, *Christian Charity*, 301).

263. Barrois, "Mediaeval Charities," 72.

264. "Visito, poto, cibo, redimo, tego, colligo, condo, consule, castiga, solare, remitte, fer, ora," in Barrois, "Mediaeval Charities," 74.

265. Aquinas, *Summa Theologiae*, 2a, 2ae, ques. 26, in Barrois, "Mediaeval Charities," 77.

266. Barrois, "Mediaeval Charities," 66.

267. Tierney, *Medieval Poor Law*, 7–8.

268. Tierney, *Medieval Poor Law*, 13.

269. Tierney, *Medieval Poor Law*, 8–9, 70.

270. Tierney, *Medieval Poor Law*, 70; Uhlhorn, *Christian Charity*, 252.

271. Tierney, *Medieval Poor Law*, 70.

272. Tierney, *Medieval Poor Law*, 70. The church fathers of the late Roman Empire had admonished people to give a tenth or more, but the Second Synod of Macon (A.D. 583) made it binding; see Uhlhorn, *Christian Charity*, 259–60.

273. Nolf, *La réforme de la bienfaisance publique à Ypres au seizième siècle*, xi.

274. Tierney, *Medieval Poor Law*, 71–73.

275. For the 5 percent figure, see R. H. Snape, *English Monastic Finances in the Later Middle Ages* (Cambridge: n.p., 1926), 110–18, as cited in Tierney, *Medieval Poor Law*, 80, 153.

276. A. Savine, *English Monasteries on the Eve of the Dissolution* (Oxford: n.p., 1909), cited in Tierney, *Medieval Poor Law*, 80–81, 153.

277. Tierney, *Medieval Poor Law*, 91–92.

278. Canon 32, in Schroeder, *Disciplinary Decrees*, 269, 573, cited in Tierney, *Medieval Poor Law*, 83.

279. Tierney, *Medieval Poor Law*, 84, 93, 114.

280. Orme and Webster, *English Hospital*, 131.

281. Tierney, *Medieval Poor Law*, 86, 114.

282. Orme and Webster, *English Hospital*, 131–32, 134–36.

283. Tierney, *Medieval Poor Law*, 96–97, 104.

284. Gavitt, *Charity and Children in Renaissance Florence*, 1, 33.

285. Orme and Webster, *English Hospital*, 128–29.

286. Tierney, *Medieval Poor Law*, 111–13, 116.

287. Tierney, *Medieval Poor Law*, 109–11, 115–16.

288. Rotzetter, Van Dijk, Matura, *Un chemin d'évangile*, 240.

289. Congar, *Lay People in the Church*, 35–36.

290. Martimort, "The Disappearance of Deaconesses and the Memory of Them That Remained in the Twelfth and Thirteenth Centuries," in Martimort, *Deaconesses*, 217–28. "By the end of the tenth or eleventh centuries, deaconesses had pretty much disappeared in the East" (Martimort, *Deaconesses*, 183). "Balsamon, Patriarch of Antioch about 1070 states that deaconesses in any proper sense had ceased to exist in the Church though the title was borne by certain nuns" (Thurston, "Deaconesses," 652).

291. Martimort, "Reappearance of Deaconesses among Women Religious," in Martimort, *Deaconesses*, 229–40.

292. Peter Lombard, *Sentences*, as quoted in Echlin, *Deacon in the Church*, 84–85.

293. Echlin, *Deacon in the Church*, 83.

294. Echlin, *Deacon in the Church*, 87.

295. Aquinas, *Summa Theologiae*, 3a, ques. 67, art. 1, in vol. 57: *Baptism and Confirmation (3a.66–72)*, ed. and trans. James Cunningham (New York: Blackfriars with McGraw-Hill, 1975), 57.

296. Aquinas, *Summa Theologiae Supplementum Tertiae Partis*, ques. 30, art. 1, cited in Echlin, *Deacon in the Church*, 88–89.

297. Echlin, *Deacon in the Church*, 87.

298. Cooke, *Ministry to Word and Sacraments*, 278.

299. Deanesly, "Archdeacons of Canterbury," 2–3.

300. Bingham, *Antiquities of the Ancient Church*, 1:97.

301. Echlin, *Deacon in the Church*, 86–87.

302. Bligh, "Deacons in the Latin West," 427.

303. H. I. Marrou, "L'origine orientale des diaconies romaines," in *Ecole Français de Rome: Mélanges d'Archéologie et d'Histoire* 57 (1940): 95–142, in Barrois, "Mediaeval Charities," 66.

304. Walker et al., *History of the Christian Church*, 268, 273.

305. Edward Echlin stated that "the task of prophets and teachers, and therefore of *episcopoi* and deacons, was to preach . . ." (*Deacon in the Church*, 17). James Barnett states in his 1995 edition of *The Diaconate* that "preaching was not a function of the diaconate in the early Church" (xiii).

CHAPTER THREE
THE REFORMATION

MARTIN LUTHER

The birth of Martin Luther in 1483 in Eisleben, Saxony, heralded a new age. The Reformation eliminated intermediaries—be they priests or saints—between God and the individual. Luther proclaimed that all Christians had open access to God, open access to Scripture, and every Christian is both saint and sinner. These teachings had profound implications for church office that even today have not been fully worked out by Protestants.

When the church, already divided east and west, resisted the reform for which Luther called and instead splintered into confessional groups, there was a shift in the ownership of church property in Protestant regions. Many buildings and endowments passed into the hands of governments, which were ruling on behalf of the fledgling churches. In some regions, during the transition from dependence on the church of Rome, the new confessional churches lost control of the property accumulations of centuries. In Catholic regions, too, there was a trend toward increased government control of church property.

In regions that accepted the Reformation, religious orders and confraternities were disbanded or gradually disappeared. This had profound implications for church-run social welfare and education. Priests, friars, and nuns had been the teachers, social workers, and nurses of the Middle Ages. Protestant cities and local governments had to reorganize hospitals and schools and find new staff from among the laity. Consequently, laypeople were important for the functions of social work and teaching in the newly organized churches.

In addition, Luther advocated for educated pastors whose key role was preaching the Gospel. His criticism of bishops and priests as they had evolved by the end of the medieval period centered on the fact that they placed other tasks before preaching. Thus Luther said in 1520 in his treatise "The Babylonian Captivity of the Church":

> The priesthood is properly nothing but the ministry of the Word—the Word I say; not the law, but the gospel. . . . Whoever, therefore, does not know or preach the gospel is not only no priest or bishop, but he is a kind of pest to the church, who under the false title of priest or bishop, or dressed in sheep's clothing, actually does violence to the gospel and plays the wolf [Matt. 7:15] in the church.

> Therefore, unless these priests and bishops, with whom the church abounds today . . . realize that they are not priests or bishops, and bemoan the fact that they bear the name of an office whose duties they either do not know or cannot fulfill, and thus with prayers and tears lament their wretched hypocritical life—unless they do this, they are truly the people of eternal perdition.[1]

Luther said of the medieval "sacrament" of ordination:

> If it is anything at all, [it] is nothing else than a certain rite whereby one is called to the ministry of the church. . . . According to what the Scriptures teach us, what we call the priesthood is a ministry. So I cannot understand at all why one who has once been made a priest cannot again become a layman; for the sole difference between him and a layman is his ministry.[2]

For Luther the preaching office was the highest office in Christendom. He also stated what he thought was the proper role of the deacon. He said that the deacon's ministry was to distribute the church's aid to the poor so the priests could give themselves more freely to prayer and to the Word. Luther described them in "The Babylonian Captivity of the Church":

> The diaconate is the ministry, not of reading the Gospel and the Epistle, as is the present practice, but of distributing the church's aid to the poor, so that the priests may be relieved of the burden of temporal matters and may give themselves more freely to prayer and the Word. For this was the purpose of the institution of the diaconate, as we read in Acts 5 [6:1–6].[3]

Luther implied that because deacons could relieve them of temporal matters, priests and bishops had no excuse for not praying, studying, and preaching. This, then, was the position Luther took on the diaconate in the early years of the Reformation before the decisive break with Rome. Later there were opportunities to put his ideas into practice as Lutheran churches organized throughout Germany.

Luther went back to Scripture and to the early church to suggest that deacons play a role in poor relief. One might have thought this ideal would have been realized in the medieval period by proto-Protestant groups that had begun to emerge in the thirteenth century and were considered heretical by the Catholic Church. These groups had pastors or priests with assistants who resembled medieval deacons. These groups included the Waldensians (named after Peter Waldo [d. 1225] and centered in Northern Italy and Southeastern France) and the Hussites of Moravia (named after John Hus [1374–1415], who was burned at the stake by the Council of Constance). Waldensians had *minores* or *iuniores* who accompanied their *barbe* (pastors) on preaching tours. After the Reformation, the Waldensians adopted deacons on the Swiss model. Hussites had assistants to the priests who accompanied them on missionary journeys, taught, preached, assisted in administration of Communion, and baptized if necessary. The care of the poor was not in the hands of the deacon, but a committee of three people oversaw poor relief.[4]

Within Lutheranism, one might have expected that deacons would have emerged on the model of the early church as Luther outlined, but these expectations were only partially fulfilled.[5] Lutheran churches would have deacons, but not every church. In many places the work of a deacon was done by someone who did not bear the title. This was the case in Wittenberg, where Luther lived and had his first concrete opportunity to implement his ideas on social welfare. Wittenberg initiated a welfare system that was to set the tone for future Protestant churches as they formed. The reforms in Wittenberg came so early in the course of the Reformation that use of the word *deacon* to refer to those who worked with the poor might have invited confusion with the late medieval diaconate of which Luther did not approve. In his lectures of 1528, Luther did endorse the value of deacons:

> Now follows about the deacons: *serious*. There were deacons who also at one time preached. From Acts: *they established seven*, who presided over the church in providing for the poor and widows. These deacons sometimes also preached, e.g., Stephen, and were admitted to other offices of the church although the chief task was to provide for the poor and widows. This custom already long ago went out of use. In the papal church the subdeacon is the one who reads the gospel; the distribution of aid and the care of the poor are relegated to hospices *hospitalia*.

According to the truth of the thing there ought to be chaplains and common chests. It would please me more if the doorkeepers had the business of feeding the poor rather than we. The cause I have recently said: because the eyes of all are on us. There ought to be deacons of the church who ought to serve the bishop and to rule the church in external things according to his counsel.[6]

On January 24, 1522, six years before the above quotation, the Wittenberg city council passed a church order that organized a welfare system. This order provided for (1) people to do the work of deacons as Luther had described them in "The Babylonian Captivity of the Church" and (2) a common chest to assist the poor. The common chest, which was an actual chest that held both current donations and property from the pre-Reformation church, was typical of areas that became Protestant. In Wittenberg, funds for the common chest initially were to be gathered from discontinued religious endowments. Money from the chest was to help the poor, support orphans, make low-interest loans to artisans that would be forgiven if they could not repay, provide dowries for poor women, and educate poor boys so there would be people to preach the Gospel and to govern the state. Begging was outlawed in Wittenberg. The magistrates were to select people to run the common chest: two from the city council, two from the citizens at large, and a secretary. The secretary collected money, supervised distribution of aid, and kept the books.[7]

When this ordinance was passed, Luther was at the Wartburg Castle, where he had been since May 1521 after his excommunication by Pope Leo X and his banishment by Emperor Charles V. Therefore, it is difficult to attribute the church order directly to Luther. Credit has often gone to Andreas Bodenstein von Karlstadt, who was in the city and three days after the ordinance was passed published a supportive tract: "There Should Be No Beggars among Christians."[8] However, Luther was not without influence in Wittenberg during this time period. He was in constant communication, and the Protestant social welfare program in Wittenberg already may have been initiated before he left town. On January 11, 1521, the city council paid a Wittenberg carpenter for a chest with three keys that met the description of a chest mentioned in an undated Wittenberg document: *Ordnung des gemeinen Beutels*, usually referred to as the *Beutelordnung*.[9]

The Wittenberg *Beutelordnung* provided for a chest to be placed in the parish church and locked with three keys. Weekly collections were to be placed therein. The mayor was to have one of the keys, and four stewards of the chest were to have the other two keys. The collections, which formerly had been for the hospital, were now to be for all the needy of the congregation. The stewards were to be elected from each quarter of the town and were to be honest and prosperous citizens. The stewards were to visit the poor, meet on Sundays after the sermon to decide to whom to allocate money, and account for their financial transactions to the mayor, the city councillors, and the pastor. The ordinance provided for the purchase and stockpiling of grain and firewood.[10] The idea of a common chest spread rapidly. Within two years, by 1523, there were provisions for common chests in Augsburg, Altenburg, Breslau, Kitzingen, Leisnig, Nuremberg, Regensburg, and Strasbourg.[11]

At least one authority, Carter Lindberg, credits Luther with assisting the city council to pass the *Beutelordnung* in late 1520 or early 1521. Hermann Barge attributed the *Beutelordnung* to Karlstadt, but a copy exists with additions and corrections in Luther's hand.[12] If the 1520–1521 dating of the *Beutelordnung* is accurate, Luther appears to have been active in the initiation of a reformed welfare system in Wittenberg at an early date. This thesis is substantiated by a letter of Ulscenius to Capito dated November 30, 1521, describing a purse for assistance to the poor that the Wittenberg magistrates established following Luther's advice.[13] Whatever conclusion one reaches on the contributions of Karlstadt versus those of Luther to welfare reform in Wittenberg, it is clear that both were influential and had similar ideas about providing for the poor. The welfare reform in Wittenberg came before the split between the two men. It is not surprising that they shared similar opinions.

As for Luther, his ideas on meeting the needs of the poor were formulated well before welfare reform in Wittenberg. Already during the indulgence controversy in 1517 he stated in the "Ninety-five Theses": "Christians are to be taught that he who gives to the poor or lends to the needy does a better deed than he who buys indulgences."[14] Luther also criticized the indulgence hawkers for robbing the people of needed resources. To those who complained that welfare is open to abuse, he replied: "He who has nothing to live should be aided. If he deceives us, what then? He must be aided again."[15]

Although Luther advocated helping the poor, he opposed begging, especially by mendicant orders whose members begged as an act of merit.[16]

> This unrestricted universal begging is harmful to the common people. I have figured out that each of the five or six mendicant orders[17] visits the same place more than six or seven times every year.[18]

Luther's solution to the problem of mendicancy was that every city should look after its own poor. In his address "To the Christian Nobility of the German Nation," he proposed the following:

21. One of the greatest necessities is the abolition of all begging throughout Christendom. Nobody ought to go begging among Christians. It would even be a very simple matter to make a law to the effect that every city should look after its own poor, if only we had the courage and the intention to do so. No beggar from outside should be allowed into the city whether he might call himself pilgrim or mendicant monk. Every city should support its own poor, and if it was too small, the people in the surrounding villages should also be urged to contribute, since in any case they have to feed so many vagabonds and evil rogues who call themselves mendicants. In this way, too, it could be known who was really poor, and who was not.

There would have to be an overseer or warden who knows all the poor and informs the city council or the clergy what they need. Or some other better arrangement might be made.[19]

Besides criticizing the mendicant orders, Luther castigated others whom he felt shirked their responsibilities toward society, especially the confraternities, of which there were twenty or twenty-one in Wittenberg.[20] In his 1519 treatise "The Blessed Sacrament of the Holy and True Body of Christ, and the Brotherhoods," Luther criticized the confraternities for the degenerate nature of their social gatherings:

And the brotherhood is also supposed to be a special convocation of good works; instead it has become a collecting of money for beer. What have the names of Our Lady, St. Anne, St. Sebastian, or other saints to do with your brotherhoods, in which you have nothing but gluttony, drunkenness, useless squandering of money, howling, yelling, chattering, dancing, and wasting of time? If a sow were made the patron saint of such a brotherhood she would not consent.[21]

Elsewhere Luther saw the positive potential of the confraternities: "But if there were a brotherhood which raised money to feed the poor or to help the needy, that would be a good idea."[22]

Luther suggested that the debts of the poor be canceled, and like the Catholic Church, he opposed usury. He proposed a 4 to 5 percent ceiling on interest and composed a "Sermon on Usury" (1519) and an "Admonition to Clergy That They Preach against Usury" (1541). He suggested that pastors refuse absolution and the Sacrament to usurers who did not repent. After his death, however, in 1564–1565 a pastor in Rudolstadt refused Communion to two parishioners who lived by usury, and the theological faculties of Wittenberg, Leipzig, and Jena found fault with the pastor, who had to leave town.[23] The issue of usury was one of the ways in which Luther emphasized the connection between the Lord's Supper and ethics, as did other reformers after him, such as John Calvin.[24] On the practical level, the Wittenberg *Beutelordung* provided that the high-interest loans of burdened citizens be refinanced at 4 percent interest.[25]

It is no wonder, then, that Luther took an active role in the reform of social welfare in Wittenberg. His interest in welfare reform also extended elsewhere. On September 25, 1522, he visited the parish of Leisnig in electoral Saxony while the city was undergoing reform. The congregation subsequently took over the church properties and asked Luther for his advice on their welfare ordinance. Luther approved their plan and wrote a preface for the ordinance.[26]

The social welfare plan for Leisnig differed from that of Wittenberg because it gave the parish assembly primary responsibility. At its annual meeting in January, the parish was to elect a board of trustees for a common chest: two from the nobility, two from the city council, three from the town citizens, and three from the peasants. This board, which would meet every Sunday, was responsible not only for the poor but also for the schools, the maintenance of church buildings, and the salaries of the pastors and custodians. Beyond the original endowments for the common chest from the pre-reform era, each family was to contribute according to its means, a provision that was closer to compulsory taxation than other Lutheran church orders, which maintained the principle of voluntarism. Luther suggested that Leisnig establish schools for boys and girls in monastery buildings. Unfortunately for the parish assembly, the city council would not turn over the properties and endowments of the pre-Reformation church to the directors of the common chest. Instead, the city council gained control of the chest. Luther favored the parish regaining control and wrote a letter to Elector Frederick on the parish's behalf.[27]

When city councils took over endowments, as in the case of Leisnig, the money and property were not necessarily lost. This was usually better than endowments going to private citizens, as happened in Scotland, for example, where John Knox (1505–1572) complained that much of what had been intended for the poor fell into other hands during the shift to Protestantism.[28] When regions of Europe became Protestant, it was a temptation for the families of people who had willed bequests to the church and for others to attempt to retrieve the endowments. Luther felt that if the families of the original donors were needy, some of the property of the church should be returned to them.[29]

Despite the attempts of private individuals to benefit from the changes in property ownership brought about by the Reformation, much church property came under governmental control. When a Lutheran or Reformed church replaced the Church of Rome, it was thought natural that its property should remain in local hands to be used as the endowment originally had intended: for the poor, clergy salaries, or as schools. Protestants did discontinue the Masses and prayers for the dead attached to these bequests, of course. When governments took over the supervision of property, the revenues of church endowments sometimes were used for other purposes, such as self-defense or even war. Lausanne auctioned church property to pay public debts, for example, and the city council of Zurich argued that the battle of Kappel in which Huldrych Zwingli (1484–1531) died had been fought for the sake of the church. Also in Zurich, the property of monasteries was placed in the hands of a new overseer elected from the city council, the *obmann*. Sometimes income was used for church needs, at other times for civic needs. In the long run, the power of governments to tax to finance education and social welfare may have offset initial losses from the diversion of church revenues at the time of the Reformation.[30]

Lutherans have been accused of cooperating too freely with the move toward state control of churches, but in the case of Leisnig, Luther attempted to protect the rights of the parish despite the city council's opposition. On other occasions he supported cooperation between church and state in social welfare, as appeared to have been the case in Wittenberg. Luther did not differentiate between church and state in a modern way. In the sixteenth century, at the local level, people had a sense of community in which all were members of one church and state. Parish and government functions, responsibilities, and personnel overlapped. Thus Luther could appeal to the Christian nobility of the German nation to reform the church.

Lutherans also have been accused of quietism and apathy toward the society that surrounds them.[31] This was not true at the beginnings of Lutheranism, and one can argue that it never has been true. Luther personally preached, exhorted, and corresponded with civic officials throughout his life, encouraging them to provide for the poor and for schools.[32] Other early Lutheran leaders did likewise. Johannes Bugenhagen (1485–1558) was particularly influential in this regard.

JOHANNES BUGENHAGEN

Luther's confessor and friend and the pastor of the city church in Wittenberg (1522–1558), Johannes Bugenhagen was called on to write church orders for new Lutheran churches in northern Germany and Scandinavia.[33] A church order is a constitution for a church in a specific geographic area (city, state, or nation). It typically consists of norms or guidelines that describe church organization in its broadest dimensions, including liturgy, education, and poor relief. Many regions that became Protestant composed such orders or requested outsiders to do so. Bugenhagen was especially prolific in this regard. He wrote or edited church orders for Braunschweig (1528), Hamburg (1529), Lübeck (1531), his home region of Pomerania (1535), Denmark (1537), Schleswig-Holstein (1542), Braunschweig-Wolfenbüttel (1543), and Hildesheim (1544).[34]

Bugenhagen's welfare programs differed in detail from those in Wittenberg and Leisnig, though they were similar in overall conception. Bugenhagen felt that care of the poor should begin at home with families and friends, but private help was sometimes insufficient. Hence there was a need for communal poor relief. The poor chest was, in effect, an extension of the family.[35]

In the church order for Braunschweig (1528), Bugenhagen's first and an example for the rest, there were at least two differences from the church order in Wittenberg: (1) The people who were doing the work of deacons were called deacons; and (2) there were two common chests recommended for large parishes rather than one. The first chest was the poor chest for the those in need; a second chest, the church chest, provided for church supplies and repairs; the salaries of preachers, sacristans, and organists; and housing for preachers and schoolmasters. Deacons chosen by the council and members of the commune were in charge of the chests. There were to be three deacons for the poor chest and four for the church chest. Both sets of deacons had similar responsibilities for money, record keeping, and accountability to an "Honorable Council" and the "Ten Men." The sets of deacons differed because the four deacons of the church chest had "authority from the commune in company with the council to appoint a preacher." The deacons of the church chest also were referred to as treasurers and overseers. One of the deacons of the church chest had to be a member of the council.[36]

Deacons of the poor chest were to meet once a week to deliberate, determine who could be on the poor rolls, and distribute aid. The poor chest was to be funded from bequests, freewill offerings put in the chest (located in the church), offerings previously made for the dead or at weddings, fees for ringing the bells when someone died (above what was owed to the sexton), collections taken by the deacons after the sermon in bags to which a bell was attached, and whatever else people could devise to fund the chest. If the deacons ran short, they were to alert the preacher, who was to appeal to the people. There was to be a reserve for emergencies, such as an outbreak of the plague or a need to buy grain.[37]

The church chest inherited its revenues and possessions from the pre-reform church: all goods, memorials, and benefices as they became vacant. Meanwhile, holders of benefices were to contribute fees they formerly had paid to the celebrant for saying Mass. It was hoped that guilds and brotherhoods would give the church chest what they previously had spent on candles, memorials, vigils, Masses for the dead, wine, and oblations. A periodic contribution called the Ember-penny belonged to the chest. The parish priest and council of the district also were expected to contribute.[38]

With the two chests, Bugenhagen provided for a division of revenues between those for the poor and those for clergy, teachers, staff, and buildings. This may have served as a protection for the poor who thus were not on the same budget as salaried church personnel.

Bugenhagen's subsequent church orders were a variant on Braunschweig's with adjustments for the local setting. The Hildesheim and the Braunschweig-Wolfenbüttel orders had a common chest rather than a separate church chest and poor chest.[39] The number of deacons for the poor chest varied: five or six for Pomerania, six for Braunschweig-Woffenbüttel and Hildesheim, twelve for Hamburg and Lübeck. Deacons were to be elected by the previous deacons, city councils, or representatives from the parishes and city councils guided by the criteria in Acts 6:3 ("Pick out from among you seven men of good repute, full of the Spirit and of wisdom") and 1 Timothy 3:8–13. The deacons were volunteers, but Bugenhagen suggested that paid assistants be hired from among the poor, if possible, one as a messenger and another as a secretary. The deacons were to aid the local worthy poor, screening potential welfare recipients for moral rectitude, financial need, and local residency. Strangers could be helped as an exception, for example, if they were ill. This appeared to be a necessary provision because begging was opposed and private almsgiving discouraged. Priests of the pre-Reformation church could be supported, if necessary, but young priests were to be given temporary assistance until they found other employment. The poor chest could support local hospitals if their endowments were inadequate.[40]

These were provisions Bugenhagen wrote into his church orders. How much of this was implemented is a question that can be resolved by research into the documents of the period: deacons' account books, legal documents, and church records. Archival records for the poor chests in Braunschweig indicate that the city had working poor chests by the end of 1528, the year the church order was written.[41] Scholars have not determined whether Bugenhagen's ideas were put into effect wherever he worked. Much investigative work remains to be done, not only in the cities and territories where Bugenhagen worked but also elsewhere.

DEACONS AND SOCIAL WELFARE WITHIN LUTHERANISM

Bugenhagen's church orders are but one example of Protestant poor relief. Other cities and states reorganized welfare. In some regions the people who were responsible for welfare were called deacons; in others they were not. Whatever their title, whether *kastenheren* or *vorweser*, their duties with the poor were similar. Already in 1526, the reform of the church of Hesse associated deacons with the care of the poor, but this was not the case in Protestant churches elsewhere.[42] Terminology associated with ministry and the diaconate within Lutheranism was complicated by the fact that, besides being associated with social welfare, the word *deacon* came to designate an assistant minister in Germany. Arthur Piepkorn asserted that "the term *diaconus/Diakon* in the Lutheran documents of the 16th century . . . must be understood as referring to ordained priests serving as curates or assistants to the rector of a parish."[43]

As with so many practical issues, Luther and Lutherans seemed to care more about the substance of matters than outward forms. The crucial issue in social welfare was providing for the poor, not the title of those who did that work. It also could be that Luther's emphasis on justification by grace alone through faith de-spiritualized poverty, as Carter Lindberg has argued, and that Protestants thus were freed to see poverty as a social evil rather than as an ascetic ideal. Therefore, they could take a practical approach to alleviating poverty.[44] Carter Lindberg states that Augustine's doctrine of charity had endorsed poverty as a "favoured status for the Christian life." It took Luther to break down an unhealthy symbiotic relationship between rich and poor that the early and medieval church had enabled by acknowledging almsgiving as atoning for sin.[45] On the other hand, others would suggest that the Protestant understanding of grace being received, not earned, deprived Protestants of motivation to be charitable because the giving of alms would no longer contribute to one's salvation. It had often been repeated that charity wipes away sin.[46]

Perhaps the most famous Lutheran welfare system was that of Nuremberg. Its welfare legislation was read widely and became a model of reform elsewhere. Its ordinances were published in Berlin, Basel, Leipzig, and

Strasbourg. It may have influenced Catholic Ypres. Even Emperor Charles V asked for a draft of the Nuremberg welfare legislation before issuing his own ordinance of 1531, which he urged the cities of the Low Countries to adopt. Reform in Nuremberg began while the city was still Catholic and the imperial diet was meeting there in the spring of 1522. Nuremberg had restrictions on foreign beggars and badges for legitimate local beggars dating from the fourteenth century, but the city council was embarrassed by its inability to keep beggars away from the important people in the city for the diet. The council asked two men, who later became the directors of poor relief, to study the situation. It passed an ordinance on July 24, 1522, appointing additional directors beneath the two chief directors. Salaried officers for each of the four wards of the city were to identify the worthy poor and provide them with special labels. The council erected collection boxes in churches and had collection plates and later collection bags passed in church. After the city formally broke with Catholicism in March 1525, the city council appropriated church endowments and property and created a common chest.[47]

ZURICH AND HULDRYCH ZWINGLI

As Protestant churches evolved in other regions of Europe, similar forms of social welfare reorganization developed. In Zurich, an early leading Reformed city, the city council centralized the welfare system and took it under its own control. Beginning in 1520, the year after Huldrych Zwingli came as priest and preacher to the city, Zurich gradually restricted begging in a series of ordinances. The first of these ordinances, a statute "On Poor Relief" (September 8, 1520), allowed for begging but established a system of poor relief too. It provided for "worthy, pious women who stand at the doors of the three parishes [every Sunday] at times of divine services, when people most frequently go into the churches, and there collect alms from the people in closed purses."[48] The Mandate of January 1523 required resident beggars to wear a badge to distinguish them from foreigners, prohibited residents from housing foreign beggars for more than a night or two, and prescribed punishment for parents who sent their children to beg and consumed the proceeds in taverns.[49] In 1524, the city council suppressed the convents and monasteries and subsequently took over their possessions, turning over some of the buildings for poor relief.[50]

The capstone ordinance of 1525, the *Almosenordnung*, attempted to bring poor people off the streets by providing a large kettle of "cornmeal, barley, or other grain" each day in front of the former Dominican cloister.

At the ringing of the bells, it would be distributed along with stewed fruit. Sick people also were allocated wine, commonly thought to be good for them in this era. The ordinance forbade begging entirely: "It is further agreed that henceforth all begging in the city of Zürich, whether by residents or foreigners, shall cease."[51] The *Almosenordnung* placed responsibility for the common chest and poor relief in the hands of four persons from the Great and Small Councils of the city and a secretary. These men were not called deacons. The four councilmen were referred to as custodians and the secretary as a steward. From each of the seven watches of the city they were to appoint a priest and a pious layman to determine who deserved poor relief. The legitimate "house poor" and no more than eight poor students in each school were to wear identification badges, which they were to turn back to the custodians when they no longer needed relief. Zurich served as a model for other Swiss cities, such as Berne, when they became reformed.[52]

Zwingli did not insist that welfare officers be called deacons. The liturgy of Zurich of the same year as the *Almosenordnung* retained the use of the word *deacon* or *lector* to refer to an assistant in liturgy. This was also true of other Protestant liturgies of the early Reformation, which may reflect a holdover from the terminology of the Catholic Mass. The Zurich liturgy read as follows:

> Now the deacon or lector says: The Lord be with you.
>
> *The people respond*: And with thy spirit.[53]

We have seen how up to eight students received aid from Zurich's Reformed welfare system. Because there was no university in Zurich at the time of the Reformation, who were these students? Both before and after the Reformation, Zurich provided a Latin school for what the modern world would consider secondary education. After the Reformation, however, Protestant pastors needed more education. As a reformer with a humanist education, Zwingli envisioned more preparation in the original languages of the Old and New Testaments for Protestant pastors than a traditional Latin school curriculum provided. When Zwingli reformed Zurich, he got the city council to agree to theological education under his leadership two years before the Mass was abolished at Easter 1525.[54]

The salaries for the exegetes, or teachers, of the biblical text in Zurich's "theological school" were to come from the benefices from the former canons, who were allowed to stay in the city after the Reformation and retain the incomes from their benefices. Thus Zwingli's educational program for pastors took several years to get off the ground. The program was called prophesying and started on a daily basis in 1525 in two large churches in the city that still exist today: the Grossmünster and the Fraumünster. The study began in the morning. The exegetes read texts from the Bible in the original languages, in Latin, and in German. There was discussion or debate of the texts rather than lectures. Zwingli himself was one of the teachers. The so-called "prophesying" was free to both clergy and laity.[55]

After Zwingli's death, Heinrich Bullinger (1504–1575) led education in Zurich in a more institutionalized direction. He was keenly aware that there were 130 posts for pastors to staff in the city and country. Therefore, Bullinger reorganized the Latin schools of the city into four and later five levels. The boys entered Latin school at about the age of 13, studied Latin and Greek, and began Hebrew in the highest level. They completed their years at the Latin school at about the age of 17 or 18.[56]

For those Zurich students who wanted more education than the city's educational institutions of the sixteenth century could provide, Zurich's solution was to send its students to institutions elsewhere. There students could continue their theological education or study other subjects, such as medicine. Some families financed this education on their own. The city also granted scholarships for study outside of Zurich, mainly to students who intended to become ministers.

Among these young men from Zurich who received city support, there was a decided preference for schools in German-speaking areas, at least between 1562 and 1591, when records are available. Most of these scholarship students matriculated in Basel, which had become Reformed in 1529. The next largest number went to Heidelberg, followed by Marburg and Wittenberg. Geneva was seventh in rank behind the city of Luther, which is surprising, considering the fact that Geneva was within the Reformed tradition of the Swiss cantons and Wittenberg was Lutheran.[57]

Strasbourg and Martin Bucer

In Strasbourg, preaching of welfare reform began before the Protestant Reformation. John Geiler von Kaysersberg, a powerful preacher of the late fifteenth and early sixteenth century, urged a new system of poor relief and suggested that only people incapable of work should receive such relief. The city took considerable responsibility for the funding and administration of welfare. In the 1520s, Strasbourg dissolved the monasteries and abolished the Mass. For teachers' salaries the city used canonical prebends (the incomes used to support the priests or canons of a cathedral or church) as in Zurich. A committee of the magistrates, whose members were called *almosenherren*, was created, with an administrator of poor relief, called the *almosenpfleger*, and nine helpers, each of whom was responsible for a parish. The city authorities took over distribution of poor relief and asked that contributions be handed over to them. A weekly allowance was to be delivered to each needy home. There was to be no begging, but there were no deacons either, despite the efforts of the Strasbourg reformer, Martin Bucer (1491–1551).[58]

Basil Hall called Bucer "the theologian of diakonia" because he gave service to humanity a fundamental place and his writings are permeated with the church as a serving community.[59] Bucer had come to Strasbourg in 1523, and in 1531 he helped prepare the first formal ecclesiastical ordinance for the city.[60] It provided for lay committees, the *Kirchenpfleger*, in each parish that were responsible for the clergy and for improving the moral standards and religious life of the people. In 1532, the *Kirchenpfleger* recommended amendments to the ordinances that deacons and deaconesses be elected to care for the sick and needy following the example of the early church.[61]

Bucer often included deacons in his concept of ministry and church office, though in 1539 he spoke of three orders and deacons were missing.[62] Bucer frequently wrote of two kinds of ministry: one belonging to bishops and presbyters and the other to deacons. In a treatise on ordination that he probably wrote in 1549, Bucer said:

> According to the teaching of the Holy Spirit, the ministries of the Church are of two kinds. One consists of the administration of the word, sacraments and discipline of Christ, which belongs especially to bishops and presbyters; the other of the care of the needy, which was formerly entrusted to persons who were called deacons.[63]

In his work on the Book of Ephesians, Bucer wrote of deacons alongside evangelists, doctors, and pastors (bishops and presbyters).[64]

Despite Bucer's espousal of the diaconate and the suggestion of the *Kirchenpfleger* that Strasbourg establish deacons, the city did not do so. Instead, the suggestion came to fruition in an ecclesiastical constitution that another Strasbourg reformer, Wolfgang Capito (1478–1541), drew up for the Frankfurt Magistrate in 1535. It resembled the Strasbourg ordinance except that a specific provision was made for deacons and the *Kirchenpfleger* were called elders.[65]

ENGLAND

Later, Bucer attempted to influence the English church. He went to England in April 1549 at the invitation of Thomas Cranmer (1489–1556), archbishop of Canterbury.[66] Bucer was in exile from Strasbourg, where he had urged rejection of the terms of the Augsburg Interim (June 30, 1548) that had been imposed on German Protestants by Charles V, the victor in the Schmalkald War. Bucer's treatise on ordination, quoted above, may have influenced the English church, but his *De Regno Christi* (*On the Kingdom of Christ*) did not make its full impact because of his subsequent death and the death of the young king, Edward VI (1537–1553).[67]

In the section on poor relief in *De Regno Christi*, Bucer spelled out the duties of deacons more than he had done previously. Every church was to have deacons. All alms for the poor were to be directed through them. Deacons were to survey the poor carefully and assess their needs, visiting them and summoning them. There was to be no begging. Because the deacons were busy with the poor and with "discipline among the rest of the Christians," the care of the properties of the church and the collection of income belonged to "the office of subdeacons and administrators." However, deacons were to keep good records, both of the money at their disposal and of the poor, and to render their accounts to the bishop and presbytery.[68] In concluding the section on poor relief, Bucer charged the church with the responsibility for the education and nurture of all Christians:

> The churches must provide that all persons baptized into Christ should from childhood be properly educated and learn decent skills so that each one according to his portion may be able to contribute something to the common good and prove himself as a true and useful member of Christ.[69]

In 1553, Thomas Cranmer proposed a reform of church law in England in which he emphasized the role of the deacon in social service to the needy while maintaining the diaconate within the medieval grades of clerical office and the archdeacon. The timing was poor. Mary Tudor (1516–1558) took the throne and burned Cranmer at the stake on March 21, 1556, without accepting his reforms, of course.[70]

After the death of Queen Mary on November 17, 1558, her half sister, Elizabeth, came to the throne in England and accepted Cranmer's liturgy as contained in the *Book of Common Prayer*. Bucer's *De Regno Christi* had just been printed in 1557 in Basel.[71] It is difficult to tell to what extent this book reached England. In any case, Elizabeth wanted an English church with bishops and a hierarchy responsive to her rather than decentralized decision-making and deacons with disciplinary powers as Bucer proposed. There were new poor laws enacted during Elizabeth's reign, however, and some authors feel Bucer may have influenced them.[72]

JOHN CALVIN

Bucer's ideas on deacons and also on discipline in the church were destined to be more fully realized through his friends. One of these was the French-born reformer of Geneva, John Calvin (1509–1564).[73] During Calvin's sojourn in Strasbourg (1538–1541), he witnessed their social system and was impressed with Bucer's ideas. Calvin already had described the office of deacon in his first edition of the *Institutes of the Christian Religion* (1536):

> This was the office of deacons: to attend to the care of the poor and minister to them; from this they took their name. For they are so called, as ministers. Then Luke added an account of their institution. Those they had chosen, he says, they ordained in the presence of the apostles: praying, they laid their hands upon them [Acts 6:6]. Would that the church today had such deacons, and appointed them by such a ceremony; namely, the laying on of hands. . . . I contend that it is dishonorable to seek from the example of those whom the apostolic church ordained as deacons a testimony for these very ones whom our opponents present to us in their doctrine. They say that it is the office of their deacons "to assist the priests; to minister in everything done in the sacraments, that is, in baptism, in chrism, in paten, and in chalice; to bring in the offerings and lay them upon the altar; to set the Lord's Table and cover it; to carry the cross and to pronounce the gospel and epistle to the people." Is there one word here of the true ministry of deacons?[74]

When Calvin returned to Geneva in 1541, he included the office of deacon in the ecclesiastical ordinances that he wrote for the city.

The draft of these ordinances stated that there are "four orders of office instituted by our Lord for the government of the church."[75] These are pastors or ministers, doctors (teachers), elders, and deacons. Calvin derived this four-part division from the Bible and the early church and also, it seems evident, from his own experience before settling permanently in Geneva. During his student days, he lived in Catholic France, where he had been born. Then Calvin lived in reformed Basel (1535–1536) until he came to Geneva for his first stint in the city (1536–1538) before being expelled and coming to Strasbourg at the invitation of Bucer to head the church for French-speaking refugees. This gave Calvin a variety of institutional models. In universities in France and elsewhere, doctors were professors,

Reformed Strasbourg had *Kirchenpfleger*, whom Capito called elders when he wrote his recommendation for the Frankfurt magistrates. In addition, Calvin was familiar with the ideas of Bucer on deacons and on discipline. William Bouwsma feels that Bucer, almost a generation older than Calvin, was a father figure for him, which might have enhanced his credibility, though Calvin was not uncritical of Bucer.[76]

Within the plurality of ministry in the ecclesiastical ordinances of Geneva, pastors were responsible for preaching, elders for discipline, deacons for money, and doctors for teaching. Thus elders were responsible for some of the discipline within the church that Bucer had assigned to deacons. Within this division of labor there was overlap. Both elders and ministers were on the consistory, a disciplinary body, and all four offices had a part in nurturing the flock. Deacons were designated to assist in offering the cup at Communion, but the records of the Consistory reveal that, in fact, elders assisted in offering the cup in Calvin's Geneva.[77] Calvin advocated the "laying on of hands" on deacons and on ministers of the Word of God, though he implied in a sermon on Acts 6:1–3 that the laying on of hands was not yet practiced in Geneva:

> St. Luke reports in this passage that, after they had elected deacons, the apostles laid their hands on them to show that they had been dedicated to God (as in all the sacrifices made under the law it was necessary to lay on hands, as we see discussed in Moses). The apostles kept that order. And even today, it would not be a bad idea if we had this ceremony; for if we reject human superstitions and inventions, that is not to say that we despise what is of God and His apostles. When it is a question of electing a minister of the Word of God (according to the fashion St. Luke shows here, that they laid their hands on the deacons), there ought to be a solemn declaration that these are no longer private persons, free to act according to their own will, but that they must be wholly dedicated to the service of God.[78]

Earlier in the same sermon Calvin included deacons among the ministers of the Word of God:

> Because, as soon as the apostles knew that murmuring was beginning in the church, they called together all the multitude of the faithful to elect deacons (as they called them). This word simply means "minister." Those who have some task of serving in the church, whether of distributing alms or preaching, are rightly called ministers, and all the apostles had this name in common. And all those who have the task of administering in the church are rightly called ministers of the Word of God, but the church names "deacons" without adding modifiers to the word, those who are charged with the poor.[79]

Yet Calvin and the other pastors of Geneva were explicit about the exclusive roles of the four offices in the church. For example, the Company of Pastors of Geneva preferred that deacons take charge of finances in the church. In a letter to the churches of Normandy, the Company of Pastors stated:

> We add yet this word, that it seems to us that in such a case, and generally, it is good that those who are committed to administer the Word are not embroiled in investments or receipts, but that one keeps them soberly and honestly, either by the means of the deacons (which really would be the better) or by other means, according to the circumstance of time and place.[80]

In the above reference, those who "administer the Word" (apparently the pastors) are distinguished from the deacons.

It is clear that Calvin thought that the office of deacon was important alongside the pastors, doctors, and elders, and he put his beliefs into action. Within months of his return to Geneva, Calvin had managed to write a plurality of office into the laws of the city. According to the chronicler Michel Roset, Calvin appeared before the city council on September 13, 1541, and asked that the ecclesiastical order be put in writing. Already on November 20 this was accomplished and passed by the general council of the city.[81]

The four-part division that Calvin laid out in the *Ecclesiastical Ordinances* was to endure not only in that city but also as a model for churches reformed on the model of Geneva throughout Europe, the British Isles, and the world. In Scotland, the 1561 *Book of Discipline* included deacons. With the consent of the ministers and elders, deacons were to gather the alms and distribute them. John Knox (1505–1572), the reformer of Scotland, had lived in Geneva.[82]

Why was it that Calvin not only theorized about the configuration of church office but also was able to put it into effect? His legal training, a doctorate in law, and the trust that the city council of Geneva placed in him at this point in his career aided him, as did his theological preparation and his strategic position in 1541 when changes in the city council since 1538 made councilmen eager to entice him back to Geneva from Strasbourg. How far this trust extended in 1541 was evidenced by the fact that not only did Calvin rewrite Genevan church law when he returned, but he also was called on to recodify the city's legal system.

Besides describing the four offices of the church, the *Ecclesiastical Ordinances* laid out the duties and institutional structures of each office. Some of the institutions Calvin described were yet to be initiated in Geneva, such as the consistory, and some already were functioning, such as the social welfare system.

Social welfare in Geneva had been centered around the general hospital in the former convent of Saint Claire since its creation in 1535 during the Reformation in Geneva. It provided not only for the institutionalized poor but also for those at home, for whom there was a weekly dole of bread. The Genevan hospital was directed by a committee of trustees or procurators who were chosen by the smallest and most powerful council of the city from its own membership and from that of the city's Council of Sixty and Council of Two Hundred. The procurators met weekly (on Sundays at 6 A.M., before the sermon) and oversaw the management and finances of the hospital. They hired a hospital manager, the hospitaler, to do the actual day-to-day work. He and his wife made purchases and dealt with servants, outpatients, and the people housed in the hospital who were orphans, as well as some of the poor, sick, or disabled in the city.[83]

It was this institution and the plague hospital that Calvin described in the *Ecclesiastical Ordinances* under the section entitled "The Fourth Order of Ecclesiastical Government, That Is, the Deacons." Calvin had an ongoing interest in the general hospital and how it functioned. In 1545, he requested the city council to put the hospital's accounting in order, to list the revenue in writing, and to keep track of those who were given assistance.[84] In December of that same year, Calvin suggested that the poor of the hospital be given a craft.[85] Eventually the silk industry was brought to the hospital.[86]

The procurators and the hospitaler of the city hospital were already doing the work of deacons before Calvin gave them that title in the *Ecclesiastical Ordinances* of 1541. Their job descriptions fit neatly into the model for the two kinds of deacons that Calvin felt existed in the ancient church:

> The one deputed to receive, dispense and hold goods for the poor, not only daily alms, but also possessions, rents and pensions; the other to tend and care for the sick and administer allowances to the poor.[87]

Calvin found a biblical basis for this two-part division of the diaconate in Romans 12:6–8:

> Having gifts that differ according to the grace given to us, let us use them: if prophecy, in proportion to our faith; if service, in our serving; he who teaches, in his teaching; he who exhorts, in his exhortation; he who contributes, in liberality; he who gives aid, with zeal; he who does acts of mercy, with cheerfulness.

In interpreting this text, Calvin described what has sometimes been called the double diaconate:

> When Paul speaks here of givers, he does not mean those who give their own possessions, but (technically) the deacons who are charged with the distribution of the public property of the Church. When he speaks of those who show mercy, he means widows and other ministers, who were appointed to take care of the sick, according to the custom of the ancient Church. The functions of providing what is necessary for the poor, and of devoting care to their attention, are different.[88]

Calvin built his interpretation of Romans 12:8 on steps in exegesis taken by Johannes Oecolampadius (1482–1531), the reformer of Basel, and Bucer, who associated the "gifts" in Romans 12:6–8 with functions in the church and ultimately with offices.[89]

From a functional point of view, this insistence on two types of diaconal care had the advantage of describing well the division of labor of Genevan welfare and of other cities. It also made a place for women within Calvin's theory of the diaconate.[90] Calvin saw the only appropriate public office of women in the church as that of caring for the poor.[91] He wrote in *Institutes of the Christian Religion* that

> [w]omen could fill no other public office than to devote themselves to the care of the poor. . . . There will be two kinds of deacons: one to serve the church in administering the affairs of the poor; the other, in caring for the poor themselves.[92]

Calvin looked back to the office of widow in the New Testament and early church and saw it as a female diaconate whose absence he regretted in contemporary Geneva.[93] He felt Phoebe in Romans 16:1–2 was a deacon, exercising the ministry described for the widows of 1 Timothy 5:9–10.[94]

The deacons whom Calvin described in the *Ecclesiastical Ordinances* of Geneva were not the only deacons in the city, though they were the only ones present in 1541. Others were created later as a response to the problem of what to do with the foreign poor in the city. By the middle of the 1540s, the general hospital was no longer able to handle all the social welfare needs in the city. This was primarily because the press of foreign refugees coming to Geneva from Catholic countries in an effort to find freedom of religious expression was overwhelming the social welfare resources of the city. A typical sixteenth-century reaction to such a dilemma would have been to have attempted to expel impoverished foreigners because then, as now, poor relief was geared to local residents. In June 1545, the Genevan city council was preparing to remove foreigners from town. Then Calvin announced to the council a large legacy to the poor from a recently deceased man, David Busanton, a wealthy refugee whom Calvin apparently was able to encourage to remember the poor.[95] Busanton's bequest came at a strategic moment, making it possible for poor foreigners to stay in Geneva without overwhelming the city's welfare system.

Tradition has it that others added to Busanton's gift, and a fund for refugees was created, the French Fund or Fund for Poor Foreigners. The pastors of Geneva could draw on this fund to avoid burdening the general hospital of Geneva with the foreign poor. In the early years, this fund may have been managed by the pastors of Geneva, but eventually the administration was given to foreign businessmen and people with inherited wealth who had come to Geneva to be a part of the Reformed church. These individuals were from Catholic France and regions where French was spoken. The fund seems to have been reorganized under their leadership in 1549, though their first surviving account book in the archives of Geneva dates from September 30, 1550.[96] The French Fund attracted some notable figures as its deacon-administrators. For example, Jean Budé, son of Guillaume Budé, renowned humanist at the court of Francis I in France, was among the first to keep the records of receipts and disbursements.[97]

In the earliest years, those in charge of the French Fund seem to have been called simply administrators of the fund. They were first formally referred to as deacons in the account books of July 1554 at an election at Calvin's house.[98] The legal documents of Geneva about that time call them "administrators and deacons of the fund for the poor foreigners."[99] Deacon appears to have been their enduring title. Their work and numbers increased with the growth in the refugee population. In the 1550s, the fund appeared to have added collectors to help gather money. The French Fund relied on an international network of resources, and gifts came in from other countries, especially France. The money was used for the poor, but it also sent books and pastors into France and paid a man to transcribe Calvin's sermons as he preached, a project that was hoped would raise money for the poor through their eventual sale. The fund had the rights to profits from the sale of Theodore Beza's (1519–1605) translation of the Psalms. The French Fund endured to the middle of the nineteenth century, and after its dissolution, the office of deacon in Geneva survived.

The principle of encouraging a foreign refugee community to provide for its own poor proved to be a sound one. Other ethnic communities in Geneva (Italian, English, and German) established their own relief funds. Deacons mentioned in sixteenth-century Genevan documents usually were associated with one of these refugee funds. The title of deacon did not catch on as quickly for the procurators and hospitalers of the general hospital, perhaps because the city hospital already was functioning when the *Ecclesiastical Ordinances* were written. Toward the end of the sixteenth century, the word *deacon* came into greater use with reference to hospital personnel, but such usage did not appear to change their responsibilities or accountability. The hospital, the procurators, and the hospitalers continued to rely on the city council for money and direction.[100]

From Geneva, Calvin's model of the diaconate spread as Reformed churches were founded. The deacons of the new churches managed local church funds, dealt with the poor, and often took on additional duties. During Queen Elizabeth's reign, there was a deacons' fund in Sandwich, England, similar to the one in Geneva. It aided the refugees from the Low Countries, where there was religious warfare.[101] There were also deacons in the Stranger Church for French in London.

ANABAPTISTS

Reformed churches outside Switzerland were not the only persecuted denomination in the sixteenth century. Anabaptists (Rebaptizers) were also an illegal minority. The Anabaptist movement arose, in part, out of Reformation Zurich. Its early adherents were well-educated people of the city who became convinced that infant baptism was no Baptism at all and that the rite should wait until someone was old enough to ask to be baptized. Anabaptists, like Zwingli, felt that practices not authenticated by clear biblical example should be eliminated from church life. Because Anabaptists did not recognize any Scripture passages that record infant baptism, they felt that Zwingli should advocate "believers' baptism."[102] He would not. In January 1525, Zurich held a public debate and decided that everyone must have their infants baptized within eight days or be exiled.[103] Advocates of believers' baptism took matters into their own hands. On January 21, 1525, they baptized (or rebaptized) one another in a ceremony in the home of Felix Manz, a scion of a patrician family who had studied in Basel and was teaching in the Academy of Zurich. With that act of defiance against the authorities, they called down the wrath of church and state. Zurich already had arrested and exiled some Anabaptists. When the city could not repress the group, it issued an edict on March 7, 1526, that "every one who baptized another would be drowned without mercy." The city also condemned Manz to death.

> Because he has baptized, against Christian regulations . . . because he and his followers have thereby separated themselves from the Christ-

ian congregation and have riotously joined themselves together, as a schism, and are trying to organize themselves as a self-made sect, under the appearance and cover of a Christian congregation; because he has rejected capital punishment . . . because such doctrines are injurious to the general custom of Christendom and lead to scandal, tumult, and rebellion against the government, to the disturbance of the universal peace, brotherly love, and civic unanimity, and to all manner of evil.

Therefore Manz shall be handed over to the executioner, who will bind his hands, place him in a skiff, bring him to the lower Hüttli, move his bound hands over his knees, and push a stick between his knees and elbows, and will thus bound, cast him into the water, and let him die and corrupt in the water, and that thus he shall have satisfied justice and right. And his goods will be confiscated by my lords.[104]

On his way to his death, Manz sang, "Into your hands, Lord, I commend my spirit." He was drowned on January 27, 1527.[105] George Williams gave him the epitaph of "the first 'Protestant' martyr at the hands of Protestants."[106]

Persecution of the Anabaptists spread beyond Zurich. Many fled, seeking refuge wherever they could find it. Parts of Eastern Europe, such as Moravia, provided shelter.[107] In the northern provinces of the Low Countries, which were struggling for independence from Spanish rule, the Anabaptists found a less hostile environment than other parts of Europe. Some adherents made their way to Russia and eventually to the New World, where the Anabaptists live on, preserving their language and way of life in what are today Amish, Hutterite, or Mennonite communities.

In the sixteenth century, as today, many Anabaptists were pacifists, refusing military service and the taking up of arms. They disdained civil government, considering it part of an evil world from which they desired to separate themselves. They would take no oaths and rejected membership in inclusive state-supported denominations, forming instead "gathered" churches of "true believers" (wheat from which the tares had been removed, in effect). Anabaptists excluded or banned those who failed to conform to standards, an exclusiveness that cost them friends. Although some people recognized them as honest hardworking folk, Anabaptists were persecuted, especially after the takeover of the city of Münster in 1534 by a group of radical revolutionaries who, though out of character with most other Anabaptists, caused Europeans to fear that this might happen again.[108]

There were exceptions to the disdain of civil government within the Anabaptist movement. For example, Claus-Peter Clasen called Balthasar Hübmaier (1485–1528) "the outstanding Anabaptist spokesman of a sober political philosophy."[109] Hübmaier had a more accepting attitude toward civil government than many Anabaptists: "A Christian may with a good conscience be a judge and a council member to judge and decide in temporal matters. . . . A Christian may . . . bear the sword in God's stead against the evildoer and punish him."[110] Despite this, Hübmaier was burned at the stake outside Vienna on March 10, 1528. His wife was drowned in the Danube a few days later.[111]

The Anabaptists gave prominence to the New Testament ministry of the deacon. The Hutterite Chronicle identified their probable role in the baptism ceremony at Felix Manz's Zurich home in 1525:

> George Cajacob [*Blaurock*] arose and asked Conrad [Grebel] to baptize him. . . . And when he knelt down with that request and desire, Conrad baptized him, since at that time there was no ordained deacon (*diener*) to perform such work.[112]

Diener in this passage could also be translated as "minister." Other titles used among Anabaptist and Mennonite groups for those who dealt with the poor were *Armendiener* or, in Dutch, *Armendienaer* ("minister to the poor") and *Almosenpfleger* ("keeper of the alms"). The Anabaptist-Mennonite movement established the office of deacon as an ordained office.[113]

Deacons were to have important roles among the Anabaptists in meeting the economic needs of the community. The separation of Anabaptists from established churches and civil governments would have made integration into state welfare systems difficult, so they strove to become self-sufficient and to meet their needs within their own communities. To this end, Anabaptists established common funds in early congregations in Strasbourg, Esslingen, Passau, Kaufbeuren, in the Tyrol, and possibly in Zurich, Basel, and Appenzell.[114]

Although Anabaptists helped one another, they usually left the ownership of property in private hands. Early on, however, there was a movement among some Anabaptists toward community property. This effort was reflected in the following 1527 church order from the Tyrol region of Austria, reputed to have been written by Hans Schlaffer, leader of an Anabaptist congregation at Rattenberg.

Discipline of the Believers: How a Christian is to Live

> Every brother and sister shall yield himself in God to the brotherhood completely with body and life, and hold in common all gifts received of God (Acts 2 and 4; I Cor. 11, 12; II Cor. 8 and 9), [and] contribute to the common need so that brethren and sisters will always be helped

(Rom. 12); needy members shall receive from the brotherhood as among the Christians at the time of the apostles.[115]

Those congregations that owned goods in common were known as communal or communistic Anabaptists.[116] The Tyrolian government killed Schlaffer (February 3, 1528) and broke up the Anabaptist congregation at Rattenberg, killing many. The survivors fled to Moravia.[117]

In 1528 a group of Anabaptists in Moravia began the practice of community goods by choosing "ministers of temporal needs (deacons)" who spread out a cloak on which everyone laid their earthly possessions.[118] They also established a *Bruderhof*, or brother house, which was a communal house and farm, owned and run collectively under the doctrine of strict community property encouraged by the Tyrolian leader Jacob Hutter.[119] Hutter was burned at the stake by Austrian authorities in 1536, but gave his name (Hutterite) to the movement.

Hutterite communities had two types of *diener*: (1) the *Diener der Notdurft*, translated by George Williams as "deacon of welfare," and (2) the *Diener des Wortes* (deacon [or minister] of the Word). There were two kinds of this latter form of deacon: an apostle sent out to preach and the minister of the Word who remained in the community.[120] The duties of the ordained deacons of welfare in a Hutterite community included buying and selling for the community and overall economic management.[121] The *Diener des Wortes* appears to have been more of a pastor or preacher. Early Anabaptists replaced martyred ministers quickly (sometimes within the hour), thus they were unable to establish strict educational requirements.[122] Some Anabaptist groups allowed women in the role of deacon, and deaconesses became important in many congregations. This influenced Brownists, Plymouth Brethren, other English Independents, and the deaconess movement of the nineteenth and twentieth centuries.[123]

Under the leadership of the ex-priest Menno Simons (1496–1561), Mennonites were pacifists. Most Anabaptists would not tolerate magistrates as members of their communion, but Menno did not reject magistrates.[124] Menno said of the office of magistrate: "I believe that it is of God, and that it is our duty to revere it, to honor and to obey it, in all things which are not contrary to the Word of God."[125] Menno died a natural death.

Anabaptists shared the sixteenth-century Protestant enthusiasm for deacons serving the poor. Some Anabaptists gave deacons a larger role in preaching and teaching than did Luther, Bucer, and Calvin, though ambiguities in terminology and translation sometimes contribute to an apparent telescoping of roles. Within some Anabaptist groups in the seventeenth century, church office appeared to become well-defined and hierarchical, as would be reflected in the Confession of Dordrecht (1632).

THE PROTESTANT DIACONATE

The next chapter will cover the development of the diaconate from the late sixteenth through the early nineteenth centuries, building on the changes of the Reformation era. In the sixteenth century, Protestants had broken with the medieval view of the diaconate as a transitional office leading to the priesthood. They had attempted to restore deacons to the functions and roles they had held in Scripture and the early church: helping the poor. This meant giving deacons a role in social welfare.

Luther set the tone for these changes by criticizing the functions of the medieval deacon in favor of those of the deacon of the early church. He also insisted, with Karlstadt, that there should be no beggars among Christians. When Luther had an opportunity to influence welfare reform in Wittenberg, however, he did not appear to insist on the title of deacon for the welfare administrators. As Lutheranism spread to northern Germany and Scandinavia, Johannes Bugenhagen, Luther's pastor and friend, included deacons in his church orders for these regions.

Meanwhile in Zurich, the Reformation in the Swiss Reformed tradition of Zwingli remodeled the welfare system of the city without including deacons in that work. In 1536, however, another leader of the Reformed Reformation, John Calvin, in his first edition of *The Institutes of the Christian Religion*, favored deacons who tended the poor as did those identified in Acts 6:6. Martin Bucer wanted the city of Strasbourg to install deacons in its newly reformed social welfare system, but he was unsuccessful both there and in England, where Elizabeth I wanted a church hierarchy closer to the medieval model of a deacon than deacons that either Bucer or, later, the Puritans would suggest.

After a sojourn in Strasbourg, Calvin, Bucer's friend, included deacons in the plural ministry of Geneva. Calvin wanted deacons to be a separate office with responsibilities for money and the poor. Instead of direct handouts to the poor, individuals were supposed to channel their contributions through the deacons. The deacons of Calvin and his successor, Theodore Beza, were recruited largely from the business or leisure classes. They did not preach. Few of them ever became pastors. One type of deacon was essentially administrative and the other dealt directly with the poor. The widows of the New Testament fit into the second type of deacon. The diaconate was the one office in the church that Calvin advocated for women, but deaconess did not become a formal office in Geneva. In 1541, at the time the *Ecclesiastical Ordinances* of Geneva were written, deacons basically were the renamed administrators of the hospital and its hospitaler, who fit conveniently into Calvin's conception of two types of deacons, or a double diaconate. Later, separate refugee funds came into existence in Geneva, each administered by its own deacons. Geneva's pattern became a model for Reformed churches as they spread. Deacons helped those churches survive in regions where they did not have state support.

On the issue of deacons and social welfare, Luther and Calvin were similar because they both (1) looked to Scripture and the early church for their model of the diaconate, (2) thought of the seven chosen to help the poor in Acts 6:1–6 as the first deacons, (3) preferred deacons who were active in poor relief to the medieval diaconate, (4) disparaged the liturgical roles of deacons in the Catholic Church, (5) were actively interested in civic welfare programs, (6) and wanted begging abolished. Luther and Calvin differed because (1) though Luther felt the church should have deacons engaged in poor relief, he appeared neither to implement that directly nor to stand in the way of Bugenhagen's doing so. Calvin, however, insisted on deacons in the church and thought of the plural ministry in which they had a part as the approved ecclesiastical order of the New Testament. (2) Calvin believed in a double diaconate, sanctioned, he claimed, in Scripture.

Timing may have had something to do with the differences between the two reformers. In the 1520s when Luther helped with the welfare program in Wittenberg, there were no Protestant deacons. By the time Calvin wrote the first edition of *The Institutes of the Christian Religion* in 1536, there were Protestant deacons in some parts of the Germanies. Therefore, when he put his ideas into practice in the Genevan *Ecclesiastical Ordinances* of 1541, he was able to build on the ideas of Bucer and the model of Strasbourg. Calvin was not embarrassed to follow in the footsteps of his predecessors in the Protestant Reformation. He saw himself as continuing the Reformation along the lines of those who had gone before. He admired Luther, but the office of deacon was more important to Calvin. This emphasis proved to be a blessing for the growth of Reformed churches despite their status as a persecuted minority.

The Anabaptists also had deacons who served in crucial financial and social roles. For example, Hutterite deacons had economic responsibility for an entire Hutterite community. Many Anabaptist deacons had pastoral duties, others had served as deacons before they became pastors, and some appear to have been the pastors of the community.

Among sixteenth-century Protestants, many of the roles that deacons had assumed in the liturgies of late antiquity and the medieval period were abandoned or transferred to the pastor. Luther set the tone for these changes by criticizing the functions of the medieval deacon in the Mass. A liturgical role that Protestant deacons often retained was the offering of the cup at Communion, a tradition that dated at least to Justin Martyr's second-century description of the liturgy. Some Protestant deacons also took the collections in church.

Before concluding this consideration of the diaconate in the Reformation churches of the sixteenth century, it is important to consider the developments within Catholicism. One can then compare the diaconate and social welfare in Protestantism and Catholicism and set both within the context of other forces and influences in the sixteenth century.

CATHOLICISM

Catholics of the Reformation or Counter-Reformation eras did not change deacons from the medieval model, but the Council of Trent, which was called by the pope to reform the church and to meet the challenge of Protestantism and which met from 1545–1563, did discuss the diaconate. In June 1563, the bishop of Ostuni called for a restoration of the functions of the deacon and subdeacon along the lines of the diaconate before the modifications of the Middle Ages:

> I desire the function of the subdeacon and deacon, diligently collected from the writings of the fathers and decrees of the councils, to be restored and put to use, especially the functions of deacons. The Church has always used their services, not only in ministering at the altar, but in baptism, in care of hospitals, of widows, and of suffering persons. Finally, all the needs and concerns of the people are mediated to the bishop by deacons.[126]

A common interpretation of what happened at Trent was that there was considerable opposition to broadening diaconal functions on the grounds that "the diaconate was instituted not for service of profane tables but for ministry at the altar!"[127] There was also sentiment against deacons preaching, though in practice few deacons preached. The council was concerned with maintaining the major and minor orders and the cursus honorum. However, William T. Ditewig, the executive director of the Committee on the Permanent Diaconate of the National Conference of Catholic Bishops, maintains that attendees at the Council of Trent supported a renewal of the diaconate that the pope did not follow through upon.[128] The end result was that the diaconate remained a step on the way to the priesthood. A canon of the Council of Trent stated that "[i]f anyone says that beside the priesthood there are not in the Catholic Church other orders, both major and minor, by which, as by certain steps, advance is made to the priesthood, let him be anathema."[129]

In the decree on "Reformation," the council was concerned that deacons and priests be ordained in their 20s with an interval between the two orders. It proposed 23 as a minimum age for deacons and 25 years of age for priests. Also a man should serve at least one year as a deacon, unless the bishop judged otherwise.[130]

After the Council of Trent, the functions of the deacons remained essentially as they had been in the medieval period with primarily liturgical roles, but the needs of the poor in the sixteenth century challenged Catholics, as they did Protestants. Before the Reformation, socially conscious people had called for welfare reform. Confraternities, with their charitable functions, had proliferated.[131] The houses of the Brothers and Sisters of the Common Life (founded in Deventer by Gerard Groote in the 1370s and 1380s as communities of laymen and laywomen dedicated to service to God and society) had spread through the Low Countries, the Rhineland, and Westphalia, and into southern and central Germany, and even into France. They influenced Luther, Erasmus, and Calvin.

All these developments provided a degree of justification for the argument that some aspects of the Catholic Reformation predated the Protestant movement. By 1500, a society existed in Genoa, Italy, aimed at prayer, personal sanctification, and practical charity. By 1517, it had moved to Rome, where, as the Oratory of Divine Love, it attracted officials of the papal court. Two members of this Oratory—Gaetano Thiene (1480–1547) and Gian Pietro Caraffa (born 1476, Pope Paul IV, 1555–1559)—established an order of secular priests bound by a rule but at work in the world. The Theatines were confirmed by the pope in 1524. The concept behind the order spread. The Clerks Regular of the Somaschi, confirmed by the pope in 1540, were founded by a nobleman of Venice who also founded hospitals, orphanages, and a home for fallen women. The chief work of the Somaschi, like that of their founder, was the care of the poor and the sick. They ran hospitals in Venice, Milan, Como, and Verona. Resembling the Somaschi were the Hospitallers of St. John of God. Their founder, St. John of God (1495–1550), was Portuguese but lived mainly in Spain. He worked with the sick in Granada. From him and his followers, an order arose that gained papal approval in 1572. They have founded hospitals throughout the world. Three laymen founded the Clerks Regular of St.

Paul, or the Barnabites, named after their church in Milan. Recognized by the pope in 1533–1535, the Barnabites became famous for their evangelical open-air meetings. They aided Charles Borromeo (1538–1584) in his missions in the archdiocese of Milan.[132]

Borromeo was a reforming bishop of the Catholic Reformation who founded seminaries and worked with the poor and sick. Among his many activities on behalf of parish life, Borromeo advocated frequent confession of one's sins to a priest and the establishment of confessionals in parish churches, an institution that spread with the Catholic Reformation. He was not alone as a reforming bishop. In Verona, Gian Matteo Giberti, bishop from 1524–1543, resided in his diocese and tended to its needs. He encouraged absentee priests to return to serve their parishes, founded orphanages and poorhouses, and established the Confraternity of the Blessed Sacrament. It was characteristic of the Catholic Reformation that concern for the material well-being of the poor accompanied the evangelical and doctrinal thrust.[133]

Philip Neri (1515–1595) of Florence founded a movement in Rome in which he personally worked for the sick and poor. He also established a confraternity to minister to pilgrims in Rome. In 1556 Neri began an oratory for prayer, Scripture reading, lectures or sermons, and music by composers such as Palestrina. From this music, composed for sacred use, came the oratorio. In 1575 the pope recognized a community of secular priests known as the Congregation of the Oratory.[134]

In addition to reforming bishops and new societies, old orders, such as the mendicant friars, reformed and put forth new shoots. The friars encouraged confraternities and often joined them, serving as their clergy, to the consternation of the parish clergy.[135] Of the mendicant friars, the Franciscans were historically vulnerable to division because of the difficulty of adhering to absolute poverty. In the mid-fourteenth century, the Observance, a subgroup within the Franciscans intent on returning to the original rule, emerged alongside a nonreformed Conventual group. This division spread to other friars. When Luther joined the Augustinians, he chose the Observant wing.[136]

Intent on a life of prayer, itinerant preaching, and charitable work, Observant Franciscans of the sixteenth century adopted a habit with a four-pointed hood. From the Italian name for this hood, they became known as the Capuchins and were authorized by the pope in 1528. Despite the fact that their vicar-general from 1538–1541, Bernardino Ochino (1487–1564), left and became a Protestant, the preaching missions of the Capuchins were to become a major force in the reconversion of Protestants during the Counter-Reformation.[137]

These new groups that formed in the first half of the sixteenth century combined prayer, preaching, and charitable activities. Women had their place in this reforming movement, too, as new and reconstituted orders for women appeared. In 1535, Angela Merici (ca. 1474–1540), already at work among the poor, sick, and uneducated in Italy, gathered a group of lay-women who dedicated themselves to charitable work and religious education of girls. The Ursulines spread into France and eventually to the New World.[138]

Catholic religious orders engaged in evangelism and missions in the sixteenth century, not only to confront Protestantism but also to address the needs of the world. Catholics of the Reformation era moved beyond Europe well before Protestants. Franciscans and Dominicans were particularly active as missionaries, as was a society of priests recognized by Pope Paul III in 1540 and known as the Society of Jesus or the Jesuits.

Ignatius Loyola (1491–1556), a Spaniard of a knightly family, founded the Jesuits after discovering during a lengthy convalescence from leg wounds that he wanted to take up the priestly vocation. During his studies in Paris, Loyola gathered other men who, in 1534, took vows of chastity and poverty. In Rome during the winter of 1538–1539, they served the sick and poor, and the next year they obtained papal recognition with the support of Cardinal Gasparo Contarini (1483–1542). The Jesuits pledged obedience to superiors and to the pope.[139]

With the advent of the Reformation, efforts to improve the situation of the poor continued in Catholic regions as it did in Protestant areas. For example, Juan Luis Vives (1492–1540), a Spanish Catholic of Jewish origins, proposed a comprehensive welfare system for the city of Bruges in the Low Countries (January 6, 1526).[140] He suggested a census of the poor to assess need, followed by state assistance in a system in which poor people would work, even the disabled and the blind.[141] Vives also wanted to outlaw begging. Although his ideas were not immediately implemented by Bruges, they were thought to have been a model for reforms elsewhere.[142]

Vives was a Christian humanist, that is, a teacher and scholar whose interests lay in the humanities: history, literature, poetry, rhetoric, and languages. At the time of the Reformation, many younger humanists became Protestant, such as Philipp Melanchthon (1497–1560) and John Calvin. Vives did not, but he and other Catholic humanists, like their Protestant counterparts, continued to advocate changes in the institutions, life, and morals of church and society. Vives was interested in suggestions for reform, especially the reform of education but also the reform of social wel-fare.[143] He was not alone. In England, the humanist Thomas More (1478–1535) described an imaginary society called Utopia in which no one went hungry. In Lyons, a humanist led in efforts to work for welfare change before the city became Protestant.[144]

The Catholic Church was not sanguine about proposals for welfare reform. The bishop of Sarepta accused the plan that Vives had written for Bruges of being heretical, a product of the Lutheran sect. The Sorbonne, or University of Paris, found fault with a plan for welfare reform for the city of Ypres in the Low Countries because it reassigned the administration of poor relief from religious groups to the government.[145] The Council of Trent condemned using civil authorities as primary administrators of poor relief and attempted to bring confraternities under closer diocesan super-vision.[146] Proposals to eliminate begging met with opposition from men-dicant orders and from those who identified laws against mendicancy with Lutheranism. Even in Catholic regions where begging was outlawed, exceptions were often made for the mendicant orders.

Those in the Catholic Church who opposed change were unable to thwart strong pressure for centralization, rationalization, and laicization of welfare in the sixteenth century. Before the Reformation, Catholic cities already had moved in that direction and would continue to do so, alongside their Protestant counterparts.

SUMMARY

The sixteenth century brought to a head reforming tendencies in social welfare. Some feel that the century was the beginning of a new era in poor relief. Others feel the reforms were a product of cumulative changes in the medieval period. Still others thank the Renaissance, with its humanists and new business practices, for welfare reform.[147] Some attribute changes in welfare administration to the Protestant Reformation, but research in social reform in Catholic areas has rendered denominational theories less tenable. Original documents of the period reveal similarities in Catholic and Protes-tant welfare.[148] This is not to say that the theological rationale that the Protestant reformers gave to welfare reform did not play its role. It is dif-ficult to argue that the Reformation did not speed up reform at the practi-cal level.[149] Yet the circumstances of the era brought pressure for change in welfare administration in both Catholic and Protestant regions. Catholics tended to work within existing structures, such as confraternities;[150] Protes-tants needed to create new structures.

There was a great desire by governments to find a system of welfare administration that worked. As cities established new systems, they would write ordinances. These would be printed and sold. The printing press enabled the ideas of one city to be copied by others, and reforms crossed denominational lines.

A typical reform was to establish a central welfare system or a hospital. Sometimes the new institutions coordinated or replaced existing multifaceted systems, but sometimes they paralleled the old. Many plans involved hiring an administrator to manage the institutions, do the purchasing, hire the servants, and keep the books. The administrator was often responsible to a committee of the government or to a board of trustees that provided income, audited the books, and made policy decisions.

Although a centralized system such as this could be set up in either Catholic or Protestant regions, the changes in property ownership that accompanied the Reformation forced many cities to act. Scholars differ as to how much credit should be given to differences in theological beliefs as a factor in social reform. Protestant areas had to make changes in the financing and staffing of social welfare and schools. This often involved the formation of a common chest and the use of laypeople as teachers and social workers. Protestants also needed to fill in the social welfare functions that Catholic confraternities had provided. With the Reformation, civil government had an opportunity to take control of the property of the church and its monasteries. Although this happened to some extent in Catholic regions, the switch was not as sudden and often not as thorough.

Overall, the Protestant Reformation acted as a catalyst to reforms that already were in process, so it is little wonder that poor relief in many Catholic and Protestant regions shared common features: offering aid to the indigent, encouragement to work or a job for the able-bodied, a handout sufficient for a day for travelers, special consideration for the "shamefaced poor" who had fallen from prosperity to hard times, loans to deserving artisans, provision of dowries to enable poor women to marry, aid to students, poor boxes in churches to receive contributions, attempts to suppress or control begging, and support for orphans, widows, and the disabled. There were also similar qualifications for welfare recipients because both Catholics and Protestants wanted to help the "deserving poor" who were worthy, honest, appreciative, morally upright, and conscientious about religious observance.

Although it certainly can be argued that Protestantism from Luther forward waged a consistent war against begging, it would be difficult to prove that Protestants were any more successful than Catholics at eradicating it.

Some analysts of the period have argued that Protestant social welfare was less effective than that of the Roman Catholics, and they have suggested that people were more willing to give to the poor when they thought such donations were a meritorious work that could contribute to a better life in the world to come.[151] That one denomination's welfare system was more or less successful than another's is difficult to substantiate because of the lack of adequate statistics in this period and the research that remains to be done in the surviving documentation.

It is true that Protestant theology eliminated the concept of an accumulation of merit for deeds well done, but this theological shift toward justification by faith was not necessarily a reason for a less successful welfare system. Some welfare systems seemed to work better after the Reformation. This may well have been true in Geneva. Crucial factors in the success of post-Reformation welfare in any given region seem to have been (1) the size of the endowment from the medieval period, (2) the presence or absence of a refugee community, (3) the organizational skills of the collectors of contributions and how widely they solicited funds, and, of course, (4) the prosperity of the population on which they had to draw.

It is difficult to ignore the testimony of contemporaries, however, some of whom were outspoken on the relative success or failure of their own systems of poor relief. A Catholic bishop of seventeenth-century Nîmes remarked that the Protestants were putting the Roman Catholics to shame. The Protestants had no beggars, took a collection every Sunday, and taxed themselves to provide for their needy.[152]

On the other hand, Catholics had their great successes too. There was, for example, the fabulously wealthy Catholic Fugger family of Augsburg, Germany. This family built the *Fuggerei*, a town-within-a-town of houses for less advantaged people. It still exists. The full social and educational impact of the Catholic Reformation came in the seventeenth and eighteenth centuries when the recommendations of the Council of Trent took effect on education and welfare and when the new religious orders of the Counter-Reformation, such as the Jesuits, had matured. But that is the story of the next chapter.

There is a difference of opinion on the success of social welfare in England in the sixteenth century as it moved from partial dependence on monasteries and convents to each parish taking full responsibility for its own poor. W. K. Jordan, who has studied English wills, believes that philanthropy was successful, especially within the Puritan community. Puritans were obliged to endow lectureships and finance ministers to guarantee the kind of preaching and teaching they wanted, and Puritans supported the poor, prisoners, and education as well.[153]

By the time the first reformers had died in the late sixteenth century, Europe had moved further toward centralization, rationalization, and laicization of social welfare. The Protestant Reformation had hurried changes already in progress, especially in the direction of civic control and the outlawing of begging. This did not mean that the church was no longer active in welfare, but it did mean that church and state often combined efforts.

Many of the deacons of the new Protestant churches combined roles in church and state. To the twenty-first-century observer, many of these deacons, where they existed, appeared to have been primarily civic officials who administered community benevolence with the blessing of the church. Because the magistrates controlled the property and often had the final say in how funds were collected and expended, it is difficult to see these Protestant deacons otherwise. However, a church or its pastor often had a say in choosing who the deacons would be, even if they were selected, in part, from among the city councillors. It is also possible that the title of deacon might have made it easier to find volunteers for this task from among those who wanted to give time and energy to church-related activities. Although recruitment of deacons was often difficult, a church connection for welfare administrators and social workers may have made a difference.

The true test of the Protestant deacon was in those denominations that found themselves an illegal minority, such as the Anabaptists and the Reformed churches outside of Switzerland and Scotland. Without the aid of the state, church members were dependent on one another for mutual assistance, and deacons facilitated this assistance.

The type of deacons who controlled money independent of the magistrates also existed in areas where Protestantism was legal, such as in Calvin's Geneva. There the funds for the various refugee groups were collected privately and administered by their own deacons. These independent deacons' funds provided the church with money to spend as it saw fit without the official sanction of the state. In Geneva this proved to be convenient for the illegal export of Bibles and Psalters to Catholic countries and the sending of ministers and messengers. It would have been awkward for the city of Geneva, striving to maintain independence, to have been involved officially in actions that could have called down the wrath of its Catholic neighbors, especially France and Savoy. Independent deacons' funds gave the church an opportunity to launch a missionary endeavor to its neighbor states and to maintain a network of support and refuge for Reformed churches in Catholic areas.

By the late sixteenth century, the diaconate in the church had gone in two main directions: (1) The new Protestants had reinstituted deacons who were involved in social welfare and the care of the poor. This was the ideal deacon within the Reformed tradition and in some regions where Lutheranism prevailed. (2) The Catholic Church, and to an extent the Church of England, retained deacons on the model of the medieval diaconate. The Anabaptists fit into both categories because they gave their deacons financial duties but also some pastoral responsibilities. Some Anabaptists encouraged a period in office as a deacon before becoming a pastor.

The model of the diaconate in the late sixteenth century through the nineteenth century built on that of the sixteenth century, but it also matured and changed. New forces in the church, such as Pietism on the continent of Europe and Methodism in the British Isles, sparked interest in social welfare and education. This is the story of the next chapter.

NOTES

1. Luther, "Babylonian Captivity of the Church," trans. in *Three Treatises*, 248–49. The Latin text of the original treatise, "De Captivitate Babylonica Ecclesiae," is in WA 6:497–573. See also Grimm, "Luther's Contributions to Poor Relief," 229. For excerpts from Luther, John Calvin, Huldrych Zwingli, Martin Bucer, and welfare legislation from this era, see Krimm, *Quellen zur Geschichte der Diakonie*, vol. 2: *Reformation und Neuzeit*.

2. Luther, "Babylonian Captivity," in *Three Treatises*, 248–49.

3. Luther, "Babylonian Captivity," in *Three Treatises*, 249.

4. Ross, "Deacons in Protestantism," 429.

5. Maurer, *Historical Commentary on the Augsburg Confession*.

6. "Iam sequitur de diaconis. 'Graves.' Diaconi fuerunt, qui etiam aliquando praedicaverunt. Ex Act.: 'constituerunt 7,' qui praeessent ecclesiae in providendis pauperibus et viduis. Illi diaconi etiam aliquando praedicavere ut Stephanus et admissi ad alia officia ecclesiae, quamquam sit providere pauperes et viduas praecipuum. Iste ritus iam diu exolevit. In ecclesia Papistica: qui Evangelium legit, subdiaconus, distributio rerum et cura pauperum relegata ad hospitalia. Secundum rei veritatem debent esse caplani et cistae communes. Mihi magis placent, ut ostiarii haberent substantiam alendorum pauperum quam nos. Causam nuper dixi: quia omnium oculi in nos. Debent diaconi ecclesiae, qui debent subservire Episcopo et ad ejus consilium regere ecclesiam in externis rebus" (WA 26:59; trans. in McKee, *Calvin on the Diaconate*, 178).

7. Grimm, "Luther's Contributions to Poor Relief," 225–26; Lindberg, " 'There Should Be No Beggars among Christians': Karlstadt," 322–23.

8. For an English translation, see Carter Lindberg, " 'There Should Be No Beggars Among Christians,' An Early Reformation Tract on Social Welfare by Andreas Karlstadt," in Lindberg, *Piety, Politics, and Ethics*, 159–66. The tract is the second half of a larger work concerned with images, *Von abtuhung der Bylder und das keyn Bedtler unther den Christen seyn sollen*, in Hans Lietzmann, ed., *Kleine Texte für Theologische und Philologische Vorlesungen und Übungen* 74 (Bonn: A. Marcus & E. Weber, 1911).

9. An English translation of this document is in Durnbaugh, *Every Need Supplied*,

217–18; for the German text, see Hermann Barge, trans., *Andreas Bodenstein von Karl-stadt*, 2 vols. (Leipzig: Friedrich Brandstetter, 1905, repr. ed., 1968), 2:Appendix 13; Leitzmann, *Kleine Texte*, 74.

10. Lindberg, " 'There Should Be No Beggars': Karlstadt," 326–27.

11. Lindberg, "Luther on the Use of Money," 19.

12. Barge, *Karlstadt*, 1:382.

13. Lindberg, " 'There Should Be No Beggars': Karlstadt," 326.

14. LW 31:29.

15. Martin Luther, as quoted in Lindberg, "Luther on Poverty," 90.

16. LW 45:285–87.

17. Franciscans, Dominicans, Augustinians, Carmelites, and Servites.

18. Luther, "To the Christian Nobility," in *Three Treatises*, 81.

19. Luther, "To the Christian Nobility," in *Three Treatises*, 80–81.

20. Lindberg, " 'There Should Be No Beggars': Karlstadt," 316.

21. LW 35:68.

22. Luther, "To the Christian Nobility," in *Three Treatises*, 84.

23. Lindberg, *Beyond Charity*, 118.

24. Lindberg, "Luther's Concept of Offering," 252.

25. Lindberg, "Luther on Poverty," 89, 91, 94–95.

26. See LW 45:159–94; Grimm, "Luther's Contributions to Poor Relief," 229.

27. LW 49:45–47 (WABr 3:124–26).

28. The year 1560 was decisive. On August 24, the Scottish Parliament outlawed Catholi-cism. See Spitz, *Protestant Reformation*, 280.

29. Luther, "Ordinance of a Common Chest," LW 45:173.

30. Innes, *Social Concern in Calvin's Geneva*, 56; Baker, *Bullinger and the Covenant*, xx.

31. Lindberg, "Ministry and Vocation of the Baptized," 385.

32. See, for example, "Luther's Letter to the Mayors and Aldermen of All the Cities of Germany in Behalf of Christian Schools [1524]," in Painter, *Luther on Education*, 169–209; as well as Luther's "Dedicatory Letter to the Honorable Lazarus Spengler, Counselor of the City of Nuremberg [1530]" and "Sermon on the Duty of Sending Children to School," in Painter, *Luther on Education*, 210–71.

33. Lane, "Poverty and Poor Relief," 1.

34. Critical editions of all but the Danish order and that of Schleswig-Holstein are in Sehling, *Die evangelischen Kirchenordnungen*.

35. Hendel, "Care of the Poor," 527.

36. "Der Ebarn stadt Brunswig christlike ordeninge to denste dem hilgen evangelio, christliker leve, tucht, frede, unde eynicheit. Ock darunder vele christlike lere vor de borgere. Dorch Joannem Bugenhagen Pomeren bescreven. 1528," in Sehling, *Die evangelischen Kirchenordnungen*, 1:348. The Braunschweig church order can be found in abbreviated form in English as "Church Order of Brunswick, 1528," in Kidd, *Documents Illustrative of the Continental Reformation*, 230–33.

37. Kidd, *Documents Illustrative of the Continental Reformation*, 231.

38. Kidd, *Documents Illustrative of the Continental Reformation*, 231–32.

39. Lane, "Poverty and Poor Relief," 85–86.

40. Hendel, "Care of the Poor," 528–30.

41. Hendel, "Care of the Poor," 531n21.

42. "Cap. xii. *De infirmorum Visitatione* of "Reformatio ecclesiarum Hassiae, 20 Oct.

1526," in Kidd, *Documents Illustrative of the Continental Reformation*, 227.

43. Piepkorn, "Sacred Ministry and Holy Ordination," 558.

44. Lindberg, "Luther on Poverty," 88–89.

45. Lindberg, "Through a Glass Darkly," 39.

46. Mollat, *Poor of the Middle Ages*, 259.

47. Grimm, "Luther's Contributions to Poor Relief," 223, 229–31.

48. "Statute: 'On Poor Relief' (September 8, 1520)," trans. in Smiar, "Poor Law and Out-door Poor Relief in Zürich," 214.

49. Smiar, "Poor Law and Outdoor Poor Relief in Zürich," 208–22.

50. Smiar, "Poor Law and Outdoor Poor Relief in Zürich," 149–51.

51. "Almosenordnung (January, 1525)," trans. in Smiar, "Poor Law and Outdoor Poor Relief in Zürich," 223–32 (translated from the original).

52. Smiar, "Poor Law and Outdoor Poor Relief in Zürich," 224–26, 228–30.

53. "Action or Use of the Lord's Supper: A Memorial or Thanksgiving of Christ as It Will Be Begun in Zurich at Easter in the Year 1525," in Thompson, *Liturgies of the Western Church*, 152. "Ietz spreche der diacon oder läser: Der herr sye mit üch. Antwurte das volck: Und mit dinem geyst" ("Action oder bruch des nachtmals, gedechtnus oder dancksagung Christi, wie sy uff osteren zu Zürich angehebt wirt, im jar 1525," in Egli et al., *Zwinglis sämtliche Werke*, 4:19).

54. Meylan, *La haute école de Lausanne*, 14; Maag, *Seminary or University?* 129–30.

55. Maag, *Seminary or University?* 130–32; Meylan, *La haute école de Lausanne*, 14–15.

56. Maag, *Seminary or University?* 133–34.

57. Maag, *Seminary or University?* 138–39.

58. Chrisman, *Strasbourg and the Reform*, 42–44, 69–78, 235–40, 272, 279–80.

59. Hall, *Humanists and Protestants*, 128; Basil Hall "Diakonia in Martin Butzer," in McCord and Parker, *Service in Christ*, 89.

60. Chrisman, *Strasbourg and the Reform*, 209.

61. Hall, "Diakonia in Martin Butzer," 209–10.

62. McKee, *Calvin on the Diaconate*, 134n53.

63. Martin Bucer, "The Restoration of Lawful Ordination for Ministers of the Church," in Wright, *Common Places of Martin Bucer*, 254.

64. Martin Bucer, *Enarratio Epistolae D. Pauli Ephesios*, Basel (1562), as referred to in Hall, *Humanists and Protestants*, 137–38.

65. Chrisman, *Strasbourg and the Reform*, 226.

66. For a thorough biography of Thomas Cranmer, see MacCulloch, *Thomas Cranmer*.

67. For Edward VI and the details surrounding his death and the succession of first Lady Jane Grey (1537–1554), then Edward's older sister, Mary Tudor, to the throne, see Loach, *Edward VI*.

68. "The Sixth Law: Poor Relief," in *De Regno Christi*, in Pauck, *Melanchthon and Bucer*, 306–15.

69. Pauck, *Melanchthon and Bucer*, 315.

70. Sachs, "Thomas Cranmer's *Reformatio Legum Ecclesiasticarum*," 147–48, 153, 158, 161, 163, 211.

71. Pauck, *Melanchthon and Bucer*, 170.

72. Wright, *Common Places of Martin Bucer*, 25.

73. Bernoulli, *Das Diakonenamt bei Calvin*.

74. Calvin, *Institution of the Christian Religion*, 235.

75. For an English translation of the *Draft Ecclesiastical Ordinances: September & October 1541*, see Reid, *Calvin*, 58–72.

76. Bouwsma, *John Calvin*, 21–24.

77. The uncertainty about elders is because the *Draft Ecclesiastical Ordinances* use another term, as does a contemporary chronicler, Michel Roset. Roset says of Communion: *"Que les Ministres la distribuent en l'église, les tables estant près la chaire; que nul ne donne le calice que les commys ou diacres"* ("That the ministers distribute it in the church, the tables being close to the pulpit; that nobody give the chalice except the committed ones or deacons") (*Les Chroniques de Genève*, 293). According to how one reads these phrases, the "committed ones" could be the deacons or others committed to the task. In French *les commys* are agents, assistants, or employees. In sixteenth-century Geneva, however, the word may have been the civil equivalent for elder, just as *procureur* (*procurator*) was the civil equivalent for deacon; see McKee, *Calvin on the Diaconate*, 129n38. The *Draft Ecclesiastical Ordinances* also mention three coadjutors who aided and assisted five ministers in their duties; see *Draft Ecclesiastical Ordinances*, in Reid, *Calvin*, 62. The registers of the Consistory, however, reveal that elders were designated to administer the wine at Communion (4 September 1561, AEG, *Registre du Consistoire*, vol. 18, folio 122).

78. John Calvin's sermon on Acts 6:1–3, fol. 186, trans. in McKee, *Calvin on the Diaconate*, 155.

79. Calvin's sermon on Acts 6:1–3, fol. 184, trans. in McKee, *Calvin on the Diaconate*, 151–52.

80. From *"Lettre de la Compagnie des Pasteurs de Genève aux Églises de Normandie"* ("Letter of the Company of Pastors of Geneva to the Churches of Normandie"), 30 November 1564, in Kingdon, *Registres de la Compagnie des Pasteurs de Genève*, 2:140; trans. in Olson, *Calvin and Social Welfare*, 225n3.

81. Fazy, *Les Chroniques de Genève*, 288, 290–91: "Calvin . . . exhorta la Seigneurie que la police ecclésiasticque fut réduicte par escript, & que gens feussent députez pour l'entendre. . . . La police ecclésiastique demandée par les Ministres fut passée en Conseil Général le vingtiesme de novembre en édict perpétuel, sans nulle contredicte." ("Calvin . . . exhorted the Seigneury that the ecclesiastical order be reduced to writing, and that people be deputized to tend to it. . . . The ecclesiastical order demanded by the ministers was passed in the General Council the twentieth of November in a perpetual edict with no one contradicting it.").

82. Ross, "Deacons in Protestantism," 432.

83. Kingdon, "Social Welfare in Calvin's Geneva," 52, 55–57.

84. The registers of the city council record that "[f]ollowing the request of Monsieur Calvin, minister, it has been ordered that the procurators of the hospital should lay down, in writing, all the revenue of the said hospital and those to whom one distributes alms, and then that the Lord Syndic Curteti, together with the deputies committed previously in such a case, should proceed to put order in such a case" (March 9, 1545, AEG, *Registres du Conseil*, vol. 40 [February 8, 1545–February 7, 1546], fol. 42).

85. Calvin's suggestion for an industry for the poor is in AEG, *Registres du Conseil*, vol. 39, fols. 84 verso–85.

86. For the silk industry at the hospital, see Mottu-Weber, "Des vers à soie à l'Hôpital en 1610," 44–49.

87. *Draft Ecclesiastical Ordinances*, in Reid, *Calvin*, 64.

88. John Calvin, CO 49:240, trans. in McKee, *Calvin on the Diaconate*, 195.

89. McKee, *Calvin on the Diaconate*, 191–94.

90. For Calvin's position on the role of women in the church, see Douglass, *Women, Freedom, and Calvin*.

91. Hammann, *L'amour retrouvé*, 252.

92. Calvin, *Institutes of the Christian Religion*, 2:1061.

93. John Calvin, sermon 39, 1 Timothy 5:7–12, in CO 53:475, quoted in McKee, *Calvin on the Diaconate*, 215–16.

94. McKee, *Calvin on the Diaconate*, 213–14.

95. On June 15, 1545, the city council of Geneva had ordered the poor out of town: "Ordered, that the two patrols newly constituted should assemble all the poor foreigners toward Rive and that each of them be given alms of bread and then a command to no longer return to Geneva" (AEG, *Registres du Conseil*, vol. 40, fol. 42). The registers of the city council of Geneva of June 25, 1545, state that Calvin "reported the death of a Frenchman, Monsieur David, who died in his house and willed to the poor of Strasbourg one thousand ecus and to the poor of Geneva one thousand ecus" (AEG, *Registers du Conseil*, vol. 40, fol. 161).

96. For a more detailed account of the French Fund and the deacons of Geneva, see Olson, *Calvin and Social Welfare*. For the origins of the fund, see especially chapter 2.

97. Olson, "Les amis de Jean Calvin," 99–102; Olson, "Friends of Jean Calvin," 161–65.

98. "The year beginning in the month of July 1554, Thursday, the fifth of the said month, July, the Company being assembled at the home of Monsieur Calvin, after having invoked the name of God, were elected deacons for the administration of the goods of the poor" (AEG, *Archives hospitalières*, Kg 15 [July 1554–July 1555], 1, translated in Olson, *Calvin and Social Welfare*, 226n12).

99. From the title of a notarial act of 2 March 1564 (AEG, *Not. Ragueau*, 7:8).

100. Olson, *Calvin and Social Welfare*, 31–32.

101. Moens, "Relief of the Poor Members," 321–38.

102. George Williams, "The Beginnings of the Anabaptist Reformation: Reminiscences of George Blaurock, an Excerpt from the Hutterite Chronicle 1525," in Williams, *Spiritual and Anabaptist Writers*, 42–43.

103. Williams, *Radical Reformation*, 121.

104. Dosker, *Dutch Anabaptists*, 31, 34–35.

105. "*In manus tuas, domine, commendo spiritum meum*," quoted in Dosker, *Dutch Anabaptists*, 35.

106. Williams, "Beginnings of Anabaptist Reformation," 45n15.

107. Lumpkin, *Baptist Confessions of Faith*, 35–36.

108. Dosker, *Dutch Anabaptists*, 41.

109. Clasen, *Anabaptism*, 177.

110. Balthasar Hübmaier, "Concerning the Sword, 1527," in Klaasen, *Anabaptism in Outline*, 248. For a translation of the entire document, see Balthasar Hübmaier, "On the Sword," in Vedder, *Balthasar Hübmaier*, 279–310.

111. Lumpkin, *Baptist Confessions*, 36.

112. George Williams translates *diener* as "deacon," emphasizing the importance of that role to the Anabaptists; see Williams, "Beginnings of Anabaptist Reformation," 44n11.

113. See *The Mennonite Encyclopedia: A Comprehensive Reference Work on the Anabaptist-Mennonite Movement*, s.v. "Deacon."

114. Clasen, *Anabaptism*, 189.

115. "Ordnung der Gemein, wie ein Christ leben sol," in Lumpkin, *Baptist Confessions*, 33.

116. Peter Klassen, "The Development of Communal Anabaptism," in Klassen, *Economics of Anabaptism*, 50–63; Packull, "Beginnings of Tyrolian Anabaptism," 719.

117. Lumpkin, *Baptist Confessions*, 31–32.

118. Wenger, *Glimpses of Mennonite History and Doctrine*, 58–59.

119. Lumpkin, *Baptist Confessions*, 36–37; Clasen, *Anabaptism*, 191.

120. Williams, *Spiritual and Anabaptist Writers*, 276n8.

121. Ulrich Stadler, "Cherished Instructions on Sin, Excommunication, and the Community of Goods, ca. 1537," in Williams, *Spiritual and Anabaptist Writers*, 280.

122. The Schleitheim Confession (1527) provided that if "a pastor were banished or led to the Lord [through martyrdom] another shall be ordained in his place in the same hour so that God's little flock and people may not be destroyed" (Sattler, *Schleitheim Confession of Faith*, in Spitz, *Protestant Reformation*, 93.

123. *Mennonite Encyclopedia*, s.v. "Deaconesses."

124. The testimony on Mennonites allowing members to be magistrates is mixed. See, for example, Lumpkin, *Baptist Confessions*, 115: "The Mennonites regarded the holding of magisterial office as incompatible with membership in the church."

125. Dosker, *Dutch Anabaptists*, 211.

126. *Concilium Tridentinum: Diariorum, actorum, epistolarum, tractatuum, nova collectio* 9 (Freiburg: Görres-Gesellschaft, 1901), 589, quoted in Echlin, *Deacon in the Church*, 100.

127. Echlin, *Deacon in the Church*, 100–101.

128. William T. Ditewig, executive director of the Committee on the Permanent Diaconate of the National Conference of Catholic Bishops, telephone conversation with author, 21 August 2003.

129. *Enchiridion Symbolorum Definitionum et Declarationum de rebus fidei et morum* (1772), ed. Henricus Denzinger and Adolfus Schonmetzer, 23d ed. (New York: n.p., 1965), 413, quoted in Echlin, *Deacon in the Church*, 104.

130. J. Waterworth, ed. and trans., *The Canons and Decrees of the Council of Trent* (London: n.p., 1848), 185, in Echlin, *Deacon in the Church*, 104–5.

131. Flynn, *Sacred Charity*, 16.

132. Dickens, *Counter Reformation*, 68–71.

133. Dickens, *Counter Reformation*, 53–54, 123.

134. O'Connell, *Counter Reformation*, 104–5.

135. Flynn, *Sacred Charity*, 117.

136. Dickens, *Counter Reformation*, 64–65.

137. Dickens, *Counter Reformation*, 71.

138. Dickens, *Counter Reformation*, 73–74.

139. Dickens, *Counter Reformation*, 75–82.

140. Juan Luis Vives, "On Assistance to the Poor," in Tobriner, *Sixteenth-Century Urban Report*, 33–57.

141. Vives, "On Assistance to the Poor," 37–38, 41, in Tobriner, *Sixteenth-Century Urban Report*, 5–6.

142. Tobriner, *Sixteenth-Century Urban Report*, 9, 11, 14–15.

143. Alves, "Christian Social Organism," 3–21.

144. Davis, "Poor Relief, Humanism, and Heresy," 17–64.

145. Tobriner, *Sixteenth-Century Urban Report*, 18.

146. Tobriner, *Sixteenth-Century Urban Report*, 15, citing Carl E. Steinbicker, *Poor Relief in the Sixteenth Century* (Washington, D.C.: Catholic University of America, 1937), 195–222. See also Flynn, *Sacred Charity*, 118.

147. Davis, "Poor Relief, Humanism, and Heresy," 17–64.

148. Brucker, "Bureaucracy and Social Welfare in the Renaissance," 1–21; Gutton, *La société et les pauvres*; Pullan, *Rich and Poor*.
149. Ole Peter Grell and Andrew Cunningham, "The Reformation and Changes in Welfare Provision in Early Modern Northern Europe," in Grell and Cunningham, *Health Care and Poor Relief*, 11.
150. Nicholas Terpstra, "Confraternities and Public Charity: Modes of Civic Welfare in Early Modern Italy," in Donnelly and Maher, *Confraternities and Catholic Reform*, 97.
151. Chrisman, *Strasbourg and the Reform*, 280.
152. Bishop Godeau in his *Discours sur l'établissement de l'Hôpital général*, as quoted in Pugh, "Social Welfare and the Edict of Nantes," 375.
153. Jordan, *Philanthropy in England*.

CHAPTER FOUR

FROM THE PROTESTANT REFORMATION TO THE NINETEENTH CENTURY

This chapter will trace the changes in deacons and in social welfare from the Protestant Reformation through the early nineteenth century, beginning with the European continent and moving out to the British Isles and the New World. These two and a half centuries after the deaths of the major reformers—Luther (1546), Bucer (1551), Melanchthon (1560), and Calvin (1564)—were a time of settling in and development of Reformation implications for the diaconate. The pressures of the late medieval period to centralize, rationalize, and laicize institutions continued and were manifested in a growth in the institutionalization of the poor in hospitals, orphanages, poorhouses, and various other homes. Characteristic of these centuries were periodic religious revitalization and revival closely connected with efforts to alleviate the conditions of the poor and untutored.

The diaconate during the Protestant Reformation had proved to be an important and versatile office. Deacons had critical responsibilities for social welfare in some churches and regions. Whether working with the state or independent of it, they controlled money and wielded influence. Some deacons were among the most influential church and community leaders of the day. Deacons continued in their social welfare roles after the Reformation, but that era caused changes in Protestant church-state relations that had a long-range effect on deacons. In many regions during the Reformation era, churches had lost control of property that had been turned over to governmental bodies. Even where the state continued to administer the property as the original donors had intended, social welfare or education increasingly became a function of the state. Those who dealt with the poor under government auspices came to be thought of as administrators, trustees, or workers with the poor rather than as deacons. Deacons survived within the church, but their roles changed.

Catholic regions participated in the gradual trend toward centralization, rationalization, and laicization of social welfare that was characteristic of the late medieval and early modern era, but because these regions were not forced into a dramatic shift in control of property from church to government, they could evolve more slowly than some Protestant regions toward separation of church and state in education and social welfare. Government in a Catholic country such as France, for example, continued to use the church to meet the welfare needs of the poor throughout the old regime. Bishops or archbishops served as permanent chairpersons of the boards of city hospitals, and those in religious vocations—priests, brothers, and nuns—staffed hospitals and schools.[1]

Because Roman Catholic deacons had largely liturgical roles, changes in social welfare administration bypassed them. Catholic social concern manifested itself through the foundation of new religious orders and lay societies dedicated to the poor. Even after the French Revolution and Napoleonic era (1789–1815), the state relied heavily on the church in the areas of welfare and education. In Protestant regions, too, the church often worked alongside the government or was used by it for education and social welfare. Distinctions between "church" and "state" characteristic of modern times were distinctions that earlier eras tended not to make. They were a product, to a large extent, of the Enlightenment and post-Enlightenment era of the eighteenth century and beyond.

Until the late eighteenth century, the challenges of caring for the poor were similar to those of the medieval period. Society's social needs remained much the same in the late sixteenth, seventeenth, and early eighteenth centuries. People depended on the land and harvested meager crops that yielded only a portion per bushel of seed grain compared to modern yields. Crops were vulnerable to blight, drought, and storm. Most people were involved in agriculture and were dependent on good weather for food. Periodic food shortages caused by crop failures were common until the agricultural and industrial revolutions, which began in the eighteenth century, revolutionized productivity. The wars of the post-Reformation era were also a hardship. Then the industrial revolution began to draw people into factories and cities. Urban life and the altered working conditions influenced the church's institutions and the diaconate.

WAR AND ITS AFTERMATH: PIETISM

As the first generation of reformers came to the end of their lives, the Peace of Augsburg in 1555 brought the Lutheran struggle for legal recognition to a close, but wars of religion dominated the latter half of the sixteenth century in France and the Netherlands. By the end of the century, King Henry IV of France (1553–1610, became king 1589), a Huguenot turned Catholic, had proclaimed the Edict of Nantes (1598), granting his former coreligionists a measure of religious toleration and participation in government alongside their Catholic compatriots.[2] By 1609, a twelve-year truce effectively ended the war in the Netherlands. The Spanish formally were to recognize the Protestant northern provinces as independent in 1648, but by 1618, Europe was again at war.

The Thirty Years' War (1618–1648) was ostensibly a war of religion and politics, but it had economic and social effects as well, especially where the battles were fought in the Germanies. By the first half of the seventeenth century, Lutheranism in the Germanies had become closely associated with the state and, some would say, had lost vigor as a result. Others would attribute the malaise to the war itself, the catastrophic decline in population, and the disorienting devastation.

After the war, in the latter seventeenth century, the church was responsive to reform. Philipp Jacob Spener (1635–1705), a Lutheran pastor, was instrumental in revitalizing congregational life in Germany through small-group meetings for Bible study, prayer, discussion of the Sunday sermon, and mutual help. Pietism, as this movement was called, included social, educational, and evangelical endeavors, especially in the last decade of the seventeenth century when it became associated with a newly founded German university in Halle, Saxony, under the influence of August Hermann Francke (1663–1727), a Lutheran pastor and professor.[3] Francke founded schools, an orphanage, a publishing house, a bookstore, and a pharmacy to serve the poor and others in need and to train pastors and teachers. He also provided free meals to university students.[4]

Pietism spread from Germany to the Scandinavian countries, but despite a warm evangelical concern at home, Pietists were not initially interested in world missions. This was an aspect of church work that Protestant churches in general had neglected. Then two of Francke's students at Halle accepted an invitation from King Frederick IV of Denmark (1699–1730) to become the first Protestant missionaries in India (1706).[5] Soon the University of Halle became a center for training missionaries. In 1742, it sent Henry Mühlenberg (1711–1787) to America at the request of three congregations in Pennsylvania.[6] Halle sent a succession of twenty-four ministers to help meet the need for Lutheran pastors in North America during the half century beginning in 1742.[7]

Pietists were active in service, *diakonia*, but were less concerned with the use of the title of deacon for people who aided the poor. In parts of Germany, deacon, as a title, had come to apply to assistant pastors.[8] For example, in 1690 Francke accepted a call as "deacon" to Erfurt, though the authorities expelled him the next year because he had roused the opposition of Erfurt's clergy by introducing pietistic practices. Francke moved on to become pastor of a congregation at Glaucha, near Halle.[9]

Pietism produced some outstanding individuals and even took under its wing Christians of other persuasions than Lutheran, such as the *Unitas Fratrum* or Bohemian Brethren. These were Czech Protestants who were descended from the followers of John Hus. In the 1720s they sought refuge in Saxony from persecution in Moravia. Their immigration was made possible because of the goodwill of a Pietist landowner, Count Nikolaus Ludwig von Zinzendorf (1700–1760), who allowed them to start a village, called Herrnhut, on his land. Some of the Brethren sought to organize their own church, but Zinzendorf, with his Pietistic model of a church within a church, strove to hold them within the state church of Saxony.[10] Despite his efforts, Zinzendorf was banished from Saxony in 1736 because of ecclesiastical complaints. By 1745, the Moravian church was organized with its own bishops, elders, and deacons. Saxon authorities allowed Zinzendorf to return to Saxony in 1747, and the Moravian body accepted the Augsburg Confession and was recognized as part of the Saxon state church in 1749. After Zinzendorf died in 1760, the Moravians broke with Lutheranism. The Moravians, like the Pietists at Halle, made a tremendous contribution to missions in the eighteenth century. They and their mission in colonial Georgia made a decisive impact on John Wesley and the Methodist movement in England.

The rise of Pietism in the latter half of the seventeenth century followed the Thirty Years' War. The war may have contributed to conditions that fostered the development of this movement within Lutheranism. But the war had a more immediate religious impact: The end of the war and the Peace of Westphalia (October 27, 1648) acknowledged the Reformed Church (as churches reformed on Swiss models were called) as a legitimate denomination in the Germanies alongside Lutheranism and Catholicism.

Early Reformed and Presbyterian Churches

Reformed churches were not new to the Germanies. They already had spread there in the sixteenth century, notably in the southwest. The Heidelberg Catechism, one of the great confessional statements of modern Reformed churches, was from the Palatinate, where Elector Frederick III (1559–1576) was sympathetic to the Swiss Reformation. He had it written by two Reformed theologians: Kaspar Olevianus (1536–1587) and Zacharias Ursinus (1534–1583). Frederick adopted the Heidelberg Catechism in 1563.

The Peace of Augsburg of 1555 had offered no protection to churches in the Germanies that had been reformed on the Swiss model. Both Catholics and Lutherans objected to tolerating them, and their existence had contributed to the formulation of the Formula of Concord (1577), which subsequently was included in the *Book of Concord* (1580). Nevertheless, the Reformed influence continued to spread to Nassau (1577), Bremen (1581), Anhalt (1597), part of Hesse, and in 1613 to the electoral house of Brandenburg, though most of the inhabitants of Brandenburg remained Lutheran.

The Swiss Reformation had an impact on the theology and worship of the Reformed churches in the Germanies, perhaps more than on their discipline, though the Consistory, or church court of Geneva, and its diaconate also spread. Reformed churches had at least two models for social welfare administration: (1) The Genevan model gave deacons responsibility for money and for the poor within an ecclesiastical structure that also included pastors, elders, and doctors (teachers). (2) The Zurich model substituted state or city officials for deacons as welfare officers. Reformed churches of the Rhineland and Westphalia had deacons.[11]

The diaconate also spread with the Reformed Church into France and from there to the Low Countries (modern-day Belgium and the Netherlands). Deacons became a part of some Eastern European churches. The Protestant exiles from England during the reign of the Catholic Queen Mary Tudor (r. 1553–1558) established deacons for the care of the poor in their communities in Frankfurt and Geneva.[12]

John Knox (born sometime between 1505 and 1515; died, 1572) and his friends used the Genevan model of the diaconate after he returned to Scotland in 1559 from exile in Geneva. Marian exiles also brought the ideal of a Reformed diaconate back to England after the death of Queen Mary, but they were unable to persuade Queen Elizabeth I (1558–1603) of its efficacy for the Church of England. Scotland and England thus provided a contrast in receptivity to Reformed Church structures from Geneva.

When the Reformation was established in Scotland in 1560, the Reformed state church was the Presbyterian church or the Kirk. Its organizational manual, the Book of Discipline of 1561, included deacons. Scottish deacons became regular members of the Session, or governing body of the local church, along with elders, and they sometimes shared their disciplinary functions and other responsibilities with them, such as distributing bread and wine at Communion. With the consent of the ministers and elders, deacons were to gather the alms and to distribute them.[13] As a state church, the Kirk became responsible for the poor and sick on a national scale.[14] If this had worked out in practice, it would have been a step forward from the Middle Ages, but several factors militated against it. Among them, Scotland was an extremely poor country in early modern times, lacking in wherewithal.

In England, the exiles who were returning from the continent after the reign of Mary Tudor joined Protestants of Puritan persuasion to agitate for the Reformed model of church office in an attempt to purify the Church of England of "papal" practices. Thomas Cartwright (1535?–1603), who was the Lady Margaret Professor of Divinity at Cambridge University until he was removed from his professorship for his nonconforming views, blamed the continued existence of so many rogues and vagabonds in England on the lack of deacons for the poor.[15] Elizabeth was not kindly disposed to the changes Puritans suggested. She did not want the decentralized polity of the European Reformed churches nor of the Scottish Presbyterians in England. Elizabeth wanted to rule the Church of England through her bishops.

POOR RELIEF IN BRITAIN

Elizabeth administered poor relief through the parishes of the Church of England rather than through deacons. The connection of poor relief with the parochial system in England had precedents in the Middle Ages, but during that era, the medieval poor could look both to the parish and to the monastery for help.[16] The post-Reformation poor had only the parish and, of course, private philanthropy, which could be generous but was rarely sufficient to meet every need. During the course of Elizabeth's reign, voluntary contributions for poor relief were supplemented by taxation at the parish level, what was called "parish rates."[17]

Elizabeth's Poor Law of 1601 relied on the parish to administer poor relief through churchwardens and overseers of the poor, a role that many Puritans would have liked to have reserved for deacons. Churchwardens were lay parish officers with responsibility for parish property and alms. Some Puritans would have been satisfied with grafting the Presbyterian system on to the existing episcopal structures of the Church of England, but Elizabeth was unwilling.[18] Walter Travers, a Puritan and former Cambridge scholar, stated that "little change is needed to turn collectors, churchwardens and sidesmen into elders and deacons, for the deacon's office is but to distribute the church's alms."[19] Instead, the terminology of the Poor Law of 1601 provided that "the churchwardens of every parish, and four, three, or two substantial householders[, are] . . . to be nominated yearly in Easter week or within one month after Easter, [and they] shall be called overseers of the poor of the same parish." They were charged with the oversight of the collection of money within the parish, including taxation, and of dispensing it for the parish poor. The overseers of the poor arranged for poor children to be apprenticed and provided work to the unemployed, when possible. They also worked closely with the justices of the peace.[20] Therefore, the overseers of the poor had diaconal duties without the title of deacon.

In Scotland, a 1579 poor law similar to the English law because it provided for overseers of the poor never effectively got off the ground. The administration of poor relief fell to the Kirk Session, the local church council, on which deacons sat.[21] Thus the Scottish system of poor relief was closer to the Reformation ideal of deacons involved in social welfare than the English system, but some would argue that the Kirk had other priorities. According to Rosalind Mitchell, "the Sessions . . . spent more time on disciplining sexual offenses than on relief." [22] Further studies of Session records would be needed to prove or disapprove this statement, but Scotland lacked a strong tradition of organized poor relief on which to build. Mitchell estimates that the 1575 and 1579 founding statutes of the Old Scottish Poor Law (modeled on the English Act of 1572) did not become even approximately effective in the lowland parishes until 1649.[23]

PURITANS AND CIVIL WAR IN ENGLAND

Meanwhile, in England, Puritans objected to the role of the deacon as prescribed in the Book of Common Prayer, the liturgical book of the Church of England. They called him a subpriest, "which never came from heaven," in contrast to the deacon of Scripture whose office "consisteth only in the oversight of the poor."[24] The Puritans in England were never able to persuade Elizabeth of their vision of church office, and to the extent that they could, the Puritans arranged it locally and clandestinely as a church-within-a-church.[25]

Forty years after Elizabeth's death in 1603, the Puritans had an opportunity to reconstruct the Church of England along Presbyterian or Reformed lines. During the civil wars in England (1642–1646, 1648), Parliament called an assembly to meet at Westminster on July 1, 1643, to advise it on the reform of the church:

> Many Things Remain in the Liturgy, Discipline, and Government of the Church, which do necessarily require a further and more perfect reformation than as yet hath been attained; and whereas it hath been declared and resolved by the Lords and Commons assembled in Parliament, that the present Church-government by archbishops, bishops, their chancellors, commissaries, deans, deans and chapters, archdeacons, and other ecclesiastical officers depending upon the hierarchy, is evil, and justly offensive and burdensome to the kingdom, a great impediment to reformation and growth of religion, and very prejudicial to the state and government of this kingdom; and that therefor they are resolved that the same shall be taken away, and that such a government shall be settled in the Church as may be most agreeable to God's holy word, and most apt to procure and preserve the peace of the Church at home, and nearer agreement with the Church of Scotland, and other Reformed Churches abroad; and, for the better effecting hereof, and for the vindicating and clearing of the doctrine of the Church of England from all false calumnies and aspersions, it is thought fit and necessary to call an Assembly of learned, godly, and judicious Divines, who, together with some members of both the Houses of Parliament, are to consult and advise of such matters and things, touching the premises, as shall be proposed unto them by both or either of the Houses of Parliament, and to give their advice and counsel therein to both or either of the said Houses.[26]

In its *Form of Church-Government*, the Westminster Assembly recommended: "Deacons as distinct officers in the church. . . . Whose Office is perpetual. . . . To whose Office it belongs not to preach the Word or administer the Sacraments, but to take special care in distributing to the necessities of the poor."[27] As for its influence on England, time and the course of events passed the Westminster Assembly by. Oliver Cromwell (1599–1658) and his Protectorate replaced the executed King Charles II (1649).

The civil war and interregnum brought forth new denominations in England, some of which continue in existence, such as the Society of

Friends or Quakers. In 1660 the monarchy and the Church of England were restored. Therefore the war did not bring a Puritan or a Presbyterian regime to England; neither did it resolve the needs of the poor. Appeals to reform the poor laws and eliminate begging in England continued.[28]

Stranger Churches

During her reign, Elizabeth I had resisted the polity of the Reformed Church within the Church of England, but she was willing to allow it within the foreign Protestant communities on English soil. The so-called "stranger churches," which consisted of foreigners resident in England, were first established in London in 1550 during the reign of Edward VI (r. 1547–1553). The development of these churches were aided by Thomas Cranmer, archbishop of Canterbury and primate of the Church of England. After Mary Tudor ascended the throne (r. 1553–1558), many members of these churches fled to the continent of Europe for safety.[29] When Elizabeth I became queen, some of these refugees returned and petitioned for the reestablishment of their churches.

By 1560 foreign Protestant churches—Dutch and French—were operative again in London as separate congregations. Many of those who had taken refuge on the continent during the reign of Mary Tudor had returned. They were enthusiastic about the Reformed churches and pastors they had known in Europe. In fact, Nicolas Des Gallars, a member of the Venerable Company of Pastors of Geneva, was called to head the French congregation in London, thus establishing a strong link with Geneva.[30]

In 1561 the town council of Sandwich, England, and the Privy Council sought from the "Church of Strangers" in London twenty Dutch families skilled in making types of cloth new to England. These workers formed a foreign Protestant church in Sandwich. "Stranger Churches" were subsequently founded in Norwich (1565) and Maidstone, Southhampton, and Stamford (1567). These churches were, in effect, daughter churches of the foreign Protestant church in London. They maintained ties with it.[31]

Under her bishops, Elizabeth permitted the foreign Protestant churches to retain their Reformed organizational structures. Thus besides pastors, the "stranger churches" could elect elders and deacons. The elders served with the pastors on the congregational consistory that governed the local church.[32] The deacons collected and disbursed the congregation's charity. The church order of John a Lasco, the first superintendent of the Dutch- and French-speaking congregations in London, included deacons who aided refugees and the poor. The deacons were established in office by a ceremony of laying-on of hands, as were ministers.[33]

Examining just one of these churches more closely, namely, the deacons' fund in Sandwich, England, one finds that it was remarkably similar to the deacons' fund in Geneva. It aided refugees from persecution and religious warfare in the Low Countries.[34] Deacons on the Reformed model of Geneva were not welcomed all over England, however. The foreign Protestant churches were an exception.

The foreign Protestant churches in London provided an example of how deacons, as a group of officers meeting together regularly within a congregation, could become a faction. In 1563 a pastor from the continent became minister to the Dutch Stranger Church in London. He decreed that a father who wanted his child baptized had to submit a declaration by two people who would act as witnesses with the intent of ensuring that the child was of parents entitled to church membership. The deacons objected to this practice and withdrew from the church. The conflict was settled with the help of other churches, even some across the English Channel, but only after people favorable to the deacons were elected as deacons and members of the Consistory. The pastor was suspended from the ministry for a while in 1570. By 1576, the appointment of godparents in the London church was left to the individual.[35]

This quarrel over the issue of godparents exemplifies how the officers of the various European Reformed churches maintained contact with one another and sought out one another to solve problems. These international contacts were important to the survival of new Reformed churches because many of them were an illegal minority in areas that were still Catholic, such as France. The existence of the Reformed churches was precarious. They needed the support of one another, and at times their members had to flee. Reformed churches developed a tradition of supplying members with what they needed to get them to the next Reformed church. In this way people could go from one church to the next as they made their way to safety. Deacons facilitated these financial arrangements.

THE LOW COUNTRIES AND EMDEN

The situation for the diaconate and for the church in the Low Countries is more complex and interesting than the old historiography, which tended to treat Calvinism as a monolith, would allow. Scholarly work on deacons and social welfare in the Low Countries during the last twenty years warrants more than a passing reference, but to make sense, deacons and social welfare need to be set within the context of a larger political and religious history.[36]

In the early sixteenth century, the Low Countries were a part of the Holy Roman Empire, which from 1519 was under the Habsburg emperor Charles V (1500–1558). Although Charles attempted to suppress Anabaptism and Lutheranism in the Low Countries, as in the rest of his empire, he failed. However, Charles got along with the people of the Low Countries better than his son and successor, Philip (1527–1598), would.[37] In part this was because Charles was born in Ghent and raised in Brussels, which meant he was not alien to the people of the Low Countries, though the Germanies and parts of Eastern Europe were also a part of his empire. Charles also had inherited Spain in 1516 when his mother was judged mentally incompetent. He spent most of the years of his reign there.[38]

Although Protestantism had appeared in the Low Countries in the first half of the sixteenth century when Charles was emperor, it was after he abdicated the throne in 1555 to his son, Philip, that Protestantism came into its own. Philip, better known as Philip II, king of Spain, did not honor the prerogatives that the burghers of the Low Countries had come to feel were their own, and he was little inclined to tolerate any divergence from the Catholic Church.[39] Therefore, a rebellion arose. Calvinist rebels in the northern provinces of the Netherlands, led by William of Orange, were to establish a Dutch Republic, but after the Spanish Fury of unpaid troops at Antwerp in 1576 had killed thousands, William tried to unite all the provinces, whatever their religious convictions, in a common front against Spain in the Pacification of Ghent. The Pacification could not resolve religious differences, however, and the alliance split into the seven northern provinces of the Netherlands, which declared independence from Spain in 1581, and the southern provinces, which remained loyal to the Habsburgs and were the precursor to modern Belgium.[40] Because of the northward migration of the adherents of the Reformed churches during the upheaval, Protestants became strong in the northern provinces of the Low Countries. The southern provinces tended to remain Catholic in religious allegiance, but many in the northern provinces remained loyal to Catholicism as well, even in areas where the Catholic Church was outlawed, a fact that has failed to be sufficiently appreciated. In effect, in many regions Catholicism was unofficially tolerated. A degree of religious diversity was allowed in the northern provinces of the Netherlands that was unusual for the sixteenth century. Not only Catholics survived there but also Anabaptists.[41]

Because of this situation, Charles Parker would argue that the Reformed Church in the Netherlands never became a state church because other churches claimed the allegiance of many of the people. At best the Dutch Reformed Church was, he would say, "the sanctioned public ecclesiastical institution."[42] How one categorizes the Reformed Church depends on how one defines "state church." A modern understanding of a state church is a church that is supported by the state (though other denominations are allowed to exist). If ministers of a particular denomination are paid by the state and the church buildings are maintained by the state, one can reasonably argue that that church is a state church. This would have been true of Reformed churches in the Netherlands where they received state support in the sixteenth century, though the magistrates did not guarantee the Reformed Church a monopoly on religious allegiance. The lack of such a monopoly frustrated Reformed pastors, especially when it came to dealing with the Anabaptists.[43]

The fact that all citizens in the state were not communing members of the Reformed Church left that denomination in a different situation than Reformed churches in some parts of Switzerland where everyone was thought of as a church member. The reaction of the Reformed Church in the state of Holland was to attempt to form a pure community among its church members, much as Puritans would attempt to do in New England in the seventeenth century. Nonmembers were excluded from the celebration of the Lord's Supper, which was not unusual in early modern times. Also, in many regions, the Reformed churches and their deacons, operating with limited resources, preferred to serve the poor of their own church community who were in good standing, to the disappointment of magistrates who needed all citizens to be served.[44]

The newly Protestant states resolved the problem of meeting the needs of all the poor in various ways at the local level, as Andrew Pettegree has pointed out. In some cities, such as Dordrecht, the deacons of the Reformed Church were given a leading role in municipal charity, as well as the resources to meet that need. This solution was attractive to Rotterdam also. In other cities, such as Haarlem, the deacons of the Reformed Church took care of church members, while others were left to the responsibility of the city magistrates. In still other cases there was a cooperative endeavor, but not one without tensions.[45] Delft was an example of a city in which deacons and municipal officials eventually came to terms when deacons were forced, for lack of resources, to cooperate with a municipality-wide welfare system.

In Delft prior to the Reformation, magistrates and the Catholic Church had worked cooperatively to provide relief to all poor citizens, but after Delft officially had accepted the Reformed Church in 1572, the denomination chose to concentrate its charity on church members, as it had done prior to 1572. Money was collected through donations and offerings in church services, but as early as 1578, this did not provide enough income because the magistrates had taken over the property and endowments from the Catholic Church. Deacons asked for help from the magistrates, but they were unsuccessful in getting adequate subvention. In 1614, after years of resistance from the Reformed Church, the diaconate was incorporated into a citywide centralized poor relief institution that had been created in 1597 by the magistrates. Because all regents of this institution were obliged to be members of the official church, however, the Reformed Church influence continued and deacons had considerable influence over charity.[46]

What is amazing about the Reformed Church in the Netherlands to an historian is the persistence with which individual congregations attempted to achieve a diaconate that was dedicated to social welfare much like the Genevan diaconate, despite a political and economic context that was different from Geneva. This is not to say that the Dutch looked directly to Geneva for inspiration in the same way as many French Protestants might have done. For the Reformed congregations in the Netherlands, the so-called *Moederkerk*, or mother church, was in Emden, a German port city, sometimes known as "Geneva of the North." There were similarities between Emden and Geneva. Both cities harbored large populations of refugees in the sixteenth century, and both cities had several categories of deacons, some dedicated to helping the local poor and others dedicated to helping foreigners.[47] Unlike Geneva, however, the Lutheran Reformation had come to Emden before the Calvinist or Reformed Reformation.

The Lutheran Reformation had been introduced into Emden by the resident counts during the rule of Count Enno (1528–1540). In 1543, however, his successor, Countess Anna (r. 1540–1558), had named as superintendent of the Emden church Jan Laski (1499–1560), an Italian-educated humanist bishop of Poland who in 1540 had renounced Catholicism and had lost his benefices.[48] Although Laski was tolerant of other Protestants, he favored Calvinist ecclesiastical polity, and he steered Emden in that direction.[49] During the Augsburg Interim (1548–1552), Emden's churches closed rather than accept Catholic ritual.[50] Like Martin Bucer, Laski went to England with the blessing of Archbishop Thomas Cranmer. In England, Laski was active in the foundation of the "Stranger Church" for refugees from the continent and was appointed superintendent in 1550 by the boy-king, Edward VI. This great Reformed experiment was suspended in 1553. With the accession of Mary Tudor, Laski and members of his congregation fled England and returned to the continent and to Emden itself. Emden was about to experience a crescendo of religious refugees, mainly from the Low Countries, fleeing religious oppression. Emden became a hub of Protestant printing, much like Geneva.

The social welfare system of Emden was confronted with the needs of the poorer refugees, and the city's poor relief institutions evolved dramatically.[51] From the Low Countries, nascent Reformed congregations looked to Emden.[52] Although Laski ended his days organizing the Calvinist church in Poland, Emden continued as a model of a Reformed church and in 1571 hosted a formative synod—the Synod of Emden—which set a Calvinist standard of organization and theology for the Dutch Reformed Church to come.[53]

Swiss Influence and France in the Sixteenth Century

In 1562 the wars of religion that were to occupy France in the latter half of the century broke out. By that time, Lutherans in the Germanies were safe under the provisions of the 1555 Peace of Augsburg, which gave Lutherans legal status in regions where the rulers were Lutheran. In those areas, Lutherans had a claim to state-supported education, clerical salaries, social welfare, and building maintenance. Reformed churches in France and the Low Countries were in quite a different situation in the sixteenth century because they frequently had to rely on their own resources to support themselves and their poor. Financing was critical. Deacons and their funds played an important role in keeping these Reformed churches alive as a viable minority.

However much the Reformed churches were interconnected, the ideal of a four-part ministry of pastors, doctors, elders, and deacons was not always realized outside of Geneva. Although the title of an office sometimes was lost as Reformed churches spread, the functions remained of preaching, teaching, discipline, and diaconal care for the disadvantaged. Churches in other countries often abridged the fourfold ministry of Calvin's model of church government in Geneva. When Swiss models of church government spread to Germany and elsewhere, geographic and historical conditions modified these models to fit local contexts. The office of doctor, in the sense that it existed in Geneva to designate theological professors, tended to drop away when the community lacked institutions of higher education.

In some areas there were no deacons, so financial responsibilities sometimes fell on elders. On the other hand, where there were deacons, their
tasks could shift toward those of pastors, especially if a church had no pastor, as happened in France under persecution. If there was a shortage of
pastors in an area, the deacons sometimes broadened their concerns from
a preoccupation with finances and social welfare to function more as assistant ministers. For example, for a time in the sixteenth century, in addition
to caring for the poor, deacons in France were in charge of small religious
meetings, consistory registers, lists of members, and baptismal and marriage lists. In 1559 the First National Synod, or gathering, of representatives of Reformed churches in France permitted deacons to conduct
services at which they would read from the Bible and pray.[54] However,
deacons were not to preach or administer the sacraments.[55] The Synod of
1559 also recognized a form of church government that included deacons
with elders and pastors as members of consistories at the level of the local
congregation, thus giving deacons a role in church government.[56] Deacons,
along with elders and pastors, also served as representatives to synods at the
provincial and national level and to colloquies organized for several congregations in a local area.[57] In March 1561, a national synod of the
Reformed Church of France at Poitiers restricted deacons to public assistance, more along Genevan lines. Whether or not they could hold public
catechisms remained in dispute for some time, with some wanting to reduce
deacons to welfare officers and debar them from presenting opinions on
contentious doctrinal points. Others wanted to allow deacons a role in
church government and theological discussion.[58] Deacons often rose to a
position of real leadership in France, in contrast to Geneva where they were
excluded from the actual government of the church. Calvin's successor in
Geneva, Theodore Beza (1519–1605), and some leaders in the French
Reformed Church viewed these changes that augmented the role of deacons as temporary and hoped to return to the pattern established in
Geneva. They made attempts to reduce the powers of deacons and to limit
them to social welfare.[59]

The French Reformed diaconate retained a degree of diversity to meet
the needs of congregations in France. French deacons were active in cate-
chizing, and despite proscriptions, some of them preached, as had some
deacons of the early church. A certain number of French Reformed deacons
went on to become pastors. Thus Glenn Sunshine feels that the French diaconate was influenced, in part, by the Roman Catholic model of the deacon, but that was probably less an influence than the practical needs of
French congregations, which were sometimes without a pastor.[60] Moreover,

Protestants retained many precedents from the early church as part of their own diaconal heritage, especially when particular practices were mentioned in the Bible. There was precedent in the early church and in the Bible for preaching and teaching by deacons. If one accepts as deacons the seven selected in Acts 6:1–6 to lighten the load of the apostles by serving tables and seeing to it that the Hellenist widows were not neglected in the daily distribution, then the first deacons also preached. In Acts 7 are found Stephen's last words before martyrdom, words that certainly are a long discourse and could be considered a sermon. The next chapter of Acts records the fact that Philip "opened his mouth and . . . told him [the eunuch] the good news of Jesus" (Acts 8:35). After that event, Philip preached the Gospel to all the towns till he came to Caesarea (Acts 8:40).

It is difficult to argue that these early church practices were "Catholic," not Protestant, though it was true that Reformed deacons in Geneva devoted themselves more particularly to social welfare than did those in France. Perhaps, biblically speaking, when it came to the tasks of deacons, the French Reformed Church got it right and Calvin got it wrong. Finally, deacons in Geneva in the sixteenth century, who were role models for deacons in Reformed churches elsewhere, were often mature men of wealth and influence, men who had property and businesses to manage. They were at a stage in life where they were less likely to become pastors. That would change to some extent as time went on and it became more difficult to recruit deacons.

WOMEN AS DEACONS

Although there was no public office of widow in Calvin's Geneva, nor any female deacons, women were not completely excluded from the diaconate as Reformed churches spread elsewhere. And women certainly were not excluded from diaconal service in the Reformed Church. For several centuries, however, their presence in a diaconal office was the rare exception, dependent on the decisions of regional churches. Wessel on the Rhine was such an exception. The first general Reformed synod of the lower Rhine and the Netherlands in 1568 approved women as deacons of the sort that care for the sick:

> Especially in larger cities, it will be best to elect two classes of deacons, of which one class will take up the work of collecting alms and distributing the same, and the other shall attend especially to the sick. We also deem it appropriate that, in these places, women should be lawfully chosen for this work.[61]

Eleven years later (1579), Wessel took the next step toward women deacons by inquiring of the Synod

> [w]hether it would not be well in the Churches and congregations, wherever it is necessary and the customs allow, especially for the sake of the timid women, that the office of deaconesses [*sic*] should be again instituted, because it has not yet been introduced in any reformed manner.[62]

Where instituted, deaconesses (1) served as nurses for women, (2) bought and sewed cloth, and (3) cared for the poor. The tendency of the Reformation era to equate female deacons with widows may have stood in the way of the continuation of this office, however, because some of the deaconesses were under 60 years of age or married, conflicting with the biblical description of widows. Apparently the election of female deacons died out in Wessel by the early seventeenth century.[63]

FRANCE IN THE SEVENTEENTH AND EIGHTEENTH CENTURIES

Even without women deacons, the social welfare role of deacons in France was important. For almost a century after the Edict of Nantes in 1598, the Reformed Church was legal in France, but it was a minority church with only limited support from the government. The Reformed Church lost this legal existence in 1685 when Louis XIV (1638–1715) revoked the Edict of Nantes, depriving Protestants of their right to be Protestant in France. Even before that date, there were inducements for them to convert to Catholicism. Sometimes this took the form of discrimination against Protestants in social welfare. The Reformed Church tried to make it possible for its poorer members to stay within the church without suffering economic consequences. It attempted to meet the financial needs of individual Protestants over and above what the government provided.

Lyons and Nîmes provide examples of how Reformed churches attempted to protect the poor in their midst from discrimination and inducements to convert to Catholicism. Lyons was predominantly Catholic before the revocation of the Edict of Nantes. It had an influential Reformed church and a wealthy Protestant minority. Nîmes, on the other hand, was predominantly Protestant with a poor Catholic minority. In both cities poor relief was an area of religious conflict.[64]

Over the course of the seventeenth century, conformity to Catholic religious practices as a condition of welfare developed in France. The state gave evidence of its negative attitudes toward the Reformed Church by insisting that its title be *Religion prétendue réformée*, the Religion that Pretends to be Reformed. Privately, people continued to speak of the Reformed churches without negative qualifiers.

There were other ways in which life for Protestants became increasingly difficult in seventeenth-century France. In 1613, in Lyons, under the influence of the Catholic Reformation, the *Aumône générale*, the welfare agency, began to require the poor to attend Mass and a catechism class at the weekly distribution of bread. After 1645 all employees and contractors of the city charity hospital had to be Catholic. In 1672 the hospital required people who did not know Catholic doctrine to agree to accept religious instruction as a condition of admission to the hospital. There were cases of Protestants abjuring their faith to gain admittance to the hospital. By 1670 persecution had driven the Reformed Church to care for its own sick in private homes, using its own funds to pay for doctors, medicine, and care.[65]

In Nîmes there is no indication of religious pressure of the kind employed in Lyons against Protestants seeking poor relief. Nîmes was in Protestant hands from 1570–1632. During this period, Protestants controlled poor relief. The city government and the consistory, the governing body of the Reformed Church, cooperated with each other. For example, the city worked in conjunction with the consistory to arrange housing for the poor in private homes during cold weather. At the city hospital a Protestant theology student served as a teacher to the children and provided religious instruction. In accordance with the Edict of Nantes, Catholics were admitted to the hospital, but priests were not allowed to visit nor to administer the sacraments.[66]

This domination of social welfare by the Protestants changed after 1632 when Catholics entered city government in Nîmes. Catholics gradually came to dominate the city hospital. They substituted a priest for the Protestant theology student who served as a teacher. They secured a majority on the hospital board. In 1654 the Protestants were allowed to build their own hospital, but in 1667 it was united with the Catholic hospital. As in Lyons, the Reformed Church moved Protestants into private homes for care.[67]

In 1678 Protestants were excluded from city government in Nîmes. The Reformed Church took on additional expenses for Protestant poor relief. It circumvented restrictions on Protestant education by renting a room and helping support a teacher. Children of the poor paid no fee to attend this school. Meanwhile, Catholic city officials used about a quarter of the funds for the poor to support the mendicant orders. Both Catholics and Protestants used money to encourage conversion or to prevent people from abjuring the faith.[68]

In 1685 King Louis XIV revoked the Edict of Nantes and forced Protestants in France to convert to Catholicism. The Protestant church, or *temple* (the term French Protestants use for their churches to distinguish them from Catholic churches, which are *églises*), was closed in Nîmes in September 1685.[69]

Through all this, the Reformed churches of Lyons and Nîmes attempted to meet the increasing demands upon their resources. They supplemented public relief to Protestants at the beginning of the seventeenth century. Later, they attempted to replace it entirely by church relief. The Reformed churches handed out bread and money both extraordinarily and on a regular basis. They provided clothing, shelter, work, books, school fees, medicine, and care. They apprenticed young people to teach them a trade and dowered women who were marrying Protestant men. The Reformed churches retrained monks and friars who became Protestant, helped set people up in business, and made loans.[70]

Reformed churches also provided aid to traveling Protestants to enable them to reach the next church. Lyons was beset with refugees because of its location on the Rhone River, an escape route to Geneva for French Protestants. Also, in Lyons the climate dictated that the Reformed church secure coal and blankets for the poor. It also provided furniture and burials. The location of the Protestant temple for Lyons also made it necessary to hire a boat for the two-and-a-half-hour trip to attend religious services.[71]

The Reformed churches of both Lyons and Nîmes sent aid to smaller churches and sometimes to distant churches. Both helped prisoners and assigned women to visit the sick. In Nîmes these women were organized as "dames de la charité" for fund-raising, a title they may have taken from Catholic organizations of the same name. The Reformed church of Nîmes released prisoners by paying their debts and attempted to help those rowing on the galleys.[72]

These acts of service became a great burden to the churches, especially when government assistance from taxation ceased. In the early seventeenth century, public relief had aided Protestants in Lyons and Nîmes. The Edict of Nantes had provided that both Catholics and Protestants should be admitted to welfare facilities, but as the century wore on, this was honored in the breech in Lyons. At the beginning of the century in Nîmes, Protestants had benefited from the proceeds of the tax on meat, but in 1654 the meat tax was divided between Catholics and Protestants for their respective poor relief programs. The Protestant share of the meat tax ended with their exclusion from city government in 1678.[73]

Eventually the Reformed churches were thrown completely on their own resources. They met this challenge through a sophisticated system of charity and mutual support implemented by the pastors, elders, or deacons of the respective churches. Each congregation was responsible for its own poor, but they often helped one another out. They relied on pledges, fines, freewill donations, house-to-house collections, poor boxes, legacies, private hospitality, gifts of property, and goods in kind. Prosperous Protestants took the poor into their homes or assumed responsibility for the feeding and care of several poor individuals.[74]

Reformed churches sometimes went to extraordinary measures to meet their obligations to the poor. In January 1679, the Consistory of Nîmes decided to sell the property belonging to the poor fund, its endowment, which had been accumulated over the years. In December 1684, the Consistory sold the Communion silver and used pewter instead. These turned out to be fortuitous acts because in the following year the revocation of the Edict of Nantes deprived Reformed churches of their legal right to property. In addition, the property of individual Protestants who fled to avoid forced conversion to Catholicism was confiscated.[75]

With the revocation of the Edict of Nantes, it was illegal to practice the Reformed religion in France.[76] Many Protestants left the country or converted to Catholicism.[77] Those Protestants who remained in France lost civil and legal rights and had to worship clandestinely. Some sought haven in out-of-the-way places such as the Cévennes Mountains in Southeast France or in the *Midi* (Southern France). They worshiped in the "desert," as they called it: outdoors in barren and isolated places, in woods, and in caves. Reformed pastors were sentenced to death and suffered cruel martyrdoms. Protestant children were kidnapped and raised Catholic to "save their souls." The Enlightenment of the eighteenth century ameliorated the situation of Protestants in France somewhat, but their status was not regularized until the French Revolution and the era of Napoleon Bonaparte (1789–1815). Then Protestants were allowed to build church buildings again. From 1685 to the nineteenth century, however, mutual support, both financial and emotional, remained important to the survival of French Protestants.[78]

Looking at Europe as a whole, deacons and their financial roles, though sometimes performed by others, may have been more important to churches that were an illegal minority than to those churches that had state support. It is no wonder that the office of deacon spread to France and the Low Countries where minority churches were struggling for existence and recognition. Another factor in the perseverance of the office in Reformed churches was the example of Geneva. Thus John Knox affirmed the office of deacon in the Church of Scotland after his sojourn in Geneva during the Marian exile. He said of Geneva that it was "the most perfect school of Christ that ever was in the earth since the days of the Apostles. In other places, I confess Christ to be truly preached; but manners and religion to be so sincerely reformed, I have not yet seen in any other place."[79] Certainly Calvin's strong feelings on the importance of the office of deacon must also have had a role in its retention in the Reformed churches of Europe and in the Presbyterian Church of Scotland. Calvin's following extended beyond these churches because he also influenced the theology of the Church of England, though not its polity, and had an impact on the Baptist churches of England as they emerged in the seventeenth century.

Baptists and Mennonites

English Baptists were influenced by Anabaptists from the continent of Europe. The Anabaptists fed the nonconformist movement of those who despaired of being able to eradicate Catholic practices from the Church of England and who separated from the church, becoming known as Separatists. Puritans, on the other hand, remained in the Church of England and continued to try to purify it from within.

Out of the company of John Smyth, an English Separatist leader, emerged the first General Baptist Church. Smyth and his congregation fled persecution in England and sought refuge in Amsterdam. There he and his followers were baptized in 1608 or 1609. Smyth attempted to join the Mennonites; to facilitate this "merger," in 1609 he wrote a "Short Confession of Faith in XX Articles." More than a decade before the Mennonite Confession of Dordrecht, this confession included widows among the deacons.

> That the ministers of the church are, not only bishops ("Episcopos"), to whom the power is given of dispensing both the word and the sacraments, but also deacons, men and widows, who attend to the affairs of the poor and sick brethren.[80]

Although Smyth's Twenty Articles did not mention relationships with the civil government, he and other English in the Netherlands were willing to accept Menno Simon's views of respect toward the civil government. Evidence in support of this is their signatures on the 1610 "A Short

Confession of Faith," which was practically a reproduction of the Mennonite Waterland Confession of 1580:

> Worldly authority or magistry is a necessary ordinance of God, appointed and established for the preservation of the common estate, and of a good, natural, politic life, for the reward of the good and the punishing of the evil; we acknowledge ourselves obnoxious, and bound by the Word of God to fear, honor, and show obedience to the magistrates in all causes not contrary to the Word of the Lord. We are obliged to pray God Almighty for them, and to thank the Lord for good reasonable magistrates, and to yield unto them, without murmuring, beseeming tribute, toll and tax.[81]

Smyth died in August 1612, and union was accomplished with the Mennonites on January 20, 1615.

After the death of John Smyth and the union of the English Baptist Separatists with the Mennonites, a statement of belief served to unify Mennonite Anabaptists and summarize the roles of deacons and deaconesses among them. Deacons and deaconesses were to serve as caretakers of the needy and assistants in attending to other necessities of the church. This statement of belief was the Confession of Dordrecht or Dort (April 21, 1632):

> That all places be well provided with deacons (to look after and care for the poor), who may receive the contributions and alms, in order to dispense them faithfully and with all propriety to the poor and needy saints. Acts 6:3–6. And that also honorable aged widows should be chosen and ordained deaconesses, that they with the deacons may visit, comfort, and care for, the poor, feeble, sick, sorrowing and needy, as also the widows and orphans, and assist in attending to other wants and necessities of the church to the best of their ability. I Tim. 5:9; Rom. 16:1; James 1:27.[82]

The Confession of Dordrecht also allowed "fit" ordained deacons a role in teaching and exhortation:

> Concerning deacons, that they, especially when they are fit, and chosen and ordained thereto by the church, for the assistance and relief of the elders, may exhort the church (since they, as has been said, are chosen thereto), and labor also in the Word and in teaching.[83]

Besides deacons, the confession provided for bishops, pastors, leaders, and elders.

Meanwhile, before the union with the Mennonites, some of the English transplanted to the Netherlands had returned to London in 1611 and founded the first Baptist church in England.[84] Because some Puritan congregations decided against infant baptism, Baptist groups emerged. In the decade of the 1630s, the Particular Baptists arose in England, so named because they believed in God's particular election of some to eternal life. In this they followed the theological convictions of many seventeenth-century English Calvinists. The confessions of faith of the Particular Baptists included deacons but did not mention women in that office.[85] The Orthodox Creed that the General Baptists of 1679 published in London also lacked mention of women as deacons. Perhaps the early attempts of General Baptists to associate with the Mennonites in the Netherlands had encouraged them initially to use women as deacons to replicate Mennonite polity.[86]

The inclusion of the deacon in Baptist polity was ultimately at the expense of the office of elder. Baptist deacons eventually took on the elders' governing responsibilities. This tradition carried over into the New World.

North America

In 1638 Roger Williams (1604?–1683) founded the first Baptist church in Providence, Rhode Island, which is today called First Baptist Church in America. After Williams's departure from the congregation, elders served the church as lay pastors until the arrival of a college-educated pastor in 1771. Today, however, the church has no elders; the board of deacons is its church council.[87]

Likewise, churches founded in New England by Puritans and Separatists eventually would consider the elder and deacon redundant, despite separation of these two offices in the Cambridge Platform (1648), the recognized standard of Congregationalism in Massachusetts throughout the colonial period.[88] The Cambridge Platform considered the ordinary offices in the church to be that of elder and deacon. Elders consisted of pastors, teachers, and "ruling elders";[89] deacons, who were to receive the offerings and keep the treasury of the church, were in charge of the temporal goods of the church. The congregation elected these officers and ordained them by imposition of hands. If pastors changed congregations, the Cambridge Platform recommended reimposition of hands:

> *Church Officers*, are officers to one church . . . Hee that is clearly loosed from his office-relation unto that church wherof he was a minister, cannot be looked at as an officer, nor perform any act of *Office* in any other church, unless he be again orderly called unto *Office*: which when it shall be, wee know nothing to hinder, but *Imposition of hands* also in

his *Ordination* ought to be used towards him again. For so Paul the Apostle received *Imposition of hands* twice at least, from Ananias. Acts. 9. 17. & Acts. 13, 3.[90]

The Cambridge Platform made a provision for "*ancient widdows* (where they may be had) to minister in the church, in giving attendance to the sick . . . & others."[91] The office of widow remained theoretical in New England, however, though there had been at least one in the London Church in Amsterdam, as described by Governor Bradford:

> She honored her place and was an ornament to the congregation. She usually sat in a convenient place in the congregation, with a little birchen rod in her hand, and kept little children in great awe from disturbing the congregation. She did frequently visit the sick and weak, especially women, and, as there was need, called out maids and young women to watch and do them other helps as their necessity did require; and if they were poor, she would gather relief for them of those that were able, or acquaint the deacons; and she was obeyed as a mother in Israel and an officer of Christ.[92]

Although the office did not disappear, the ordination of deacons declined in Massachusetts. In "Ratio Disciplinae" (1726), Cotton Mather stated that he thought this change was because deacons had come to have no significant responsibilities in the church beyond that of aiding in the Communion service, but it may have been caused by a lack of enthusiasm within Congregationalism for detailed adherence to the Cambridge Platform. For example, an installation ceremony for pastors who changed congregations replaced reimposition of hands.[93]

In time, Congregational deacons took on responsibilities in the governance of the churches that could conceivably have been those of ruling elders. Elders disappeared entirely in many churches, except to the extent that pastors were considered elders, leaving a twofold pattern of church office that consisted of pastors and deacons. By 1700 few New England Congregational churches had officers other than pastors and deacons.[94] In colonial New England the title of deacon was of some importance, as evidenced by the inclusion of that title on the name plaques on portraits of colonial men and on street and road signs such as Deacon Haynes Road in Concord, Massachusetts.

Another office was to develop within North American churches, that of trustee. In many regions of North America, civil law required trustees to hold and transfer property.[95] Thus they became part of the organizational structure of many American churches, Lutheran as well as Congregational, Presbyterian, and Baptist.[96] The trustees of a congregation managed the property of the church, a task that otherwise could have remained with the elders or deacons. In Presbyterian churches that had trustees, it was sometimes at the expense of the office of deacon.[97]

Presbyterian and Reformed Churches

Calvin's fourfold pattern of church office continued to evolve in the Old World. In Scotland, as elsewhere, the office of doctor dropped out of church organizational structures, leaving pastors, elders, and deacons. When the Westminster Assembly in England (1643–1649) recommended against including deacons on Sessions (church councils) and construed the role of deacons more narrowly within the area of social welfare, Scottish practice generally conformed. In the seventeenth century, deacons were a regular institution in Scotland, but they often were prospective elders. In some churches elders performed diaconal duties. In the eighteenth century, Sessions tended to take over diaconal responsibilities.[98] Thus by the time Scottish immigrants arrived in the New World, deacons had disappeared in some congregations. Therefore, some churches in the New World founded by Scottish immigrants had pastors, elders, and deacons; others omitted the office of deacon.[99]

The Presbyterian Church in the United States of America organized in 1788 with a General Assembly at the national level. This assembly contained synods that were subordinate to it, which in turn were composed of presbyteries of congregations in geographic proximity to one another.[100] In the preliminary discussions of drafts of the church's constitution, or "Form of Government," at least two presbyteries were unhappy with the 1786 draft because it lacked a section on the election and ordination of deacons and elders. The 1787 draft provided for election by any method decided upon by the individual congregation. Deacons and elders were to be set apart by prayer without the imposition of hands.[101] The imposition of hands was added in 1879 among Presbyterians in the South.[102]

Deacons were found in some of these early Presbyterian churches but not in others. Some churches used trustees, especially in the North, though trustees also could be found in the South. For example, the Rocky River Church in North Carolina had trustees, but the Sugar Creek Church, also in North Carolina, called the men responsible for finances "Collectors." This term was used by Presbyterian churches in Ireland before 1717 and by the Reformed Church of Geneva during the time of Calvin to refer to the men who collected money for the deacons of the French refugee fund.[103]

The opinion of some Presbyterians was that deacons were lower than elders, and a "lower office" is included in those above it.[104]

There is some evidence that the office of deacon in France lapsed in Reformed churches despite the importance of social welfare to their continued existence as a minority.[105] This decline may have begun as early as the seventeenth century. One author points out that in 1620 there was a list of elders but not of deacons for the Reformed Church at Charenton, which served Paris. Therefore, he assumes there were no deacons.[106] In the case of individual congregations, judgment might depend on research into the archival documents of the period, especially contracts conserved by the notaries in which reference to deacons is often found.

The fate of deacons and elders in Scotland, France, and New England in the seventeenth and eighteenth centuries reveals a tendency for the two offices to merge in churches in which both served together on sessions, consistories, or local church councils. An overlapping of duties appears to have facilitated the elimination of one of the two offices. In Scotland and France the office of deacon suffered, whereas in New England the office of elder disappeared in many Congregational and Baptist churches. This point should not be pushed too far, however, because the organization of Reformed churches as prescribed by the Synod of Emden (1571) placed deacons on consistories with pastors and elders, and both offices survived when Dutch Reformed churches spread to the New World.[107] In the Reformed Church in America, which is of Dutch origin, deacons are considered part of the consistory.[108]

In Geneva deacons continued their active role in social welfare in the seventeenth and eighteenth centuries. The city's deacons met separately from elders and pastors. Calvin originally had designated as deacons the trustees and administrator of the Geneva city hospital. In addition to this native institution, foreign refugees from Italy, France, England, and German-speaking regions founded congregations in Reformed Geneva with deacons' funds to provide for church services in their own languages and to aid their compatriots.[109] These foreign refugees collected their own funding, some of it internationally. The Italian, German, and French Funds continued into the nineteenth century.[110]

Deacons of the *Bourse Française*, or French Fund, remained especially active because of persecution in France both before and after the revocation of the Edict of Nantes. In the seventeenth century, Geneva experienced a "Second Refuge" of French Protestants, so named because the city had absorbed a "First Refuge" of French Protestants during the sixteenth century. The deacons of the French Fund had the primary responsibility for these poor refugees from France. The deacons managed to meet the crisis of the enormous influx of refugees of the era with the help of the city government, which gave them grain and required the Italian Fund to give them money, but primarily the French Fund relied on private donations.[111] Beginning in 1685, the deacons also drew on the capital of the fund.[112] They had accumulated an endowment through gifts and legacies over the years. At the time of the revocation of the Edict of Nantes, the deacons of the French Fund reimbursed the city hospital for care of their sick poor, but from 1703–1798, the deacons of the French Fund had their own hospital on the Bourg-de-Four in what is today the old city of Geneva.[113]

LUTHERANS

In the parts of Europe that were Lutheran, the role of deacons varied. The title of deacon was used both for administrators of poor relief and for assistant pastors, depending on the region. Johannes Bugenhagen preferred calling welfare officers deacons. He helped formulate church orders for Denmark and parts of the Germanies. These deacons primarily disseminated government funds because the state had taken over church property and endowments at the time of the Reformation. Regions without such deacons provided poor relief through administrators who were, in many ways, the counterparts of Bugenhagen's deacons but lacked the title. In time the title of deacon tended to fall into disuse for welfare officers who disseminated state funds.

The situation for Lutherans who lived in areas where they were not in the majority was different. This was the case with Lutherans in the Low Countries. The civil government did not support Lutherans there, and they did not constitute a state church. Instead, they were a small minority, which was a contrast to the situation for Lutherans whose churches in other Northern European countries were established by law. In 1597 the Lutheran church of Amsterdam prepared a church order or constitution providing for a consistory consisting of a pastor, elders, and deacons. Other Lutheran congregations in the United Provinces of the Netherlands adopted this church order in the early seventeenth century, then brought it to the New World by way of early immigrants to territory claimed by the Dutch along the Hudson River.[114]

Lutherans in London, England, a small minority of the population, adopted the church order from the Netherlands for use in St. Mary's (Savoy) Lutheran Church. From there it was carried to the colony of Georgia. Therefore, the church order of the Lutheran church of Amsterdam influenced American Lutheranism directly from the Netherlands and indirectly by way of London. German Lutheran congregations in Pennsylvania had elders and deacons.[115] Presumably because of the presence of elders and deacons, Theodore Tappert stated that "Lutheran congregational organization in the Netherlands had to some extent been patterned after Reformed models, and the influence of Dutch and German Reformed polity may be presupposed in America too."[116] He could also have looked to Lutheran deacons in the church orders of Bugenhagen for a model.

Henry Mühlenberg came to the New World in 1742. In London and later in the colony of Georgia, he had become acquainted with a Lutheran church order that included deacons and elders before he met them again in Pennsylvania.[117] Records of annual conventions of the Pennsylvania Ministerium dating from 1748 list elders and deacons from local congregations in attendance with pastors.[118] The attendance roster for the convention of 1750 lists more than thirty members of church councils and seven deacons but only five preachers and two catechists.[119] In 1750 there were few ordained Lutheran pastors, but their numbers increased in the decades that followed. The Revolutionary War period made meetings difficult and cut into the attendance of lay delegates at the annual convention of the Ministerium of Pennsylvania. In 1775 there was no convention at all.[120] At the 1776 and 1777 conventions, only nine pastors attended.[121]

The 1781 constitution of the Pennsylvania Ministerium gave lay delegates from congregations a peripheral role at synodical meetings, but a second constitution of 1792 rectified the situation by providing that delegates of the congregations should be regular members of the synod with a voice and a vote alongside ordained ministers and licensed candidates.[122] The 1781 constitution officially called the mutual association of ministers "An Evangelical Lutheran Ministerium in North America" and every meeting "a Synodical Meeting." Even after the reforms of 1792 provided for greater lay participation, the ministers met together after the general meeting of the synod to make decisions about the qualifications of those who wanted to preach and to become members of the ministerium.[123]

The 1792 constitution provided insight into the internal organization in the German Lutheran congregations in Pennsylvania and adjacent states. The constitution stated that every delegate claiming a vote had to present "a certificate of election from his ministers, elders and deacons; that is, from the Church Council."[124] These church councils, as described in the constitution, consisted of deacons and elders. Thirty years earlier, Henry Mühlenberg had helped St. Michael's Church in Philadelphia ratify a constitution that became a model for other congregations on the Atlantic seaboard. This constitution included a church council of six elders and six deacons. Deacons served for two years and elders for three. The congregation elected these men from thirty-six nominees proposed by the church council. There were also trustees, as required by civil law.[125]

More pressing than the need for lay officers for these colonial churches was the need for pastors. The first Lutheran laypeople arrived in North America before pastors did. They organized into congregations and even selected elders and deacons. Then pastors came from Europe in response to the appeals of the laypeople or on their own, but there were not enough pastors. Therefore, in the colonial era, American Lutherans relied heavily on lay preachers. Sometimes schoolmasters would conduct services, occasionally itinerant ministers would do so, and often people who set themselves up as preachers would administer the sacraments without examination or certification.[126]

In addition to schools for children, the certification of pastors was a primary concern of the early synods into which Lutheran congregations in North America organized themselves on a geographic basis. The Ministerium of Pennsylvania described "the preachers who wander about unordained and uncalled, a disgrace to our religion."[127] The pastors of the early Lutheran Pennsylvania Ministerium wanted educated pastors whose theological orthodoxy could be verified. The ministerium wanted those who were ordained to know ancient languages and theology, but such an education was difficult to acquire. The colonies and early United States had no Lutheran theological seminaries until the nineteenth century. Lutheran ministers were educated either in Europe or were apprenticed to pastors in North America who tutored them privately.

This system of informal apprenticeship sometimes functioned well. With a good teacher, an individual could do well. William Kurtz, a candidate for ordination in 1760, was examined in theology in Latin orally and in writing. He was

> required to open the Greek Testament to the third chapter of I Corinthians and explain it in Latin, which was done satisfactorily without hesitation. Afterwards the 117th Psalm was given to him in Hebrew, and he was asked to translate it into Latin, *ex tempore*, according to the genuine literal sense, which again was done readily and skillfully. Further, he was also required to treat the second Psalm similarly.[128]

This young man might have been somewhat of an exceptional case because he was under the wing of his father, John Nicholas Kurtz. The elder Kurtz had been sent from Halle to Pennsylvania in 1745 and had served as an assistant until he was ordained a pastor in 1748 at the first convention of the Philadelphia Ministerium.[129]

If the ministerium had required of everyone the language skills of John Kurtz's son, the Lutheran Church in the colonies would have been unable to meet the needs of the pioneers. The Pennsylvania Ministerium attempted to keep its standards for ordination high, but it allowed men other than ordained pastors to serve congregations, to preach, and even to administer the sacraments under ministerial supervision. In 1748, when the Pennsylvania Ministerium began annual conventions, the church had two categories of individuals ministering in congregations: preachers and assistants, the latter being the post John Kurtz had held. This two-tiered system allowed for a period of training and observation before a man was ordained as a pastor.[130] At the 1750 convention of the Pennsylvania Ministerium, however, Mühlenberg still called the men who had been ordained in 1748 assistants, but they were listed with the preachers.[131] There was also a category of "catechist," the post William Kurtz was to hold before he was ordained pastor in 1760.[132]

The qualifications and duties of a catechist were outlined in the 1792 ministerial regulations of the German Evangelical Lutheran congregations in Pennsylvania and adjacent states. The regulations provided that a catechist's walk and conversation must be blameless; "he must be at least twenty years old; have acquired a systematic knowledge of Christian doctrines and ethics; he ought to possess some knowledge of human nature, manifest a gift of speaking, and above all things a practical knowledge of experimental religion." His official duties were to preach, "catechize the young, baptize, visit the schools and the sick, attend funerals and instruct the confirmands." The ministerium examined and licensed the catechist. He could not exercise his official duties in a congregation other than his own, and he was under the supervision of an ordained minister who would administer the Lord's Supper to his congregation.[133] Eventually the catechist might become a pastor if he passed the necessary examinations.

The Pennsylvania Ministerium was frequently beset with requests by isolated congregations either to ordain their catechists as pastors or to allow these catechists more responsibility, especially the right to give Communion. For example, Augusta County, Virginia, sent its catechist three hundred miles and requested that the ministerium ordain him "because their children not being baptized are growing into heathenism, and the older persons, when they die, because of the absence of any ordained preacher, must depart without the Lord's Supper, and thus be without this refreshment of the soul even on their death beds."[134] H. George Anderson estimated that "six out of seven pioneer pastors in western Pennsylvania began their ministries before they had been recognized by any synod," but the ministerium was hesitant to ordain men of uncertain qualifications or limited education.[135] Even with the support of his congregation, a catechist could return repeatedly to the ministerium to seek ordination but still not meet the group's standards. The alternative for some catechists was to give them additional responsibilities without ordination. This was done in 1763, for example, with a catechist for a congregation "in and about Conowago across the Susquehanna." He was allowed to give Communion to sick people in extreme necessity.[136]

The Pennsylvania Ministerium preferred to have only ordained ministers administer Communion. Neighboring pastors periodically offered Communion in the congregations of catechists. In 1768 the ministerium withdrew the privilege of administering the sacraments from a catechist who moved within what was considered reasonable range of Yorktown, where there was a Swedish preacher.[137]

Ministers were expected to travel at least once a year to annual meetings. As the frontier expanded, the distance on horseback to these meetings became one reason for the formation of new synods. In addition to this annual event, ministers also traveled to serve the needs of congregations. In 1805 the Synod of Pennsylvania appointed traveling preachers to serve a number of congregations and decided to pay them forty dollars per month.[138]

Another solution to the problem of the pastor shortage was the licensed candidate. This was an interim step between catechist and pastor. As described in the first Constitution of the Ministerium of the Evangelical Lutheran Church of North America, in force in 1781, the licensed candidate was allowed all the privileges of a pastor within a specified geographic area: "Candidates who have received licenses are allowed to preach, to catechize, to administer the Holy sacraments." Candidates underwent a brief examination in the ancient languages and theology before receiving a license good for one year. At the end of the year, the candidates either could undergo a stricter written examination to qualify for ordination or they could ask to have their license extended by the synod.[139]

Licensed candidates administered Communion without ordination, which was acceptable to the Pennsylvania Ministerium. In 1814, however, the secretary of the Carolina Ministerium (formed in 1791) wrote the Pennsylvania Ministerium to report that several of its members doubted "whether any one had the right to administer the Holy Communion without the laying on of hands or ordination." The secretary wanted information from church history, other sources, and the Bible on this point. The Pennsylvania Ministerium requested each of its ordained preachers to "present in writing to next year's Ministerium his opinion."[140] The following year at its annual convention, the Pennsylvania Ministerium declared unanimously that a written permit was as valid as the laying on of hands and that candidates who were licensed could "perform all ministerial acts."[141]

In connection with this, however, the Pennsylvania Ministerium decided to introduce "another class or order of preachers," that of deacon. This was to be an ordained position for men who fell short of the requisite languages and the three years of systematic instruction from an ordained minister that was required of pastors. The Pennsylvania Ministerium ordained nine deacons in 1815.[112] The proposal for a "rank of preachers with the title of Ordained Deacons" already had surfaced in Pennsylvania in an 1812 motion in the ministerial transactions at the synodical meeting. The proposed addition of deacons to the constitution at that time provided that the deacon, when advanced to be a pastor, should be ordained by a "second laying on of hands." In 1816, the year after deacons were introduced, the Pennsylvania Ministerium decided that a second ordination was unnecessary.[143] A "simple declaration of the assembled pastors" was sufficient "to advance him to the office of pastor":

> If a preacher [has] already received formal ordination as deacon, by the laying on of hands, no further formal laying on of hands shall be deemed necessary to advance him to the office of a pastor; that, therefore, a simple declaration of the assembled pastors, through the President or Senior of the Ministerium, shall be regarded as sufficient for this purpose.[144]

In 1820 thirteen deacons were advanced to the grade of pastor through a public declaration and a handshake, and six candidates were ordained deacon. The customary examination before ordination was omitted because of "a lack of time, and other urgent business."[145]

Alongside these ordained deacons, lay deacons and elders continued to serve in the Lutheran congregations. The office of catechist declined, however. No catechists were listed in attendance at the synodical meeting of 1816 and only two the following year. In contrast, there were twelve deacons in attendance.[146]

Not all Lutheran ministers were as enthusiastic about "a graded ministry" as the Pennsylvania Ministerium. As other synods spun off from the synod of Pennsylvania, they abolished the "grade" of deacon, for example, the Ohio Synod (1818) and the Maryland-Virginia Synod (1820). A plan proposed by the Ministerium of Pennsylvania for a General Synod to coordinate the various geographic synods provoked objections to a proposal that this General Synod would fix grades of the ministry for participating synods. There was fear of a multiplication of ranks. The supporters of the General Synod responded by limiting its prerogatives to offering "well considered advice" to the individual member synods.[147]

Summary

In early Lutheranism in North America before 1820, there were at least two types of deacons: the lay deacon and the ordained clerical deacon. When the Ministerium of Pennsylvania began meeting in 1748, some of the lay deacons were congregational delegates to the annual conventions. These deacons often took responsibility, alone or with the elders, to request the ministerium for pastors or for expansion of the responsibilities of the catechists assigned to their congregation. At several early annual conventions, the deacons carried the sacred vessels into the church for the worship services that preceded the meetings.[148]

Ordained deacons formally became a part of the Pennsylvania Synod in 1815 as the result of a decision to create another class or order of preachers. These deacons constituted a grade between licensed candidates and pastors, a transitional step that resembled the deacon in the Catholic and Episcopal traditions. The year after the Pennsylvania Synod introduced ordained deacons, it dropped ordination of pastors for those who already had been ordained as deacons. In the 1820 convention, deacons were recognized as pastors with a handshake.[149]

In the early years of Lutheranism in North America, there are some hints that the two conceptions of deacons (as lay and as transitional to the pastorate) might have existed simultaneously. For example, Henry Mühlenberg was well aware of lay deacons in Pennsylvania, but after John Kurtz had been ordained a pastor in 1748, Mühlenberg referred to him as a deacon and an assistant.[150] Perhaps this was a fallback to the terminology used in Germany.

There was at least one other man whom the Pennsylvania Ministerium called a deacon after he had been mentioned as a preacher: J. J. Roth, a former Roman Catholic student who was listed as a preacher in an account of the 1762 convention. At that convention the pastors examined him for correct doctrine, after which "[h]e was earnestly exhorted and requested to wait for his reception into our fellowship until further information, and then in fervent prayer commended to the Lord."[151] The 1763 convention referred to this man as Deacon Roth, then received him into the minis-terium "with the right hand" after reading a letter testifying to "his upright-ness in life" and a letter from inhabitants of Allentown who wanted him as their preacher.[152]

The above examples would seem to indicate that Lutherans in North America drew on the two models of the diaconate in the Christian church (as lay and as transitional to the pastorate), using each or both at the same time as convenience dictated. Colonial Lutheran churches also performed diaconal service. Family members handled many social problems, and local congregations attempted to care for their own. For example, members of early congregations along the Delaware and Hudson River valleys were asked to give toward relief of the poor.[153]

Soon attention was given on a larger scale to the plight of orphans and the needs of widows, especially the widows of pastors. In 1737 Salzburg Lutherans, with help from abroad, founded an institution for orphans that also housed forsaken adults.[154] In 1750 the Ministerium of Pennsylvania appointed a guardian for newly arrived orphans whose parents had been lost at sea. These guardians "shall see to it that such orphans do not lose their possessions at the hands of deceivers and unjust persons."[155] In 1773 Mühlenberg presented a plan to the twenty-sixth convention of the Penn-sylvania Ministerium to found what he called an "orphan institution" for "aged, helpless, poor United Preachers, school teachers, their widows and orphans." He suggested that "capable subjects might be prepared there in the necessary languages and knowledge" to enter a seminary that the synod planned to start in Philadelphia. Each member of the ministerium agreed to "contribute his mite from his scanty support" toward the home, but it, like the seminary, remained in the planning stages at this time.[156]

The Pennsylvania Ministerium received legacies, gifts, and even a box from Europe containing books, money, and clothing designated for orphans, schoolteachers, and preachers.[157] Synodical meetings granted small sums of money to widows and "aged" pastors and made loans to men who wanted to become preachers.[158] One project of the proposed General Synod, besides the foundation of a theological seminary, was an institution for orphans and widows. A theological seminary at Gettysburg, Pennsyl-vania, was founded in 1826.[159]

CATHOLICS

In the Roman Catholic Church, after the Council of Trent, the office of deacon continued to be preparatory to the priesthood. Religious orders, parishes, and lay societies continued their concern for the poor as they had in the Middle Ages. The Council of Trent did attempt to reform hospitals and confraternities.[160] But new institutions also emerged for the poor. The Society of Jesus (1540) and others followed up on the educational recommendations of the Council of Trent. Seminaries for men studying for the priesthood and new secondary schools and colleges moved the Counter-Reformation forward.[161] Catholic missions expanded around the globe on the crest of Spanish and Portuguese exploration and discovery.

During the Counter-Reformation, confraternities came under attack as lay organizations of social welfare. Complaints against the confraternities at Trent were similar to those Martin Luther had made earlier in the century when he criticized them for feasting, drinking, and spending money on entertainment rather than on the poor. Luther said, however, that brotherhoods truly dedicated to social welfare could be a good thing. The reformers at Trent complained that the charity that confraternities administered was sporadic, ill-coordinated, and misdirected. They resented the independent spirit of the confraternities and the control that the mendicant orders—such as the Franciscans—had over the organizations. Already at mid-century, a priest had complained that "with so many brotherhoods, the laymen are in such firm control that they order the priests around as if they were day-laborers."[162] In 1556 the ecclesiastical community in Spain complained to Pope Paul IV of confraternities that "bury [their members] with tall crosses without calling the parish priest, and administer the sacraments to whomever asks for them."[163]

The Catholic reformers wanted coordination, centralization, and supervision of confraternities. Therefore, in 1562 and 1563, the last sessions of the Council of Trent attempted to bring confraternities and hospitals under tighter ecclesiastical control. The church needed the cooperation of governing authorities to enforce new regulations that mandated episcopal supervision, auditing of accounts, elimination of overlapping activities, and appointment of secular priests to replace mendicant friars as confraternity chaplains.[164]

In Spain, Philip II moved quickly to enforce the decrees of the Council of Trent. The government wanted to consolidate small hospitals, each serving a few needy, and to control confraternity endowments. Some confraternities had acquired considerable property through gifts and wills. At the local level, magistrates wanted beggars off the streets, especially in times of plague and famine.[165] In 1604 Pope Clement VIII issued a decree, *Quaecumque*, that reinforced episcopal control of confraternities.[166] A bishop could redirect the charitable contributions of testators if he decided that funds were needed elsewhere.[167]

Sometimes confraternities were successful in resisting changes imposed upon them because many people continued to want to deal with the poor directly through their confraternity, and welfare was still largely dependent on voluntary contributions. Governments needed the goodwill of contributors to make poor relief work. For example, some hospitals with no endowment depended on ongoing gifts of time and money that could potentially be lost if the hospitals were dissolved because they were small or inefficient.

Confraternities also met social needs. People were attached to the ritual and festivity they provided, their help in times of illness, and the presence of confraternity brothers and sisters at funerals. Confraternities cared for members and nonmembers too, especially widows, some of whom joined at reduced fees. Membership in many confraternities was open to women and the poor; in some cases, even children could be members. There were some confraternities that had only female members, especially those who gave help at childbirth.[168]

Famine, plague, and the beginning of economic decline in Spain in the 1590s created needs that no welfare system could resolve. It was not until the Enlightenment touched Spain in the mid-eighteenth century that confraternities were seriously challenged there. The confraternity system remained strong in Spain until at least the end of that century.[169]

Confraternities north of the Pyrenees typically were neither as numerous nor as pervasive. In Spain they were particularly tenacious, but elsewhere, too, they remained an important ingredient in social welfare, at least until the French Revolution in 1789.[170] Confraternities did change after the Council of Trent, however, as Rome attempted to centralize and control them. The Counter-Reformation church fined confraternities that spent alms and bequests on drink and food. It frowned on excessive feasting, drinking, and social life that accompanied outdoor religious processions. The church encouraged oracular confession, frequent Communion, and devotional practices such as the use of the rosary.[171]

The church of the Counter-Reformation redirected confraternity practices, established new confraternities, and supported those it favored. Catholic reformers were both founders and members of confraternities. The newly founded Society of Jesus (1654), the Jesuits, promoted frequent Communion. Arch-confraternities that were favored by Rome replicated themselves elsewhere, for example, the Misericordia, with its hospitals and funeral services. New confraternities formed, dedicated to the sacraments, especially the Mass, the Sacred Heart of Jesus and of Mary, the relief of souls in purgatory, the spread of Christian doctrine through education of the young, and the conversion of Protestants.[172] Besides the doctrinal and devotional interests of the confraternities of the Counter-Reformation, they continued to be concerned with the poor and even took on new responsibilities. For example, during the sixteenth century, an increased awareness of the needs of orphans moved some confraternities to redirect their concern toward needy children.[173]

In 1617 Vincent de Paul founded a confraternity in France whose members visited the poor, especially the sick poor. Some of these Ladies of Charity came from the highest echelons of society.[174] In fact, charity became fashionable, and the queen herself ministered to hospital patients.[175] The Ladies of Charity brought food and consolation, but they also hoped to encourage the poor to make a general (complete) confession to a priest.[176] Religion and social welfare intertwined. Eventually, the Association of the Ladies of Charity spread throughout the world.[177]

At the other end of the social spectrum, Vincent de Paul and Louise de Marillac, a widow who worked with him, recruited country girls to work with the poor. In 1633 the two formed the Daughters of Charity from a group of young women who assisted Louise de Marillac and gathered in her home. Vincent de Paul composed their rule. To avoid being cloistered, as the Council of Trent desired for women religious, which would remove them from the homes of the poor, the Daughters of Charity sidestepped immediate formal recognition as a traditional religious order. In 1638 they began to care for abandoned children or foundlings. Eventually they became known as the Grey Sisters because of the color of their garb.[178]

Some groups that had been active among the poor accepted enclosure in convents, for example, the Ursulines of Paris. They were cloistered in 1612, but they continued their work in the education of girls. In fact, Ursuline convents multiplied.[179] François de Sales (1567–1622), titular bishop of Geneva, and Jeanne de Chantal (1572–1622) established the Order of the Visitation (also known as the Salesian Sisters) from women who were visiting the poor and the sick much like the original Ursulines. In 1618 the Salesian Sisters became a religious order devoted to educating girls.

Vincent de Paul also was interested in education for men who were studying for the priesthood. He conducted retreats for them, founded a seminary, and created minor and major seminaries to separate boys from adult men during their seminary training. In 1625, Vincent de Paul founded the Congregation of the Mission, also known as Lazarists or Vincentians, to preach to poor rural people. The Vincentians also conducted seminaries.[180]

Vincent de Paul's friends and concerns were broadly based. He did what he could to alleviate the misery of galley slaves, organized wartime relief, and left a legacy of concern for the poor that is evident today in urban Vincent de Paul stores, which are similar to those of the modern Salvation Army.[181] He is perhaps the most famous man of the Counter-Reformation. Vincent de Paul was deeply influenced by other Counter-Reformation figures: François de Sales and Cardinal Pierre de Bérulle (1575–1629), who adapted the Oratory of Philip Neri to French needs and founded schools. It was out of the milieu of the French version of the Italian Oratory that John Eudes (1601–1680) created the Congregation of the Good Shepherd for the care of fallen women. After him, the Catholic Reformation in France produced other fruit. For example, John Baptist de la Salle (1651–1719), a canon of the Cathedral of Rheims, resigned his comfortable post, opened a normal school (1684), and founded the Institute of the Brothers of Christian Schools.[182]

Vincent de Paul helped make France the leader of the Counter-Reformation in the seventeenth century just as Italy had been in the sixteenth, though Italians continued to found new orders, such as the Redemptorists or Congregation of the Most Holy Redeemer, which was founded in 1732 to preach to the poor. Even before the Counter-Reformation, Italian social welfare institutions such as the *Monti di Pietà*—credit institutions for the poor—had spread to France.[183] Throughout Catholic Europe there was an interest in the poor as part of the Counter-Reformation.

INSTITUTIONALIZATION OF THE POOR

Social welfare of the seventeenth and eighteenth centuries had other dimensions than the founding of religious orders and confraternities for education and poor relief. Centralization and rationalization of welfare administration led to the founding of hospitals, orphanages, and homes for the poor. The goals of these institutions were many-faceted: to empty the streets of the poor, to eliminate begging, to distribute social welfare more equitably, to educate and rehabilitate the poor, and to reform them. Some institutions specialized in particular diseases or social needs, for example, contagious or noncontagious illness, foundlings or legitimate orphans. Some of these welfare institutions had a disciplinary or reformatory side.

There was opposition to new institutions. Some people viewed institutionalization of the poor as incarceration, a sentiment shared by many poor people because welfare institutions tended to restrict the freedom of their inhabitants, to insist that they work, and to enforce religious observation. Some people of the era were unsympathetic to attempts to restrict begging, considering it a natural right. One bishop stated that "it is the part of the magistrate to clear the streets of beggars; it is my duty to give alms to all who ask."[184]

Some people attributed this seventeenth- and eighteenth-century movement to institutionalize the poor to Protestants. Charles Dickens immortalized the horrors of the welfare institutions within which he had lived as a child in England in his nineteenth-century novels, but Catholic Paris matched or surpassed Protestant countries in discipline of the poor through hard labor, corporal punishment, and compulsory piety.[185] In Geneva a separate section of the hospital, called the "discipline," was created in 1631 as a place of punishment for the poor. Even the deacons of the French Fund for refugees asked that people be incarcerated there. Both Catholics and Protestants placed the poor in institutions and expected a degree of conformity and religious devotion from them.[186]

Plans to permanently confine the poor spread throughout France and Holland in the seventeenth century and into England in the early eighteenth century. England established its first workhouse in 1697 in Bristol.[187] In Italy and France, some welfare institutions resembled penal monasteries. In Venice, institutions for recovering prostitutes were religious houses.[188] The tradition of religious orders for repentant women, Magdalenes, endured in conjunction with homes for women and adolescents.

Institutionalization of the poor had both positive and negative sides. It was well underway before the eighteenth century brought revolutionary changes to the setting within which social welfare operated.

The Industrial Revolution and Methodism

The eighteenth century brought both an agricultural and an industrial revolution. Farmers in the Low Countries initiated better methods in agriculture and husbandry that made more food available. These improvements spread to England. The English textile industry led the world in industrialization in the latter half of the century. The industrial revolution created jobs, and people left farms to work in factories. Undesirable working conditions and crowded living in cities brought new problems, but medical advances lowered the death rate and population soared. The Church of England was unprepared to meet the challenges of the industrial revolution and urbanization. Its clergymen were reticent to move from rural vicarages to urban slums. The Church of England, nevertheless, produced evangelists who were intent on bringing the Gospel to the poor wherever they lived. The most famous of these were John Wesley and his younger brother, Charles (d. 1788), a hymn writer.

John and Charles Wesley were born in 1703 and 1707 to a rector of the Church of England and his wife. The brothers both attended Oxford. John became a fellow of Lincoln College in 1726, the year after he was ordained a deacon. In 1728 he was ordained a priest in the Church of England.[189] At Oxford the brothers gathered a group of like-minded friends, called the Holy Club, for prayer and Bible study, and this group also pledged to help the needy and destitute. The members of this club were nicknamed the Methodists because of the group's methodical ways. John Wesley read the Greek New Testament intensely, visited prisoners in jail, communed weekly, and fasted on Wednesdays and Fridays.[190] In 1735 John and Charles sailed to the colony of Georgia as missionaries for the Society for the Propagation of the Gospel in Foreign Parts. Their stay was short: Charles returned in 1736, and John was back in England in 1738.[191]

As missionaries, the brothers were impressed by Moravians, in part because a Moravian in London was instrumental in the inner conversion of the brothers in May 1738. John Wesley records experiencing a sense of trust in Christ and an assurance of sins forgiven. He experienced this as Luther's preface to his translation of the Book of Romans was read at a meeting on Aldersgate Street near St. Paul's Cathedral after evening prayer. Shortly thereafter John left for Germany to visit Zinzendorf and Herrnhut. John was back in England in September and began a career of evangelism and preaching.[192]

Although John Wesley remained a member of the Church of England throughout his life, he often preached outdoors and created an organizational structure within that church that functioned well in an urban society. It consisted of Methodist societies of small groups that met once or twice a week. Neighboring societies formed circuits that were served by traveling preachers. Conferences met regularly. John Wesley headed the structure at the national level. The movement spread internationally. Laypeople held office and also preached. Members led disciplined lives of prayer, Bible study, charity, and stewardship.[193]

At first, Methodists in London were part of a Moravian group, but they separated from it in 1740 after a leader of the London Moravians suggested that a person who developed doubts should separate from the sacraments and prayer and await God's renewal. With his more activist approach, Wesley found this unsatisfactory; thus the Methodists in London founded their own society, and Methodism and Moravianism went their own ways.

The formal split from the Church of England came after John Wesley's death in 1791. Although John did not want to separate from the Church of England, the Methodist movement had difficulty persuading bishops of the Church of England to ordain some of their candidates for the priesthood. Because John Wesley was not a bishop, he was not authorized to ordain others. Nevertheless, one day in 1784 he ordained Richard Whatcoat and Thomas Vasey for service in North America as deacons. The next day John Wesley ordained them as elders (pastors). He then ordained Thomas Coke, a priest in the Church of England, as superintendent with authority to ordain. John Wesley stated that he felt "providentially called at this time to set apart some persons for the work of ministry in America."[194] These ordinations affronted the episcopal authority of the Church of England, but John Wesley had become convinced that a bishop and a presbyter are essentially one order with different tasks, that is, a priest or elder such as himself is of the same order as a bishop. In certain circumstances, John Wesley said, a presbyter such as himself had the right to ordain.[195]

In the same year, John Wesley also organized a conference of one hundred ministers to direct the Methodist movement and hold the property of the Methodist societies and their chapels after his death. The Methodists had become a church within a church, but Methodism evolved into a denomination on its own and experienced further divisions in the nineteenth century.[196]

John Wesley cared for both the souls and the bodies of the poor. Amid a busy preaching schedule he visited the poor, raised money, opened a dispensary for the sick, started a loan society, founded a home for widows and a school for children, and opposed slavery. He gave unstintingly of his time and money.[197]

Socially active and engaged, the Methodists nevertheless left the diaconate much as it had been in the Church of England—a transitional step toward becoming a priest. When John Wesley abridged the *Book of Common Prayer* as a service book for North America, he retained deacons, though he changed the titles of bishops and priests to superintendents and elders. British editions of Wesley's service book retained this threefold ministry until the mid-nineteenth century.[198] Although practices varied in early Methodism, the American church practiced a two-step ordination of deacons and elders. Some ministers were deacons only a day before becoming ordained elders. This probationary period as a deacon eventually lengthened into two years or more.[199]

The issue was complicated by the presence of offices within Methodism whose roles resembled those of deacons in some Reformed and Lutheran churches. Chief among these were the stewards. Methodists had society stewards, circuit stewards, and stewards of the poor. Society stewards were the treasurers of the local church fund. The stewards of the poor prepared the Lord's Supper and ensured that a collection for the poor was taken at the sacrament. The circuit stewards were financial officers and leaders in the groupings of Methodist societies into circuits.[200]

In addition to stewards, Methodism had local lay preachers. John Wesley had initially been reticent to allow laypeople to preach, but his mother suggested that he might be impeding the work of the Holy Spirit. Therefore, lay preachers became important in the movement. In North America, the Methodist church ordained these preachers into what was, in effect, a permanent form of the diaconate "to perform all the duties of a pastor" in a local area to which they were appointed. District committees on ordained ministry licensed these local preachers.[201]

Of course, not all English reform at this time was the result of John Wesley or his influence. In the eighteenth century, hospitals were established in tremendous numbers, especially for the sick but also for foundlings and prostitutes. The influence of Methodism spread beyond the movement to John Wesley's friends and admirers, people such as John Howard (1726–1790), who labored for the reform of prisons in England, Scotland, Ireland, and on the continent of Europe.[202]

EVANGELICALS

Not all who were influenced by the revival of the eighteenth and early nineteenth centuries left the Church of England when the Methodists separated from it. Those who remained within the Church of England became the core of an evangelical movement. They were known as Evangelicals and were active in good causes both within the church and across denominational lines, particularly in the voluntary societies of the late eighteenth and early nineteenth centuries. They included the Religious Tract Society (1799), the Church Missionary Society (1799), and the British and Foreign Bible Society (1804). Evangelicals tried to regulate child labor in the emerging factories and to protect chimney sweeps. They promoted education of the poor.[203]

Evangelicals were particularly well-suited to causes that required legislative reform because the passage of the Test Act in 1673 required that civil officeholders, including members of Parliament, had to commune in the Church of England. This excluded Nonconformists and Catholics from civil office. The Test Act was repealed in 1828.[204] Evangelicals within the Church of England included prominent and powerful people, male and female. A number of them lived in Clapham, a suburb of London, which gave its name to a group of devout Anglicans whose influence surpassed their numbers.

Members of the "Clapham Sect" were active in the campaign against the slave trade. Most effective was William Wilberforce, the Claphamite member of Parliament. Three years after his 1784 "conversion," Wilberforce began a prolonged battle against slavery that resulted in the abolition of the slave trade in 1807 and the abolition of slavery itself throughout British dominions in 1833.[205] Through the efforts of Wilberforce and other Evangelicals, Parliament altered the charter of the East India Company in 1813 to allow missions within the Company's territories. The Anglicans set up an episcopal establishment in India, including a bishop and three archdeacons.

With the rise of the industrial revolution in England, poor children worked in factories six days a week from dawn to dusk. This left Sunday for their education. In 1780 Robert Raikes (1735–1811), an Evangelical layman, began a Sunday chool in Gloucester that met from 8 A.M. until 8 P.M. with breaks to attend church. Five years later in London, the Society for Promoting Sunday Schools formed. In 1791 a similar society formed in Philadelphia.[206] The enthusiasm for Sunday schools spread quickly and included German-speaking Lutherans in North America who were motivated, in part, by a desire to continue teaching their children the German language.[207]

VOLUNTARY AND MISSIONARY SOCIETIES

Voluntary societies tended to address themselves to areas of service that denominations had neglected, such as foreign missions. Some missionary societies were concentrated in particular denominations. For example, such was the case with the Baptist Missionary Society of England (1792). Voluntary societies often attempted to appeal across denominational lines. The (London) Missionary Society (1795) started as an interdenominational organization but gained largely Congregationalist support. In time denominations would take up particular projects of the voluntary societies.

The missionary societies, like the Sunday school movement, spread beyond England. The Netherlands Missionary Society organized in 1797. Germans and Swiss supported a school at Basel to train missionaries (1815).

The Danish Missionary Society dates from 1821, the Berlin and Paris societies from 1824, the Rhenish Missionary Society from 1828, the Swedish from 1835, the Leipzig Evangelical Lutheran Mission and the North German Missionary Society from 1836, and the Norwegian and the Finnish from 1842.[208]

Already in the seventeenth century in North America before these missionary societies were formed, John Campanius, a Swedish pastor on the Delaware from 1643 to 1648, had reduced a Native American dialect to writing and translated Luther's Small Catechism into the language. It was printed in 1696 at Swedish royal expense. Lutheran ministers in New York also worked among the Native Americans.[209] The Great Awakening in America that began in 1734–1735 with Jonathan Edwards (1703–1758) in Northampton, Massachusetts, also provoked a concern for evangelism among Native Americans.

These eighteenth-century beginnings of mission among Native Americans expanded in the nineteenth century into an American concern for foreign missions. In 1810 Congregationalists formed the American Board of Commissioners for Foreign Missions. It attracted the support of Christians of other denominations. Lutherans occasionally supported its work but were more preoccupied with home missions and the frontier at this time. The Foreign Missionary Society of the Evangelical German Churches in the United States formed in 1837.[210]

The nineteenth century witnessed the further growth of voluntary societies and the spread of foreign missions. Lutherans in North America would take an increased interest in the causes they promoted and would join them or form organizations of their own. As Germany began to grapple with the industrial revolution and its accompanying social problems, new forms of deaconesses and deacons would emerge in that country and spread throughout Northern Europe, into North America, and to other parts of the world. This is the story of the next chapter.

SUMMARY

From the death of the major reformers of the Protestant Reformation to the early nineteenth century, the diaconate evolved. The Reformation had brought a break from the deacons of the medieval church who were transitional to the priesthood. After the first flush of the Reformation, lay deacons as welfare officers continued in some regions, but gradually they appeared more to be agents of the state. In Scotland, lay deacons retained an important role in the sixteenth and seventeenth centuries because they administered welfare, and the Scottish poor law did not function effectively without them. In Geneva, the deacons of the poor refugee funds continued their important role in welcoming expatriates.

In regions where Protestant churches were in the minority, as was the case with Reformed churches in France and the Low Countries in the sixteenth century, deacons remained important because of their key financial roles, but in some regions, Reformed church deacons tended to take on the functions of the pastor, especially where pastors were in short supply, as in France. In many places where deacons served on church councils or sessions along with elders, one or the other office was lost. Lay elders succumbed to deacons in Congregational and Baptist churches in New England. By the nineteenth century, deacons had lost out to elders in Scotland. Reformed churches from the Netherlands in the New World were the exception. Deacons survived alongside elders. Likewise, Lutheran churches that came to the New World from the Netherlands brought both elders and deacons with them. The early records of these churches attest to their activities both locally and at the synodical level.

In parts of Germany, the word *deacon* came to refer to assistant pastors, and this terminology was also carried to the New World. Henry Mühlenberg and his colleagues in the Ministerium of Pennsylvania sometimes used it in that way. In 1815, after Mühlenberg's death, they created a grade of deacon between the licensed candidates for the ministry and the ordained pastors. There was some discomfort with this development, however, and new synods formed in Ohio and Virginia-Maryland abolished the office of deacon as transitional to the ministry.

Catholics and the Church of England retained the medieval diaconate, to the disgust of Puritans in England, but both churches cared for the poor—England through its church wardens and overseers of the poor and the Catholic Church through its confraternities and religious orders stimulated by the Counter-Reformation. In the eighteenth century, as Methodism grew and became independent of the Church of England, it retained deacons on the Anglican pattern, but in actual fact, many of their duties had been absorbed by stewards and other officers.

The reformers of the Protestant Reformation had tried to recreate deacons as they had found them in the early church, but changes in society and culture during the intervening years had made it impossible to exactly replicate the deacon of the past. The two hundred and fifty years after the death of the major reformers saw development and change in the Reformation model of the diaconate to adjust to the needs of society and of the church. Each denomination retained or changed its diaconate to fit its own particular needs, though there were standard patterns based on the precedents of the past. The evolution of deacons would continue in the nineteenth and twentieth centuries and produce new forms.

NOTES

1. McCloy, *Government Assistance in Eighteenth-Century France*, 183–84.

2. Wanegffelen, *L'Édit de Nantes*.

3. Heinz Renkewitz, "Der diakonische Gedanke im Zeitalter des Pietismus," in Krimm, *Das diakonische Amt der Kirche*.

4. Bodensieck, *Encyclopedia of the Lutheran Church*, vol. 2, s.v. "Francke, August Hermann."

5. Bartholomäus Ziegenhalg (1683–1719) and Heinrich Plütschau (1678–1747); see Neill, *History of Christian Missions*, 228–31.

6. The quest for preachers was mentioned in the record of the first convention of the Pennsylvania Ministerium held in August 1748 at Philadelphia, see *Halle'sche Nachrichten*, n. e. pp. 150, 151; o. e. 76, 77, in *Documentary History of the Evangelical Lutheran Ministerium of Pennsylvania*, 3. Colonial Lutherans wanted to secure ministers, to build a church, and to establish schools for their children; see Theodore Tappert, "The Church's Infancy, 1650–1790," in Nelson, *Lutherans in North America*, 30, 44.

7. Tappert, "Church's Infancy," 44.

8. Ross, "Deacons in Protestantism," 430.

9. Bodensieck, *Encyclopedia of the Lutheran Church*, s.v. "Francke."

10. Aland, *History of Christianity*, 2:255–57.

11. Ross, "Deacons in Protestantism," 431.

12. Burn, *Livre des anglois à Genève*, 12–13; Ross, "Deacons in Protestantism," 433.

13. Ross, "Deacons in Protestantism," 432–33.

14. Henderson, *Presbyterianism*, 87–88.

15. George Yule, "The Puritans," in McCord and Parker, *Service in Christ*, 126.

16. Mackay, *English Poor*, 111.

17. "A compulsory poor rate (1572)," Document 15, in Pound, *Poverty and Vagrancy*, 96–97.

18. Pearson, *Cartwright and Elizabethan Puritanism*, 262.

19. *Seconde Parte of a Register*, i:170, quoted in Yule, "Puritans," in McCord and Parker, *Service in Christ*, 125.

20. "The Poor Law Act of 1601," Document 17, in Pound, *Poverty and Vagrancy*, 98–99.

21. Mitchison, "Making of the Old Scottish Poor Law," 62.

22. Rosalind Mitchison, "Poor Relief and Health Care in Scotland, 1575–1710," in Grell and Cunningham, *Health Care and Poor Relief*, 222.

23. Mitchison, "Poor Relief and Health Care in Scotland," 221, 225.

24. Quotation from *A Seconde Parte of a Register*, I:127, 130, in Yule, "Puritans," 125.

25. For a thorough account of Puritans in sixteenth-century England, see Collinson, *Elizabethan Puritan Movement*.

26. From an ordinance calling the assembly into existence, as quoted in Leith, *Assembly at Westminster*, 24–25.

27. Ross, "Deacons in Protestantism," 433–34.

28. Thomas Lawson, "An Appeal to the Parliament, Concerning the Poor, That There

May Not Be a Beggar in England (1660)," in Durnbaugh, *Every Need Supplied*, 177–80.

29. Pettegree, "Stranger Community in Marian London," 41–44.

30. Olson, "Family, Second Marriage, and the Death of Nicolas Des Gallars," 75–76.

31. Pettegree, *Foreign Protestant Communities*, 141–42, 263–64.

32. Olson, "Des Gallars and the Genevan Connection of the Stranger Churches," 43.

33. Olson, "Des Gallars and the Genevan Connection of the Stranger Churches," 202.

34. Moens, "Relief of the Poor Members," 321–38.

35. Pettegree, *Foreign Protestant Communities*, 243–52.

36. For an example of such work on social welfare and deacons in the Low Countries, see subsequent footnotes and these additional authors and works: Grell and Cunningham, "The Reformation and Changes in Welfare Provision in Early Modern Europe," in Grell and Cunningham, *Health Care and Poor Relief*, 1–16; Hugo Soly, "Continuity and Change: Attitudes towards Poor Relief and Health Care in Early Modern Antwerp," in Grell and Cunningham, *Health Care and Poor Relief*, 84–107; Guido Marnef, "The Changing Face of Calvinism in Antwerp, 1555–1585," in Pettegree, Duke, and Lewis, *Calvinism in Europe*, 145–47; Parker, *Reformation of Community*.

37. *The Encyclopedia of the Reformation*, s.v. "Pacification of Ghent."

38. *The Oxford Encyclopedia of the Reformation*, s.v. "Charles V."

39. *The Oxford Encyclopedia of the Reformation*, s.v. "Charles V" and "Philip II of Spain."

40. *The Oxford Encyclopedia of the Reformation*, s.v. "The Pacification of Ghent."

41. Charles H. Parker, "Public Church and Household of Faith: Competing Visions of the Church in Post-Reformation Delft, 1572–1617," *The Journal of Religious History* 17, no. 4 (December 1993): 419.

42. Parker, "Public Church and Household of Faith," 418.

43. Andrew Pettegree, "Coming to Terms with Victory: The Upbuilding of a Calvinist Church in Holland, 1572–1590," in Pettegree, Duke, and Lewis, *Calvinism in Europe*, 174–75.

44. Parker, "Public Church and Household of Faith," 419–20.

45. Pettegree, "Coming to Terms with Victory," 170–71.

46. Parker, "Public Church and Household of Faith," 421–23, 426–38.

47. Fehler, *Poor Relief and Protestantism*, 2, 19.

48. *The Encyclopedia of Protestantism*, s.v. "Emden" and "Laski, Jan."

49. For recent essays on Jan Laski, see Christoph Strohn, *Johannes a Lasco*.

50. *The Oxford Encyclopedia of the Reformation*, s.v. "Emden."

51. For the evolution of social welfare in sixteenth-century Emden, see Fehler, *Poor Relief and Protestantism*.

52. Fehler, *Poor Relief and Protestantism*.

53. *The Encyclopedia of the Reformation*, s.v. "Emden, Synod of," and "Laski, Jan."

54. Kingdon, *Geneva and the Consolidation of the French Protestant Movement*, 41.

55. Article 24 of the 1559 *Discipline ecclésiastique* of the Reformed churches of France, as quoted in Sunshine, "Geneva Meets Rome," 335.

56. Henderson, *Presbyterianism*, 78, 100.

57. Kingdon, *Geneva and the Consolidation of the French Protestant Movement*, 42.

58. Léonard, *History of Protestantism*, 2:132n5, 139–41.

59. Kingdon, *Geneva and the Consolidation of the French Protestant Movement*, 41.

60. Sunshine, "Geneva Meets Rome," 344–46.

61. Golder, *History of the Deaconess Movement*, 32.

62. Golder, *History of the Deaconess Movement*, 32.

63. Doumergue, *Jean Calvin*, 5:304–7.

64. Pugh, "Social Welfare and the Edict of Nantes," 349.

65. Pugh, "Social Welfare and the Edict of Nantes," 355, 357, 360–61.

66. Pugh, "Social Welfare and the Edict of Nantes," 353–54.

67. Pugh, "Social Welfare and the Edict of Nantes," 354–55, 362–65.

68. Pugh, "Social Welfare and the Edict of Nantes," 365–66.

69. Pugh, "Social Welfare and the Edict of Nantes," 362–68.

70. Pugh, "Social Welfare and the Edict of Nantes," 351–55, 360–65, 368.

71. Pugh, "Social Welfare and the Edict of Nantes," 353–61.

72. Pugh, "Social Welfare and the Edict of Nantes," 352, 366–67.

73. Pugh, "Social Welfare and the Edict of Nantes," 366.

74. Pugh, "Social Welfare and the Edict of Nantes," 352–53, 368.

75. Pugh, "Social Welfare and the Edict of Nantes," 368.

76. "The Provisions of the Edict of Revocation," in Léonard, *History of Protestantism*, 2:430–31.

77. For the refuge of French Reformed by way of Geneva, see Olivier Reverdin et al., *Genève au temps de la Révocation de l'Édit de Nante*.

78. Roelker, *French Huguenots*, 8–10.

79. In a December 1556 letter to Anna Locke, as quoted in McNeill, *History and Character of Calvinism*, 178.

80. Lumpkin, *Baptist Confessions of Faith*, 101.

81. *A Short Confession of Faith* (1610), in Lumpkin, *Baptist Confessions of Faith*, 111.

82. Van Braght, *Bloody Theater*, 41 (the full confession is pp. 38–44).

83. Van Braght, *Bloody Theater*, 41.

84. Lemons, *First Baptist Church in America*, 10.

85. Lumpkin, *Baptist Confessions of Faith*, 143. See also The London Confession of 1644 or *The Confession of Faith, of Those Churches which Are Commonly (though Falsely) Called Anabaptists*, in Lumpkin, *Baptist Confessions of Faith*, 153–71, specifically 166; Article 36 of the Second London Confession of 1677 or *Confession of Faith Put Forth by the Elders and Brethren of Many Congregations of Christians (Baptized upon Profession of Their Faith)*, in *London and the Country*, in Lumpkin, *Baptist Confessions of Faith*, 241–46, specifically 287.

86. *An Orthodox Creed, or a Protestant Confession of Faith Being an Essay to Unite and Confirm All True Protestants in the Fundamental Articles of the Christian Religion, Against the Errors and Heresies of Rome* (London, 1679), in Lumpkin, *Baptist Confessions of Faith*, 319.

87. Lemons, *First Baptist Church in America*, 19, 25.

88. Walker, *Creeds and Platforms of Congregationalism*, 185.

89. "Of *Elders* (who are also in Scripture called *Bishops) Some* attend chiefly to the ministry of the word, As the *Pastors & Teachers. Others,* attend especially unto *Rule,* who are therfore called *Ruling Elders* ("The Cambridge Platform," in Walker, *Creeds and Platforms of Congregationalism*, 211).

90. Walker, *Creeds and Platforms of Congregationalism*, 213, 216–17.

91. Walker, *Creeds and Platforms of Congregationalism*, 214.

92. Quoted in Walker, *History of Congregational Churches*, 3:230.

93. Walker, *History of Congregational Churches*, 222–23, 229, 239.

94. Walker, *History of Congregational Churches*, 220.

95. Tappert, "Church's Infancy," 55.

96. Tappert, "Church's Infancy," 55; McKee, *Diakonia*, 87, 135n9.

97. Thompson, *Presbyterians in the South*, 1:520–21.

98. Henderson, *Presbyterianism*, 81–86.

99. Thompson, *Presbyterians in the South*, 1:520; McKee, *Diakonia*, 134–35nn7–8.

100. Loetscher, *Brief History of the Presbyterians*, 76–77.

101. Trinterud, *Forming of an American Tradition*, 298–99.

102. Thompson, *Presbyterians in the South*, 2:417–18.

103. Thompson, *Presbyterians in the South*, 1:520–21.

104. James Scouller, "History of the United Presbyterian Church of North America," in Alexander et al., *History of the Methodist Church*, 217.

105. Ross, "Deacons in Protestantism," 432.

106. Henderson, *Presbyterianism*, 79, citing a Dr. Pannier.

107. E. T. Corwin, "History of the Reformed Church, Dutch," in Corwin et al., *History of the Reformed Church*, 14–15.

108. Ross, "Deacons in Protestantism," 434.

109. Bernoulli, *Das Diakonenamt bei Calvin*, 15–16.

110. Olson, "Social Welfare," 155–68.

111. Cécile Holtz, "La Bourse française de Genève et le Refuge de 1684 à 1686," in Reverdin et al., *Genève et la Révocation*, 439–500, see especially, 443, 449, 478, 484.

112. Holtz, "La Bourse française de Genève," 486.

113. Grandjean, "La Bourse Française de Genève," 55–57.

114. Tappert, "Church's Infancy," 5–9, 53–54.

115. Tappert, "Church's Infancy," 53–54.

116. Tappert, "Church's Infancy," 54.

117. Tappert, "Church's Infancy," 54.

118. First Convention, Philadelphia, August 15, old style; August 26, new style, 1748, *Hallesche Nachrichten*, n. e. pp. 150, 151; o. e. 76, 77, in *Documentary History of the Evangelical Lutheran Ministerium of Pennsylvania*, 3; Second Convention, Lancaster, June 4, 1749, "Paster Handschuh's Diary," *Hallesche Nachrichten*, n. e. pp. 538–39; o. e. 404–6, in *Documentary History of the Evangelical Lutheran Ministerium of Pennsylvania*, 25. Subsequent conventions also record the presence of elders and deacons; see *Documentary History of the Evangelical Lutheran Ministerium of Pennsylvania*, passim.

119. Third Convention, Providence, June 17, 1750, *Hallesche Nachrichten*, n. e. pp. 471–73, in *Documentary History of the Evangelical Lutheran Ministerium of Pennsylvania*, 29–30.

120. Twenty-Eighth Convention, 1775, Omitted, "Mühlenberg's Journal," 1774–1775, pp. 697–98, in *Documentary History of the Evangelical Lutheran Ministerium of Pennsylvania*, 149.

121. Twenty-Ninth Convention, Yorktown, October 6ff., 1776; Thirtieth Convention, New Hanover, May 25ff., 1777, "Mühlenberg's Journal," 1776–1777, in *Documentary History of the Evangelical Lutheran Ministerium of Pennsylvania*, 150–51.

122. "Constitution of the Ministerium of the Evangelical Lutheran Church of North America, in Force in 1781" and "Constitution of 1792: Ministerial Regulations of the German Evangelical Lutheran Congregations in Pennsylvania and the Adjacent States," in *Documentary History of the Evangelical Lutheran Ministerium of Pennsylvania*, 171–72, 253–54.

123. "Constitution of 1781" and "Constitution of 1792," in *Documentary History of the*

Evangelical Lutheran Ministerium of Pennsylvania, 165, 256–58.

124. "Constitution of 1792," in *Documentary History of the Evangelical Lutheran Ministerium of Pennsylvania*, 253–54.

125. Tappert, "Church's Infancy," 54–55.

126. Tappert, "Church's Infancy," 32, 53; Nineteenth Convention, Philadelphia, June 10–13, 1766, "Mühlenberg Journal," MS. I. 21 p. 73 f., a part of the protocol, in *Documentary History of the Evangelical Lutheran Ministerium of Pennsylvania*, 85.

127. Thirteenth Convention, Lancaster, October 19–20, 1760, Ms. in Archives, *Hallesche Nachrichten*. o. e. 854 fl. Halle Doc. 121–67, in *Documentary History of the Evangelical Lutheran Ministerium of Pennsylvania*, 49.

128. Thirteenth Convention, Lancaster, October 19–20, 1760, Ms. in Archives, *Hallesche Nachrichten*. o. e. 854 fl. Halle Doc. 121–67, in *Documentary History of the Evangelical Lutheran Ministerium of Pennsylvania*, 56–57.

129. Henry Mühlenberg reported on August 14, 1748: "After the sermon, Provost Sandin, Pastors Brunnholtz, Hartwig, Handschuh and I, together with the candidate, Mr. Kurtz, who was to be ordained, took our places around the altar, and three Reformed preachers were witnesses. The delegates from all the congregations again formed a semi-circle, one of us read the formula of ordination, offered prayer at the close, and with the other preachers laid his hand upon the candidate, and thereby consecrated him to the holy ministry" (Pastor Mühlenberg's Report, 1748. H. N., n.e. pp. 392–93; o.e. 284–86, in *Documentary History of the Evangelical Lutheran Ministerium of Pennsylvania*, 8). See also Tappert, "Church's Infancy," 49.

130. First Convention, 1748, *Hallesche Nachrichten*, n. e. pp. 150, 151; o. e. 76, 77, in *Documentary History of the Evangelical Lutheran Ministerium of Pennsylvania*, 3.

131. Third Convention, 1750, "Pastor Mühlenberg's Report of His Official Transactions," 1750, *Hallesche Nachrichten* (n. e.) 507, 595 f. (o. e.) 352–54; *Hallesche Nachrichten*, (n. e. pp. 471–73), in *Documentary History of the Evangelical Lutheran Ministerium of Pennsylvania*, 27, 29.

132. Third Convention, 1750, *Hallesche Nachrichten* (n. e. pp. 471–73), in *Documentary History of the Evangelical Lutheran Ministerium of Pennsylvania*, 29. Thirteenth Convention, 1760, MS. in Archives, *Hallesche Nachrichten*. o. e. 854 fl. Halle Doc. 121–67, in *Documentary History of the Evangelical Lutheran Ministerium of Pennsylvania*, 45.

133. "The Constitution of 1792," in *Documentary History of the Evangelical Lutheran Ministerium of Pennsylvania*, 251–52.

134. See Henry Mühlenberg's summary in his journal, Nineteenth Convention, 1766, MS. I. 21 p. 73f., a part of the protocol, in *Documentary History of the Evangelical Lutheran Ministerium of Pennsylvania*, 84.

135. H. George Anderson, "Early National Period, 1790–1840," in Nelson, *Lutherans in North America*, 82.

136. Sixteenth Convention, Philadelphia, October 16–19, 1763, "Pastor Mühlenberg's Diary," 1763, *Hallesche Nachrichten*, 1122ff.; MS.; Supplemented by Halle Doc. II. 1575ff., in *Documentary History of the Evangelical Lutheran Ministerium of Pennsylvania*, 74–75.

137. Twenty-First Convention, New Hanover, November 6, 1768, "Mühlenberg's Diary," 1768–1769. MS. pp. 16ff., in *Documentary History of the Evangelical Lutheran Ministerium of Pennsylvania*, 93.

138. Fifty-Eighth Convention, "Transactions of the Evangelical Lutheran Synodical Meeting, Held at Germantown, June 9th and the Days Following, 1805," in *Documentary History of the Evangelical Lutheran Ministerium of Pennsylvania*, 356–57.

139. *Documentary History of the Evangelical Lutheran Ministerium of Pennsylvania*, 174.

140. Sixty-Seventh Convention, Easton, June 5–8, 1814, in *Documentary History of the Evangelical Lutheran Ministerium of Pennsylvania*, 471.

141. Ministerial meeting, Sixty-Eighth Convention, Frederichtown, Tuesday afternoon, May 23, 1815, in *Documentary History of the Evangelical Lutheran Ministerium of Pennsylvania*, 482.

142. Ministerial meeting, Sixty-Eighth Convention, Tuesday and Wednesday, May 23–24, 1815, in *Documentary History of the Evangelical Lutheran Ministerium of Pennsylvania*, 482–83.

143. Sixty-Fifth Convention, Carlisle, May 24–27, 1812, in *Documentary History of the Evangelical Lutheran Ministerium of Pennsylvania*, 444; Sixty-Ninth Convention, 1816, in *Documentary History of the Evangelical Lutheran Ministerium of Pennsylvania*, 494.

144. Ministerial Meeting, Sixty-Ninth Convention, 1816, in *Documentary History of the Evangelical Lutheran Ministerium of Pennsylvania*, 494.

145. Seventy-Third Convention, Lancaster, May 28–June 1, 1820, in *Documentary History of the Evangelical Lutheran Ministerium of Pennsylvania*, 565–67.

146. Sixty-Ninth Convention, Philadelphia, Trinity Week 1816, in *Documentary History of the Evangelical Lutheran Ministerium of Pennsylvania*, 486; Seventieth Convention, Yorktown, June 2, 1817, in *Documentary History of the Evangelical Lutheran Ministerium of Pennsylvania*, 498.

147. "The General Synod is authorized by and with the approval of a majority of the particular Synods or Ministeriums proper, to fix grades in the ministry which are to be generally recognized" ("Proposed Plan for a Central Union of the Evangelical Lutheran Church in the United States of North America, Baltimore, 1819," in *Documentary History of the Evangelical Lutheran Ministerium of Pennsylvania*, 543). See also Anderson, "Early National Period," 114–16, 118–19.

148. See, for example, the Twenty-First Convention, 1768, "Mühlenberg's Diary," 1768–1769. MS. pp. 16ff., in *Documentary History of the Evangelical Lutheran Ministerium of Pennsylvania*, 88.

149. Ministerial meeting, Seventy-Third Convention, Lancaster, June 1, 1820, in *Documentary History of the Evangelical Lutheran Ministerium of Pennsylvania*, 567.

150. See "Pastor Mühlenberg's Reports of His Official Transactions, 1749, 1750," in *Hallesche Nachrichten*, n. e. pp. 492–93, 507, 595, f., o.e. 329–30, 352–54, in *Documentary History of the Evangelical Lutheran Ministerium of Pennsylvania*, 24, 27.

151. Fifteenth Convention, Philadelphia, June 27–29, 1762, "Report of the Preachers' Conference in June, 1762, Prepared by Pastor Handschuh." H. N. 954 (Sup. II. Doc. II. 1245), MS. "Mühlenberg's Diary," in Archives, in *Documentary History of the Evangelical Lutheran Ministerium of Pennsylvania*, 61, 65.

152. Sixteenth Convention, Philadelphia, October 16–19, 1763, "Pastor Mühlenberg's Diary," 1763. H. N. 1122ff.; MS; Supplemented by Halle Doc. II. 1575ff., in *Documentary History of the Evangelical Lutheran Ministerium of Pennsylvania*, 68, 71–72.

153. Tappert, "Church's Infancy," 72.

154. Tappert, "Church's Infancy," 72.

155. Third Convention, 1750, *Hallesche Nachrichten*, n. e. pp. 471–73, in *Documentary History of the Evangelical Lutheran Ministerium of Pennsylvania*, 31–32.

156. Twenty-Sixth Convention, Philadelphia, June 12–15, 1773, "Mühlenberg's Journal," Sept. 1772–June 1774, pp. 108ff., in *Documentary History of the Evangelical Lutheran Ministerium of Pennsylvania*, 145.

157. Sixteenth Convention, 1763, "Pastor Mühlenberg's Diary," 1763. H. N. 1122ff.; MS.; Supplemented by Halle Doc. II. 1575ff., in *Documentary History of the Evangelical Lutheran Ministerium of Pennsylvania*, 80–81.

158. Synodical Meetings: Sixty-Fifth Convention, 1812; Sixty-Sixth Convention, Reading, June 13–16, 1813; Sixty-Eighth Convention, 1815; Sixty-Ninth Convention, 1816, in *Documentary History of the Evangelical Lutheran Ministerium of Pennsylvania*, 441–42, 458, 483, 492.

159. Anderson, "Early National Period," 128.

160. For a book on the Council of Trent and its impact that revises the accepted traditional views of Hubert Jedin, see O'Malley, *Trent and All That*.

161. O'Malley, *First Jesuits*.

162. Cited in William Christian, *Local Religion in Sixteenth-Century Spain* (New Jersey: n.p., 1981), 166, quoted in Flynn, *Sacred Charity*, 117.

163. Quoted from the General Archive of Simancas, *Patronato Real*, Caja 16, folio 86, in Flynn, *Sacred Charity*, 118.

164. Flynn, *Sacred Charity*, 102, 117–18.

165. Flynn, *Sacred Charity*, 102–3, 119.

166. *Dictionnaire de spiritualité ascétique et mystique doctrine et histoire*, s.v. "Confréries."

167. Flynn, *Sacred Charity*, 119.

168. Flynn, *Sacred Charity*, 10, 21, 23, 32, 55–56, 95, 97–102, 104–5, 108–12.

169. Flynn, *Sacred Charity*, 138–41.

170. *Dictionnaire de Spiritualité*, s.v. "Confréries."

171. Pullan, "Catholics and the Poor," 31.

172. Flynn, *Sacred Charity*, 5; *Dictionnaire de spiritualité*, s. v. "Confréries."

173. Flynn, *Sacred Charity*, 58.

174. *New Catholic Encyclopedia*, s.v. "Ladies of Charity."

175. Dickens, *Counter Reformation*, 179.

176. Pullan, "Catholics and the Poor," 29.

177. *New Catholic Encyclopedia*, s.v. "Ladies of Charity."

178. *New Catholic Encyclopedia*, s.v. "Vincent de Paul, St."

179. Dickens, *Counter Reformation*, 74.

180. Dickens, *Counter Reformation*, 178; *New Catholic Encyclopedia*, s.v. "Vincent de Paul, St."

181. *New Catholic Encyclopedia*, s.v. "Vincent de Paul, St."

182. Dickens, *Counter Reformation*, 173–76.

183. Pullan, "Catholics and the Poor," 23.

184. The remark of an Asturian bishop, quoted in Joseph Townsend, *A Journey through Spain*, 3 vols. (London: n.p., 1791), 2:9, quoted in Flynn, *Sacred Charity*, 112.

185. Pullan, "Catholics and the Poor," 19.

186. Genequand, "La prison de Saint-Antoine," 52–54. The deacons asked that Catherine Chevalier be incarcerated in the chamber of discipline. She had been brought up with the funds of the *Bourse Française* and had committed larcenies; see AEG, *Archives hospitalières*, Ka 6, "Livre de Memoire commenceé le premier mars 1680 et finy le 30e decembre 1691" (November 12, 1683), 217.

187. Flynn, *Sacred Charity*, 110, 173n140.

188. Pullan, "Catholics and the Poor," 32.

189. Cragg, *Church in the Age of Reason*, 141–42.

190. Cragg, *Church in the Age of Reason*, 141–42.

191. Cragg, *Church in the Age of Reason*, 142.

192. Cragg, *Church in the Age of Reason*, 142–43.

193. Cragg, *Church in the Age of Reason*, 145–47.

194. Harnish, *Orders of Ministry*, 23.

195. Harnish, *Orders of Ministry*, 27.

196. Harnish, *Orders of Ministry*, 149–51.

197. Harnish, *Orders of Ministry*, 147–49; Wesley, *Journal of John Wesley*, 261–62.

198. Gordon S. Wakefield, "Diakonia in the Methodist Church Today," in McCord and Parker, *Service in Christ*, 182.

199. Keller, Moede, and Moore, *Called to Serve*, 1.

200. Wakefield, "Diakonia in the Methodist Church Today," 183–84.

201. [The United Methodist] *Book of Discipline* (1984), par. 406.1, 2, as quoted in Keller, Moede, and Moore, *Called to Serve*, 1.

202. Cragg, *Church in the Age of Reason*, 133.

203. Cragg, *Church in the Age of Reason*, 152–54, 156.

204. Cragg, *Church in the Age of Reason*, 55, 134–35, 170.

205. Cragg, *Church in the Age of Reason*, 154–55.

206. Cragg, *Church in the Age of Reason*, 131–32.

207. Anderson, "Early National Period," in Nelson, *Lutherans in North America*, rev. ed. (1980), 138.

208. Arthur R. Suelflow and E. Clifford Nelson, "Following the Frontier, 1840–1875," in Nelson, *Lutherans in North America*, 200.

209. Anderson, "Early National Period," 72–73.

210. Suelflow and Nelson, "Following the Frontier," 200–201.

CHAPTER FIVE

THE NINETEENTH CENTURY
NEW FORMS OF DEACONS
AND DEACONESSES IN EUROPE

As the industrial revolution spread to Europe in the first half of the nineteenth century, it brought with it the urbanization and congested living conditions that England already had begun to experience. The churches focused more attention on the cities, and new forms of the diaconate came into being.

Europe experienced the industrial revolution later than England. One reason for this delay was that English manufacturers protected their new inventions and were not eager to transplant them to the continent. Also the French Revolution and Napoleon (1789–1815) kept Europe preoccupied. War may have produced a need for armaments, but it hindered the development of an industrial revolution of the English sort. Not until 1815 was Europe able to defeat Napoleon definitively and win a peace conducive to industrial progress on the continent.

After the Napoleonic wars, conditions in Europe were difficult. Warfare had left women widowed and children orphaned. The conservative governments that Metternich and the leaders of Europe had established at the Congress of Vienna (1814–1815) were not receptive to innovation or changes in society. To compound the problems of the poor, population soared and illegitimate births increased. For example, in Hamburg in the years 1826–1835, one out of five births was illegitimate.[1]

The industrial revolution brought with it the problems of urbanization, while it weakened the guild structure. By 1856 in Hamburg, 85 percent of goods manufactured for export came out of factories rather than guild shops. Mechanization threw artisans out of work, for example, weavers in the textile industry. Even those who had jobs often lived at a marginal level. A surplus of workers kept factory wages low. Legislation against association, strikes, and public demonstrations hampered the organization of labor unions, which took some time to get off the ground. Thus in the early decades of industrialization, unions were not present to struggle for higher wages and to replace some of the mutual help that guilds had offered to their members. The city governments could not fill the gap. Hamburg, for example, had a welfare system that was the envy of Europe in the late eighteenth century, but the city was unable to cope with the greater demands of an industrialized society.[2]

In the first half of the nineteenth century, cities were crowded. They lacked both planning and plumbing. The enlarged cities concentrated urban dwellers close to their centers because of the difficulties of transporting people from outlying areas in these days before the automobile. The neighborhoods of the poor were densely populated and filthy. Often whole families lived in a single room. The lack of running water and modern sewage systems made these cities ready targets for disease. Life expectancy in Europe was lower in urban areas than in the country. Cholera swept the cities of Europe as it has recently swept areas of Latin America. Yet people, especially the young, flocked to the cities despite the lack of a job or a place to stay, hoping to better their lot.

The United States, like Europe, experienced the industrial revolution later than England, and New England textile mills continued to use waterpower even after mills in England had shifted to steam. During the course of the nineteenth century, North America would catch up to England in many areas. With a Western frontier to absorb expansion, the United States did not suffer from population pressures equivalent to those of the Old World. However, the role of the United States as a safety valve for the surplus population of Europe contributed to overcrowding in U.S. urban areas because many immigrants settled in cities.

In both the Old World and the New there was a need to resolve the problems of urban life. Solutions to particular problems came through the efforts of countless individuals who were active in private and public spheres. Some of this work was accomplished by people working together in voluntary societies that were organized to address a wide variety of needs, from schools to temperance. Some of these groups were more political in nature than others because the problems they sought to cure required government action, such as the extension of suffrage and the abolition of child labor, of the slave trade, and of slavery.

The church was a major part of the endeavor to meet society's problems in the nineteenth century, though it was not always the organized church *per se*; rather, its members often took the lead. Leaders of reform, in turn, interested their respective denomination in the causes they espoused. Efforts that began outside denominational frameworks sometimes moved within. For example, this was true of the Sunday school movement and, in North America, of the support for world missions.

In some European countries after the Franco-Prussian War of 1870–1871, the conservative attitudes in government, society, and even in the churches alienated from Christianity the industrial masses and those affiliated with labor unions and social-democratic organizations. By the end of the century, many people remained formally affiliated with a church but concentrated their creative energies elsewhere. This effected Catholicism in France and Protestantism in Germany. On the other hand, earlier in the nineteenth century, the Inner Mission had risen out of German Protestantism, and Catholics had revived old religious orders, established new ones, and founded new lay organizations.

After the fall of Napoleon in 1814 and 1815, the Catholic Church experienced renewal. In 1814 the pope revived the Society of Jesus (the Jesuits), which had been suppressed in the eighteenth century, and both France and Spain readmitted Jesuits. New Catholic religious orders and organizations of brothers and secular priests focused on social service, education, and missions. In 1816 in Provence, France, Charles de Mazenod (1782–1861), the future bishop of Marseilles, began the Oblates of the Immaculate Heart of Mary. Its members served both in France and in the mission field. In 1868 Charles Lavigerie (1825–1892), archbishop of Carthage, began the Society of Missionaries of Our Lady of Africa, or the White Fathers, named after the white robes they wore to resemble the Muslims among whom they first worked in North Africa. The White Fathers also served south of the Sahara. In 1822 Pauline-Marie Jaricot (1799–1862) originated an effort in Lyons, France, to collect from a number of friends a centime a week for missions. This led to the organization of the Society for the Propagation of the Faith, which subsidized orders, societies, and congregations that sent missionaries. In 1868 Italian youth banded together to support the church, which developed into the organization known as Catholic Action and eventually spread beyond Italy. Catholic Action varied from diocese to diocese but involved the laity in the service of society through evangelism, promotion of Catholic schools, political action, and other activities. The work of evangelism and charity in the Catholic Church in the nineteenth century largely bypassed the office of deacon, which remained a transitional office for men on their way to becoming priests.[3]

Within Protestantism, each country produced its own constellation of nineteenth-century reformers. Names and methods differed, but reform leaders knew about one another, copied one another's work, and sometimes worked together. There was considerable fertilization across denominational lines and some cooperation among denominations. Movements and institutions that began in one country sometimes spread to others. This was true of England and of Germany, for example.

England had led the industrial revolution and was an early leader in reforms to correct the abuses produced by changing manufacturing processes. Reform in England had roots in the late eighteenth century, but in the period immediately after the Napoleonic wars, England was a part of the conservative reaction of Europe. Within several years, under pressure from reformers, England became receptive to change. As early reformers died, others stepped in to take their place. Women were accepted in benevolent work. John Howard's concern for the conditions of the prisons in the eighteenth century continued in the person of the Quaker Elizabeth Fry (1780–1845).[4] There were also new areas of reform. In the latter half of the nineteenth century, nursing became a dignified profession, in part through the efforts of Florence Nightingale. Many ideas and institutions spread beyond England, such as the Young Men's Christian Association, founded in London in 1844 by George Williams (1821–1905). The YMCA had formed to provide Christian fellowship and to meet the needs of men moving to the cities for work. It was followed by the Young Women's Christian Association. In 1855 the World Alliance of the YMCA came into being, and in 1894 the World Alliance of the YWCA followed suit. William Booth (1829–1912), attempting to meet the needs of the urban poor, formed the Salvation Army (developed in 1878 and named in 1880). It was destined, like the YMCA and YWCA, to spread around the world, as would the later-founded Boy and Girl Scouts.

Germany, like England, had suffered from the conservative reaction in Europe after the Napoleonic wars. From England, Germany had inherited the Sunday school and the nineteenth-century version of the Mission Society and the Bible Society, though German Pietism already had produced both missionaries and the world's oldest Bible Society. August Hermann Francke at Halle and Karl Hildebrand (Baron von Canstein [1667–1719]), worked together to produce a Bible inexpensive enough for the common person to afford. Canstein obtained money and lent his name to the resulting Bible society, the *Cansteinsche Bibelanstalt*, which was founded in 1710.[5]

THE INNER MISSION

Germany made its own unique contribution in urban work: the Inner Mission, a program of social action and evangelism. Inner Mission work began with rescue houses for children who were neglected or abandoned during the Napoleonic wars. Johannes Falk in Weimar founded the first such house in 1813. He also founded the Society for Friends in Need (*Verein der Freunde in der Not*), a society to promote the founding of these rescue homes. Sixteen rescue homes were founded from 1813 to 1830, forty-eight from 1830 to 1847, and 290 from 1848 to 1867.[6]

In 1833 in Hamburg, Johannes Wichern founded *Das Rauhe Haus*, a home for vagrant boys, in connection with a Sunday school initiated under English influence.[7] Wichern educated and trained the boys and gathered them into family-type groups of twelve to fourteen boys with a *Bruder*, a surrogate older brother.[8] The *Bruder* was a new type of deacon. Despite some hesitation on the part of Wichern, the men came to be called deacons.[9] In 1839 Wichern founded a *Bruderhaus* to train deacons for work in jails, slums, and other places where many pastors of the era would not go.[10] This movement spread, and deacons were trained in other centers, too, sometimes in conjunction with their female counterparts, who were called deaconesses.[11] In Karl Rahner's *Diaconia in Christo*, published in 1962, Herbert Krimm reported that there were fifteen brother houses in Germany with 4,550 deacons and candidates, in addition to establishments in Scandinavia, Holland, and Switzerland.[12]

Wichern's all-encompassing vision of social action and evangelism had its roots in Pietism.[13] He called for a mission of the church to society.[14] Like John Wesley, he wanted to reach the cities of Germany, which were, like England's, overpopulated and undersupplied with churches. Some outstanding people became involved in the Inner Mission.[15]

The Inner Mission met people's needs through a variety of institutions and programs, many of which arose independently of one another: seamen's missions, hostels, hospices, halfway houses, prison visitation, Christian literature and tract distribution, homes for young women to rescue them from prostitution, and deaconess institutions. This is to name but some aspects of this many-faceted effort to meet the needs of nineteenth-century German society. From Germany, the Inner Mission movement spread to the Netherlands and Scandinavia.[16]

In 1848 the Wittenberg *Kirchentag* (church conference) adopted Wichern's program, leading to the formation of the Central Committee for Inner Mission of the German Evangelical Church (*Zentralausschusses für die*

Innere Mission der deutschen evangelischen Kirche). In 1848 the City Mission, *Stadtmission*, was founded and in 1854 the Hostels of the Homeland (*Herbergen zur Heimat*).[17]

The nineteenth-century leaders of the German Inner Mission movement popularized the term *diakonia* with reference to work among the delinquent, displaced, illiterate, and sick.[18] There were societies for caring for the sick, hospitals, evangelistic publications, and the People's Mission (*Volksmission*). The Inner Mission also included youth work. The Young People's Missionary Society (*Missions-jünglingsverein*), a society for evangelical young people, began in 1823 in Bremen-Gemarke and grew to two hundred similar societies by 1870. In 1833 in Berlin, the *Christlicher Verein Junger Männer* organized (similar to what would later be the Young Men's Christian Association [YMCA] in England). From it came work with university students: the Christian Students' Mission (*Christliche Studentenmission*). In 1897 the *Deutsche Christliche Studenten-Vereinigung* formed from the two groups.[19] In many regions Inner Mission work drew Lutherans and the Reformed into cooperative endeavors. To some German Christians this was unacceptable. Conservatives tended to dislike the lay leadership in the Inner Mission (for example, Wichern was never ordained a minister).[20]

By 1849 Wilhelm Löhe (1808–1872) was creating the Society for Inner Mission according to the Lutheran Church (*Gesellschaft für Innere Mission im Sinne der lutherischen Kirche*).[21] Löhe was pastor of the village parish at Neuendettelsau, Bavaria. He founded a house to train missionaries, a home mission society to distribute literature, and an entire constellation of charitable institutions.[22] Löhe organized the North American mission (1841) that contributed so many pastors to Germans in the New World, especially to The Lutheran Church—Missouri Synod and the Iowa Synod.[23]

DEACONESSES AND THEODORE FLIEDNER

As the Inner Mission produced a new form of the diaconate for men, it also established a new form for women. The same year that Wichern founded the *Rauhes Haus*, the first newly released woman prisoner entered what was to become the halfway house of Theodore Fliedner (1800–1864). It was located in Kaiserswerth on the Rhine River, which was a mile and a half below Düsseldorf in territory subject to the kings of Prussia.[24] In 1835 Fliedner founded a knitting school there. In 1836 a kindergarten and a school for nurses followed.

Fliedner was pastor of a small Evangelical congregation in Kaiserswerth, which was a predominantly Roman Catholic town.[25] After the factory in which his parishioners worked went bankrupt in 1822, Fliedner traveled throughout Holland and England in 1823 and 1824 to collect money for his church.[26] In England he became acquainted with Elizabeth Fry, and on his return, he founded the first German society for improving prisons: the Prison Society of the Rhineland and Westphalia (1826). The establishment in 1833 of a halfway house for released female convicts was a natural outcome of that society's work.[27] Fliedner established other institutions at Kaiserswerth that grew from his general interest in the poor and the examples of charitable institutions he had seen in England and Holland. The knitting school he had started in 1835 for poor children became a kindergarten, then an elementary school.[28] In conjunction with the educational program, Fliedner offered training to women who wanted to become teachers. He founded, as he had means and personnel to staff them, an orphanage (1843), a shelter for mentally challenged and epileptic women (1848),[29] and a mental hospital (1852).[30]

Just as Wichern's work produced a new deacon, Fliedner's produced the new deaconess. Because of his contact with British philanthropy, Fliedner was committed to involving women in charity in Germany, where he felt they had been wrongfully excluded from the work of the church. He anticipated opposition but circumvented it. Fliedner found precedent in the past for women church workers. For the title of deaconess he took inspiration from Mennonite deaconesses in Holland whose work with the poor he referred to as an institution of primitive Christianity that deserved imitation.[31]

Fliedner's Kaiserswerth deaconesses were primarily nurses, an area in which there was an acknowledged need and a precedent for women's work, at least in wartime. Women had worked in military hospitals in the war of liberation from Napoleon in 1813–1815, and hospital conditions in general in Europe were deplorable. Kaiserswerth nurse-deaconesses initiated structured professional nursing care.[32] Women as nurses were less objectionable to Germans at this time than female teachers, against whom there was opposition. Fliedner, however, had the support of the Government Board of Education for his teacher-training institution. By 1844 the education of teachers at Kaiserswerth expanded beyond kindergarten to elementary school.[33] Eventually it would train teachers for girls' high schools.[34] But every deaconess was given nurse's training during her probation, regardless of what she went on to do later.[35]

Many students who trained as teachers at Kaiserswerth never became deaconesses because Fliedner allowed women who did not intend to become deaconesses to board and study at his institution for a fee.[36] In his promotional literature for the teacher-training institution, Fliedner specifically invited single women and widows to apply "to make themselves into useful members of society."[37] Women who were attracted to the teaching profession because of its autonomy in the classroom may also have been less attracted to a permanent commitment to the community life of a deaconess, which was similar to that of a Catholic nun.

Fliedner was accused of recreating in his deaconesses a religious order similar to those that had been disbanded at the time of the Protestant Reformation. At Kaiserswerth his deaconesses called one another sister, lived together in a motherhouse, wore distinctive garb, woke and slept at the same time, served a period of probation before being formally admitted to the community, were guaranteed lifelong support, and received only room, board, and pocket money for their labors. The deaconesses attended morning and evening prayer in the chapel and also went there to meditate, read the Bible, or pray during a quiet half hour, the *Stille halbe Stunde*, which became traditional in deaconess institutions.[38] For their spiritual life, Fliedner assembled a collection of hymns and a manual of Bible readings. Kaiserswerth deaconesses adopted a dark blue dress.[39] The symbol of the community became a dove carrying an olive branch. It was depicted either in white (as on the blue flag that floated over the banks of the Rhine at the Kaiserswerth properties) or in gold (as on the pin that was presented to the deaconess upon her consecration).[40] Their workday was long. One deaconess described a day in training as "so apportioned that from mornings at five o'clock until evenings at six the powers of both soul and body are perpetually in motion."[41] In 1851 when Florence Nightingale wrote a booklet supporting Kaiserswerth, the sisters rose at 5 A.M. and went to bed at 10 P.M.[42]

Fliedner was accused of attempting, through his deaconesses, to imitate and compete with the Catholic nursing orders, especially the Sisters of Charity or the Sisters of Mercy, who were having tremendous success in the Germanies at this time. Fliedner wrote to Elizabeth Fry on December 2, 1839, that the Sisters of Charity were like a "flood everywhere . . . in Protestant countries and hospitals . . . where they endeavor artfully to place their church in the best possible light to make proselytes of the sick and poor."[43]

On the other hand, Kaiserswerth deaconesses did not take lifelong vows. They committed themselves for only five years at a time. They were not cloistered, whereas some Catholic religious orders were. Deaconesses could keep any private fortune they might have from their family and pass it on to others after their death, which was not true of many Catholic religious orders, especially those founded before the French Revolution (1789).[44] Kaiserswerth deaconesses could choose to leave the deaconess community to marry, though their special garb, especially the white bonnet, was soon out of style and may have made them less attractive to men. The garb also may have rendered their work as unmarried women out in the community more acceptable, especially for the visiting nurse or for the deaconess who helped in parish work, an endeavor begun in 1844.[45]

The deaconess community at Kaiserswerth presented little threat to family structures in Germany at this time because though it took women out of the marriage market, there was a surplus of unmarried women and few vocational alternatives for them.[46] Many women sought employment as servants or burdened their fathers and brothers with their care. Thus many deaconess candidates came from large families, had lost a parent or two, or had been raised by or had raised siblings.[47] The deaconess community provided such women a family environment, security, and a vocation. In fact, it was much like a family. Florence Nightingale said the institution stood "in the place of a parent to the Deaconesses."[48] Yet women were not allowed entry without the consent of their parents or guardians. The deaconesses called Fliedner and his wife "father" and "mother," and they were encouraged to confide in them. They also called one another "sister," a title they assumed after consecration as deaconesses.[49] At first Fliedner had frequent contact with the deaconesses informally, but as the community grew larger, regular Monday evening gatherings were instituted during which Fliedner shared letters and news of deaconesses working elsewhere.[50]

The women whom Kaiserswerth attracted conformed to this regimen. At first many who joined the motherhouse were young women from rural or artisan families. Regulations limited admissions to women who were 18 to 40 years of age. The autobiographies that they were required to write on admission reveal that many of them had been servants.[51] The first deaconess, Gertrude Reichard, was an exception. She was the daughter of a physician and skilled as a nurse.[52] Although he has been criticized for being paternalistic, Fliedner provided these women with training, a secure future, and a role in the church.[53] The deaconess community grew rapidly. Within a decade of its founding in 1836, the annual report indicated there were 101 deaconesses.[54]

A secret of Fliedner's success with the deaconess movement was that from the beginning he looked to others for help. His relationship to the deaconesses might appear paternalistic to women more than a hundred and fifty years later, but according to a contemporary woman of some accomplishment, Florence Nightingale, one of his great strengths was that Fliedner was willing to delegate authority.[55] He apparently also was receptive to strong women because at the beginning of his deaconess project, Fliedner offered the office of superintendent of the community to Amalie Sieveking (1794–1859), who was the daughter of one of the first families of Hamburg and famous in her own right as a philanthropist.[56]

AMALIE SIEVEKING AND BENEVOLENT VISITING

The religious awakening in Germany during and after the French occupation had touched Amalie Sieveking and introduced her to the work of the Sisters of Charity in France through a biography of Vincent de Paul. During the 1831 cholera epidemic, Sieveking volunteered her services among the female patients at the infirmary of St. Ericus in Hamburg. After initial resistance by the medical service, she acquired a reputation as a heroine.[57] Sieveking would have been Fliedner's immediate subordinate, had she accepted his offer, but after some hesitation, she turned him down in 1837.[58] Her charitable endeavors took another direction.

Amalie Sieveking believed that the enforced domesticity and round of social activities of upper-class women in the nineteenth century limited their talents and potential contribution to the contemporary world. Unmarried herself, many of the women with whom she associated were married and came from her own elevated social milieu. There was no question of them becoming deaconesses. She felt, however, that they should be engaged in activity on behalf of the poor. To that end, in 1832, with twelve other women in Hamburg, she founded the Female Association for the Care of the Poor and Sick (*Weiblicher Verein für Armen- und Krankenpflege*). The women of this association committed themselves to at least one, preferably two, calls each week to the households of impoverished invalids who had been recommended by the public poor relief administration. They were to provide practical, material, and spiritual help to the poor, and every visit included Bible reading and prayer. This was called benevolent visiting.[59] The women also agreed to meet with other members of the association at least once each week to assess their visits.

Florence Nightingale later questioned the efficacy of such visits to people in ill health by visitors who had no training as nurses, but the benevolent visitors of Hamburg were women of means.[60] They distributed clothing, food, and work assignments, such as repairs, maintenance, sewing, and knitting.[61] Sieveking also established inexpensive housing for the poor and founded a children's hospital.[62] Another society in Hamburg was formed by Charlotte Paulsen for women of a lower social stratum, small-businesswomen, and artisan women. It provided job counseling for the poor, day care for their children, and training and positions as domestic servants.[63]

Sieveking's model provided inspiration for women's societies for the poor elsewhere in Germany. By 1842 there were more than fifteen affiliate societies. By 1848 there were fifty-five, forty-five of which were within Germany.[64] Such societies became a charitable outlet for women who were not interested in a vocation as a deaconess or who were married and not allowed to become one. In his *Fliegende Blätter*, Wichern praised this "voluntary effort of Christian women" as "one of the most distinctive evidences of social regeneration of our times."[65]

Innovative she might have been, but Amalie Sieveking was also authoritarian and elitist. She effectively limited the membership in her benevolent visiting society to women in her own social milieu who shared her religious convictions. In contrast, Fliedner initially tended to draw women from the other end of the social spectrum. Sieveking criticized Fliedner's policies for being too monastic, though her own initial goal had been to found a religious order much like the Catholic Sisters of Charity. Later, Wilhelm Löhe freely admitted that the nineteenth-century deaconess was a Protestant copy of the Sisters of Mercy.[66] Sieveking accused Fliedner of being reluctant to release deaconesses to get married.[67] Florence Nightingale claimed the contrary, stating in a booklet she wrote about Kaiserswerth in 1851 that

> [t]he Christian liberty of the Deaconess is carefully preserved. Even during the five years, for which a Deaconess engages herself after her solemn consecration in the Church, should marriage, or her parents, or any important duty claim her, she is free, she is never held fast to conclude the term of years. The Institution may thus be said to be a school for wives as well as for sisters, as no one can suppose that these women are not the better fitted for the duties of wives and mothers by their education here.[68]

Florence Nightingale may have been unable to judge accurately Fliedner's true attitude toward releasing deaconesses because her stay in Kaiserswerth was so short. She was there from July 31 to August 13, 1850, and from July 6 to October 7, 1851. The booklet in which she wrote the above quotation placed Kaiserswerth in an attractive light because Fliedner had asked her to write it in English to acquaint England with the deaconess community.[69]

Despite Sieveking's criticism of Fliedner, his deaconess movement was a phenomenal success, both in its rapid growth and in Fliedner's ability to avoid antagonism. In contrast, Sieveking's movement was subject to criticism. Ladies of her class did not customarily visit the homes of the poor.[70] Baron Kaspar von Voght (1752–1839), a welfare reformer in Hamburg, doubted whether a group of "wives, mothers, housekeepers, sisters, and daughters" could perform these tasks: "The work of sisters of charity is suitable only to persons who are completely alone in the world and can devote themselves exclusively to their calling."[71] Kaspar von Voght may have expressed the opinions of many of his era concerning the mutually exclusive roles of single and married women, which may possibly be a reason the unmarried Kaiserswerth deaconess was more acceptable in the nineteenth century than married women working with the poor.

There were other reasons for the ready acceptance of the deaconesses in contrast to other relief efforts of nineteenth-century women. Chief among these was the fact that Fliedner's deaconesses worked under the umbrella of the church whereas some other women's organizations did not. The state church officially recognized the office of deaconess. Legally the institution of the diaconate was a corporate entity overseen by the Rhine-Westphalian province of Prussia's state church: the Prussian United Church. This body was a union of Lutheran and Reformed churches that had been instigated in 1817 by Frederick William III (1797–1840).[72]

Fliedner was aided considerably by the help he received from the state. He was on good terms with Frederick William IV, king of Prussia, who in 1835 as crown prince expressed enthusiasm for the "revival of the order of deaconesses in our Church" as an object for which he had longed for many years.[73] Fliedner and the deaconess community received gifts from the crown to help their work. For example, Frederick William IV gave them an unused hospital barrack at Kaiserswerth with a beautiful garden for use as a mental hospital for women. It opened in 1852.[74] Eventually a statue of Crown Prince Frederick holding a child was erected at Kaiserswerth in commemoration of an 1884 visit when he had allowed a young child in his arms to play with the medals on his chest.[75]

With the friendship of the monarch, the deaconess community at Kaiserswerth weathered the reaction after the liberal revolution of 1848 failed in its attempts to democratize Prussia and unite the Germanies into one nation under the king of Prussia. Other German women's organizations and their benevolent projects and educational programs did not fare so well. In Hamburg the school of Charlotte Paulsen disbanded. Earlier, Paulsen's religious convictions had been a factor in Amalie Sieveking refusing her membership in the benevolent visiting society. Now, under criticism for offering no formal instruction in religion, the support for Paulsen's school withered away.

A school order of August 7, 1851, attacked secular education, stating that schools organized along the principles of Friedrich Froebel, who believed Christian dogmatics had no place in the classroom, could not be tolerated.[76] While Froebel's program was coming under attack, Fliedner's kindergarten program, with its Christian component, thrived. He wanted education to include religious instruction and to penetrate every village. He wanted education to begin with 2- and 3-year-old children. By 1854, 638 women had received teacher training at Kaiserswerth.

One scholar has suggested that Fliedner's administrative and financial gifts were well suited to the efficient bureaucracy of Prussia.[77] It may well have ingratiated him with the Prussian court. The very appearance of the buildings and grounds at Kaiserswerth suggested orderliness and stability. New buildings, such as the deaconess house, tended to be large, solid structures with evenly spaced windows and a symmetry of style disturbed only by the conflicting architecture of the older buildings to which some of them were attached.[78]

In the first twenty-five years of its existence as a deaconess community, Kaiserswerth had expanded amazingly, and this was accomplished without a substantial endowment. The operating budget was funded by fees from patients and students and by donations, as well as by the sale of books and periodicals. There was a graduated fee schedule of sorts. At the mental institution, for example, the spaciousness of an individual's accommodations influenced the fees. First-class patients who wanted two rooms paid five times as much as third-class patients. Even the orphanage charged because the orphans were from parents of the educated middle class who could pay, though a few orphaned children of teachers and pastors were admitted without a fee or for a smaller amount.[79] In addition, churches took up collections for Kaiserswerth. Families of the rich, where deaconesses served as nurses or teachers, also gave generously.[80] In time, the famous Kaiserswerth calendar would be sent out by the hundreds of thousands annually.[81]

THE SPREAD OF THE DEACONESS MOVEMENT BEYOND KAISERSWERTH

If Fliedner's deaconess movement had focused only on Kaiserswerth, it would have had limited impact, but the institutions there were training schools as well as benevolent in their own right. Within a few years of the inception of the deaconess community, the sisters were working elsewhere. Trained nurse-deaconesses were in demand, as were later parish workers

218_DEACONS AND DEACONESSES THROUGH THE CENTURIES

and teachers. In January 1838, the hospital at Elberfeld requested help, and Fliedner sent two deaconesses. In 1839 deaconesses were sent to a hospital in Frankfurt and to Kirchheim in Württemberg; others were sent to Barmen in 1842 and to Berlin in 1843.[82]

Within a decade of its founding, a majority of the Kaiserswerth deaconesses were working elsewhere. Fifty-six (of 101) deaconesses were in eighteen hospitals, rescue homes, orphanages, or parishes. Typically the deaconesses did not find these posts for themselves. In the tradition of the time, the city and church officials who administered hospitals and welfare institutions and the heads of families who sought private nurses approached Fliedner, much as they would approach the father of a young person if they were seeking a servant or an apprentice,[83] These institutions or families provided the deaconesses they took on with room and board, but the woman's salary returned to the motherhouse, which eventually would provide her with a place of retirement.

London was the first city outside the continent of Europe to which Kaiserswerth deaconesses were sent. In 1846 Fliedner brought four deaconesses to London to work in a new hospital for Germans in Dalston. There, in the home of the Prussian ambassador, he met Samuel Gobat, who had been appointed by Frederick William IV as Protestant bishop of Jerusalem. In 1850 when Jerusalem was in the midst of an epidemic, Gobat wrote to Fliedner and asked for two deaconesses. Fliedner received the letter in Berlin and shared the contents with Frederick William IV. The king and Fliedner decided that four deaconesses would be better than two. Frederick William paid for the deaconesses' travel to Jerusalem and gave them his houses in the city for their use as hospitals. The deaconesses admitted patients of all religions and also visited the poor and sick in the city. They educated and trained Arab children, especially girls. From Jerusalem, their work spread to other parts of the Middle East and North Africa: Smyrna, Alexandria, Beirut, Cairo, and Constantinople.[84]

Soon the dispatch of two to four deaconesses to meet a given need was not enough. Motherhouses began elsewhere and took on probationers of their own. In 1851 Florence Nightingale reported that "the system for the practical training of Deaconesses has spread in all directions. In Paris, Strasbourg, Echallens (in Switzerland), Utrecht, and England, the institution exists. . . . From all parts of Germany, from Constantinople, and even from the East Indies, requests for Deaconesses are constantly pouring in." Fliedner and the deaconess community at Kaiserswerth responded as best they could.[85] Of course, both the Inner Mission and the deaconess movement made an impact on Protestant communities in neighboring German-speaking Austria.[86]

Kaiserswerth deaconesses helped deaconess communities elsewhere in Europe, assuming the direction of some of the new motherhouses. In 1861, the twenty-fifth anniversary of the reception of the first deaconess, Fliedner organized a General Conference of all deaconess motherhouses. It was to meet every third year. By the time of its second meeting in 1864, Fliedner was dead.[87] By 1864 the deaconess community at Kaiserswerth and its deaconesses in the field had extended their work to include poorhouses, elementary schools, nurseries, infirmaries, hospices, rescue homes, boarding-houses, retreat centers, prison work, homes for servant girls, and hospitals for the mentally challenged, for epileptics, and for children. The growth in the last half of the nineteenth century was prodigious. In less than fifty years after the founding of Fliedner's General Conference, there were at least fifty motherhouses in the Kaiserswerth Union, and there were more than fourteen thousand deaconesses.[88]

After Fliedner's death, his second wife, Caroline Bertheau-Fliedner, continued as superintendent of the deaconess house at Kaiserswerth (1843–1883). She followed Fliedner's first wife in that position.[89] Caroline was from an old Huguenot family.[90] Before her marriage to Fliedner, Caroline had been overseer of the hospital in Hamburg and a pupil of Amalie Sieveking.[91] Fliedner's first wife, Friederika Muenster (1800–1842), had shared with Fliedner an interest in prison work. In fourteen years of marriage, Friederika had borne him ten children, seven of whom had died during her lifetime.[92] He said of her:

> In my first wife, Friederika Muenster, who was taken from me in April, 1842, the Lord had given me a faithful helper in this labor of love, and especially for the care of the prisoners. After having gratuitously served in the Rescue House at Düsseldorf, for several years, as assistant in taking care of neglected children, she was about to devote herself to the care of the prisoners in the prison of Düsseldorf, when the Lord led her to me (1828).[93]

Friederika played a key role in Fliedner's decision to found a deaconess institution, and she was a mediating influence in Fliedner's relationship with the women at Kaiserswerth.[94] He had rigorous standards and could be impatient with them.

Friederika's death on April 22, 1842, was a blow to Fliedner, but he did not take long to marry Caroline in May of the next year.[95] This could be perceived as ironic because Fliedner was living among the deaconesses whom he expected to remain unmarried to pursue their vocation. But in addition to his personal desire for a wife, Fliedner needed help with the work among the deaconesses. The leadership of the deaconess community was a team effort. In addition, marriage probably gave him an aura of respectability in the nineteenth-century world as he worked among so many single young women.

As superintendent of the deaconess community after Fliedner's death, Caroline Bertheau-Fliedner did not have the sole charge of Kaiserswerth. Nineteenth-century property laws and customs expected men to head institutions, and Fliedner's son-in-law, Pastor Dr. Julius Disselhoff, took over for the next thirty-two years.[96] The work at Kaiserswerth grew under his leadership both in the number of deaconesses and in the physical plant. In 1865 a preparatory school opened for girls who intended to become dea conesses, a foundation that other deaconess homes copied. By 1871 the institution had taken over a fourth of the town of Kaiserswerth and presented imposing structures on the horizon. The Paul Gerhard Home, a home for invalid women, was established in 1876. Disselhoff died in 1896.[97]

The deaconess movement truly fit the spirit of what was acceptable in nineteenth-century women's work, so it spread rapidly. Not all the leadership came from Kaiserswerth. In 1833 in Berlin, Pastor Johannes Gossner of the *Bethlehems-Gemeinde*—a convert to Protestantism who had influenced Amalie Sieveking in founding her benevolent visiting society when he had lived in Hamburg—founded a *Krankenverein*, a women's society for the care of the sick.[98] He already had founded a similar society for men.[99] In 1836 the women's society rented a house in which to care for some of their patients and built a permanent establishment. This was the Elizabeth Hospital (1837), named after the queen of Prussia, who was its protectress.[100] It became a center for the care of sick women. The members of Gossner's society for the care of the sick continued to visit people in their homes. Eventually, a deaconess home was built next to the hospital, but Gossner avoided the word *deaconess* himself and preferred to call the members of his group *Pflegerin*. He thought of them as nurses. They were not as tightly organized as deaconesses, though they wore a uniform. Gossner died in 1858.[101]

Another deaconess community that began with a society for the care of the sick was that of Strasbourg, a city that became part of a united Germany in the nineteenth century. After World War I, Strasbourg became part of France. The impetus for founding the society, the *Dienerinnenverein* (1836), was the shame felt by Franz Heinrich Härter (1797–1874), a Protestant pastor, because the city could not find Protestant women to serve in the hospital, though Catholic nuns were available.[102] The members of the *Dienerinnenverein* visited poor sick women on Sundays. When several women volunteered to work full time, Härter founded a deaconess home in 1842. Härter was a man of many charitable interests. Besides training nurses, he also educated teachers and founded a servants' training school, a reform school, a nursery, a kindergarten, and a home for the elderly.[103]

The Strasbourg deaconess community was unique for the time because it was governed by a committee of women, whereas most deaconess institutions had men on governing boards or in some position of oversight. Like many other deaconess institutions, the Strasbourg community had a full-time male pastor, but he was only an adviser. A turn of the century historian of the deaconess movement, Christian Golder, called the Strasbourg deaconess community "a female democracy."[104] Another deaconess home founded in the 1840s was that of Dresden (1844).[105] It was part of the state church in Saxony.

In Prussia, Frederick William IV, Fliedner's supporter, wanted to build a chain of benevolent institutions. In 1845 he began building a hospital in Berlin. Two years later the deaconess home Bethanien opened under the protectorate of his wife, Elizabeth.[106] The management was entrusted to a head deaconess (*Oberin*). Bethanien admitted for training unmarried women and widows between the ages of 18 and 36. It became the central deaconess home for East Prussia. The sisters of Bethanien served on the battlefields during the German wars of unification: the 1864 war with Denmark over Schleswig-Holstein, the 1866 war with Austria, and the 1870–1871 Franco-Prussian War.[107]

The deaconess community at Bethanien crossed socioeconomic lines, indicating that the vocation of deaconess was attracting women of the higher echelons of society. This is not surprising because deaconesses were becoming involved in increasingly respected tasks and had responsibilities that other women did not have. The head deaconess, or *Oberin*, had a particularly important charge. Women virtually became hospital administrators—responsible to a board of managers or trustees—where they were in charge of a deaconess community that staffed a hospital.

Attracted to the deaconess community at Bethanien was Anna, Countess of Stolberg-Weringerode (1819–1869). Daughter of the Count of Stolberg, who had been a friend of Fliedner's, Anna desired to serve the sick. She entered Bethanien in 1852, and after she completed her probation in 1855, Anna became head deaconess. In that position she worked with her brother Eberhardt, whom Frederick William IV had appointed commander of a hospital order he had founded, the *Johanniterordern*, or Order of

Malta. When Eberhardt established new hospitals, Anna sent out deaconesses. The two instituted twenty-four hospitals and infirmaries. Eventually Bethanien took charge of all the hospitals of the Order of Malta. Anna died in 1869 after serving in an epidemic of typhus in Prussia (1868). She willed a part of her large inheritance to her motherhouse. The king himself placed a wreath on her casket and escorted her mother in the funeral cortege. Before Anna's death, another Berlin deaconess community, that of the Elizabeth Hospital, also had appointed a countess as head deaconess (1867): Anna, Countess of Arnim.[108]

WILHELM LÖHE AND NEUENDETTELSAU

After the revolutions of 1848, the foundation of motherhouses accelerated: Wroclaw (Breslau) and Königsberg (Kaliningrad) in 1850 and Ludwigslust and Karlsruhe in 1851. The best known of the decade of the 1850s was probably that of Neuendettelsau, Bavaria (1854), because of its founder, Wilhelm Löhe, the third of those whom Herbert Krimm calls the "Three Great Ones" in reference to the Inner Mission and diaconate of the nineteenth century.[109] Originally, Löhe had not intended to found a motherhouse but only to train people for service and encourage such activity at the congregational level. To that end he encouraged the formation of the *Lutherische Verein für weibliche Diakonie* (Lutheran Association for the Female Diaconate) in 1853. He hoped this action would be replicated elsewhere. That purpose was not fully realized, but in 1854, a deaconess community began at Neuendettelsau when several deaconesses moved into rooms rented in an inn. Löhe took out a loan and bought a house for them.[110]

Once the deaconess community was established, Löhe encouraged a full spiritual life for the sisters. Besides regular community worship, he suggested daily private prayer in this pattern: In the morning, a yielding of self to God; in the forenoon, praise and thanksgiving; at the hour of Christ's death (three o'clock), preparation for one's own death; and in the evening, self-examination. Löhe considered private oral confession of one's sins in the Lutheran tradition to a pastor or another Christian to be an important discipline. "The present generation has grown so bold," he said, "because it no longer confesses."[111]

Löhe conceptualized the deaconess as a "[m]aiden betrothed to God," a longstanding Catholic way of viewing nuns, a perspective not shared by all others involved in the deaconess movement.[112] Löhe dismissed a deaconess when she became engaged to marry because he felt betrothal and the diaconate did not fit well together. Yet he did not ask the deaconesses to agree to remain unmarried, which he thought was wrong. However, he did exact from them a promise of uprightness. They were to speak to the pastor of their motherhouse as soon as it seemed that they intended to marry. During Löhe's life, there were 163 deaconesses consecrated. Forty-five percent of them resigned, many to marry.[113]

In Catholic Bavaria, Löhe had fund-raising problems that Fliedner, who had the financial support of the kings of Prussia, did not have. Yet the deaconess community at Neuendettelsau grew. There was also a deacons' institution, though it had considerably fewer deacons than there were deaconesses. With this staff, it was possible to establish a hospital, an institution for the mentally challenged and one for epileptics, houses for the education of women, a manual-training school, a place for the preparation of communion wafers, and in time, a retreat for invalid or sick deaconesses.[114] The work eventually expanded beyond the town itself. Deaconesses staffed hospitals and institutions elsewhere, much as the Kaiserswerth deaconesses did. The deaconess community at Neuendettelsau drew a wider spectrum of women than those who had initially come to Kaiserswerth. For example, the daughters of pastors joined.[115]

The deaconess movement met needs in health and social welfare that governments had not yet fully addressed. The movement as a whole grew enormously in the latter half of the nineteenth century with more new motherhouses than can be described or even mentioned.

EXPANSION IN THE 1850S AND 1860S

About the same time as the founding of the deaconess community at Neuendettelsau, a movement for the foundation of a deaconess motherhouse was stirring in Stuttgart, the capital of Württemberg. There was a public appeal in 1853, which led to the purchase of a house.[116] Eight deaconesses moved in. The queen of Württemberg took the institution under her protection, and the royal family gave financial support. At first there was no hospital, and the Stuttgart deaconesses went to Strasbourg for nursing training. Besides nursing, the Württemberg deaconesses worked in parishes, kindergartens, and homes for children, adolescents, servants, and women.[117]

Also in the 1850s, deaconess motherhouses were founded in Augsburg (1855), in Halle on the Saale (1857), in Darmstadt (1858), and in Speyer (1859). The impulse for founding these motherhouses came mainly from Kaiserswerth, which also initially supplied most of the head deaconesses, though the first head deaconess of the *Elisabethenstift* in Darmstadt came from the Bethanien home in Berlin.[118] The German states supported these endeavors. King Frederick William IV made the first donation to Speyer. Prince Karl of Hesse's wife, Elizabeth, was the patroness of the *Elisabethenstift* in Darmstadt, which was named after her.[119]

State support continued in the 1860s. The motherhouse Betheseda (1860) in Hamburg was built on land donated by the state. Queen Maria contributed 150,000 marks to the *Henrietta Stift* (1860) in Hanover. The year 1860 also saw the founding of a motherhouse in Craschnitz, Silesia. In the decade of the 1860s, deaconess homes were founded in Danzig (Gdansk, 1862), Kassel (1864), Posen (Poznan, 1865), and Frankenstein (1866). The latter was the third such home in Silesia. Bethanien in Breslau (1850) and a motherhouse in Craschnitz (1860) already were in operation. A deaconess home was founded in Altona in 1867, the first in Schleswig-Holstein, and one in Bremen in 1868. In that year and the next, two institutions were founded in Stetten (Szczecin): Salem (1868) and Bethanien (1869).[120]

Before the end of the decade, a center of deaconess work was founded near Bielefeld in Westphalia (1869). In five years it was replaced with a larger institution named Sarepta. A constellation of institutions followed that ultimately covered fifteen hundred acres. Together, the institutions sometimes were called "the hill country of Judah" because many of them had biblical names. Besides the home for deaconesses, the brotherhood of the Maltese Cross had a home, which was called Nazareth. The original motherhouse became an infirmary for women, the *Marienstift*. The building named Bethel housed female epileptics, and the name Bethel was applied to the entire establishment at Bielefeld. Other buildings included Hephata (for contagious diseases), Nain (for sick young men), Tabor (for invalid men), Bersaba and Bethanien (for patients from the upper classes), Emmaus (for mentally challenged girls), Zoar and Ophra (for mentally challenged boys), Morija (for mentally ill men), Magdala and Betheseda (for mentally ill women), Sichem (men's infirmary), Bethlehem (bookstore), and Sunem (bookbindery and salesroom). The complex also included three parsonages and Zion's church, which seated twelve hundred people.

The Westphalian motherhouse, like Kaiserswerth, had branches both within the Germanies and in other countries. These were located in Berlin, Brussels, Paris, Nice, Metz, Lemgo, Arolsen, and Zanzibar (East Africa). In contrast, the deaconess community in Altona concentrated its work in Schleswig-Holstein. During the era when Hitler controlled Germany, the directing sister and the pastor at Bethel defied attempts by the Nazis to exterminate the patients and residents of the institution—individuals whom Hitler considered useless to the state.[121]

THE MORAVIANS

While this growth was occurring within the German state churches, the deaconess movement spread to the Moravians. In a sense the movement had a head start in Moravia because in 1745 Count Zinzendorf had consecrated deaconesses, who assisted in worship, served the women of the Moravian community, performed the ceremonial act of foot washing, and oversaw the training of girls. These deaconesses, however, did not live in a motherhouse. By the 1840s, these women were no longer called deaconesses, though the office endured.

In 1842 Hermann Plitt became excited by Fliedner's model of deaconess work. More than two decades later, in 1864, Plitt rented the upper story of a dwelling in the village of Pawlowitsky, which was dedicated on May 6, 1866, as the *Heinrichstift*. One of its first two nurses trained at Kaiserswerth. Helped by a revival among the Moravians, an orphanage and a home for the elderly also were established. The *Heinrichstift* itself dedicated a new building on September 28, 1870. Plitt's work received gifts from members of the royal family, and branch stations began in 1879. The *Heinrichstift* was moved to Niesky and opened under the name Emmaus on July 3, 1883. In October 1897, in keeping with the Moravian tradition of foreign missions, the first missionary deaconess went to India and worked chiefly among lepers. In 1898, the motherhouse joined the Kaiserswerth General Conference.[122]

THE 1870S TO 1890S

The decade of the 1870s saw growth and new challenges. Germans continued to give their money and their daughters to the deaconess movement. They founded new motherhouses and erected large buildings to replace old ones. In 1870 deaconess institutions were founded in Braunschweig and in Frankfurt on the Main. During the Franco-Prussian War (1870–1871), thirty different motherhouses supplied more than eight hundred deaconesses to work on the battlefields and in 230 field hospitals. After the war, Empress Augusta sent the cross of merit to women of Kaiserswerth. Field Marshall General von Moltke showed special interest in the *Oberlinhaus* at Nowawes (1874) in suburban Potsdam.

In addition to the *Oberlinhaus*, the following deaconess houses were founded during the 1870s: Wroctaw [Breslau] (1873), Flensburg (1874), the Paul Gerhardt-Stift in Berlin (1876), Ingweiler (1877), and Bethlehem at Hamburg (1877). In 1878 Friedrich Wilke founded a children's hospital, and when he failed to find a motherhouse to take charge, he established one. His entire constellation comprised the Naemi-Wilkestift, Hospital, and Evangelical Lutheran Deaconess Institution in Guben. In 1889 it came under the auspices of the Evangelical Lutheran Church in Prussia. It did not join the Kaiserswerth Union of motherhouses. Besides the mother-house, there was a hospital, an institution for the mentally ill, a school for the deaf and dumb, a refuge for children, and twenty-two branch stations that included a training school for girls, a nursery, two homes for conva-lescents, and six schools for children.[123]

In the 1880s and 1890s, the deaconess movement continued to grow through institutions at Mannheim (1884), Berlin (the Magdalen hospital, 1888), Kreuzberg (1888), Groningen (1888), Sobernheim (1889), Witten (1890), Oldenburg (1890), Leipzig (1890), Michowitz (1891), Eisenach (1891), Frankfurt on the Oder (1891), Wiesbaden (1896), and Borsdorf near Leipzig (1896). Both private and state support continued. For exam-ple, the first deaconess home in Leipzig came into being through the efforts of Dr. Pank, an active church member. He organized a union of societies dedicated to caring for the poor and the sick through deaconesses. In 1890 he issued a call for prospective deaconesses, interviewed women, and selected eight. As the number of deaconesses grew, they served the hospi-tals and private families of Leipzig as nurses and in 1892 founded a kinder-garten. In 1895 the city council gave the deaconesses land on which to build a complex of buildings that included a new motherhouse.[124]

OVERVIEW

The foundation of the deaconess community of Leipzig followed a famil-iar pattern in the founding of deaconess communities. The initiative came from the grass roots. A wealthy or influential man, often a pastor, would become interested in alleviating the distress of the sick, handicapped, and abandoned where he lived. He would rally others around him, both men and women. They would form a society or a union of societies dedicated to the care of the sick or to the establishment of a deaconess community that would address social welfare needs. The society would engage in a fund-raising campaign and establish a hospital or a deaconess home or both. Because deaconesses staffed hospitals, their homes often were founded in connection with hospitals. Sometimes the deaconess home preceded the hospital; sometimes the deaconess home and the hospital came into being at about the same time; and sometimes the hospital came first. For example, the Danzig deaconess home developed from a children's hospital.[125] At some point, the royal family or the state would take an interest in the project and donate property or offer financial support out of goodwill but also because the deaconesses and their institutions were doing social welfare work. Deaconesses served the interests of the state and of the community.

Deaconesses, then, were in demand and typically did not have to seek work. The decision of whether or not the deaconesses would respond positively to a particular request for help lay with the motherhouse and its pastor or superintendent, who operated under the auspices of a board of directors. Because of the nature of nineteenth-century society, many decisions were in the hands of the men who served the deaconess communities rather than in the hands of the women themselves. Although men held the ultimate supervision of deaconess institutions, the practical aspects of work and life in the motherhouse left a great deal of responsibility to the deaconess community itself, especially to the head deaconess. Nevertheless, the men involved with the deaconess communities were often better remembered than the women, at least in histories of the deaconess movement or of Lutheranism written near the turn of the twentieth century.[126] Research on many of these women remains to be done.

Some of the men involved with the deaconess movement in the nineteenth century were outstanding individuals in their own right. They had interests beyond the deaconess communities they served, especially in the area of Inner Mission. Some of these men were authors or editors; most were pastors. Some were laymen of influence or wealth, such as Friedrich Wilke.[127] Besides the men already mentioned—Theodore Fliedner, Johannes Gossner, Wilhelm Löhe, Franz Heinrich Härter, Hermann Plitt, and Friedrich Wilke—there were Friedrich von Bodelschwingh, Theodor Schäfer, Karl Wilhelm Theodor Ninck, and Gerhard Uhlhorn.

Friedrich von Bodelschwingh (1831–1910) was a miner and a farmer before he became a pastor.[128] He served a congregation in Paris (1858) before becoming superintendent at Bielefeld in Westphalia in 1872. For thirty years von Bodelschwingh led that institution's phenomenal growth and sent forth more than a thousand deaconesses and deacons. He related closely to the German East African Society. Perhaps encouraged by his cosmopolitan experiences, the motherhouse at Bielefeld had branch institutions in Paris, Nice, Metz, Berlin, Lemgo, Arolsen, Brussels, and Zanzibar. Recognized by the emperor for his achievements, it was said of von

Bodelschwingh that he had a "gift of soliciting aid in so kind and gentle a manner that he [was] seldom refused."[129]

Theodor Schäfer (born 1846) was, like von Bodelschwingh , a pastor in Paris before he became superintendent and pastor of the deaconess community at Altona in Schleswig-Holstein in 1872, the same year that von Bodelschwingh became superintendent at Bielefeld. Schäfer wrote in support of Inner Mission and the diaconate.[130] Concern for the disadvantaged was a family tradition. Schäfer's father had founded the home for the blind in Friedberg, Hessen.[131]

Pastor Karl Wilhelm Theodor Ninck founded Bethlehem, the deaconess home in Hamburg. It served only the poor, and wealthy families could rarely secure a nurse from the institution. The result was that the Bethlehem home relied more on donations than did other motherhouses, which relied on income from paying patients and residents. Ninck was a man of many talents. Pastor of a large congregation, he supported the Bremen North German Mission; reorganized the Netherland Tract Society; founded a seaman's mission; and edited a magazine for families, *Nachbar*, and a periodical, *Deutscher Kinderfreund*. Despite Ninck's broad interests, the Bethlehem deaconesses established no branches until after his death (December 17, 1887).[132]

Gerhard Uhlhorn (1826–1901), spiritual director of the *Henrietta Stift* and a court preacher in Hanover, was a prolific author of religious and historical books.[133] His work on charity in the ancient world contributed to this book.

By the end of the nineteenth century, some German women wanted to be nurses but did not want to become deaconesses. The Evangelical Diaconate Society opened a home for these women in Zehlendorf, near Berlin, in October 1899. The city's hospitals were used for training, and the society gave women an opportunity for a year of voluntary service and training. Many participants continued beyond the year and became sisters of the Evangelical Diaconate Society, but they were not formally deaconesses. Eventually these women received a pension. The sisters also entered new phases of social work: schools for girls from cultured circles, social clubs for working girls, and a home for students. The deaconess motherhouses resented that the Evangelical Diaconate Society had included the word *diaconate* in the organization's title.[134]

But the deaconess movement had little to fear from competing organizations in the nineteenth century. From Germany the deaconess movement spread through branch institutions and filial motherhouses, one of which was founded in Zwickau by the Dresden deaconess institution.[135] The inspiration of the German model also resulted in the founding of motherhouses in other countries. Many of these deaconess communities joined the Kaiserswerth Union of motherhouses.

THE DEACONESS MOVEMENT
OUTSIDE GERMANY

FRANCE

One of the earliest deaconess communities outside Germany emerged in France. Antoine Vermeil, a pastor of the Reformed Church of France, founded the first deaconess institution in Paris on November 6, 1841, less than ten years after the beginning of the deaconess movement at Kaiserswerth. Because the beginning of the deaconess community in Paris occurred so soon after the foundation of Kaiserswerth, it would be difficult to assume that German influence predominated.

Born March 19, 1799, in Nîmes, Vermeil was the descendant of a Huguenot family. For many years he had wanted to renew the diaconate as it was in the early church. As a young man, he became pastor of the French congregation in Hamburg in 1823.[136] This Reformed church exercised an influence over the circle to which Amalie Sieveking belonged.[137] Vermeil's stay in Hamburg was brief, however. The next year he accepted a call to the Reformed church in Bordeaux, where he founded several benevolent institutions.

In 1840 Vermeil accepted a call to Paris, where Elizabeth Fry had formed a society to visit women at the Saint Lazare prison. These women needed a halfway house when they were released, so Vermeil and the society opened one in the Saint Antoine suburb of Paris on November 6, 1841. A friend of Vermeil's from Bordeaux, Mademoiselle Malvesin, was the first deaconess of the society and became its superintendent. The work of the society expanded to include a nursery, a children's hospital, and a training and reform school for girls.[138] Within four years, the building was too small. Vermeil found a larger property and erected a central deaconess institution for the Reformed Church of France. In Paris, deaconesses dressed in black.[139] Before his death on October 8, 1864, Vermeil passed the leadership of the deaconess movement in France to his friend, Pastor Louis Valette (born May 24, 1800), who trained deaconesses for parish work.[140]

Under Valette, the French deaconesses nursed those who fought in the Franco-Prussian War of 1870–1871. The sisters established at their school a hospital for the sick and wounded of any faith. After Valette's death on

October 20, 1872, the directorship of the institution fell to four pastors, two Reformed and two Lutheran. Increased funding after the Franco-Prussian War made it possible to establish a hospital for women in September 1873.[141] In 1874 a deaconess home in Paris began under the control of the Lutheran Church to train parish deaconesses.[142]

By the turn of the century, motherhouses and their branches extended throughout France. There were Protestant hospitals at Uzès, Marseilles, Audincourt, La Rochelle, and Montauban; orphanages at Orleans and Montauban; homes for the elderly at Nanterre, Montauban, Bordeaux, and Lyons; an industrial school at Livron; and a convalescent home for young boys at Versailles. In addition, there was a kindergarten in Paris. A Lutheran pastor founded a second deaconess home in Paris in 1874.[143]

Switzerland

Only one year after the foundation of Antoine Vermeil's deaconess home in Paris, another pastor, Louis Germond (died September 11, 1866), founded a deaconess home in Echallens, Switzerland (1842). It closed and then reopened in 1852 at Saint Loup, where an infirmary for women and children with chronic diseases and an institute for scrofulous children developed. The Saint Loup deaconesses wore brown.[144] The influence of this deaconess home spread throughout French-speaking Switzerland and beyond. Its branches included a hospital in Lausanne and a station in Cannes, France.[145]

Deaconess institutions in the German-speaking parts of Switzerland also began early in the overall movement. In Bern, the deaconess movement emerged from a women's benevolent visiting society that was organized in 1836. In 1842 the most prominent member of that society, Sophia Wurstemberger, visited Kaiserswerth and England, where she stayed with Elizabeth Fry. On returning to Switzerland, Sophia struggled with her family, who were reluctant to allow her to work alongside women of inferior social rank and to dedicate herself to the care of the poor and the sick. Finally they consented but declared that she could expect no financial assistance. She lived for eighteen years in rented rooms in Bern with the women with whom she worked. In 1862 they were able to buy a home. From Bern their work spread to more than forty hospitals. Sophia married a man who took charge of the deaconess work in Bern in the 1850s, John F. Daendliker (1821–1900). Sophia died in 1878.[146]

A deaconess institution in Neumünster near Zurich arose in November 1858 through the fund-raising efforts of an evangelical society. On June 6, 1869, the deaconesses founded a home for the elderly. By 1903, the community had twenty-six hospitals, a children's rescue home, and four homes for servant girls.[147]

Influential people were associated with some of these Swiss deaconess homes. At Riehen, near Basel, the president of the city council headed the deaconess institution for twenty years. Theodore Fliedner, son of the founder of Kaiserswerth, was rector at Riehen for three years before he left in 1879 to manage the Paul Gerhardt-Stift in Berlin. The Riehen deaconesses worked in more than thirty-five hospitals.[148] The home at Zurich started as a daughter house of Riehen but eventually became independent of it.[149]

THE NETHERLANDS

In the Netherlands, as in Switzerland and France, deaconess work began early. In fact, it was there and in England during a June 1823 trip that Theodore Fliedner found inspiration for his work at Kaiserswerth:

> In both of these countries I became acquainted with a number of benevolent institutions for both the body and the soul; schools, and educational institutions, poor houses, orphanages and hospitals, prisons and societies for the improvement of prisoners, Bible societies, Missionary societies, etc. . . . I returned home in August 1824 . . . with deep shame that we men of Germany had permitted the women so far to outstrip us in Christian charity, and especially that we cared so little for the prisoners.[150]

As the result of a second trip in 1827, Fliedner wrote:

> In the churches [of the Dutch Mennonites] there are deaconesses who are elected and controlled by the Official Board of the Church, and whose duty it is to look after the poor of their own sex. They visit the huts of the poor, distribute what clothing they have received, see that the girls find employment as servants, etc. Neither they nor the deacons are paid; they belong to the most respectable families of the church, and they undertake this work, which requires considerable sacrifice of time, etc., with the greatest readiness. Other Evangelical Confessions ought of right to imitate this praiseworthy and Christian practice.[151]

Besides this Mennonite model of deaconess work, women were active in the founding and support of deaconess institutions in the Netherlands. The queen herself was the protector of the deaconess home in The Hague, which was dedicated in 1865. In Utrecht, several women initiated a society that founded a deaconess motherhouse on the Kaiserswerth model, the first one in Holland. This motherhouse sent two deaconesses to Kaiserswerth for training and, when they returned, opened a hospital in November 1844.

One woman built a children's hospital in Utrecht in 1860. A rest home for deaconesses and for elderly women appeared in 1875. In 1903 the head deaconess was Countess Anna Von Bylandt Rheydt.[152]

In 1874 in Haarlem, A. J. M. Teding Van Berkhourt, a young woman, began caring for people in her home who suffered from epilepsy. In 1880 a building was erected in her garden for the care of her patients. It soon became too small, so she appealed to friends for help. They formed a society and expanded to nearby Heemstede. The presence of male patients at the facility created a need for men to do some of the tasks that nineteenth-century deaconesses considered indiscreet, such as bathing. Friedrich von Bodelschwingh of Bielefeld came to the aid of the Heemstede deaconesses until they could build their own deacons home to provide male nurses. Van Berkhourt founded a deaconess home in 1887, and in 1888 the Haarlem deaconesses began a children's home. In 1889 they sent deaconesses to Amsterdam to begin parish work, and in 1891 they founded the Reformed deaconess institution in that city. Lutherans already had founded a motherhouse in Amsterdam in 1880. In Haarlem, the Reformed deaconesses added a rescue home for girls in 1894 and a home for the elderly and for the chronically ill in 1897. Several deaconesses from Haarlem went to the Dutch East Indies.[153]

In Arnheim, the queen mother was the patroness of the deaconess motherhouse that opened August 3, 1884. The house had its origin in the consistory of the Reformed church of Arnheim. D. Disselhoff was rector of the institution until he returned to Kaiserswerth in 1900 to be co-rector. His father, Julius Disselhoff, had become the superintendent at Kaiserswerth after Theodore Fliedner had died.[154]

A deaconess motherhouse opened in Groningen in 1888. The deaconess institution in Rotterdam emerged in 1892 from the work of two parish deaconesses and the money of two anonymous women. A group of pastors formed a deaconess society and institution in 1900 in Zeeland. At the turn of the century, the Dutch still were building new deaconess institutions.[155]

SCANDINAVIA

The deaconess movement spread to the Scandinavian countries in the mid-nineteenth century. Stockholm, Sweden, had a motherhouse by 1851. This institution, Ersta, was intended principally for training nurses.[156] Its first superintendent was Sister Maria Cederschiöld, a deaconess trained at Kaiserswerth. Within two years, an orphanage and a girls' home opened, followed in 1858 and 1860 by rescue homes for girls, and subsequently a housekeeping school to train these girls for domestic service. A rest home opened in 1884, then an infirmary for the chronically ill.[157] The mother-house Ersta was followed by Samariterhemmet in 1882, a motherhouse in Uppsala.[158]

In the nineteenth century, there was only one diaconal institution for men in Scandinavia. It was founded in 1898, and from 1905 it was located outside Stockholm at Stora Sköndal, Farsta. Male deacons were few in Sweden, and they often worked as social workers. Some were parish clerks.[159]

In Denmark, the royal family was instrumental in initiating the dea-coness movement, especially Princess (later Queen) Louisa (died Septem-ber 29, 1898) and Queen Caroline Amelia. Because of their efforts, the deaconess home in Copenhagen opened in 1863. Bishop Martinson super-vised the growth of the institution. A member of Denmark's privy counsel was president of the board of directors. With the support of the court and other influential people, the deaconess home never lacked backing. The Danish church supported it through an annual general collection. Con-nected with the motherhouse were hospitals, schools, a girls' home, an infirmary, a colportage society (to distribute religious literature), a home for epileptic girls, and a rescue home for women. The deaconesses worked throughout Denmark in parishes and benevolent institutions.[160]

The movement to establish deaconesses in Norway, inspired by the German model, was active in the 1850s, as was the Inner Mission move-ment. In 1855 an Oslo professor, Gisle Johnson (1822–1894), shaped an Inner Mission organization. The Norwegian Seamen's Mission formed in 1864.[161] The society for home missions in Christiana (Oslo) also promoted the deaconess endeavor. The first superintendent of Lovisenberg, the motherhouse in Christiana, which was founded in 1868, was Cathinka Guldberg, a woman trained at Kaiserswerth. Lovisenberg was important for the development of modern nursing in Norway, and nursing was the chief emphasis of Norwegian diaconal work. Deaconesses in Norway also worked with children and engaged in educational and social work.[162]

There was also a deacons home or "fatherhouse" in Oslo that dated from 1890. This facility trained male deacons, who were considered male nurses, though their training also included theology and social science.[163] The deacons initially worked primarily in the institution's hospital.[164]

Finland also was receptive to the Inner Mission and the organization of diaconal work as inspired by Theodore Fliedner. In Finland deaconesses concentrated on nursing.[165] A deaconess motherhouse in Helsingfors (Helsinki), Finland, opened in September 1867 through the efforts of

Madame Aurora Karamsin (Karamzin), who had visited Fliedner in Germany. Karamsin worked in cooperation with ministers and academics. The first directing sister of the motherhouse was Amanda Cajander, a widow who had been trained in St. Petersburg because Finland had passed from Sweden to Russia in 1806. Cajander founded a children's hospital in 1869.[166] That same year, the Hackman family founded a deaconess institution in Vyborg that qualified its first deaconess in 1872, a year before the first deaconess was to be qualified from Helsinki.[167]

Finnish women did not take immediately to the deaconess movement. Some favored the less-restrictive model of the Evangelical Diaconate Association in Germany. The Helsinki deaconess home had only eleven sisters in 1882 when Deaconess Lina Snellmen became directing sister. Nevertheless, deaconesses served in six hospitals and managed a poorhouse. Aurora Karamsin provided ongoing financial support. The Inner Mission Society founded a training center for parish workers at Sortavala in Karelia in 1894. It never had motherhouse rules, but it did have deaconesses.[168] A deaconess house was founded in Oulu in 1896.[169]

RUSSIA

The deaconess motherhouse of St. Petersburg, Russia, grew out of an evangelical hospital that had been founded in 1859 rather than out of the Russian Orthodox Church. The hospital and the deaconess home were under one roof, a different arrangement from that found in the motherhouses in Europe. The emperor of Russia, Alexander II, supported the work of the deaconesses financially. Along with the empress and the imperial household, he often visited the deaconess institutions: the hospital, primary school, children's home, and rest home. The motherhouse in St. Petersburg supplied a deaconess to direct diaconal work in Moscow.[170]

Deaconess institutions elsewhere in the Russian Empire opened in the 1860s. Deaconesses from Neuendettelsau helped in Saraton, where the Alexander Asylum opened in 1865, and in Tallin (in Estonia, formerly the city of Revel), where a deaconess institution opened on May 23, 1867. Deaconess institutions opened in Mittau in 1865, in Riga in 1866, and in Viborg (Karelen) in 1869. The deaconess home in Mittau was a daughter of the motherhouse in Dresden. Bethel in Viborg grew out of a children's home and was the result of a large donation from the Hackman family.[171]

AUSTRIA AND HUNGARY

In Hungary, deaconess work began in 1866 in Budapest. There four deaconesses from Kaiserswerth inaugurated a hospital that nursed soldiers during the Austro-Prussian War. At this time Hungary was linked to Austria in the Austro-Hungarian Empire. The German Reformed Church originated the hospital and also founded an orphanage. Most of the deaconesses in Hungary were drawn from other countries.[172]

In Austria, the Evangelical congregation at Gallneukirchen founded a deaconess institution in 1872 with two deaconesses who had received their training at Stuttgart. Eventually they established a hospital, a place for the mentally ill, a home for epileptics, an orphanage, and a rescue home.[173] Their work spread elsewhere in Austria with parish deaconesses in Meran, Tyrol (December 13, 1885), and an orphanage and rescue home in Rechersdorf (1880).[174]

THE METHODISTS

The deaconess institutions described so far have been primarily Lutheran or Reformed institutions or both, in keeping with the original institution at Kaiserswerth. In countries where these denominations dominated, the deaconess houses attempted to maintain an "active yet independent connection with the state church," as prescribed in the constitution of the deaconess motherhouses connected with Kaiserswerth. However, the deaconess movement also spread to the so-called Free Churches, the denominations independent of state support.[175] This was true of the Methodists.

In the nineteenth century, Methodism spread to the Germanies and to German-speaking Switzerland. In Germany in mid-century, the Methodist Episcopal Church organized. At this same time, Methodist women were joining deaconess motherhouses of other denominations, and some were lost to Methodism, which concerned the denomination's leadership. In reaction, a Methodist minister in Calw, Württemberg, used deaconesses as nurses and organized a society. Methodist churches in Frankfurt on the Main, Pforzheim, Karlsruhe, and Bremen followed suit. However, the denomination voted down a proposal at the Annual Conference of 1874 in Schaffhausen, Switzerland, that it support a deaconess program. Four members of the conference then met separately and organized an independent society of deaconesses, the *Bethanienverein*, or Bethany Society Faced with this *fait accompli*, the Methodist Annual Conference endorsed the new society. Work formally began in April 1876 with one deaconess living in the parsonage in Frankfurt on the Main. Most German Methodist deaconesses engaged in caring for the sick,[176] but the women had problems finding hospitals in which to train. The Frankfurt deaconesses used the academic hospital in Heidelberg for training. In 1885 they opened their own hospital in Frankfurt, which was partially funded from a door-to-door solicitation. Methodist deaconesses also trained and worked in Berlin.[177] Methodist deaconesses in Germany wore black.[178]

In 1885 the Bethany Society sent deaconesses to St. Gallen, Switzerland, and in 1887 to Zurich. In 1878 the Frankfurt Methodist deaconesses expanded to Hamburg. There they initially had problems with fundraising because they lacked an association with the state church. They countered this problem by pointing out that the Methodist Church had denied them support in 1874, and they were not, therefore, under the denomination's official direction. Hamburg publicly recognized their deaconess home, Bethany, as a charitable institution in 1886. The city gave the Methodist deaconesses land for a hospital and a new deaconess house (dedicated September 14, 1893). In 1892 the deaconesses helped in a cholera epidemic in Hamburg. In Berlin in 1888 the city council permitted a house-to-house collection for the purchase of property for a deaconess home in the city.[179] The Methodist deaconess work was independent of the conference and self-supporting.[180]

The Bethany Society ventured outside German-speaking areas on October 31, 1890, when it stationed two French-speaking deaconesses in Lausanne, Switzerland. In 1897 the Bethany Society sent deaconesses to Strasbourg and to Vienna, Austria. In 1900 a station began in Pforzheim in the Grand Duchy of Baden. Because of small numbers and a relative lack of hospitals in Germany and Switzerland, many Methodist deaconesses engaged in private nursing. Beginning in 1889, they worked in parishes, where they nursed the poor, conducted societies for young women, engaged in mission work, and opened nurseries for the children of working mothers.[181]

The Bethany Society of Germany helped to bring about the adoption of deaconess work in the Methodist Episcopal Church in the United States. The Methodist deaconesses in Germany provided an example to encourage the 1888 General Conference in the United States to take steps to support such work.[182]

The Martha and Mary Society of the Wesleyan Synod, a second society of Methodist deaconesses in Germany, began work with one deaconess on February 4, 1889, in Nuremberg. In 1890 a branch station began in Munich. In 1892 work began in Vienna and in Magdeburg. In 1899 a filial institution began in Heilbronn. The society was blessed with the considerable financial support of the Baroness of Langenau, a convert to Methodism and the widow of an ambassador of the Austrian emperor. The baroness died February 24, 1902, after the Wesleyan Synod had amalgamated with the Protestant Episcopal Church.[183]

Methodist churches in Sweden began employing sisters in city mission work in the nineteenth century, but it was not until 1900 that a Methodist deaconess society formed in Gothenburg. The society employed Anna Kajser, a nurse from Gothenburg. At the 1901 Annual Conference of the Methodist Church, Bishop Vincent consecrated Kajser as the first Methodist deaconess in Sweden.[184]

BAPTISTS

The Baptist Church in Germany founded the Martha Deaconess Society in Berlin in February 1885. This society focused especially on finding women for nursing and missions. Not until two years later, however, did the society find a deaconess, whom it employed as a parish nurse. Others joined her, forming a deaconess community named Bethel. From Berlin the German Baptist deaconesses spread to Hanover, Württemberg, Königsberg (Kaliningrad), Zurich, and eventually to India and Cameroon.[185]

EVANGELICAL ASSOCIATION
IN GERMANY AND SWITZERLAND

In June 1886 the Evangelical Association in Germany and Switzerland met in Essen on the Ruhr. One result of the meeting was the foundation of the deaconess institution at Elberfeld. Members of the association formed a society to raise funds for deaconess work, built a hospital at Elberfeld (1890), and founded institutions in Berlin (1887), Hamburg (1888), Strasbourg (1889), Dresden (1891), Stuttgart (1896), and Karlsruhe (1900). Betheseda deaconesses also were in charge of a hospital in Solingen. They engaged in parish work in Elberfeld, Gelsenkirchen, Dortmund, Barmen, Stuttgart, Karlsruhe, and Reutlingen. They worked among the poor and sponsored Sunday schools, women's groups, and manual-training schools for children. One Elberfeld deaconess worked in Philadelphia, Pennsylvania, in a home for the elderly. This society maintained a rest home for deaconesses at Friedrichrode in the Thuringian Forest. In 1889 the society founded a second motherhouse in Strasbourg with two deaconesses from Elberfeld. The connection between the two groups was severed in 1892, and the Strasbourg house maintained stations in Zurich, Colmar, and Mühlhausen. The supporting society for the Strasbourg house was the Betheseda-Verein für allgemeine Krankenpflege im Elsass und in der Schweiz.[186]

SUMMARY AND ANALYSIS

Many motherhouses founded in the nineteenth century joined the Kaiserswerth Union. Besides German institutions, the Kaiserswerth Union included motherhouses from countries such as France, Switzerland, Russia, the Netherlands, the Scandinavian countries, and the United States.[187]

From Europe the deaconess movement spread to the British Isles and to the New World, where it took a shape of its own. Before tracing that story, consider the success of the deaconess movement on the continent: Why did the deaconess movement have such phenomenal growth in its first seventy years? Clearly it had an enormous appeal to nineteenth- and early twentieth-century women. This may be explained, in part, by the lack of vocational opportunities for single women, particularly in Germany. Revivals within the church had a role in moving women to this work. The fields of labor in which deaconesses engaged also attracted recruits because they were areas of obvious need to which women could dedicate themselves in a lifetime of service.

Deaconesses had a degree of independence, though the motherhouse was the final arbiter of what they did and where they worked. In addition, the motherhouse, even with its restraints, offered the promise of lifelong companions, female bonding, and security in old age. The Kaiserswerth deaconesses remembered particularly the afternoon coffee hour and tried to replicate the *Kaiserswerther Kaffee* when stationed elsewhere.[188] Each sister's birthday was celebrated,[189] and a sense of sisterhood was encouraged. Women stationed in outlying branches received newspapers and correspondence, a tradition begun by Theodore Fliedner. Some motherhouses paid special attention to connections among the sisters. For example, the motherhouse near Bielefeld in Westphalia sent every deaconess a letter each month and the *Westfaelische Sonntagsblatt* each week. The deaconesses held an annual conference and rotated women back to the motherhouse after prolonged periods in the field.[190]

Nineteenth-century society was receptive to the deaconess movement, though it often resisted other kinds of women's work or manifestations of independence. The respectability conveyed by the deaconesses' connection with the church clearly was a factor in this receptivity, as was the willingness of the movement to fit into society without threatening the status quo. Because deaconesses remained unmarried, they sidestepped protests that a woman's place was in the home with her husband and children. In addition, the motherhouses connected with Kaiserswerth did not accept "fallen" women. Although widows were accepted, many communities accepted only those who were childless. Families might have found it convenient to have their unmarried female relatives housed in a deaconess motherhouse rather than with siblings or other family members. Also in allowing a daughter to become a deaconess, the family often gained a nurse, and if the deaconess was needed to nurse a parent, the motherhouse allowed her to go.[191]

The nineteenth century saw the rise of modern nursing and social work, which, in addition to parish work and teaching, was what deaconesses did. There was tremendous need for nurses and social workers, functions that deaconesses pioneered. Because many deaconess hospitals were small, they were easy to establish. The lack of modern technology and equipment enabled the use of a relatively small building as a hospital, for example, a family home was adequate. Thus homes were common gifts to deaconess societies and could serve as a catalyst for the foundation of a hospital.

It is amazing, however, that there was not more resistance to deaconesses on the grounds that they were Protestant nuns, especially given the support that Martin Luther and the reformers of the sixteenth century gave to marriage and the reformers' criticism of vows of celibacy. The fact that the deaconesses did not take lifelong vows but only a formal commitment of five years at a time may have circumvented that opposition. Deaconesses also could keep inherited wealth and pass it on. Some deaconesses married or left the community, which may have obscured the fact that so many remained unmarried. Deaconesses were, in fact, encouraged to think of their vocation as lifelong. The constitution of the motherhouses connected with Kaiserswerth that was adopted by the thirteenth conference of September 18–19, 1901, stipulated that "[t]he Sisters are to realize more and more that the calling of a deaconess is to be their life work" and "[t]he Mother House expects of a deaconess, just as parents do of their children, that if she receives a proposal of marriage, before deciding on the same she should notify her superiors and receive their advice."[192]

Deacons had developed considerably since the sixteenth century. The nineteenth century made real Luther's vision that deacons should be involved in social welfare and work with the poor, but the nineteenth century also produced unmarried female deaconesses who were obligated to remain single if they wanted to continue as deaconesses. Luther might have rejected the mandatory celibacy aspect of the office. What, then, had happened to deacons in the Reformed tradition?

REFORMED CHURCHES

Many Reformed churches adopted the new forms of the deaconess and deacon that emerged from Kaiserswerth and from Hamburg in the nineteenth century. The Prussian Union Church oversaw the Kaiserswerth motherhouse, and Prussia's state church was a union of Lutheran and Reformed elements. Kaiserswerth lay within both traditions. Members of Reformed churches that were not part of a union with Lutherans supported the deaconess movement, for example, in Switzerland, the Netherlands, and France. Many Reformed churches, however, also retained the diaconate as an office for laymen who were chosen from individual congregations to work on a volunteer basis. This followed the vision of John Calvin and other early leaders of Reformed churches. There were calls for the revival of deacons in Scotland and elsewhere in the nineteenth century, but by then the state had stepped into social welfare and the role of deacons was limited. In Geneva, the funds for the poor merged with the city hospital. The deacons of the poor funds disappeared briefly but were reconstituted within the church.

In the nineteenth century, there were periodic attempts to revive deacons in Scotland as the Scottish church split and new Presbyterian churches were organized. Thomas Chalmers reinvigorated the diaconate to serve the urban poor, but as time went on, the state increasingly took over social welfare. The Free Church of Scotland, founded in 1843, elected deacons for life and ordained them. Some deacons were elected for a specific term of years and in that case were not ordained. Deacons administered all the temporal affairs of a congregation. The United Presbyterian Church in Scotland, formed in 1847 from eighteenth-century Secession groups, assigned administration of poor funds to the Session (the congregational governing board) and usually appointed managers to look after congregational finances.[193]

In the first half of the nineteenth century, a change in the internal politics of Geneva brought into power a government that was unsympathetic to private welfare funds focused on aid to Protestants. The government wanted to combine the French Fund with the hospital, in effect dissolving the fund. The French Fund attempted to resist, but in 1849 the Council of State gave the assets of the French Fund to the city hospital, an act that continued to cause rancor a half century later.[194] Deprived of resources, the deacons of the fund met for the last time on September 14, 1849.[195] The Italian Fund voluntarily turned over its capital in 1869 to the Hospice général or General Hospice, the renamed General Hospital.[196]

Undaunted by this setback, the Reformed Church of Geneva instituted a new diaconate within a year of the dissolution of the French Fund. The church attempted to avoid the appearance of instituting a Protestant welfare fund in opposition to that of the state. The deacons were closely tied to the pastors, some of whom had indicated a desire for help with the care of the poor and the surveillance of the city's youth. The regulation instituting the new system reads as follows: "Diaconates are instituted by the Consistory in the city of Geneva in order to look after, in concert with the pastors, religious and moral interests and the works of charity."[197]

The deacons were selected by the Consistory, the governing body of the Genevan church, which was composed of pastors and laypeople. The deacons were to serve six-year terms and were assigned to one of five sections of the city with nine other deacons and three or four pastors. The deacons were charged with aiding the pastors with religious education and the youth, with calling attention to the religious and material needs of which they were aware, with seeking resources for charitable work, with distributing aid, and with whatever else might aid the religious and moral life of the parish.[198] The deacons and pastors in each section of the city were to meet regularly and elect a president. Once a year, the deacons were to meet with the Consistory and render an account of their work.[199]

Within the first fifty years of their existence, the Genevan deacons helped establish a laundry for the poor, attempted to get city businesses to close on Sundays, requested the health department do something about poor housing, helped found an establishment for unruly children, founded a placement service for Protestant domestic servants, complained to the city about the braying of donkeys outside the church during services, recruited children for religious instruction, established meetings for boys on Sunday evenings and singing lessons for children, helped the women run classes in sewing and religion for girls, established evening classes to help students with schoolwork, established lending libraries, helped run a dispensary for women, and established an auxiliary of women charged with helping the deacons visit families.[200]

The Genevan deacons of the latter half of the nineteenth century broadly followed Calvin's conception of the diaconate. They were nonsalaried volunteers who were members of the Genevan church. They had jobs or lived from family wealth. Genevan deacons were male.

Calvin had wanted a revival of the New Testament office of widow. In modern times there were deaconesses on the Kaiserswerth model in Geneva (unmarried women in full-time service) who were connected to the Reformed churches. Some of these women came from the German-speaking areas of Switzerland. Home St. Pierre, a former deaconess home, still remains in the old city on the court of the church that was the cathedral in medieval times.

NOTES

1. Catherine M. Prelinger, "Prelude to Consciousness: Amalie Sieveking and the Female Association for the Care of the Poor and the Sick," in Fout, *German Women in the Nineteenth Century*, 122.

2. Prelinger, "Prelude to Consciousness," 122–24.

3. For a more extensive discussion of these nineteenth-century Catholic congregations, societies, and movements, see Latourette, *Christianity in a Revolutionary Age*, 1:336–48.

4. Beyreuther, *Geschichte der Diakonie*, 60–61.

5. *Lexikon für Theologie und Kirche*, s.v. "Bibelgesellschaften"; Aland, *History of Christianity*, 2:263, 345–46.

6. Aland, *History of Christianity*, 2:347–48.

7. Gerhardt, *Johann Hinrich Wichern*, 3 vols.; for some of Wichern's correspondence, see Beyreuther, *Geschichte der Diakonie*, 93; and Krimm, *Quellen zur Geschichte der Diakonie*, 2:166–98.

8. Lendtke, *Wicherns Bedeutung*.

9. For Wichern's hesitation to call the brothers "deacons," see Schering, *Erneuerung der Diakonie*, 66ff. See also Frederick Herzog, "Diakonia in Modern Times, Eighteenth-Twentieth Centuries," in McCord and Parker, *Service in Christ*, 141n5.

10. Herzog, "Diakonia in Modern Times," 141.

11. Rünger, *Die männliche Diakonie*, 71–236.

12. Krimm, "Der Diakon in den Evangelischen Kirchen," in Rahner and Vorgrimler, *Diaconia in Christo*, 198.

13. Gohde and Haas, *Wichern erinnern*.

14. "Der Prophet ohne Gemeinde," in *Gesegnetes Werk* (Berlin: Wichern-Verlag Herbert Renner, 1948); Gerhardt, *Wichern und sein Werk*.

15. Lohbeck, *Andreas Bräm*.

16. Bergendoff, *Church of the Lutheran Reformation*, 213.

17. Aland, *History of Christianity*, 2:348–49.

18. Collins, *Diakonia*, 8.

19. Aland, *History of Christianity*, 2:349–50.

20. Bergendoff, *Church of the Lutheran Reformation*, 210–11.

21. For Löhe on the Inner Mission, see Götz, *Wilhelm Löhe*, 73–77; Merz, "Löhe und die Innere Mission," 226–31. For Inner Mission and deaconess work, see Kressel, *Löhe: Ein Lebensbild*, 59–67; Schäfer, *Löhe*, 179–207.

22. Eichner, *Wilhelm Löhe*, 85–132; Kressel, *Löhe als Prediger*, 137–39; Kressel, *Löhe der lutherische Missionär*; Delitzsch, *Vier Bücher von der Kirche*.

23. Schaaf, "Löhe's Relation to the American Church"; Heintzen, *Love Leaves Home*.

24. Lenker, *Lutherans in All Lands*, 121, 135, 137–38.

25. For a short biography of Theodore Fliedner, see Wentz, *Fliedner the Faithful*; Sticker, *Theodor Fliedner*.

26. Nightingale, *Institution of Kaiserswerth*, 11.

27. Pierard, "Bedfellows of Revival," 24.

28. Herzel, *One Call*, 22.

29. Herzel, *One Call*, 22.

30. Lenker, *Lutherans in All Lands*, 135, 137–38.

31. Herzog, "Diakonia in Modern Times," 141–42, 142n2.

32. Rasche, "Deaconess Sisters," 103.

33. Lenker, *Lutherans in All Lands*, 123, 135.

34. For more on the subject of nineteenth-century girls' schools, see Joanne Schneider, "Enlightened Reforms and Bavarian Girls' Education," in Fout, *German Women in the Nineteenth Century*, 55–71; Schneider, "Das Schülerlebnis der bayerischen Mädchen," 205–18.

35. Golder, *Deaconess Motherhouse*, 84–85.

36. Nightingale, *Institution of Kaiserswerth*, 32n.

37. Prelinger, *Charity, Challenge, and Change*, 168.

38. Bancroft, *Deaconesses in Europe*, 83–84.

39. Meyer, *Deaconesses* (2d ed.), 35, 40.

40. Bancroft, *Deaconesses in Europe*, 91.

41. Sophie Eberle, quoted in Prelinger and Keller, "Function of Female Bonding," 2:322.

42. Nightingale, *Institution of Kaiserswerth*, 22.

43. Quoted in Prelinger, *Charity, Challenge, and Change*, 19, 27n39.

44. The Sisters of Notre Dame de Namur, founded on February 2, 1804, are among those who can inherit property and pass it on to someone other than the order itself; from Anne O'Donnell, sister of Notre Dame de Namur and professor, Catholic University, interview by author, Philadelphia, Pennsylvania, 7 September 2003.

45. Lenker, *Lutherans in All Lands*, 145.

46. Prelinger, *Charity, Challenge, and Change*, 20–21.

47. Prelinger and Keller, "Function of Female Bonding," 2:321.

48. Nightingale, *Institution of Kaiserwerth*, 23.

49. Rasche, "Deaconess Sisters," 106.

50. Nightingale, *Institution of Kaiserswerth*, 23–24; Vossen, *Florence Nightingale*.

51. Prelinger, *Charity, Challenge, and Change*, 18, 21.

52. Prelinger and Keller, "Function of Female Bonding," 2:322.

53. For more on the deaconess and deacon homes as paternal and patriarchal, see Jäger, *Diakonie als christliches Unternehmen*, 128–29.

54. Prelinger, *Charity, Challenge, and Change*, 21.

55. Nightingale, *Institution of Kaiserswerth*, 16.

56. Prelinger, *Charity, Challenge, and Change*, 22, 30.

57. Prelinger, "Prelude to Consciousness," 121, 123; Beyreuther, *Geschichte der Diakonie*, 61.

58. Prelinger, "Prelude to Consciousness," 126, 131nn28, 35; Prelinger, *Charity, Challenge, and Change*, 22, 32.

59. Prelinger, "Prelude to Consciousness," 118–19, 123–24.

60. Nightingale, *Institution of Kaiserswerth*, 28–29.

61. Prelinger, *Charity, Challenge, and Change*, 37.

62. Golder, *History of the Deaconess Movement*, 41.

63. Prelinger, *Charity, Challenge, and Change*, 81–84.

64. Prelinger, *Charity, Challenge, and Change*, 43.

65. Johann Wichern, *Fliegende Blätter aus dem Rauhen Haus*, 4 (1847), 228, quoted in Prelinger, "Prelude to Consciousness," 126.

66. Wilhelm Löhe, *Von der Barmherzigkeit* (1860; 2d ed., 1877), 164, cited in Shober, *Treasure Houses of the Church*, 20.

67. Prelinger, *Charity, Challenge, and Change*, 22–23, 32, 41–42.

68. Nightingale, *Institution of Kaiserswerth*, 23.

69. Nightingale, *Institution of Kaiserswerth*, 33–34.

70. Prelinger, *Charity, Challenge, and Change*, 39.

71. Heinrich Sieveking, "Zur Geschichte der Geistigen Bewegung in Hamburg nach den Freiheitskriegen," *Zeitschrift des Vereins für Hamburgische Geschichte* 38 (1927): 141, quoted in Prelinger, *Charity, Challenge, and Change*, 38.

72. Prelinger, *Charity, Challenge, and Change*, 12, 22.

73. Frederick William IV, as quoted in Golder, *History of the Deaconess Movement*, 44.

74. Lenker, *Lutherans in All Lands*, 138.

75. Golder, *History of the Deaconess Movement*, 68.

76. Friedrich Froebel (1782–1852), founder of the modern kindergarten, believed that children should be educated without teaching them Christian dogmatics.

77. Prelinger, *Charity, Challenge, and Change*, 22.

78. See the etching of the deaconess house at Kaiserswerth (1861) in Lenker, *Lutherans in All Lands*, 131.

79. Lenker, *Lutherans in All Lands*, 137.

80. Meyer, *Deaconesses*, 36.

81. Golder, *History of the Deaconess Movement*, 66–67, 73–74.

82. Lenker, *Lutherans in All Lands*, 145.

83. Prelinger, *Charity, Challenge, and Change*, 21.

84. Golder, *History of the Deaconess Movement*, 70–71; Lenker, *Lutherans in All Lands*, 606–7.

85. Nightingale, *Institution of Kaiserswerth*, 10, 32.

86. For a history of the deaconess movement in Austria, see Reiner, *Das Amt der Gemeindeschwester am Beispiel der Diözese Oberösterreich*.

87. Fliedner died October 4, 1864. See Wacker, *Deaconess Calling*, 68; for Fliedner's correspondence see Krimm, *Quellen zur Geschichte der Diakonie*, 2:198–229.

88. The figures for 1910 are fifty motherhouses and 14,945 sisters, according to Thiele, *Diakonissenhäuser im Umbruch der Zeit*, 26. The number of motherhouses that he records as being members of the Kaiserswerth Conference is lower than the seventy-five that Christian Golder records for 1901; see "Statistics of the Evangelical Deaconess Mother Houses belonging to the Kaiserswerth Conference, 1901," in Golder, *History of the Deaconess Movement*, 603–4.

89. For Fliedner's wives, see Sticker, *Friederike und Karoline Fliedner*.

90. Bancroft, *Deaconesses in Europe*, 72.

91. Golder, *History of the Deaconess Movement*, 50.

92. Spaeth, *Deaconess and Her Work*, 47.

93. Theodore Fliedner, as quoted in Golder, *History of the Deaconess Movement*, 49.

94. Pierard, "Bedfellows of Revival," 24; Sticker, *Friederike Fliedner und die Anfänge der Frauendiakonie*.

95. Wacker, *Deaconess Calling*, 66.

96. Golder, *History of the Deaconess Movement*, 64.

97. Lenker, *Lutherans in All Lands*, 64–65, 140–42.

98. Golder, *History of the Deaconess Movement*, 83; Prelinger, *Charity, Challenge, and Change*, 32–33.

99. For correspondence between Theodore Fliedner and Gossner, see Krimm, *Quellen zur Geschichte der Diakonie*, 2:205–6.

100. Weiser, *Love's Response*, 45.

101. Golder, *History of the Deaconess Movement*, 83–84.

102. Bancroft, *Deaconesses in Europe*, 93–94.

103. For excerpts from Franz Heinrich Härter, see Krimm, *Quellen zur Geschichte der Diakonie*, 2:354–61.

104. Golder, *History of the Deaconess Movement*, 81.

105. Weiser, *Love's Response*, 45.

106. Bancroft, *Deaconesses in Europe*, 72.

107. Golder, *History of the Deaconess Movement*, 75–76.

108. Golder, *History of the Deaconess Movement*, 77–79, 84.

109. Herbert Krimm, "Erneuerung im 19. Jahrhundert?" in Krimm, *Das diakonische Amt der Kirche*, 355.

110. Krimm, "Erneuerung im 19. Jahrhundert?" 91–92, 113. Works on or by Löhe include Shober, "Loehe: Witness of the Living Lutheran Church," 98–99; Kantzenbach, *Wilhelm Löhe*; Beyreuther, *Geschichte der Diakonie*, 76; Kantzenbach, *Wilhelm Löhe die Kirche in ihrer Bewegung Mission Diakonie*. For correspondence by Löhe on Neuendettelsau, see Löhe, *Etwas aus der Geschichte des Diaconissenhauses Neuendettelsau*.

111. Löhe, quoted in Weiser, *Love's Response*, 136–37.

112. Wacker, *Deaconess Calling*, 101.

113. Shober, *Treasure Houses of the Church*, 27–28, 37, 44, 103–4.

114. Shober, "Loehe: Witness of the Living Lutheran Church," 101, 104. For Wilhelm Löhe and deaconesses, see Götz, *Wilhelm Löhe*, 84–114; Kressel, *Löhe: Der lutherische Christenmensch*, 61–66; Shober, *Löhe: Ein Zeuge lebendiger lutherischer Kirche*, 83–92.

115. Matthies, *Wilhelm Löhe*, 103–5.

116. Frederick Weiser lists the founding date as 1854; see *Love's Response*, 46.

117. Golder, *History of the Deaconess Movement*, 99–101.

118. Golder, *History of the Deaconess Movement*, 113–34.

119. Golder, *History of the Deaconess Movement*, 114.

120. Golder, *History of the Deaconess Movement*, 113–15.

121. Golder, *History of the Deaconess Movement*, 84–88, 99; Weiser, *Love's Response*, 46; Weiser, *To Serve the Lord*, 11.

122. Golder, *History of the Deaconess Movement*, 106–11.

123. Golder, *History of the Deaconess Movement*, 111–12, 114–18.

124. Golder, *History of the Deaconess Movement*, 103–5, 118.

125. Golder, *History of the Deaconess Movement*, 96, 114–15.

126. Golder, *History of the Deaconess Movement*, passim; Lenker, *Lutherans in All Lands*, passim.

127. Golder, *History of the Deaconess Movement*, 111–12.

128. For selections from Bodelschwingh, see Krimm, *Quellen zur Geschichte der Diakonie*, 2:448–53.

129. Golder, *History of the Deaconess Movement*, 88–89; Beyreuther, *Geschichte der Diakonie*, 141–51.

130. For example, Schäfer, *Die Geschichte der weiblichen Diakonie*; Schäfer, *Wilhelm Löhe*.

131. Golder, *History of the Deaconess Movement*, 96–99.

132. Golder, *History of the Deaconess Movement*, 101–3.

133. Golder, *History of the Deaconess Movement*, 105–6.

134. Golder, *History of the Deaconess Movement*, 122–25.

135. Golder, *History of the Deaconess Movement*, 119–21.

136. Golder, *History of the Deaconess Movement*, 208–9; Weiser, *Love's Response*, 45.

137. Prelinger, *Charity, Challenge, and Change*, 32.

138. Bancroft, *Deaconesses in Europe*, 125, 127–32.

139. Meyer, *Deaconesses*, 40.

140. Golder, *History of the Deaconess Movement*, 209–12.

141. Golder, *History of the Deaconess Movement*, 212–13.

142. Bancroft, *Deaconesses in Europe*, 139.

143. Golder, *History of the Deaconess Movement*, 213–14.

144. Meyer, *Deaconesses*, 40.

145. Golder, *History of the Deaconess Movement*, 215–16; Weiser, *Love's Response*, 45.

146. Golder, *History of the Deaconess Movement*, 217–18.

147. Golder, *History of the Deaconess Movement*, 219–20.

148. Golder, *History of the Deaconess Movement*, 220–21.

149. Bancroft, *Deaconesses in Europe*, 104.

150. Theodore Fliedner, quoted in Golder, *History of the Deaconess Movement*, 221–22.

151. Golder, *History of the Deaconess Movement*, 222.

152. Lee, *As among the Methodists*, 19; Golder, *History of the Deaconess Movement*, 222–26.

153. Golder, *History of the Deaconess Movement*, 226–29.

154. Golder, *History of the Deaconess Movement*, 229.

155. Golder, *History of the Deaconess Movement*, 229–32.

156. Frederick Weiser lists 1849 as the date of its founding; see *Love's Response*, 45–46.

157. Golder, *History of the Deaconess Movement*, 248.

158. Brodd, "Deacon in the Church of Sweden," 103.

159. Brodd, "Deacon in the Church of Sweden," 103.

160. Brodd, "Deacon in the Church of Sweden," 245–47; Weiser, *Love's Response*, 45–46.

161. Bachmann and Bachmann, *Lutheran Churches in the World*, 410.

162. Golder, *History of the Deaconess Movement*, 247–48; Weiser, *Love's Response*, 46; "The Deaconess Institutions in Scandinavia: Norway," *Diakonia News* 78 (July 1990): 16–17.

163. Meland, "Deacon in the Church of Norway," 65–67.

164. Meland, "Deacon in the Church of Norway," 67.

165. Pohjolainen, "Deacon in the Evangelical-Lutheran Church of Finland," 143–44.

166. "The Deaconess Institutions in Scandinavia: Finland," *Diakonia News* 78 (July 1990): 18; Golder, *History of the Deaconess Movement*, 237–38.

167. Pohjolainen, "Deacon in the Evangelical-Lutheran Church of Finland," 142.

168. "The Deaconess Institutions in Scandinavia: Finland," 18; Golder, *History of the Deaconess Movement*, 237–38.

169. Pohjolainen, "Deacon in the Evangelical-Lutheran Church of Finland," 145.

170. Golder, *History of the Deaconess Movement*, 232–36.

171. Golder, *History of the Deaconess Movement*, 239–41; "Deaconess Institutions in Scandinavia: Finland," 18.

172. Golder, *History of the Deaconess Movement*, 242–43.

173. Bancroft, *Deaconesses in Europe*, 105.

174. Golder, *History of the Deaconess Movement*, 243–45.

175. "Constitution," in Golder, *History of the Deaconess Movement*, 570.

176. Bancroft, *Deaconesses in Europe*, 112.

177. Golder, *History of the Deaconess Movement*, 128–34, 136.

178. Meyer, *Deaconesses*, 40.

179. Golder, *History of the Deaconess Movement*, 134, 136–42; Bancroft, *Deaconesses in Europe*, 113–14.

180. Meyer, *Deaconesses*, 39.

181. Golder, *History of the Deaconess Movement*, 141–46.

182. "Journal of the General Conference of 1888," 435, and "Report IV," 246, 292, in Golder, *History of the Deaconess Movement*, 151–52.

183. Golder, *History of the Deaconess Movement*, 152–58.

184. Lee, *As among the Methodists*, 23–24.

185. Golder, *History of the Deaconess Movement*, 165–68.

186. Golder, *History of the Deaconess Movement*, 159–65.

187. See "Statistics of the Evangelical Deaconess Mother Houses belonging to the Kaiser-swerth Conference, 1901," in Golder, *History of the Deaconess Movement*, 603–4. These statistics listed seventy-five motherhouses in the conference with 14,501 sisters.

188. Prelinger and Keller, "Function of Female Bonding," 324.

189. Meyer, *Deaconesses*, 35.

190. Golder, *History of the Deaconess Movement*, 90–91.

191. "Constitution of the Deaconess Mother House Connected with the General Confer-ence of Kaiserswerth Adopted by the Thirteenth General Conference on the 18th and 19th of September, 1901," in Golder, *History of the Deaconess Movement*, 571–72.

192. "Constitution of the Deaconess Mother House Connected with the General Confer-ence of Kaiserswerth," in Golder, *History of the Deaconess Movement*, 571–72.

193. Henderson, *Presbyterianism*, 83–85, 87–88, 140.

194. At the general meeting of the deacons of Geneva on November 27, 1900, Henri Heyer expressed regret that the French Fund had been absorbed by the General Hospice; see Église Nationale Protestante de Genève, *Les Diaconies de la ville de Genève*, 10, 61.

195. Grandjean, "La Bourse Française de Genève," 58–60.

196. Heyer, *L'Église de Genève*, 74nn1, 75.

197. "Règlement sur l'institution de Diaconies dans la ville de Genève du 4 avril 1850. Le Consistoire, Vu les rapports de MM. les Pasteurs . . . plusieurs d'entre eux expriment le voeu d'une institution de diacres chargés de les seconder dans le soin des pauvres et la surveillance de la jeunesse. . . . Des diaconies sont instituées par le Consistoire dans la ville de Genève, pour s'occuper de concert avec les pasteurs des intérêts religieux et moraux, et des oeuvres de bienfaisance." ("Regulation on the institution of diaconates in the city of Geneva of 4 April 1850. The Consistory saw the reports of Monsieurs the pastors . . . several among them express the desire for an institution of deacons charged with assisting them in the care of the poor and the surveillance of the youth. . . . Dia-conates are instituted by the Consistory in the city of Geneva in order to look after, in concert with the pastors, religious and moral interests and the works of charity.") (Église Nationale Protestante de Genève, *Les Diaconies de la ville de Genève*, 27).

198. "Les diacres sont chargés d'aider les pasteurs dans la surveillance de l'éducation religieuse de la jeunesse, de signaler les besoins religieux et matériels qui viennent à leur connaissance, de prendre part à la recherche des ressources pour les oeuvres de bienfaisance, à la distribution des secours, et généralement à tous les efforts ayant pour object la moralité de la paroisse et tendant à y propager la vie chrétienne." ("The deacons are charged with aiding the pastors in the surveillance of religious education of the youth, with signaling the religious and material needs that come to their atten-tion, with taking part in the search for resources for charitable works, with the distrib-ution of aid, and generally with every effort that has as its object the morality of the

parish and tends to propagate the Christian life.") (Église Nationale Protestante de Genève, *Les Diaconies de la ville de Genève*, 28).

199. Église Nationale Protestante de Genève, *Les Diaconies de la ville de Genève*, 28.

200. Louis Johannot, "L'activité des Diaconies de 1850 à 1900," in Église Nationale Protestante de Genève, *Les Diaconies de la ville de Genève*, 36–46.

CHAPTER SIX

The Nineteenth Century

NEW FORMS OF THE DIACONATE
IN THE BRITISH EMPIRE AND NORTH AMERICA

Deaconess work in Britain began with members of the Church of England; only later did it spread to Methodists and Scottish Presbyterians. In many ways England appeared to be a fertile field for the deaconess movement. Women there already were engaged in similar work under the inspiration of leaders of the Church of England—such as Hannah More (1745–1833)—and the Society of Friends—such as Elizabeth Fry (died 1845). There also was the example of Catholic nuns, whom the British encountered on the continent during the Napoleonic Wars. British women were active in the antislavery movement, missionary work, the temperance movement, and the Salvation Army. John Wesley tore down barriers that had prevented women from serving as church officers, prayer leaders, and Sunday school teachers, though Methodists, coming out of the Church of England, did not initially allow women in the ministry.[1]

Although England allowed women's charitable work, the deaconess movement did not grow as large there as it did on the European continent. One author suggested that this was because of the "less-restricted position" of women in England, inferring, perhaps, that English women could become active in society without becoming deaconesses.[2] In the field of nursing, for example, Florence Nightingale trained at Kaiserswerth, but she neither became a deaconess nor used the deaconess movement as a vehicle for making nursing a profession in England. She said of the Church of England: "She gave me neither work to do for her, nor education for it."[3] A woman could become a nurse in England without becoming a deaconess.

A smaller portion of English deaconesses were nurses than on the continent.

THE OXFORD MOVEMENT

There were other factors at work in nineteenth-century England that discouraged the development of the deaconess movement. One of these was the Oxford Movement, named after the university where it began in the 1830s. In keeping with the Romanticism of the early nineteenth century and its appreciation for the medieval church, this movement emphasized Anglicanism's Catholic rather than Protestant heritage and stressed the historical continuity of the church and the apostolic succession of bishops. The Oxford Movement spread beyond the university and brought elements in the Church of England closer to the Church of Rome in belief and practice. It produced some actual conversions to Catholicism, such as that of John Henry Newman (1801–1890), after whom Catholic university centers in North America have been named. Newman became a Catholic on October 9, 1845, and a cardinal in 1879. In the late nineteenth century, the Oxford Movement would inspire a revival of reverence for the saints, fasting, clerical celibacy, and Roman Catholic liturgical practices in the Church of England, which Episcopalians call "high church" as opposed to more Protestant "low church" practices.

A concern for the poor and neglected was part of this "high church" movement in the Church of England, as was the formation of religious orders on the model of Roman Catholic monks, nuns, and friars. These Anglican orders were called sisterhoods and brotherhoods, and they provided a communal life for English men and women who desired such an existence. These developments coincided with the foundation of homes for deacons and deaconesses in Europe.

In the early 1840s, Theodore Fliedner came to London from Kaiserswerth with four deaconesses for the German hospital, but this was a foreign import of the deaconess movement.[4] In the mid-1840s, on the wave of the Oxford Movement, Edward B. Pusey (1800–1882), a leader in the Anglo-Catholic Movement, founded a sisterhood in the suburbs of London at Park Village West, Regent's Park. This was an indigenous development.[5] Despite hostility to "Puseyite nunneries," religious communities spread in the Church of England and continue to the present. Some of these communities are contemplative, some are active in the world, and others are mixed.[6] By 1875 there were eighteen sisterhoods in the Church of England in ninety-five centers. Ten years later there were about thirty sisterhoods and more than 1,300 sisters. The sisters performed the same functions as deaconesses: They were nurses, teachers, social workers, and parish workers, especially in Anglo-Catholic parishes. In 1875 there were more than a thousand sick in their care, and they provided the entire staff for three London hospitals. These sisters nursed people in their homes, helped more than a thousand former prostitutes, and taught six thousand children.[7] Like Roman Catholic nuns, the Church of England sisterhoods took perpetual vows, wore a nun's garb, and lived in communities with mother superiors to whom they owed obedience. The sisterhoods grew much faster in England than the deaconess movement.

Members of brotherhoods in the Church of England were similar to Roman Catholic brothers or monks. The work of some of the English brotherhoods was similar to that of the deacons of the Inner Mission movement in Germany, but the men were not called deacons. Similar to the Roman Catholic model, the diaconate in the Church of England was an office for men on the way to becoming priests.

BIBLE WOMEN, PARISH MISSION WOMEN, CHURCH ARMY WOMEN, MISSIONARIES

What the Oxford Movement did on the "high church" end of the spectrum of English church life to attract men and women into full-time service, the Salvation Army and, to some extent, the Young Men's and Young Women's Christian Association did on the "low church" end of the spectrum. In addition, the Church of England offered opportunities for women to serve, diminishing the pool of candidates for the role of deaconess. Church work in Victorian England was largely philanthropic, but there also were some women in paid positions. Volunteers were largely "leisured women" who were Sunday school teachers, parish visitors of the poor and shut-ins, girls' club organizers, and members of societies to support foreign missions or temperance. Bible Women, parochial mission women, Church Army Mission women, and foreign missionaries were paid.[8]

Bible Women were poor people who reached out to even poorer people. The Bible Women movement began in the 1850s at the instigation of Ellen Henrietta Raynard (1810–1879), a philanthropist and longtime member of the Bible Society. She founded the London Female Bible and Domestic Mission or Raynard Mission. It trained poor women to work among the poor and paid them, in the early period, ten shillings each week for five hours a day, five days a week. These women of humble social rank visited the very poor and evangelized those whom the church had failed to reach. Bible Women did much the same work in parish visitation as the wealthier volunteers but at a lower social level. In 1858 there were seven Bible Women; in 1867 there were 234. In 1868 Ellen Raynard started a nurses' division, which for some Bible Women added three months of hospital training to the customary three-month training period. The movement was nonsectarian but received substantial support from the Church of England.[9]

Bible Women and parochial mission women were parallel groups, but the parochial mission women had closer ties to the Church of England. Caroline Jane Talbot (1809–1876) founded the parochial mission movement in 1860. She wanted work with the poor to be an integral part of the Anglican Church. Parochial mission women and Bible Women sold Bibles, visited the poor, established soup kitchens and clothing clubs, and extended the ministry of the clergy working in the parish. In the 1880s, there were more than two hundred Bible Women and more than two hundred parochial mission women working in London.[10]

The Church Army was inspired by the Salvation Army. Both organizations were known for their street-level approach. Church Army literature proclaims it as "a worldwide Society of Evangelists that started in England in 1882 as a domestic mission arm of the Anglican Church."[11] A women's branch of the Church Army developed in 1887. These women were not supposed to preach, but they provided nursing care, assisted at meetings, organized sea missions and medical missions, visited women's prisons, and attempted a mission to barmaids. The first women who joined were single and from the middle-class, but soon the Church Army was recruiting among shop workers and domestic servants.[12] (The Church Army would spread across the world in the twentieth century. Its current U.S. headquarters is in Pittsburgh, Pennsylvania.)[13]

Thus in the last half of the nineteenth century, English women could enter paid church work as Bible Women, parochial mission women, or Church Army women. These three groups recruited from the lower classes. Some middle-class women sought to become foreign missionaries, but the two largest Anglican missionary societies were hesitant to send women abroad unless they were the wives or sisters of male missionaries. In 1867 the Society for the Propagation of the Gospel (S.P.G.) finally assigned an unmarried female missionary to Madagascar, and she took up her post in 1874. In the 1890s, the S.P.G. began training unmarried women on a larger scale, but it was not until the twentieth century that it sent these women abroad as a general policy. The Church Missionary Society accepted unmarried women as missionaries earlier. In 1819 it sent two women to

Sierra Leone, but not until the 1880s did it recruit women on a large scale.[14]

In addition, there were various opportunities for women generated by volunteer organizations. An association of women called the Sisters of the People worked in London. Twelve of the sisters lived together in Katherine House; the others resided in their own homes as "out sisters." The Prison Gate Mission, founded in 1866, met prisoners as they were released and offered them food and employment.[15]

THE DEACONESS MOVEMENT IN ENGLAND

Despite these alternate channels of church work for women, a deaconess movement did arise in England in the mid-nineteenth century. In 1858 the Convocation of Clergymen of the Church of England applauded the progress made and considered the question of establishing rules and regulations for deaconesses in the Church of England. The convocation appointed a committee to study the matter. Thirteen years later, in 1871, the Church of England finally embodied the deaconess in its church organization and defined her as "a woman set apart by a bishop under that title, for service in the Church."[16]

While the Church of England was reviewing the issue of deaconesses (1858–1871), the movement continued to develop, helped along by the power of individual bishops to allow movements within their own dioceses that did not exist everywhere in the church. William Pennefather, a priest of the Church of England, and his wife, Catherine, visited Theodore Fliedner in Kaiserswerth in 1860. Upon their return to England, the Pennefathers founded the Training Home for Female Missionaries. In 1861 the bishop of London sanctioned designating these women as deaconesses. Only a few were episcopally admitted to the office, and they worked chiefly in British colonies.[17] Also in 1861, Elizabeth Ferard and two other women (Ellen Meredith and Anna Wilcox) began to live together under common rules, including dedication to worship and works of mercy; thus they effectively began a community of deaconesses. On St. Andrew's Day 1861, the deaconess institution opened, though the women were not yet formally recognized as deaconesses by the Church of England.[18]

In 1862 Dean J. S. Howson of Wells, a diligent supporter of English deaconesses and a lecturer at Cambridge, published *Deaconesses or the Official Help of Women in Parochial Work and in Charitable Institutions*.[19] This was followed by *Deaconesses in the Church of England* (1880) and *The Diaconate of*

Women (1886). Although Howson advocated "setting apart" deaconesses by the imposition of hands, he found

> no proof that the earliest Deaconesses were necessarily chosen for life, or necessarily precluded from marriage, or even necessarily everywhere appointed by laying on of hands. . . . If women are professionally and officially employed in works of religion and charity under the direction of the clergy, and if they have the general recognition of the Bishops, this sufficiently satisfies the conditions of the Primitive Female Diaconate.[20]

In 1862 A. C. Tait, bishop of London, who later became archbishop of Canterbury, set apart Elizabeth Ferard, a member of an old Huguenot family who was connected to Tait by marriage, as the first deaconess in the Church of England.[21] He issued to her "Deaconess License Number 1" on July 18, 1862. Bishop Tait had visited Kaiserswerth on August 14, 1855.[22] His action in setting apart Elizabeth Ferard as a deaconess established a model in the Church of England for bishop initiative in the commissioning of deaconesses. These women then served under the bishop in his diocese at his behest and became diocesan deaconesses, many of whom engaged in parish work. Elizabeth Ferard had intended that deaconesses share a common life, but the great majority of deaconesses in England were "unattached."[23] The phrase "non-community deaconesses" described these women, who differed from the sisters of Kaiserswerth in their living arrangements and because they were responsible to a bishop.[24]

Elizabeth Ferard experienced community living after the death of her mother. She visited Kaiserswerth on September 12, 1856, and returned to Kaiserswerth from August 28, 1858, through at least December 13.[25] At Kaiserswerth she had wanted to learn nursing but was switched from department to department to "observe."[26] When Ferard was distressed by the disagreeable aspects of nursing, Fliedner commented that a deaconess institution could not succeed in England "until English ladies gave up the expectation of having everything disagreeable done by servants."[27] In fact, unlike Kaiserswerth, Elizabeth Ferard felt that it was better if deaconesses were taken from the better educated ranks of society.

Ferard's community became the North London Deaconess Institute.[28] By 1863 the community, modeled after Kaiserswerth, had three deaconesses, six candidates, and eight assistants. The institute adopted a modification of Kaiserswerth dress and rules,[29] and Fliedner sent a Kaiserswerth deaconess to train the sisters, though morning and evening prayer were from the *Book of Common Prayer* of the Church of England. Time also was set aside for private prayer and meditation. First, a woman became a provisional sister; then she spent two years as a candidate before admission to the order. The first deaconesses worked as nurses, parish workers, and teachers. The deaconess society took charge of the nursing department at the Great Northern Hospital, worked in parishes "of great poverty," and took charge of an infants' and girls' school. The supply of deaconesses could not meet the demand.[30]

The North London Deaconess Institute was not the first religious community of women in the Church of England. By the mid-1870s, six dioceses of the Church of England had deaconess training homes. The number of deaconesses in England increased slowly, however. Twenty years after the commissioning of Elizabeth Ferard, there were only sixty deaconesses.[31] There was some resistance to so-called "Popish Communities." To meet such charges, the deaconesses emphasized the advantages of community life and the absence of vows or of seclusion from friends and society. In 1869 the title of the North London Deaconess Institute was changed to the London Diocesan Deaconess Institution, clarifying its role as an integral part of the London diocese. It also trained some unattached deaconesses who worked under the authority of the bishop.[32]

In 1873 the community of deaconesses moved to St. Andrew's House, Tavistock Crescent, Westbourne Park, the address that readers for years became accustomed to seeing on *Diakonia News*.[33] In 1877 the facility's chapel was built.[34] St. Andrew's House remained the home of the community until February 2002.[35] The community founded a seaside convalescent home at Westgate, Kent, in 1876, which later was called St. Michael's.[36] By 1878 deaconesses were working in five dioceses outside London and training women for the Church of England, not only for London.[37] In 1887 the community of deaconesses adopted the "Day Hours of the Church of England," which, with almost daily Eucharist, brought the community into the worship stream of traditional religious orders, which recited the Daily Office. The title of Head Sister was changed to Mother Superior.[38]

When nursing became a profession with specialized training and attracted more women, the London Diocesan Deaconess Institution gave it up, as did other religious communities. In 1888 their nursing home, St. Gabriel's, became an "industrial school for girls." The sisters also gave up control of schools after the state became increasingly responsible for education. Elementary education in England was made free for all in 1891.[39] The deaconesses also expanded into the world. In the 1880s, Sister Edith went to New Zealand to found a deaconess community that became a sisterhood in Christchurch, which survived into the modern world.[40] In 1888 deaconesses were sent to Japan, and in 1894 they were sent to South Africa.[41]

English deaconess institutions had larger numbers of associates who worked like deaconesses but without the length of commitment of a deaconess. In a book published in 1890, Jane Bancroft, an American supporter of the deaconess movement, observed that the deaconess movement in England attracted women of a higher social status than those in Germany. Some of the English deaconess homes employed servants to do housework whereas German deaconesses did their own housekeeping.[42] In the latter half of the twentieth century, however, the situation in the Deaconess Community of St. Andrew was different. When Sister Teresa (Joan White) came to the community in 1970, the deaconesses were doing almost all the domestic work in the house. The only outside staff were two part-time cleaners. In the 1980s and 1990s, the deaconesses had caretakers for the infirm when none of the deaconesses were capable of lifting them, but only in the late 1990s did the community employ a female cook, whom they worked alongside in the kitchen.[43]

By the end of the nineteenth century, diocesan deaconess institutions in the Church of England included Bedford and Chester (1869), Canterbury (1874), Salisbury (1875), Winchester (at Portsmouth) (1879), East London (1880), Durham (1883), Rochester (1887), which joined with Southwark (1891), Exeter (1890), and Llandaff in Penarth (1893). After the foundation of the Rochester Deaconess Institution, noncommunity deaconesses increased.[44]

Besides these diocesan deaconesses, there were those of William Pennefather (died 1873). While rector of Christ's Church at Barnet, he began an outreach centered around annual ecumenical conferences (1856). In 1864 Pennefather moved to St. Jude's Church in Mildmay Park in London, and his projects relocated with him. At first he trained women as foreign missionaries, but after 1866, the training was directed more toward work in England. Pennefather initially called the women he trained "sisters." Later he called them deaconesses.[45]

Advocates of episcopal admission of deaconesses in the Church of England considered Pennefather's deaconesses to be different from what Anglican deaconesses should be, especially because Pennefather came to ignore denominational distinctions and accept women from various Protestant groups.[46] A Lambeth Conference[47] (1897) committee on "The Relation of Religious Communities to the Episcopate" stated that "care should be taken to prevent the application, within the limits of our Communion, of the term 'Deaconess' to any woman other than one who has, in accordance with primitive usage, been duly set apart to her office by the Bishop himself."[48] An Anglican deaconess abbreviated this to read: "Where a bishop will not ordain, there is no deaconess."[49] At first the Church of England commissioned, or "set apart," deaconesses. In the mid-twentieth century it ordained them.

Pennefather's movement prospered, despite its limited support from the Church of England. A motherhouse was built in 1870. The community at Mildmay included a hospital, a nursing home, a probation house, a junior deaconess home, a home for elderly workers, a home for children, a home for servants, and a large conference hall for the gatherings of the Mildmay Conference of pastors and church workers. The hall also housed a night school, a library, and Bible classes. Like Kaiserswerth, Mildmay also trained people who did not become deaconesses. In 1884 those being trained at Mildmay for foreign work transferred to Kennaway Hall, Stoke Newington. Women from Mildmay worked among prostitutes, sponsored a refuge on Trinity Street for young women, established homes for convalescents in Barnet and Bright, set up a registry for the unemployed, and staffed a hospital in Bethnal Green. By 1899 the Mildmay Mission had 250 deaconesses and nurses.[50] It had stations in Malta, Jamaica, and Hebron.[51] Jane Bancroft, the Methodist supporter of deaconesses, stated that no deaconess institution "will perhaps furnish more practical models for American Methodism" than that of Mildmay.[52]

By the end of the nineteenth century, the only English motherhouse that maintained membership in the Kaiserswerth Union was at Tottenham, a suburb of London. Michael Laseron, who was born in Königsberg [Kaliningrad], founded this deaconess home in 1877 to staff a home and hospital for children that he and his wife had established after the death of their only child in 1855. The first sister of this motherhouse was from Bethanien, the deaconess home in Berlin. The first head deaconess was from Kaiserswerth. The institution adopted the garb, regulations, and government of Kaiserswerth. Deaconesses trained at Tottenham superintended hospitals in England, Scotland, Ireland, Palestine, and Sierra Leone. In addition to hospital nursing and private nursing, the deaconesses of this community had an orphanage, a girls' home, night schools, sewing schools, kindergartens, and a school for servants.[53]

The British Empire and Commonwealth

Anglican churches founded deaconess institutions throughout the British Empire and Commonwealth. The first Anglican deaconess in South Africa was Cecile Isherwood. She came from England and was ordained at the age of 20, after volunteering for service in 1883. She helped found St. Peter's Home in Grahamstown and the Community of the Resurrection, which was organized as a sisterhood but made no claim to be a deaconess community. In 1894 the sisterhood set up the Grahamstown Training School to train teachers. These women exercised considerable influence on education in South Africa.[54]

Deaconess work in Australia began in Melbourne in 1884 with the founding of a training school. The first Anglican deaconess in Australia was ordained on July 16, 1886.[55] The Anglican deaconesses of Australia did rescue work in the slums, worked in parishes, and were responsible for a children's home and a home for female prisoners. The community developed along the lines of a sisterhood, then closed for lack of recruits some years later. In 1891 the largest of the Australian deaconess institutions was founded in Sydney. It was a training school, and the deaconesses were involved in Christian education, social work, and, at the beginning, nursing. Connected to this training school were a number of institutions, including a children's home and a home for poor women. Several deaconesses also worked in Tasmania.[56]

According to Janet Grierson, historian of the Anglican deaconesses, the Kingston [Jamaica] Deaconess Institution was founded in 1889, but the Anglican Deaconess Order, Diocese of Jamaica, celebrated a centenary on November 14, 1990. The Kingston Deaconess Institution was staffed primarily by women trained at Mildmay. The deaconesses from the Kingston institution were active in founding schools and educational work.[57]

In Canada in 1893, Mildmay-trained volunteers helped establish the Church of England Deaconess and Missionary Training House in Toronto. The Methodist Episcopal Church also founded a deaconess home in the city (1894), and the Presbyterians founded a deaconess training school. Thus Toronto was a center of deaconess work in Canada.[58] Also in 1893, Sister Edith Mellish of the London Diocesan Deaconess Institution founded a community of deaconesses in Christchurch, New Zealand. The sisters engaged in teaching and nursing.[59]

In 1896 Bishop Matthew of Lahore (now Pakistan) initiated deaconess work for the Protestant Episcopal Church of India with the ordination of Deaconess Katherine Beynon, the daughter of a British major general in Rajputana. Beynon became the first head of the Society of St. Hilda, a group dedicated to educational and pastoral work. Although the first sisters came from England, Indian women also became deaconesses.[60]

Already in the nineteenth century, like their Methodist counterparts, Anglican deaconesses from the British Isles and Episcopal deaconesses from North America had begun to work around the world, even beyond the sphere of British influence. In 1889 the London Deaconess Institution sent Margaret Butler to Japan, where she was the sister in charge of the St. Hilda's Mission in Tokyo. Although Japan's deaconesses came largely from the United States, deaconesses from England did significant work in China. In 1897 the deaconess house St. Faith's was founded in Peking. Deaconesses staffed schools and dispensaries in China and engaged in evangelism work.[61]

METHODISTS AND BAPTISTS IN ENGLAND

Among the Methodists in England, deaconess work began later than similar efforts in the Church of England. There also were Baptist deaconesses in Bloomsbury. In 1888 Hugh Price Hughes, a Methodist minister, and his wife, Catherine, rented a house near the British Museum that was large enough for twelve women. Hughes preferred to call the women "sisters" rather than "deaconesses." Recent centenary celebrations, however, considered 1890 rather than 1888 to be the year Methodist deaconess work began in England.[62] By 1891 the house was too small, and the sisters moved to Viceroy Square. These women ministered to people in the slums of London. They visited homes, conducted kindergartens and nurseries, maintained a home for servant girls and a labor bureau, conducted boys' and girls' clubs and youth groups, and established temperance societies and a "Sheen Society" to collect and distribute clothing. The Methodist sisters invited poor people into their own household for meals.[63]

In 1890 Thomas Bowman Stephenson, a Wesleyan Methodist pastor, organized deaconess work and training in connection with care for orphans that eventually became the National Children's Home. The Wesleyan Deaconess Order had training schools in London and Leicester. They used city hospitals as training sites for nurses. The Wesleyan Methodist sisters served throughout England and in South Africa, New Zealand, and Ceylon (Sri Lanka). The annual reports described their work as that of a "nurse, teacher, visiter [sic], even preacher when necessary."[64] The year he founded the Deaconess Order, Stephenson had suggested that preaching might be necessary for the deaconesses in the context of their work in villages, though the title "Wesley Deaconess-Evangelist" was not used officially until 1901, when it was applied to Sister Jeanie Banks.[65] From 1896 until she died in 1932, Deaconess Banks was engaged in "evangelistic work" that included nursing and open-air preaching, but the Wesleyan deaconesses were not an order of preachers.[66] In 1908 only two of the 160 Wesleyan deaconesses conducted evangelistic services: Jeanie Banks and Helen Fieldson.[67]

In 1891 another minister, T. J. Cope, founded the United Methodist Free Church deaconesses.[68] This denomination was the result of an 1857 amalgamation of three groups that had separated from the Wesleyan Methodist Church earlier in the nineteenth century: the Protestant Methodists (1827), the Methodist Association (1835), and the Wesleyan Reformers (1857).[69]

SCOTLAND

The General Assembly of the Church of Scotland established a deaconess institution in Edinburgh in 1887 through the efforts of the Reverend Archibald Hamilton Charteris (1835), professor of biblical criticism at Edinburgh University, and his Christian Life and Work Committee. The first deaconess, Lady Grisell Baillie, was installed on December 9, 1888. Thus the Scottish deaconesses, from their inception, were a part of the Presbyterian Church of Scotland. Besides the deaconess home, there was a hospital (1894), an orphanage, and St. Ninian's Mission House for inner-city work.[70]

The 1899 yearbook of the Church of Scotland indicates that Scottish deaconesses were "set apart." They promised "as a deaconess of the Church of Scotland to work in connection with that Church, subject to its Courts, and in particular to the Kirk-session of the parish" in which they worked. The women received two years of training, one of which was in the deaconess hospital. Afterward they served in one of the deaconess institutions, in a parish, or in the mission field.[71] In 1903 there were twenty-six deaconesses, six of whom were in foreign missions.[72]

LUTHERAN DEACONESSES IN NORTH AMERICA

From Europe and the British Isles the deaconess movement of the nineteenth century spread to the New World. Those who attempted initially to transplant the movement in North America followed the European model. Such was the case with William Alfred Passavant, the name associated with the founding of the deaconess movement among Lutherans in North America.

Passavant, a member of a French Huguenot family, was born on October 9, 1821, in Pennsylvania. He attended Jefferson College in Canons-

burg, Pennsylvania, and the Lutheran Seminary at Gettysburg, Pennsylvania, from which he was graduated in 1842. The Maryland Synod licensed
Passavant on October 17, 1842, and he became pastor of the First English
Lutheran Church in Pittsburgh, Pennsylvania, in 1844. He was the key
mover behind the organization of the Pittsburgh Synod (January 15, 1854).
In 1846, when Passavant was 24 years old, he went to London as a delegate
of the Evangelical Alliance, an ecumenical group. He was impressed by the
benevolent institutions in the city, especially a Jewish orphanage.[73]

Passavant visited Theodore Fliedner in Kaiserswerth and made
arrangements with Fliedner to establish deaconesses in North America.
Passavant signed the register at Kaiserswerth on October 11, 1846.[74] In his
annual report of January 1847, Fliedner indicated that Passavant "laid the
matter on our conscience with such urgency that we could but promise to
send out a number of sisters as soon as it should be possible."[75] The new
institution in the United States was to be a station of the Kaiserswerth
Motherhouse.[76] There is no concrete evidence that Passavant left money to
facilitate this, as some authors have suggested.[77] Before March 1848 and in
preparation for the deaconesses from Germany, Passavant rented a house
in Allegheny, Pennsylvania (now part of Pittsburgh), for a hospital. The
revolutions of 1848 in Europe intervened, so Passavant opened the hospital without deaconesses in January 1849. He personally recruited two
patients from a boat carrying soldiers from the Mexican War. It was the first
Protestant hospital in the United States west of the Allegheny Mountains.[78]

A cholera epidemic developed in June, and the Sisters of Charity
refused cholera victims as patients. Passavant accepted them, but Allegheny
drove the hospital out. The institution moved to a former girls' school in
Lacyville, which is now part of Pittsburgh.[79] Meanwhile, Fliedner resigned
his parish in Kaiserswerth and went to Berlin to request help from Frederick William IV, including money for a trip to the United States and the
release of Elizabeth Hupperts, the directing sister of the children's station
in Berlin, to become directing sister in Pittsburgh. Frederick William
agreed, and Fliedner took Hupperts and three other sisters to America: the
recently consecrated Paulina Ludewig, Luise Hinrichsen, and Elizabeth
Hess.[80]

Upon arriving in Pittsburgh in July 1849, the group found the hospital
ready and one probationer in place, Catharina Louisa Marthens, a member
of Passavant's congregation. Americans found the German deaconesses'
garb strange and confused them with Catholic nuns. The deaconesses were
attacked by the press. Some sources claim that public opinion forced them
to give up their deaconess garb temporarily.[81] Passavant said that "time . . .

will be necessary to wear away the prejudices even of the pious, and suffer them to look upon the Institution with favor."[82]

Nevertheless, the work moved ahead. In April 1852 an orphanage opened. On May 28, 1850, Passavant consecrated Catharina Louisa Marthens, which was the first consecration of a deaconess in the United States.[83] Upon her consecration as a deaconess, Marthens became known as Sister Louisa. On June 17, 1850, there was an organizational meeting to form a motherhouse for the deaconesses. Elizabeth Hupperts became matron of the house, and Passavant was named its director. Passavant bought property at Zelienople for an Orphans' Farm School for boys, which began in May 1854. Pastor Gottlieb Bassler supervised the school, and Sister Louisa supervised the orphanage for girls in Pittsburgh. In November 1855 G. C. Holls, who had been trained by Johannes Wichern at his *Rauhe Haus*, became housefather and headmaster at the Orphan's Farm School. That same year Passavant resigned his pastorate to devote himself full time to the institution's work, which consisted of the hospital, the orphanage, and the farm school.[84]

Passavant, Bassler, and Holls hoped to establish a training center for brothers (deacons) in connection with the Orphans' Farm School. Johannes Wichern promised six of his men from Europe, but the U.S. Civil War delayed their arrival until April 1863. Their suggestions for the institutions were not followed, however, and the men soon returned to Europe. Thus died an attempt to establish male deacons in the United States on the model of European Inner Mission.[85]

In 1861, during the Civil War, Passavant offered the services of the deaconesses, an offer the U.S. government accepted through the auspices of Dorothea Dix. Elizabeth Hupperts, Mary Keen, and Barbara Kang went to the front and nursed sick soldiers until Passavant had to recall them because of a shortage of deaconesses. The last to leave, in the fall of 1863, was Sister Barbara Kang, so valued by Dorothea Dix that she remembered her in her will.[86]

Passavant recalled Sister Barbara so she could be the matron of a hospital (dedicated August 3, 1863) that he had founded in a remodeled farmhouse in Milwaukee, Wisconsin. It was the first institution of Protestant deaconesses outside Pennsylvania. The Lutheran Deaconess Motherhouse and a congregation was organized for these women in 1893.[87] In July 1865 Passavant, with the help of deaconesses, opened a hospital in Chicago, but the building burned in the 1871 Chicago fire. The hospital reopened in 1885 as Passavant Memorial Hospital, but it did so without deaconesses.[88]

Meanwhile, the establishment of orphanages continued. In March 1859 Sister Louisa helped open an orphanage for St. Michael's Church in Germantown, Pennsylvania. Cramped for space, the girls' orphanage in Pittsburgh moved to Rochester, Pennsylvania, on November 8, 1861. In August 1869 the building of the Wartburg Farm School at Mount Vernon, New York, began. G. C. Holls became its director. In 1870 Sister Louisa went to Jacksonville, Illinois, to work in a new orphanage. It failed as an orphanage but changed to a hospital, and Sister Louisa remained as directing sister. Deaconesses from Milwaukee maintained this hospital until 1902.[89]

In Milwaukee on December 29, 1891, Passavant arrived in a wheelchair to help consecrate three deaconesses: Caroline Ochse, Martha Gensike, and Katharine Foerster. These three women became the nucleus of the Milwaukee motherhouse, which had been organized at the October 29, 1893, meeting of the Board of the Institution of Protestant Deaconesses, the last meeting of the group that Passavant attended.[90] At the consecration of the Milwaukee deaconesses, Passavant had been moved to tears because the consecration of deaconesses had been all too rare for him. At the end of his life, the Institution of Protestant Deaconesses had five deaconesses and a number of probationers, which was the same number that he had started with when Fliedner brought four women from Germany to join the one who had stepped forward from Passavant's own Pittsburgh congregation. Three of these four deaconesses from Germany had quit the work. A number of American women had come forward but not lasted beyond their probation. Others had been consecrated but left, including some European women. In thirty-five years, from 1849 to 1884, sixteen candidates entered the Pittsburgh institution. Some of these married; others found the life uncongenial. Of those who were consecrated deaconesses, most terminated their affiliation within nine years of service.

From the perspective of numbers, the deaconess movement had barely sustained itself.[91] But when one considers the institutions Passavant founded, he left a strong legacy: the Institution of Protestant Deaconesses, chartered in Illinois and Pennsylvania; orphanages at Mount Vernon, New York, and Rochester and Germantown, Pennsylvania; the Farm School at Zelienople; the motherhouse and hospital at Milwaukee; and hospitals in Chicago and Jacksonville, Illinois. Passavant died on June 4, 1894, nursed by two of his deaconesses.[92]

Critics have blamed Passavant for recruiting so few deaconesses, suggesting that he spread his efforts over too many institutions, thus not concentrating enough on the deaconesses under his care. One problem was that some of his deaconesses had less ecumenical conviction than he had.

One potential probationer, Franziska Harder, who came from a Lutheran congregation in Fort Wayne, Indiana, left because Passavant conducted open Communion services. Two deaconesses, sensitized by her example, followed.[93]

Passavant also failed to recruit many deaconesses because the institution he founded was a foreign import. Henry Jacobs, in a nineteenth-century history of Lutheranism, said that "the church was not ready for the work when introduced by Dr. Passavant." He was suspected of a "secret inclination toward Romanism."[94] The introduction of deaconesses took time to take hold, and the denomination gave Passavant moral support but not wholehearted financial backing. Champion of the cause, Passavant complained of the lack of opportunity for higher education for women. He wrote in 1852:

> We have seven theological seminaries, four classic schools, five colleges for the education of our young men, and for our women two seminaries *on paper*. That shows what little importance is attached to the education of women. Our attitude so far in this question is neither Scriptural nor just to the female sex or the Church of Christ itself.[95]

The story of deaconesses in North America was not over with the death of Passavant. The 1880s and 1890s would be more propitious for the recruiting of deaconesses in the United States than the three previous decades had been. The deaconesses at Milwaukee continued the work of the Institution of Protestant Deaconesses. Magdalene Steinmann came from Philadelphia in 1896 to be *Probemeisterin*, or training sister. The Milwaukee motherhouse was bilingual: German and English. Deaconess candidates had to be Lutheran, in good health, between 28 and 40 years of age, and they had to have the consent of their parents.[96]

With the organization of a training program in Milwaukee, the number of women in the Institution of Protestant Deaconesses grew. The largest concentration of deaconesses was at the Milwaukee hospital. By 1899 there were six deaconesses and twenty probationers.[97] In that same year, William Passavant Jr., son of the founder of the Institution of Protestant Deaconesses, became rector at Milwaukee. Deaconesses served at the Passavant Memorial Homes for epileptics at Rochester, Pennsylvania, and Passavant Memorial Hospital in Jacksonville, Illinois (until 1902). The institution also maintained the Passavant Hospital at Pittsburgh and the orphan homes at Zelienople. In 1894 the institution began publication of the *Annals of the Institution of Protestant Deaconesses*.[98]

Neuendettelsau Deaconesses
in the United States

There were deaconesses in the United States other than those of the Passavant-inspired Institution of Protestant Deaconesses. Some of these women were Lutheran. In 1857 and 1858, Wilhelm Löhe sent several deaconesses to the Iowa Synod. Of these deaconesses, two in succession became housemother at Wartburg Theological Seminary in Dubuque, Iowa. In 1859 there were five deaconesses from Neuendettelsau in the United States. A report from Neuendettelsau about 1860 indicated they had all married.[99]

There was a second attempt to establish Neuendettelsau deaconesses in Iowa Synod institutions in the late 1860s. In response to an 1868 appeal from Pastor Johannes Dörfler to help found a motherhouse in Toledo, Ohio, under the auspices of the Iowa Synod, in 1870 supportive individuals formed an Association for Works of Beneficence. Löhe promised to send money and two deaconesses, but the Franco-Prussian War of 1870–1871 intervened, placing demands on the nursing services of the Neuendettelsau deaconesses. Löhe died January 2, 1872, but ties between Neuendettelsau and the Iowa Synod continued. In 1872 Anna Lutz was sent to Neuendettelsau to train to be matron of Dörfler's orphanage. She fell ill after she returned to the United States. In 1869 Sister Louise Adelberg of Neuendettelsau became housemother of St. John's orphanage near Buffalo, New York, though she eventually returned to Neuendettelsau.[100]

Neuendettelsau influenced other deaconess establishments in North America, providing personnel, worship practices, and training. The first full-time training sister recruited for the deaconess training school that opened in Philadelphia in 1889 was Magdalene Steinmann, a deaconess from Neuendettelsau. The liturgy at Neuendettelsau became a model for this Philadelphia motherhouse.[101] Catherine Dentzer, an American who became the second training sister at the Milwaukee motherhouse in 1900, had taken a special course at Neuendettelsau. Just as some U.S. deaconesses went to Kaiserswerth for training, they also went to Neuendettelsau.[102]

The Philadelphia Motherhouse

The Philadelphia motherhouse emerged from the German hospital in that city (incorporated in 1860 and opened in 1866) through the efforts of a wealthy immigrant patron, John Lankenau. Born in Bremen, Germany, on March 18, 1817, Lankenau had come to the United States in 1836. He married Mary Joanna Drexel in 1848 and joined the board of the German Hospital in Philadelphia in 1866, three years after the death of his father-in-law, Francis M. Drexel, who had been treasurer of the board. Lankenau became the board's president in 1869. His wife died in 1873 and his only son, Francis, in 1877.

In 1878 Lankenau took it upon himself—at the suggestion of his daughter, Elise—to establish a home for the elderly in his wife's memory. After Elise died in 1882, Lankenau moved ahead on his project. He attempted to get deaconesses from Germany and finally persuaded a small sisterhood in Iserlohn, Westphalia, to come to Philadelphia. Seven deaconesses arrived on July 19, 1884. Ground was broken in 1886 for an enormous neo-Gothic structure that was to house a deaconess motherhouse, a children's hospital (1889), and elderly Protestants of German descent. In 1888 the Mary J Drexel Home and Philadelphia Motherhouse of Deaconesses was dedicated, and the Kaiserswerth General Conference voted it conditional membership. The first consecration of deaconesses took place in 1889. In 1890 a girls' school opened on the fourth floor. There was also an evening school for boys (1892) and a kindergarten (1893).[103] By 1899 the Philadelphia motherhouse had thirty-one deaconesses and forty probationers.[104]

The deaconesses worked primarily as hospital nurses and, in the early years, engaged in some private nursing. They did all the nursing at the German Hospital in Philadelphia until 1899, when the hospital board opened a school of nursing. Deaconesses also were teachers and parish workers. Their work resembled that of European motherhouses, except that they were not engaged in foreign missions or the rescue of prostitutes. In 1890 the Philadelphia deaconesses began a nursery in Germantown, which in 1894 became a home for children under 5 years of age. Philadelphia deaconesses served at the hospital in Easton, Pennsylvania, and at St. John's in Allegheny, Pennsylvania, which opened as a home in September 1893 and as a hospital in May 1896. St. John's was sponsored by the Joint Synod of Ohio.[105]

The interior order of the Philadelphia motherhouse resembled a European deaconess institution—from the cleanliness to the garb that Jane Bancroft described in a book published in 1889 as "black, with blue or white aprons, white caps and collars." The *Deaconess Messenger*, a newsletter of the Philadelphia motherhouse, described the garb as blue cotton imported from Germany.[106] Even the bricks of the building were from Europe. The deaconesses were German or of German descent and spoke German in the house rather than English. To enter they had presented certificates of Baptism and letters from their parents, their pastors, and their employers, as well as personal autobiographies. After a preliminary screening of about six weeks that eliminated many of them, the women became probationers for about a year, then "help-sisters" or subsisters for two or three years. After all this, the women were consecrated deaconesses with an imposition of hands. Once consecrated, the women had a right to their own bedroom; before that they slept in a common dormitory in beds separated by curtains. The women in the motherhouse rose early, ate simply, and had no food available to them between meals. They were not allowed to go home to visit their families for their first two years in the motherhouse, except in the event of an emergency.[107] Deaconesses of the motherhouse were expected to be obedient to their superiors: "If you have been ordered to do something it will be done, and done exactly as you were ordered to do it."[108]

With the Philadelphia motherhouse, deaconesses came into their own among Lutherans of German descent in North America. With sound financing and a dynamic patron, the Philadelphia motherhouse experienced a success that Passavant never realized. Lankenau involved key pastors on the board. The president of the Lutheran General Council, Spaeth, a man active in the Ministerium of Pennsylvania,[109] was a founder of the motherhouse and an active supporter.[110] The Ministerium of Pennsylvania took the motherhouse under its wing, and the General Council also gave its support. Many of the deaconess candidates came from congregations of the ministerium. John Lankenau died in 1901.[111]

NORWEGIAN LUTHERAN DEACONESSES IN THE UNITED STATES

Other Lutheran groups in North America besides the Germans began deaconess work in the nineteenth century. The Norwegians established three motherhouses in the United States in the nineteenth century: one in Brooklyn, New York; Minneapolis, Minnesota; and Chicago, Illinois. The first of these was in Brooklyn.

The deaconess work in Brooklyn, New York, began with Elizabeth Fedde, a deaconess from Norway, who responded to a request to meet the needs of poor Norwegian immigrants in the United States. The initiative behind this appeal lay with Anna Bors, wife of the Norwegian consul general, and Andreas Mortensen, pastor of the Norwegian Seamen's Mission Church in Brooklyn. Elizabeth Fedde was born in Norway in 1850 and entered the motherhouse in Christiana (Oslo) in 1873. Before coming to the United States, she superintended a hospital in Troms, in northern Norway. She arrived in the United States on April 8, 1883. Along with interested laypeople and pastors, she formed the Voluntary Relief Society for the Sick and Poor among the Norwegians in New York and Brooklyn on April 19. She established her headquarters in a home next to the Seamen's Mission Church. From there, she visited the poor and provided "outdoor relief," which was help for the needy, short of providing housing. Fedde cleaned; washed; sewed; did home nursing, including maternity care; tried to find people employment; placed children in foster care; raised funds and distributed money, clothing, and food; visited mental institutions and prisons; and arranged burials. Fedde's actions demonstrate that when a deaconess entered a home in need, she often took over the care of the entire household. In 1885 the society for the Norwegian sick and poor incorporated. On March 1, 1885, it opened a nine-bed hospital.[112]

Elizabeth Fedde's life was a unique chapter in the history of the deaconess movement in the United States because of her personal inspiration and leadership of the deaconess community and hospital in Brooklyn and her role in the early deaconess community in Minnesota. In Brooklyn she started a training program for deaconesses. On May 16, 1885, the first candidate arrived; another came in March 1886. Both left, creating a temporary hiatus. In 1888, when the General Council of the Lutheran Church met in Minneapolis, Minnesota, Fedde spoke to a group with whom William Passavant had met. He suggested that "the way to start deaconess work was with a deaconess."[113] A gentleman offered a new house on Hennepin Avenue free for two years. Fedde agreed to stay and equip a hospital and deaconess home. Two probationers joined her, and they began work on November 11, 1898, with four rooms for patients. Fedde returned to Brooklyn in May 1889 for the groundbreaking of a thirty-bed hospital on Forty-sixth Street and stayed until two deaconesses from Norway arrived in July. When Fedde returned to Minneapolis that same month, she discovered that the board of trustees of the deaconess hospital had dissolved. However, Professor Georg Sverdrup of Augsburg Seminary reorganized the board, and the Norwegian Deaconess Institution incorporated on August 17, 1889. Located in the heartland of Scandinavian immigration, it would attract more deaconesses than the group in Brooklyn to which Elizabeth Fedde returned in January 1891.[114] By 1899 the Norwegian Lutheran Deaconess Institute in Minneapolis had eleven deaconesses and twenty probationers.[115]

In Brooklyn, two deaconesses were consecrated on April 19, 1892. Fedde was able to obtain state aid for the hospital, so on November 15, 1892, the hospital incorporated under the name Norwegian Lutheran Deaconesses' Home and Hospital. The deaconess community grew with the hospital, ranging in size from thirteen to fifteen sisters. Fedde returned to Norway in 1896. To an extent unparalleled in the other nineteenth-century Lutheran deaconess communities in the United States, the Norwegian deaconess community was built through the efforts of one woman. By 1899 the Norwegian Lutheran Deaconess Home and Hospital in Brooklyn had six deaconesses and seven probationers.[116] Not until 1905 would there be a rector of the Brooklyn hospital. The Reverend E. C. Tollefson came shortly after it expanded to ninety beds in 1903 and 1904.[117]

Elizabeth Fedde did not have a free reign, however. She recorded in her diary on June 20, 1885, that the Lutheran Hospital in Manhattan did not want her to call on patients because they thought pastors, not women, should give spiritual care. A board also supervised Fedde's work, and she was not allowed to be a member. Sometimes there was disagreement between her and the board. She wrote in her diary on April 7, 1885: "Board meeting and I have been left in a powerless position. This is the hardest time I have had in America. . . . I have the whole board against me and I wish I were dead." In March 1886 the members of the board refused to let her admit paying students unless she consulted with them. In 1892 it refused her desire to make the Chicago deaconess home a station of the Brooklyn home.[118]

The vicissitudes of immigration history played an important role in the next chapter of the Norwegian Deaconess Institution in Minnesota. Ingeborg Sponland, a deaconess from Norway, came to the United States to bring her parents home, but the trustees of the deaconess home in Minneapolis asked her to remain and become sister superior of a new hospital, which was dedicated September 1, 1891. Sponland agreed and stayed until 1904. The number of deaconesses grew under her leadership. The community was able to provide nurses for a hospital in Grand Forks, Hillsboro, and Fargo, North Dakota, as well as Crookston and Austin, Minnesota. Minneapolis deaconesses served in children's homes in Beloit, Iowa, and Paulsbo, Washington. One worked in Madagascar.[119]

Chicago became the third Norwegian Lutheran deaconess center in the United States. On November 3, 1885, a Norwegian Lutheran Tabitha Society formed, consisting of women involved in charitable work. Six years later, a faction within that society recruited three deaconesses from Minneapolis to staff a Norwegian Lutheran Deaconess Home and Hospital (November 3, 1891). The institution burned in August 1893. Then on February 17, 1896, a Norwegian Lutheran Deaconess Society formed, and on September 17 of the same year, a Norwegian Lutheran Deaconess Home and Hospital incorporated. It opened on May 22, 1897, under the direction of Sister Anna Tofte, who came from the motherhouse in Norway and remained in that post until November. Ingeborg Oberg, a probationer from Minneapolis, succeeded Tofte, the first woman to be consecrated a deaconess from the Chicago motherhouse (November 20, 1898). The next year the Norwegian Lutheran Deaconess Home of Chicago had eight probationers in addition to its one deaconess.[120]

SWEDISH LUTHERAN DEACONESSES IN NORTH AMERICA

Deaconess work among Swedish Lutherans in the United States began through the efforts of a Swedish immigrant educated in the States, E. A. Fogelstrom (1850–1909). Fogelstrom attended Augustana College and Seminary in Illinois. In 1879 he became a pastor in Omaha, Nebraska. In 1886 he decided to establish a Lutheran hospital in the city, which he hoped to maintain with deaconesses. The next year building began, and Fogelstrom sent Bothilde Swenson, a woman from his congregation, to the Philadelphia motherhouse for deaconess training. Before the completion of the hospital, a need for a children's home emerged because a couple in Fogelstrom's congregation died in August 1887, leaving their four children (all under the age of 7) without care. Thus a room in the church basement became the first children's home with Fredina Petersen, a Sunday school teacher, serving as the first housemother.

On October 8, 1887, The Evangelical Lutheran Immanuel Association for Works of Mercy organized. The next year four more women went to Philadelphia for deaconess training, and the association incorporated without the word *Lutheran* in the title. This intentional step was meant to encompass "all evangelicals" and attract members of wealth from a larger pool of those interested in the institution. The hospital opened December 29, 1890, and the next year the Immanuel Deaconess Institute, a deaconess home and training school, opened. According to Lucy Rider Meyer, a contemporary supporter of the deaconess cause, English was to be the official and preferred language of this Swedish-American Deaconess Institute.[121] The first deaconess consecrated was Bothilda Swenson in April 1891. The following January the deaconesses organized as a congregation with Fogelstrom as their pastor.[122] Meanwhile, the Minnesota Conference of the Swedish Lutheran Augustana Synod opened a hospital in St. Paul in 1883. It closed in 1884 but reopened March 8, 1892, under the leadership of Sister Fredina Peterson of Omaha. By 1899 Betheseda Hospital in St. Paul, Minnesota, had four sisters.[123]

Fogelstrom sought broader denominational support for his work. To that end he encouraged those members of the board of trustees of the hospital in Omaha who were not members of the Augustana Synod to step down in January 1894. The synod president, Dr. Sward, and the president of the synod's Nebraska Conference, Pastor Swenberg, replaced two of these board members. In 1896 the synod met in Omaha and observed the institutions more closely. By 1899 the Immanuel Deaconess Institute of Omaha, Nebraska, had thirteen deaconesses and twelve probationers. In 1904 there was an official affiliation between the Augustana Synod and the deaconess work in Omaha.[124]

THE GENERAL SYNOD
AND THE BALTIMORE MOTHERHOUSE

Formal denominational support for the Lutheran deaconess movement in the United States came slowly. Instead, philanthropic individuals, interested pastors, and societies for the promotion of deaconess work took the initiative. An exception was the Baltimore deaconess home, which was organized by the General Synod, which was the first U.S. intersynodical body among Lutherans. Formed from the old "Muhlenberg Churches," it was unable to attract new Lutherans from Europe. Some synods never joined; others withdrew. The tensions associated with the Civil War provoked the withdrawal of several synods to form the United Synod of the South. Confessional disagreements led other synods to form the General Council in 1867. Despite its struggle, the General Synod took the initiative as a body to sponsor the deaconess movement.[125]

The initiative within the General Synod occurred on March 13, 1883. The North Branch Conference of the Susquehanna Synod decided to consider a need for an "Order of Deaconesses in our Church." In 1885 the request came before the General Synod, which set up a study committee and subsequently a Board of Deaconess Work (1889). The board's initial plan was to send U.S. women to Kaiserswerth for free training, which Julius Disselhoff promised to provide. In 1893 the first deaconess candidate left for Germany, but few of the candidates spoke German, thus the Philadelphia Motherhouse became the center for the training of nurses in the General Synod.[126] In 1895 the Deaconess Board incorporated as the Deaconess Board of the General Synod of the Evangelical Lutheran Church in the United States of America.[127]

With six candidates in training in 1895, the issue of housing became critical. The synod accepted the offer of a large house in Baltimore to

house the women free of charge for three years. The first Baltimore deaconesses were consecrated in the First English Church on October 23,
1895. They engaged in home nursing and opened an industrial school for
children in January 1896, which was followed by an evening school for
black children. Plans for a hospital went awry, but the deaconesses began
parish work in New York City in 1897. They entered foreign missions in
1898, the same year that the Baltimore motherhouse incorporated (February 25) and the Kaiserswerth Conference accepted them (September). The
sponsorship of the General Synod gave the deaconesses a publicity opportunity in the periodicals of the church, as well as the support of the
Women's Home and Missionary Society and the Luther League. By 1899
the Baltimore Motherhouse and Training School had ten deaconesses and
twelve probationers.[128]

Lutheran deaconess organizations in the United States functioned
autonomously, though they did help one another. The Philadelphia motherhouse decided to formalize this spirit of cooperation by hosting a meeting in September 1896 of representatives of the other Lutheran
motherhouses in the United States. Omaha, Milwaukee, and Baltimore
sent delegates. Minneapolis sent statistics. Brooklyn declined the invitation.
Thus began a regular Conference of Evangelical Lutheran Deaconess
Motherhouses in America (every one to four years), which offered a forum
for the discussion of common problems, challenges, terminology, and procedures, such as training, publicity, relationships to the church, and the
transfer of deaconesses from one institution to another. On the latter point,
the conference simply accepted the procedure of the Kaiserswerth Conference of motherhouses: accepting transfers of deaconesses from other
conference motherhouses only upon the recommendation of the motherhouse of origin. One aspect of the conference unsatisfactory to later generations was that the men involved in the Lutheran deaconess movement
made the speeches at the gatherings rather than the women.[129]

INTERDENOMINATIONAL DEACONESS ASSOCIATIONS
AND HOMES IN NORTH AMERICA

Lutherans were not the first in the United States to organize a deaconess
conference. In July 1890 Dr. Spaeth spoke at Chautauqua, New York, to the
third interdenominational deaconess convention, an organization of
Methodists. In 1894 in Dayton, Ohio, a conference of Protestant deaconess houses formed. It was interdenominational in composition, though
largely German.[130] Members of denominations other than Lutheran were

promoting the deaconess movement in the United States. Some of these efforts were interdenominational in scope, particularly on a local level where several churches in a city would rally to support a hospital drive and form a society to promote deaconesses to staff it. The people involved in these efforts tended to be German immigrants or of German background.

Among the oldest of the interdenominational deaconess homes was the German Deaconess Home and Hospital in Cincinnati, Ohio, which arose out of the activity of the Evangelical Society for Deaconess Work and the Care of the Sick, founded in 1888. In 1890 the Cincinnati home provided the first two deaconesses for Dayton, Ohio, and Friedrich von Bodelschwingh of Bielefeld in Germany provided the next two. In 1894 the Dayton home took on, as a station, the recently founded Protestant Deaconess Home and Hospital of Evansville, Indiana (1892), but in 1898 the deaconess home in Dayton dissolved, leaving its hospital to be staffed by professional nurses. Meanwhile, the Evansville project prospered and enjoyed a broad base of support that included local pastors from the Evangelical St. Lucas Church, the First German Methodist Church, and the First Evangelical Reformed Church. It also received the support of a Ladies' Deaconess Aid Society, a Young Ladies' Deaconess Aid Society, and charitable organizations in the city. Before the dissolution of the deaconess home in Dayton, its superintendent, the Reverend C. Mueller, delivered a lecture on October 22, 1894, that motivated the formation of a society to support a Protestant deaconess home and hospital in Indianapolis, Indiana. The new institution was dedicated on April 3, 1899. There was also a home for the elderly and a training school for nurses. In 1899 two deaconesses trained in Dayton took charge of a deaconess home in Lincoln, Illinois. Further cross-fertilization occurred when the deaconess home in Cincinnati provided two deaconesses for a home and hospital in Buffalo, New York, which opened October 23, 1895, under the auspices of a recently founded deaconess society (January 26, 1895). The society recruited Ida Tobschall, the directing sister of the Cincinnati deaconess institution and a native of Buffalo, to head the new home and hospital, which was dedicated on November 28, 1896. The hospital also included a home for the elderly. The deaconesses also nursed in private homes and operated a nursery for children. The rector of the Dayton deaconess home, Carl Mueller, took a step toward cooperation among these deaconess homes when he called together representatives of the German Protestant Deaconess Homes in America to form the Protestant Deaconess Conference. This group met for the first time October 15, 1894. Christian Golder, the author of *A History of the Deaconess Movement*, was president of this organization for a time.[131]

All these interdenominational deaconess institutions were founded through the efforts of pastors, trustees, and deaconess societies whose membership numbered in the hundreds. But there were other interdenominational deaconess endeavors that centered on a single founder. Such was the case in Chicago, Illinois, and Berne, Indiana.

In Chicago, a German-born philanthropist was largely responsible for the founding of the Betheseda deaconess home in 1895, though he worked with other people of German descent in the city. Frank F. Henning was born in Prussia on May 3, 1840. As a young man, he encountered the Methodist Church in Wisconsin. In 1880, under the influence of the evangelist Dwight L. Moody, Henning resolved to found a German Protestant Hospital in Chicago. Thus he spearheaded the organization and incorporation of a hospital association (December 17, 1883) and the Betheseda Deaconess Society (February 4, 1886). Henning also founded a German-American hospital on October 1, 1896.[132]

In Berne, Indiana, J. A. Sprunger, a Mennonite pastor, founded an interdenominational deaconess home in February 1890. It was under the control of the deaconesses themselves, as members of a United Deaconess Association, which was unusual in this era. The deaconesses had an orphanage in Berne, but their motherhouse moved to Chicago in June 1890, where they established a maternity and rescue home. A branch hospital opened in 1894 in Cleveland and another in Detroit. Deaconesses worked in Evansville, Indiana; Indianapolis; and Bloomington, Illinois. Three went as missionaries to Africa and two to Turkey. Eighteen deaconesses left in 1897 and established a home in Chicago. Within the first decade of the twentieth century, the Sprunger deaconess homes collapsed, but individual deaconesses continued to work in foreign missions and at the orphanage in Berne, Indiana.[133]

NON-LUTHERAN DEACONESSES OF GERMAN EXTRACTION IN NORTH AMERICA

Besides these interdenominational efforts, churches from various denominations of German background supported deaconess work in North America. As early as 1866, Jane Bancroft asserts that J. Dixon Roman, a layman from Hagerstown, Maryland, tried to interest the German Reformed Church in the office of deaconess.[134] The German Reformed Church in Cleveland, Ohio, founded a Society for the Christian Nursing of the Sick and Poor (July 2, 1892), but the three young women it sent for hospital training were lost to the society. On November 15, 1893, Catherine

Broeckel, a deaconess from Neumuenster, Switzerland, took over the society, and the project prospered. These Cleveland deaconesses established a home for the elderly and a hospital, which later became Fairview Park Hospital. The deaconesses also engaged in private nursing. Deaconesses of the German Reformed Church also organized the German Deaconess Home and Hospital in Buffalo, New York (1895). The first English-speaking deaconess home of the Reformed Church of the United States was opened in 1899 in Alliance, Ohio, as a deaconess institute and hospital.[135]

German Baptists incorporated the Deaconess Society of the German Baptists of Chicago and Vicinity in 1897. The society engaged two deaconesses who had been trained in Philadelphia and in Dayton.[136]

The German Evangelical Synod of North America established deaconess institutions in Lincoln, Nebraska, and St. Louis, Missouri. In Nebraska in 1887, the German Evangelicals founded a Tabitha Institute, which had an orphanage and added a deaconess home in 1889. On March 18, 1889, at St. Peter's Evangelical Church, St. Louis, Missouri, an Evangelical Deaconess Association organized (the *Evangelischer Diakonissen-Verein*). A widow donated money that rented and renovated a house at 2119 Eugenia Street. This became the first Deaconess Hospital and Home. The first deaconesses were Katharine Haack, a minister's widow, and Lydia Daries, Haack's stepdaughter, both of whom were trained nurses. In 1892 the directors bought property at the corner of West Belle Place and Sarah Street and built a hospital. Katharine Haack was appointed head deaconess. When the directors decided to turn the management over to a minister of the German Evangelical Synod in 1897, Haack objected, resigned, and left the institution along with several other deaconesses. Nevertheless, in 1902 there were twenty-two deaconesses in the home, ten of whom were consecrated. Besides working in their hospital and the Good Samaritan Hospital of St. Louis, these deaconesses nursed at an institution for epileptics in Marthasville, Missouri, and did charity work in St. Louis and the surrounding areas in Missouri and Illinois.

Within thirty years after the founding of the Evangelical Deaconess Association, members of the Evangelical Synod had established institutions (usually titled "Evangelical" or "Evangelical Deaconess" Home or Hospital) in Evansville, Indiana (1892); Lincoln, Illinois (1902); St. Charles, Missouri (1905); Faribault, Minnesota (1908); Milwaukee, Wisconsin (1910); Chicago, Illinois (1910); Louisville, Kentucky (1911); Baltimore, Maryland (1912); Marshalltown, Iowa (1913); East St. Louis, Illinois (1915); Detroit, Michigan (1917); and Cleveland, Ohio (1919).[137]

In 1899 the Evangelical Association, formed in the 1840s when German immigrants of Lutheran and Reformed backgrounds began working together, appointed a commission to draft plans for managing deaconesses. Deaconess work began on a small scale in Chicago, Cleveland, Toronto, and Berlin, Ontario.[138]

The character and composition of the above institutions exemplify the central role that people of German descent made in the deaconess movement in the United States. German women from other North American denominations—Methodists, for example—also became deaconesses. The Methodist editor of *Christliche Apologete*, A. J. Nast, stated near the turn of the twentieth century that deaconess work in North America appealed "with particular force to the German mind and German sentiment in contrast with the prevalent ideas of woman's emancipation, which in these times have obtruded themselves upon us in so marked a manner."[139] Writing before women had the right to vote, Nast, like others in the New World and the Old, found deaconess work acceptable, whereas other forms of women's work were not.

THE PROTESTANT EPISCOPAL CHURCH

The Protestant Episcopal Church in America began deaconess work in the mid-nineteenth century, as did Lutherans. However, as in England, sisterhoods attracted a larger number of candidates than the deaconess institutions did. In the early years of deaconess work in the Episcopal Church, it was sometimes difficult to distinguish a deaconess community from a sisterhood because of the similarity of titles and lifestyles. Ordinarily, though, deaconesses retained full control of their own property whereas sisters relinquished it.[140]

William Augustus Muhlenberg, an Episcopal clergyman and a descendant of the Muhlenberg family that had organized Lutheranism in North America, was an early promoter of deaconesses in the Episcopal Church.[141] After contact with deaconesses in Europe, he wrote a pamphlet titled "The Institution of Deaconesses in the Evangelical Church" and in 1845 began an organization in New York in association with the Church of the Holy Communion, of which he was rector. Except for minor details, the rules for Muhlenberg's Sisters of the Holy Communion were taken from Fliedner in Germany. Muhlenberg insisted that these women were not like the Sisters of Charity or "Anglican" sisterhoods, which were imitations of Roman Catholic orders. Muhlenberg provided for four classes of sisters: united sisters, living in the house of the sisterhood; associate sisters, living in their respective homes; probationers; and serving sisters, "who are qualified only to do the more laborious work of the household." Their house, next to the church, was nearing completion in 1853.[142] The sisters agreed to three-year renewable terms. They taught school, managed a home for the elderly, directed an orphanage and a girls' school, and opened a dispensary that was the beginning of St. Luke's Hospital in New York.[143] Out of Muhlenberg's efforts, the Sisterhood of St. Mary was formed in 1863.[144]

Other communities of women in the Episcopal Church in America were more like Catholic sisterhoods than Muhlenberg's. Some of these communities were branches of sisterhoods in England; others were indigenous to the United States. The Episcopal Church had deaconess communities, but a few communities of women attempted to be a cross between a sisterhood and a deaconess community.

In 1855 in St. Andrew's congregation in Baltimore, two women volunteered to nurse the poor. At first they worked out of a room in the parish house. In 1857 the bishop of Maryland, William Whittingham, "set apart" but did not "ordain" Adeline Blanchard Tyler and five others as the first U.S. Episcopal deaconesses.[145] St. Andrew's Hospital emerged from this community. Other bishops followed Whittingham's example. In 1864 Richard Hooker Wilmer of Mobile, Alabama, set apart three women who began work under his direction. In 1872 Bishop A. N. Littlejohn founded the Deaconess Organization of the Diocese of Long Island. These deaconesses worked in congregations, especially in Brooklyn. In 1887 Bishop Potter of New York City set apart Julia Ferneret as the first deaconess of his diocese.[146]

The order of deaconess was officially recognized in the Episcopal Church in America in 1889. Church canons stipulated that a deaconess was not a deacon, the first level of ordained ministry, which at the time was an exclusively male role.[147] In 1889 the General Convention of the Episcopal Church adopted a canon on deaconesses requiring that they receive religious training. Because there were no motherhouses that provided training in the German sense, Bishop H. C. Potter of New York established a training school in 1890. It was not a deaconess institution per se but a training school with a two-year course, and it charged fees. Graduates could join a sisterhood or a deaconess community or work independently under the direction of a bishop. Likewise, the Church Training and Deaconess House (1891) in Philadelphia educated both deaconesses and lay workers.[148] Nineteenth-century Episcopal deaconesses served in parishes, health clinics, schools, recreation programs, settlement houses, church hospitals, children's homes, girls' schools, and Chinese and Japanese missionary posts.[149]

THE METHODIST EPISCOPAL CHURCH

In North America, women were active in promoting deaconess work. Perhaps in no denomination were they more prominent than in the Methodist Episcopal Church. Deaconess work in the Methodist Church in America began decades later than it did among Lutherans in the United States, but it grew with amazing speed. Precursors to the deaconess movement in the Methodist Church included the Female Missionary Society (1819), the Ladies' and Pastors' Christian Union (1868), the Woman's Foreign Missionary Society, the Woman's Home Missionary Society (1880), and a Training School for Missions in Chicago (1885).[150] Methodist women were Sunday school teachers, benevolent visitors, and activists in the temperance movement.

The Ladies' and Pastors' Christian Union sprang from the efforts of Anna Wittemeyer. During the Civil War, she organized bands of women to work among the wounded. After the war, Wittemeyer settled in Philadelphia and organized the Ladies' and Pastors' Christian Union (March 1868) to continue work among the needy. She and her colleague, Susan M. D. Fry, traveled around the country advocating the establishment of hospitals, orphanages, and homes for the elderly. Wittemeyer and Fry founded societies to look after the poor and to visit prisoners. Susan Fry was herself an exceptional woman who had held a chair at Illinois Wesleyan University. In 1872 the Methodist Church recognized the Ladies' and Pastors' Christian Union, and Anna Wittemeyer visited Kaiserswerth. She and Susan Fry became advocates for the deaconess cause in the United States.[151]

In 1880 the Woman's Home Missionary Society organized under the presidency of Lucy Ware Webb Hayes, the wife of Rutherford B. Hayes, president of the United States (1877–1881). When the Ladies' and Pastors' Home Missionary Union was dissolved, the Woman's Home Missionary Society carried on some of its work. The society was a financial backer of the Chicago School for City and Home and Foreign Missions (October 20, 1885).[152]

The Chicago Training School, as the Chicago School for City and Home and Foreign Missions was called, trained people to work in the church, especially in the city. The curriculum consisted of courses in the Bible, doctrine, church history, elocution, music, teaching, and nursing. In 1887 when a group of students stayed on at the school and worked over the summer, the Chicago Deaconess Home began, almost spontaneously, though it retained ties with the Training School. It was the first Methodist deaconess home in America, and the Chicago Training School was the first school for deaconesses in the Methodist Episcopal Church. The school trained Christian workers and contributed personnel to foreign and home missions, as well as to the many deaconess establishments of the Methodist Church. Out of the deaconess home emerged Wesley Methodist Hospital, established in 1888–1889. The Chicago Training School was founded by Lucy Rider Meyer.[153]

Lucy Rider, a Vermont farm girl, was graduated from Oberlin College in 1872. She worked for the Illinois Sunday School Association from 1880 to 1884 and taught at the Northfield School in Massachusetts from 1884 to 1885. Because she understood the need for a training school for Christian workers, she founded the Chicago Training School in 1885, the same year in which she married Josiah Shelly Meyer of Chicago, a YMCA secretary. He later worked full time with her at the school. Lucy Meyer Rider wrote on deaconess work and contributed to the *Message*, a publication of the Chicago Training School first issued in January 1886. Out of her writing efforts emerged *The Missionary and Deaconess Advocate*, which later was shortened to *The Deaconess Advocate*. In 1888 the *Message* facilitated the formation of a Deaconess Aid Society to support the Chicago Home.[154]

The Chicago Training School sent deaconesses to help establish deaconess homes in other parts of the country. By 1890 Lucy Rider Meyer stated that eight of the ten workers who had gone to other deaconess homes were superintendents of those homes.[155] Within eighteen years of its founding, the Chicago Training School had educated almost two thousand young women, seven hundred of whom entered deaconess work and one hundred and sixty of whom entered mission work.[156] More information on the Chicago Training School and other training schools can be found in Mary Agnes Dougherty's *My Calling to Fulfill: Deaconesses in the United Methodist Tradition*. This publication of the Women's Division of the General Board of Global Ministries of the United Methodist Church is evidence of continuing support for the deaconess movement by the women of the United Methodist Church.[157]

One of the attractions of deaconess service to students of the Chicago Training School was that Lucy Rider Meyer treated deaconesses like the educated women they were. She stated that the deaconess in the Chicago home needed to perform "only the lightest forms of household service . . . rarely exceeding . . . half an hour," in contrast to Germany where more manual labor was required of deaconesses. She saw the role of motherhood as central to the work of deaconesses:

The world wants mothering. Mother-love has its part to do in winning the world for Christ as well as father-wisdom and guidance. The deaconess movement puts the mother into the church. It supplies the feminine element so greatly needed in the Protestant Church, and thus is rooted deep in the very heart of humanity's needs.[158]

Meyer's philosophy was that a deaconess was not a recluse and that a deaconess home was "only a working basis, a place having the comforts of a true home." A deaconess was expected to do that which was assigned to her, however, and to wear the black or dark grey dress prescribed by the community. Lucy Rider Meyer was frank about the difficulties of life in a deaconess community. She wrote in her history of deaconesses:

> The moulding [sic] into one family of mature women coming from different homes, and with tastes and habits already well fixed, is not an easy matter and does not take place in a day; but it does take place at last, as a result of what St. Augustine calls the "dear and sweet habit of living together."[159]

The work of the Chicago Training School for Missions moved the Methodist preachers of the city to ask the 1888 General Conference of the Methodist Church to recognize deaconess work as an institution of the church. The Annual Conference of Bengal, India, sent a petition, too, hoping that deaconesses in India would be given permission to administer the sacraments to women who were so strictly secluded from men that a male pastor could not visit them. The General Conference referred the matter to a committee chaired by James M. Thoburn, a missionary to India, an advocate of the deaconess cause, and a friend of the Chicago Training School.[160] In the preface to its remarks, Thoburn's committee pointed out that "[i]n some of our congregations Sisters are already employed, performing the work of deaconesses without being called so, and their number could be increased if we were to organize the workers. We believe that God is in this movement, and the Church ought to recognize this fact."[161] Recognize them Methodists did by incorporating into the Discipline of the Church the following words:

> The duties of the deaconesses are to minister to the poor, visit the sick, pray with the dying, care for the orphan, seek the wandering, comfort the sorrowing, save the sinning, and, relinquishing wholly all other pursuits, to devote themselves in a general way to such forms of Christian labor as may be suited to their abilities.[162]

No vow was to be exacted of any deaconess, and they were to be free to leave at any time. The church, through a board, would issue certificates to deaconesses on the condition that they were more than 25 years of age and had served a two-year probation. In June 1889 three deaconesses from the Chicago Training School were consecrated, the first such consecrations in the Methodist Episcopal Church in the United States.[163]

Formal recognition was a great help to the Chicago Training School. In December 1888, after the General Conference's action, a deaconess convention convened at the Chicago Training School to make further plans for the coordination of deaconess work in the Methodist Church. It formulated a "Plan for Securing Uniformity in the Deaconess Homes of the Methodist Episcopal Church" that recommended a uniform for the deaconesses, a three-month probationary phase for prospective deaconesses, a maximum age of 40 years for admission, and a two-year course of study. The Methodist Episcopal Church was to hold all the property acquired by the deaconess homes. The deaconess convention, which was to meet annually, convened in 1889 in Ocean Grove, New Jersey, and in 1890 at Chautauqua, New York.[164]

The General Conference did not intend that deaconess work should belong to any one group in the church, but the Woman's Home Missionary Society assumed that it would be under its aegis. In October 1888, a few months after the adjournment of the General Conference of the Methodist Church, Jane Bancroft, a leader in the Woman's Home Missionary Society, attempted to garner the support of the society for the deaconess movement. The society formed a deaconess committee with Bancroft as chairperson. The next year it evolved into a Deaconess Bureau. The society employed deaconesses for its work and developed training schools around the country.[165]

In 1892 and 1896, the General Conferences of the Methodist Church maintained the rules adopted in 1888, but by 1900 there were at least three different organizational structures. (1) There were Methodist deaconess institutions under the Deaconess Bureau of the Woman's Home Missionary Society and (2) other institutions governed by local boards, whose deaconesses belonged to the Methodist Episcopal Deaconess Society (organized in 1895). (3) In addition, there were Methodists of German extraction in the United States who belonged to the European *Bethanien Verein*, the *Martha-Maria Verein*, or who were under the Central Deaconess Board of the Methodist Episcopal Church in the United States, which was organized in 1897 to have authority over German deaconess institutions.[166]

In 1900 the General Conference placed deaconess work under the board of Methodist bishops, which in turn assigned supervision of all deaconess work in a district to the district superintendent. When working alone, a deaconess was to be "under the direction of the pastor of the Church" in which she worked. When in a deaconess home, she was to be "subordinate to, and directed by the superintendent placed in charge." A candidate for a license as a deaconess was to be unmarried, more than 23 years of age, have given two years of continuous probationary service, have passed an examination as to religious qualifications, and have a certificate of good health from a physician.[167] The deaconess had to wear a prescribed uniform to protect her in the city, normally a black dress with white trim.[168]

The Methodist deaconess work was now under the control of the Board of Bishops, but other groups within the church remained involved, especially the Woman's Home Missionary Society. The Deaconess Bureau of the Woman's Home Missionary Society came into being largely through the efforts of women interested in the deaconess cause. Prominent among them were two women of extraordinary ability: Jane and Henrietta Bancroft, daughters of a New England pastor.

In 1871 Jane Bancroft was graduated from Emma Willard's Seminary in Troy, New York, and the next year from the State Normal School in Albany, New York. She obtained a doctorate from Syracuse University and became professor of French and dean of the Woman's College at Northwestern University in Evanston, Illinois (1877). From 1886 to 1888, Jane Bancroft studied abroad. While in Zurich, Switzerland, she became interested in deaconesses. In the spring of 1887, she visited the deaconess institution of Antoine Vermeil in Paris. She also visited hospitals and institutions in England. The Mildmay Deaconess Home in London impressed her. She went to Kaiserswerth before returning to the United States in 1888.

Upon her return to the United States, Jane was instrumental in the formation of the Deaconess Committee of the Woman's Home Missionary Society (subsequently the Deaconess Bureau). As chairperson of this committee, Jane Bancroft traveled around the country, founding deaconess associations and homes. The first home under the society's auspices opened in January 1890 in Detroit, Michigan. The second institution opened in May 1890 in Washington, D.C., with funds raised by Jane Bancroft. This was the Lucy Webb Hayes Deaconess Home and National Training School, dedicated to the deceased wife of the ex-president of the United States. (Lucy Webb Hayes had served as president of the Woman's Home Missionary Society.) With the offer of a rent-free house, the deaconess home opened. Jane Bancroft was also influential in the founding of a deaconess home and training school in San Francisco, California (1895).[169] In

1891 Jane organized the Deaconess Society of the California Conference of the Methodist Church. By the end of the year, it had opened a deaconess home. In 1893 the home was transferred to the Woman's Home Missionary Society. Through her efforts, deaconess homes in Philadelphia, Baltimore, Buffalo, Pittsburgh, Los Angeles, Washington, D.C., Brooklyn, and Denver came into existence. In the spring of 1891, she married George Robinson, a prominent lawyer in Detroit, but she continued to work on behalf of the deaconess movement and gave generous financial support.[170]

Jane Bancroft's sister, Henrietta, was field secretary for the Deaconess Bureau of the Woman's Home Missionary Society. She was graduated from Albany State Normal College; Cornell College, Iowa; and the University of Michigan. She studied at Oxford University in England, in Paris, and in Strasbourg. She held a chair of English language and literature at Cornell College and was later professor and dean of the woman's college of the University of Southern California. She was elected preceptress of Albion College and professor of English language and literature. She gave up her position in 1898 to travel in support of the deaconess cause.[171]

The deaconesses experienced an advantage from the sponsorship by the Woman's Home Missionary Society: fundraising.[172] The society's work in promoting the deaconess cause was prodigious. In 1892 the society founded deaconess work in Baltimore, Maryland; a deaconess home and training school in Brooklyn, New York (June 15); and a home in Des Moines, Iowa, that received a legacy of $22,000 from the Bidwell family. In 1895 the Methodist Episcopal Church in Iowa cooperated with the Woman's Home Missionary Society to found the Iowa Methodist Hospital, which adjoined the Bidwell Deaconess Home. In conjunction with the hospital and home there was also a Bible training school. On February 7, 1893, the Woman's Home Missionary Society opened a deaconess home in Knoxville, Tennessee. In 1894 William Sibley gave $10,000 toward a hospital in Washington, D.C., in memory of his wife. The Sibley Hospital was under the auspices of the Woman's Home Missionary Society as was the Rust Training School, housed in a separate building from the Lucy Webb Hayes Deaconess Home. In 1895 the society received a building in Urbana, Illinois, and the Cunningham Deaconess Home and Orphanage opened. In 1896 Lucy Rider Meyer and Bishop William Ninde helped organize a deaconess hospital in Kansas City, Kansas. After visiting the facility in 1898, Henrietta Bancroft and other women of the Woman's Home Missionary Society encouraged the founding of a training school to provide the nurse-deaconesses with religious education. In 1901 the first class graduated.[173]

The training school in Kansas was one of three nineteenth-century national training schools affiliated with the Woman's Home Missionary Society. The other two were in Washington, D.C., and San Francisco. In 1896 a deaconess from Chicago began work in Los Angeles. The Woman's Home Missionary Society added deaconesses and rented a house for them. In 1897 Elmira Christian gave homes to the Brooklyn Methodist deaconesses, which they used to open a kindergarten and a training school. On October 9, 1897, Methodist deaconess work began in Colorado with a visiting deaconess connected with the Woman's Home Missionary Society. The next year, a house was rented in Denver for the deaconesses. On February 10, 1899, the Woman's Home Missionary Society inherited a home in Rensselaer, New York, as well as money for its repair. It became the Elizabeth Wellington Griffin Home, named after its founder. In July 1899 the Woman's Home Missionary Society founded a deaconess home in Newark, New Jersey, and the society also began deaconess work in Puerto Rico and Hawaii.[174]

In 1895 the Methodist Episcopal Deaconess Society organized to form a bond between deaconesses and to hold property for disabled deaconesses. Headquartered in Chicago, many of the deaconesses whom it coordinated belonged to institutions that had come into being through the efforts of local individuals, associations, or Methodist conferences. The Methodist Episcopal Deaconess Society helped open schools, orphanages, and hospitals.[175]

The institutions that Methodists founded and staffed with deaconesses included hospitals, training schools for Christian workers, orphanages, children's schools, industrial schools, a young women's school, homes for the elderly, and rest homes for deaconesses. Deaconesses were nurses, child-care workers, social workers, singers, teachers, stenographers, physicians, editors, evangelists, and superintendents of homes and hospitals. In keeping with the thrust of the Chicago Training School, Methodist deaconesses were active in work among immigrants in the inner city. Individual philanthropists, many of them women, collaborated with local associations and Methodist conferences to found these Methodist charitable institutions. Prominent among these institutions were hospitals.[176]

Also in 1888, a number of people met in Cincinnati to organize a deaconess home in the residence of James P. Gamble of Proctor and Gamble. He offered a rent-free building and money to found the Elizabeth Gamble Deaconess Home and Christ Hospital. The deaconesses worked in the hospital and throughout the city distributing food and clothing, finding work for the unemployed, conducting Sunday schools and kindergartens, visiting prisoners, sponsoring an Italian mission, and doing "Travelers' Aid" work among young women new to the city to save them from prostitution. Deaconesses from the Gamble home headed new deaconess homes and worked for local churches in Ohio, Kentucky, and Indiana.[177]

In 1891 two deaconesses began mission work in Minneapolis. The following year a gift from Mrs. S. H. Knight made it possible to organize the Asbury Methodist Hospital and Rebecca Deaconess Home, which was incorporated in 1893. The Methodist bishop in Minneapolis became chairman of the board.[178]

Two deaconesses from the Chicago Training School moved to Spokane, Washington, in April 1892, and in 1896, the Maria Beard Deaconess Hospital was incorporated. On February 6, 1896, a fourteen-bed hospital in Boston opened its doors in conjunction with the New England Deaconess Home and Training School that had been founded November 20, 1889, through the efforts of the New England Conference of Methodists.[179] The training school provided deaconesses and also female missionaries to China, Korea, Japan, India, and South America.[180]

The Methodist Conference of the State of Indiana took the first steps in 1898 and 1899 to establish a deaconess home and hospital in Indianapolis. Deaconesses engaged in city mission work while they waited for the hospital to be built. In 1911 a home opened for six deaconesses who were doing parish and mission work in Indianapolis.[181]

Thomas Tippy, a millionaire, made it possible to open the first Protestant hospital in Seattle, Washington, on March 1, 1900, under the auspices of the Methodist Episcopal Church. That same year the Wilkinson Memorial Institute opened on May 24 in Peoria, Illinois, as a deaconess home and hospital. Methodists also began a deaconess hospital in Jeffersonville, Indiana; the Ensworth Deaconess Home and Hospital in St. Joseph, Missouri; and the Watts de Peyster Hospital, a children's hospital in Verbank, New York, which was managed by the Deaconess Society of the New York Conference of Methodists.[182]

The list of Methodist deaconess hospitals was imposing, and some of them, such as the New England Deaconess Hospital, eventually would become famous for research and teaching, for nursing schools, and for excellent patient care.[183] Hospitals were only a fraction of the Methodist deaconess institutions, however. For example, an orphanage opened in Lake Bluff, Illinois, in 1895 and the Deaconess Home for Old People in Edgewater, Illinois, in 1898. That same year the Jennings Seminary, a school for young women, opened in Aurora, Illinois, with deaconesses serving as teachers. The Chicago Training School furnished the teachers for Chaddock College for young men in Quincy, Illinois, which opened September 20, 1900. The deaconesses had rest homes and vacation houses in the East and Midwest and the National Deaconess Sanitarium for pulmonary diseases in Colorado Springs, Colorado.[184]

In the Methodist tradition, deaconesses were active in inner-city work among the poor and among immigrants. Jane Bancroft held up the example of the deaconesses of East London for deaconesses in U.S. cities to emulate.[185] Deaconesses visited people in their homes, brought food and clothing to them, and even washed their dishes and cleaned their houses. Through this work, U.S. deaconesses, who were typically from rural backgrounds or the parsonage, became aware of society's problems. Confronted with the exploitation of women and children and the problems of alcoholism, Methodist deaconesses in the United States were opposed to child labor and were active in the temperance movement. Their deaconess homes became employment agencies, especially for domestic servants. Deaconesses met young women as they arrived in the city at train stations and found them safe boardinghouses, seeking to protect them from those who sought to enlist them in prostitution. Deaconesses also opened clubs for young men and women, sponsored mothers' circles, and established kindergartens and nurseries.[186]

With inner-city work as a focus, many Methodist deaconess homes had no particular institution attached to them except a training school or rooms for classes or activities. This was different from Lutheran deaconess homes, many of which were associated with hospitals. For example, Methodists established a home and training school in New York City in 1889 without a hospital. Women who wanted training as nurses received it in local hospitals. This same pattern occurred in other Methodist deaconess homes. Sometimes the presence of deaconesses in a city was the catalyst for the establishment of a deaconess home. This was the case in Buffalo, New York (1890); Pittsburgh, Pennsylvania (1892); and Providence, Rhode Island, where deaconesses from the Boston Training School came to work in 1893 and a home opened for them in 1895. At other times local Methodists desired deaconesses and established a home to attract them. Such was the case in Grand Rapids, Michigan, where Methodist preachers met on February 19, 1891, to initiate such a project. A training school was added to the Grand Rapids deaconess home in 1897. In Sioux City, Iowa, on May 22, 1899, a field secretary of the Woman's Home Missionary Society addressed a group gathered to consider founding a deaconess home, and by August the institution opened. Sometimes a large donation precipitated the founding of a deaconess home. Such was the case in 1893 in Milwaukee, Wisconsin, and in 1899 in Normal, Illinois, where women donated houses. Sometimes a Methodist conference initiated the founding of a deaconess home. Such was the case in 1897 in Jersey City, New Jersey, and in March 1898 in Wichita, Kansas. Methodists also founded deaconess homes in Freeport, Illinois (1892); Toronto, Canada (1894); Fall River, Massachusetts (1894); La Crosse, Wisconsin (founded 1895 but opened 1899); Pueblo, Colorado (1898); and Bridgeport, Cleveland, and Columbus, Ohio.[187]

Methodist deaconesses were noteworthy for their work among immigrants of diverse ethnic backgrounds in the cities—Bohemians and Italians, for example. In 1900 W. H. Riley, an African American Methodist pastor in Cincinnati, founded a deaconess home and training school for African American women. The school closed in 1905. But there already were African American deaconesses from some of the other Methodist institutions. In the South, the African Methodist Episcopal Church founded a deaconess home in 1901. The ethnic group most active in organizing Methodist deaconess institutions of their own in North America, however, were the Germans.[188]

When the Methodist Episcopal Church first established deaconess institutions, German Methodists entered these English-speaking establishments, but they were attached enough to their language to desire German motherhouses. The donation of a house in St. Paul, Minnesota, made it possible to establish the Elizabeth Haas Deaconess Home on January 12, 1891. After only seven years, it ceased to exist. Meanwhile, Isabella Thoburn, a deaconess from the Chicago Training School, provided the impetus for the establishment of the German Deaconess Institute in Chicago in 1892. The next year in Brooklyn, New York, the Bethany Deaconess Home and Hospital began under a deaconess from the Bethany Society of Hamburg, Germany. In Louisville, Kentucky, the deaconess home and hospital began work in 1895.[189]

When Germans in the Methodist Episcopal Church formed a Central Deaconess Board in 1897, it gave its blessing to a new German deaconess motherhouse in Cincinnati. This community had formed in 1896 when the Gamble Deaconess Home released Louise Golder and several deaconesses to form a core community for a new German-speaking home. Louise, an immigrant from Germany in 1877, was the sister of Christian Golder, a Methodist of German descent and author of *A History of the Deaconess Movement in the Christian Church*. The Central Deaconess Board asked the other German Methodist deaconess homes to affiliate with this community. German Methodist deaconess homes thus belonged to the Central Deaconess Board of the United States, the Bethany Society, or the Martha-Mary Society of Germany.[190]

The Cincinnati deaconess home incorporated as the German Methodist Deaconess Home and Bethesda Hospital. The home was a success both in recruitment of deaconesses and in ability to establish branch hospitals and homes in Terre Haute, Indiana; Milwaukee and La Crosse, Wisconsin; Kansas City, Missouri; Pittsburgh, Pennsylvania; and Los Angeles, California. The East German Conference of the Methodist Episcopal Church was active in founding the Bethany Deaconess Home and Hospital Society in Brooklyn, New York. Emmanuel Deaconess Society organized in 1897 in Chicago and moved to Kansas City, Missouri, in 1901. At the turn into the twentieth century, German Methodists had thirty institutions in the United States and Europe with four hundred deaconesses, including probationers.[191]

Deaconesses in North American Methodism emerged shortly after single women began to go abroad as foreign missionaries. Training schools, such as the one in Chicago that educated deaconesses, also trained women to be missionaries. Some deaconesses went abroad as missionaries. Isabella Thoburn, was the first U.S. Methodist woman employed as a missionary abroad to become a deaconess. She was the sister of John Thoburn, a missionary who promoted the deaconess cause and eventually became bishop of India and Malaysia. Isabella Thoburn was born in 1840 and was graduated from a women's seminary in Wheeling, West Virginia. In 1866 she became principal of a school for girls in Farmington, Ohio. The formation of a Woman's Foreign Missionary Society in Boston enabled her to become a missionary. In January 1870 she and Clara Swain, a female physician, left for India under the auspices of the society. Isabella Thoburn founded a girls' school in India.

In 1886 Isabella Thoburn returned to the United States because of her health. After two years, she took charge of the first deaconess home of the Methodist Episcopal Church in Chicago. Also in 1888, the Elizabeth Gamble Home in Cincinnati asked her to become superintendent. There she oversaw the founding of Christ Hospital. After two years in Cincinnati, she returned to India, now wearing the gray dress of a Methodist deaconess. She died of cholera on September 1, 1901. By then deaconesses were employed in many parts of India in evangelism efforts, schools, orphanages, and benevolent institutions, but deaconess work did not become an indigenous movement. Many Indian women were training and worked in the church, but they were called "Bible Women."[192]

The Woman's Foreign Missionary Society in the Southern Church of the United States was instrumental in founding the first institution for preparing deaconesses for work in the Methodist Episcopal Church. This institution was Scarritt Bible and Training School, which was founded in 1892 in Kansas City, Missouri, though it moved in 1924 to Nashville, Tennessee. This institution was founded largely through the efforts of Belle Harris Bennitt, a woman from a wealthy Kentucky family.[193]

At the turn of the century, there were almost two thousand deaconesses in America. In an article published in 1901, Lucy Rider Meyer stated that there were 1,160 deaconesses and probationers in the Methodist Episcopal Church in America.[194] In a 1903 book, Christian Golder estimated that there were twelve hundred Methodist deaconesses, an average increase in deaconesses of 26 percent per year in that denomination for the previous twelve years.[195] The deaconess movement in the Methodist Church was a greater numerical success than in other U.S. denominations. With such a late start (1888 as compared to 1849 for Lutherans) in the United States, why were the Methodists so successful in recruiting deaconesses?

Several factors contributed to their success: (1) the Methodist training schools; (2) the positive attitude toward the English language; (3) the emphasis on inner-city work; (4) the willingness to work with people of diverse ethnic backgrounds; (5) the denomination's size, nationwide distribution, and preponderance of women; and (6) the denomination's early acceptance of women in leadership roles in the church. Taking each of these in turn:

Methodist training schools. The Methodist training schools for Christian workers were an ingenious approach to the training of women and the recruitment of deaconesses. They were noncollegiate schools for laypeople who wanted to enter service for the church. Bible study was the principal preoccupation in the schools, but this was alongside courses of study that led toward nursing, missions, work as a pastor's assistant, work in settlement houses, teaching in Sunday schools, or directing church music programs. Thus there were courses in bookkeeping, medicine, domestic science, and sacred music.[196]

Sixty such training schools opened in the United States in the twenty-five years from 1880 to 1915. In many of these schools, enrollment was open to adults at least to the age of 40, a traditional ceiling for the admission of a deaconess. Educational requirements were flexible; typically they admitted non-high school graduates. The course of study was usually free or inexpensive and lasted about two years—no more than in training schools for teachers, secretaries, and nurses of this era. Opportunities for hands-on experience were available in the cities in which the schools were located, focusing especially on "religious calling" to deliver food, clothing, Bibles, and tracts, as well as a kind word and a helpful hand.[197]

Many deaconesses were recruited from these training schools, and the names of some schools implied their purpose, for example, the New England Deaconess Training School. The schools followed an old tradition and admitted other people. For example, Fliedner's school at Kaiserswerth admitted young women who did not intend to become deaconesses, especially those who wanted to become teachers. Lay education was not Fliedner's major thrust, however, as it was in some of the U.S. Methodist training schools. It was possible in many of the religious training schools in the United States that were located in major cities to live at home and commute to school, thus cutting expenses. This freedom was in contrast to the confinement of deaconess candidates in the Lutheran motherhouse in Philadelphia.[198]

The English language. Whereas most Methodist deaconess homes used English as their primary language, in the Philadelphia Motherhouse the deaconesses initially spoke German and worked primarily among the patients in the German Hospital in Philadelphia. Norwegian and Swedish Lutheran deaconesses in the United States spoke Scandinavian tongues, though the Swedish-American Deaconess Home (Immanuel in Omaha, Nebraska) established English as its primary language from the beginning. Norwegian-Americans relied on deaconesses from the Norwegian Mother House in Christiana (Oslo, Norway) to provide the early leadership for their deaconess movement in the United States. A number of the deaconesses returned to Norway for retirement. In this same ethnocentric spirit, German Methodists insisted on motherhouses of their own, training German-speaking women to work among German immigrants, but they were a minority among Methodist deaconesses.

Inner-city work. Methodist deaconesses in the United States worked in the city as social workers, which was a pressing need in the late nineteenth century. The deaconesses had hospitals, too, but many Methodist deaconess homes were unaffiliated with any hospital, orphanage, or home for the elderly. A significant number of deaconesses lived and worked on their own or with one or two other deaconesses. This was true especially in the foreign mission field. Although motherhouses would continue to be founded in the twentieth century, in many ways they were an institution of the nineteenth century and became less attractive to modern women who saw them as confining.

Work with diverse people-groups. The work of Methodist deaconesses in the cities brought them into contact with a variety of people from diverse ethnic groups in the new immigrant communities. The Methodist deaconesses did not limit their activities to individuals of the same denomination or of the same ethnic background, though specific Methodist deaconess communities did surface to address the needs of particular immigrant groups, such as the German-speaking deaconess homes.

Denominational size and large number of female members. A major factor in the success of the Methodist deaconess movement was the size of the denomination, which experienced rapid growth in the nineteenth century. Methodist circuit riders, who would not have met Lutheran or Presbyterian educational standards for entry into the ministry, had spread Methodism westward with the frontier. Thus the Methodist Church was national in scope in contrast to more ethnically centered denominations that focused on one nineteenth-century immigrant group. Also many Methodists were women and, therefore, potential candidates for deaconess recruitment. An 1872 contributor to the *Ladies Repository*, a magazine read by many Methodists, stated that there were seven hundred thousand women in the Methodist Church—or two hundred thousand more women than men.[199] One might question the statistics on the number of women in the Methodist Church, but the fact that women were in the majority was or would be true of other denominations as well. Improved medical techniques had made childbirth safer than in earlier centuries when it was a major killer of young women, especially those pregnant with their first child. Thus women were living longer.

Women in leadership roles. Methodists traditionally had been receptive to the laity and to the work of women in the church because John Wesley's mother, Susannah, had done evangelical home preaching when her husband, an Anglican parson, was out of the house. Methodist women, like other Protestant women in the nineteenth century, organized to accomplish their goals. The Woman's Home Missionary Society became an advocate of the deaconess movement and gave it financial support. The Woman's Foreign Missionary Society sent the first deaconess missionary abroad. The Methodist deaconess cause had extraordinary well-educated female leaders in Jane and Henrietta Bancroft, Lucy Meyer Rider, Isabella Thoburn, and Louise Golder, to name but a few. It is no wonder, then, that modern U.S. Methodist feminists espoused the deaconess movement in the denomination with zeal. But not only women were enthusiastic. At the turn of the twentieth century, A. J. Nast, the editor of the *Christliche Apologete*, summarized his reasons for the success of the Methodist deaconess movement:

> Methodism is especially adapted, by its very spirit and genius, to carry out this work of love with devotion, zeal, and success. The employment of the varied work and talents of the laity, and the large liberty given to women in the advancement of the kingdom of God have, from the beginning, been two leading characteristics by which Methodism differed and distinguished itself from the other denominations. Another distinction lies in its practical character. We believe that the New Testament idea of the female diaconate was destined to reach its complete and diversified realization in no other Church so readily as in the Methodist Church.[200]

CONGREGATIONALISTS AND BAPTISTS

Deaconess work of the Inner Mission variety in Congregational churches began in the twentieth century, though interest emerged earlier. In 1900 the Illinois State Association of Congregational Churches at Oak Park appointed a committee to look into means for training young women for work in the church. The next year the committee was offered a building in Dover, Illinois. Chicago businessmen endorsed the effort, and a house was rented in the city as a deaconess training home.[201]

Since the seventeenth century, Baptists historically have had congregational deaconesses in some of their churches, for example, in Bristol, England. However, records of seventeenth-century Baptists in the American colonies make no reference to deaconesses. Baptist deaconesses in eighteenth-century North America were primarily found among the Separate Baptists, though a few Particular Baptist churches had deaconesses, as did some of the Tunker (German Baptist) churches in Pennsylvania. There was an apparent decline in deaconesses in Baptist churches in the nineteenth century as deacons, in addition to their concern for the poor, took on more administrative, management, and business responsibilities in congregations.[202]

The Baptist Church in America first attempted to found a deaconess institution in 1894 in New York. Two congregations—the Second German Baptist Church and the English-speaking Amity Church—established the Baptist Deaconess Society of the City of New York. They opened a home in 1895 on West Fifty-Fourth Street that shared space with the Amity Theological School, a nondenominational school for Christian workers. There deaconesses received Bible training, but they went to a city hospital for training in nursing. The women also engaged in parish work. The first deaconess was consecrated in 1897. Shortly after the turn of the century, there were seven consecrated deaconesses and five probationers. They wore uniforms like those of the Methodist deaconesses, except they were dark blue rather than black. Similar efforts were made in Chicago, Illinois; Dayton, Ohio; and Philadelphia, Pennsylvania, at the end of the nineteenth century.[203] The strongest deaconess work among Baptists was among German Baptist deaconesses. In most Baptist churches in the United States, the word *deaconess* referred to a volunteer chosen to serve within the congregation's fellowship, a female version of the male deacon in the congregation. Often the deaconess had restricted responsibilities because the male Baptist deacon had considerable responsibility in church governance.[204]

PRESBYTERIANS

Among the Presbyterians, A. T. McGill at Princeton Theological Seminary recommended the revival of the office of deaconess, but his proposal ran afoul of Presbyterian polity in the nineteenth century, which required that deacons be male.[205] Isolated congregations set apart women from the congregation as deaconesses, however, and eventually deaconesses of the motherhouse variety became acceptable to many Presbyterians and worked in some congregations.[206] In 1914 the Presbyterian School of Christian Education was founded in Richmond, Virginia. Although not destined to train deaconesses, it resembled the training schools that Methodists and others were establishing to train lay workers alongside deaconesses.[207]

SUMMARY AND ANALYSIS

In North America, the deaconess movement had guarded success in the nineteenth century. Deaconess homes often numbered only a few sisters. This was partly the result of the dispersion of U.S. deaconesses in many locations, but it also was the result of fewer overall numbers of deaconesses. Some motherhouses in Europe could number deaconesses in the hundreds, and some had whole constellations of charitable institutions built around them, such as Kaiserswerth or Bielefeld.

The success of European deaconess homes as compared to their North American counterparts is sometimes attributed to a lack of religious devotion on the part of American women or too great a spirit of independence. Instead, one should consider the relative ease that American women had in entering the professions of nursing and teaching without becoming deaconesses. The deaconesses in North America were not pioneers in the same way deaconesses in the Germanies had been. To a young German woman in the nineteenth century, becoming a deaconess held forth the prospect of a more exciting and challenging life than she otherwise might experience in her parents' home or working as a servant. It provided her with vocational mobility. This is not to detract from the religious devotion and self-sacrificing spirit of many of these European women.

Also, the deaconess movement in North America in the nineteenth century was perhaps too imitative of Europe. This was especially true of Lutheran deaconesses. The retention of the European languages and customs was at first an attraction to immigrant girls who entered these institutions, but in the long run, the immigrants ran out, and a transition was necessary to forge a genuinely American institution. Some denominations did better at this than others. The Methodists, with their deaconess social workers and inner-city work, were especially adapted to an urbanizing United States. Methodist training schools and an open attitude toward educating religious laypeople with no prior commitment to the deaconess cause were good recruiting devices. Women's societies also played no small part in the success of the Methodist deaconess movement.

Of course, the deaconess movement was only one part of the story of deacons in North America in the nineteenth century. As Catholics continued their centuries-old tradition of treating the diaconate as transitional to the priesthood, the social welfare functions held by deacons in the early church were now in the hands of Catholic religious orders, parish priests, and bishops. North America also developed new congregations and societies dedicated to an active life in the community. Elizabeth Seton, a convert to Catholicism, inaugurated the Sisters of Charity, a religious community that pioneered Catholic education of children in the United States. The Catholic Church in America made the decision to commit itself to parochial schools staffed with nuns and brothers. This was possible because the nineteenth century was a great age of Catholic vocation. Some countries, such as Ireland, exported priests to serve new immigrant communities in the United States. There were many more Catholic nuns than there were Protestant deaconesses.[208]

Within U.S. Protestantism, many denominations continued to select deacons within individual congregations for volunteer part-time service. These denominations passed this tradition to new denominations, such as the Adventists and the Shakers. Shakers had deacons and deaconesses who took care of household and business problems in their communities. Elders and elderesses dealt with spiritual issues, and the communities also had male or female trustees.

Some Protestant churches in which the office of deacon had lapsed in the seventeenth or eighteenth centuries attempted to revive it in the nineteenth century. For example, in the 1840s there was an increased emphasis on the office of deacon in the Presbyterian Church in America, especially in the South. However, many individual congregations were slow to take steps toward the election of deacons. Presbyterian deacons in the South typically had responsibility for the temporal affairs of churches—at the expense of concern for the poor, some would say. In accord with the Scottish Second Book of Discipline, Presbyterians in the American South in 1879 provided for the ordination of deacons and stipulated that they should "especially relate [not only] to the care of the poor [but also] to the collection and distribution of the offering of the people for pious uses, under the direction of the Session."[209]

Changes in the office of deacon were to come in the next century, especially in the 1960s. However, the first part of the twentieth century was a continuation of the nineteenth, as far as deacons and deaconesses were concerned.

NOTES

1. Golder, *History of the Deaconess Movement*, 170–77.

2. Golder, *History of the Deaconess Movement*, 177.

3. Florence Nightingale, quoted by H. U. Weitbrecht Stanton, "The Modern Revival and Development of Deaconess Life and Work: Womanhood of the Modern Age," in *Ministry of Women*, 197.

4. Jane Bancroft gives 1842 as the date for Fliedner's arrival with "four sisters"; see *Deaconesses in Europe*, 146. Christian Golder gives 1846; see *History of the Deaconess Movement*, 178.

5. Baldwin, "Deaconess Community of St. Andrew," 217–18.

6. Baldwin, "Deaconess Community of St. Andrew," 215, 218.

7. Heeney, *Women's Movement in the Church of England*, 63.

8. Heeney, *Women's Movement in the Church of England*, 10, 19–24, 27–34, 36–45.

9. Heeney, *Women's Movement in the Church of England*, 46–49; Bancroft, *Deaconesses in Europe*, 160.

10. Heeney, *Women's Movement in the Church of England*, 52–55.

11. Church Army USA, *Heart of God for the Broken*, [2].

12. Heeney, *Women's Movement in the Church of England*, 55–57.

13. Church Army, USA, 210 W. North Avenue, Pittsburgh PA 15212-4625 (888/412-5442).

14. Heeney, *Women's Movement in the Church of England*, 58–61.

15. Bancroft, *Deaconesses in Europe*, 160–65.

16. Golder, *History of the Deaconess Movement*, 179.

17. Stanton, "Modern Revival and Development of Deaconess Life and Work," 189–90.

18. Baldwin, "Deaconess Community of St. Andrew," 215, 220.

19. Howson, *Deaconesses*.

20. Howson, quoted in Stanton, "Modern Revival and Development of Deaconess Life and Work," 186.

21. Grierson, *Deaconess*, 21.

22. "Kaiserswerth and London," *Diakonia News* 87 (November 2000): [5].

23. Baldwin, "Deaconess Community of St. Andrew," 216.

24. Stanton, "Modern Revival and Development of Deaconess Life and Work," 187.

25. "Kaiserswerth and London," [5].

26. Sister Teresa [Joan White], electronic mail, 16 August 2003.

27. Baldwin, "Deaconess Community of St. Andrew," 219.

28. Baldwin, "Deaconess Community of St. Andrew," 220–22.

29. Grierson, *Deaconess*, 21; Bancroft, *Deaconesses in Europe*, 152.

30. Baldwin, "Deaconess Community of St. Andrew," 220–22.

31. Stanton, "Modern Revival and Development of Deaconess Life and Work," 70.

32. Baldwin, "Deaconess Community of St. Andrew," 222–24.

33. Baldwin, "Deaconess Community of St. Andrew," 224.

34. Baldwin, "Deaconess Community of St. Andrew," 228.

35. Sister Teresa, electronic mail to author, 13 August 2003.

36. Baldwin, "Deaconess Community of St. Andrew," 229.

37. Baldwin, "Deaconess Community of St. Andrew," 224.

38. Baldwin, "Deaconess Community of St. Andrew," 226, 228.

39. Baldwin, "Deaconess Community of St. Andrew," 224–25.

40. Sister Teresa, electronic mail to author, 13 August 2003.

41. Baldwin, "Deaconess Community of St. Andrew," 224–25.

42. Bancroft, *Deaconesses in Europe*, 154, 157.

43. Sister Teresa, electronic mail, 13 August 2003.

44. Bancroft, *Deaconesses in Europe*, 187, 204; Stanton, "Modern Revival and Development of Deaconess Life and Work," 24; Golder, *History of the Deaconess Movement*, 183.

45. Stanton, "Modern Revival and Development of Deaconess Life and Work," 189; Bancroft, *Deaconesses in Europe*, 166–70, 173.

46. Golder, *History of the Deaconess Movement*, 187.

47. Lambeth Conferences are periodic gatherings of the bishops of churches of the worldwide Anglican community.

48. Quoted in [Mary] Siddall and Barker, "The Ministry and Order of Deaconesses," in *Ministry of Women*, 202–3.

49. Siddall and Baker, "Ministry and Order of Deaconesses," 205.

50. Heeney, *Women's Movement in the Church of England*, 69.

51. Stanton, "Modern Revival and Development of Deaconess Life and Work," 189–90; Golder, *History of the Deaconess Movement*, 186–90.

52. Bancroft, *Deaconesses in Europe*, 166.

53. Bancroft, *Deaconesses in Europe*, 158–59; Golder, *History of the Deaconess Movement*, 184–85.

54. Grierson, *Deaconess*, 100.

55. "Australian Anglican Diaconal Association," *Diakonia News* 78 (July 1990): 30.

56. Grierson, *Deaconess*, 101–2; Golder, *History of the Deaconess Movement*, 463–64.

57. "The Anglican Deaconess Order," *Diakonia News* 78 (July 1990): 6; Grierson, *Deaconess*, 103.

58. Golder, *History of the Deaconess Movement*, 462–63, 474; Grierson, *Deaconess*, 104.

59. Grierson, *Deaconess*, 105.

60. Grierson, *Deaconess*, 106; Golder, *History of the Deaconess Movement*, 464–65.

61. Grierson, *Deaconess*, 107–8.

62. Golder, *History of the Deaconess Movement*, 191–95; "Methodist Diaconal Order 100 Years," *Diakonia News* 78 (July 1990): 21.

63. Golder, *History of the Deaconess Movement*, 195–98.

64. Golder, *History of the Deaconess Movement*, 198–201; "Methodist Diaconal Order, Methodist Church of Great Britain," *Diakonia News* 78 (July 1990): 28.

65. Warner, "Wesley Deaconess-Evangelists," 179, 187.

66. Warner, "Wesley Deaconess-Evangelists," 179, 186–89.

67. Warner, "Wesley Deaconess-Evangelists," 188–89.

68. Warner, "Wesley Deaconess-Evangelists," 176.

69. Warner, "Wesley Deaconess-Evangelists," 176n4.

70. Stanton, "Modern Revival and Development of Deaconess Life and Work," 194, 201–7; Bancroft, *Deaconesses in Europe*, 189–203.

71. "The Book of the Church of Scotland," 74, in James Cooper, "Deaconesses in the Established Church of Scotland," Appendix XIII, in *Ministry of Women*, 216–17.

72. Golder, *History of the Deaconess Movement*, 204.

73. Golder, *History of the Deaconess Movement*, 249–50; Weiser, "Serving Love," 1–2, 14.

74. Weiser, "Serving Love," 2–3.

75. *Zehnter Jahresbericht über die Diakonissen-Anstalt zu Kaiserswerth am Rhein, vom 1. Januar 1846 bis 1. Januar 1847 . . . in Das Erste Jahr-Zehnt der Diakonissen-Anstalt zu Kaiserswerth am Rhein, vom 13. Oktober 1836 bis 1. Januar 1847 . . .* (Kaiserswerth: Diakonissen-Anstalt, n.d.), 183–84, in Weiser, "Serving Love," 5.

76. "A Brief History of the Lutheran Deaconess Motherhouses in America," in *Proceedings and Papers of the Seventh Conference of Evangelical Motherhouses in the United States* (Philadelphia: Edward Stern, 1908), 32.

77. Golder, *History of the Deaconess Movement*, 251; Weiser, "Serving Love," 6.

78. Golder, *History of the Deaconess Movement*, 7; "History of the Lutheran Deaconess Motherhouse at Milwaukee," [1].

79. Weiser, "Serving Love," 7–8.

80. Fliedner, "Journey to North America," 31–41; Weiser, "Serving Love," 8.

81. Lee, *As among the Methodists*, 29; Weiser, "Serving Love," 8–9, 12–13, 28–29.

82. Quoted in Muhlenberg, *Two Letters on Protestant Sisterhoods*, 28.

83. "Brief History of the Lutheran Deaconess Motherhouses in America," 33.

84. Henry Jacobs, *A History of the Evangelical Lutheran Church in the United States*, The American Church History Series Consisting of a Series of Denominational Histories Published under the Auspices of the American Society of Church History, vol. 4 (New York: Christian Literature Co., 1898), 386–87; Weiser, "Serving Love," 11–14, 24.

85. Weiser, "Serving Love," 14, 24–25.

86. Weiser, "Serving Love," 39–41; "History of the Lutheran Deaconess Motherhouse at Milwaukee," [1].

87. "History of the Lutheran Deaconess Motherhouse at Milwaukee," [1]; Weiser, "Serving Love," 41–43.

88. Weiser, "Serving Love," 42.

89. Weiser, "Serving Love," 25–26, 42–43; *Mary J. Drexel Home and Philadelphia Motherhouse*, 43.

90. "History of the Lutheran Deaconess Motherhouse at Milwaukee," [1]; Weiser, "Serving Love," 43.

91. "Brief History of the Lutheran Deaconess Motherhouses in America," 33; Weiser, "Serving Love," 32–34, 43.

92. Jacobs, *History of the Evangelical Lutheran Church*, 387; Weiser, "Serving Love," 43–44.

93. Weiser, "Serving Love," 33–34.

94. Jacobs, *History of the Evangelical Lutheran Church*, 387.

95. William Passavant, *The Missionary* (1852), in Golder, *History of the Deaconess Movement*, 44–47, 255–56.

96. Weiser, "Serving Love," 96–98.

97. *Proceedings and Papers of the Third Conference of Evangelical Lutheran Deaconess Motherhouses in the United States, Omaha, Neb., October 4 and 5, 1899* (Philadelphia: Edward Stern, n.d.), 5–6.

98. Weiser, "Serving Love," 98–99.

99. Weiser, "Serving Love," 35; Spaeth, *Deaconess and Her Work*, 72.

100. Spaeth, *Deaconess and Her Work*, 72–75; Weiser, "Serving Love," 35–36.

101. Bachmann, *Story of the Philadelphia Deaconess Motherhouse*, 13–14.

102. "Brief History of the Lutheran Deaconess Motherhouses in America," 35.

103. Wolf, *Lutherans in America*; Bachmann, *Story of the Philadelphia Deaconess Motherhouse*, 5–14; *Mary J. Drexel Home and Philadelphia Motherhouse*, 6–15, 19–28, 34–38; Bancroft, *Deaconesses in Europe*, 210; Bachmann and Bachmann, *Lutheran Churches in the World*, 377.

104. *Proceedings and Papers of the Third Conference of Evangelical Lutheran Deaconess Motherhouses*, 5.

105. Bachmann, *Story of the Philadelphia Deaconess Motherhouse*, 19; Wacker, *Deaconess Calling*, 127; Weiser, "Serving Love," 58–59.

106. Bancroft, *Deaconesses in Europe*, 210; *The Deaconesses Messenger* 1 (1890), in Weiser, "Serving Love," 59.

107. Sister Bertha Mueller to Frederick S. Weiser, February 22, 1960, in Weiser, "Serving Love," 55, 59–60, 71–72; Bachmann, *Story of the Philadelphia Deaconess Motherhouse*, 12.

108. Spaeth, *Deaconess and Her Work*, 156.

109. The Ministerium of Pennsylvania had joined with other Lutheran synods in 1867 to form the General Council after breaking away from the General Synod over its 1864 admission to its ranks of the Franckean Synod, which did not subscribe to the Augsburg Confession. The Missouri Synod, the Iowa Synod, and the Joint Synod of Ohio did not join the General Council, though they participated in a preliminary meeting December 12–14, 1866, with the Pennsylvania Ministerium; the New York Ministerium; the Pittsburgh Synod; the Minnesota Synod; the English Synod of Ohio; the English District Synod of Ohio; and the Wisconsin, Michigan, Canada, and Norwegian Synods. See August Suelflow and E. Clifford Nelson, "Following the Frontier, 1840–1875," in Nelson, *Lutherans in North America*, 234–37.

110. Weiser, "Serving Love," 53–63.

111. *Mary J. Drexel Home and Philadelphia Motherhouse*, 32; Weiser, "Serving Love," 63–67.

112. Elizabeth Fedde, "Diary, 1883–38," trans. and ed. Beulah Folkedahl, *Norwegian-American Studies and Records* 20 (1959), 170, 173, in Everson, "Demise of a Movement," 2; Weiser, "Serving Love," 74–77.

113. From N. N. Ronning and W. H. Lien, *They Followed Him: The Lutheran Deaconess Home and Hospital, 1889–1939* (Minneapolis: The Lutheran Deaconess Home and Hospital, 1939), 39, quoted in Lagerquist, *From Our Mother's Arms*, 68.

114. Weiser, "Serving Love," 76–78, 79–80; Bancroft, *Deaconesses in Europe*, 211.

115. *Proceedings and Papers of the Third Conference of Evangelical Lutheran Deaconess Motherhouses*, 6.

116. *Proceedings and Papers of the Third Conference of Evangelical Lutheran Deaconess Motherhouses*, 7; Weiser, "Serving Love," 78, 80.

117. Weiser, "Serving Love," 79.

118. Fedde, "Diary," in Everson, "Demise of a Movement," 173, 185, 188, 191.

119. *Proceedings and Papers of the Seventh Conference of Evangelical Lutheran Deaconess Motherhouses*, 46; Weiser, "Serving Love," 81.

120. *Proceedings and Papers of the Third Conference of Evangelical Lutheran Deaconess Motherhouses*, 7; Weiser, "Serving Love," 82.

121. Meyer, *Deaconesses*, 54.

122. Bachmann, *Story of the Philadelphia Deaconess Motherhouse*, 17; Weiser, "Serving Love," 86–89.

123. *Proceedings and Papers of the Third Conference of Evangelical Lutheran Deaconess Motherhouses*, 5; *Proceedings and Papers of the Seventh Conference of Evangelical Lutheran Deaconess Motherhouses*, 44.

124. "Brief History of the Lutheran Deaconess Motherhouses in America," 5; Spaeth, *Deaconess and Her Work*, 78; Weiser, "Serving Love," 90–91.

125. Weiser, "Serving Love," 105.

126. Weiser, "Serving Love," 105–9; Bachmann, *Story of the Philadelphia Deaconess Motherhouse*, 18.

127. "Brief History of the Lutheran Deaconess Motherhouses in America," 40.

128. *Proceedings and Papers of the Third Conference of Evangelical Lutheran Deaconess Motherhouses*, 6; Weiser, "Serving Love," 109–12.

129. *Proceedings and Papers of the First Conference of Evangelical Lutheran Deaconess Motherhouses*, 3–39; Bachmann, *Story of the Philadelphia Deaconess Motherhouse*, 18.

130. Weiser, "Serving Love," 128.

131. Golder, *History of the Deaconess Movement*, 273–87, 291, 302–4.

132. Golder, *History of the Deaconess Movement*, 287–91.

133. Golder, *History of the Deaconess Movement*, 300–301.

134. Bancroft, *Deaconesses in Europe*, 24, 211.

135. Rasche, "Deaconess Sisters," 97, 99; Golder, *History of the Deaconess Movement*, 291–95, 472.

136. Golder, *History of the Deaconess Movement*, 299–300.

137. Rasche, "Deaconess Sisters," 96–98; Golder, *History of the Deaconess Movement*, 296–99.

138. Golder, *History of the Deaconess Movement*, 302.

139. Quoted in Golder, *History of the Deaconess Movement*, 446; Lee, *As among the Methodists*, 42.

140. Meyer, *Deaconesses*, 58.

141. In the United States, the umlaut tended, over time, to drop out of the Mühlenberg family name.

142. Muhlenberg, *Two Letters on Protestant Sisterhoods*, iv, vi, 25–26.

143. Golder, *History of the Deaconess Movement*, 449–51.

144. Spaeth, *Deaconess and Her Work*, 82.

145. Hein and Shattuck, *Episcopalians*.

146. Hein and Shattuck, *Episcopalians*; Bancroft, *Deaconesses in Europe*, 212–16; Golder, *History of the Deaconess Movement*, 451–61; Grierson, *Deaconess*, 97.

147. Hein and Shattuck, *Episcopalians*.

148. Grierson, *Deaconess*, 97–98.

149. Hein and Shattuck, *Episcopalians*.

150. Meeker, *Six Decades of Service*, 1–8.

151. Meeker, *Six Decades of Service*, 1, 3–4; Golder, *History of the Deaconess Movement*, 307–11.

152. Meeker, *Six Decades of Service*, 4–8, 97; Lee, *As among the Methodists*, 32–34.

153. Meyer, "Mother in the Church," 11–14; Meyer, *Deaconesses*, 85, 160, 195, 218–20, 225–29.

154. Horton, *High Adventure*, 1–99; Lee, *As among the Methodists*, 31–35; Meyer, *Deaconesses*, 86–97, 114, 207; Golder, *History of the Deaconess Movement*, 315–20, 341–46; Keller, Moede, and Moore, *Called to Serve*, 32.

155. Meyer, *Deaconesses*, 140.

156. Golder, *History of the Deaconess Movement*, 345–46.

157. Dougherty, *My Calling to Fulfill*, 94–180.

158. Lucy Rider Meyer, quoted in Horton, *Burden of the City* (1904), 145–46, quoted in Keller, Moede, and Moore, *Called to Serve*, 32.

159. Meyer, *Deaconesses*, 71, 73–74, 77, 148, 192, 236–37.

160. Golder, *History of the Deaconess Movement*, 311–16, 320; Bancroft, *Deaconesses in Europe*, 221.

161. Preface to the resolutions of Thoburn's committee in Golder, *History of the Deaconess Movement*, 320–21. This quotation is worded differently in Bancroft, *Deaconesses in Europe*, 222–23.

162. Lee, *As among the Methodists*, 37.

163. Meyer, *Deaconesses*, 205.

164. Bancroft, *Deaconesses in Europe*, 226; Golder, *History of the Deaconess Movement*, 331–32; Meyer, *Deaconesses*, 75–79, 167.

165. Lee, *As among the Methodists*, 48–49.

166. Golder, *History of the Deaconess Movement*, 428.

167. Quoted from additions to the Discipline of the Methodist Church, in Golder, *History of the Deaconess Movement*, 334–39.

168. Keller, Moede, and Moore, *Called to Serve*, 27.

169. Letzig, "Deaconesses Past and Present," 30.

170. Bancroft, *Deaconesses in Europe*, 226–27; Meeker, *Six Decades of Service*, 91–95, 102; Golder, *History of the Deaconess Movement*, 322–28, 339, 362–63, 387–88.

171. Meeker, *Six Decades of Service*, 93–94; Golder, *History of the Deaconess Movement*, 328–30.

172. For a thorough list of Woman's Home Missionary Society projects, see Meeker, *Six Decades of Service*, 91–368.

173. Golder, *History of the Deaconess Movement*, 326, 362–67, 369–70, 376–77, 383–90; Meeker, *Six Decades of Service*, 98–106; Lee, *As among the Methodists*, 38.

174. Lee, *As among the Methodists*, 38; Golder, *History of the Deaconess Movement*, 367, 369–70, 390.

175. Golder, *History of the Deaconess Movement*, 339–40.
176. Meyer, "Mother in the Church," 14–15.
177. J. M. Buckley, *A History of Methodists in the United States*, 6th ed. (New York: Charles Scribner's Sons, 1897), 679; Lee, *As among the Methodists*, 40; Golder, *History of the Deaconess Movement*, 354–62; Bancroft, *Deaconesses in Europe*, 226.
178. Bancroft, *Deaconesses in Europe*, 226; Golder, *History of the Deaconess Movement*, 373–76.
179. Gaintner, *New England Deaconess Hospital*, 8.
180. Golder, *History of the Deaconess Movement*, 370–72, 386.
181. Golder, *History of the Deaconess Movement*, 393–95; Meeker, *Six Decades of Service*, 325.
182. Golder, *History of the Deaconess Movement*, 397–98, 400–401.
183. Gaintner, *New England Deaconess Hospital*, 17–21.
184. Meeker, *Six Decades of Service*, 324–25; Golder, *History of the Deaconess Movement*, 349–53, 407–9.
185. Bancroft, *Deaconesses in Europe*, 242.
186. Keller, Moede, and Moore, *Called to Serve*, 32–35.
187. Golder, *History of the Deaconess Movement*, 367–69, 380–82, 395–96, 399–400, 402–6.
188. Golder, *History of the Deaconess Movement*, 377, 379, 409–13; Meeker, *Six Decades of Service*, 107.
189. Golder, *History of the Deaconess Movement*, 429–32; Lee, *As among the Methodists*, 40.
190. Lee, *As among the Methodists*, 42–44; Golder, *History of the Deaconess Movement*, 427–28, 432–38.
191. Golder, *History of the Deaconess Movement*, 435, 438–48; Lee, *As among the Methodists*, 42–43, 45.
192. Lee, *As among the Methodists*, 40, 104; Golder, *History of the Deaconess Movement*, 413–25.
193. Keller, Moede, and Moore, *Called to Serve*, 39.
194. Keller, Moede, and Moore, *Called to Serve*, 26; Meyer, "Mother in the Church," 14.
195. Golder, *History of the Deaconess Movement*, 484.
196. Keller, Moede, and Moore, *Called to Serve*, 40–41.
197. Keller, Moede, and Moore, *Called to Serve*, 40–41; Prelinger and Keller, "Function of Female Bonding," 326–27.
198. Prelinger and Keller, "Function of Female Bonding," 326–27; Keller, Moede, and Moore, *Called to Serve*, 40–41.
199. Quoted in Golder, *History of the Deaconess Movement*, 306.
200. A. J. Nast, quoted in Golder, *History of the Deaconess Movement*, 447.
201. Golder, *History of the Deaconess Movement*, 465–67.
202. Deweese, "Deaconesses in Baptist History," 52–55.
203. Deweese, "Deaconesses in Baptist History," 55; Golder, *History of the Deaconess Movement*, 472–74.
204. Thomas, *Deacon in a Changing Church*, 114.
205. Thompson, *History of the Presbyterian Churches*, 229.
206. Bancroft, *Deaconesses in Europe*, 217–19.
207. For a history of this institution, see McComb, *Presbyterian School of Christian Education*.
208. Latourette, *Christianity in a Revolutionary Age*, 1:160.
209. Thompson, *Presbyterians in the South*, 1:521–22; 2:417–20.

CHAPTER SEVEN
THE TWENTIETH CENTURY
DEACONESSES AND DEACONS

The shape of the diaconate in the church responded to the tremendous changes of the twentieth century, but the beginning of the century continued the institutions, lifestyle, and world of thought of the late nineteenth century. Deacons on the Inner Mission model thrived. Deaconess communities grew. New communities were established. In some regions, growth continued until World War II, but by the post-World War II era, the deaconess movement appeared to have peaked, and the deaconess movement had problems with recruitment.

The lifestyle of industrialized nations had undergone dramatic changes with the advancement of technology. These changes were true especially for women, who in the twentieth century entered the world of work outside the home in ever increasing numbers. Some deaconess communities made an adjustment to the modern world, survived, and even thrived. Others died out entirely.

Parallel to these developments in the deaconess movement, denominations that had elected deacons from their lay membership continued to do so, and some individual churches that did not have deacons at all, or that had allowed the office to lapse, revived it. The diaconate continued as a step to the priesthood within Roman Catholicism and within the worldwide Anglican Communion that included Episcopalians in the United States. Likewise, many Methodist groups continued the diaconate as a stage before becoming a minister (elder). In the 1960s to the 1980s, Catholics, Episcopalians, and Methodists also supported a permanent life-long diaconate that was not a step to the priesthood or to becoming a minister. In 1993 in the United States, United Methodists did away with the transitional deacon.

Ecumenical discussions among various Christian groups led to a desire to resolve differences in the configuration of the diaconate among those churches that elected lay deacons from the local congregation, those churches that had no deacons at all, and those churches whose deacons were either on their way to becoming ministers or were considered permanent. The need to resolve differences in church office became particularly acute when churches united or when Lutheran synods merged. Some new denominations tolerated a benign federalism whereby each individual congregation continued to do what it had done before the merger with regard to deacons, though the practices within the denomination varied as a result. Other denominations sought greater conformity among participating congregations and faced the problem of finding a solution to church office that pleased everyone. One way to postpone the decision of what to do about deacons and other church offices and to attempt to arrive at consensus was to inaugurate a study of ministry, which is what the ELCA did. This placed pressure on those involved in the study to come up with an acceptable solution without alienating the denomination's constituency.

Older denominations, such as the United Methodist Church, also considered changes in church office and initiated studies. When these studies encompassed other aspects of church office, as with the study by the ELCA, the diaconate sometimes took second place to denominational concerns about bishops, ministers, and other church officers. Nevertheless, deacons did enter into consideration.

To facilitate consideration of the complexities of the diaconate in the modern world, this book has three chapters on the twentieth century. The first covers deaconesses and deacons of the type who emerged after the work of Fliedner, Wichern, and the Inner Mission in the nineteenth century. The second chapter covers the permanent diaconate after World War II, concentrating on Catholic, Episcopal, and United Methodist churches. This chapter also includes the deacons and deaconesses of Germany and Scandinavia, who in effect became permanent deacons as they were integrated into national church programs and as their mother- and father-houses were turned into institutions for diaconal education for the Scandinavian Lutheran churches. The third chapter covers contemporary trends in diaconal ministry in Lutheran and other denominations, as well as ecumenical dialogue among church bodies.

This first of three chapters on the twentieth century includes the history of many women because of their extensive involvement in the deaconess movement, but there are also deacons of the Inner Mission variety. In the post-World War II world, women were allowed to become deacons in some denominations, and the use of inclusive terminology to refer to deacons and deaconesses came into greater use. The international diaconal associations of the postwar era reflect that change.

This chapter begins with a brief survey of changes in society and culture in the twentieth century, the context within which the diaconate functioned. It then considers the diaconal movement in North America, in Europe, and in the rest of the world. It ends with the international diaconal organizations of the post-World War II era.

IMPACT OF SOCIETY AND CULTURE
ON THE DIACONATE

The cultural milieu has influenced the diaconate in every age. The modern diaconal movement emerged, in part, out of a revival in the church in the nineteenth century and a need to meet problems of industrialization and urbanization. In the twentieth century, cities continued to grow and nations continued to industrialize, so, too, the basic patterns of life of the nineteenth century continued. Within this milieu, the deaconess movement flourished.

Although there were problems in late nineteenth-century society, many of them were on the way to being solved, especially in the area of technology, where an improvement as simple as the introduction of modern plumbing and a pure water supply could revolutionize the comfort and health of thousands. Many people were convinced that humankind could solve most of its own problems. For a few years the late nineteenth-century optimism continued into the next century, but two world wars and a depression dominated the first half of the twentieth century. World War I (1914–1918) jolted Europe out of its complacency and changed the way people lived. Confronted by the horrors of war and what he saw as the reality of human sin, the Swiss theologian Karl Barth made his internal transition from the religious liberalism of the late nineteenth century to neoorthodoxy. For him and for others, the bubble of optimism and self-sufficiency burst.

With the men off to war, women entered the workforce in unprecedented numbers. Some of them staffed the munition plants. Although many of these women returned to housewifery after the war, they had gained the vote in the United States and elsewhere. There was no going back to what had been before. Women used their political power. They were a major force in the prohibition of alcoholic beverages in postwar United States. Confronted with the problems of alcoholism in the inner city, deaconesses advocated Prohibition. Already in 1896, *The Deaconess Advocate*, the journal of the Chicago Training School, supported the Prohibition Party, though the journal criticized the party's failure to support women's suffrage.[1]

During World War II (1939–1945), women entered the workforce again. After the war, they remained as a permanent feature in the workplace. In the 1960s and beyond, women routinely entered professions that previously had been almost exclusively male, such as medicine, law, and the ministry (in many denominations). More and more married women with children worked outside the home. The changing face of the workforce had its impact on the deaconess movement. Single women who formerly had been attracted to the possibility of a fulfilling life of service as a deaconess now could have a satisfactory professional life while being married and raising children. Recruitment of deaconesses lagged in many regions after World War II. Nevertheless, the deaconess movement established new institutions even as the old ones failed.

LUTHERAN DEACONESSES AND DEACONS

Among Lutheran synods in the United States, the deaconess movement had varied success, though by European standards it was never numerically large. Some Lutheran synods in North America, such as the Missouri Synod, had no deaconess program at the beginning of the century but developed one later.[2] Other Lutheran synods had deaconess programs throughout the first half of the century but lost them after that. The general story in the early decades of the twentieth century was one of the expansion of deaconess programs already in existence and the founding of new programs. Some of these programs, as in Europe, had deacons associated with them.

Beginning in chronological order, in 1902 the Augustana Synod expanded its deaconess program by founding a motherhouse in St. Paul, Minnesota, where it owned Bethesda Hospital. The sisters were nurses in the hospital but also served parishes, a home for the elderly, a children's home, and foreign missions. In 1930 the Bethesda Deaconess Home merged with the Immanuel Deaconess Institute in Omaha, Nebraska. Bethesda Hospital took over the vacated quarters in St. Paul.[3]

In 1903 Pastor Jens Madsen led Danish American Lutherans to found a Lutheran Deaconess Institute and a tuberculosis sanatorium in Brush, Colorado (which in 1907 was named Ebenezer Mercy Institute).[4] There Madsen established both a male and female diaconate and added a home for the elderly (1907) and a small hospital (1915).[5] He also founded *Una Sancta*, a journal supportive of the liturgical movement. Madsen's wife had trained at Immanuel Deaconess Institute, Omaha, Nebraska.[6]

Bethel in Germany inspired the institutions at Brush and also an institution for persons with mental retardation and epilepsy in Axtell, Nebraska.[7] In 1913 at Axtell, K. G. William Dahl and the Augustana Synod founded the Bethpage Inner Mission Association of Nebraska.[8] Like Madsen in Colorado, Dahl instituted both the male and female diaconate.[9]

Missouri Synod Lutherans became involved in deaconess work as individuals in several places but chiefly in Fort Wayne, Indiana, in 1919, though this was hardly the beginning of their charitable work. By the turn of the century, the Missouri Synod had eight orphanages, the earliest established in 1868, and five homes for the aged, the earliest dating from 1875. By World War I, the Missouri Synod had added three more homes for the elderly. Missouri Synod Lutherans established a school for the deaf at Detroit in 1874. Two decades later, Pastor August Reinke of Chicago conducted services for those unable to hear or speak; other Midwest cities followed his example. The Missouri Synod assumed responsibility for this work in 1896 and had three missionaries to the deaf within a year. Like other synods in the United States, the Missouri Synod established charitable institutions separately from the deaconess movement.[10] The synod rejected an appeal by Pastor F. W. Herzberger at the 1911 general convention in St. Louis to take on the deaconess cause. The deaconess movement organized without synodical sponsorship but with the help of individuals from within the Missouri Synod.[11]

THE LUTHERAN DEACONESS ASSOCIATION

Deaconess work began on a permanent basis in Fort Wayne, Indiana, in 1919, initiated by individuals from within the Evangelical Lutheran Synodical Conference, which encompassed Midwestern German Lutherans. This conference was a federation of Lutheran synods committed to the confessional documents of *The Book of Concord* (published in 1580), especially the Augsburg Confession. In 1872 the Evangelical Lutheran Synodical Conference formed from the Missouri, Wisconsin, Illinois, and Norwegian Synods and the Joint Synod of Ohio. All of these synods were unaffiliated with the General Synod and the General Council. The Evangelical Lutheran Synodical Conference met periodically and attempted common efforts in social welfare and missions. By the time of the establishment of a deaconess program in 1919, the Ohio and Norwegian Synods had dropped out and the Slovak Synod had joined.[12]

In July 1919 a deaconess association organized and asked the Lutheran Hospital in Fort Wayne to accept deaconess candidates in its nursing school. The Lutheran Deaconess Association of the Evangelical Lutheran Synodical Conference of North America incorporated under the laws of Indiana on April 10, 1920. The first president was Pastor Philip Wambsganss, a son of one of the four deaconesses that Passavant brought to the United States from Europe in 1849. The Lutheran Deaconess Association (LDA) was a "free-standing Lutheran organization to train and support deaconesses." It had branch hospitals and training schools at Hot Springs, North Dakota, and at Beaver Dam (1922) and Watertown, Wisconsin.[13] The training school at Watertown opened on April 15, 1925, and combined with an institution for the mentally challenged and epileptics already in existence.[14] Freestanding Lutheran organizations were not unusual at the time. Clara Strehlow (1895–1985), a graduate of the school's first deaconess class, helped found the deaconesses' own Lutheran Deaconess Conference and served as its president from 1934–1938.[15]

Deaconesses were paid professional female workers in the Missouri Synod.[16] Most of the deaconesses were nurses, as were Lutheran deaconesses across the country. In 1935 the Wisconsin and North Dakota schools closed, replaced by a unified program at Fort Wayne. After 1935 a woman had to complete her professional training for teaching, nursing, or social work before entering a year of deaconess training at Fort Wayne. In 1941 the deaconess training expanded to two years, and the field of parish work opened for deaconesses.[17]

In 1943 the deaconess training moved within Indiana to the university associated with the Evangelical Lutheran Synodical Conference, Valparaiso University. The LDA remains on this campus today. The motherhouse concept, in the usual sense, was gone, but there were annual conferences.[18] In 1946 the training program included a college education with a baccalaureate degree and a major in religious education. The number of deaconess candidates grew. In 1957 a dormitory and hall were built for the women. The common dormitory served to some extent as a motherhouse because the deaconess students lived together with a deaconess director, and there was a kitchen, a dining room, and a chapel with stained-glass windows.[19] In 1958 Clara Strehlow became the first director of this training program and continued in the position until her retirement in 1963.[20] Also in 1958, a fifth year was added to deaconess training: a one-year internship.[21] The deaconess students also had a sorority, Pi Delta Chi, and were integrated into campus life at Valparaiso University.[22]

During the 1950s and early 1960s, the LDA was in close relationship with the LCMS. The graduates were assigned through the LCMS Council of Presidents; all the deaconesses were serving in the LCMS; and the deaconesses were listed as such in LCMS statistics. Several requests were made to the LCMS to take over the program, but the denomination was content to let the Lutheran Deaconess Association remain freestanding. Further involvement would have involved financial responsibilities.[23]

In 1969 the LDA became inter-Lutheran. At that time the LCMS was in altar and pulpit fellowship with the ALC. In 1975 the LDA revised its articles of incorporation and its bylaws to express its inter-Lutheran character. Thus when the Association of Evangelical Lutheran Churches (AELC) took final steps to organize in December 1976, a number of deaconesses of the LDA were in congregations that became part of the AELC.[24] Some deaconesses had found jobs in other Lutheran churches. However, the 1979 version of the LDA articles still stated that a purpose of the LDA was "to serve the church, with primary reference to The Lutheran Church—Missouri Synod," and it welcomed as a member "any person who supports the aims of the Lutheran Deaconess Association, Inc., and evidences this support with a contribution of $10.00 or more."[25] A 1989 presentation to the ELCA study of ministry revealed that the LDA maintained a liaison with the Department of Higher Education of the LCMS, which it still maintains, and with the Division of Ministry of the ELCA. The members of the board of directors of the LDA are approximately half LCMS and half ELCA.[26] For example, the current (May 2005) thirteen-person board of directors of the LDA is composed of deaconesses, pastors, and laypeople, five of whom are from the LCMS and seven of whom are from the ELCA. One member is from the Evangelical Lutheran Church in Canada. An ELCA Division of Ministry staffperson attends the biannual board meetings of the LDA in an advisory capacity.[27]

Deaconesses of the LDA can remain deaconesses in full-time service even after marriage. They serve several Lutheran bodies, including some who serve within the LCMS. But the LCMS requires that its ministers of religion be graduated and certified by a synodical university after completing a synodical course of study or the equivalent as determined by a colloquy committee. Valparaiso is a freestanding Lutheran university and is not an LCMS institution. Deaconesses of the LDA who already had been listed by the LCMS as deaconesses before this 1986 ruling went into effect were grandfathered (or grandmothered) in, but new LDA deaconesses who wish to be rostered with the Synod must apply to the LCMS colloquy committee, which decides what, if anything, the candidate must do to be rostered, for example, coursework at a synodical university or a paper on doctrine.[28] LDA deaconesses who apply for the colloquy procedure often have a call to an LCMS congregation and being rostered with the Synod is a condition of employment.[29] The deaconess also may seek to be rostered on her own, though it is not required.[30] To serve in chaplaincy for the LCMS, the deaconesses must be rostered.[31]

Deaconesses of the LDA are also active in the ELCA. Some of them have enrolled at seminaries and have been ordained pastors within that denomination. Although the deaconesses of the Deaconess Community of the ELCA, formerly of Gladwyne, Pennsylvania, cannot remain deaconesses if they seek ordination as pastors, some deaconesses of the LDA at Valparaiso are deaconesses and pastors at the same time.[32] These deaconesses are officially on only one roster for the ELCA—that for ordained pastors. Deaconess-to-pastor is not a typical career path, however. In addition to deaconesses who are ELCA pastors, other LDA deaconesses were rostered in the early years of the ELCA as AELC deaconesses (21); commissioned church staff in The American Lutheran Church, a denomination formed in 1960 from a merger of the ALC with other Lutheran synods (4); LCA lay professionals (8); and ELCA associates in ministry (8).[33] These categories reflect the fact that the ELCA honored the rosters inherited from its predecessor churches until the ELCA created new rosters after the completion of its study of the ministry in 1993. LDA deaconesses are on all three current ELCA rosters as ordained ministers, as diaconal ministers, and as associates in ministry.[34] For example, Louise Williams, the executive director of the Lutheran Deaconess Association, is on the ELCA roster of associates in ministry.[35] There were also LDA deaconesses who were not rostered by the ELCA but who were related to it.

As of October 19, 1990, the LDA had fifty-one of its deaconesses working (for pay or as volunteers) in ELCA parishes and twenty-seven in ELCA agencies or institutions. At this same time, the LDA had fifty-eight deaconesses working in LCMS parishes, forty in LCMS agencies and institutions, and five in LCMS missions. The LDA had fifty-two deaconesses in nonchurch-related agencies and institutions.[36] LDA deaconesses also were serving in the Evangelical Lutheran Church in Canada in the latter half of the twentieth century.[37]

The LDA had approached the ELCA "seeking to become a related organization," though this would not exclude work in the LCMS. As a result of its study of the ministry, the ELCA Division for Ministry decided not to establish a more formal relationship with the LDA, though the two organizations maintain a collegial working relationship.[38]

Lutheran Deaconess Conference deaconesses work in ecumenical and secular agencies, such as soup kitchens, that are not directly affiliated with a Lutheran church.[39] One recent graduate is a medical student at the Mayo Clinic Medical School in Rochester, Minnesota.[40] Lutheran Deaconess Conference deaconesses work wherever a deaconess can be effective.

The Lutheran Deaconess Association and the Lutheran Deaconess Conference have an independent spirit, perhaps as a result of their relative autonomy. They do not receive financial support "through the budget of any church body or of Valparaiso" University.[41] Besides paying the salaries of the three deaconesses on staff at Valparaiso, Indiana, the LDA pays for its own utilities and secretarial staff. The university pays the deaconesses for classes they teach at the university, which are open to all Valparaiso students.[42] The university also provides work-study student helpers and computer support for the association.[43] The LDA uses modern fund-raising techniques, such as a phonathon, to support its programs.[44] Difficult as it must be at times, the financial autonomy of the LDA has been one of the secrets of its success. This autonomy makes the organization less vulnerable to the vicissitudes of university or denominational budgets.

In 1992 the Lutheran Deaconess Conference had approximately 425 deaconesses,[45] and 419 in 2005, which is phenomenal in an age when many deaconess associations are losing numbers.[46] In its 1992 promotional literature, the LDA stated that it had sent out more than six hundred deaconesses. Some of them, of course, were deceased.[47] By May 2005, the LDA had sent out more than 700 deaconesses.[48] In 2002 there were twenty-three students in training,[49] and by 2005 the number of students had increased to thirty-one (excluding from that number some who were on leave),[50] almost exactly the same number of students as the LDA had had enrolled in 1992.[51]

Until the fall of 2004, there were four educational programs that a woman could enter to become an LDA deaconess: (1) Undergraduate students who wanted to become a deaconess majored in theology as part of a Bachelor of Arts program, or they (2) took a minor in theology and pursued a professional degree: a Bachelor of Social Work, a Bachelor of Science in Elementary Education, a Bachelor of Science in Nursing, or a Bachelor of Arts in Music.[52] (3) Deaconess students who already have a bachelor's degree could take either a master of arts degree with a theology and ministry concentration or take two semesters plus a summer session at Valparaiso University in a plan of study that included a full complement of theology courses. (4) Women who could not leave their place of residence for a long term of study at Valparaiso could become a deaconess through a nondegree program developed through an individual learning contract. Students pursuing a bachelor's degree in either of the first two programs were admitted to the deaconess program at the start of their junior year. They could take their first two years of college at an institution other than Valparaiso.[53] In 2005, there were three deaconess students in plan 1, five in plan 2, and two in plan 3.[54]

Most of the women in plan 4 were older and had served in church and community. The minimum age for plan 4 was envisioned as 35. This plan involved study in the student's home area or at Valparaiso University for a short time, "meetings with deaconesses, and regular contact with the Lutheran Deaconess Association staff" with whom the candidate establishes an individualized program.[55] There was an annual weeklong seminar at Valparaiso that the plan 4 students attended during their course of study. For the academic year 1992–1993, there were ten students in plan 4,[56] and in 2005, there were twelve students.[57] The LDA had to limit the number of women in plan 4 because it required the deaconess staff at Valparaiso to dedicate significant time to mentoring and individualized attention. Thus there were more applicants for plan 4 than could be accepted.[58] An internship was part of the deaconess training program for students in plans 1, 3, and 4. Students in plan 2 chose between an internship and a year of reflection, which was a year in which the students worked full-time in their profession and met regularly with a deaconess consultant.[59]

In 2005 the deaconesses in formation ranged from 20 years old to 63 years old. The average age of deaconesses in formation in all four programs and the New Design was 40, but that was because 25 percent of the women were between 55 and 64 years old, which balanced the 25 percent at the other end of the age spectrum who were 20 to 24 years old, the traditional age for acquiring a higher education (immediate high school graduates). In between the two extremes in age range, about 20 percent of the women were 25 to 44 years old and 30 percent were 45 to 54 years old. About one-half of these deaconesses in formation were married and one-half were single. All were Lutheran, nineteen from the LCMS and twelve from the ELCA, a split of about 60 percent from the LCMS and 40 percent from the ELCA.[60]

The LDA offers scholarship assistance.[61] Financial assistance for deaconess students also is available through Valparaiso University, which gives an automatic grant in aid of $500 per semester to full-time junior and senior deaconess students and to some of the plan 3 students.[62]

The LDA attempts, in its own words, to "remain flexible in order to be responsive to changing circumstances in each new age."[63] In 1981 it completed a self-study that resulted in the development of plan 2, which allows deaconess students to pursue a professional degree in elementary education, nursing, or social work, or a bachelor's degree in music while taking eighteen credit hours in theology.[64] Under its "six essential characteristics" for the 1980s, the LDA admitted that flexibility might require diaconal "service both inside and outside institutional church structures."[65] The association accepted as one of its goals the encouragement of laypeople (who were not members of the diaconate) in their diaconal work. The LDA established the *Diakonia en Cristo* Lay Ministry Award for a layperson, either male or female, engaged in diaconal service "to human need without seeking recognition or reward."[66] Also in the 1980s, the LDA inaugurated a fourth study plan that was suitable for women who wanted to become deaconesses but were unable to pursue full-time studies at Valparaiso University.[67] The association offered gatherings for mothers that the Aid Association for Lutherans helped fund.[68] This led to a "seven-session video discussion series" called "The 'M' Is for Me . . . A Discussion for Mothers."[69] The LDA currently offers "Caring for the Care Givers," which helps congregations to set up programs.[70]

The publications of the LDA are informative and well illustrated. A recent booklet to encourage the laity in their diaconal ministry is entitled *Celebrating Servants: God's People at Work, a Devotional Guide for Congregation Committees and Groups*.[71] The association regularly publishes *The LDA Today: A Newsletter of the Lutheran Deaconess Association* and *Lutheran Deaconess Association Connections*.[72] Formerly, the LDA published *Diaconalogue: A Quarterly Publication of the Lutheran Deaconess Association, Inc., to Enhance the Dialogue and Exchange among People with Diaconal Hearts*.[73] The literature includes children. There also are colorful contemporary pamphlets geared to different age levels entitled *A Deaconess! What's That? Deaconesses Serve . . . To Make a Difference Today!* In these pamphlets, young children are invited to request a letter from a deaconess. Middle-school children and older are invited to find out how to become a Lutheran deaconess at the organization's web site (www.valpo.edu/lda) or through e-mail correspondence.[74]

One strength of the LDA program, and also that of the Concordia Deaconess Program that emerged at River Forest, Illinois, is association with a Lutheran university, thus exposing college women to the deaconess programs at an age when they select vocations and college majors. The connection of each deaconess association with only one Lutheran university, however, makes it necessary for women who want to become deaconesses through that association to spend time at that university to undergo training. Plan 4 and the New Design of the LDA provide a way around that constriction, as does the colloquy program of the Concordia Deaconess Program.

The LDA at Valparaiso, Indiana, is attempting to minimize geographic barriers to becoming a deaconess in its New Design, an innovative curriculum that enables women who are students at other institutions to become part of the LDA program. This flexibility has brought applications from women in their 30s and 40s. The New Design requirements include a formation in theology, clinical pastoral education, practical fieldwork experience, and an internship, in addition to professional formation in a field of the student's choice. The New Design began in fall 2004 with ten students, only one of whom was at Valparaiso University. It allows undergraduate and graduate students studying at other schools and seminaries to become LDA deaconesses without switching institutions. The New Design also accommodates nontraditional students of any age. These deaconesses in formation attend an orientation week and annual weeklong seminars, as well as short courses or retreats at Valparaiso University or elsewhere at times of the year when their own educational institutions, if they are studying elsewhere, are not in session.[75] There is an online component, and the deaconess candidates maintain contact with the LDA and are mentored by LDA deaconesses.[76] Practical field experience of three to four hours per week is performed where the candidates live.[77]

The New Design is for all deaconess candidates, including Valparaiso students. It incorporates ideas from the four educational plans but is more individualized. It allows a woman to combine any undergraduate major with the coursework required to become a deaconess.[78] The New Design was formed in consultation with educators, psychologists, church leaders, and more than one hundred people who contributed their ideas.[79] The New Design includes psychological testing as part of the application process, a requirement for those who will be rostered in the ELCA. This is both a screening procedure and a way of providing guidance to students who enter the program.[80] This is not new to the LDA, which used psychological testing thirty years ago but has not used it recently.[81]

At Valparaiso, the deaconesses strive to maintain a community identity within the university. On a weekly basis, deaconess students gather for the Eucharist and have breakfast together. They meet with other church vocation students at Valparaiso University every other week. They take retreats and belong to a service sorority, Pi Delta Chi, that meets weekly or biweekly.[82] This activity is facilitated by the Center for Diaconal Ministry, which was dedicated in November 1986 at the annual meeting of the LDA.[83] The Center for Diaconal Ministry houses the offices of the LDA and provides a place for deaconesses to meet.[84] Currently three deaconesses work at the offices in Valparaiso: Louise Williams, executive director; Diane Marten, director of education and formation; and Lisa Polito, director of public relations and development. In addition, there are two office staffpersons.[85]

The LDA holds an annual meeting that is open to anyone who supports the association. There is also an annual deaconess conference for the deaconess community, which includes deaconesses in formation, and deaconesses attend from around the country. In 2004 this conference was at Augsburg College in Minneapolis, Minnesota, and in 2005 it was in Colorado.[86] Deaconesses also meet in regional conferences, which helps to maintain a sense of community.[87] In certain areas of the country where there are deaconesses from other deaconess associations (such as the Concordia Deaconess Association), they sometimes meet together.[88]

As the Lutheran Deaconess Conference evolved within its sixty-year history, some deaconesses in the 1970s became uncomfortable with its ecumenical endeavors: the change from serving only the LCMS to serving all Lutheran church bodies and the idea of ordaining women, specifically some deaconesses, as pastors. In 1976 "some concerned deaconesses submitted a petition to the Board of Higher Education of The Lutheran Church—Missouri Synod." They wanted the establishment of a deaconess program at a synodical school. In 1977 the Synod received seventeen memorials to study or assume responsibility for the deaconess program. The convention voted that the LCMS Board of Higher Education should study the matter and report to the 1979 synodical convention (Resolution 6–12). In 1979 the Synod received eighteen memorials supporting a synodical deaconess program.[89] At its July 1979 convention, the LCMS resolved to expand the deaconess program and establish a training program at Concordia College (now Concordia University), River Forest, Illinois.[90]

The Concordia Deaconess Program

In the fall of 1980, the Concordia Deaconess Program began at Concordia College, River Forest, Illinois, with twelve students enrolled. In the decade that followed, the annual enrollment for some years averaged two or three times that number:

River Forest Deaconess Student Enrollment
Numbers in parentheses indicate nontraditional students.

1980–1981………12 (0)	1986–1987………22 (5)
1981–1982………33 (2)	1987–1988………26 (7)
1982–1983………36 (4)	1988–1989………25 (9)
1983–1984………39 (4)	1989–1990………26 (13)
1984–1985………26 (1)	1990–1991………26 (12)
1985–1986………24 (3)	1991–1992………28 (14)[91]

Graduates

1983………6	1988………2
1984………10	1989………6
1985………6	1990………6
1986………6	1991………3
1987………7	1992………6[92]

The program consists of five years of education, one of which is an internship between the junior and senior years.[93] During their junior and senior years, in addition to other courses at Concordia University, the deaconesses in formation do fieldwork in parishes and institutions of the LCMS.[94] The students major in theology and minor in church music, sociology, psychology, or social service, with a concentration in counseling, education, languages, early childhood education, Hispanic ministry, music, urban ministry, or youth work. The women also can design their own concentration.[95] The deaconess certification program coordinates with the requirements for a Master of Arts degree.[96] Some Concordia Deaconess Program interns work in Spanish-speaking areas. The Concordia Deaconess Program, in partnership with the LCMS Board for Mission Services and Wheatridge Ministries, established two internships, one in Miami working with Hispanics and the other in Guatemala. The Guatemalan internship is the first foreign internship of the Concordia Deaconess Program and is a two-year internship.[97]

CONCORDIA DEACONESS PROGRAM INTERNSHIP PLACEMENTS

1981–1982	9	1987–1988	6
1982–1983	10	1988–1989	6
1983–1984	8	1989–1990	4
1984–1985	8	1990–1991	6
1985–1986	7	1991–1992	8
1986–1987	2	1992–1993	.........8[98]

In keeping with the original hesitation concerning the ordination of women as pastors, the "Deaconess Field Work Manual" states that "[t]he deaconess role is not parallel to nor aspiring to the Office of the Public Ministry. Therefore, it is not considered appropriate for deaconesses to participate in functions of that Office."[99]

Upon completion of their preparatory program, deaconesses are certified for service in the LCMS. The Synod arranges for first placements through its Council of Presidents.[100] In 1992 there were thirty-seven deaconesses from this program serving in the congregations, institutions, hospitals, and agencies of the LCMS.[101] As of January 20, 1992, they worked in parishes, as missionaries (in Japan, Thailand, and Taiwan), in refugee resettlement, for Lutheran Social Services (two with the aged and two with the developmentally disabled), in Hispanic and African American ministry, as a Lutheran camp director, as a women's dormitory director, at the Dakota Boys Ranch, in LCMS district ministries (deaf, older adults, social, prison), as the director of the deaconess program, and in chaplaincy (at Bethesda in Watertown and in a home for the aged). There were thirteen deaconesses on leave who had previously served. These women were considered to be on "candidate" status. In addition, two deaconesses had retired, and three were waiting for placement. Thirteen deaconesses were married but still active as deaconesses; two had young children at home.[102]

It is possible for women who already have a bachelor's degree to become deaconesses through the Concordia Deaconess Program.[103] There are no age or health limitations. The numbers in parentheses on the table of the student enrollment of the Concordia Deaconess Program (p. 316) reveal the growing popularity of the deaconess program for nontraditional students who attend college at a later age or who are second-degree or second-career women. On January 20, 1992, half of the twenty-six students enrolled were nontraditional students. The average age of the students was 30, the mean was 23, and the range was from 18 to 58 years of age.[104]

In the fall of 2003, the Concordia Deaconess Program had twenty-five undergraduate students and thirty-three colloquy students. By 2005, the twenty-fifth anniversary of the Concordia Deaconess Program, there were more than 140 graduates. Since 2000, the program had graduated eight to eleven women each year. Students were serving internships in Illinois, Indiana, Michigan, Wisconsin, California, Oklahoma, Guatemala, Venezuela, Germany, and England.[105]

The deaconesses from the Concordia Deaconess Program become members of the Concordia Deaconess Conference, an organization of some of the deaconesses of the LCMS.[106] Membership is contingent on holding membership in no other deaconess conference.[107] The conference manages an endowment fund and is active in preparing promotional materials for the deaconess program: brochures, a display, and a video entitled *Deaconess: Privileged to Serve*.[108] As of March 31, 2005, the Clara Strehlow Endowment had $109,000.[109]

The Concordia Deaconess Conference meetings are important to maintaining a sense of unity among the deaconesses despite their disparate locations and lack of a motherhouse.[110] Beginning in 1989, they held a conference each year. Before that, the deaconesses met twice a year.[111] In 2005, there were fifty active members in the Concordia Deaconess Conference, eighteen deaconess candidates, and five emeriti members.[112] Their uniform and insignia encourage a sense of identity: a navy blue suit with a white blouse or a navy blue dress, both with a Concordia Deaconess Conference cross on the left shoulder and the design repeated in a pin worn on the left lapel.[113] Rather than having a retirement center, the deaconesses are members of the Concordia Health Plan.[114]

In July 1989 the LCMS in convention adopted a resolution to change its constitution, upon ratification by the congregations, to declare deaconesses eligible for synodical membership. Previously only congregations, pastors, and teachers were "official" members.[115] The Synod also adopted resolutions to amend the bylaws to establish procedures to certify deaconesses (Resolutions 3–11A, 3–18A, 3–19). In 1990 the congregations of the LCMS ratified the change by a vote of 2,300 to 207.[116] Therefore, deaconesses of the LCMS are rostered as "Ministers of Religion—Commissioned."[117] However, "in their own minds," they are also "consecrated," a term deaconesses hold dear. For many early deaconesses, the service of consecration concluded their studies and signaled their readiness for service in the church. As part of the service, the women made their vows to be faithful in this service. The deaconesses also received a deaconess pin. The long history of the word *consecration*, which means "to set apart"—in this case, to set apart for service in the church—within the deaconess community reveals a strong belief that their whole lives are encompassed by this vocation.

The LCMS Board for Higher Education and the deaconesses of the Concordia Deaconess Conference proposed a colloquy program to allow "mature women with church work experience" and "deaconesses from denominations or training programs outside the Missouri Synod" to obtain LCMS deaconess certification without going through the entire educational program required of someone with only a high school diploma. The 1992 Pittsburgh convention of the LCMS approved the colloquy program.[118] The colloquy process enables deaconesses of the LDA to become members of the LCMS. Since the 1986 synodical convention, new graduates of the Lutheran Deaconess Association program at Valparaiso University could not be certified in the LCMS because of a requirement that synodical workers graduate from a synodical school. Although there is no formal relationship between the Lutheran Deaconess Association and the Concordia Deaconess Conference and Program, the deaconesses of the Missouri Synod in both groups do occasionally meet and talk.[119] Moreover, Kristin Wassilak, director of the Concordia Deaconess Program, and Louise Williams, executive director of the Lutheran Deaconess Association, have maintained cordial and cooperative relations.[120]

In 2002 Kristin Wassilak prepared an informative paper for a Task Force on Deaconess Education titled "A Developing Theology for the Female Diaconate: A Paper for Discussion."[121] It contains a brief but detailed history of the diaconate in the LCMS, particularly with regard to women.[122] Wassilak alludes provocatively to the diverse use of the words *deacon* and *diaconate* in the LCMS, the existence of district programs for deacons and congregational boards of deacons/deaconesses,[123] and the self-identification of the Lay Ministry Program at Concordia University Wisconsin as a program "[t]o provide certification for the position of lay ministry/diaconate in The Lutheran Church—Missouri Synod."[124] The paper suggests that the Synod could well consider the value of a diaconate for both genders.[125]

Despite more than two decades of a deaconess program at Concordia University, River Forest, the university's Board of Directors made a decision during the 2002–2003 school year to halt new admissions at both the graduate and undergraduate level and to diminish the directing deaconess's salary.[126] They were seeking funding of $1.5 million for an endowed chair to pay the annual expenses of maintaining the deaconess program so it could be reopened for admissions. This closure left women of the LCMS without a synodically supported program designed for prospective deaconesses who have no bachelor's degree. It also effectively eliminated the alternate route or colloquy program that had been approved by the 1992 Pittsburgh convention for becoming a deaconess of the LCMS.[127]

However, with a new president for Concordia University, River Forest, the deaconess program was reinstated and is accepting new admissions. A certification program enables women, many of whom have a bachelor's degree but who do not necessarily want to seek a master's degree, to become deaconesses. The colloquy program is alive and well, enabling women from other deaconess programs to become LCMS deaconesses.[128] In addition, a Deaconess Council has come into being. It is comprised of the president of the Concordia Deaconess Conference; the Rev. John Fale of LCMS World Relief/Human Care; and the deaconess staff and faculty of Concordia University, River Forest, and of the two other LCMS institutions now preparing deaconesses: the seminaries in St. Louis, Missouri, and Fort Wayne, Indiana.[129]

LCMS Seminary Diaconal Programs

A recent development in the LCMS is the establishment of seminary-based graduate programs for deaconess formation. With the encouragement of the deaconesses themselves, Concordia Theological Seminary at Fort Wayne, Indiana, and congregations of the LCMS presented resolutions to the 2001 synodical convention asking the denomination to permit and encourage the founding of deaconess programs at the seminaries of the church. The resolutions passed overwhelmingly, and in the fall of 2002, Concordia Seminary in St. Louis began such a program with the encouragement of the LCMS Board for Higher Education. Concordia Theological Seminary in Fort Wayne, Indiana, opened such a program in the fall of 2003 under the leadership of Dr. Arthur Just. Deaconess Theresa List, a graduate of the River Forest diaconal program, was the first assistant to the dean of the Graduate School for Diaconal Studies at Concordia Seminary, St. Louis. Deaconess Gloria DeCuir, the first graduate of the program at Concordia Seminary, St. Louis, took over after Theresa List. Seminary faculty also teach the students.[130] There were two more graduates of the program at St. Louis expected in 2005.[131]

Students entering these graduate deaconess programs are required to have a bachelor's degree. Successful candidates graduate with a master's degree.[132] If they intend to be certified as deaconesses in the LCMS, the women must be members of the denomination. If they are married, their husbands must be members as well. At Concordia Seminary in St. Louis there is no psychological examination for admission, but there is a personal entrance interview with the Deaconess Program Committee and a personal exit interview before beginning an internship. At Concordia Theological Seminary in Fort Wayne there is at present no psychological examination for admission either.[133]

At St. Louis, deaconess candidates prepare for a master's degree. Students meet weekly for devotions and ten times a year for what is called character formation. Fieldwork is a requirement: "approximately 4 hrs/week (40 hrs/quarter) of supervised practical training for two academic years (six quarters)" in parish or institutional settings, supervised by a pastor or deaconess. The deaconesses in formation also serve an internship of nine to twelve months.[134] In sum, the students spend two years in academic study in addition to the year in an internship. Concordia Seminary, St. Louis, also offers deaconess certification through the Hispanic Institute of Theology.[135]

The educational requirement and the length of time to complete the deaconess program is similar at Concordia Theological Seminary, Fort Wayne, Indiana, to the master's level program at Concordia Seminary, St. Louis. At Fort Wayne, the women earn a master of arts in theology. They are housed in Phoebe House, a refurbished building that has the capacity to house seventeen women. Except for six classes designed especially for them as future deaconesses, the students take courses with the Master of Divinity students. In 2003–2004, there were nine entering deaconess students, and in 2004–2005 fourteen more entered the program. The numbers continue to grow. Ten to twenty students are expected for 2005–2006.[136]

Upon completion of the program and receiving a call, deaconesses are rostered with the LCMS and can become members of the Concordia Deaconess Conference along with graduates of the St. Louis and River Forest diaconal programs. The deaconesses wear the same pin and uniform: a navy blue suit, dress, or pantsuit with a distinctive cross stitched on the shoulder. The deaconesses are salaried and members of the Concordia Health Plan.[137]

There were 124 deaconesses rostered in the LCMS in 2002. This includes deaconesses who graduated from Concordia University, River Forest; deaconesses who have been rostered through the colloquy process; and deaconesses who graduated from the program at Valparaiso University and were rostered before the colloquy process was initiated.[138] In August 2003 there were 132 deaconesses rostered in the LCMS, of whom 92 were active, 25 were candidates, and 15 were emeriti.[139] In May 2005 there were 155 deaconesses rostered in the LCMS, of whom 99 were active, 20 were candidates, 15 were emeriti, and 17 were noncandidates, that is, not currently seeking a call.[140] Deaconesses rostered in the LCMS belong to one of two deaconess associations or to none at all, if they choose not to join. Most do join either the Concordia Deaconess Conference or the Lutheran Deaconess Association. The decision of which association to join is usually based on whether the deaconess graduated from Concordia University, River Forest, or from Valparaiso University. Current members of the Concordia Deaconess Conference are largely graduates of the deaconess program at Concordia, River Forest. As mentioned, deaconesses who are members of the Concordia Deaconess Conference cannot have membership in other deaconess associations. The Lutheran Deaconess Conference is larger, with a deaconess membership of 419, but it has been in existence longer than the Concordia Deaconess Conference, which has a membership of 73.[141]

About half of the LCMS deaconesses serve in congregations. (Deaconess Kristin Wassilak, director of the Deaconess Program, Concordia University, River Forest, estimates that "roughly 1 percent of the LCMS congregations have a deaconess on staff."[142]) Other deaconesses serve in the institutions of the church or in secular institutions in the name of the LCMS, for example, as chaplains in a hospital or a prison.[143] However, almost every deaconess employed by an LCMS district has been released because of funding cuts in the last few years.[144]

These deaconesses have been flexible and inclusive as to which church workers should be considered deaconesses or deacons. For example, the deaconesses were in favor of including parish nurses under the name "deaconess." To be a nurse is historically a strong diaconal role. Some deaconesses proposed expanding their ranks to include female commissioned ministers of religion in the LCMS.[145]

Within the first two years of the initiation of graduate programs at Concordia Seminary, St. Louis, and Concordia Theological Seminary, Fort Wayne, approximately 20 women enrolled.[146] A share of the prospective deaconesses' expenses are met by the denomination through the seminaries and through the students' own districts,[147] whereas the expenses of students pursuing a Master of Divinity degree are subsidized almost entirely through donations designated for the education of future LCMS pastors.[148]

With the establishment of the graduate programs at the seminaries in St. Louis and Fort Wayne, the educational choices for prospective deaconesses in the LCMS would seem to have increased if it had not been for the decision of the Board of Directors of Concordia University, River Forest, to halt new admissions to its deaconess program. This not only eliminated undergraduate options for becoming a deaconess in the LCMS, it also effectively eliminated the alternate route or colloquy program for becoming a deaconess that had been approved by the Synod. Women who were not within commuting distance of the St. Louis and Fort Wayne seminaries and wanted a synodically sponsored diaconal formation program were left bereft.[149] Dr. Andrew Bartelt, vice president for academic affairs at Concordia Seminary, St. Louis, indicated that

> Concordia Seminary is certainly looking into appropriate ways of being of greater service to our church. If that means we pick up the alternate route and colloquy programs, we are willing to do what the church needs. If it is deemed better to do that through other agencies, we stand ready to support whatever decisions will best serve the needs of the deaconess programs.[150]

Amid this upheaval, some might ask whether a graduate program is necessary for every deaconess in every field of endeavor. Surely a graduate degree will be useful to many, but whatever else she does, the deaconess of the LCMS is not allowed to preach or administer the sacraments. Some of them do take on the responsibility of congregations that have no regular pastors, but in those situations, supply pastors preach and administer the sacraments. Also, many women would like to begin their diaconal preparation at the undergraduate level when they are making their vocational choices and before they are married and have a family to limit their mobility. As this book goes to press, the issue of the education of deaconesses in the LCMS will probably not yet be fully resolved, though admissions to the deaconess program at Concordia University, River Forest, have been reestablished.

DEACONESSES IN NORTH AMERICAN LUTHERANISM

Although members of the LCMS became involved in deaconess work later (1919) than other Lutheran synods, training programs have prospered. Looking at deaconesses as a whole in the Lutheran synods through the statistics of the conferences of the Lutheran deaconess motherhouses in North America, the original deaconess institutions peaked in numbers of sisters between 1908 and 1944. The three Norwegian-American institutions peaked early: Brooklyn at twenty-three in 1908 (nineteen of whom were probationers);[151] Chicago at seventy-four in 1912 (fifty-one were probationers); and St. Paul at twenty-eight (sixteen were probationers);[152] Minneapolis at forty-eight in 1914 (thirty-three were probationers);[153] Brush, Colorado, at seven in 1924;[154] Fort Wayne at seventy-three in 1933,[155] Baltimore at seventy-seven in 1935;[156] Milwaukee at sixty-four in 1935 and 1936;[157] Philadelphia at 127 in 1936;[158] Axtell at sixteen in 1940;[159] and Omaha at seventy-seven in 1944.[160] Later, some of the above deaconess institutions merged. The deaconess institutions at Philadelphia, Baltimore, and Omaha came together at Gladwyne, Pennsylvania.

The total number of deaconesses associated with the above Lutheran institutions seemed to peak at 482 about 1940, before the United States entered World War II.[161] However, the meetings of the conferences of the Lutheran deaconess motherhouses from which these statistics were gleaned were not annual. Moreover, the Lutheran Deaconess Association at Fort Wayne moved its headquarters to Valparaiso, Indiana, where it continued to prosper. In the 1970s and 1980s, some of the deaconesses helped formulate the Concordia Deaconess Program at Concordia College, River Forest, Illinois. Both of these groups did well in recruitment. The Lutheran Deaconess Association's 419 deaconesses approaches the overall total of the other Lutheran deaconess institutions between the world wars.[162]

Rather than looking only at the overall picture of the deaconess movement within North American Lutheranism, it is useful to compare the relative success of the movement in the various synods. Those churches that together formed the LCA, which included people of German ancestry, had strong deaconess programs. Those church bodies had an advantage in deaconess work because of the sound foundations of the nineteenth century, the support that John Lankenau gave to the Philadelphia motherhouse, and the General Synod's sponsorship of the center in Baltimore. The church bodies that formed the LCA in 1962 had trained 515 deaconesses throughout the years. The LCMS started deaconess work relatively late as compared to the other Lutheran synods in North America, but the LCMS made solid headway. Synods with a constituency of members of Norwegian or Danish ancestry had fewer deaconesses. The Norwegian Americans had their greatest success with the deaconess movement in Chicago and Minneapolis, a center of Scandinavian immigration, but the Norwegian deaconess movement died out in the 1960s and 1970s. The Danes never attracted significant numbers in Colorado.[163]

THE LUTHERAN CHURCH IN AMERICA AND ITS PRECURSORS

The deaconess communities in Baltimore and Philadelphia flourished in the twentieth century and cooperated in deaconess education. The Philadelphia motherhouse provided nursing training for Baltimore deaconesses. The Philadelphia motherhouse conducted its training in German until the rectorate of Carl Goedel (1893–1906), the last German rector.[164] The Baltimore deaconesses opened a school for church workers in 1910. In addition to educating deaconesses, parish workers, missionaries, church secretaries, and educators also studied at this institution. When the United Lutheran Church in America organized in 1918, it administered the Baltimore motherhouse through its Board of Deaconess Work. Throughout the various church mergers, the ties between the motherhouses in Philadelphia and Baltimore remained. They were strengthened in 1947 when the Board of Deaconess Work of the United Lutheran Church in America, which operated the Baltimore center, began a formal relationship between the two. At that point, deaconesses of the Philadelphia motherhouse, like those of the Baltimore community, held an office in the church. The two communities merged on January 1, 1963, in conjunction with the 1962 formation of the LCA.[165]

Between the 1895 founding of the Baltimore motherhouse and the 1962 merger with the Philadelphia motherhouse, 165 Baltimore deaconesses were consecrated. The two groups of deaconesses adopted a common garb, a common cross, and a common motherhouse at Gladwyne, Pennsylvania, to which the Philadelphia deaconesses had already moved in 1953 when Mary Ethel Pew had donated a large residence. The center at Gladwyne provided a facility for guest ministry, or what is commonly called in Catholic circles a retreat center, to which people could come and share meals and worship with the deaconess community.[166] Even deaconesses of other denominations thought affectionately of the house at Gladwyne because in recent years it was what remained of what could be called a traditional motherhouse community. Deaconesses of several different generations lived together, and the retired sisters could live in community as they grew older, which many had anticipated when they first became a deaconess.[167]

On January 1, 1966, the deaconesses from Omaha, Nebraska, joined those from Philadelphia and Baltimore in the "Deaconess Community of the Lutheran Church in America," bringing the number of deaconesses to 202.[168] From 1963, when the merger between the Baltimore and the Philadelphia (Gladwyne) deaconesses took place, through 1983, fifty women were set apart as deaconesses. Seven of them were later ordained ministers of Word and Sacrament. Eight decided to do something else. The remaining thirty-five served as deaconesses: fourteen as parish workers, ten in health and social service, and six working for church agencies, including the diaconate itself.[169] By 1984, the hundredth anniversary of the deaconess community, 565 women had been "set apart to the office of deaconess" and had served in more than 336 parishes and 221 agencies and institutions.[170]

Auxiliaries to support the deaconess communities developed. In 1938 the Philadelphia Deaconess Association formed. In 1979 it reorganized as the Auxiliary of the Deaconess Community of the Lutheran Church in America. It handled promotion, publication of *The Deaconess*, and liaison with individual congregations. By 1984 there were about one thousand members.[171] The auxiliary remained active as the Auxiliary of the Deaconess Community of the Evangelical Lutheran Church in America.[172]

There were changes in the education, remuneration, dress, and lifestyle of deaconesses that accompanied the organizational changes of motherhouses and deaconess communities. Deaconess training increasingly moved out of the motherhouse. Educational standards gradually improved, especially after World War II. In 1942 Baltimore required two years of college education for its deaconesses, but Philadelphia required none, unless it was necessary for the chosen profession of the deaconess. In the 1950s, a joint program of college education and deaconess training emerged, consisting of three years of education plus two years of training in a deaconess school. This program yielded a college degree and a certificate from the motherhouse. Nursing candidates received medical training and parish secretaries learned secretarial skills in lieu of a college education. The schools at Philadelphia and Baltimore merged in Baltimore in 1963. Soon the deaconess school was entirely displaced as deaconess training was integrated into the four years of college life.[173]

In 1965 the deaconess school system closed. About a thousand women had graduated from these schools. Besides their undergraduate work, deaconess social work candidates took theological courses at a seminary, while parish workers obtained a Master of Arts in Religion. Arrangements for education made with the seminary in Philadelphia lasted until 1970. An experimental baccalaureate-level program began at Muhlenberg College, and the Lutheran School of Theology in Chicago provided education between 1976 and 1980.[174]

The program asked prospective deaconesses to complete two to four years of college before joining the deaconess community. Then the candidates were to come to the deaconess center at Gladwyne, Pennsylvania, for a three-month seminar. The 1991 seminar took place during the summer; four women took part, one of whom had attended a previous summer, had completed a master's degree in religion, and was about to begin an internship.[175]

In the 1950s the arrangements for payment for the professional education of a United Lutheran Church deaconess candidate depended on whether she chose to receive the salary she earned directly or to follow the traditional "cooperative plan" of returning her salary to the deaconess community and living on an allowance, much like Catholic nuns. Deaconesses who were not on the cooperative plan contributed a portion of their salary to support the deaconess center. For deaconesses on the cooperative plan, the expense of the scholarships for their education was forgiven at the rate of a year of tuition, room, and board for every two years of deaconess service. For salaried deaconesses, one year of tuition was forgiven for each year of service, but they paid for their own room and board.[176] In 2003 in the deaconess program of the ELCA, students paid for their own education, but they could be granted funds from a "Fiftieth Anniversary Fund," which could be forgiven at a fixed rate through service as a deaconess.[177]

In 1950 the wearing of the deaconess garb in the United Lutheran Church was tied to the plan of reimbursement that each deaconess chose. Those who remained on the cooperative plan wore the garb. Those who chose the salaried plan had the option to wear the uniform or not. An altered garb had been adopted in 1944.[178] The present garb of the deaconesses of the ELCA, into which the United Lutheran Church eventually merged via the LCA, is a black dress with a white collar and a budded cross pin as insignia. There also is a working dress of grey or blue with a white collar. Most ELCA deaconesses, however, wear civilian clothes.[179] Some of them do not even own any garb.[180]

By 1960, the year that deaconesses were accepted as part of the pension plan of the LCA, only about 10 percent of the women had entered the salaried plan. The plan became increasingly popular among newly consecrated deaconesses, however, and by 1978 nonsalaried deaconesses had virtually disappeared in the LCA. Thus the "cooperative plan" was ended.[181] The deaconesses in the pension plan lifted a burden from the LCA of directly supporting future retired sisters, who, with the decline in the numbers of new candidates, were a significant part of the deaconess communities just as retired sisters were in Catholic religious orders. The LCA continued to support the deaconesses of Immanuel at Omaha, Nebraska, however, because it had taken on the responsibility for these Augustana Synod deaconesses in the 1962 merger with that church body.[182] Present ELCA deaconesses are paid by the institution to which they are called and contribute 4 percent of their income to the deaconess community.[183]

Retired deaconesses are not obliged to make this contribution to the community.[184]

The 1958 and 1959 meetings of the Augustana Synod had made the wearing of the deaconess garb optional, had required Augustana deaconesses to be salaried, and had allowed them to marry without resigning from the diaconate.[185] After its formation, the LCA also dealt with the question of the marriage of its deaconesses. Deaconesses had been allowed to marry before, of course, but if they did so, they had to resign from the diaconate. In 1969 the LCA allowed deaconesses to continue in their mode of service after marriage, as long as they remained in full-time service. By October 1976 deaconess students were allowed to be married. In 1982 the requirement that deaconesses remain in full-time service was changed to allow them to continue as deaconesses in part-time service if they worked at least twenty hours each week.[186] As of January 9, 1992, the Deaconess Community of the Evangelical Lutheran Church in America had eleven married deaconesses and twelve deaconesses with children, some of whom were widows, one of whom was a foster parent, and one of whom was a single adoptive parent. None of these deaconesses or their children were living with the deaconess community at Gladwyne.[187]

Ordination of deaconesses to the ministry of Word and Sacrament became possible in 1970 when the LCA ordained women as pastors. Women were not allowed to be pastors and deaconesses at the same time, however, because it would result in holding more than one church office simultaneously. Some deaconesses became pastors; therefore, they had to resign from the diaconate.[188] Currently under study is whether deaconesses on the ELCA deaconess roster can also be on the roster as associates in ministry.[189]

THE EVANGELICAL LUTHERAN CHURCH IN AMERICA

In 1987, before the creation of the ELCA, the LCA deaconess community based at Gladwyne, Pennsylvania, had 123 deaconesses, 47 of whom were in full-time active service.[190] With the formation of the ELCA, the Gladwyne deaconess community was formally recognized on January 1, 1988, as the Deaconess Community of the Evangelical Lutheran Church of America. However, the ELCA placed a hold on setting apart new deaconesses, pending the conclusion of a study of ministry and church office.

The Deaconess Community of the Evangelical Lutheran Church in America relates to the ELCA through its Division for Ministry. According to the bylaws, the director of the Division for Ministry is invited to attend each biennial meeting of the Deaconess Assembly. The Board of the Division for Ministry must approve all amendments to the bylaws of the community. The bylaws protect the property of the Deaconess Community of the Evangelical Lutheran Church in America, stipulating that none of the community's real estate can be sold without a majority vote of the Deaconess Assembly or a two-thirds vote by mail.[191]

The moratorium on the setting apart of new deaconesses displeased the deaconess community. An appeal was referred to the Church Council of the ELCA and denied on March 1, 1989.[192] After this rebuff, Diakonia of the Americas and the Caribbean supported the Deaconess Community of the Evangelical Lutheran Church in America with a motion passed at its August 7–14, 1989, conference:

> Whereas the Deaconess Community to the Evangelical Lutheran Church in America (ELCA) may continue to recruit, prepare, invest, and place deaconess candidates in appropriate positions but the setting apart to the Office of Deaconess will await the completion of the ELCA Study of Ministry in 1994; and, whereas it is our conviction that this inequity in recognition of the parallel paths of ministry—word and service and word and sacrament—is incompatible with the pattern of Christ's ministry which encompassed the totality of the needs of all of the people of God, therefore it is moved and seconded that the organization of Diakonia of the Americas and Caribbean (DOTAC) make known its affirmation and support of the concerns of the Deaconess Community as they address this issue within the ELCA.[193]

Although the Deaconess Community of the ELCA was unsuccessful in its hope to reinstate the setting apart to the Office of Deaconess, the candidates for the office of deaconess could be invested by the community with their garb and the title "sister." Thus deaconess work continued. The ban on the setting apart to the Office of Deaconess was lifted by the churchwide assembly of the ELCA of 1993.

On February 10, 1991, the executive director of the ELCA Division for Ministry, Joseph Wagner, installed Sister Nora Frost as directing deaconess.[194] Sister Collette Brice, the director of education and interpretation of the Deaconess Community, reported that as of January 9, 1992, there were more than one hundred deaconesses. About half of them were working as deaconesses full-time or part-time for the ELCA or ecumenical bodies with which the ELCA had fellowship. Deaconesses from this community also were working for the Evangelical Lutheran Church in Canada, as they had done during the era of the LCA and prior to the formation of the ELCA. New candidates continued to express interest in becoming deaconesses.[195]

A big change for the Deaconess Community was the sale of its house at Gladwyne, Pennsylvania. On November 1, 2002, the Deaconess Community moved to the ELCA headquarters in Chicago. The sale of the deaconess center at Gladwyne had been discussed by the Deaconess Community since at least the 1998 assembly. When the move finally occurred, seven retired deaconesses had to be moved to nursing homes.[196] Three moved into independent living situations, two of whom are living together.[197] Even deaconesses in communities other than that of the ELCA regretted the sale of the last of the "motherhouses" in the United States to which women, who had entered the diaconate in anticipation of a life in a community, could retire and where active deaconesses could gather.[198] The move provided new opportunities for the deaconess community, however. The deaconesses gave Lutheran Social Services forty beds, forty-five garbage bags of linens, several dozen lamps, storage units, filing cabinets, desks, chairs, conference tables, and boxes of household items.[199] On February 28, 2003, shortly after the move to Chicago, Nora Frost resigned as directing deaconess to care for her father.[200]

In Chicago the Deaconess Community rents space for its headquarters as a separately incorporated body because it is not supported financially by the ELCA. However, it has an endowment that dates from the time of the generous nineteenth-century benefactor John Lankenau. Also, the Friends of the Deaconess Community supports the deaconesses.[201] With the exception of the office in Chicago and a cottage in the Poconos, the ELCA Deaconess Community has no house or deaconess center.[202]

The deaconess program remains approximately the same, however. Summer seminars probably will be replaced by a series of formation retreats.[203] Candidates for the deaconess community must meet the educational requirements of their individual professions, which ordinarily means possession of a bachelor's degree. A deaconess candidate also can be a registered nurse, a licensed practical nurse, or have an associate's degree in early childhood education, for example.[204] Candidates spend two years or less, if they have prior preparation, in theological studies at a seminary. Some obtain a master's degree from a seminary. Some women may decide to become pastors at this point.[205] They have clinical pastoral training, often overlapping with their seminary experience. Candidates also participate in a Diaconal Ministry Formation Event that is offered each year at the ELCA Center for Diaconal Ministry Preparation at Lutheran Theological Seminary at Gettysburg, Pennsylvania.[206] The ELCA deaconesses have commissioned and are funding a January term course on *Diakonia*, which prospective deaconesses and others attend at the Southern Seminary of the ELCA in Columbia, South Carolina.[207] Candidates are accepted into the sisterhood through investiture before their internship or as early as their second year at a seminary.[208] They spend a year in an internship.[209] Financial aid is available from the Deaconess Community. Most candidates have received a master's degree; some have doctorates.[210]

The Directory of Candidacy of the ELCA Division of Ministry reported on February 21, 2005, that there were sixty-five consecrated deaconesses in the ELCA, thirty-seven of whom were active (six of whom were on leave) and twenty-eight of whom were retired. Five women had been invested, three of whom were awaiting their first call and two of whom were serving internships. Four women had been approved for the candidacy process.[211]

The opportunity for temporary diaconal service without commitment to a lifetime as a deacon or deaconess arose in the post-World War II era. In Germany in 1954, Hermann Dietzfelbinger, the rector of the motherhouse in Neuendettelsau, asked young people to serve for one year, which met with remarkable success. Three years later, the Deaconess Community at Gladwyne brought the idea of a diaconal year of service before the church. The Associates in Diaconal Service began as a volunteer program of the United Lutheran Church in America and was administered by the Gladwyne deaconesses. With the formation of the LCA, the program continued for those who were willing to work for the church for a year without salary in a congregation, school, home for the aged, children's home, camp, conference center, or social service agency. By 1984, 350 associates had served. Eleven of these had decided to make the diaconate their career. The program remained active through the Deaconess Community of the ELCA.[212] In August 1991 sixteen men and women in the Diaconal Year Program participated in orientation at Gladwyne. The group included teachers, a music educator, a nurse, and people from other walks of life. Three continued to serve for a second, fourth, or fifth year.[213] In 2002–2003, there were five people in the Diaconal Year Program. As of June 10, 2002, there were three people in the program for 2003–2004.[214]

THE AMERICAN LUTHERAN CHURCH

The deaconess movement among the Scandinavian and German Lutherans who formed the American Lutheran Church (ALC) in 1960 was not as numerically successful as that of the LCA. The ALC formed through a merger of the Evangelical Lutheran Church (which had owned the Chicago Deaconess House and which was associated with the Brooklyn Motherhouse), the United Evangelical Lutheran Church (associated with the Lutheran deaconesses of Brush, Colorado), and the American Lutheran Church (in which the Milwaukee Motherhouse congregation was a member).[215] None of these motherhouses ever reported more than seventy-four deaconesses. Chicago had that number in 1912.[216]

The demise of Norwegian Lutheran deaconesses in North America was a particularly poignant tale. They had a small but energetic beginning through the work of deaconesses from Norway, including Elizabeth Fedde and Ingeborg Sponland in Brooklyn, Minneapolis, and Chicago. After 1953, however, no new deaconesses were trained at these centers. Between 1946 and 1958, a commission of the Norwegian Evangelical Lutheran Church tried to bring new life to the deaconess movement. It trained and commissioned six deaconesses, then abandoned the task.[217] In 1960 at the time of the merger of the Evangelical Lutheran Church (Norwegian), the American Lutheran Church (German), and the United Evangelical Lutheran Church (Danish) into the ALC, the Norwegian Lutheran diaconate had trained no more than 150 to 175 deaconesses during its existence in the United States.[218] In 1979 Anna Bergeland, the last deaconess of the home and hospital in Minneapolis, died. Only a remnant remained of the Norwegian-American deaconesses.[219] Why did the Norwegian Lutheran deaconesses in the United States die out whereas other groups of deaconesses survived? For example, deaconesses thrived in the Methodist church, the LCA, and the LCMS.

Susan Corey Everson of California Lutheran University, director for education for women in the ALC from 1981 to 1986, blamed the demise of the Norwegian Lutheran deaconesses on two factors: (1) the lack of church support and (2) the lack of powerful representation of deaconesses on governing boards. Deaconesses lacked control over their finances, their property, and their own survival as an organization.[220]

In the 1880s the deaconess movement among Norwegian Americans had gotten off to a brave start apart from synodical structures. It continued to be vigorous into the first decades of the twentieth century. Deaconess communities gradually established closer ties with the organized church. In 1904 the Chicago Deaconess Home became the property of the United Norwegian Lutheran Church. In 1917 the deaconess home in Brooklyn associated loosely with the Evangelical Lutheran Church that had formed in that same year from a merger of the Norwegian Lutheran Church in

America, the Norwegian Synod, and the Hauge Synod. The deaconess home in Minneapolis affiliated loosely with the Lutheran Free Church.[221]

Synodical mergers were not always to the advantage of the deaconesses. Ingeborg Sponland, head deaconess at Minneapolis (1891–1904) and Chicago (1906–1938), regretted the dissolution of the Auxiliary Board of the old Deaconess Society that occurred with the 1917 merger because the church women on the board had raised funds for the deaconesses. It took time to recover that support, but by 1929 ladies' aid societies from Minnesota, Wisconsin, the Rocky Mountain District, and North and South Dakota had raised $45,446 for the Chicago home. Church women continued to be willing to support the deaconess movement financially into the 1950s, but they were less willing to become deaconesses themselves.[222]

Some pastors within the church discouraged young women who professed an interest in a vocation as a deaconess.[223] Many clergy lacked enthusiasm: "The diaconate is far from the most popular subject in the church and according to the interests of the pastors, it will not fare well," the Rev. H. B. Kildahl wrote to Dr. Magnus Dahlen on April 26, 1948, before a convention of the Evangelical Lutheran Church (the name for the Norwegian Lutheran Church beginning in 1946).[224] Deaconesses complained of problems with individual pastors. Both Elizabeth Fedde and Ingeborg Sponland recorded that pastors thought that pastors, not women, should provide spiritual care. Sponland said, "I'm sorry to say that some of the pastors even worked against us."[225] The problem continued at least into the 1940s when a deaconess observed that a pastor had objected to her organizing Bible study classes.[226]

By the mid-twentieth century, the various Norwegian Lutheran synods were not overwhelmingly behind the deaconess movement. The deaconesses also confronted obstacles in their own governing boards. The history of the relationship of Ingeborg Sponland, head deaconess at Minneapolis and at Chicago, to her boards is a case in point. Leading spirits of the Lutheran Free Church had founded the Lutheran Deaconess Home and Hospital in Minneapolis, though there was not an organic connection between the motherhouse and the Lutheran Free Church.[227] In Minneapolis in 1904, Sponland wanted a new hospital and better working conditions. When the board did not provide these, she became head deaconess at the deaconess home in Chicago (1906–1936). There she worked well with H. B. Kildahl, the president of the board of the home and hospital, who was supportive of the deaconess community. He complained, however, of the other board members: "They talk Deaconess Home but seem to think Hospital." He wanted a separate board established for the deaconess home and training center to protect the interests of the deaconesses, but the rest of the hospital board refused.[228]

The power that the Chicago deaconess home and hospital board had over the deaconesses was apparent in 1936 when the board overruled the deaconesses' choice of a Caroline Williams to replace Sponland as head deaconess. Williams had thirty years of juvenile court experience in Chicago. Instead, the board members chose Marie Rorem, a younger woman whom they perceived as being "more closely allied with the hospital." The board borrowed from the deaconess pension fund and even attempted to sell the hospital against the wishes of the deaconesses.[229] In 1954 the board wanted to sell the building to St. Mary's Hospital, which was located across the street. Board members talked with Monsignor Barnett of the Archdiocese of Chicago, who responded to them that "[t]he order of sisters controlling St. Mary's is somewhat autonomous and, except on very broad policy matters, generally handles their own affairs."[230] The sisters of St. Mary's, unlike the deaconesses, controlled their own hospital. They were not interested in buying the deaconesses' hospital building.

In the 1960s the deaconess hospital "moved" when the Lutheran General Hospital opened in Park Ridge, Illinois; however, the word *deaconess* did not appear in the new hospital's name. The deaconess training program was dropped. Fourteen years before, the Board of the Chicago Deaconess Home and Hospital had sent a telegram to the convention of the Evangelical Lutheran Church in Minneapolis, asking the church to assume responsibility for the diaconate. J. A. Aasgaard, the church president, supported the deaconess program, and the Evangelical Lutheran Church agreed to take it on and formed a committee. In 1948 the committee recommended the creation of a training school for deaconesses and other church workers in the Minneapolis-St. Paul area. In 1951 the head deaconess at Chicago reported twenty-four inquiries concerning how to become a deaconess. The Evangelical Lutheran Church elected a permanent commission on the diaconate. The commission recommended that the synod hire a deaconess to promote the cause and to find property for the establishment of a school. In 1952 the commission asked the church to allocate $100,000 to a training school for deaconesses. The church allocated $47,000, but the commission did not buy property and in April 1953 planned instead to locate on a church college campus. The commission recommended that

> [w]e do not draw from the Church's educational staff and funds to set up a new school, which would likely be inferior in standards and opportunities to existing facilities. That we not concentrate on selecting one central home for our students. That instead we work out individual pro-

grams with each student according to his [*sic*] educational needs and aims. . . . [T]hat deaconess students live with the larger group and not isolate themselves in any way.[231]

Other deaconesses had survived without a motherhouse, but this was not to be the case with the Evangelical Lutheran Church deaconesses.

In 1954 Shirley Barns, who was serving as fieldworker for the ELC deaconess program, began a summer institute at Luther Seminary in St. Paul at which women interested in the diaconate or in church-related work could study. The five women who attended the eight-week Christian Service Institute that summer were the first women to study and live on the seminary campus. Five deaconesses were consecrated in 1955. By 1960 the enrollment of the institute had increased to thirty-nine, but Sidney Rand, the new director of higher education in the church, allowed men to enroll in the Christian Service Institute. Thus it became a lay training institute.[232]

With the 1960 merger that formed the ALC, the plans to found a deaconess center were abandoned, and the diaconate office closed. The commission was assigned to two church boards that absorbed it into a lay certification effort.[233] The diaconate among Norwegian Lutherans in the United States never ended formally. The church allowed the deaconess project to fade away in the 1960 merger. Loren Halvorson, who served in the Higher Education Department after the merger, stated of the diaconate: "No one was deeply committed in the leadership of the church and there was no grass roots demand for it. . . . We all felt, let's honor it as a program that once developed and pursue what seemed to be the growing edge."[234]

The Brooklyn and Minneapolis deaconess homes, not being closely allied to the church, were unaffected by the attempts to revitalize deaconess training in the 1950s; Brooklyn and Minneapolis had ceased training deaconesses. Concern there now focused on the school of nursing and the hospital, as was the case with so many other deaconess programs.[235]

Deaconesses of the Lutheran Deaconess Motherhouse in Milwaukee became members of the ALC when it formed in 1960, along with deaconesses of Norwegian-American and Danish-American descent. As the Norwegian-American deaconesses suffered from this transition so, too, did the Milwaukee deaconesses: "It was during the reorganizational period that our identity seems to have gotten lost." Among the deaconess institutions that formed the ALC, the Milwaukee motherhouse was, in many ways, the hardiest. It had a long history. In 1863 William Passavant founded the hospital in Milwaukee. In 1891 he consecrated three deaconesses there, two of whom had received much of their training in Europe, according to J. F. Ohl, rector of the deaconess motherhouse, Milwaukee Hospital, who wrote in 1894.[236] In 1893 the Lutheran Deaconess Motherhouse had formed, though Ohl would date it to the 1891 consecration of the first three deaconesses.[237] In 1927 the congregation of Lutheran Deaconesses at Milwaukee became a member of the Iowa Synod, and in 1933 it was accepted by the ALC. In 1934 it began a communion wafer bakery that remained in operation until 1980, at which time it was producing eight million wafers annually. In 1935 and 1936 the number of sisters peaked at sixty-four.[238]

The deaconesses were self-supporting and received "no remuneration from the church" as a group, though many of the deaconesses did receive their higher education with support from the motherhouse. On December 31, 1975, however, the congregation of the Milwaukee community of deaconesses dissolved because of the "diminishing sisterhood." In 1976 they ceased promotional activity, "decided to conserve their assets," and referred future applicants to other Lutheran deaconess groups. As for the retirement plan of the individual deaconesses, some of them were on the ALC Pension Plan because they had worked for the church in the mission field, for example. Others were to be supported by a trust.[239]

Why did deaconess candidates fail to come forward in sufficient numbers to keep the Milwaukee program going? Some of the responsibility may lie with the motherhouse itself. The Milwaukee deaconess community failed to make the changes in garb and salary that other deaconess communities made in the post-World War II era. The 1989 report of Sister Rose Kroeger of the Lutheran Deaconess Motherhouse in Milwaukee to the Task Force on the Study of Ministry of the ELCA stated that: "Ours was a cooperative, non salaried [sic] plan, whereby we received a monthly allowance." The rule that the sisters must gather at Christmas ended only in the 1960s. The garb became optional in 1975, the year the congregation dissolved, and it was worn rarely by those who remained in 1989.[240]

Nevertheless, the Lutheran Deaconess Motherhouse at Milwaukee "witnessed the consecration of 95 of its' [sic] members, the last in June 1977." In 1989 the deaconesses were still serving the church in Milwaukee, Pennsylvania, Texas, California, Iowa, and New Guinea. The deaconesses were particularly strong in hospital work, not only in Milwaukee, where a deaconess served until 1980, but at hospitals in Pittsburgh, Pennsylvania; San Antonio, Texas; Saginaw, Michigan; and Puyallup, Washington. They were not only active in nursing but also in occupational therapy, public relations, dietary work, administration, and the heading of departments. The deaconesses also worked in social agencies and in parishes.[241]

Although the deaconess movement in the ALC faded away, the movement in the LCA continued. By 1978, however, LCA deaconesses were apprehensive that their institutions or survival might be threatened by ambiguity within the denomination about the diaconate. They asked for greater autonomy in churchwide structures. In 1979 they had voting representatives on boards, controlled their own finances, and elected their own directing deaconess. They also had a stronger financial base than that exhibited by the deaconesses of the Evangelical Lutheran Church. The LCA deaconesses had patrons. They had student deaconesses in their program. Not until the 1980s and the merger that formed the ELCA did they run into problems with recruitment that some might consider serious. The LCA deaconesses were concerned about how the new church would affect them and their plans.[242]

The deaconess movement in the LCA and its predecessor church bodies experienced greater success in the postwar era than the predecessor bodies of the ALC. This was especially true during the 1950s when there was a revival in numbers of women entering deaconess work just as recruitment of Scandinavian-American deaconesses was faltering. The efforts of the Evangelical Church in America to respond to the need to strengthen the deaconess program were too little and too late. Beginning prior to World War II, the deaconesses at Chicago appealed in vain for adequate money from their board to strengthen their training and recruitment. The deaconess program was taken over by the church in 1946, but the Commission on the Diaconate took years to get a program off the ground. The attempt in the 1950s to give prospective deaconesses theological education at Luther Seminary in St. Paul, Minnesota, was diverted into a lay education movement. The deaconesses did not have a sufficient dedicated endowment to fund extensive recruitment efforts without denominational support, and some deaconesses felt that it was more appropriate to wait for women to come to the program than to actively recruit, sometimes for fear of interfering with the divine call. Women of the Evangelical Lutheran Church gave a measure of financial support but did not become deaconesses. As the training programs faltered, with a degree of sadness incumbent deaconesses referred prospective candidates elsewhere for diaconal training.

EUROPE

The deaconess movement within North American Lutheranism had never been as large as that in Europe, where nineteenth-century roots were deeper and where the motherhouse concept of the diaconate originated.

The motherhouse form of the diaconate remained strong in the early twentieth century in Europe and elsewhere. New motherhouses were founded, some in predominantly Roman Catholic countries such as Poland, where a motherhouse officially was founded in 1923.[243] In a 1966 publication on deaconesses of the World Council of Churches, Paul Philippi asserted that in 1901 there were 75 motherhouses with 14,500 sisters; in 1926 there were 106 motherhouses with 28,900 sisters; and in 1955 there were 91 motherhouses with 33,000 sisters.[244] In the second half of the twentieth century, however, motherhouses had problems with recruitment of new deaconesses. Nevertheless, at the time of a June 1992 international assembly of deaconesses and deacons in Nova Scotia, there were reported to be more than one hundred deaconess motherhouses in Germany.[245] That same year a comprehensive history of Protestant deaconesses in Austria was published that recorded the impact the movement had made in that country.[246]

For some observers, the motherhouse form of organization, initiated in Germany, was the genius of the deaconess movement, a replacement for the family and the nurturer of a godly life.[247] For many, the positive benefits of life in a motherhouse outweighed any disadvantages to women in terms of restrictions on their lifestyle, their freedom of movement, and their right to marry and remain deaconesses. This way of thinking was in accord with values of the nineteenth and early twentieth century, but women of the latter half of the twentieth century were less attracted to the deaconess motherhouses than women of earlier generations. This was despite the role of deaconesses during World War II.[248] Their service in institutions and hospitals was indispensable,[249] and some deaconesses were heroic in their efforts to protect the patients under their charge. The institutions at Bielefeld were an example. The persons with mental retardation and other handicaps there were prime targets for the Nazi program of extermination, but the administration at Bielefeld was able to protect these people.

After World War II, many motherhouses had problems with recruitment. Faced with a lack of new deaconesses, some sisterhoods made changes to involve the sisters in administration, decision-making, and their own placement, but some of these changes in Germany were late chronologically as compared with the United States or Scandinavia.[250] On April 25, 1990, the Sisterhood of the Evangelical Diakonie Association, Berlin-Zehlendorf, decided to allow the sisters "to receive a monthly salary as would commonly be paid for their work, and then give a contribution to the sisterhood" as an alternative to the old plan of receiving free room and board and a "cooperative salary" set by the sisterhood. This association was founded in 1894 not as a deaconess motherhouse but to give Protestant girls diaconal training after their schooling and before marriage. In 1990 there were more than three hundred married sisters in the association. The change in remuneration approved in 1990 was made with the comment that "this new scheme is particularly in the interest of many younger sisters . . . who would like the financial possibility of structuring their own lives with more independence and freedom." Sisterhoods in North America and Scandinavia made such changes decades earlier.[251]

The advanced age of the inhabitants of some European deaconess motherhouses, as in some Catholic convents, made it difficult for them to support and care for one another, to the extent that, in some cases, outside groups, such as the Red Cross, had to take over.[252] As an example, 1968 was the year of the most recent entry of a new sister into the Evangelical Deaconess Motherhouse, Frankenstein in Wertheim/Main, as indicated by its 1985 list of sisters.[253] The retired Lutheran bishop of Magdeburg, Werner Krusche, former chairman of the Federation of Protestant Churches in the German Democratic Republic, expressed concern at the declining number of people entering diaconal service: "It is a sign of spiritual poverty in our parishes, that the number of women and men, who are motivated by their faith and are ready to engage themselves professionally in diaconal institutions, is not sufficient."[254]

Although many deaconess programs have abandoned the motherhouse style of organization, the attraction of European sisterhoods indicates that communal life for women still has a place within Protestantism. For example, the presently interdenominational community of Deaconesses of Reuilly thrives in Versailles, France, having adopted garb after World War II that resembles that of Catholic cloistered nuns. The deaconess community of Reuilly, founded in 1841, is named after the part of Paris where the deaconesses founded a hospital.[255] Both the deaconesses of Reuilly and the deaconesses of Strasbourg, a community founded in 1842, wore traditional European deaconess bonnets in the nineteenth century, but in the 1940s, the deaconesses of Reuilly adopted a veil, the first Protestant sisterhood to do so.[256] Then they adopted garb that resembled that of Catholic sisters and have maintained this mode of dress to the present, even after Catholic sisters modernized their dress at the Second Vatican Council in the 1960s. In 1982 the Lutheran deaconesses of Strasbourg adopted garb similar to that of the deaconesses of Reuilly and of cloistered nuns.[257]

The necrologies list deceased deaconesses yearly,[258] but at Kaiserswerth, where the nineteenth-century German deaconess movement was founded, the institutions live on into the twenty-first century with their deaconesses and rich archives of the deaconess movement.[259] The Kaiserswerth association of motherhouses continued with a new administrator (October 1, 1991) and a new administrative secretary (February 1, 1991).[260] The Kaiserswerth Association gave 10 percent of what was needed to build a new motherhouse for the 180 to 200 deaconesses of the Hungarian Protestant churches. The state in Hungary had dissolved seven motherhouses.[261]

Modern motherhouses of the Kaiserswerth style in Germany educate and train young people for service in hospitals, homes for the aged, schools, and training centers, though these young adults do not intend to become deaconesses or deacons. This is what the original institutions at Kaiserswerth had done. Aspects of deaconess training are built into these programs: the experience of living and learning together, religious education, and seminars.[262] Although Kaiserswerth itself, where the deaconess movement in Germany was founded, is depleted in its number of deaconesses, laypeople who are not deaconesses are present and active in responsible positions. The main building is being renovated.[263]

The reunion of East and West Germany encouraged plans to gather sisters from throughout Germany and to unite deaconess associations. The Sisterhood of the Evangelical Diakonie Association, Berlin-Zehlendorf, held a conference on April 16, 1990. Six hundred sisters from East and West Germany attended. The Kaiserwerth Association of German Deaconess-motherhouses of West Germany and the Association of Kaiserswerth-style Motherhouses of East Germany decided to create a joint association with a joint board that met for the first time June 6–7, 1990.[264]

SCANDINAVIA

In the mid-nineteenth century, the Inner Mission movement and deaconess communities in the style of those founded by Fliedner had spread from Germany into Scandinavia. In the Scandinavian countries, additional motherhouses were built in the early decades of the twentieth century, and after that deaconess and deacon training institutions were founded.[265] Scandinavians became familiar with the persons and institutions of deaconesses and deacons. Based on that solid beginning, modern diaconal programs in Scandinavia are successful.[266] We will consider, in turn, the development of the deaconesses and deacons in each Scandinavian country.

DENMARK

In Denmark, as was indicated in chapter 5, the royal family was instrumental in initiating the deaconess movement, especially the women of the royal family. A deaconess home in Copenhagen opened in 1863. With the support of the court and other influential people, the home had backing over time. The Danish church supported deaconesses through an annual collection. The deaconesses worked throughout Denmark in parishes and benevolent institutions.[267] Denmark had at least two deaconess houses in Copenhagen and institutes for deacons in Aarhus and Filadelfia, Dianalund.[268]

NORWAY

The modern Norwegian deacons, who are such an integral part of the Church of Norway, emerged like those in the Danish church from a strong tradition that dates to the Inner Mission movement of the nineteenth century, the Lutheran Reformation itself, and the transitional deacon of the medieval church. A 1607 Norwegian Church Order described the deacon as one who served the "poor and crippled." Liturgically, he read the Introit, the Collect, the Epistle, the Gospel, and the Creed. He assisted at services and wore a black gown, but no liturgy for the ordination of deacons is extant, if there was an ordination.[269]

When the Inner Mission movement spread to Norway, it prospered and laid a foundation for the modern diaconal program in Norway. Even in 1990, the original deaconess motherhouse—Lovisenberg in Oslo, which was founded in 1868—had about 250 deaconesses. In the first two decades of the twentieth century, this institution inspired two other institutions: one in Oslo and the other in Bergen. In 1906 in Oslo, women who had trained at Lovisenberg but who were not deaconesses formed an independent fellowship. In 1916 they obtained their own hospital and home, Menighedssoaterhjemmet. Originally this institution was midway between a school of nursing and a deaconess institute, but it came to resemble a deaconess institution. It is known in English as the Menigh Deaconess Home. The Bergen Deaconess Home began as an affiliate of the Lovisenberg Institute, but in 1918 it became independent. The Bergen Deaconess Home acquired its own training school. A pietistic revival in western Norway influenced this institution. There was a hospital, a nursing school, and a geriatric center. Deaconesses worked in parishes and homes for children and the aged.[270]

Shortly after World War II, deaconesses in Norway began receiving salaries, though they contributed a percentage to the deaconess institute. They could rent an apartment from the institute, then pay for room and board. Social security met their retirement and health care needs. There was a trend for deaconesses to become parish workers or social workers in Norway, though there were still deaconesses who were nurses.[271]

Deacons and deaconesses working in congregations were the forerunners of home nursing offered by government entities and the inspiration of the renewal of the diaconate in the Church of Norway. In 1974 there were still 254 parish nurses employed by local parishes or by the diaconate. They had been consecrated in their training institutions and motherhouses. In 1978 only fifty deacons worked as parish deacons. Approximately 430 worked in family counseling, in prisons, or in missions. The largest group of deacons headed health and social institutions, as they do today.[272]

SWEDEN

Like Norway, Sweden has a history of the diaconate that goes back to the Protestant Reformation of the sixteenth century and earlier to the medieval church. One of the earliest Swedish reformers, Olaus Petri (1493–1552), was a deacon from 1520 to 1539, when he was ordained a priest.[273] In Sweden during the Reformation there was no effort to introduce a diaconate focused on charitable work. The diaconate was transitional to the priesthood. The period as a deacon before becoming a priest lasted about a year and a half.[274] After the monasteries and religious orders were dissolved at the end of the sixteenth century, parishes and civil magistrates took over the responsibility for charitable work.[275] Ordination to the diaconate in Sweden ceased in the middle of the seventeenth century.[276]

Two hundred years later, the Inner Mission came to Sweden as it did to Norway. The first Swedish motherhouse for deaconesses, Ersta, was established in Stockholm in 1851, seventeen years earlier than the first Norwegian motherhouse. This was followed by three other motherhouses: Samariterhemmet in Uppsala in 1882, Vårsta in Härnösand in 1912, and Bräcke in Göteborg in 1923.[277] Deaconesses were nurses, teachers, and parish workers.[278] They also worked in the larger community, but they were bound to their motherhouse and lived in poverty, chastity, and obedience.[279] Motherhouses founded hospitals, schools, and social institutions, and ran homes for the elderly, the destitute, and the disabled.[280] The number of people entering the diaconate declined sharply in the 1960s. The motherhouse system dissolved in the 1960s and 1970s.[281]

The motherhouses were transformed into centers for diaconal education and training in pastoral care.[282] There are monasteries and religious communities in Sweden where a communal life is lived, but the numbers therein are fewer than those who enter the modern Swedish diaconate.[283]

Sweden was to have more applicants in the 1970s than it could admit to the twenty places at each of its five deacon and deaconess schools.[284] As in Norway, the motherhouses were never integrated into the official church. Nevertheless, priests superintended the institutions and bishops chaired the boards.[285] The Swedes became fond of their deaconesses, and the idea of the diaconate for many Swedes from the 1850s to at least the 1960s was associated with the motherhouses.[286] Like deacons, by the 1960s Swedish deaconesses could marry and continue to hold their office and title.[287]

Founded in 1898, the diaconal institution for men relocated in 1905 outside Stockholm at Stora Sköndal, Farsta. Male deacons were few in Sweden in the early years. They worked as social workers and parish clerks.[288] In addition, for a little more than ten years from 1925 to 1936, male deacons (*pastorsdiakoner*) were episcopally ordained in the Church of Sweden to aid the priests, especially in pastoral counseling and preaching, but they were not canonically integrated into the Church of Sweden. Male deacons lived on voluntary subsidies.[289] The diaconate was transformed into a church office in Sweden in 1942.[290]

FINLAND

In 1990 *Diakonia News* reported that Finland had the largest deaconess institution in Scandinavia and also the one most recently founded. These were two different institutions. The largest was the Helsingfors (Helsinki) Deaconess Institute, which had 1,500 deaconesses. Founded in 1867, it started slowly. As mentioned, it had only eleven sisters in 1882 when Deaconess Lina Snellmen became directing sister. During her 41-year incumbency in that position (1882–1924), the number of sisters rose to 265. At first the work concentrated in the hospital, but sisters were sent to workhouses, parishes, and other institutions and hospitals. Affiliated with the Helsingfors Deaconess Institute was a home for people with tuberculosis, a hospital, homes for children, a domestic science school, and institutions for people with epilepsy or mental retardation.[291]

As of 1990, the "youngest," that is, most recently founded, deaconess institution in Scandinavia was reported to be at Björneborg (Pori), Finland. It was founded in 1949 and had a school for training deacons, deaconesses, and health and social workers rather than a motherhouse. There were 384 deaconesses in Finland in 1987, the year that the Church of Finland ordained its first female pastors.[292] A somewhat older Finnish diaconal institution was the Lutheran Institute, which was founded in Järvenpää in 1936 just prior to World War II.[293] The institute educated deacons.

Finland also had two deaconess institutions that moved from areas that became part of the Soviet Union after World War II. These were the Lahti Deaconess Institute, founded in Viborg (Karelen) in 1869, and the Pieksämäki Deaconess Institute, which moved after World War II from Sortavala, where it had been founded in 1894.[294] In 1990 *Diakonia News* reported that the Lahti Deaconess Institute had about 850 deaconesses. The Pieksämäki Deaconess Institute had about 1,000 deaconesses. It never had motherhouse rules and was part of a large center for work with the mentally challenged, people with epilepsy, and those who were chronically ill.[295] Deacons also were trained at Pieksämäki for social work.[296] The Oulu Deaconess Institute at Oulo (Uleaborg) was founded in 1896 on principles similar to those of Pieksämäki and had about 750 deacons and deaconesses in 1990.[297] In Finland the title "deaconess" today means a female deaconess with a nursing background.[298]

THE DIACONATE IN NON-LUTHERAN PROTESTANT CHURCHES

The deaconess movement in non-Lutheran Protestant churches flourished in the early twentieth century, and some denominations that had not had diaconal programs initiated them. Diaconal programs in the British Isles and the New World thrived. The overall numbers of deaconesses increased for a time, but in the second half of the twentieth century, recruitment problems surfaced. New diaconal programs were begun, nevertheless, and beginnings that had been made in Africa, Asia, and Latin America came to fruition. Many diaconal programs included both men and women. International federations of deacons also came into being.

Of the non-Lutheran denominations, Methodism continued to be prominent in the world diaconal movement, but this was less true in Methodism's country of origin, England, than in the United States and other countries that Methodist world missions had touched. In 1933 in England, various strands of deaconesses within Methodism came together as "Wesley deaconesses." In 1978 the Methodist diaconal order in Great Britain closed candidature because of fewer recruits, but in 1987 it was reopened to both men and women. On June 24, 1990, the year of the hundredth anniversary of Methodist deaconesses in England, the president of the Methodist Conference of Great Britain ordained two men and two women at the annual Methodist Conference. These were the first ordinations of the renewed order in Britain among British Methodists.[299]

THE UNITED METHODIST CHURCH
IN NORTH AMERICA AND ITS PRECURSORS

In North America, the Methodist deaconess movement expanded in the early twentieth century based on its strong beginnings in the late nineteenth century. After first being recognized in the Methodist Episcopal Church by the 1888 General Conference, the deaconess movement spread through various branches of Methodism. The Methodist Episcopal Church, South, authorized the Office of Deaconess in 1902 and consecrated its first five deaconesses in 1903, the same year that the Methodist Episcopal Church began training overseas deaconesses in the Philippines under Winifred Spaulding, former superintendent of the Deaconess Training School in Kansas.[300] The Methodist Protestant Church authorized the deaconess office in 1908.[301] By 1915 sixty Methodist religious training schools, which trained deaconesses and other church workers, had opened in the United States.[302] Methodists attracted new recruits and disputed the advisability of deaconess work under the Woman's Home Missionary Society or under the General Conference of the Methodist Church in works such as Isabelle Horton's *The Burden of the City* and the Woman's Home Missionary Society's *The Early History of Deaconess Work and Training Schools for Women in American Methodism, 1883–1885.*[303]

The 1939 Uniting Conference brought the three branches of Methodism in the United States into a single unified body, the Methodist Church.[304] The deaconess program was standardized. Methodists had more than a thousand deaconesses in the United States at this time, more than double the number of Lutheran deaconesses.[305] The education of Methodist deaconesses moved from training schools to church colleges, and after 1959 deaconesses were salaried and free to marry and retain their status as deaconesses.[306] Denominations that later would unite with Methodists also had deaconesses: the United Brethren in Christ since 1897 and the Evangelical Association/United Evangelical Church since 1903.[307] The Deaconess Program Office of the United Methodist Church is in New York City.[308] The Committee on Deaconess Service reported "a renewed interest in the Office of Deaconess" among persons making a mid-career change. Methodist deaconesses were in communication with deaconesses throughout the world. For example, in the early 1990s, deaconesses and home missionaries of the United Methodist Church sent $3,659 to deaconesses in the Philippines in an area devastated by the Mount Pinatubo eruption and flooding.[309]

In 1995 Deaconess Betty Purkey became executive secretary of the Deaconess Program Office of the General Board of Global Ministries of the United Methodist Church in New York City. She retired in June 2003 but remained in a half-time consultative capacity for one year. Becky Dodson Lauter, a deaconess candidate awaiting commissioning, became the new executive secretary. Her mother was a retired deaconess with more than twenty-two years of active service.[310]

The Methodist Church granted full clergy rights to women in 1956,[311] but deaconess work in the United Methodist Church continued. In 1988 a National Association of Deaconesses and Home Missionaries of the United Methodist Church formed, and it meets every other year.[312]

From 1980 to 1995, thirty-nine women were commissioned to the office of deaconess. This was during a period when they felt their future in the United Methodist Church was uncertain because of ongoing studies of ministry in the denomination. United Methodist deaconesses were revitalized by the adoption of The Study of Ministry by the 1996 General Conference, which recommended no change in the status of United Methodist deaconesses. Only one or two of the women opted to become deacons, which was another option.[313] The *Book of Discipline of the United Methodist Church* states simply: "There shall be in the United Methodist Church the Office of Deaconess."[314] Deaconesses are commissioned by a bishop. They can work for any United Methodist board or agency, but they can also serve in agencies or programs other than those of the United Methodist Church.[315]

The deaconesses of the United Methodist Church are active in communication and recruitment efforts through literature; a video called *Love, Justice, and Service: The Ministry of Deaconesses*; and "Discernment Events."[316] There are a variety of recent articles about Methodist deaconesses, some in a traditional vein about deaconesses in health care professions: "Deaconesses Bring Healing," for example.[317] Others are less traditional, such as one article written by a bishop of the United Methodist Church who reflected on his positive experience with deaconesses as college professors when he was a student in an historically black college of the United Methodist Church.[318]

Modern Methodist deaconess recruitment addresses "women of all ages and backgrounds, married, single—including those widowed or divorced seeking a mid-life career change." It invites prospective candidates to contact the Mission Personnel Program Area, General Board of Global Ministries of the United Methodist Church.[319] Some recent prospective deaconesses have been nontraditional students of mature years, some entering the program after their retirement from other professions.[320]

Between 1996 and 2004, eighty-six women were commissioned as deaconesses in the United Methodist Church, and more are becoming deaconesses. Women come in with a bachelor's degree or its equivalent. Prospective deaconesses have an interview (at which the executive secretary is present), psychological testing, and a psychological interview in New York City. They must complete five courses: Old Testament, New Testament, history of the United Methodist Church, United Methodist doctrine and polity, and theology with an emphasis on mission. They can bring some of these courses with them into the preparation program, but since 2002 courses also have been offered in short intensive segments at the Alma Mathews House in New York City by faculty of Drew and the New York Theological Seminary. The tuition is paid by the Deaconess Program Office of the United Methodist Church with funds from the Women's Division of the United Methodist Church.

The program to become a deaconess averages two or three years but can be completed in less time if one already has some of the core courses. Beyond their coursework, prospective deaconesses have a week of training, usually immediately prior to commissioning, which is typically in the spring or fall. The prospective deaconesses must secure a job in either a helping profession or a church-related vocation, though the deaconesses emphasize that being a deaconess is not a job. Being a deaconess is a relationship of service through the church and lasts for a lifetime. Some deaconesses who are able serve without pay. For many, however, their employer pays their salary and pension. The United Methodist *Book of Discipline* provides that "each deaconess shall enroll in a pension plan."[321]

There is no mandatory retirement for a deaconess. Some women work into their 70s. In February 2005 there were 115 active deaconesses and 116 who were retired in the United Methodist Church. Deaconesses are considered lay members of the United Methodist Church as are Home Missioners, who are laymen with positions equivalent to those of deaconesses. Home Missioners came out of the tradition of the Evangelical United Brethren, which had home missionaries. Since January 1, 2005, the education of Home Missioners has been coordinated by the Deaconess Program Office of the Board of Global Ministries of the United Methodist Church.[322]

Within the years since the 1996 restructuring of the General Board of Global Ministries, the finances of the deaconess program have improved. There is an advisory committee for the Deaconess Program Office. The salary of the executive secretary of the Deaconess Program Office is paid by the General Board of Global Ministries of the United Methodist Church, which also provides the office in New York City. In addition, the deaconess program receives funds from the United Methodist Women.[323]

Modern Methodist deaconesses are active in international diaconal organizations, for example, DOTAC (Diakonia of the Americas and the Caribbean) and Diakonia, the international diaconal association.[324] In keeping with the early foundation of deaconess work in India and elsewhere in the nineteenth century, Methodist churches founded deaconess work abroad, for example, in Fiji. In 1953 two Fijian women began training in Melbourne, Australia. When they returned to Fiji, three women donated money for property on which to build a deaconess house. Fijian Methodist deaconesses work among women and with children and young people; they also preach. Fijian Methodist deaconesses can marry. In July 1987 they had ten women in training and five probationers.[325]

MENNONITES IN NORTH AMERICA

Deaconess work on the Kaiserswerth pattern developed in the General Conference Mennonite Church with headquarters in Newton, Kansas, under the encouragement of the Rev. David Goerz. He had appealed to the 1890 General Conference to support deaconess work, but it was not until 1900 that Frieda Kaufman, the first candidate, came forward. In 1903 the board of directors of Bethel College in Newton led in organizing the Bethel Deaconess Home and Hospital Society. In 1908 a hospital was dedicated and the first three deaconesses ordained. From 1911 to 1930 Mennonites made efforts to develop training schools in five other locations—for example, in Mountain Lake, Minnesota—as a station of the Bethel Deaconess Hospital in Newton, Kansas. In the 1930s and 1940s, there was a plateau in the Mennonite deaconess population. There were thirty deaconesses and probationers in 1928 and that same number in 1942. Then numbers declined, but these figures are deceptive. Many Mennonite deaconesses became missionary nurses and were no longer counted as members of the diaconate because they were supported by the church's board of foreign missions.[326]

ORTHODOX CHURCHES

The Orthodox Church in Russia considered the possibility of an Orthodox order of deaconesses in the mid-nineteenth and early twentieth century. There were Orthodox nuns, but deaconesses were perceived as more active in the community than nuns. In 1910, after failing to receive the approval of the Holy Synod for the foundation of an order of deaconesses, the Grand-Duchess Elizaveta Fyodorovna obtained permission from the czar, her brother-in-law, for the foundation of a monastic nursing community in Moscow, the Martha-Maria community. The grand-duchess was originally from Hesse-Darmstadt and was a convert from Lutheranism. She and some twenty others embarked on work among the poor of Moscow, but the community did not survive the Russian Revolution of 1917 and the murder of its founder in 1918.[327]

In the twentieth century, the Greek Orthodox Church had deaconesses. In Athens the Apostolic Diakonia of the Church of Greece founded a college for deaconesses and social workers. From November 21, 1957, it had its own building, constructed with the help of the World Council of Churches. Its purpose was to train deaconesses and social workers for the Greek Orthodox Church to be assistants to pastors and to engage in social welfare work. A Preparatory School for Deaconesses preceded this college (1952–1954).[328]

Other Orthodox churches were calling for a revival of the "apostolic order of deaconesses." The 1988 Rhodes Inter-Orthodox Theological Consultation of the Place of Women in the Orthodox Church and the Question of Ordination for Women stated that "the revival of women deacons in the Orthodox Church would emphasize in a special way the dignity of woman and give recognition to her contribution to the work of the Church as a whole." The second International Orthodox Women's Consultation on "Church and Culture" that met in 1990 at the Orthodox Academy, Crete, emphasized "the urgency of a creative restoration of the diaconate for women," a response to the vital needs of our churches.[329]

It was hoped that this restoration would also lead to a renewal in the male diaconate, "not merely in liturgical roles or as a step to the 'higher ranks' of the clergy" but with extension into the social sphere in the spirit of the ancient tradition of the diaconate. It was suggested that deacons could serve parishes without priests, open closed churches, lead monastic communities that had no priests, and perform social work in connection with pastoral care, "anointing the infirm, counseling the faithful, ministering to the sick, confined, and imprisoned, and bringing them Communion."[330]

In the 1990s some Russian Orthodox deacons were doing social outreach in Moscow.[331]

PRESBYTERIAN CHURCHES

The deaconess movement in churches of the Reformed and Presbyterian tradition spread in Europe and in the British Isles, Australia, New

Zealand, Canada, the United States, and other parts of the world through the world missions movement. Presbyteries of the Presbyterian Church of Scotland continued to "commission" deaconesses. Scottish deaconesses who took a full theological course were licensed to preach but not to administer the sacraments, apparently as a concession before the ordination of women as ministers. The 1962 Church of Scotland Deaconess Board Scheme for Deaconesses provided that

> [a] Deaconess may be licensed to preach the Word. The regular preaching of the Word and regular participation in the conduct of public worship by Deaconesses shall belong only to Deaconesses so licensed. . . . A Deaconess must . . . be commissioned by the Presbytery, and, in the case of a Deaconess qualified and trained to preach the Word, be licensed by the Presbytery.[332]

The General Assembly of the Church of Scotland in 1990 determined that the diaconate of the Church of Scotland was part of the courts of the church with the same voting rights as the ordained ministry.[333]

Although the Church of Scotland spoke of commissioning deaconesses, the Presbyterian Church of New Zealand used the word *ordination* for deaconesses from the beginning (1904), in line with the Presbyterian Church of Victoria (Australia). The United Church of Canada "designated" deaconesses. Recruits were few.[334]

THE UNITED CHURCH OF CHRIST

Although the deaconess work within Congregationalism (1901) never became a large enterprise, it fared better in the German Reformed Church (1892) and the Evangelical Synod (1889), precursors to the United Church of Christ. The German Reformed Church began deaconess work in Cleveland, Ohio (1892), and Buffalo, New York (1895). The Evangelical Synod of North America began with the Tabitha Institute in Lincoln, Nebraska, and the Evangelical Deaconess Home and Hospital in St. Louis, Missouri (1889). Between 1892 and 1919, twelve deaconess institutions were founded in the synod. The Evangelical Deaconess Hospital of St. Louis reached its peak of 147 deaconesses in 1937.[335] It was the only one of the Evangelical and Reformed deaconess institutions to prosper after World War II. In 1952 St. Louis deaconesses helped organize the Conference of Deaconesses of the Evangelical and Reformed Church, but the St. Louis institution discontinued recruitment of deaconesses in the 1950s.[336] This was not the end of deaconesses in the Evangelical and Reformed Church, however. The denomination continued to commission deaconesses.[337]

FINANCING THE DEACONESS MOVEMENT

When one surveys diaconal work in North American Protestant denominations, one is struck by the divergence in financing. No group has or receives as much as its members could use because service is a bottomless task and the needs of humankind are vast. Nevertheless, there is a considerable spectrum in financing of diaconal work among the denominations, complicated further by the fact that some deaconess groups are independent. There is, for example, the Lutheran Deaconess Association, which started as a movement within the LCMS and is now an independent deaconess association with a training program centered at Valparaiso, Indiana. Independence allows this organization freedom of action, but it also means that raising funds must be a conscious part of the program. The LDA does have some endowment.[338] On the other end of the spectrum are the deaconesses of the United Methodist Church, whose General Board of Global Ministries provides office space in New York City, pays the salary of the executive secretary of the program, and more.[339] Somewhere in between fall deaconess communities that have denominational support but not much money, if any, from the denomination. For example, the ELCA welcomed the deaconesses to the church headquarters in Chicago when their Gladwyne, Pennsylvania, center closed, but the deaconesses pay rent for their office space. Much of this has to do with how much money a denomination has, but it also has to do with priorities, organizational structures, and a tradition of support for deaconess communities.

In many ways, deaconess communities are less of a potential financial drain because many deaconesses are salaried, which means the institutions for which the deaconesses work pay their wages and often their pensions. Deaconess communities have promotional and educational needs, however. Deaconesses themselves contribute financially to their deaconess communities and associations, but given the service nature of deaconess work, resources are limited. The Deaconess Community of the ELCA expects each working deaconess to contribute 4 percent of her salary to the community. The Deaconess Community also has an endowment that dates to the nineteenth century.[340]

Some denominations or educational institutions support deaconesses through funding all or part of their education. The LCMS supports the educational program of the deaconesses indirectly through its seminaries. For example, Concordia Seminary in St. Louis pays the salary of the deaconess in charge of the educational program at the seminary and also provides her office space, as it would to anyone on the seminary faculty or staff.

Also, students accepted into the deaconess program can apply for financial aid. On the other hand, at the undergraduate level, the deaconess program at Concordia University, River Forest, Illinois, was closed to admissions for awhile awaiting financing.[341]

Another avenue of support that can be cultivated is that which comes from women and women's organizations. The women of the United Methodist Church give millions of dollars annually to missions and designate some of that to the United Methodist deaconess program.[342] There has been a long tradition of support for deaconesses among Methodists. The Methodist deaconess movement was initiated in the nineteenth century with the backing of the women of the church. LCMS women also have been helpful to deaconesses, particularly at the local level through support of individual deaconesses or candidates and their needs.

One can ask what financing has to do with the success or lack of success of a deaconess program. The question also may be raised whether the best-funded program is the most successful. That would be difficult to ascertain, and no one would claim it to be so. Some programs are frugal but successful. Nevertheless, a deaconess program does need the support of its constituents, and it does need to fund education for its candidates. The failure of the deaconess program in the American Lutheran Church is one example of a denomination backing away from a program that might have succeeded. Not every group can go it alone and realize its full potential.

Deacons, Deaconesses, Diaconal Ministers

Within the last decade, the word *deaconess* has become less popular in some denominations. It has been replaced by "diaconal sister" or "diaconia sister" and "diaconal minister" or "deacon" (which could encompass men and women).[343] For example, in 1990 *Diakonia News* commented on changes in the theological education of "diaconal ministers" within the "Order of Diaconal Ministries of the Presbyterian Church in Canada."[344] In February 1986 the Australian Anglican Deaconess Conference became the Australian Anglican Diaconal Association because women were being ordained as deacons.[345]

In many denominations it is now possible for women to be ordained deacons. This is true both of churches that choose lay deacons from the congregation for part-time service, such as the Presbyterian Church (U.S.A.), and of churches with a tradition of deaconess programs, such as the United Methodist Church and some churches within the worldwide Anglican Communion. Although the Church of England had deaconesses since at least 1862 (when the bishop of London set apart Elizabeth Ferard), the ordination of women as deacons on a par with men is relatively recent within the Anglican Communion.[346]

ANGLICAN CHURCHES

Historically, even when describing deaconesses within the Church of England, many preferred saying they were "set apart" rather than ordained. The 1897 Lambeth Conference, a gathering of bishops of Anglican churches, acknowledged deaconesses, but there was no official recognition of their duties and status. A deaconess was still defined generally as "a woman set apart by a Bishop, under that title, for service in the Church."[347] Some authors, such as Deaconess Cecilia Robinson at the turn of the century, wrote of deaconesses as members of an "Order" in the church, but many people in the Church of England, especially among the clergy, resisted any implications that deaconesses were a "holy order within the church" or members of the clergy rather than of the laity.[348]

The status of deaconesses in the Church of England took a step forward in 1920 when a Lambeth Conference gave deaconesses fuller recognition. The bishops resolved that "the Order of Deaconesses is for women the one and only Order of the Ministry which has the stamp of Apostolic approval, and is for women the only Order of the Ministry which we can recommend that our Branch of the Catholic Church should recognize and use."[349] The next Lambeth Conference of 1930 reiterated the same statement almost word for word.[350] In the 1920s Anglican churches increasingly used the expression "ordination" to refer to the setting apart of deaconesses.[351] When the 1923–1925 Convocations of the Church of England formally restored the Order of Deaconesses in the Church of England, the women were "episcopally ordained with prayer and the laying-on of hands."[352] The 1930 Lambeth Conference used the terminology "Ordination of Deaconess."[353] The 1948 Lambeth Conference reiterated the resolutions of 1920 and 1930 that "the Order of Deaconesses is for women the one and only Order of the ministry . . ."[354]

Statistics for the number of deaconesses in Anglican churches in these early decades are inaccurate, but in 1918 there were no fewer than 340 in the dioceses of England and Wales. However, the first deaconess of the Episcopal Church of Scotland was not set apart until 1917. The decade of the 1920s, with a total of 140 deaconesses recruited, was one of active recruitment of deaconesses in England. Recruitment peaked in 1927 and 1928 with fifteen and sixteen women each year, respectively, then declined for a generation. In the 1960s recruitment averaged nine per year, which was twice that of the 1950s. The 1970s, with 180 for the decade, surpassed even the 1920s.[355] Archbishop of Canterbury Robert Runcie stated that in 1976 there were 121 deaconesses licensed in the Church of England. By 1980 there were 285.[356] By January 1987 Sister Teresa of the Community of St. Andrews estimated that there were more than one thousand deaconesses, most of whom became deacons that year when the Church of England allowed women to be ordained deacons.[357]

Numbers alone tell only part of the story. There also were changes within the deaconess communities. The community initiated by Elizabeth Ferard (after 1868 called the London Diocesan Deaconess Institution) came more to resemble other sisterhoods. For example, the community adopted rules for religious life and instead of speaking of "sisters" and "trainees" referred to "Postulants, Novices, and Sisters." After the introduction of a new chaplain, Fr. Bickersteth, in 1917, the community moved from one that had emphasized no vows to one that accepted vows of poverty, chastity, and obedience. The superior and some of the sisters resigned.[358] The final steps toward the religious life were taken in 1930 when Fr. Horner was appointed chaplain. The annual vows of poverty, chastity, and obedience became life vows for the deaconess upon her ordination after a two-year novitiate. The sisters tied three knots in their girdle to symbolize their vows and wore a plain gold ring like other religious orders.[359]

The deaconesses of the Community of St. Andrew did not become cloistered by any means and served in the world. They continued some of their work of the nineteenth century and initiated new projects, for example, a home for the aged (1919) and a training school for mentally challenged girls (1912). In 1934 the community took charge of the diocesan orphanage at Bedford, St. Albans. Parish work remained a key occupation and a central part of the work of the deaconess community.[360] Brian Heeney, an historian of women's work in the Church of England, particularly praises the deaconesses for their work in the parishes as he compares them to other sisterhoods in England.[361] A seemingly indefatigable younger deaconess from the United States, Sister Teresa (Joan White), the youngest deaconess in the Community of St. Andrew today, became active in national and international diaconal circles. She was the long-time editor of *Diakonia News: Newsletter of Foundation Diakonia World Federation of Diaconal Associations and Diaconal Communities* (1987–2002), of *Distinctive Diaconate News* (1981 to the present), and of *Distinctive News of Women in Ministry* (1994 to the present). She was also a member of the General Synod of the Church of England (1995–2000).[362]

St. Andrew's House became an oasis in an increasingly lively and challenging London neighborhood. The sisters extended their hospitality for retreats, and women other than deaconesses stayed at St. Andrew's House, some for months. The influence of the community extended beyond their numbers. The community was never large. In 1899 there were thirty-four members of the community. In 1961 there were thirty-two sisters and four novices.[363] In 1987 there were twenty members of the Deaconess Community of St. Andrew, of whom ten were ordained deacons; thus they changed their name to the "Community of St. Andrew." The community had eight members as of August 13, 2003, but no one was living in St. Andrew's House, which was being refurbished.[364]

Meanwhile, head deaconesses of the various houses in the Church of England organized an association in the first decade of the twentieth century. In 1918 a deaconess conference was held, which became an annual event and encouraged interaction among the various groups of deaconesses. A smaller group formed, the Chapter of Deaconesses, which consisted of representatives from the various institutions. In 1967 a Central House for the Order of Deaconesses was established at Hindhead for meetings, prayer, and retreats. The house closed in 1976. In 1967 the Diaconal Association of the Church of England joined an international association of diaconal associations called Diakonia, as did the Accredited Layworkers Association.[365]

Outside the British Isles, deaconesses within the worldwide Anglican Communion built on the foundations of the nineteenth century. The New York Training School for Deaconesses continued to educate both deaconesses and lay workers. By 1912 it had trained deaconesses who served in twenty-two dioceses in the United States, Mexico, Japan, China, and the Philippine Islands. The New York Training School for Deaconesses closed in 1948. By 1917 the Church Training and Deaconess House in Philadelphia had trained seventy deaconesses and eighty-seven lay workers, many of whom worked overseas. In the early twentieth century, training schools on a smaller scale than those in Philadelphia and New York opened in San Francisco, California; Minneapolis, Minnesota; New Orleans, Louisiana; Chicago, Illinois; and Berkeley, California. In 1928 and 1929 the movement peaked with 224 deaconesses, exclusive of candidates and of those who were retired.[366] By 1950 there were 164 deaconesses.[367] In 1954 a Central House for Deaconesses opened in Sycamore, Illinois, and subsequently moved to Evanston, Illinois, where it could use facilities at Seabury-Western Theological Seminary. In 1964 deaconesses were allowed to marry

356__D<small>EACONS AND</small> D<small>EACONESSES THROUGH THE</small> C<small>ENTURIES</small>

without vacating their appointment as deaconesses. With few candidates for training in the late 1970s, the Central House for Deaconesses closed.[368]

In Australia the deaconess movement grew and spread.[369] In Melbourne, an interdenominational missionary college, St. Hilda's House, began in 1902. In 1922 it became an Anglican training house for female missionaries and deaconesses. It remained that until it closed in 1978. In the 1940s deaconesses of a community in the diocese of Gippsland, known as the Diocesan Order of Bush Deaconesses, were taking charge of churches, except for functions that only a priest could perform. In the 1970s in that diocese, a deaconess was rural dean, overseeing a group of parishes. In 1941 the All Australia Deaconess Conference was founded.[370]

In New Zealand in 1914, the bishop of Waiapu invited Esther Brand, a deaconess of the Rochester Institution in England, to take charge of a rescue home. She trained deaconesses, parish workers, and missionaries. In 1931 St. Faith's House of Sacred Learning opened in Christchurch to train both deaconesses and lay workers. It closed in 1943 for lack of recruits. A deaconess house opened in Auckland in 1966 in part as a result of the 1974 decision of the General Synod of the Province to recognize the order.[371]

In Canada, the Church of England Deaconess and Missionary Training House in Toronto prospered and sent graduates to the dioceses of the Canadian church and to countries such as China, Japan, and India. Deaconesses also came directly from England to places such as Calgary. Some deaconesses worked on reservations for the native peoples of Canada, for example, among the Sioux in Manitoba, where Deaconess Winifred Stapleton took most of the services in the mission church, including funerals and baptisms. The Canadian church, like that of Australia, was willing to give liturgical functions to deaconesses, perhaps, in part, because they had a personnel shortage in outlying regions.[372]

The history of Anglican deaconesses in Africa was not one of great numbers but one of individuals and mission stations. Off the coast of Africa, Anglican deaconesses had a small mission in Madagascar, but most of their work was in South Africa where deaconesses engaged in missions such as the St. Agnes Mission, Zoar, which was founded in the 1920s. Deaconesses started a school, opened a dispensary, and trained a Zulu woman as the first non-European deaconess in the diocese of George. The liturgical opportunities for deaconesses in South Africa varied greatly from one diocese to another. In George they preached, led services, and baptized. In Grahamstown they were not allowed to do so.[373]

In Jamaica, after a solid start in education and the direction of an orphanage near Kingston, the number of deaconesses dwindled. By World

War II, all the British deaconesses had returned to England or had died. The government bought the property of the deaconess house in Kingston, but with the encouragement of the bishop, the work began again in 1957 in new premises with six deaconesses from England. These women emphasized the training of Jamaican women for church work. However, most of the training of deaconesses and other church workers moved to the Theological College of the West Indies. Both Jamaican and British deaconesses worked in schools, youth work, Sunday schools, and parish work.[374] Jamaican deaconesses were ordained as deacons in the early 1990s, then as priests.[375]

In India, the deaconess work begun at Lahore (now Pakistan) prospered. The Society of St. Hilda continued its educational work and opened membership to lay workers. Members worked among neglected children and orphans and at St. Faith's Children's Home in Rawalpindi. They did parish work. The schools and orphanage flourished. The society itself came to an end in 1963, leaving behind a few surviving members.[376]

Deaconesses from England also went to other parts of India. At Madras in 1913, St. Faith's House was founded as a center for church work and as a training school. It closed officially in 1948 with the inauguration of the Church of South India. At first, in this united church, deaconesses became members of an order of sisters.[377]

In China in the 1920s and 1930s, Anglican deaconess work prospered. Deaconesses came from England, the United States, and Canada. From the 1930s on, there were Chinese deaconesses. Some of the non-Chinese deaconesses withdrew from the country during World War II. Of those who stayed, some were interned. The war also created a shortage of Anglican priests. This placed the church in a difficult situation. Sometimes a deaconess was available to serve a parish and a priest was not.[378]

The situation of the female deaconess in the worldwide Anglican Communion was complicated by the fact that for most of the history of these churches the male deacon could proceed to the priesthood but the female deaconess could not. In some parts of the Anglican Communion any suggestion that deaconesses function in a role that could be considered "priestly" met with resistance. Some people feared that giving deaconesses the liturgical tasks of deacons might be the "thin end of a wedge" that would open a door for them to enter the priesthood. For a long time, deaconesses in many Anglican churches were not allowed to perform some of the traditional roles of deacons, such as reading the Gospel in church or helping to distribute Communion.[379] In 1941 the Church of England allowed that "(i) In case of need [the bishop can authorize a deaconess] to read the services of Morning and Evening Prayer and the Litany, except those portions reserved to the priest, and to lead in prayer; (ii) to instruct and preach, except during the service of Holy Communion."[380] From then on, the Church of England moved gradually in the direction of giving deaconesses a greater liturgical role, for example, removing the limitations on preaching in 1973.[381]

The 1968 Lambeth Conference recommended that the diaconate be open to men and women. The Church of England hesitated to allow women to become deacons, however, though joint theological training of men and women had already begun in some theological colleges.[382] Churches within the Anglican Communion in the rest of the world moved faster to expand the diaconate. In many ways, the Anglican Church of China had given Chinese deaconesses the status of deacons when it began ordaining women to the order in the 1930s. In the 1960s and 1970s, Anglican bishops in the rest of the world began to recognize deaconesses as deacons. In the United States in 1964, when deaconesses were allowed to marry, the Episcopal Church stated that they were "ordered," not "set apart," for ministry in the church. James Pike, the bishop of California, said in 1965 that he would recognize Phyllis Edwards, already a deaconess, as a deacon and list her as a member of the clergy. The 1970 Episcopal General Convention at Houston passed a canon (church law) doing away with differences between deacons (male) and deaconesses, allowing women to seek ordination as a deacon.[383] This affected training, so women were allowed to study at theological seminaries alongside men. Other Anglican churches permitted deaconesses to be ordained deacons: Korea, Canada, and Kenya in 1968; New Zealand in 1972; Uganda in 1973; Japan in 1974; and Central Africa in 1976. In 1971 Bishop Snell of the Church of Canada ordained two deaconesses as deacons at St. John's, York Mills. As late as 1980 in the British Isles, however, only Wales had decided to ordain women to the diaconate, but the next decade saw additional churches making this move.[384]

On February 9, 1986, women were first ordained deacons in the Anglican Church in Australia. This occurred in Melbourne. There were those that argued that "the Deaconess Order" was a separate "*lay* Order for women." Some of those who were ordained deacons already were deaconesses. In 1989 many deaconesses in Sydney were ordained deacons.[385]

In February 1987 women were ordained deacons in the Church of England. That previous month there had been more than one thousand deaconesses in the Church of England, the most ever. Twenty of these deaconesses were members of the Deaconess Community of St. Andrew. Most of the deaconesses in the Church of England became deacons, at least

635. Ten of the twenty deaconesses in the Deaconess Community of St. Andrew were ordained as deacons, at which time the community changed its name to the "Community of St. Andrew."[386] By 1990 there were 1,100 female deacons in the Church of England, according to an international newsletter of diaconal associations.[387]

By then, what some had feared had come about in some Anglican churches: Allowing women to be deacons had been a prelude to their ordination as priests. A deaconess was the first woman to be ordained a priest in an Anglican church. Lei Tim-oi, a Chinese woman, was ordained a priest under unusual circumstances. A graduate of Union Theological Seminary, Canton, where she had passed with honors the full theological course that the Anglican clergy took, in 1941 Lei Tim-oi was ordained a deaconess. During World War II, she was in charge of a congregation in Macao, a Portuguese colony forty miles from Hong Kong. Ronald Hall, her bishop, sent a Chinese priest to Macao once a month to supplement Lei Tim-oi's pastoral duties, but after the Japanese occupation, it was impossible to continue this arrangement.[388] On June 4, 1943, Bishop Ronald Hall wrote Archbishop of Canterbury William Temple, informing him that rather than depriving a congregation of 150 people of the sacraments, he had given Lei Tim-oi permission to celebrate the Lord's Supper. Hall stated that he hoped that at the next Lambeth Conference there would be a clear majority in favor of experiments in provinces that had an acute shortage of priests.[389]

Archbishop of Canterbury Temple wrote back that Hall's action was "manifestly exceptional," but that it could be "terminated when the emergency is past," whereas if he ordained a deaconess to the priesthood, he would be doing something of which "the effects would be permanent and could not be terminated."[390] By the time this letter reached Hall, he had ordained Lei Tim-oi a priest. Apparently, he was influenced in this decision by a 1941 visit to New York and to Reinhold Niebuhr and his wife, who was Anglican. Two days after the ordination of Lei Tim-oi, on January 17, 1944, he wrote Archbishop Temple:

> On St. Paul's Day I ordained a Chinese Deaconess as a priest in the Church of God . . . . I have licensed her to serve as a priest in my diocese. . . . My reason was not theoretical views of the equality of men and women but the needs of my people for the sacraments and the manifest gift of the pastoral charisma. . . . I do not expect you to approve.[391]

Archbishop Temple did not approve but withheld official comment until the Anglican bishops of China could have a chance to act. Because of the war, however, they could not meet. Temple died. His successor, Archbishop Fisher, tried to get Hall to suspend Lei Tim-oi. Archbishop Fisher was concerned about "ecumenical repercussions on the Orthodox" and schism in the Anglican Communion. The news of the ordination of a woman had created a furor among some Anglicans. Archbishop Fisher wrote a letter disapproving of Hall's actions to Arnold Scott, the presiding bishop of the Chinese bishops. In March 1946 the Chinese House of Bishops met in Shanghai and passed the following resolution:

> That this House regrets the uncanonical action of the Bishop of Hongkong [sic] in ordaining Deaconess Lei to the priesthood; and, having understood that Deaconess Lei has already placed in his hands her resignation from her priestly ministry, this House requests the Bishop of Hongkong [sic] to accept it.[392]

Deaconess Lei did not resign her priestly orders but ceased to practice them.[393] She went back to the work of a deaconess. The 1948 Lambeth Conference received a proposal from the General Synod of the Church of China for the Diocese of South China "that for an experimental period of twenty years a deaconess might . . . be ordained to the priesthood." The proposed Chinese canon was rejected.[394] The time had not come, the Lambeth Conference said.[395] Twenty-five years later, however, the Anglican Church of China was among the first of the worldwide Anglican Communion to ordain women to the priesthood. On November 28, 1971, Bishop Gilbert Baker of the diocese of Hong Kong (all that was left organizationally of the Anglican Church of China) ordained two women priests: Jane Hwang and Joyce Bennett.[396] He ordained another woman in 1973.

In 1974 four bishops, on their own, ordained eleven female priests in Philadelphia, and the General Convention of the Episcopal Church in the United States regularized these ordinations in 1976. The Anglican Province of the Indian Ocean decided to ordain female priests in 1974. Canada ordained female priests in 1975 and New Zealand in 1976, the same year that Kenya decided to ordain female priests. One by one, the churches within the Anglican Communion began to ordain women as priests.[397]

INTERNATIONAL ASSOCIATIONS OF DEACONS AND DEACONESSES

The Kaiserswerth General Conference (*Kaiserswerther Generalkonferenz und Verband*), founded in 1861, can be considered the oldest international diaconal association, but it did not meet all the needs of the twentieth century. In 1923 an *International Verein für Innere Mission und Diakonie* was founded.[398] In 1946 a World Federation of Deaconess Associations met in Utrecht, the Netherlands, and in 1947 in Riehen, Switzerland, just before the inauguration of the World Council of Churches in 1948 in Amsterdam. The World Federation of Deaconess Associations was the precursor body to Diakonia, the World Federation of Diaconal Associations and Diaconal Communities, an organization intended "to further ecumenical relationships between diaconal associations in various countries; to reflect on the nature and task of *diakonia* in the New Testament sense and to further the understanding of it; to strengthen a sense of community among associations and sisterhoods; to render mutual aid; to undertake common tasks."[399] The president of Diakonia in 2005 was Deaconess Louise Williams, executive director of the Lutheran Deaconess Association, centered at Valparaiso University, Indiana.[400]

Diakonia has contact and interaction with the World Council of Churches.[401] It publishes a newsletter that is a rich source of information on the current status of diaconal movements in the world today: *Diakonia News*, formerly known as the *Newsletter of the World Federation of Diaconal Associations and Sisterhoods* but now known as the *Newsletter of Foundation Diakonia World Federation of Diaconal Associations and Diaconal Communities*. The July 1990 issue carried news of diaconal associations in Africa, Madagascar (the Malagasy Republic), Suriname (formerly Dutch Guiana), Jamaica, Brazil, Japan, Indonesia, India, the Philippines, and, of course, Europe and North America. Denominations represented included Lutheran, Reformed, Methodist, Anglican, Roman Catholic, and Orthodox.[402]

Diakonia has member diaconal associations from throughout the world. It includes sixty-five individual associations or federations of many associations in some thirty-six countries. The member associations include about "23,000 women and men . . . male and female deacons and diaconal ministers as well as deaconesses, diaconal sisters, and female church workers."[403] An international assembly of Diakonia occurs every four years. An assembly met June 19–26, 1992, in Wolfville, Nova Scotia, Canada. In 2001 the assembly met July 5–11 at the University of Queensland, Brisbane, Australia.[404] In 2005 it met in Durham, England.[405] Diakonia aids various diaconal projects through "Diak-Aid.[406]

There are three regions in Diakonia: DRAE (Africa and Europe); DAP (Asia and the Pacific); and DOTAC (the Americas and the Caribbean), originally called DOTA (Diakonia of the Americas),[407] which have assemblies every four years[408] attended by both deacons and deaconesses. In 1992 DOTAC's president was Louise Williams, executive director of the Lutheran Deaconess Association.[409] A DOTAC conference was held August 9–14, 1989, at the University of the West Indies, Kingston, Jamaica, and was hosted by the Anglican Deaconess Order of the Diocese of Jamaica and the Deaconess Order of the Wesley Deaconesses of the Methodist Church in the Caribbean and the Americas.[410] In 2001 the president was Deacon Linda M. Ervin of the United Church of Canada, and DOTAC was advertising simultaneous translation into Portuguese, Spanish, English, and French at its June 22–26, 2002, conference in Winnipeg, Canada.[411]

Diakonia is one of three main diaconal associations in Europe. The other two are (1) the European Conference of Deacons (EDC), founded by deacons from Scandinavia, Switzerland, Germany, and the Netherlands;[412] and (2) the Roman Catholic International Diaconate Centre (IDC or IDZ), formerly in Freiburg-im-Breisgau, Germany, but now based in Rottenburg, Germany.[413] Diakonia relates to these and other diaconal associations through mutual attendance at conferences and service on one another's boards.[414] The secretary of Diakonia has been on the board of the International Federation of Inner Mission and Diakonia (IFIM), an association founded in 1922 that is primarily German.[415]

Diakonia also engages in ecumenical dialogue. It sends representatives to gatherings of the Permanent International Ecumenical Consultation of Religious Superiors. DOTAC and the Leadership Conference of Women Religious (Catholic) exchange representatives at some of their meetings.[416] The willingness of Roman Catholics to relate to other denominations after the Second Vatican Council (1962–1965) led to the formation of Koinonia-Diakonia, which offered opportunities for Catholics, Orthodox, and Protestants who are committed to diaconal service to interact with one another.[417] In 1976 Koinonia-Diakonia held its first major encounter at l'Arbrèsle, France.[418] The European Conference of Deacons was a partner in Koinonia-Diakonia, which ceased in the early 1990s, though the European Conference of Deacons, which canceled its 2002 meeting because of the death of its leader, lived on. Germans are the largest constituency of the European Conference of Deacons, but there are also deacons from Switzerland, Denmark, Norway, Sweden, the Netherlands, and other countries of Europe.[419]

In 1971, five years before the first Koinonia-Diakonia gathering, Kaire, a group that offers some members of Diakonia opportunities to interact with members of religious sisterhoods, met for the first time at Bossey, near Geneva, Switzerland.[420] Kaire meetings involve people from Catholic,

Anglican, Orthodox, and Protestant sisterhoods in addition to members of Diakonia. March 9–11, 1990, a Kaire meeting took place in a Catholic convent and a deaconess house in what had been East Germany.[421] The 2002 Diakonia calendar listed a June 3–10 Kaire meeting in Monastery-Bose, near Magnano, Italy.[422]

By the final decade of the twentieth century, the deaconesses and deacons of the Inner Mission model had evolved considerably since their beginnings in the nineteenth century. As the work in which they engaged (nursing, social work, and teaching) became professionalized, deaconesses and deacons also became professional. They were better educated. Some of the communities of deacons and deaconesses had become part of the institutional church, sponsored by particular denominations or affiliated with them. Individual communities of deaconesses and deacons were in contact with one another. International organizations of deaconesses and deacons had formed. Some deacons and deaconesses of the Inner Mission model had come to resemble the permanent diaconate that some churches emphasized beginning in the 1950s and 1960s.

The subject of the next chapter is the permanent diaconate in the Catholic Church, the perpetual or vocational deacon in Episcopal churches, the diaconal minister and deacon in Methodist churches, and the career deacons and deaconesses of the Lutheran churches of Germany and the Scandinavian countries.

NOTES

1. Keller, Moede, and Moore, *Called to Serve*, 34.
2. The German Evangelical Lutheran Synod of Missouri, Ohio and Other States was founded in 1847. The word *German* was omitted in 1917. In 1947 the name became The Lutheran Church—Missouri Synod. See Wentz, *Basic History of Lutheranism*, 202.
3. Steininger, "History of the Female Diaconate," 80.
4. Steininger, "History of the Female Diaconate," 82–83.
5. Kirsch, "Deaconesses in the United States since 1918," 231.
6. Weiser, *Love's Response*, 68.
7. Weiser, *To Serve the Lord*, 14.
8. Steininger, "History of the Female Diaconate," 85.
9. Eugene Fevold, "Coming of Age, 1875–1900," in Nelson, *Lutherans in North America*, 300; Weiser, *Love's Response*, 68–69.
10. Fevold, "Coming of Age," 301.
11. Steininger, "History of the Female Diaconate," 86.
12. Carl S. Meyer, "The Missouri Synod and Other Lutherans before 1918," in Meyer, *Moving Frontiers*, 246–47, 260–62, 265; August Suelflow and E. Clifford Nelson, "Following the Frontier, 1840–1875," in Nelson, *Lutherans in North America*, 247–51; Fred W. Meuser, "Facing the Twentieth Century, 1900–1930," in Nelson, *Lutherans in North America*, 379.

13. "Articles of Incorporation of the Lutheran Deaconess Association, Inc., as Amended May, 1975 and November, 1979" (Mimeographed); "Lutheran Deaconess Association, Inc., Valparaiso, Indiana: Presentation to Task Force on the Study of Ministry, Evangelical Lutheran Church in America, Chicago, Illinois, October 7, 1989" (Mimeographed), [1]; Weiser, *Love's Response*, 69; Steininger, "History of the Female Diaconate," 87.

14. Hattstaedt, "History of the Southern Wisconsin District," 86.

15. Deaconess Program, Concordia College, *Strehlow Endowment Fund*.

16. Schlegel, " 'Daddy' Herzberger's Legacy," 142.

17. Roth, "Female Diaconate," 67–68; Weiser, *Love's Response*, 69, 80–81.

18. Thomas Coates and Erwin L. Lueker, "Four Decades of Expansion," in Meyer, *Moving Frontiers*, 390; Louise Williams, executive director of the Lutheran Deaconess Association, telephone conversation with author, 10 August 1992.

19. Deaconess Joyce Ostermann, president of the Concordia Deaconess Conference, telephone conversation with author, 13 August 2003.

20. Concordia Deaconess Conference and Concordia Deaconess Program, The Lutheran Church—Missouri Synod, "Our Clara . . .," in "3D: A Decade of Deaconess Dedication, 1980–1990, Our History . . ." (n.p., n.d., photocopy).

21. Lutheran Deaconess Association, "Deaconess Education Catalogue" (n.p., n.d., mimeographed), 1.

22. Weiser, *Love's Response*, 81; Weiser, *To Serve the Lord*, 13.

23. Louise Williams, executive director, Lutheran Deaconess Association, telephone conversation with author, 20 August 2003.

24. Nichol, *All These Lutherans*, 111.

25. Article 2, B, and Article 7, "Articles of Incorporation Amended, 1979," 1–2.

26. "Lutheran Deaconess Association Presentation"; "Working Draft: ELCA Division for Ministry—Lutheran Deaconess Association Understanding of Relationship" (n.p, April 1992, photocopy), 2.

27. Williams, telephone conversation, 20 August 2003; 9 May 2005.

28. Williams, telephone conversation, 20 August 2003.

29. Williams, telephone conversation, 8 August 2003.

30. Deaconess Diane Marten, director of education and formation of the LDA, Valparaiso, Indiana, telephone conversation with author, 11 August 2003.

31. Williams, telephone conversation, 20 August 2003.

32. "Working Draft," 1.

33. "Working Draft," 1.

34. Williams, telephone conversation, 8 August 2003.

35. Carol Schickel, Division of Ministry, Evangelical Lutheran Church in America, telephone conversation with author, 16 June 2003.

36. Greve, "Statistics on Ministry of Deaconesses"

37. Williams, telephone conversation, 8 August 2003.

38. "Working Draft," 1; Martin, telephone conversation, 11 August 2003.

39. Williams, telephone conversation, 8 August 2003.

40. "Deaconess, M.D.," *The LDA Today: A Newsletter of the Lutheran Deaconess Association* 8, no. 2 (Fall 2002): 1.

41. See the brochure "Among You as One Who Serves" (Lutheran Deaconess Association, Valparaiso, Indiana, n.d.).

42. Williams, telephone conversation, 8 August 2003.

43. Marten, telephone conversation, 11 August 2003.

44. Marten, telephone conversation, 11 August 2003; "Phonothon," *Lutheran Deaconess Association* (Spring 1990): [4].

45. Marten, telephone conversation, 27 April 2005.

46. Williams, telephone conversation, 8 August 2003.

47. See the brochures "Among You as One Who Serves" and "Becoming a Deaconess Isn't for Everyone" (Lutheran Deaconess Association Center for Diaconal Ministry, n.d.); "Deaconess Ministry Yesterday and Today" (Lutheran Deaconess Association, Valparaiso, Indiana, July 1987).

48. Williams, telephone conversation, 9 May 2005.

49. Louise Williams, "From My Perspective . . ." *The LDA Today: A Newsletter of the Lutheran Deaconess Association* 3, no. 2 (Fall 2002): 2.

50. Marten, telephone conversation, 24 February 2005.

51. Williams, telephone conversation, 10 August 1992.

52. "The Lutheran Deaconesses [*sic*] Association," *Diakonia News* 78 (July 1990): 5.

53. Lutheran Deaconess Association, "How Can I Become a Deaconess?"; Lutheran Deaconess Association Center for Diaconal Ministry, "Deaconess Education Catalogue," 3–4, 6–10, 12–13.

54. Marten, telephone conversation, 24 February 2005.

55. See "New Educational Program" in the periodical of the *Lutheran Deaconess Association* (Fall 1988): [3], or "Plan 4" in the brochures "How Can I Become a Deaconess?" or "Could a Deaconess Serve with Us?" (Lutheran Deaconess Association, n.d.), 1.

56. Louise Williams, telephone conversation with author, 14 August 1992.

57. Marten, telephone conversation, 24 February 2005.

58. Marten, telephone conversation, 11 August 2003.

59. Lutheran Deaconess Association Center for Diaconal Ministry, "Deaconess Education Catalogue," 3–4, 7–10, 12–13.

60. Marten, telephone conversation, 24 February 2005.

61. Marten, telephone conversation, 24 February 2005.

62. Lutheran Deaconess Association, "How Can I Become a Deaconess?"; Williams, telephone conversation, 9 May 2005.

63. Lutheran Deaconess Association, "Excerpts from 'A Proposal,' " 3.

64. Lutheran Deaconess Association Center for Diaconal Ministry, "Deaconess Education Catalogue," 2.

65. Lutheran Deaconess Association, "Excerpts from 'A Proposal,' " 3–4.

66. "Diakonia en Christo Lay Ministry Award," *Lutheran Deaconess Association* (Spring 1990): [2]; "Diakonia en Christo Award," *Lutheran Deaconess Association* (Fall 1987): [3]; "Diakonia Award," *Lutheran Deaconess Association* (Spring 1989): [3].

67. "New Educational Program," [3].

68. "Mother's Gathering," *Lutheran Deaconess Association* (Fall 1985): [3]; and (Spring 1987): [4]; "Mothers Gatherings," *Lutheran Deaconess Association* (Fall 1987): [2]; (Fall 1988): [3]; and (Spring 1989): [2].

69. "Mothers Discussion," *Lutheran Deaconess Association* (Spring 1989); "The 'M' Is for Me"—Gatherings and Materials," *Lutheran Deaconess Association* (Spring 1990): [3].

70. Williams, telephone conversation, 20 August 2003.

71. Burgess-Cassler, *Celebrating Servants*.

72. *Lutheran Deaconess Association Connections* is published by the Center for Diaconal Ministry, Valparaiso, Indiana.

73. See, for example, no. 18 (Fall 1988); "Among You as One Who Serves," *Lutheran Deaconess Association* 5 (1990).

74. Lutheran Deaconess Association, *A Deaconess! What's That? Deaconesses Serve . . . To Make a Difference Today! Kindergarten and Up* (Lutheran Deaconess Association, n.d.); *A Deaconess! What's That? Deaconesses Serve . . . To Make a Difference Today! Grade 3 and Up* (Lutheran Deaconess Association, n.d.); *A Deaconess! What's That? Deaconesses Serve . . . To Make a Difference Today! Middle School and Up* (Lutheran Deaconess Association, n.d.).

75. Williams, telephone conversation, 20 August 2003; Marten, telephone conversation, 24 February 2005.

76. Williams, telephone conversation, 8 August 2003.

77. Marten, telephone conversation, 11 August 2003; 24 February 2005.

78. Williams, telephone conversation, 8 August 2003.

79. Williams, telephone conversation, 20 August 2003.

80. Marten, telephone conversation, 11 August 2003; 24 February 2005.

81. Williams, telephone conversation, 20 August 2003.

82. Williams, telephone conversation, 20 August 2003.

83. *Lutheran Deaconess Association* (Spring 1987): [1].

84. Lutheran Deaconess Association, "Deaconess Education Catalogue," 5, 11, 14.

85. Marten, telephone conversation, 11 August 2003.

86. Williams, telephone conversation, 20 August 2003; Marten, telephone conversation, 24 February 2005.

87. Lutheran Deaconess Association, "Deaconess Education Catalogue," 10.

88. For example, St. Louis, Missouri. Williams, telephone conversation, 8 August 2003.

89. Concordia Deaconess Conference and Concordia Deaconess Program, The Lutheran Church—Missouri Synod, "Our Synod . . . ," in "3D: A Decade of Deaconess Dedication."

90. See "To Expand Deaconess Program," Resolution 6–05, Overtures 6–46 to 6–51D, in *1979 Convention Workbook* (St. Louis: The Lutheran Church—Missouri Synod, 1979), 195–97.

91. The Deaconess Program, Concordia College, River Forest, Ill., "Deaconess Program Fact Sheet" (n.d., photocopy).

92. The Deaconess Program, Concordia College, River Forest, Ill., "Deaconess Program Fact Sheet" (n.d., photocopy). Deaconess Kristin Wassilak, director of the Concordia Deaconess Program, telephone conversation with author, 6 July 1992.

93. For a more complete description of this program, see "The Deaconess Internship" (River Forest, Ill.: n.d., photocopy).

94. For a more complete description of the fieldwork, see Concordia College, River Forest, Ill., "Deaconess Field Work Manual" (1991–1992, photocopy).

95. The Deaconess Program, Concordia University, River Forest, Ill., "Undergraduate Program Fact Sheet Curriculum" (n.d., photocopy); Concordia Deaconess Program, Concordia College, River Forest, Ill., "Curriculum" (n. d., photocopy).

96. The Deaconess Program of The Lutheran Church—Missouri Synod, River Forest, Ill., "Deaconess . . . Serving the Lord and His People" (n.d., photocopy).

97. The Deaconess Program, Concordia University, River Forest, Ill., "Undergraduate Program Fact Sheet Curriculum," verso.

98. The Deaconess Program of The Lutheran Church—Missouri Synod, River Forest, Ill., "Deaconess . . . Serving the Lord and His People"; Wassilak, telephone conversation, 6 July 1992.

99. Concordia University, River Forest, Ill., "Deaconess Field Work Manual," [1].

100. Concordia College, River Forest, Ill., "Concordia Deaconess Program" (n.d.).

101. Wassilak, telephone conversation, 6 July 1992.

102. Kristin Wassilak, letter to the author, River Forest, Illinois, 20 January 1992.

103. Concordia College, River Forest, Ill., "Concordia Deaconesses [*sic*] Program."

104. The Deaconess Program, Concordia University, River Forest, Ill., "Non-Traditional Programs Fact Sheet" (n.d., photocopy).

105. Kristin Wassilak, electronic mail to author, 24 August 2003, 21 February 2005, 4 April 2005.

106. Nancy Nemoyer, director of the Concordia Deaconess Program, letter to the author, River Forest, Illinois, 15 March 1989.

107. Article 3: "Membership in the Conference is contingent upon holding membership in no other deaconess conference" (Concordia Deaconess Conference, "Constitution" [n.p.: (prior to March 15, 1989)], mimeographed).

108. Concordia Deaconess Conference and Concordia Deaconess Program, The Lutheran Church—Missouri Synod, "Our History . . . ," in "3D: A Decade of Deaconess Dedication."

109. Wassilak, telephone conversation, 31 March 2005.

110. "From the Desk of Deaconess Kristin: One in the Spirit," *Deaconess Beacon*, [3].

111. Concordia Deaconess Conference and Concordia Deaconess Program, The Lutheran Church—Missouri Synod, "Our History . . . ," in "3D: A Decade of Deaconess Dedication."

112. Deaconess Grace Rao, electronic mail to author, 31 March 2005.

113. Concordia Deaconess Conference and Concordia Deaconess Program, The Lutheran Church—Missouri Synod, "Our Cross . . ." and "Our Uniform . . .," in "3D: A Decade of Deaconess Dedication."

114. Wassilak, letter to the author, January 20, 1992.

115. Wassilak, letter to the author, January 20, 1992.

116. Concordia Deaconess Conference and Concordia Deaconess Program, The Lutheran Church—Missouri Synod, "Our Synod . . .," in "3D: A Decade of Deaconess Dedication."

117. "The Lutheran Deaconesses [*sic*] Association," 5.

118. "What in the World Is a 'Colloquy'?" *Deaconess Beacon*, n.d., [3]; The Deaconess Program, Concordia University, River Forest, Ill., "Non-traditional Programs Fact Sheet"; Wassilak, telephone conversation, 10 August 1992.

119. Wassilak, letter to the author, 20 January 1992.

120. Marten, telephone conversation, 11 August 2003.

121. Presented 28 February 2002, St. Louis, Missouri.

122. Kristin Wassilak, "A Developing Theology for the Female Diaconate: A Paper for Discussion" (St. Louis: 28 February 2002), 5–10.

123. Wassilak, "Developing Theology for the Female Diaconate," 10.

124. Concordia University Wisconsin, "Lay Ministry Programs: A Theological Education Extension Program," http://www.cuw.edu/laymin/default.htm, as quoted in Wassilak, "Developing Theology for the Female Diaconate."

125. Wassilak, "Developing Theology for the Female Diaconate," 12.

126. Kristin Wassilak, telephone conversation with author, 12 June 2003.

127. Deaconess Theresa List, assistant to the dean of the Graduate School for Diaconal Studies, Concordia Seminary, St. Louis, Mo., telephone conversation with author, 13 June 2003.

128. Wassilak, telephone conversation, 31 March 2005, and electronic mail, 21 February 2005, 4 April 2005.

129. Wassilak, electronic mail, 21 February 2005.

130. Theresa List, telephone conversation with author, 6 June 2003.

131. Gloria DeCuir, assistant to the dean of the Graduate School for Diaconal Studies, Concordia Seminary, St. Louis, Missouri, electronic mail to author, 8 March 2005.

132. Ostermann, telephone conversation, 13 August 2003; Concordia Seminary, St. Louis, *Academic Catalog 2002–2003, Concordia Seminary, St. Louis Missouri* (n.p.: n.d.), 68; Concordia Seminary, St. Louis, *Graduate School, Concordia Seminary, St. Louis: Addressing Contemporary Issues with the Historic Christian Faith* (n.p.: n.d.).

133. Ostermann, telephone conversation, 27 August 2003.

134. Concordia Seminary, St. Louis, "Deaconess Addendum to the 2002–2003 Academic Catalog" (n.p.: n.d.), [4].

135. Theresa List, "LCMS Deaconesses: Who We Are, How to Become One, and How We Can Enrich Your Congregation or Institution," *Issues in Christian Education* 39, no. 1 (Spring 2005): 26.

136. Deanna Cheadle, electronic mail to author, 9 March 2005; Sara Bielby and Arthur A. Just Jr., "Serving Christ by Serving Our Neighbor: Theological and Historical Perspectives on Lutheran Deaconesses," *Issues in Christian Education* 39, no. 1 (Spring 2005): 8, 11.

137. List, telephone conversation, 13 June 2003.

138. Ostermann, telephone conversation, 13 August 2003.

139. John O'Hara, Research Services, The Lutheran Church—Missouri Synod, electronic mail to author, 15 August 2003.

140. Tonia Burcham, electronic mail to author, 17 May 2005.

141. Marten, telephone conversation, 27 April 2005; Deaconess Grace Rao, electronic mail to author, 31 March 2005.

142. Kristin Wassilak, "Deaconesses: Engaging the Church in Diakonia," *Issues in Christian Education* 39, no. 1 (Spring 2005): 16.

143. Margaret Anderson, "The Distaff Side of Pastoral Care: The Deaconess as Chaplain," *Issues in Christian Education* 39, no. 1 (Spring 2005): 4.

144. Wassilak, "Deaconesses: Engaging the Church in Diakonia," 19.

145. Ostermann, telephone conversation, 13 June 2003.

146. List, telephone conversation, 13 August 2003; Ostermann, telephone conversation, 13 August 2003.

147. List, telephone conversation, 10 June 2003.

148. List, telephone conversation, 13 June 2003; Ostermann, telephone conversation, 13 August 2003.

149. List, telephone conversation, 13 June 2003.

150. As quoted in Theresa Jo List, assistant to the Graduate School, for Diaconal Studies, Concordia Seminary, St. Louis, letter to author, 25 June 2003.

151. *Proceedings and Papers of the Seventh Conference of Evangelical Lutheran Deaconess Motherhouses in the United States, Philadelphia, Pa., April 21–22, 1908* (n.p.: n.d.), 5.

152. *Proceedings and Papers of the Ninth Conference of Evangelical Lutheran Deaconess Motherhouses in the United States, Chicago, Ill., May 1–2, 1912* (n.p.: n.d.), 6.

153. *Proceedings and Papers of the Eleventh Conference of Evangelical Lutheran Deaconess Motherhouses in the United States, Minneapolis, Minn., May 20–22, 1914* (n.p.: n.d.), 5.

154. *The Sixteenth Conference of Lutheran Deaconess Motherhouses in America, Milwaukee, Wis-*

consin, May 20–22, 1924 (n.p.: n.d.), 6.

155. *The Twentieth Conference of Lutheran Deaconess Institutions in America, Brooklyn, N.Y., April 20–21, 1933* (n.p.: n.d.), 4. Fort Wayne statistics were first included in 1922 with a note: "Not officially connected with Conference" (*The Fifteenth Conference of Evangelical Lutheran Deaconess Motherhouses in the United States, Omaha, Nebraska, October 31 November 2, 1922* [n.p.: n.d.], 6).

156. *The Twenty-first Conference of the Lutheran Deaconess Motherhouses in America, Baltimore, MD., June 25–27, 1935* (n.p.: n.d.), 4.

157. *Twenty-first Conference of the Lutheran Deaconess Motherhouses in America*, 4. *The Twenty-second Conference of the Lutheran Deaconess Motherhouses in America, Omaha, Nebr., September 27–29, 1936* (n.p.: n.d.), 5.

158. *Twenty-second Conference of the Lutheran Deaconess Motherhouses in America*, 5.

159. *The Twenty-fourth Conference of Lutheran Deaconess Motherhouses in America, Milwaukee, Wis., Wednesday–Friday, June 19–21, 1940* (n.p.: n.d.), 15.

160. *Twenty-sixth Conference of Lutheran Deaconess Homes in America, June 19–21, 1944, Minneapolis, Minnesota* (n.p.: n.d.), 13.

161. *Twenty-fourth Conference of Lutheran Deaconess Motherhouses in America*, 15.

162. Williams, telephone call, 9 May 2005.

163. Weiser, *To Serve the Lord*, 14–15.

164. Bachmann, *Story of the Philadelphia Deaconess Motherhouse*, 21; *Mary J. Drexel Home and Philadelphia Motherhouse*, 29.

165. "Deaconess Community of the Evangelical Lutheran Church in America" (materials presented by the Deaconess Community to the Task Force on Ministry of the Evangelical Lutheran Church in America, cover letter, Sister Frieda Gatzke, 3 October 1989, photocopy), Appendix A; Weiser, *Love's Response*, 85–86.

166. See the brochure of The Deaconess Community of the Evangelical Lutheran Church in America, "A Place Apart for Personal Retreat" (n.p.: The Deaconess Community, ELCA, 1989); Weiser, *To Serve the Lord*, 15–17, 25, 31; Weiser, *Love's Response*, 85–86.

167. List, telephone conversation, 6 June 2003.

168. "Bylaws of the Deaconess Community of the Evangelical Lutheran Church in America" (materials presented by the Deaconess Community to the Task Force on Ministry of the Evangelical Lutheran Church in America, cover letter dated 3 October 1989, Sister Frieda Gatzke, photocopy), 1.

169. Weiser, *To Serve the Lord*, 15–17, 31; Weiser, *Love's Response*, 85–86.

170. Gilbert, *Commitment to Unity*, 517.

171. Weiser, *To Serve the Lord*, 29–30.

172. See the brochure of the Deaconess Community of the Evangelical Lutheran Church in America, "Auxiliary of the Deaconess Community" (The Deaconess Community of the Evangelical Lutheran Church in America, 1988).

173. Weiser, *To Serve the Lord*, 28; Weiser, *Love's Response*, 88, 113–15.

174. Gilbert, *Commitment to Unity*, 238; Weiser, *To Serve the Lord*, 28–30.

175. "1991 Candidate Seminar," *The Deaconess* 20, no. 2 (1991): [1].

176. Weiser, *To Serve the Lord*, 21, 43; Weiser, *Love's Response*, 89, 115.

177. Terance Lucas, administrative assistant of the Deaconess Community of the Evangelical Lutheran Church in America, telephone conversation with author, 10 June 2003.

178. Weiser, *Love's Response*, 89.

179. Lucas, telephone conversation, 10 June 2003.

180. Deaconess Elizabeth Steele, chairperson of the Board of Directors of the Deaconess

Community of the Evangelical Lutheran Church in America, Huron, Ohio, telephone conversation with author, 18 June 2003.

181. "Deaconess Community of the Evangelical Lutheran Church in America."

182. Weiser, *To Serve the Lord*, 21.

183. Steele, telephone conversation, 18 June 2003.

184. Lucas, telephone conversation, 10 June 2003.

185. Weiser, *Love's Response*, 90.

186. "Deaconess Community of the Evangelical Lutheran Church in America"; Weiser, *To Serve the Lord*, 16–17.

187. Sister Collette Brice, director of Education and Interpretation of the Deaconess Community of the Evangelical Lutheran Church in America, telephone conversations with author, 9 January 1992, 2 July 1992.

188. Weiser, *To Serve the Lord*, 27.

189. Lucas, telephone conversation, 10 June 2003.

190. Gilbert, *Commitment to Unity*, 317. The number of active deaconesses was listed as 44 in the ELCA, *Study of Ministry Study Edition*, 30, 30n105. The study admits that the statistics might not reflect the actual numbers.

191. Articles 1, 4.9, 8.4, 9.3, "Bylaws of the Deaconess Community of the Evangelical Lutheran Church in America" (n.d., photocopy), 1–2, 7.

192. "Deaconess Community of the Evangelical Lutheran Church in America."

193. K. Virginia Coleman, of the Diakonia of the Americas and the Caribbean, letter to Sister Frieda Gatzke, directing deaconess, Deaconess Community, the Evangelical Lutheran Church in America, 11 September 1989 (photocopy).

194. "Installation of Directing Deaconess," *The Deaconess* 20 (1991): [1].

195. Brice, telephone conversation, 9 January 1992.

196. Lucas, telephone conversation, 10 June 2003.

197. Steele, telephone conversation, 18 June 2003.

198. List, telephone conversation, 6 June 2003.

199. The Deaconess Community of the Evangelical Lutheran Church in America, "News: Deaconess Community Heaps Blessings on LSS Programs" (available from http://www.deaconess-elca.org/news.asp; Internet; accessed 9 June 2003).

200. Lucas, telephone conversation, 10 June 2003.

201. "The Deaconess Community of the Evangelical Lutheran Church in America," 1 (available from http://www.deaconess-elca.org/ministries.html; internet; accessed 9 June 2003).

202. Anne Keffer, directing deaconess of the Deaconess Community of the Evangelical Lutheran Church in America, telephone conversation, 8 March 2005.

203. Steele, telephone conversation, 18 June 2003.

204. "Candidacy for the Deaconess Community of the ELCA," (September 1999), [2].

205. Steele, telephone conversation with author, 18 June 2003.

206. [The Evangelical Lutheran Church in America], "Candidacy for Diaconal Ministry," (n.p.: n. d.), E–4.

207. Anne Keffer, telephone conversation, 8 March 2005.

208. [The Evangelical Lutheran Church in America], "Candidacy for Diaconal Ministry," (n.p.: n. d.), E–4. "The Deaconess Education Program," (photocopy), 1; and "Deaconess Candidate Formation" in the Deaconess Community of the Evangelical Lutheran Church in America (materials presented by this Deaconess Community to the Task Force on Ministry of the Evangelical Lutheran Church in America), 1.

209. See the brochure of the Deaconess Community of the Evangelical Lutheran Church in America, "The Deaconess Community of the Evangelical Lutheran Church in America" (The Deaconess Community, Evangelical Lutheran Church in America, 1989).

210. Elizabeth Steele, electronic mail, 19 June 2003.

211. Carol Schickel, director for candidacy, Division for Ministry, The Evangelical Lutheran Church in America, electronic mail to author, 21 February 2005.

212. See the brochure of the Deaconess Community of the Evangelical Lutheran Church in America, "Invest One Year . . . Be a Diaconal Associate" (n.p.: Deaconess Community of the Evangelical Lutheran Church in America, 1988); Weiser, *To Serve the Lord*, 29; "1990 DYP Director," *The Deaconess* 19 (1990): [2].

213. "Investing a Year," *The Deaconess* 20, no. 2 (1991): [2].

214. Lucas, telephone conversation, 10 June 2003.

215. Weiser, *Love's Response*, 82.

216. *Proceedings and Papers of the Ninth Conference*, 6.

217. Everson, "Demise of a Movement," 3.

218. Weiser, "Serving Love," 84.

219. *The Minneapolis Star* (7 February 1979): 7, cited in Everson, "Demise of a Movement," 1, 7.

220. Everson, "Demise of a Movement," 6–7.

221. Weiser, *Love's Response*, 75.

222. Ingeborg Sponland, *My Reasonable Service*, 65, 75, 143–45, cited in Everson, "Demise of a Movement," 8, 31n39.

223. Interview, Eileen Eckberg, 10 May 1979, in Everson, "Demise of a Movement," 30n31.

224. Archives, Luther Northwestern Seminary, St. Paul, Minn., quoted in Everson, "Demise of a Movement," 9.

225. 20 June 1885, Fedde, "Diary," 185; Sponland, *Reasonable Service*, 44, 61, quoted in Everson, "Demise of a Movement," 9.

226. Interview, Ella Knutson, Minneapolis, Minn., 9 May 1979, in Everson, "Demise of a Movement," 9.

227. Kirsch, "Deaconesses in the United States since 1918," 221.

228. Letter from H. B. Kildahl, n.d., in W. M. F. Deaconess Secretary's Notebook; Letter from H. B. Kildahl to the Board of Charities, ELC, n.d., in Commission on the Diaconate file (Luther Northwestern Seminary Archives), in Everson, "Demise of a Movement," 14–15, 31nn49–50.

229. Everson, "Demise of a Movement," 16–18.

230. Minutes, the quarterly Board Meeting, Lutheran Deaconess Home and Hospital, Sept. 15, 1955 (Luther Northwestern Seminary Archives), in Everson, "Demise of a Movement," 14.

231. "Recommendations, The Commission on the Diaconate" (n.d.). See also Minutes, Meeting of Commission of the Diaconate, 14 February 1953, and an article in the *Lutheran Herald* (2 June 1953), in Everson, "Demise of a Movement," 20–22, 19.

232. Everson, "Demise of a Movement," 22–24.

233. Interview, Prof. Loren Halvorson, n.d., in Everson, "Demise of a Movement," 25.

234. Interview, Halvorson, in Everson, "Demise of a Movement," 17, 24–25.

235. Interview, Halvorson, in Everson, "Demise of a Movement," 25, 33n84.

236. Ohl, *Deaconesses and Their Work*, 13.

237. Ohl, *Deaconesses and Their Work*, 13.

238. *The Twenty-first Conference*, 4; *The Twenty-second Conference*, 5.

239. "History of the Lutheran Deaconess Motherhouse at Milwaukee," [1–2].

240. "History of the Lutheran Deaconess Motherhouse at Milwaukee," [1–2].

241. "History of the Lutheran Deaconess Motherhouse at Milwaukee," [2].

242. Everson, "Demise of a Movement," 26–27.

243. "Poland," *Diakonia News* 78 (July 1990): 12.

244. Paul Philippi, "The Continental Mother-House Organization of Deaconesses," in Faith and Order Secretariat, *The Deaconess*, 37–38.

245. Wassilak, telephone conversation, 6 July 1992.

246. Reiner, *Das Amt der Gemeindeschwester am Beispiel der Diözese Oberösterreich.*

247. See, for example, Golder, *Deaconess Motherhouse.*

248. See, for example, Strohm and Thierfelder, *Diakonie im "Dritten Reich."*

249. See, for example, Müller und Siemen, *Warum sie sterben müssten*; and Lauterer, *Liebestätigkeit für die Volksgemeinschaft.*

250. Philippi, "Continental Mother-House," 39–40.

251. "Evangelical Diakonie Association, Berlin-Zehlendorf," *Diakonia News* 78 (July 1990): 15–16.

252. For example, the Evangelical Deaconess Motherhouse Frankenstein in Wertheim/Main. For information on this establishment, see *Jahresgruss 1988 aus dem Evang. Diakonissenmutterhaus "Frankenstein" in Wertheim am Main* 178 (December 1988).

253. *Schwesternverzeichnis des Evangelischen Diakonissenmutterhauses Frankenstein in Wertheim/Main, 1985* (n.p.: 1984), 5.

254. From *Der Ring*, Informationsblatt der v. [sic] Bodelschwinghschen Anstalten, 10 (October 1989), in "East Germany," *Diakonia News* 78 (July 1990): 13.

255. "Finding Inner Life in an Outside Tent," *One World* 75 (April 1982): 17–18.

256. Lambin, "Le costume des diaconesses," 359–61, 368.

257. Lambin, "Le costume des diaconesses protestantes," 598, 607, 617–19.

258. *Jahresbericht über die Diakonissen-Anstalt Kaiserswerth* 121 (13 October 1956–1957): 33.

259. For an example of twentieth-century promotional and recruitment literature, see *Der Direction der Diakonissenanstalt. Was, wann, wie, wer, wo, warum: Fragen und Antworten und noch zu Beantwortende Frage de Diakonissenanstalt Kaiserswerth* (Essen: Essener Druckerei Gemeinwohl, n.d.).

260. Pastor Fr. Reinhold Lanz was the director and Matron Erna Carle was the administrative secretary; see "Germanic Diakonia: Changes in Personnel," *Diakonia News* 78 (July 1990): 12.

261. "Hungary," *Diakonia News* 78 (July 1990): 11.

262. "Motherhouses—Training Centres of the Church in Germany," *Diakonia News* 78 (July 1990): 13.

263. Sister Teresa [Joan White], electronic mail, 24 August 2003.

264. "The German Sisterhoods after the Opening of the Wall," *Diakonia News* 78 (July 1990): 15.

265. Hagemann, *Diakonissen.*

266. Olesen, *Diakonien i kirkens historie.*

267. Golder, *History of the Deaconess Movement*, 245–47; Weiser, *Love's Response*, 45–46.

268. Bachmann, *Lutheran Churches in the World*, 397.

269. Meland, "Deacon in the Church of Norway," 63–64.

270. "The Deaconess Institutions in Scandinavia: Norway," *Diakonia News* 78 (July 1990): 16–17.

271. "Deaconess Institutions in Scandinavia: Norway," 17.

272. Meland, "Deacon in the Church of Norway," 67–68.

273. Brodd, "Deacon in the Church of Sweden," 98.

274. Brodd, "Deacon in the Church of Sweden," 99–101.

275. Brodd, "Deacon in the Church of Sweden," 99.

276. Brodd, "Deacon in the Church of Sweden," 101.

277. Brodd, "Deacon in the Church of Sweden," 103.

278. Brodd, "Deacon in the Church of Sweden," 104.

279. Brodd, "Deacon in the Church of Sweden," 104, 133.

280. Brodd, "Deacon in the Church of Sweden," 104, 132.

281. Brodd, "Deacon in the Church of Sweden," 131.

282. Brodd, "Deacon in the Church of Sweden," 112, 133.

283. Brodd, "Deacon in the Church of Sweden," 132.

284. Elmund, *Den kvinnliga diakonin i Sverige*.

285. Brodd, "Deacon in the Church of Sweden," 103.

286. Brodd, "Deacon in the Church of Sweden," 104, 134.

287. Philippi, "Continental Mother-House," 40.

288. Brodd, "Deacon in the Church of Sweden," 103.

289. Brodd, "Deacon in the Church of Sweden," 106.

290. Brodd, "Deacon in the Church of Sweden," 108.

291. "Deaconess Institutions in Scandinavia: Finland," 18.

292. "Deaconess Institutions in Scandinavia: Finland," 18; Pohjolainen, "Deacon in the Evangelical Church of Finland," 168.

293. Pohjolainen, "Deacon in the Evangelical Church of Finland," 145.

294. Pohjolainen, "Deacon in the Evangelical Church of Finland," 145; "Deaconess Institutions in Scandinavia: Finland," 18.

295. "Deaconess Institutions in Scandinavia: Finland," 18.

296. Pohjolainen, "Deacon in the Evangelical Church of Finland," 145.

297. "Deaconess Institutions in Scandinavia: Finland," 18.

298. Pohjolainen, "Deacon in the Evangelical Lutheran Church of Finland," 141.

299. "Methodist Diaconal Order 100 Years" and "Methodist Diaconal Order, Methodist Church of Great Britain," *Diakonia News* 78 (July 1990): 21, 28.

300. Lee, *As among the Methodists*, 104.

301. Mission Education and Cultivation Program Department, General Board of Global Ministries, The United Methodist Church, *Office of Deaconess*; Betsy K. Ewing, "The Ministry of Deaconesses in the Free Church Tradition Such as the Methodists in the United States," in Faith and Order Secretariat, *Deaconess*, 59.

302. Keller, Moede, and Moore, *Called to Serve*, 40; for the training schools, see Dougherty, "Education," pt. 2 of *My Calling to Fulfill*, 94–180.

303. Horton, *Burden of the City*; Woman's Home Missionary Society, *Early History of Deaconess Work*.

304. Dougherty, *My Calling to Fulfill*, 208.

305. Letzig, "Deaconesses," 30; *The 24th Conference*, 15.

306. Dougherty, *My Calling to Fulfill*, 17–18; Gifford, introduction to *American Deaconess*

Movement, [15]; Weiser, *Love's Response*, 67.

307. Letzig, "Deaconesses," 30.

308. Deaconess Program Office, General Board of Global Ministries, the United Methodist Church, 475 Riverside Drive, New York, New York 10115. Telephone: 1-800-654-5929.

309. Grinager, "Report to National Program Division Plenary."

310. Betty Purkey, executive secretary of the Deaconess Program Office of the General Board of Global Ministries of the United Methodist Church, telephone conversation with author, 12 June 2003.

311. Ewing, "Ministry of Deaconesses," 63.

312. "National Association of Deaconesses and Home Missionaries of the United Methodist Church," *Diakonia News* 78 (July 1990): 6.

313. Purkey, telephone conversation, 12 June 2003.

314. Paragraph 1313, *The Book of Discipline of the United Methodist Church 2000* (The United Methodist Church, 2000), 538.

315. Purkey, telephone conversation, 12 June 2003.

316. Purkey, telephone conversation, 12 June 2003.

317. Coudal, "Deaconesses Bring Healing," *Response* (February 2003): 30–32.

318. White, "From the Bishop," *Hoosier United Methodist News* (May 2000): n.p.

319. Mission Education and Cultivation Program Department, *Office of Deaconess*.

320. Purkey, telephone conversation, 12 June 2003.

321. Paragraph 1313, *The Book of Discipline of the United Methodist Church 2000* (Nashville: UMPH, 2000), 539; Becky Dodson Lauter, executive secretary of the Deaconess Program Office of the General Board of Global Ministries of the United Methodist Church, telephone conversation, 18 February 2005.

322. Purkey, telephone conversation, 12 June 2003.

323. *Deaconesses: A Movement for Laywomen Who Feel Called to Serve God Full-Time through the United Methodist Church* ([New York]: General Board of Global Ministries, the United Methodist Church, n.d.).

324. Purkey, telephone conversation, 12 June 2003.

325. "Deaconesses of the Methodist Church, Fiji," *Diakonia News* 78 (July 1990): 9.

326. Kirsch, "Deaconesses in the United States since 1918," 335–41.

327. Hackel, "Mother Maria Skobtsova," 265–66.

328. Evangelos Theodorou, "The Ministry of Deaconesses in the Greek Orthodox Church," in Faith and Order Secretariat, *Deaconess*, 30.

329. "Orthodox Reports," *Diakonia News* 78 (July 1990): 26.

330. "Orthodox Reports," 26.

331. Sister Teresa [Joan White], electronic mail, 16 August 2003.

332. "Extracts from the Church of Scotland Deaconess Board Scheme for Deaconesses (1962)," in Faith and Order Secretariat, *Deaconess*, 81.

333. "United Kingdom Liaison Group," *Diakonia News* 78 (July 1990): 20.

334. Jean Fraser, "Deaconesses in Churches of the Reformed and Presbyterian Tradition," in Faith and Order Secretariat, *Deaconess*, 52, 54–56.

335. Kirsch, "Deaconesses in the United States since 1918," 334.

336. Rasche, "Deaconess Sisters," 96–99, 108–9.

337. Kirsch, "Recent Trends in Deaconess Work," 32.

338. Schickel, telephone conversation, 16 June 2003.

339. Purkey, telephone conversation, 13 June 2003.

340. Steele, telephone conversation, 17 June 2003.

341. List, telephone conversation, 13 June 2003.

342. Purkey, telephone conversation, 13 June 2003.

343. "Koinonia-Diakonia," *Diakonia News* 78 (July 1990): 24.

344. "The Order of Diaconal Ministries, the Presbyterian Church in Canada," *Diakonia News* 78 (July 1990): 7.

345. "Australian Anglican Diaconal Association," *Diakonia News* 78 (July 1990): 30.

346. Heeney, *Women's Movement in the Church of England*, 68.

347. H. U. Weitbrecht Stanton, "The Modern Revival and Development of Deaconess Life and Work—Womanhood of the Modern Age," Appendix X, in *Ministry of Women*, 190.

348. Robinson, *Ministry of Deaconesses*, 1–15.

349. "Lambeth Conference Resolution Forty-Eight," (1920), in V. Nelle Bellamy, "Participation of Women in the Public Life of the Church from Lambeth Conference 1867–1978," *Historical Magazine of the Protestant Episcopal Church* 51, no. 1 (1982): 89.

350. Resolution 67: "The Order of *Deaconesses* is for women the one and only Order of the ministry which we can recommend our branch of the Catholic church to recognize and use" (Bellamy, "Participation of Women," 91).

351. Grierson, *Deaconess*, 51, 59.

352. Cited in Sister Joanna [Baldwin], "The Deaconess Community of St. Andrew," 227.

353. Resolution 68: "The Ordination of a Deaconess should everywhere include Prayer by the Bishop and the Laying on of Hands, the delivery of the New Testament to the candidate, and a formula giving authority to execute the office of a Deaconess in the Church of God" (Bellamy, "Participation of Women," 91).

354. Resolution 114, in Bellamy, "Participation of Women," 93.

355. Grierson, *Deaconess*, 36–37, 57, 71.

356. Robert Cantuar, foreword to Grierson, *Deaconess*, [v].

357. Sister Teresa [Joan White], electronic mail, 13 August 2003.

358. Sister Joanna [Baldwin], "Deaconess Community of St. Andrew," 227.

359. Sister Joanna [Baldwin], "Deaconess Community of St. Andrew," 228.

360. Sister Joanna [Baldwin], "Deaconess Community of St. Andrew," 229–30.

361. Heeney, "Women's Struggle for Professional Work and Status," 333.

362. Sister Teresa [Joan White], electronic mail, 13 August 2003.

363. Heeney, "Women's Struggle for Professional Work and Status," 230.

364. Sister Teresa [Joan White], electronic mail, 13 August 2003.

365. Sister Teresa [Joan White], electronic mail, 13 August 2003.; Grierson, *Deaconess*, 53–55, 71.

366. Kirsch, "Deaconesses in the United States since 1918," 344.

367. Hein and Shattuck, *Episcopalians*, 127.

368. Grierson, *Deaconess*, 99.

369. Rodgers, "Attitudes to the Ministry of Women in the Diocese of Sydney," 73–82.

370. Grierson, *Deaconess*, 102–3.

371. Grierson, *Deaconess*, 105–6.

372. Grierson, *Deaconess*, 104–5.

373. Grierson, *Deaconess*, 99–101.

374. Grierson, *Deaconess*, 104; "Anglican Deaconess Order," *Diakonia News* 78 (July 1990): 6.

375. Sister Teresa [Joan White], electronic mail, 13 August 2003.

376. Grierson, *Deaconess*, 106.

377. Grierson, *Deaconess*, 106–7.

378. Grierson, *Deaconess*, 108.

379. Grierson, *Deaconess*, 59.

380. Convocation Resolutions 1939–1941 [from a leaflet issued in 1941 by the Council for the Order of Deaconesses]: "Status and Functions of Deaconesses, Resolutions as Passed by Both Houses of Both Convocations [Canterbury and York], 1939–1941," Appendix 1, in Grierson *Deaconess*, 118–19.

381. Grierson, *Deaconess*, 68. See also, "Canons D 1; D 2; D 3; C 15,1 (Including Revision, March 1979)," Appendix 2, in Grierson *Deaconess*, 121.

382. Grierson, *Deaconess*, 95; Resolution 32, Clause (a), in Grierson, *Deaconess*, 111.

383. Hein and Shattuck, *Episcopalians*, 139–40.

384. Grierson, *Deaconess*, 99, 105–6, 108, 112, 116.

385. Rodgers, "Deaconnesses [sic] and the Diaconate," 46.

386. Sister Teresa [Joan White], electronic mail, 13 August 2003.

387. "United Kingdom Liaison Group," *Diakonia News* 78 (July 1990): 20.

388. See the letter of Ronald Hall, bishop of Hong Kong, to William Temple, archbishop of Canterbury, in Paton, "Chinese Deaconess," 265; Grierson, *Deaconess*, 108.

389. Paton, "Chinese Deaconess," 263–65.

390. See the letter of William Temple to Ronald Hall in Paton, "Chinese Deaconess," 265.

391. Paton, "Chinese Deaconess," 266–67.

392. Paton, "Chinese Deaconess," 270.

393. Sister Teresa [Joan White], electronic mail, 16 August 2003.

394. Resolution 113, in Bellamy, "Participation of Women," 92–93.

395. Resolution 115, in Bellamy, "Participation of Women," 93.

396. Paton, "Chinese Deaconess," 270–71.

397. Grierson, *Deaconess*, 113.

398. Brodd, "An Escalating Phenomenon," 12.

399. Weiser, *To Serve the Lord*, 30.

400. Williams, telephone conversation, 9 May 2005.

401. "Diakonia and the World Council of Churches: 1948–1973," *Diakonia News* 78 (July 1990): 21–22.

402. *Diakonia News* 78 (July 1990): 3–30.

403. Framo, "Retiring President's Report," 1.

404. Framo, "Retiring President's Report," 1.

405. "England in 2005," *Diakonia News* 88 (November 2001): 14; Sister Teresa [Joan White], electronic mail, 13 August 2003.

406. See, for example, the projects listed under "Diak-Aid," *Diakonia News* 78 (July 1990): 314; "Marilyn J. Clark Memorial," *Deaconess and Home Missionary News and Views* (December 1991): [2].

407. Sister Teresa [Joan White], electronic mail, 13 August 2003.

408. Sister Teresa [Joan White], electronic mail, 13 August 2003; Brice, telephone conversation, 2 July 1992.

409. Williams, telephone call, 12 August 1992.

410. "Kingston," *Diakonia News* 78 (July 1990): 4–5.

411. "Diakonia of the Americas and the Caribbean," *Diakonia News* 88 (November 2001): 30.

412. Brodd, "Escalating Phenomenon," 13.

413. "About the International Diaconate Centre," available from http://www.kirchen.de/drs/idz/en/idz/ (accessed 11 June 2003).

414. "Koinonia-Diakonia," *Diakonia News*, 24–25.

415. "Diakonia and the World Council of Churches: 1948–1973," *Diakonia News* 78 (July 1990): 22.

416. "Kaire!" *Diakonia News* 78 (July 1990): 27.

417. "Koinonia-Diakonia," 23.

418. "Diakonia and the World Council of Churches," 22.

419. Sister Teresa [Joan White], electronic mail, 13 August 2003.

420. "Diakonia and the World Council of Churches," 22.

421. "Kaire!" 27.

422. "The Diakonia Calendar, 2002," *Diakonia News* 88 (November 2001): [46].

CHAPTER EIGHT
PERMANENT DEACONS

The era from World War II to the present brought changes in the diaconate. The war and its aftermath brought a desire to reaffirm the church's mission to the poor and disadvantaged. This focused attention on deacons as a symbol of the servant ministry of the church in some denominations. Ecumenical dialogues also raised the issue of church office. Shortages of pastors in some denominations encouraged a search for alternative ways to staff parishes. All this brought to the forefront the role of the deacon.

The next two chapters will consider deacons in the world from the period after World War II to the present. First, the role of deacons in various denominations will be surveyed, then consideration will be given to ecumenical dialogue that involves deacons. The book will end with a brief survey of the diaconate over the centuries. The following denominations and their counterparts in Europe, the British Isles, and the rest of the world will receive attention: Catholic, Episcopalian, Methodist, Lutheran, Presbyterian, Reformed, Unitarian, Mennonite, Orthodox, and Seventh Day Adventist. This chapter will concentrate on Catholic, Episcopal, Methodist, German, and Scandinavian Lutheran deacons. Chapter 9 will concentrate on developments in other denominations and dialogue among churches.

In the immediate post-World War II era, Europe, North America, and Asia were occupied with economic recovery and political attempts to avoid future wars. Allied representatives met in San Francisco, California, in 1945 to organize the United Nations. In June 1947 the United States launched the Marshall Plan, the recovery program that extended economic aid to war-devastated Europe. Likewise, the Christian church initiated cooperative endeavors. Well before World War II, world denominational associations had come into being, including the World Methodist Coun

379

cil in 1881 and the Lutheran World Federation in 1923. In 1948 the World Council of Churches was organized.

The Christian church flourished in many ways in the immediate postwar era. Attendance was high in many denominations, especially in the United States, at least through the 1950s. Parochial schools prospered. Catholic men and women took up vocations as priests and nuns, but this fell off. The decade of the 1960s, with the war in Vietnam, was a turning point. Even before that war accelerated to involve the United States on a large scale, the Catholic Church had begun its Second Vatican Council (1962–1965). That council made changes in traditional Catholic practices and along with the social reform movements of the 1960s was critical in restoring deacons to renewed prominence.

CATHOLICS

In Europe a movement arose within the Catholic Church to revitalize the diaconate as a permanent ministry, not merely as a transition to the priesthood. In the years following the end of World War II, Wilhelm Schamoni and Otto Pies, two priests who had been prisoners at Dachau during the war, urged the ordination of married deacons.[1] In 1951 Hannes Kramer, a social worker, became convinced that God had called him to be a deacon, so he formed a diaconate circle (*Diakonatskreis*) at the Social Workers Seminar at Freiburg im Breisgau.[2] The German Caritas, a Catholic welfare organization much like Catholic Charities in the United States, gave support, and interest spread. Pope Pius XII was sympathetic, though, on October 5, 1957, he still believed the time was not ripe for a restoration of the diaconate.[3]

There was considerable writing about the diaconate in Europe, mainly in French and German, for example, Paul Winninger, *Vers un renouveau du diaconat*, and Josef Hornef, *Kommt der Diakon der frühen Kirche wieder?*[4] Karl Rahner also began writing on the subject. In 1959 the International Diaconate Circle was organized with headquarters in Freiburg, from which much of the work was done to promote "the restoration of the diaconate as a lifetime ministry."[5]

In the pre-preparatory phase for the Second Vatican Council, the idea of the permanent diaconate was discussed. Caritas International sponsored a petition for restoration sent to all the council fathers in July 1959.[6] Karl Rahner and Herbert Vorgrimler edited *Diaconia in Christo*, an influential book on deacons with authors from throughout the world.[7] There were 101 proposals to the council concerning the diaconate, ninety of which were in favor of permanent deacons. Several commissions, particularly the prepara-tory commission *De Sacramentis*, which included Rahner, proposed a per-manent diaconate (1961).[8] The issue became part of the council agenda.

During the second session of Vatican II, the council fathers debated the question of restoration of the diaconate from October 4–16, 1963. A major-ity of them voted for the restoration of the diaconate as a "distinct and per-manent order" on October 30, 1963.[9] There was opposition from a minority, which included Cardinal Spellman of New York, who opposed it in the press on the grounds that permanent deacons were unnecessary. Other opponents were concerned that allowing married men to become deacons would erode clerical celibacy.[10]

On November 21, 1964, the restoration of the diaconate was promul-gated as part of the Dogmatic Constitution on the Church.[11] Local author-ities, with papal approval, could decide whether it actually would be restored in their region.[12] Married men of mature age and younger celibate men could become permanent deacons. Young married men would not be allowed to become deacons.

> At a lower level of the hierarchy are deacons, upon whom hands are imposed "not unto the priesthood, but unto a ministry of service." For strengthened by sacramental grace, in communion with the bishop and his group of priests, they serve the People of God in the ministry of the liturgy, of the word, and of charity. It is the duty of the deacon, to the extent that he has been authorized by competent authority, to admin-ister baptism solemnly, to be custodian and dispenser of the Eucharist, to assist at and bless marriages in the name of the Church, to bring Viaticum to the dying, to read the sacred Scripture to the faithful, to instruct and exhort the people, to preside at the worship and prayer of the faithful, to administer sacramentals, and to officiate at funeral and burial services. Dedicated to duties of charity and administration, let deacons be mindful of the admonition of Blessed Polycarp . . . It per-tains to the competent territorial bodies of bishops, of one kind or another, to decide, with the approval of the Supreme Pontiff, whether and where it is opportune for such deacons to be appointed for the care of souls. With the consent of the Roman Pontiff, this diaconate will be able to be conferred upon men of more mature age, even upon those living in the married state. It may also be conferred upon suitable young men. For them, however, the law of celibacy must remain intact.[13]

Thus the restoration of the permanent diaconate emerged out of the Second Vatican Council.[14] On June 18, 1967, Pope Paul VI issued *Sacram Diaconatus Ordinem* (The Sacred Order of Deacons: General Norms for Restoring the Permanent Diaconate in the Latin Church), an apostolic letter by which the permanent diaconate was restored to the church. He described two kinds of permanent deacons: (1) men of 25 years of age or older who have studied three years in a college of formation, remain celibate, and engage in full-time service; and (2) men of 35 years of age or older who have studied an unspecified amount of time, who work as deacons alongside their professions, who could be married but who could not remarry if widowed. If married, they needed the consent of their wives to become deacons.[15] One reason for an older age of ordination for permanent deacons was that it allowed the marriage of the prospective deacons to be of longer duration and to have proved its stability.[16]

On April 28, 1968, the first ordination of permanent deacons took place in Cologne.[17] In April 1968 the United States Conference of Catholic Bishops voted to authorize restoration of the diaconate and petitioned the Holy See. Pope Paul VI granted permission within four months.[18] In November 1968 the U.S. Conference of Catholic Bishops created the Bishops' Committee on the Permanent Diaconate, which is headquartered in Washington, D.C.[19] Meanwhile, in December 1968, the first ordination of permanent deacons outside of Germany took place in Douala, Cameroun.[20] In the United States, the Bishops' Committee on the Permanent Diaconate received four proposals for diaconal training programs within two months of the committee's formation, and Archbishop Fulton Sheen ordained the first permanent deacon on June 1, 1969, in Rochester, New York. The second and third permanent deacons were ordained in May 1970.[21] Thirteen programs were in operation by spring 1971, training permanent deacons, especially those from the category of mature men. That same year the Bishops' Committee on the Permanent Diaconate published guidelines for the formation and ministry of deacons. On August 15, 1972, Pope Paul VI issued *Ad Pascendum*, an "Apostolic Letter Containing Norms for the Order of Diaconate." By 1984 more than three-fourths of the dioceses in the United States had diaconal programs, and the guidelines for the formation and ministry of deacons were revised.[22]

As of January 1992, there were 17,856 permanent deacons in the Catholic Church in 105 countries.[23] In 2003 there were approximately 30,000, and more are in training.[24] Permanent deacons in the United States comprise almost half of the world total. As of January 1, 1992, there were 10,120 deacons in the United States, according to Deacon Samuel M. Taub, who at the time was executive director of the Bishops' Committee on the Permanent Diaconate.[25] Of these deacons, 50 percent were concentrated in twenty-seven dioceses.[26] By 2005, there were about 15,000 permanent deacons in the United States, an increase of 24 percent in the

United States from 1998 to 2004.[27] This was an average of more than one deacon for every two parishes.[28] In reality, more than one out of three Catholic parishes in the United States reports having a deacon.[29] Permanent deacons serve in every state of the Union and in the District of Columbia. They serve in almost every diocese.[30] Only six of 196 dioceses in the United States have no deacons.

The number of permanent deacons in the United States has been gradually increasing, and the pool of deacon candidates has increased since 1975. The candidates were hovering around 2,000 per year,[31] but in 2003 the number was 2,800. In 2005 there were 3,225 candidates as compared to 3,285 students studying for the priesthood in major seminaries in the United States. Most dioceses have formation programs for the permanent diaconate. There is a national association of deacon directors with 350–400 members. The association has met annually since the early 1970s. Some dioceses cannot accept all the applicants. The deacons are growing older, but most permanent deacons are still active, 86 percent in 1999.[32] Of the remaining 14 percent, 7 percent were retired and 7 percent were inactive or on leave.[33]

Who are these permanent deacons? They are members of the one Order of Deacon in the Catholic Church. The church uses the terms "transitional" to describe a deacon who is called to the priesthood and will be ordained presbyter (priest) and "permanent" to describe a man who is ordained deacon for life and is not called to the priesthood.[34] A permanent deacon in the Catholic Church worldwide is a baptized man of at least 25 years of age (if unmarried) and 35 years of age (if married) who has gone through a period of formation and has been ordained to the diaconate. Some Catholics, like some Episcopalians, would prefer candidates for the priesthood to move directly to ordination as a priest without a phase as deacon. This would eliminate the "transitional" deacon, leaving only deacons who would see the diaconate as a lifelong vocation.[35]

Most permanent deacons are ordained for the diocese in which they serve, though transfer from one diocese to another is possible if the bishop of the new diocese agrees.[36] Most permanent deacons are married, but in addition to the diocesan permanent deacons, there are permanent deacons who are members of religious orders. In 1991 in the United States, more than twenty years after the first permanent deacons were ordained, only thirty-eight members of religious communities were deacons.[37] Worldwide in 2005, there were 511 members of religious orders who were deacons.[38] These celibate men are the minority among permanent deacons.

A deacon in the Catholic Church is not a layperson. He is a member of the clergy as are priests and bishops, and he is a deacon whether he is doing a diaconal task or not, even while working in his secular profession.[39] The bishop determines what title, if any, should be used to address a deacon. In the Western Church, one would ordinarily address him as "Deacon" followed by his name. In the Eastern Catholic Church, he is addressed as "Father Deacon."[40] On the street, the deacon usually dresses in ordinary apparel but may wear a Roman collar and clerical dress, depending on the guidelines of the local bishop.[41] Dioceses have their own training programs for permanent deacons. The deacon's training typically involves theology, liturgy, Scripture, homiletics, canon law, counseling, field experience, and spiritual and pastoral formation.[42]

In the United States, the Catholic bishops established 35 as the minimum age of ordination for both married and celibate men who become permanent deacons.[43] According to canon law, an individual bishop can make an exception and ordain a man at 34 years of age, and a permanent deacon can be ordained even younger at the discretion of the Apostolic See.[44] According to the June 2000 report of the Bishops' Committee on the Diaconate, which has statistics on age through 1999, less than 1 percent of the permanent deacons in the United States were under the age of 40, but that is not so strange when one considers that 35 is the minimum age of ordination.[45] One can begin the formation process to enter the permanent diaconate before the age of 35, however.[46] The bishops considered setting a maximum age to enter the permanent diaconate but have not done so. In 2005 only 2 percent of permanent deacons in the United States were between the ages of 35 and 44. Fifteen percent were between the ages of 45 and 54. Thirty-four percent were between the ages of 55 and 64, and 34 percent were between the ages of 65 and 74. Fifteen percent were over the age of 75. Only 1 percent of permanent deacons considered themselves retired from their work as deacons.[47]

The candidates for the permanent diaconate are younger than the deacons themselves, though markedly older than candidates for the priesthood. Only 9 percent of candidates for the permanent diaconate were under the age of 40 in 1999. Seventy-six percent were in their 40s and 50s. Fourteen percent were between the ages of 60 and 69, and 1 percent were between the ages of 70 and 79![48]

What do deacons in the Catholic Church do, and what can they not do? They baptize; witness marriages; preside at wakes and graveside services; lead Communion services and liturgies of the Word; and bless persons, houses, rosaries, water, images of Christ, images of the Virgin Mary, and images of the saints, if they are meant for private veneration.[49] Deacons cannot celebrate the Mass or pronounce absolution. During the Mass, the deacon's place is normally to the right of the celebrant (a priest or bishop), whom the deacon assists throughout the liturgy. The deacon is vested in a white alb, a full-length white vestment with long sleeves that is gathered at the waist; a stole, which is worn on his left shoulder and across his chest; and a dalmatic, a wide-sleeved overgarment. The deacon may lead the congregation in the opening penitential rite. Deacons read the Gospel and lead the prayers of intercession. They may preach, and many of them do. After the consecration of the bread and wine, a deacon holds aloft the consecrated cup, whereas the celebrant holds aloft the consecrated bread. The deacon invites the congregation to exchange the greeting of peace. At Communion, he assists in distributing the bread, or if Communion is given in both kinds, he is responsible for the cup. He dismisses the congregation at the end of the Mass after the final blessing.[50] At the Easter Vigil on Holy Saturday, at the beginning of the service, the deacon carries the paschal candle in procession and sings the Exsultet, the Easter hymn that symbolizes the return of light to the world in the risen Christ, a moving beginning to the Easter Vigil.[51]

Besides their role in the liturgy, deacons minister to the sick and imprisoned; teach; counsel; instruct catechumens; lead retreats; help couples prepare for marriage; assist those seeking annulments; and work in the inner city, in hospitals, in poverty programs, and in soup kitchens. Several permanent deacons serve as professors of theology in seminaries for priests. Some edit Catholic newspapers and do administration. In 1991 in the United States, 709 deacons were engaged primarily in ministry to youth or young adults; 234 to substance abusers; 2,976 to candidates for baptism or marriage; 255 to migrant or refugee populations; 17 to battered women and children; 6 to people with AIDS; 369 were in ecumenical ministry; 483 in social justice; 1,690 were serving in nursing homes; 1,884 in hospitals; and 39 in prison ministry.[52]

According to the 1994–1995 national study on the permanent diaconate, however, the parish-based and liturgical activities of the deacons had taken precedence over broader social action activities such as prison ministries and promoting human and civil rights. Also, there were fewer "charity-related responses" to open-ended questions on the future of the diaconate.[53] This was despite the fact that in an address to permanent deacons and their wives in Detroit, Michigan, on September 19, 1987, Pope John Paul II described deacons as having a threefold ministry of the "word, the altar, and charity."[54] Many of a deacon's service responsibilities can be done by laypeople, too, and some liturgical and pastoral responsibilities as well.[55]

The bishop may request that deacons share in the pastoral care of a parish if there is a shortage of priests. In cases where there is no resident pastor, a deacon can be given the pastoral care of a parish.[56] The Code of Canon Law states:

> If, because of a shortage of priests, the diocesan Bishop has judged that a deacon, or some other person who is not a priest, or a community of persons, should be entrusted with a share in the exercise of the pastoral care of a parish, he is to appoint some priest who, with the powers and faculties of a parish priest, will direct the pastoral care.[57]

This canon also includes laypeople, whom one author entitles "Lay Pastors," an incorrect term.[58] The correct term is "lay ecclesial minister.[59]

Before one becomes a deacon in the Catholic Church, one must have exercised the ministries of lector and of acolyte for at least six months. Lector and acolyte are what remain from the ancient minor orders that also included porter and exorcist. One is no longer ordained to be a lector or an acolyte. The offices are conferred upon the recipient who is installed in these ministries. Permanent deacons, like transitional deacons, must be installed in the ministries of lector and acolyte before ordination to the diaconate.[60] The change was effected on January 1, 1973, when Pope Paul VI's "Apostolic Letter on First Tonsure, Minor Orders and the Subdiaconate" took effect. It reads as follows:

1. First tonsure is no longer conferred. Entrance into the clerical state is joined to the diaconate.

2. Orders which up to now have been called "minor" will henceforth be known as "ministries."

3. Ministries may be committed to lay Christians. They are thus no longer to be regarded as reserved to candidates for the sacrament of orders.

4. The ministries which are to be retained in the Latin Church as a whole, but adapted to today's needs, are two, that of lector and that of acolyte. The major order of subdiaconate no longer exists in the Latin Church. There is nothing to prevent acolytes being called subdeacons in this or that region, should the conference of bishops judge this opportune. . . .

7. The offices of lector and acolyte are reserved to men.[61]

Since Pope Innocent III (1210), the ceremony of first tonsure was the entrance into the clerical state. Pope Paul VI changed that. A petitioning procedure known as "Admission to Candidacy" replaced the old ceremony of the first tonsure. A man does not become a cleric until he is ordained a deacon.[62]

Both the lector and the acolyte, though not clerics, participate in liturgical celebrations, and both prepare other people to participate in the liturgy. The lector reads from the Scriptures (but not the Gospel reading). He also prepares others from among "the faithful" to read the Scriptures in liturgical celebrations. The acolyte ministers to the priest and assists the deacon, especially in the celebration of the Mass. He attends to "the service of the altar." He also can distribute Communion in case of need. He instructs "the faithful" who assist the priest and deacon in liturgical celebrations.[63] In actual fact, laypeople in the United States carry out many of the functions of lectors, acolytes, and even deacons.[64] Although they are not officially installed as lectors or acolytes, both men and women perform these functions. In most dioceses in the United States both boys and girls participate as altar servers (formerly called altar boys). An altar server in the Catholic Church is not an acolyte, who has broader responsibilities, but sometimes altar servers are referred to colloquially as acolytes.[65]

According to canon law, permanent deacons differ from those who aspire to become priests because (1) permanent deacons are required to prepare for three years whereas candidates for the priesthood are required to complete five years of philosophical and theological studies;[66] (2) permanent deacons can have a wife if they are 35 years old or older and married when they are ordained;[67] (3) permanent deacons are older when ordained, at least 35 years of age for married deacons and, unless the bishops have set a higher age (as in the United States), 25 years of age for celibate deacons in contrast to a minimum of 23 years of age for deacons who intend to become priests.[68] In actuality, in the modern world there are permanent deacons who take more than three years to complete their preparation and candidates for the priesthood who take more than the specified five years. In addition, the requirements for formation of permanent deacons in the United States have been made more stringent and are accompanied by national norms.[69]

Permanent deacons usually support themselves through their secular professions. However, increasing numbers of permanent deacons are working full time for the church. Canon 281 of the 1983 code of canon law provides for financial support for married permanent deacons and their families if they are in full-time service for the church:

> Married deacons who dedicate themselves full-time to the ecclesiastical ministry deserve remuneration sufficient to provide for themselves

and their families. Those, however, who receive a remuneration by reason of a secular profession which they exercise or exercised, are to see to their own and to their families' needs from that income.[70]

By the mid-1980s, only about 3 percent of the permanent deacons were employed full time by the church, most in education jobs as teachers or as directors of parish education.[71] In 1991, 1,740 of the permanent deacons in the United States were receiving salaries from the church. Salaries ranged from $540 to $32,000 per year; the average was about $19,289.[72] The Center for Applied Research in the Apostolate at Georgetown University is investigating just how many men work as deacons for the church. Thirty percent have full-time jobs in the church. Salaries vary, and there are no averages available today.[73] Because many men enter the diaconate after or near completion of a career, some deacons have pensions from their years of employment in another profession.[74]

Permanent deacons differ from other clerics—that is, from priests and from deacons aspiring to become priests—because permanent deacons ordinarily are not required to abstain from public office, the practice of commerce and trade, or an active role in political parties or directing trade unions. Permanent deacons, like other clerics, are expected to get permission before volunteering for the armed services, however. They are also expected to take advantage of exemptions from duties and offices that are granted to clerics by civil law, such as jury duty.[75]

Permanent deacons are required to recite daily only that part of the Liturgy of the Hours (the Divine Office) that the Episcopal Conference determines. This liturgy includes readings from Scripture, teachings of the saints, excerpts from church councils and from the church fathers, and intercessory prayers. The guidelines for the permanent diaconate in the United States oblige deacons to pray Morning and Evening Prayer each day. Transitional deacons and priests recite the whole Office.[76]

The council fathers at Vatican II expected that the permanent diaconate would be helpful in Third World nations where there were few deacons and priests.[77] In these areas catechists already were performing many of the tasks of deacons. What did happen, however, is that the permanent diaconate became larger in the United States than in the Third World.[78] The number of permanent deacons on all continents increased from 1992 to 1998 and, except for Asia, continued to do so through 2001, the last year for which statistics were available. To be specific about the rate of growth on each continent, as of January 1992, Africa had 256 permanent deacons and, in 2001, 361 in twenty-eight countries. In 1992 Central and South

America had 2,029 permanent deacons, and in 2001 Latin America had more than doubled that number to 4,453. In 1992 Asia had 94 permanent deacons, which increased to 142 in 1998 but decreased to 128 in 2001. North America (Canada and the United States) had 10,950 permanent deacons in 1992.[79] As of 2005 there were 15,000 permanent deacons in the United States.[80]

In some urban areas, deacons have been especially useful in inner-city work and among minority communities. The archdiocese of Chicago makes use of permanent deacons liberally and has more than any other area of the country. In 1992 the archdiocese of Chicago had 708 permanent deacons, and in 1999 it had 817. The archdiocese of New York came in a distant second with 289 permanent deacons in 1992 and 340 in 1999.[81] The archdiocese of Hartford [Connecticut] was third in 1999 with 319 permanent deacons.[82]

Sixteen dioceses in the United States had a formation program conducted in Spanish in 1992.[83] Spanish-speaking deacons work among people whom the church might not otherwise reach.[84] About two dozen dioceses offered a Spanish-language track in 2000, and a few dioceses offered instruction in other languages as well.[85]

Aside from the United States, Africa, Asia, and Latin America, the rest of the world's permanent deacons are in Europe (4,429 in 1992 and 9,198 in 2001), Australia, and Oceania (99 in 1992 and 180 in 2001).[86] In 1998 there were 24,063 permanent deacons worldwide, and in 2001 there were approximately 28,238. Approximately 27,720 were diocesan clergy, and approximately 520 were in religious orders.[87] Currently there are at least 31,000 permanent deacons in the Catholic Church worldwide.[88]

The worldwide statistics for the permanent diaconate and their breakdown by country come from the International Diaconate Centre (IDC) in Germany.[89] The IDC calls itself "a *movement* for the renewal of the permanent diaconate in the Catholic Church."[90] Among other things, it collects and transmits information. The 1998 and 2001 statistics are on the web site of the Secretariat for the Diaconate of the National Conference of Catholic Bishops.[91] Deacon William T. Ditewig, executive director of the Secretariat on the Permanent Diaconate of the National Council of Catholic Bishops in the United States, sits on the board of the IDC. The IDC began in Freiburg, Germany, and is currently in Rottenburg, which is in the diocese of Rottenburg-Stuttgart.[92]

In 1981 the United States Catholic Conference in Washington, D.C., published *A National Study of the Permanent Diaconate in the United States*. The avowed purpose of this project was "to assess the extent to which the vision of the United States bishops, reflected in the initial guidelines published in 1971 (*Permanent Deacons in the United States: Guidelines on Their Formation and Ministry*)" had "been realized." The study summarized the results of data collection from four questionnaires on the permanent diaconate sent respectively to the bishops, the deacons themselves, their wives, and their supervisors. The Office of Research of the National Council of Catholic Bishops collaborated in this study.[93] A plan to update the 1981 study of the permanent diaconate came to fruition in 1994–1995.[94] There has been no such national study since that time, but one is planned, though perhaps not of so vast a scope.[95] Ditewig anticipated working closely with the Center for Applied Research in the Apostolate at Georgetown University to keep statistics and information up-to-date.[96]

The central finding of the surveys in 1981 and 1994–1995, as stated in the second report, is that "the restored order of the diaconate has been hugely successful, and . . . [i]t is growing at a steady rate."[97] Although the two surveys are less than exact replicas of each other either in questions asked or in respondents questioned, there is considerable overlap. The 1994–1995 study leaves out the bishop respondents but adds members of parish councils, thus including the laity among the respondents beyond the wives of deacons.[98]

The 1994–1995 survey includes questions posed to the deacons regarding their involvement in social issues and even inquiries as to whether or not they had read particular church documents related to social justice. Most of the deacons questioned had not read these documents.[99] According to the 1994–1995 survey, permanent deacons do not receive sufficient preparation even "to use social referral agencies like Catholic Charities and the Family Life Bureau."[100] Those who conducted the survey concluded that the permanent deacon was focused primarily on service in the parish, much like the parish priest, and that neither in the training of the permanent deacon nor in the time spent functioning as a deacon is there sufficient concentration on larger church and world issues.[101] The larger vision of what an informed diaconate could be as held by those who conducted the survey is apparently a view that was not shared by the church at large because the data from lay leaders revealed that members of parish councils "view the deacon as essentially an adjunct to the pastor and primarily accountable to him."[102]

A comparison of the 1981 and the 1994–1995 surveys of the permanent diaconate is revealing. There appears to be more continuity than change. This conclusion is upheld by statistics for other years collected by the Secretariat for the Permanent Diaconate of the National Council of Catholic

Bishops. For example, the 1981 study revealed that the overwhelming majority of permanent deacons in the United States were married (89.7 percent), a trend that has continued with the number of married deacons hovering around 90 percent.[103] The permanent diaconate in the United States attracts a far larger percentage of married men than the percentage of married men within the general Catholic population.[104]

There were divorced men among the permanent deacons also, though not as large a percentage as among the male Catholic population and a far lower percentage than in the general U.S. population. To be precise, in 1999, 2 percent of the permanent deacons were divorced, whereas 91 percent were married, 4 percent widowed, and only 3 percent never married.[105] The number of widowers among the permanent deacons had more than doubled from less than 2 percent in 1981.[106] The deacons have grown older, and so have their wives.

The preponderance of married men in the diaconate is partly because the average age of permanent deacons is older than that of Catholic men in general.[107] The current average age for permanent deacons in the United States is 61, about the same as the average age for the diocesan (parish) priest.[108] In the 1981 survey, the median age of permanent deacons was 49.[109] (For comparison, in Germany as of 2003, the average age of a deacon was 41.)[110] William Ditewig states that 91 percent of permanent deacons are married today.[111]

Most permanent deacons have children. The 1981 study revealed that more than half of the deacon respondents to the questionnaire (52.9 percent) had four or more children.[112] The 1994–1995 survey did not ask how many children the deacon had but how many remained at home. The deacons averaged less than one child still living at home, so the possibility that the deacon's role will interfere with the raising of young children is considerably diminished by the life stage at which Catholic men are becoming permanent deacons.[113]

As for racial and ethnic background, in the United States Caucasians predominate, but the percent of Caucasian permanent deacons declined from 88 percent in 1981 to 79 percent in 1991 before leveling off at 80 percent white, non-Hispanic permanent deacons in 1996 and 1999.[114] Hispanic/Latino deacons are the largest minority, and there has been a gradual increase in the percentage of the total number of permanent deacons that they constitute. In 1981 Hispanic deacons represented 8.8 percent of the total, but by 1991 that had increased to 13 percent.[115] In 1996, 14 percent of the deacons were Hispanic/Latino and in 1999, 15 percent.[116] The percent of African American permanent deacons has remained relatively constant since 1981 (2.9 percent).[117] That figure increased to 3 percent in 1991 and remained at that level in 1996 and 1999.[118] The remaining 1 percent of permanent deacons in the United States in 1992 were described by Samuel Taub, commenting on 1991 figures, as Native American, Eskimo, Asian, etc.[119] By 1996, that figure had doubled: 2 percent of the permanent deacons in both 1996 and 1999 were Asian/Pacific Islanders, Native Americans, and others. The ethnic breakdown of the permanent diaconate reflects the approximate ethnic distribution of Catholic men in the United States, 35 years of age and older, in 2000.[120] Some dioceses, however, have a disproportionate number of deacons who come from racial and ethnic minorities, in contrast to the priesthood. In some dioceses, such as in Washington, D.C., there is a much larger percentage of African American permanent deacons, for example.[121]

The deacons in formation determine the future of the permanent diaconate in the Catholic Church. In 1999–2000, 79 percent of the candidates were white and non-Hispanic, 1 percent less than the percentage of ordained permanent deacons. African Americans represented 4 percent, Asians just more than 2 percent, and Native Americans under 1 percent of the candidates. The ethnicity of diaconal candidates, as of permanent deacons themselves, reflects the ethnicity of the Catholic population as a whole.[122] In the 1981 study, 58 percent of permanent deacons lived in middle-class neighborhoods, 23.4 percent in upper-class neighborhoods, and 18.3 percent in lower-class neighborhoods.[123] This information was not available in the 1994–1995 study of the permanent diaconate.

As for education, more than half of permanent deacons in the United States have a bachelor's degree and 28 percent have postgraduate education.[124] Seven dioceses require an undergraduate degree, and four dioceses require a graduate degree.[125] Most dioceses offer ongoing formation for deacons and their wives after ordination. Most dioceses require an annual retreat.[126]

The educational level of permanent deacons has increased over time and in 2000 was slightly higher than that of Catholic men over the age of 35.[127] Looking first at college degrees, the number of permanent deacons with undergraduate degrees increased from 1981 to 1999. In 1981, 12.4 percent of permanent deacons were college graduates, but ten years later, 25 percent had received college degrees.[128] In 1999, 28 percent had a bachelor's degree.[129] By 2005, 30 percent had at least that.[130] Beyond that, some permanent deacons had postgraduate work, and the number of permanent deacons with postgraduate education has been relatively high, beginning at least in 1981 when almost one-third had some postgraduate education

(31.8 percent).[131] After that initial high percentage, the number of permanent deacons with postgraduate education leveled off at about 20 percent, though the statistics are difficult to compare because in some years only postgraduate degrees were calculated and in others postgraduate education was measured.[132] To be precise, in 1991, 19 percent had postgraduate education, and in 1999, 21 percent had postgraduate degrees.[133] By 2005, 28 percent had postgraduate education.[134]

At the other end of the educational spectrum were those deacons with a high school education or less, which currently encompasses more than one-fourth of the diaconate. Figures are hard to compare in the past because in 1981 high school graduates and those with no diploma appear to have been lumped together (22.9 percent of the permanent deacons).[135] Ten years later the number who had been to high school was 27 percent, but the statistics remained unclear as to how many permanent deacons had a high school diploma.[136] By the end of the twentieth century, it was clear that the number of high school graduates had increased. By 1999, 26 percent of the permanent deacons had completed their education with high school graduation or a GED.[137]

As for those permanent deacons with less than a high school diploma or a GED, this was a separate category in 1991 when 4 percent of the permanent deacons had completed their formal education with eight grades or less.[138] In 1999 there were no figures for those who had completed eight grades or less. They were apparently included in 4 percent of permanent deacons who had less than a high school diploma and no GED degree.[139] By 2005, 1 percent had less than a high school diploma.[140] Clearly standards at the basic educational level had improved.

Between the permanent deacons with a bachelor's degree or more and those with high school education or less were deacons who had some college experience but had not earned a bachelor's degree. In 1981 that category encompassed almost one third of the permanent deacons (32.2 percent).[141] In 1991, 23 percent had "some" college, interestingly, because the percentage had gone down, perhaps because more of them were receiving degrees and had moved into the higher educational category.[142] In 1999, 21 percent of the deacons had had some college or had earned associate degrees.[143] By 2005, 26 percent had some college.[144]

Of course, the educational level of permanent deacons is typically less than that of priests. Nevertheless, the 1994–1995 study of the permanent diaconate revealed that most members of parish councils (52.4 percent) rated the homilies of deacons as about the same quality as those of priests and containing about the same content (56.7 percent).[145] However, most supervisors and directors of deacons (50.5 percent), mainly priests, considered the deacons they direct as only "somewhat" effective in preparing and giving homilies.[146] (The introductory text to the 1994–1995 study erroneously quotes the majority of supervisors as valuing the deacons' homilies as "very" effective.) The difference between the parish council members' positive evaluation of the deacons' homilies with the less favorable evaluation of the supervisors could be interpreted to imply that the deacon is doing better at preaching to the common individual than the priests might think. It could also mean that the priests are more discerning than the laity as to the quality of the homilies. The amount of preaching by deacons varies considerably. Some seldom preach; others preach frequently.[147]

Diaconal candidates are trained for a number of years before they are ordained. While they are in training, they typically meet one or two evenings a week and one weekend each month, making it possible for them to hold down another job. Formation programs vary from two to six years, but those that are two years long require prior completion of a lay ministry formation program. As of 2000, forty-seven dioceses of the 155 in the United States reporting required wives to participate in the formation program. Eight dioceses had programs for children of candidates.[148] Child care during the training classes is provided in some dioceses. In Europe, an increasing focus on the family might be a reason for the younger average age of permanent deacons.[149]

The formation of Catholic deacons in the United States is formalized into three phases: (1) aspirancy, (2) candidacy, and (3) post-ordination education, continuing for at least three years. Formation has four dimensions: human, spiritual, academic, and pastoral. There are national norms to meet. The proposal passed the Catholic bishops in June 2003 and has received papal approval.[150] The National Council of Catholic Bishops in Washington, D.C., published *A National Directory for the Formation, Ministry, and Life for Permanent Deacons in the United States* in 2005. The Episcopal Church also has recently structured its diaconal formation more formally.

As for the occupations of the permanent deacons, in the 1981 study, 64.1 percent held managerial or professional positions compared to 57.9 percent in 1994–1995; 12 percent were in clerical or sales positions as compared to 7.5 percent in 1994–1995; and 21.9 percent were in semi-skilled or skilled positions as compared to 10.9 percent in 1994–1995. The remainder in 1994–1995 were private household workers, laborers, or service workers (1.8 percent); farmers (1.1 percent); full-time deacons (6.4 percent); or other (14 percent).[151] In the 1981 survey, most of the permanent deacons had been born Catholic (84.8 percent).[152] That question was not asked in the 1994–1995 survey. In 1981 slightly more than one-fifth of permanent deacons had been enrolled in a seminary at some point in their lives, 10.4 percent for four or more years.[153] In 1991, of 1,979 candidates, 101 had been seminarians, 5 had received minor orders, and 14 had been members of a religious institute.[154] The question about seminary attendance was not asked in the 1994–1995 survey. However, the involvement of deacons in the church before becoming a deacon was high.

The typical permanent deacon was a white, middle-aged, middle-class married man with at least one child still living at home. In the 1981 study, he rarely, if ever, wore a Roman collar. He had spent two or three years in formation for the diaconate, participated in continuing education, made an annual retreat, received no salary for his work as a deacon, and devoted an average of 13.7 hours each week to his office, most of which was devoted to his ministry of charity, followed by his ministry of the Word and his liturgical ministry. The activities that he most frequently performed on a regular basis were distribution of Communion, proclamation of the Gospel, visiting the sick and the aged, and giving homilies.[155] The 1994–1995 survey did not ask about the specific allocation of a deacon's activities.

Of the 1981 respondents, 88.4 percent said they would seek ordination again, and 94.6 percent would encourage others to do so.[156] The question on whether or not the deacon would seek ordination again was not asked on the 1994–1995 survey, but 69.2 percent would have recommended the diaconate to someone else, and 29.5 percent more would have done so with reservations.[157] This was despite the fact that some deacons complained of being thought of by the laity and parish staff as either "incomplete priests" or "more advanced laity." Deacons' wives also complained about this misconception.[158]

Of the married deacons, in 1981, 35.7 percent said their wives were "very involved" in their ministry; 46.6 percent said their wives had "some involvement"; and only 11.7 percent said their wives had "little or no involvement." A wife is not necessarily expected to be involved in her husband's ministry as a deacon in the way that a Protestant pastor's wife used to be expected to take on certain roles in the congregation.[159] More than three-fourths of the married deacons in 1981 said the diaconate had strengthened their marriage.[160] The questions were phrased differently in the 1994–1995 survey, but most permanent deacons said that being a deacon had enhanced their family life, their relationship with their wives, and their relationship with their children, while 81.9 percent said that their wives had "a very clear vision of the role of the diaconate."[161]

In 1981 more than two-thirds reported family prayer as a daily or frequent practice.[162] The questions on "spirituality" on the 1994–1995 survey were focused on the individual deacon and did not ask the question about family prayer. Most permanent deacons (55.1 percent) read the Bible at least several times a week. Most deacons (72.8 percent) set aside fifteen minutes or more to meditate each day.[163] Most deacons (52.5 percent) said the rosary at least once a week or more, and most (51.1 percent) celebrated the Sacrament of Reconciliation, that is, went to confession, at least every couple of months.[164] Most deacons (59.4 percent) had a spiritual director, of whom the majority were priests (52.3 percent).[165]

In 1981, 44.8 percent of the deacons said the rule should be changed to allow widowed deacons to remarry.[166] That question was not asked on the 1994–1995 survey, but most permanent deacons (62.4 percent) said that if they lost their wives, they would either accept celibacy or consider it an obligation based on tradition.[167] Most of these men had not yet lost their wives, however, so the question was somewhat theoretical. Some deacons have been granted a dispensation from the pope to marry after the death of a wife; others have remarried without a dispensation.[168] Interestingly, of sixteen deacons who asked for a dispensation to marry again after the death of a wife, Pope John Paul II had granted the request of all sixteen.[169] Other widowed deacons, however, were turned down over the years. In 1997 rules were changed that previously had made it difficult to obtain a dispensation to remarry, and now such requests are often approved.[170]

As for the value of ordination, of the supervisors of permanent deacons surveyed in 1981, most of whom were priests, 66.7 percent felt that the deacons would not be willing to devote as much time to the ministry if they were not ordained.[171] In 1994–1995 almost the same percentage (65.3 percent) still felt that way.[172] In 1981, 65.7 percent of the supervisors said that the ministries of deacons could not be performed as well by laypersons, but in 1994–1995, after a longer opportunity for experience with permanent deacons, a smaller percentage of supervisors (55.5 percent) said that such a statement was probably or definitely true.[173] Lay leaders were less certain about the advantage of ordination for deacons. A majority (51 percent) did not consider ordination necessary for the ministries deacons performed.[174]

As for how well permanent deacons were accepted, in 1981 a majority of the supervisors, most of whom were priests, felt that 72 percent of the bishops supported and desired deacons, and 53 percent of the priests supported and desired them, but only 40 percent of the laity understood the role of the permanent deacon.[175] In 1994–1995, though only 5.7 percent of the supervisors of permanent deacons "strongly" agreed that the diocesan bishop was supportive of the permanent diaconate, 78 percent of diocesan priests were supportive (20 percent more than in 1981), and 70 percent of parishioners understood the role of deacons (30 percent more than in 1981).[176] The bottom line is that deacons can be helpful to priests at the parish level, so much so that 79.4 percent of the supervisors felt that the permanent diaconate is needed more now than when it was first restored.[177]

To return to the bishops, as for the 196 bishops surveyed in 1981, 65 percent were positive toward the permanent diaconate, though a higher percentage of those who had permanent deacons in their dioceses were positive toward them. Of 150 bishops who had experience with deacons in their diocese, 87 percent desired and supported the diaconate. Yet only 30 percent of the bishops surveyed rated their deacons as "very effective," whereas 65 percent rated them as "somewhat effective," and 69 percent detected conflict between deacons and priests. At ordination, 59 percent of the bishops gave their deacons responsibility to preach, 89 percent to baptize, and 79 percent to witness marriages.[178] The 1994–1995 study did not publish a survey of bishops on the permanent diaconate. A survey of the attitudes of bishops toward permanent deacons would be interesting.

As for deacons' wives, there was not universal acceptance of their husbands' role as deacon, especially in 1981 when 42 out of 144 wives surveyed had a negative reaction to their husbands' ministry. Of these respondents, 66.6 percent said their husbands' ministry took time from the family, and 21.4 percent said their parishes were taking advantage of their husbands. However, 97 wives reported they were involved in their husbands' ministry.[179] The open-ended responses were revealing. Not every woman felt truly welcome during the diaconal training. One wife resented her husband taking off for three-day weekends of diaconal training, leaving her to care for young children alone after working during the week.[180]

In 1994–1995, the wives of permanent deacons seemed more content. The church apparently had acted upon the less than enthusiastic response of many of the wives of deacons in the 1981 survey and improved the situation of deacons' wives. Moreover, most deacons' wives were active in the parish or diocese as lectors, extraordinary eucharistic ministers (bringing the Lord's Supper to shut-ins), catechists, and in other roles, though 48.8 percent of the wives were employed outside the home and earned a salary.[181] The vast majority of respondents (95.5 percent) had a sense of pride that their husbands were ordained ministers, had participated in the formation program by attending almost all or all formal sessions (66.2 percent), and shared in their husbands' ministry (67.4 percent).[182] Nevertheless, 43.7 percent of deacons' wives felt they had a formal ministry distinct from that of their husbands.[183] The one negative seemed to be that wives felt that most priests did not respect their husbands for their personal talents (84.7 percent) and some priests resented working with a married deacon (66.7 percent).[184] Those opinions seem to reflect negatively on priests, however, not on the deacons.

The Catholic Church has attempted to be considerate of a deacon's children. Deacon training attempts to instill in the deacon the conviction that his family must come first.[185] The guidelines for permanent deacons in the United States read as follows:

> The sacrament of matrimony preceded the sacrament of orders and thus established a practical priority in the deacon's life. Consequently, he must be able to support his wife and family before he can be acceptable as an ordained minister. The marriage bond should be enriched by the sacrament of orders. . . . The revised Code of Canon Law requires the written consent of the wife to her husband's ordination. . . . It is strongly recommended that the wife of the candidate participate as fully as possible in the entire program of formation, including taking courses, social gatherings, and retreats. A 1981 national study demonstrated that wives who participated most fully in the formation and ministry of their husbands manifested the highest degree of satisfaction and the lowest degree of stress. . . . She should have the benefit of the same extent of psychological screening as her candidate husband. There should be opportunities during the course of formation for the wives of candidates to discuss and share their insights, apprehensions, and concerns.[186]

In addition, "insofar as possible, depending on their ages, the children should be informed and involved in the formation of their candidate father."[187]

The Catholic Church appears to be a model for other denominations in the care it has taken that the responsibilities of the deacon not compromise family life and that wives and children are involved in the ministry. Perhaps this is because historically some Catholics have questioned whether it is possible to successfully combine the life and dedication of a cleric with marriage and a family.

The results of the 1994–1995 survey of the wives of deacons are significant for a church that has expected celibacy of its clerics. The wives of deacons in this survey were largely positive about the diaconate and its effect on them, on their marriages, and on family life. Often the Catholic Church has been considerate of the wives of deacons, requiring their consent for their husbands to become deacons and encouraging their attendance at formation sessions. This is not with the intention that these women become deacons, though diaconal ministry has appeared to some Catholics to be a potential role for women.[188] The support from historical precedent is strong—stronger for female deacons than for female priests.[189] One Eastern Catholic comments that in consideration of the ancient practice of the church, "there is no reason why the female diaconate, especially for consecrated virgins, could not be reinstated in the Church."[190] However, the inclusion of only consecrated virgins in the diaconate would not satisfy those women who aspire to become deacons in the Catholic Church, at least several of whom attended diaconal formation sessions with their husbands.[191]

EPISCOPALIANS AND ANGLICANS

Anglicans acted even sooner than Catholics to affirm "permanent" deacons. In 1952, under the pressure of expanding membership, the Episcopal Church added a provision for deacons, who were called perpetual, to its canons. It retained the transitional diaconate, as did the Catholic Church, but opened the diaconate to men who retained their secular occupations "with no intention of seeking advancement to the Priesthood." These men had to be 32 years old and could assist in any parish but were not to be in charge of a congregation. By 1964 that function, too, was allowed. Educational requirements for the diaconate were less than those for the priesthood. A final clause of the canon provided for a deacon who afterward decided to become a priest, which some men did. From 1952 through 1970, the year in which women were allowed to become deacons, 517 deacons were ordained under this canon.[192] The word *perpetual* was only formally used in association with the title "deacon" from 1952–1970, and what these deacons are now called depends on the diocese. Some use the term "vocational deacon." Others use the word *deacon* with no adjective.[193]

The 1970 General Convention of the Episcopal Church enacted a new canon. Deacons were expected to function directly under their bishops. The number of male deacons who used the deacon's canon to become priests, without going to a theological seminary, increased from 1973–1978.[194]

The 1979 *Book of Common Prayer*, the liturgical book of the Episcopal Church, gave deacons a central role in the church. According to Ormonde Plater, archdeacon of Louisiana and an expert on Episcopalian deacons, there were 1,440 deacons in the Episcopal Church in 1992.[195] Eleven years later there were almost one thousand more (2,272).[196] In 1992 there were more men than women in the diaconate, 60 percent male deacons (864) and 40 percent female (576).[197] By 2003 that distribution had reversed itself, and there were more female deacons (1,260) than male (1,012).[198] Already in 1992 there were more women in formation programs than men (60 percent female [207] and 40 percent male [139]). Eleven years later there were still slightly more women (233) than men (210) in formation.[199] The number of deacons in formation in the Episcopal Church had increased from 346 in 1992 to at least 443 by 2003, but it is difficult to determine an accurate figure.[200] Ormonde Plater estimates that now there are typically 500 to 600 in formation, almost double the 1992 figure.[201] It is difficult to obtain comprehensive figures because of the tendency of many churches to keep statistics only of clergy on the payroll. Thus many deacons can be left out, especially distinctive, permanent, or vocational deacons.[202] Only twenty Episcopal dioceses out of 113 have no diaconal program.[203]

In 1986 the North American Association for the Diaconate (NAAD) replaced the older National Center for the Diaconate in Evanston, Illinois. NAAD has regular meetings; makes available materials on the diaconate from authors of several denominations; and publishes books, working papers, reports,[204] a monograph series,[205] and an award-winning bimonthly newsletter, *Diakoneo: Serving Deacons and All Servant Ministers in North America*.[206] In 2005 Susanne Watson Epting was the current executive director of NAAD and Edwin Hallenbeck was its publication director. The mission statement of NAAD describes the organization as

> an association of persons and dioceses within the Episcopal Church USA and the Anglican Church of Canada whose mission is to increase participation and involvement of all baptized persons in Christ's diaconal ministry, especially by promoting and supporting the diaconate as a full and equal order.[207]

> Though an Anglican organization, the Association and the journal aim to serve deacons, diaconal ministers, and all servant ministers in North America.[208]

The North American Association for the Diaconate holds biennial conferences.[209]

Since 1995, NAAD has formally recognized deacons, publishing the names and work of specific deacons in a booklet called "Recognition of Diaconal Ministry in the Tradition of St. Stephen." The work of these representative deacons is but a small window into the world of Episcopal deacons. If space allowed, it would be a pleasure to describe their endeavors in more detail. The sixteen honorees for 2003 included a medical doctor, a lawyer, and missionaries to Nicaragua and the Dominican Republic. The honorees were involved in refugee resettlement, advocacy for the homeless, health care for the elderly, prison and urban ministry, and in the Lutheran/Anglican Anti-Racism Project in Chicago. This is a small sampling of the variety of work that Episcopal deacons do, much of it without pay.[210]

In June 1989 NAAD decided to open its membership to deacons in the Lutheran synods. Forty-two ELCA deacons were included in the 1991 directory of the association. Most of them were in the eastern United States. Twenty of them were from the ELCA New York Synod alone.[211] In 1993 the ELCA decided to consecrate diaconal ministers, but it neither called them deacons nor ordained diaconal ministers.[212] Diaconal ministers are not included in NAAD's *Directory of Deacons*.[213] According to Edwin Hallenbeck, ELCA diaconal ministers are attempting to form their own organization.[214]

Since at least the 1980s, there has been some sentiment in the Episcopal Church to do away with the sequential ordination system, that is, to do away with the transitional deacon, much as the United Methodists have done.[215] Episcopalians call the ordination of laypersons directly to the priesthood "direct ordination."[216]

The General Convention of the Episcopal Church, which meets every three years, met in Minneapolis in July and August 2003. With the support of "vocational deacons," the Standing Commission on Ministry Development proposed direct ordination.[217] To substantiate the case for direct ordination, a short work by John St. H. Gibaut was circulated at the convention, providing historically minded Episcopalians with an historical justification for direct ordination.[218] On July 30, 2003, the Standing Commission on Ministry Development held hearings at the convention on its proposals. In a packed room, comments from the floor were generally in favor of direct ordination. Although in favor of the proposal, the Rev. Wendy Smith, one of the first women to be ordained a priest in the Episcopal Church and now a rector in San Jose, California, cautioned the commission that, if direct ordination to the priesthood were to be initiated in the Episcopal Church, it behooved the church to make provision for an internship experience for prospective priests. The transitional time as a deacon has served as an internship or mentoring period for candidates for the priesthood in the Episcopal Church.[219] The General Conventions of the Episcopal Church have two chambers, the House of Bishops and the

House of Deputies, elected from the dioceses. The proposal needed to succeed in both chambers to pass.[220] It failed in the House of Bishops but may come up in a refined form at a future General Convention of the Episcopal Church.

Even as the diaconate developed in the U.S. Episcopal Church over the last decades, there also were developments among Anglicans elsewhere in the world. Already in 1958 and 1968, meetings of the bishops of the worldwide Anglican Communion of churches at Lambeth Palace in England supported "the restored diaconate," that is, an office held until death without aspiration to the priesthood. The 1968 Lambeth Conference recommended that the diaconate be open to "(i) men and women remaining in secular occupations, (ii) full-time church workers, (iii) those selected for the priesthood," and spoke of a "new role envisaged for the diaconate."[221] It also recommended that deaconesses "be declared to be within the diaconate."[222] In 1969 the Church of England opened to women the Office of Reader, the "only officially authorized lay ministry in the Church of England" at that time.[223]

In 1974, however, the Church of England's Advisory Council for the Church's Ministry published a report on the diaconate, recommending its discontinuation in the Church of England. The council suggested that eliminating the diaconate would give a clearer picture of the diaconal responsibilities of laypeople. The General Synod of the Church of England did not accept the Advisory Council's recommendations.[224]

The 1978 Lambeth Conference urged member churches to include women as deacons. The Church of England did not ordain women as deacons, however, until February 1987. By the end of 1989, there were approximately 1,116 female deacons in the Church of England. More than five hundred of these women were full-time stipendiary deacons, that is, they were paid. Of the female deacons, 756 had been deaconesses. Given an opportunity to be ordained deacon, only approximately 150 had continued as deaconesses, of whom only about 55 were active. Deaconesses were designated as "lay" members. There would be no more new deaconesses in the Church of England, except those who were in training were allowed to complete their formation as deaconesses.[225] Besides the deaconesses who were ordained deacons, many accredited lay workers were ordained in late 1987 and 1988.[226] On November 29, 1988, the Diaconal Association of the Church of England (DACE) had its first meeting.[227] DACE includes deaconesses, accredited lay workers, and Church Army members, as well as deacons. Not all who are qualified join.[228]

If they could, many of the British female deacons would have become priests like their U.S. counterparts. Some of them had the necessary education.[229] The education for the deaconesses had been the same since the early 1970s. At that time pastoral theology/fieldwork placements were required for the first time for the men. The women had done them for years.[230]

Ordaining women as priests had been the topic of conversation for some time in the worldwide Anglican Communion, initially in a negative sense. The 1920 and 1930 Lambeth Conferences of Anglican bishops, which had been so favorable to deaconesses, came out strongly against ordination of women to the priesthood despite a movement favoring it within the Church of England that had begun prior to World War I (1914–1918) and developed parallel to the women's suffrage movement.[231] The 1948 Lambeth Conference acknowledged that in "some quarters there is a desire that the question of ordination of women to the priesthood should be reconsidered," but this conference was "of the opinion that the time has not come . . ."[232] The conference of 1958 urged that "fuller use should be made of trained and qualified women,"[233] and finally, the 1968 Lambeth Conference requested "every national and regional Church or province to give careful study to the question of the ordination of women to the priesthood."[234] Meanwhile, the 1968 conference said that qualified women should "share in the conduct of liturgical worship, to preach, to baptize, and to read the epistle and gospel at the Holy Communion, and to help in the distribution of the elements."[235] By the 1978 Lambeth Conference, "the diocese of Hong Kong, the Anglican Church of Canada, the Episcopal Church of the United States of America, and the Church of the Province of New Zealand" had ordained women priests. The Lambeth Conference acknowledged "the legal right of each Church to make its own decision."[236] It said further that "[t]he holding together of diversity within a unity of faith and worship is part of the Anglican heritage."[237]

The Church of England did not yet ordain women priests, though the issue came before the General Synod in 1992 and was passed. The first women were ordained priests in the Church of England two years later.[238] The Church of England is a state church, and the issue had to pass the British Parliament. Also, women needed to be selected for ordination in the dioceses.

In 1994, 1,280 women who had been deacons for more than a year were ordained priests in the Church of England, plus approximately 93 who had been ordained deacon in 1993, rapidly depleting the number of deacons in the Church of England. Of course, each year transitional deacons are ordained in the Church of England: 379 in 1997, 468 in 1998, 481 in 1999, 569 in 2000, and 496 in 2001, of which 214 were female.[239]

A 1997–1998 survey prepared for an Anglo-Nordic Diaconal Research Project determined there were 81 active "vocational" deacons in the Church of England, among whom 26 percent were male.[240] Most of these deacons of the Church of England work without pay or for little pay, some of them almost full time.[241] Nevertheless, there is a "steady trickle" of deacon candidates: one stipendiary and four nonstipendiary for 1995; one stipendiary and three nonstipendiary for 1996; two nonstipendiary for 1997; and two stipendiary and one nonstipendiary for 1998. Thus by November 1998, the Advisory Board of Ministry of the Church of England reported that there were 114 women and 41 men who were long-term deacons, both stipendiary and nonstipendiary.[242] This was far fewer than the 1,785 in the United States that year.[243] The overwhelming majority of ministerial opportunities for deacons carry no stipend. Deacons desire more stipendiary posts in England.[244] Many individuals work part time as deacons.[245] If deacons wear clerical dress, many wear the black dress of priests, but a few wear green clerical dress, which commonly identifies the deacon in Nordic countries.[246]

To be a deacon in the Church of England, one must be at least 23 years old, baptized and confirmed, without a criminal record, of "virtuous conversation," and "a wholesome example to the . . . flock of Christ."[247] The bishop of a diocese decides whom he wants to ordain, but those ordained as deacons must have "an ecclesiastical office to take up in which to exercise their ministry."[248]

Among those deacons ordained priests were female deacons in the Church of England who had initially been deaconesses, such as Sister Teresa (Joan White), long-time editor (1987–2002) of *Diakonia News: Newsletter of Foundation Diakonia World Federation of Diaconal Associations and Diaconal Communities*. Two other deacons of St. Andrew's House, the original deaconess community of the Church of England, were ordained priests.[249] These resident priests, who could celebrate the Eucharist, facilitated the worship cycle at St. Andrew's House, but one deaconess left the house because of these changes.[250] She had, however, moved to the Community of St. Andrew from the Church of Sweden because that church ordained women.[251] A "Working Party on Women in the Episcopate" was created in the Church of England.[252] The U.S. Episcopal Church already had female bishops.

As for other churches in the Anglican Communion, in Canada in 1989 the General Synod recommended a plan to "restore" the diaconate.

Ormonde Plater indicated that by the summer of 1992 there were 64 deacons in the Anglican Church of Canada, 36 of whom were men and 24 of whom were women. There were five deacons in training—three men and two women. The Anglican ecclesiastical province of Ontario approved guidelines to restore the diaconate in its seven dioceses on October 19, 1991. This increased the number of deacons in Canada, especially in Toronto.[253] By 2003 Canada had more than tripled its number of vocational deacons to 203, according to Dutton Morehouse, editor of *Diakoneo*, which publishes the NAAD *Directory of Deacons*. Women predominated in the diaconate in Canada. (There were 111.)[254] By 2005 there were 225 names on the database of deacons of the Anglican Church of Canada, though there is no real mechanism for the Association of Anglican Deacons in Canada to keep perfect records. About 40 percent of them were male and 60 percent female.[255] The Province of Southern Africa granted permission for a diaconate that included men and women in 1983. The Episcopal Church in Scotland approved a "restored" diaconate for men in l965 and in 1986 opened it to women. In 1990 in Australia, there were 92 female deacons.[256]

The liturgical responsibilities of deacons of the Anglican Communion are similar to those of Roman Catholic deacons.[257] They are encouraged, like Catholic deacons, to recite the Daily Office, pray, read Scripture, make retreats, and confess their sins to a confessor. Whether they can preach or not depends on the local bishop, who can license baptized persons to preach. Many deacons do preach. Most deacons are parish-based rather than diocese-based, that is, they work with a specific congregation rather than for the bishop at the diocesan level. Deacons are liturgically assigned to a parish and carry out their ministry in the world outside the parish under the direction of the bishop.[258] For example, this was true of all thirty-four deacons in Rhode Island in 1992.[259] In the United States, deacons are usually nonsalaried and work about ten hours each week. They receive no housing or housing allowance, though some dioceses provide a car allowance or funds for continuing education.[260]

As with Roman Catholics, bishops in the Anglican Communion have considerable power over the diaconal programs within their dioceses, if they choose to have any. In the United States it is possible for a bishop to discontinue a diaconal program, which was done by Bishop Geralyn Wolf in Rhode Island in 1994. The program is being reinstated.[261] Bishops determine the nature of the training where there is a program. There are two alternatives for the "restored" diaconate: (1) a special school just for deacons, usually established on a part-time basis to accommodate working students, or (2) deacon training at a school of theology or ministry. A dia conal school can serve several dioceses. In Britain there is a diaconal formation program at the Bishop Otter Centre for Theology and Ministry, Chichester, which is staffed by deacons.[262] Deacons who have trained elsewhere in Britain generally have followed the same program as candidates for the priesthood.[263]

In the United States, there is an Episcopal Church School for Deacons that rents space at the Church Divinity School of the Pacific in Berkeley, California. Such an established and organized school for deacons is somewhat the exception across the country. It presents itself as "[a] pre-eminent program for the education and formation of deacons in the Episcopal Church."[264] It is an institution of the Diocese of California and is usually known by Episcopalians as the California School for Deacons.[265] It also serves two other California dioceses (Northern California and El Camino Real), thus covering California geographically from San Luis Obispo to the Oregon border. The California School for Deacons dates from 1980.[266] Admission to the school requires a bachelor's degree, an associate's degree, or sixty semester hours of lower division college credit, and it is not free.[267] The approximate cost of the three-year program in tuition and fees in 2005 was $12,000.[268] The program is designed for students employed elsewhere and offers a Bachelor of Theological Studies. Classes meet every third weekend, and in addition to a dean and administrator, twenty adjunct faculty members teach the courses. For the fall of 2003 there were approximately thirty students, with six incoming students. All the students had a professional background.[269]

In general the educational background of candidates for the diaconate in the Episcopal Church is more varied than that of candidates for the priesthood, but candidates for the "restored" diaconate take some of the same subjects as candidates for the priesthood: theology, Scripture, history, ethics, even clinical pastoral education in a hospital. Diaconal candidates spend two to four years in training but not full time. A high school diploma or its equivalent can be sufficient in some dioceses to enter the program.[270]

The 2003 canonical proposals for the diaconate that were passed at the 74th General Convention of the Episcopal Church added "diakonia and the diaconate" to the above academic study and education for deacons, as well as human awareness and understanding, spiritual development and discipline, and practical training and experience. The proposals also provided that "wherever possible, formation shall take place in community."[271] The proposals also mandated continuing education for deacons.[272] These proposals went into effect January 1, 2004. In March 2004, the program directors of the diaconal programs for the Episcopal dioceses met in Louisiana, which they have done annually for about five years. The 2004 gathering addressed the logistics of implementing the new canons in dioceses across the country, as did the April 2005 gathering.[273]

Some bishops appoint archdeacons from among the deacons to serve as directors or coordinators of diaconal programs, "providing supervision and oversight of deacons for the bishop, as director of the diaconate program." The new canons encourage the appointment of archdeacons in the Episcopal Church to "assist with diaconal programs in the formation, deployment, supervision, and support of the Deacons or those in preparation to be Deacons."[274] There are fifty Episcopal archdeacons nationwide in the United States. The archdeacons have an annual meeting. For example, in March 2004 and April 2005 they met in conjunction with the meeting of diaconal program directors. There is a duplication of roles. With the new canons, some bishops appointed as archdeacons are program directors. Other bishops retained the title of program director.[275] As in the Roman Catholic Church, the local bishop decides if and when deacons can wear clerical dress and what their title will be. They are properly addressed simply as "Deacon."[276]

UNITED METHODISTS

Methodism separated from the Church of England in the late eighteenth century as Methodists emigrating to the New World needed to ordain pastors (elders) but lacked a bishop to do so who was recognized by the Church of England as being in the historic episcopate. However, Methodists retained the transitional diaconate of the Church of England. In the nineteenth century, Methodists fragmented further both in the British Isles and in the New World. In the late nineteenth and twentieth centuries, Methodists began to reunite, even with denominations that did not bear the title "Methodist."

In the latter half of the twentieth century, the Methodist Church grappled with the office of deacon in a series of studies of the ministry that date from at least 1960. Historically, the diaconate in the Methodist churches in North America had encompassed deacons and deaconesses. The office of deacon was transitional for those who eventually would become elders (pastors). It was a permanent office for those "local pastors" who sought ordination but lacked the requisite education to become ordained elders (pastors).[277] Deaconesses were approved by the General Conference of the Methodist-Episcopal Church in 1888.[278] The first deaconesses were consecrated in 1889.[279]

In 1968 the Methodist Church united with the Evangelical United Brethren and the Evangelical Association/United Evangelical Church to form the United Methodist Church. The study committees of the Methodist Church and the United Methodist Church wanted to change or strengthen the diaconate in some way, but their proposals in this regard tended to be rejected by the General Conference. Using the title "deacon" for anyone other than the transitional deacons who intended to become elders (pastors) was less acceptable to some people than a new title. That problem was resolved by the use of the title "diaconal minister" instead of "deacon." In 1976 the General Conference accepted "diaconal ministers" within the United Methodist Church and created the Division of Diaconal Ministry within the church's General Board of Higher Education and Ministry.[280] Thus diaconal ministers joined the existing ministries of elders (pastors), transitional deacons, deaconesses, and local pastors or local preachers (persons licensed by a district Committee on Ordained Ministry to perform the duties of a pastor locally). The July 1990 issue of *Diakonia News* (the newsletter of the World Federation of Diaconal Associations and Sisterhoods) reported that the Office of Diaconal Ministry of the United Methodist Church had applied to join. *Diakonia News* also reported that there were "some 1,883 diaconal ministers of whom 1,107 are active and 550 are students. They are Christian educators, musicians, evangelists, church and community workers, church business administrators, health workers, professors, etc."[281]

As of January 29, 1992, there were 1,415 diaconal ministers in the United Methodist Church.[282] Diaconal ministers were laypeople in full-time service to the church. In addition to the above mentioned professions, they were directors of music, nurses, social workers, lawyers, and day-care workers, but they did not include all people working in those categories for the church. For example, about half of the fourteen hundred certified Christian educators were diaconal ministers. Diaconal ministers had a professional education and had completed theological courses at a seminary. Most had additional graduate work. Eighty percent of them had master's degrees in their area of specialization. Some had a master's degree in theology, but most did not have a master's of divinity. Diaconal ministers were "representative ministers" in the United Methodist Church, voting members of the Annual Conference, like the clergy, but they were not clergy.[283] They were consecrated rather than ordained, but the consecration by a bishop was almost identical to an ordination ceremony. Diaconal ministers were paid professionals.[284]

The 1988–1992 Commission for the Study of Ministry of The United Methodist Church wanted to replace the office of diaconal ministry with an order of lay consecrated deacon. The commission did not want any additional diaconal ministers consecrated. In the commission's 1992 report, current diaconal ministers and ordained deacons could remain such or become consecrated deacons if they desired and if they met the qualifications for that order. The office of deaconess would be included as an option within the order of deacon. Corresponding with these changes, the Commission for the Study of Ministry wanted to replace the term "diaconal minister" with "deacon" and relabel boards and committees of the United Methodist Church. There was no provision in the commission's plan for a local pastor becoming a deacon or for the order of the "transitional" deacon to continue.[285]

The consecrated deacon in the commission's plan was required to have a baccalaureate degree or competency equivalence and a graduate theological degree or a graduate professional degree. All would have completed "Basic Studies of the Christian Faith," including Old and New Testament, liturgy and worship, theology, church history, United Methodist studies of doctrine and polity, and coursework on the "Church and Society." Each candidate would have had at least two years of probation before consecration. No "self-avowed practicing homosexuals" would "be accepted as candidates."[286] The United Methodist Commission for the Study of Ministry envisioned deacons in a "lifelong ministry of liturgy and service." They would "assist the elders in the celebration of the sacraments," in contrast to Methodist local pastors who "perform a full range of pastoral duties . . . including the celebration of the Sacraments." The deacon would participate with elders in leading worship and "serving the needs of the poor, the sick, and the oppressed." They would be lay members of the Annual Conference who performed a nonitinerant ministry, as did the existing diaconal ministers. Unlike the elders (pastors) who could be moved from congregation to congregation, deacons would be free to seek their own places of service but could not accept them without the bishop's approval. They could serve a local congregation, a church-related agency, or another specialized ministry.[287]

The Commission for the Study of Ministry in the United Methodist Church wanted to phase out the order of ordained deacon as it existed. Except for some local pastors, the position of ordained deacon was usually transitional to becoming an elder (pastor). The commission also wanted to phase out diaconal ministers. The commission's desire was that "no further candidates for the office of diaconal minister or the order of ordained deacon should be accepted after December 31, 1992," and "candidates for elders' orders would no longer be ordained deacons prior to their ordination as elders."[288]

These proposed changes did not meet with universal enthusiasm in the United Methodist Church in 1992.[289] The suggestions of the Commission for the Study of Ministry were amended at the May 1992 Methodist General Conference. For example, the word *ordination* replaced *consecration*. The amended version was defeated 478 for and 480 against. Some people objected to the elimination of the transitional deacon. A few preferred the retention of the present title of "diaconal minister" to that of "deacon" (however foreign that might sound to people of other denominations with the exception of the United Church of Canada, the Church Uniting of Australia, the ELCA, and some Lutheran deaconesses who use that title). Still others who voted at the 1992 General Conference felt uncomfortable with the last-minute nature of the amendments to the plan that left it less than complete with reference to issues such as pensions and health care.

Another strategy might have been to suggest the retention of the transitional diaconate for people in formation as elders, at least for a while, despite inconsistencies that this might imply. Other denominations, for example, Roman Catholic and Episcopalian, have had both a transitional and a permanent diaconate. The United Methodist bishops commended the report of the Commission on the Study of Ministry "to the Church for continued study and reflection." The bishops agreed to "make a study of the theology and shape of ministry a priority in the new quadrennium" and were to "report the results to the 1996 General Conference."[290] Thus diaconal ministry in the United Methodist Church remained as it was, and the transitional deacon continued to exist. The majority of diaconal ministers appeared to approve of being ordained rather than consecrated. The deaconesses, of whom there were about 75 active and 210 retired, opted to remain lay, though some became diaconal ministers.

Four years later, "the 1996 General Conference of the United Methodist Church reordered its ministry and adopted a new Order of Deacon" in full connection.[291] The "new" Methodist deacon is ordained and is not transitional to becoming an elder (pastor). No additional diaconal ministers have been consecrated. The diaconate is no longer a preliminary to becoming an elder.

The diaconal ministers in existence in 1996 could become ordained deacons, and many did. Others remained diaconal ministers, believing that it was important to remain lay and consecrated rather than to be ordained in a denomination that had historically been so strongly committed to lay ministry. There were 508 United Methodist diaconal ministers on March 24, 2005, of whom 295 were active. There also were 1,234 ordained deacons, of whom 1,075 were active. In addition there were 1,362 in candidacy, preparing to become deacons.[292]

There are four routes to becoming an ordained deacon in the United Methodist Church. (1) First, one can receive a master's of divinity from a school approved by the University Senate of the United Methodist Church and become a deacon instead of an elder (pastor). (2) One can obtain a master's degree from a graduate theological school recognized by the University Senate and complete basic theological studies in Hebrew Bible, the New Testament, theology, church history, mission of the church in the world, evangelism, worship/liturgy, and United Methodist Studies. (3) Candidates also can get a master's degree in an appropriate area of specialization, such as in social work or counseling. If they choose non-master of divinity options, candidates must also complete the basic theological studies mentioned above.[293] (4) Finally, candidates can seek church or secular professional certification in an appropriate area rather than a master's degree. This route is available for candidates who have reached the age of 35 and have a bachelor's degree. Along with the professional certification requirements, they must complete eight semester hours of graduate academic credit and a minimum of twenty-four semester hours in the basic graduate theological studies. This works well for those who are already on the job. For example, if a candidate currently serves in youth ministry, he or she would take five courses in youth ministry and twenty-four semester hours in theological studies, in addition to his or her practical experience. There are seven such areas of specialization: youth ministry, camp and retreat ministry, older adult ministry, spiritual formation, evangelism, music ministry, and Christian education.[294]

The coursework for all four routes to becoming a United Methodist deacon must be completed at one of the thirteen United Methodist seminaries or in a seminary approved by the church.[295] There are several criteria for a seminary to be approved; for example, the institution must offer a course in United Methodist studies and it must meet standards for gender and racial-ethnic diversity. A candidate for deacon serves in a probationary status on the job for three years before being ordained.[296]

United Methodist deacons serve in many different settings, such as community centers, agencies of the church, and hospitals.[297] They are ordained and serve as staff members in an annual Methodist conference or as teachers, social workers, health care providers, or Christian educators, for example.[298] United Methodist deacons are not itinerant, as compared to the elders (pastors) who can be moved more freely than deacons. "Elders are not hired by the local church to which they are appointed," whereas "deacons are able to initiate their own employment and will be hired by the local church or agency in which they serve."[299] However, deacons, like all ordained ministers, are under the authority of a bishop who can choose not to make an appointment.

About three quarters of the United Methodist deacons are women, but more men than women are United Methodist elders (pastors). The problem for United Methodist deacons is not finding employment or a call, it is their level of compensation, which is typically less than that of United Methodist elders, though they start at the same minimum as elders. Some deacons need to accept part-time positions because full-time positions are not available within their geographic area.[300] United Methodist deacons are allowed to accept a call with no compensation. Elders (pastors) are guaranteed appointment in the United Methodist Church. Deacons are not.[301]

Liturgically, United Methodist deacons preach occasionally but are not intended to be primarily preachers. Deacons are not to preside over Communion, though they can assist an elder.[302] A resolution asking for "sacramental authority for the deacon" was presented for the 2000 United Methodist General Conference, but it was rejected by the legislative committee, as were two proposals to return to the pre-1996 ordering of ministry that required ordination as a deacon prior to ordination as an elder and included consecration of diaconal ministers.[303]

Literature on the United Methodist deacons produced by Methodists makes much of the uniqueness of this "new" office, in contrast to many denominations that emphasize the historical roots of their diaconate: "The United Methodist Church has chosen to forge something new . . . quite different from our historic office of ordained deacon and distinct from our lay office of diaconal ministers."[304]

Eliminating the ordained deacon transitional to the ordained elder was a decisive change that overthrew centuries of tradition dating to the medieval church, but the differences between the "new" Methodist deacon and the Methodist diaconal minister seem limited. Ordination to the diaconate instead of consecration to the diaconal ministry seems to loom large in the literature, but educational levels, nonitinerancy, participation in the General Conference, and compensation do not seem to have changed appreciably. Perhaps the possibility that seemed to exist of becoming a United Methodist diaconal minister without a bachelor's degree was eliminated for new deacons. Perhaps the deacon is more closely tied to the bishop than the diaconal minister.[305] One popular book, *A Deacon's Heart:*

The New United Methodist Diaconate, claims that "deacons have a heightened sense of community with one another." This appears to be inconsistent with the comment on the same page that only 16 percent of deacons listed the Order of Deacons as a "major source of support" in a 1997–1998 survey of deacons conducted by the United Methodist General Board of Higher Education.[306] Of course, this survey was taken soon after the office of the nontransitional ordained deacon had been initiated. Community may still have been in the making.

GERMANY

The type of deacons and deaconesses that came out of the nineteenth-century Inner Mission movement exists today in Europe with some twentieth-century innovations, such as diaconal married couples.[307] In Germany, there are still brotherhoods of deacons and sisterhoods of deaconesses, but there are also deacons who function as assistants to pastors and are attached to individual congregations.[308] Under the pastor's supervision, deacons help with worship, Communion, and Baptism. They work as parish workers, youth workers, or workers in special ministries, such as among the elderly.[309] These deacons can be either male or female, just as either men or women can be pastors in Germany. They are allowed to preach if they have taken a special preaching class.[310]

A pastor in Germany receives a university education, whereas a deacon does not necessarily need one. Deacons have three years of training in a diaconal school and a year of "practical" training or an internship. This difference in educational qualifications for pastors and deacons results in a two-tiered system, but it allows young people who have not prepared for university admission in a German *Gymnasium* (a college-preparatory secondary school) to go into church work. Deacons are paid less than pastors. In times of financial problems, the deacon is more likely to lose his or her job than the pastor. Some deacons are second-career people. University-trained social workers are employed by some churches in Germany. Social workers in the church do not necessarily have any special theological education beyond a course or two in religion and would not lead worship.

SCANDINAVIA

The Scandinavian diaconate is a great success story. Today in Scandinavia the diaconate survives and thrives. The Inner Mission movement of Wichern and the deaconesses of Fliedner paved the way. Those who used to be traditional deaconesses and deacons, attached to independent motherhouses and fatherhouses, have been transformed and have emerged as permanent deacons under the auspices of the Lutheran churches of Scandinavia. They are salaried, and they are organized to uphold their own economic rights vis-à-vis their employer, the church. The motherhouses have become centers of diaconal education. Some of the women call themselves deaconesses, but the conditions of life are different from the traditional motherhouse deaconess. Deaconesses and deacons in Scandinavia today can marry and have families.

NORWAY

Today there are no more consecrations in motherhouses, but the diaconate is thriving.[311] The modern Norwegian deacons are ordained by bishops or by priests on the behalf of bishops.[312] Some of the Norwegian female deacons continue to call themselves deaconesses.

In 1987 the General Synod of the Church of Norway established a "Comprehensive Diaconal Programme."[313] In 1994 the General Synod announced that it was only natural that the largest parishes should have a deacon and a catechist. Thus the synod asked for money from the government for salaries for one of each per every 10,000 church members.[314] Five years later, the ratio of deacons to parishioners as requested by the General Synod in 1994 had not been realized. Instead, there was one deacon per 16,900 church members (as compared to one pastor per 3,300 church members). A parish with 7,000 members averaged two pastors and one deacon, if there was a deacon at all. Seventy percent of those deacons were women, and the proportion of women to men in the diaconate was increasing.[315] Parishes continue to seek money to establish posts for deacons.[316]

Currently, there is no church tax in Norway, but churches receive grants from local and state governments in addition to contributions from members.[317] The Church of Norway is understaffed, not only with regard to deacons but also with regard to pastors, especially in some rural areas such as Ålen, Norway, southeast of Trondheim, where one pastor has three churches. He holds one worship service per month in each church and takes the fourth Sunday off.[318]

There were 237 posts for parish deacons in Norway in 1999.[319] Every diocese of the eleven dioceses in the Church of Norway has deacons.[320] The deacons in these posts in 1999 were relatively new, only 10 percent had been in ministry more than ten years.[321] Parish deacons have liturgical functions and can preach. When they make home visits, they can consecrate the elements for Holy Communion.[322]

In Norway, there are also posts for deacons in hospitals and prisons.[323] In addition, in 1999, approximately twenty deacons were working in a variety of autonomous institutions and organizations that have no formal links with church leadership, many of which came out of the nineteenth-century Pietist movement in Norway.[324] For the first time in August 1998, two deacons were ordained for the Norwegian Seamen's Mission, the Norwegian Church Abroad.[325] Almost all deacons are in full-time posts, and there is a Norwegian Association of Deacons that dates from 1915 that regulates working conditions, pay, leaves, and hours.[326] Before 1915 it was a branch of the fatherhouse or deacon home.[327]

There are many more diaconal candidates each year (approximately 60) than there are posts, so only a small portion of the candidates are ordained, though it is difficult to recruit deacons in the far north of Norway. The deacon's formation requires at least five years of full-time study at the higher education level. Courses include social studies, health, or education in addition to theology. Practical training is also a feature of a deacon's formation.[328] Few deacons had been ordained for work outside the church structure in 1999, though many graduates of diaconal training had taken positions in related fields or in autonomous organizations.[329]

SWEDEN

The diaconate was transformed into a church office in Sweden in 1942.[330] A 1985 restructuring of the Church of Sweden created nine commissions that supervise work under a central board. One of these nine was "Diaconia and Social Responsibility." In 1988 it was integrated into a Commission for Congregational Work.[331] This was one year after Sweden acknowledged the diaconate as part of a threefold ministry that included priests and bishops.[332] During the 1980s, deacons became more active in the liturgy: reading the Gospel, leading the prayers of the church, administering the chalice, but deacons cannot preside at the Eucharist.[333] A new liturgical form for ordination also was implemented in 1987.[334] "The Church of Sweden *ordains* bishops, deacons and priests, *consecrates* buildings and objects, and *sends out* missionaries and people to undertake various kinds of lay ministries."[335] When deacons wear a clerical shirt, it should be green.[336]

That the Church of Sweden accepts a threefold ministry is in contrast to the Church of Norway, which has been hesitant to do so, though Norway, through its bishops, ordains deacons.[337] Norway ordains catechists as well.[338] In 1985 the Norwegian bishops responded to the positive attitude toward the threefold ministry of *Baptism, Eucharist and Ministry*, the Lima Document of the World Council of Churches, with these words:

The traditional threefold ministry with Bishop, Priest and Deacon is foreign to our way of thinking. According to the Lutheran tradition there is only one ministry expressed by the service of Word and Sacrament. . . . We are afraid that a too strong emphasis on the threefold ministry in the sense of the Lima Document, will repress the plurality of the service of the Church.[339]

In Sweden in 1987, any remaining theological differences between female and male deacons were done away with. Most deacons in Sweden are female. In a church ordinance of the Church of Sweden that was adopted by the General Synod in June 1999, there is one official title, "deacon," but women can use the title "deaconess," which is common.[340] The Church of Sweden does not ordain transitional deacons, though some deacons have undertaken further studies and been ordained to the priesthood.[341]

In Sweden as in Norway, there are more candidates for the diaconate than posts, as acknowledged by Sven-Erik Brodd, a priest in the Church of Sweden and professor of ecclesiology at the University of Uppsala.[342] Brodd stated in 1999 that the church employed 26,000 people (including 2,200 people who worked at cemeteries).[343] Of these 26,000 employees, 3,400 were priests and 900 were deacons, but there are more deacons in Sweden than 900 because the Church of Sweden has ordained deacons for work outside the church, though most bishops today do not ordain deacons unless they have a post in the church.[344] There were about ninety deacons in hospital chaplaincies.[345]

Deacons are prepared for work outside a church or a church institution because they must have professional training as a condition of being accepted by a diaconal seminary, where they spend one year.[346] The most common training is medical or nursing, teaching, social work, and lay ministry.[347] In 1999 about 240 deacons were salaried outside the church, particularly in social service.[348]

The number of deacons working in parishes was increasing. Brodd stated that 50 percent of "parishes in the Church of Sweden have created posts for deacons."[349] In 1994 the activities rated as most common to deacons in a parish setting was visiting individuals in their homes (77 percent) and individual counseling (63 percent).[350] They also can work as teachers, youth leaders, or administrators.[351] Priests are paid more than deacons, but most of the deacons working in parishes had full-time positions.[352]

FINLAND

The Church of Finland has fully integrated the diaconate into its administration. A 1943 church law stated that each parish should have at least one deaconess or deacon, which was confirmed by the Finnish Church Law of 1994.[353] They are supervised by the bishop and his staff. Prior to 1990, many deacons and deaconesses were not enthusiastic about a proposal that they be given liturgical tasks, except that they wanted to be able to administer Communion in home settings, but in practice deacons and deaconesses have taken an increasingly active role in worship.[354] Increasingly, members of the diaconate read the Gospel during the service and, on rare occasions, preach.[355]

When public health care and social welfare advanced with new laws in the 1970s and 1980s, diaconal work expanded in areas of pastoral care, recreational activities, the creation of aid networks, and the international field.[356] The Finnish diaconate cooperated with secular bodies in mental health work. With the high unemployment rates in the 1990s (as much as 14.1 percent in October 1998), however, public provision of social services and health care could no longer meet needs, and people turned to their local parishes.[357] In the 1990s, 2 to 5 percent of Finnish families needed food, so deacons organized food banks.[358]

Candidates for professional diaconal training must have good physical health and pass a psychological aptitude test.[359] Diaconal education is part of higher education in Finland. Candidates study full time for three and a half to four and a half years for a bachelor's degree in social work or health care.[360] Candidates can also specialize in education.[361]

As six diaconal institutes evolved from the motherhouses, there were more applicants for diaconal training than could be admitted.[362] There are also more graduates (about one hundred each year) of diaconal training programs than can be placed in ecclesiastical institutions.[363] Those who cannot be placed in the church take positions in the public sector in fields such as health care and social work, for which they are qualified.[364] Deacons in Finland have dual vocational training, but the practice of making them deacons or deaconesses who do not work for the church and are paid by someone else was not guaranteed to last.[365]

Deacons may work in church-related posts other than parishes. The diocesan secretaries of the eight dioceses of the Church of Finland are deacons. Deacons and deaconesses also work as missionaries. They teach in the six diaconal educational institutes that evolved from the old motherhouses and that, since August 2000, constitute the Diaconal Institute of Higher Education in Finland.[366]

In 1999 the Evangelical Lutheran Church of Finland had about 1,100 deacons, of whom 90 percent were women. Of these deacons, 75 percent used the title "deaconess," the Finnish title for female deacons with a nursing background. The remaining 25 percent, male or female, had professional training in social work.[367] Most Finns belong to the Evangelical Lutheran Church of Finland, though there is also an Orthodox Church in Finland, recognized by the state, and there are smaller Protestant denominations such as Methodists, Baptists, and Seventh Day Adventists. There also is a Catholic diocese.[368]

Parishes in the Evangelical Lutheran Church of Finland can be large—more than half of the Finnish parishes have 4,000 members. Some parishes have more than "twenty full-time people involved in parish work," including several deacons, which allows deacons to specialize.[369] Specialist posts include those who work with people with various disabilities, prisoners, refugees, the elderly, or alcoholics. Since 1994, parishes with several deacons are allowed to appoint a head deacon as a team leader.[370] Most deacons and deaconesses are employed full time, but some prefer to share their job with an otherwise unemployed deacon. Some parishes can afford only part-time deacons.[371] Full-time deacons make as much as social workers and specialist nurses in the public sector. Deacons are protected by the Church Collective Labour Agreement that regulates working conditions, salary, and pensions.[372] Deacons can train unpaid volunteers to assist them.[373]

In the 1990s in Finland, there was disagreement over whether deacons and deaconesses should be considered ordained or lay. The Church of Finland set up a Diaconate Committee in November 1994 that in a 1997 report suggested two ministries, that of Word and Sacrament and that of Word and Service.[374] These same two categories were suggested by the ELCA Task Force on the Study of Ministry in its 1991 report to the Churchwide Assembly of the ELCA as the second of three options for a configuration of ministry in the ELCA.[375] The Finnish proposal suggested that the diaconate should consist of deacons, church musicians, and youth workers (education officers), all of whom would be ordained by the bishop.[376]

Finland is an example of how adequate funding and supportive legislation in a state church setting can produce a thriving diaconate.

Denmark and Iceland

As a product of the Protestant Reformation, Denmark experienced a similar history with regard to the diaconate as did Norway, Sweden, and Finland. In the nineteenth century, the Inner Mission movement and deaconesses on the style of those founded by Fliedner spread from Germany into Denmark. Denmark had two deaconess houses in Copenhagen and deacon institutes in Aarhus and Filadelfia, Dianalund.[377] Denmark hosted the 1989 and 1990 Nordic conferences for deacons and deaconesses, a regular conference that rotates from one Scandinavian country to another.[378] The Church of Denmark refrained from signing the Porvoo Declaration in 1996 to become a member of the Porvoo communion of churches.[379] The other Lutheran churches of Scandinavia and the Anglican churches of the British Isles did sign, with the exception of the Evangelical-Lutheran Church of Latvia.[380] The signatory churches agreed to full mutual recognition and interchange of priests, deacons, and bishops.[381] The Church of Denmark has appointed a group to reconsider diaconal ministry in the church.[382]

The church in Iceland established a department of diaconia late. In 1989 it had two deaconesses and a man studying at Lovisenberg in Oslo, Sweden, to become a deacon. The bishop had established a committee to determine what would be required of those seeking ordination as deacons and deaconesses.[383] In 1993 a program for training deacons was begun in the faculty of theology at Reykjavik University. Within the next four years, eighteen deacons completed training. In 1997 there were eleven deacons in Iceland.[384]

SUMMARY

Catholics and Episcopalians recovered the permanent diaconate in the decades after World War II. Episcopalians initially called them perpetual deacons. Modern Episcopalians use the term "vocational" deacon or "deacon." Methodists had some permanent deacons among their transitional deacons simply because some were not able to move on to the position of elder (pastor). In 1976, however, the United Methodists established diaconal ministers as a lay office in the church. Less than two decades later, in 1993, the United Methodist Church voted to ordain deacons and to phase out the title "diaconal minister" except for those who were already diaconal ministers and did not choose to become deacons. In 1993 the United Methodist Church also voted out the diaconate as a transitional step to becoming an elder (pastor), a move that has been proposed in the Episcopal Church and discussed in the Catholic Church.

Through all these changes, the United Methodist Church retained their deaconesses, unlike the Church of England and the Episcopal Church, which gave deaconesses an opportunity to move into the office of deacon. In the Church of England, when women were allowed to become deacons, there were some deaconesses who elected to retain the title "deaconess," but there were to be no new deaconesses besides those already in training. Only a few United Methodist Church deaconesses chose to become deacons when the opportunity presented itself within that church. The United Methodist Church supports deaconesses, especially through its women's program.

The vocational deacon is less prominent in the worldwide Anglican Communion than in the Episcopal Church in the United States. Many of those who became deacons in the Church of England and other Anglican churches have become priests. In effect, they are transitional deacons.

The modern deacons and deaconesses of Germany and Scandinavia are career or permanent deacons, though of somewhat different origins than those in the Catholic and Episcopal Churches who emerged from the transitional diaconate. The precursors of the modern German and Scandinavian deacons and deaconesses were the motherhouses and fatherhouses of the Inner Mission movement, but the rules have changed, as in Germany, where deacons and deaconesses may marry, have children, receive pay, and even become unionized. Deacons and deaconesses are fully integrated into the Lutheran churches of Germany and Scandinavia.

The next, and final chapter, will deal with contemporary trends in diaconal work and ecumenical dialogue on the diaconate.

Notes

1. Schamoni, *Familienväter als geweihte Diakone*.
2. Taub, *Permanent Deacon in the Church Today*, 2.
3. Echlin, *Deacon in the Church*, 108–9.
4. Winninger, *Vers un renouveau du diaconat*; Hornef, *Kommt der Diakon der frühen Kirche wieder?*
5. Taub, *Permanent Deacon in the Church Today*, 3.
6. Echlin, *Deacon in the Church*, 109.
7. Rahner and Vorgrimler, *Diaconia in Christo*.
8. William T. Ditewig, executive director of the Committee on the Permanent Diaconate of the National Conference of Catholic Bishops, telephone conversation with author, 19 August 2003; Echlin, *Deacon in the Church*, 109–10.
9. Taub, *Permanent Deacon in the Church Today*, 3.
10. Consejo Episcopal Latinoamericano, *El Diaconado Permanente en America Latina*; *Diaconato no Brasil*; Echlin, *Deacon in the Church*, 110–11.
11. Taub, *Permanent Deacon in the Church Today*, 4.
12. Echlin, *Deacon in the Church*, 110–13.
13. *Lumen Gentium* (Light of All Nations), or *Dogmatic Constitution on the Church*, in Abbott, *Documents of Vatican II*, 55–56.
14. Hornef and Winninger, "Chronique de la restauration du diaconat," 205–22.

15. Paul VI, *Sacrum Diaconatus Ordinem* (The Sacred Order of Deacons: General Norms for Restoring the Permanent Diaconate in the Latin Church, June 18, 1967), trans. United States Catholic Conference (n.p: n.d.); Liptak and Sheridan, *New Code*, 96.

16. Ditewig, telephone conversation, 21 August 2003.

17. Nowell, *Ministry of Service*, 9.

18. Taub, *Permanent Deacon in the Church Today*, 4.

19. In 1992, at the time of the publication of the first edition of this book, the executive director was Deacon Samuel M. Taub. The current executive director is William T. Ditewig, Ph.D., Committee on the Permanent Diaconate, National Conference of Catholic Bishops, 3211 Fourth Street, Northeast, Washington D.C. 20017-1194. Deacon Ditewig's doctoral dissertation at Catholic University on "The Exercise of Governance by Deacons: A Theological and Canonical Study" is to be published as *The Deacon as Icon of the Kenotic Christ*. Ditewig has published *One Hundred and One Questions and Answers on Deacons* (New York: Paulist Press, 2004); and with Owen Cummings and Richard Gaillardetz, *Theology of the Diaconate: State of the Question* (New York: Paulist Press, 2005).

20. Ditewig, telephone conversation, 10 June 2003.

21. Samuel Taub, letter to author, 22 July 1992.

22. Bishops' Committee on the Permanent Diaconate, *Permanent Deacons in the United States*, 1–3; Shaw, *Permanent Deacons*, 19.

23. International Center for the Diaconate, Freiburg, Federal Republic of Germany, "The Diaconate Worldwide," 1.

24. Ditewig, telephone conversation, 10 June 2003.

25. Taub, letter to author, 22 July 1992.

26. "Annual Report on the Permanent Diaconate in the United States, 1991" (Secretariat for the Permanent Diaconate of the National Conference of Catholic Bishops, 1991, photocopy), 3. This statistical report was based on returns from the directors of 155 diocesan diaconal formation programs. Data from 1984 was used for one (arch)diocese, data from 1986 for one (arch)diocese, data from 1987 for six (arch)dioceses, data from 1988 for four (arch)dioceses, data from 1989 for three (arch)dioceses, and data from 1990 for 18 (arch)dioceses who did not respond by the deadline.

27. Ditewig, telephone conversation, 10 June 2003.

28. "Permanent Diaconate Today," 1.

29. "Permanent Diaconate Today," 2.

30. "Permanent Diaconate Today," 1.

31. "Permanent Diaconate Today," 1.

32. Ditewig, telephone conversations, 21 August 2003 and 7 March 2005.

33. "Permanent Diaconate Today," 2.

34. Taub, letter to author, 22 July 1992.

35. Ditewig, telephone conversation, 21 August 2003.

36. Ditewig, telephone conversation, 10 June 2003.

37. "Annual Report on the Permanent Diaconate, 1991," 3.

38. "Worldwide Statistics on the Diaconate as of 2001," 3 (available from http://www.usccb.org/deacon/worldstats.htm; accessed 11 June 2003).

39. Ditewig, telephone conversation, 21 August 2003.

40. Ditewig, telephone conversation, 21 August 2003.

41. Libersat, *Permanent Deacons*, 21–22; Canons 266, 284, 1024, 1031–32, in Canon Law Society, *Code of Canon Law in English Translation*, 45, 49, 183–84; Liptak and Sheridan,

New Code, 111–12; Guideline 130, in Bishops' Committee on the Permanent Diaconate, *Permanent Deacons in the United States*, 47 .

42. Shaw, *Permanent Deacons*, 31; Guidelines 78–96, in Bishops' Committee on the Permanent Diaconate, *Permanent Deacons in the United States*, 32–37.

43. Guidelines 66, 141, in Bishops' Committee on the Permanent Diaconate, *Permanent Deacons in the United States*, 29, 51.

44. Canon 1031, in Canon Law Society, *Code of Canon Law*, 184.

45. "Permanent Diaconate Today," 3.

46. Ditewig, telephone conversation, 21 August 2003.

47. Ditewig, telephone conversation, 7 March 2005.

48. "Permanent Diaconate Today," 7.

49. A deacon can preside at a wake, a cemetery service, or a service in church, but he cannot celebrate a funeral Mass (Kwatera, *Liturgical Ministry of Deacons*, 70).

50. Libersat, *Permanent Deacons*, 7–8, 11, 15–16; Canons 764, 767, 834, 861, 910, 1108, in Canon Law Society, *Code of Canon Law*, 140–41, 154, 159, 167, 196; *De Benedictionibus [May 31, 1984]* (About Blessings), cited in Liptak and Sheridan, *New Code*, 114–16; Guideline 42, *Permanent Deacons Guidelines*, 20.

51. Barnett, *The Diaconate* (1981), 76–78.

52. "Annual Report on the Permanent Diaconate, 1991," 4; Ditewig, telephone conversation, 7 March 2005.

53. *National Study of the Permanent Diaconate, 1994–1995*, 4, 7.

54. Quoted in Sherman, *Deacon in the Church*, 127.

55. Libersat, *Permanent Deacons*, 10, 17; Shaw, *Permanent Deacons*, 24; Liptak and Sheridan, *New Code*, 98.

56. "Permanent Diaconate Today," 2.

57. Canon 517, in Canon Law Society, *Code of Canon Law*, 93; Guidelines 44–45, in Bishops' Committee on the Permanent Diaconate, *Permanent Deacons in the United States*, 21.

58. Chandler, *Pastoral Associate and the Lay Pastor*, 51–64.

59. Ditewig, telephone conversation, 21 August 2003.

60. Pope Paul VI, *Ministeria Quaedam* (An apostolic letter given *motu proprio*, by which the discipline of first tonsure, minor orders and subdiaconate in the Latin Church is reformed, August 15, 1972), in Flannery, *Vatican Council II*, 427–29, 431; Canon 1035, in Canon Law Society, *Code of Canon Law*, 184.

61. Paul VI, *Ministeria Quaedam*, in Flannery, *Vatican Council II*, 429, 431.

62. Paul VI, *Ministeria Quaedam*, in Flannery, *Vatican Council II*, 429, 431; Liptak and Sheridan, *New Code*, 102, 117.

63. Paul VI, *Ministeria Quaedam*, in Flannery, *Vatican Council II*, 430–31.

64. Joseph Komonchak, "The Permanent Diaconate and the Variety of Ministries in the Church," in Bishops' Committee on the Permanent Diaconate, *Diaconal Reader*, 21.

65. Ditewig, telephone conversation, 19 August 2003.

66. Canons 236 and 1032, in Canon Law Society, *Code of Canon Law*, 39, 184.

67. Canon 1031, in Canon Law Society, *Code of Canon Law*, 184.

68. Canon 1031, in Canon Law Society, *Code of Canon Law*, 184.

69. Ditewig, telephone conversations, 21 August 2003 and 7 March 2005.

70. Canon 281, in Canon Law Society, *Code of Canon Law*, 48.

71. Shaw, *Permanent Deacons*, 30.

72. "Annual Report on the Permanent Diaconate, 1991," 3.

73. Ditewig, telephone conversations, 21 August 2003 and 7 March 2005.

74. "Permanent Diaconate Today," 7.

75. Canon 89, in Canon Law Society, *Code of Canon Law*, 49; Liptak and Sheridan, *New Code*, 113.

76. Canons 276, 285–88, in Canon Law Society, *Code of Canon Law*, 47, 49; Guideline 97, in Bishops' Committee on the Permanent Diaconate, *Permanent Deacons in the United States*, 37; Libersat, *Permanent Deacons*, 8.

77. François Lepargneur, "Ein Diakonat für Lateinamerika"; Jean Perraudin, "Der Diakonat in afrikanischer Sicht I"; Bonifaas Luykx OPraem, "Der Diakonat in afrikanischer Sicht II"; François Rajaonarivo, "Diakonat für Madagaskar"; Willem van Bekkum, "Diakone in Indonesien," in Rahner and Vorgrimler, *Diaconia in Christo*, 463–500, 509–15.

78. Komonchak, "Permanent Diaconate," in Bishops' Committee on the Permanent Diaconate, *Diaconal Reader*, 22, 27, 29.

79. International Center for the Diaconate, "Diaconate Worldwide," 1; "Worldwide Statistics on the Diaconate as of 2001," 1–2 (available from http://www.usccb.org/deacon/worldstats.htm; accessed 11 June 2003).

80. Ditewig, telephone conversation, 7 March 2005.

81. Samuel Taub, telephone conversation, 13 July 1992; "Permanent Diaconate Today," 2.

82. "Permanent Diaconate Today," 2.

83. "Annual Report on the Permanent Diaconate, 1991," 4.

84. For example, Felipe Marquez, a permanent deacon in San Jose, California. See Geaney, *Emerging Lay Ministries*, 92–96.

85. "Permanent Diaconate Today," 5.

86. International Center for the Diaconate, "Diaconate Worldwide," 2; "Worldwide Statistics on the Diaconate as of 2001," 2–3.

87. "Worldwide Statistics on the Diaconate as of 2001," 3.

88. Ditewig, telephone conversation, 7 March 2005.

89. International Center for the Diaconate, "Diaconate Worldwide," 1; "Worldwide Statistics on the Diaconate as of 2001," 1–3.

90. "About the International Diaconate Centre," available from http://www.kirchen.de/drs/idz/en/idz/; accessed 11 June 2003.

91. "U.S. Catholic Bishops—Secretariat for the Diaconate," available from http://www.usccb.org/deacon/worldstats.html; accessed 11 June 2003.

92. Ditewig, telephone conversation, 21 August 2003.

93. *National Study of the Permanent Diaconate* (1981), 1, 8–9.

94. Taub, letter, 22 July 1992; *National Study of the Permanent Diaconate, 1994–1995*.

95. Ditewig, telephone conversation, 10 June 2003.

96. Ditewig, telephone conversation, 19 August 2003.

97. *National Study on the Permanent Diaconate, 1994–1995*, 1.

98. "National Conference of Catholic Bishops Diaconate Study for Parish Council Members," in *National Study on the Permanent Diaconate, 1994–1995*, 35–58.

99. "A National Study of the Permanent Diaconate Conducted by the NCCB [National Council of Catholic Bishops] Committee for the Permanent Diaconate," in *National Study on the Permanent Diaconate, 1994–1995*, 73–81.

100. *National Study on the Permanent Diaconate, 1994–1995*, 9.

101. *National Study on the Permanent Diaconate, 1994–1995*, 4, 6–9.

102. *National Study on the Permanent Diaconate, 1994–1995*, 6.

103. *National Study on the Permanent Diaconate* (1981), 55.

104. Within the Catholic population in 2000, 52 percent of the men were married, with 3 percent of the general Catholic population widowed, 12 percent divorced or separated, and 33 percent never married ("Permanent Diaconate Today," 5).

105. "Permanent Diaconate Today," 5.

106. *National Study on the Permanent Diaconate* (1981), 55; "Permanent Diaconate Today," 5.

107. "Permanent Diaconate Today," 3, 5.

108. Ditewig, telephone conversation, 7 March 2005.

109. *National Study on the Permanent Diaconate* (1981), 13.

110. Ditewig, telephone conversation, 19 August 2003.

111. Ditewig, telephone conversation, 7 March 2005.

112. *National Study on the Permanent Diaconate* (1981), 13.

113. *National Study on the Permanent Diaconate, 1994–1995*, 2–3.

114. *National Study on the Permanent Diaconate* (1981), 13; Taub, telephone conversation, 16 July 1992; "Permanent Diaconate Today," 4.

115. *National Study on the Permanent Diaconate* (1981), 13; Taub, telephone conversation, 16 July 1992.

116. "Permanent Diaconate Today," 4.

117. *National Study on the Permanent Diaconate* (1981), 13.

118. Taub, telephone conversation, 16 July 1992; "Permanent Diaconate Today," 4.

119. Taub, telephone conversation, 16 July 1992.

120. "Permanent Diaconate Today," 4.

121. Ditewig, telephone conversation, 21 August 2003.

122. "Permanent Diaconate Today," 7.

123. *National Study on the Permanent Diaconate* (1981), 13.

124. Ditewig, telephone conversation, 7 March 2005.

125. "Permanent Diaconate Today," 6.

126. "Permanent Diaconate Today," 6.

127. "Permanent Diaconate Today," 5.

128. *National Study on the Permanent Diaconate* (1981), 13; "Annual Report on the Permanent Diaconate, 1991," 2.

129. "Permanent Diaconate Today," 5.

130. Ditewig, telephone conversation, 7 March 2005.

131. *National Study on the Permanent Diaconate* (1981), 13.

132. *National Study on the Permanent Diaconate* (1981), 13; "Annual Report on the Permanent Diaconate, 1991," 2; "Permanent Diaconate Today," 5.

133. "Annual Report on the Permanent Diaconate, 1991," 2; "Permanent Diaconate Today," 5.

134. Ditewig, telephone conversation, 7 March 2005.

135. *National Study on the Permanent Diaconate* (1981), 13.

136. "Annual Report on the Permanent Diaconate, 1991," 2.

137. "Permanent Diaconate Today," 5.

138. "Annual Report on the Permanent Diaconate, 1991," 2.

139. "Permanent Diaconate Today," 5.

140. Ditewig, telephone conversation, 7 March 2005.

141. *National Study on the Permanent Diaconate* (1981), 13.

142. "Annual Report on the Permanent Diaconate, 1991," 2.

143. "Permanent Diaconate Today," 5.

144. Ditewig, telephone conversation, 7 March 2005.

145. "National Conference of Catholic Bishops Diaconate Study for Parish Council Members," in *National Study on the Permanent Diaconate, 1994–1995*, 40.

146. "National Conference of Catholic Bishops Diaconate Study for Supervisors and Directors of Deacons," in *National Study on the Permanent Diaconate, 1994–1995*, 123.

147. *National Study on the Permanent Diaconate, 1994–1995*, 4.

148. *National Study on the Permanent Diaconate, 1994–1995*, 4–5.

149. Ditewig, telephone conversation, 7 March 2005.

150. Ditewig, telephone conversation, 7 March 2005.

151. *National Study on the Permanent Diaconate* (1981), 13–14; "A National Study of the Permanent Diaconate Conducted by the NCCB [National Council of Catholic Bishops] Committee for the Permanent Diaconate," in *National Study on the Permanent Diaconate, 1994–1995*, 91.

152. *National Study on the Permanent Diaconate* (1981), 13, 57.

153. *National Study on the Permanent Diaconate* (1981), 13–14.

154. "Annual Report on the Permanent Diaconate, 1991," 2.

155. *National Study on the Permanent Diaconate* (1981), 14, 16–17.

156. *National Study on the Permanent Diaconate* (1981), 16.

157. *National Study on the Permanent Diaconate, 1994–1995*, 89.

158. *National Study on the Permanent Diaconate, 1994–1995*, 7–8.

159. Ditewig, telephone conversation, 21 August 2003.

160. *National Study on the Permanent Diaconate* (1981), 16.

161. *National Study on the Permanent Diaconate*, 64, 87.

162. *National Study on the Permanent Diaconate* (1981), 16.

163. *National Study on the Permanent Diaconate, 1994–1995*, 83.

164. *National Study on the Permanent Diaconate, 1994–1995*, 84.

165. *National Study on the Permanent Diaconate, 1994–1995*, 85.

166. *National Study on the Permanent Diaconate* (1981), 23.

167. *National Study on the Permanent Diaconate, 1994–1995*, 83.

168. "Permanent Diaconate Today," 4.

169. "Annual Report on the Permanent Diaconate, 1991," 4.

170. Ditewig, telephone conversation, 21 August 2003.

171. *National Study on the Permanent Diaconate* (1981), 37.

172. *National Study on the Permanent Diaconate, 1994–1995*, 122.

173. *National Study on the Permanent Diaconate* (1981), 37; *National Study on the Permanent Diaconate, 1994–1995*, 116.

174. *National Study on the Permanent Diaconate, 1994–1995*, 5.

175. *National Study on the Permanent Diaconate* (1981), 37.

176. *National Study on the Permanent Diaconate, 1994–1995*, 116.

177. *National Study on the Permanent Diaconate, 1994–1995*, 117.

178. *National Study on the Permanent Diaconate* (1981), 41.

179. *National Study on the Permanent Diaconate* (1981), 33–34.

180. Virginia Ratigan, "The View from Inside," in Ratigan and Swidler, *New Phoebe*, 23.

181. "A Study of Wives of Permanent Deacons by the National Conference of Catholic Bishops," in *National Study on the Permanent Diaconate, 1994–1995*, 96–97.

182. "A Study of Wives of Permanent Deacons by the National Conference of Catholic Bishops," in *National Study on the Permanent Diaconate, 1994–1995*, 98, 102, 104.

183. "A Study of Wives of Permanent Deacons by the National Conference of Catholic Bishops," in *National Study on the Permanent Diaconate, 1994–1995*, 98.

184. "A Study of Wives of Permanent Deacons by the National Conference of Catholic Bishops," in *National Study on the Permanent Diaconate, 1994–1995*, 103–4.

185. Miles, "Pastor-Deacon Relationship," 13; Sherman, *Deacon in the Church*, 107.

186. Guidelines 107–8, in Bishops' Committee on the Permanent Diaconate, *Permanent Deacons in the United States*, 40–41.

187. Guideline 112, in Bishops' Committee on the Permanent Diaconate, *Permanent Deacons in the United States*, 42.

188. Hünermann, "Conclusions Regarding the Female Diaconate," 325–33; Aubert, *Des femmes diacres*; Irene Löffler-Mayer, "Pushing for the Diaconate for Women," in Ratigan and Swidler, *New Phoebe*, 60–62; Hünermann, Biesinger, Heimbach-Steins, and Jensen, *Diakonat*.

189. Zagano, *Holy Saturday*, 87–110.

190. Slesinski, *Essays in Diakonia*, 123.

191. *National Study on the Permanent Diaconate* (1981), 91.

192. Plater, *Many Servants*, 55.

193. Ormonde Plater, telephone conversation with author, 22 July 2003.

194. Plater, *Many Servants*, 62, 67–68.

195. Ormonde Plater, telephone conversation with author, 10 June 1992.

196. Edwin Hallenbeck, executive director of the National Association for the Diaconate, electronic mail to author, 26 July 2003.

197. Plater, telephone conversation, 10 June 1992.

198. Hallenbeck, electronic mail, 26 July 2003.

199. Plater, telephone conversation, 10 June 1992; Hallenbeck, electronic mail, 26 July 2003.

200. Plater, telephone conversation, 10 June 1992; Hallenbeck, electronic mail, 26 July 2003.

201. Plater, telephone conversation, 5 March 2005.

202. Sister Teresa [Joan White], electronic mail, 16 August 2003.

203. Hallenbeck, electronic mail, 5 March 2005.

204. Ormonde Plater, ed., *Deacons in the Episcopal Church: Guidelines on Their Selection, Training, and Ministry* (Providence: NAAD, 1991); Edwin F. Hallenbeck, ed., *A Working Paper of Guidelines for Deacon Programs*, 2d ed. (Providence: NAAD, 2002); Edwin F. Hallenbeck, ed., *A Working Paper Report of NAAD Visioning Workshop: New Orleans, LA, March 18–20, 2002* (Providence: NAAD, 2002); Edwin F. Hallenbeck, *A Working Paper of Trial Liturgy for Celebration of Deacon's Ministry* (Providence: NAAD, 1996).

205. Richard F. Grein, *Baptism and the Ministry of Deacons*, North American Association for the Diaconate Monograph Series 1 (Providence: NAAD, 1987); James Lassen-Willems, *Are Deacons the Enemy?* North American Association for the Diaconate Monograph Series 2 (Providence: NAAD, 1989); Richard F. Grein, *The Renewal of the Diaconate and the Ministry of the Laos*, North American Association for the Diaconate Monograph Series 3 (Providence: NAAD, 1991); The 1986 Sindicators Meeting, *Laos and the Diaconate*, North American Association for the Diaconate Monograph Series 4 (Providence: NAAD, 1991); Ormonde Plater, comp., *Calendar of Deacon Saints*, North

American Association for the Diaconate Monograph Series 5 (Providence: NAAD, 1998); Jeffrey D. Lee, *A View from the Omnivorous Presbyterate*, North American Association for the Diaconate Monograph Series 6 (Providence: NAAD, 1991); Ormonde Plater, *Historic Documents on the Diaconate*, North American Association for the Diaconate Monograph Series 7 (Providence: NAAD, 1991); Ormonde Plater, *Music and Deacons*, North American Association for the Diaconate Monograph Series 8 (Providence: NAAD, 1995); W. Keith McCoy, *The Deacon as Para-Cleric*, North American Association for the Diaconate Monograph Series 9 (Providence: NAAD, 1998); Louise Williams, *Growing in Ministry: Formation for Diaconal Service*, North American Association for the Diaconate Monograph Series 10 (Providence: NAAD, 1999); Susanne K. Watson, *Formation of Ministering Christians*, North American Association for the Diaconate Monograph Series 11 (Providence: NAAD, 1999); Thomas Ferguson, *Lifting Up the Servants of God: The Deacon, Servant Ministry, and the Future of the Church*, North American Association for the Diaconate Monograph Series 12 (Providence: NAAD, 2001); Richard L. Jeske, *The Role of the Diaconate and the Unity of the Church*, North American Association for the Diaconate Monograph Series 13 (Providence: NAAD, 2002).

206. "Diakoneo Wins Polly Bond Award," *Diakoneo* 24, no. 2 (Eastertide 2002): 17.

207. "The Mission of NAAD," *Diakoneo* 24, no. 4 (Pentecost 2002): 1.

208. Title and Masthead, *Diakoneo* 24, no. 4 (Pentecost 2002): 1–2.

209. "Calendar of Diaconate Events," *Diakoneo* 24, no. 2 (Eastertide 2002): 20.

210. North American Association for the Diaconate, "Recognition of Diaconal Ministry in the Tradition of St. Stephen" (Toronto: n.p., June 14, 2003), 1–4.

211. *Directory of Deacons, Episcopal Church, Anglican Church of Canada, Evangelical Lutheran Church in America* (Providence: NAAD, 1991), 33–34.

212. Busse, "Development of Diaconal Ministry in the ELCA," 102.

213. "Directory of Deacons, Episcopal Church and Anglican Church of Canada, Summer 2003," *Diakoneo* 25, no. 3 (Summer 2003); Dutton Morehouse, deacon and editor of *Diakoneo*, interview by author at the 74th General Convention of the Episcopal Church, Minneapolis, Minnesota, 30 July 2003.

214. Edwin Hallenbeck, telephone conversation with author, 8 June 2003.

215. Ormonde Plater, interview by author at the 74th General Convention of the Episcopal Church, Minneapolis, Minnesota, 30 July 2003.

216. For a discussion of this issue, see Hallenbeck, *Orders of Ministry*.

217. *Reports to the 74th General Convention*, 219.

218. John St. H. Gibaut, *Sequential or Direct Ordination? A Return to the Sources*, Joint Liturgical Studies 55 (Cambridge, England: Grove Books, 2003).

219. Standing Commission on Ministry Development of the Episcopal Church, hearing, Hyatt-Regency, Minneapolis, Minnesota, 30 July 2003.

220. Plater, telephone conversation, 22 July 2003.

221. Resolution 32, in Bellamy, "Participation of Women," 94–95.

222. Resolution 32, in Bellamy, "Participation of Women," 95.

223. Martineau, *Office and Work of a Reader*, viii and 29.

224. Christine Hall, "The Deacon in the Church of England," in Borgegård and Hall, *Ministry of the Deacon*, 1:197–99.

225. Plater, *Many Servants*, 89–94, 97–98.

226. Sister Teresa [Joan White], electronic mail to author, 13 August 2003.

227. Plater, *Many Servants*, 89–94, 97–98.

228. Sister Teresa [Joan White], electronic mail, 13 August 2003.

229. Treasure, *Walking on Glass*, 32–47.

230. Sister Teresa [Joan White], electronic mail, 13 August 2003.

231. Heeney, *Women's Movement in the Church of England*, 68, 126–29.

232. Resolution 115, in Bellamy, "Participation of Women," 93.

233. Resolution 93, in Bellamy, "Participation of Women," 93.

234. Resolution 35, in Bellamy, "Participation of Women," 95.

235. Resolution 38, in Bellamy, "Participation of Women," 95.

236. Resolutions 21, 1. and 3.(a), in Bellamy, "Participation of Women," 96.

237. Resolution 7. (a), in Bellamy, "Participation of Women," 97.

238. Sister Teresa [Joan White], electronic mail to author, 4 June 2003.

239. Sister Teresa [Joan White], electronic mail, 13 August 2003.

240. Hall, "Deacon in the Church of England," in Borgegård and Hall, *Ministry of the Deacon*, 1:201–2.

241. Hall, "Deacon in the Church of England," 1:182, 195, 209.

242. "Candidates," *Distinctive Diaconate* 44 (April 1999): 3.

243. "The Anglican Communion: Statistics," *Distinctive Diaconate* 44 (April 1999): 4.

244. Hall, "Deacon in the Church of England," 201, 237.

245. Hall, "Deacon in the Church of England," 208.

246. Hall, "Deacon in the Church of England," 214; Sister Teresa [Joan White], electronic mail, 13 August 2003.

247. Hall, "Deacon in the Church of England," 226–27.

248. Hall, "Deacon in the Church of England," 226–27.

249. Sister Teresa [Joan White], electronic mail to author, 10 June 2003.

250. Sister Teresa [Joan White], London interview with author, April 2000.

251. Sister Teresa [Joan White], electronic mail, 13 August 2003.

252. "Church of England. July General Synod. The Working Party on Women in the Episcopate," *Distinctive Diaconate News* 51 (September 2002): 1; "Church of England. July General Synod. The Women in the Episcopate—Working Party," *Distinctive News of Women in Ministry* 18 (September 2002): 1.

253. "Ontario Approves Deacons for Seven Dioceses," *Diakoneo* 13, no. 5 (November 1991): 1.

254. Edwin F. Hallenbeck and Dutton Morehouse, interview by author at the 74th General Convention of the Episcopal Church, Minneapolis, Minnesota, 30 July 2003.

255. Deacon Jacquie Boutheon, Diocese of Toronto, electronic mail, 25 March 2005.

256. Plater, *Many Servants*, 99–100.

257. Plater, *Deacon in the Liturgy*.

258. Plater, *Deacons in the Episcopal Church*, 3–4.

259. Edwin Hallenbeck, letter to author, 2 July 1992.

260. Plater, *Many Servants*, 127, 137, 141, 159, 162–63, 166.

261. Hallenbeck and Plater, interview by author, 30 July 2003; Wayne Runner, rector of Trinity Church, Cranston, Rhode Island, telephone conversation with author, 5 March 2005.

262. Fanuelsen, "Education and Formation of Deacons," in Borgegård, Fanuelsen, and Hall, *Ministry of the Deacon*, 2:187.

263. Hall, "Deacon in the Church of England," 1:222.

264. The Episcopal School for Deacons, 2451 Ridge Road #114, Berkeley, CA 94709, Telephone 510/848-1723 (available from http://www.sfd.edu/; accessed 9 June 2003).

265. Plater, interview, 30 July 2003.

266. Ferguson, *School for Deacons*, [7].

267. *Catalogue 2003–2004: The Episcopal School for Deacons*, 4. Available from http://www.spd.edu/. Accessed 5 March 2005.

268. *Catalogue 2003–2004: The Episcopal School for Deacons*, 7.

269. Christopher Butler, administrator, The Episcopal School for Deacons, telephone conversation with author, 10 June 2003.

270. Plater, interview, 30 July 2003.

271. *Reports to the 74th General Convention*, 223. For a discussion of these canons, see "New Diaconate Canons," *Diakoneo* 25 (Epiphany 2003): 1, 6–7. In the same issue of *Diakoneo*, see "Commentary," 2, 4, 7.

272. *Reports to the 74th General Convention*, 224.

273. Plater, telephone conversations with author, 20 August 2003 and 5 March 2005.

274. Sec. 3, Canon 7: "Of the Life and Work of Deacons," Proposed Title Three Revisions of the *Constitution and Canons of the Episcopal Church*, in *Reports to the 74th General Convention*, 224.

275. Plater, telephone conversations, 20 August 2003 and 5 March 2005.

276. Plater, *Many Servants*, 129, 144, 160; Ormonde Plater, letter to author, 26 June 1992.

277. "Local pastors may be ordained deacons and retain that ordination for life. These persons function as elders and not primarily as deacons despite being named such" (Commission for the Study of Ministry, "Report of the Commission for the Study of Ministry, 1992," 2).

278. Lee, *As among the Methodists*, 37.

279. Meyer, *Deaconesses*, 205.

280. Yocom, "Ministry Studies," 1–4.

281. "Office of Diaconal Ministry, United Methodist Church," *Diakonia News* 78 (July 1990): 7; Keller, Moede, and Moore, *Called to Serve*, 1–2, 62.

282. Jack Roulier, Division of Diaconal Ministry of the Board of Higher Education and Ministry of the United Methodist Church, telephone conversation with author, 19 August 1992.

283. Annual Conferences in the United Methodist Church in the United States are regional conferences that meet each year. The General Conference is a national conference that meets every fourth year, the same year as the U.S. presidential election.

284. Plater, *Many Servants*, 105.

285. Commission for the Study of Ministry, "Report of the Commission for the Study of Ministry, 1992," 24–25, 34–35, 41–43.

286. Commission for the Study of Ministry, "Report of the Commission for the Study of Ministry, 1992," 22–23, 41–42.

287. Commission for the Study of Ministry, "Report of the Commission for the Study of Ministry, 1992," 21–23, 31, 41–42.

288. Commission for the Study of Ministry, "Report of the Commission for the Study of Ministry, 1992," 34–35.

289. Betty Letzig, executive director, Deaconess Program Office, General Board of Global Ministries, the United Methodist Church, letter to author, 11 June 1992; *The United Methodist Church Deaconess and Home Missionary News and Views* (December 1991): [1].

290. *Daily Christian Advocate: The General Conference of the United Methodist Church* 4, no. 12 (16 May 1992): 8.

291. Ben L. Hartley and Paul E. Van Buren, *The Deacon: Ministry through Words of Faith and*

Acts of Love (Nashville: Section of Deacons and Diaconal Ministries, General Board of Higher Education and Ministry, the United Methodist Church, 2000), 1.

292. Deacon Sharon Rubey, director of Candidacy and Conference Relations of the Division of Ordained Ministry, General Board of Higher Education and Ministry of the United Methodist Church, telephone conversation with the author, 24 March 2005.

293. Division of Ordained Ministry, General Board of Higher Education, United Methodist Church, "Theological Education for the Ordained Deacon" (n.p.: n.d.); Rubey, telephone conversation, 24 March 2005.

294. Rubey, telephone conversation, 24 March 2005.

295. The United Methodist seminaries are: Boston University School of Theology; Candler School of Theology, Emory University, Atlanta, Georgia; Claremont School of Theology, Claremont, California; Duke University, the Divinity School, Durham, North Carolina; Drew University, the Theological School, Madison, New Jersey; Gammon Theological Seminary, Atlanta, Georgia; Garrett-Evangelical Theological Seminary, Evanston, Illinois; The Iliff School of Theology, Denver, Colorado; Methodist Theological School of Ohio, Delaware, Ohio; Perkins School of Theology, Dallas, Texas; Saint Paul School of Theology, Kansas City, Missouri; United Theological Seminary, Dayton, Ohio; and Wesley Theological Seminary, Washington, D.C.

296. Deacon Joaquín García, assistant general secretary for the Section of Deacon and Diaconal Ministry, Division of Ordained Ministry, General Board of Higher Education and Ministry of the United Methodist Church, telephone conversation with the author, 17 June 2003.

297. García, telephone conversation, 17 June 2003.

298. Section of Deacons and Diaconal Ministries, *Ordained Deacon*.

299. Harnish, *Orders of Ministry*, 121.

300. Rubey, telephone conversation, 24 March 2005.

301. Rubey, telephone conversation, 24 March 2005.

302. Hartley and Van Buren, *Deacon*, 66.

303. "Appendix 6: The Impact of General Conference 2000," in Harnish, *Orders of Ministry*, 187.

304. Harnish, *Orders of Ministry*, 109.

305. Harnish, *Orders of Ministry*, 121–22.

306. Crain and Seymour, *Deacon's Heart*, 88.

307. Thiersch, *Über das Diakonenamt*.

308. Rünger, *Die Männliche Diakonie*, 71–236; Schafer, "Hundert Jahre Adelberdt-Diakonissen-Mutterhaus Kraschnitz zu Stendal," 225–33.

309. Philippi, "Le ministère du diacre," 286.

310. *Theologische Realenzyklopädie*, s.v. "Diakonie."

311. Meland, "Deacon in the Church of Norway," 66.

312. Meland, "Deacon in the Church of Norway," 89.

313. Meland, "Deacon in the Church of Norway," 79.

314. Meland, "Deacon in the Church of Norway," 69.

315. Meland, "Deacon in the Church of Norway," 70.

316. Meland, "Deacon in the Church of Norway," 91.

317. Meland, "Deacon in the Church of Norway," 78.

318. Personal interview with the pastor at Ålen, Norway, 28 June 2003.

319. Meland, "Deacon in the Church of Norway," 70.

320. Meland, "Deacon in the Church of Norway," 71.

321. Meland, "Deacon in the Church of Norway," 72.

322. Meland, "Deacon in the Church of Norway," 76.

323. Meland, "Deacon in the Church of Norway," 74.

324. Meland, "Deacon in the Church of Norway," 65, 73.

325. Meland, "Deacon in the Church of Norway," 72, 73.

326. Meland, "Deacon in the Church of Norway," 78.

327. Meland, "Deacon in the Church of Norway," 89.

328. Meland, "Deacon in the Church of Norway," 82.

329. Meland, "Deacon in the Church of Norway," 80.

330. Brodd, "Deacon in the Church of Sweden," 108.

331. Bachmann and Bachmann, *Lutheran Churches in the World*, 413–14.

332. Brodd, "Deacon in the Church of Sweden," 108.

333. Brodd, "Deacon in the Church of Sweden," 114, 136.

334. "Nordic Conference, 1989" and "Nordic Conference, 1990," *Diakonia News* 78 (July 1990): 19–20.

335. Brodd, "Deacon in the Church of Sweden," 121.

336. Brodd, "Deacon in the Church of Sweden," 131.

337. Brodd, "Deacon in the Church of Sweden," 108–9; Meland, "Deacon in the Church of Norway," 85.

338. Meland, "Deacon in the Church of Norway," 84.

339. The Bishops' Conference, autumn 1985, Case 15/85 as translated from the Norwegian, in Meland, "Deacon in the Church of Norway," 85–86.

340. Brodd, "Deacon in the Church of Sweden," 109.

341. Brodd, "Deacon in the Church of Sweden," 107.

342. Borgegård and Hall, *Ministry of the Deacon*, 1:4.

343. Brodd, "Deacon in the Church of Sweden," 109–10.

344. Brodd, "Deacon in the Church of Sweden," 109, 111.

345. Brodd, "Deacon in the Church of Sweden," 111.

346. Brodd, "Deacon in the Church of Sweden," 109, 117, 120.

347. Brodd, "Deacon in the Church of Sweden," 120.

348. Brodd, "Deacon in the Church of Sweden," 109.

349. Brodd, "Deacon in the Church of Sweden," 109.

350. Brodd, "Deacon in the Church of Sweden," 113.

351. Brodd, "Deacon in the Church of Sweden," 110, 113.

352. Brodd, "Deacon in the Church of Sweden," 115, 130.

353. Pohjolainen, "Deacon in the Evangelical Lutheran Church of Finland," 146, 163.

354. Pohjolainen, "Deacon in the Evangelical Lutheran Church of Finland," 171; "Nordic Conference, 1989: Finland," *Diakonia News* 78 (July 1990): 19.

355. Pohjolainen, "Deacon in the Evangelical Lutheran Church of Finland," 175.

356. Pohjolainen, "Deacon in the Evangelical Lutheran Church of Finland," 147.

357. Pohjolainen, "Deacon in the Evangelical Lutheran Church of Finland," 149–50.

358. Pohjolainen, "Deacon in the Evangelical Lutheran Church of Finland," 161.

359. Pohjolainen, "Deacon in the Evangelical Lutheran Church of Finland," 164.

360. Pohjolainen, "Deacon in the Evangelical Lutheran Church of Finland," 165.

361. Pohjolainen, "Deacon in the Evangelical Lutheran Church of Finland," 166.

362. Pohjolainen, "Deacon in the Evangelical Lutheran Church of Finland," 155; "Nordic Conference, 1989: Finland," 19.

363. Pohjolainen, "Deacon in the Evangelical Lutheran Church of Finland," 151.

364. Pohjolainen, "Deacon in the Evangelical Lutheran Church of Finland," 151–52.

365. Pohjolainen, "Deacon in the Evangelical Lutheran Church of Finland," 151, 156.

366. Pohjolainen, "Deacon in the Evangelical Lutheran Church of Finland," 155.

367. Pohjolainen, "Deacon in the Evangelical Lutheran Church of Finland," 141.

368. Pohjolainen, "Deacon in the Evangelical Lutheran Church of Finland," 148.

369. Pohjolainen, "Deacon in the Evangelical Lutheran Church of Finland," 149.

370. Pohjolainen, "Deacon in the Evangelical Lutheran Church of Finland," 155.

371. Pohjolainen, "Deacon in the Evangelical Lutheran Church of Finland," 162.

372. Pohjolainen, "Deacon in the Evangelical Lutheran Church of Finland," 163.

373. Pohjolainen, "Deacon in the Evangelical Lutheran Church of Finland," 162.

374. Pohjolainen, "Deacon in the Evangelical Lutheran Church of Finland," 170.

375. ELCA, *The Study of Ministry Study Edition, Report to the 1991 Churchwide Assembly* (Chicago: Evangelical Lutheran Church in America, 1991), 30–41.

376. Pohjolainen, "Deacon in the Evangelical Lutheran Church of Finland," 170–71.

377. Bachmann and Bachmann, *Lutheran Churches in the World*, 397.

378. "Nordic Conference, 1989" and "Nordic Conference, 1990," 19–20.

379. Borgegård and Hall, *Ministry of the Deacon*, 1:5.

380. Borgegård and Hall, *Ministry of the Deacon*, 1:5, 26.

381. Borgegård and Hall, *Ministry of the Deacon*, 1:26.

382. Borgegård and Hall, *Ministry of the Deacon*, 1:45.

383. "Nordic Conference, 1989," 19.

384. Fanuelsen, "Education and Formation of Deacons," 181.

CHAPTER NINE
CONTEMPORARY TRENDS

As in the medieval church, Catholics, Episcopalians, and Methodists could be said to be within the historic tradition of those churches that retained the deacon as transitional to becoming a priest or pastor, though the United Methodists eliminated the transitional diaconate in 1993. Lutherans and other denominations departed from that tradition at the time of the Reformation. However, Lutherans changed the diaconate less aggressively than Reformed and Presbyterian churches, perhaps because of the strong stand John Calvin made on that issue and because of the influence of the Genevan Reformation on Reformed denominations. In the sixteenth century, within the church orders for some of the new Lutheran churches, Johannes Bugenhagen provided for deacons who cared for the poor. By the seventeenth century at least, some Lutheran churches had deacons as assistant pastors or as men in a position of training to become a pastor. At least by the eighteenth and nineteenth centuries in some Lutheran churches, these deacons were parallel to lay deacons selected at the congregational level. Historically, Lutherans have had a wide understanding of the word *deacon*, and Lutheran diaconal work has often included individuals other than those who have that title.

LUTHERANS

The male diaconate on the Inner Mission model had a strong history in some European Lutheran churches but barely established a foothold in the United States. Lutheran congregations in North America elected lay deacons within congregations to serve on church councils or on boards of deacons. Before the LCMS was founded, the Ministerium of Pennsylvania used the word *deacon* to refer to assistant pastors, as Germans did in the eighteenth century. In 1815 the Ministerium of Pennsylvania began to ordain men as deacons who were in transition to becoming pastors, but as synods spun off from Pennsylvania, they objected to what they called a "graded ministry." As the Lutheran synods in the United States came into being, they adopted divergent models. Some Lutheran synods had no deacons at all. Some had lay deacons elected by the congregations. Some of these deacons functioned more like elders in the Presbyterian tradition.

The Lutheran Church—Missouri Synod

The LCMS organized in 1847 with pastors and teachers in key roles. Many congregations had elementary schools.[1] By 1864 an institution for training teachers had been established. The teacher was omnicompetent, a jack-of-all-trades in congregational activities who was somewhere between the pastor and the parishioner, a general assistant who could be called upon for many types of service. Being a teacher and highly respected, he might function as a deacon, depending upon his personality, interests, and abilities. A teacher, or another lay leader, properly supervised, can perform some of the functions of the office of public ministry when a congregation is without a pastor.[2] In the words of C. F. W. Walther: "The offices of school-teachers, who have to teach God's Word in their schools, almoners, sextons, leaders of singing at public worship, and others, are all to be regarded as ecclesiastical and sacred, for they take over a part of the one ministry of the Word and support the pastoral office."[3]

A congregation, if it had a staff of male and female teachers and laypeople taking on responsibilities that a deacon could fulfill, might not feel a need for specially trained deaconesses, but in the twentieth century, congregations and pastors in the LCMS began to see what trained deaconesses could do by way of assisting a pastor outside the chancel.

After World War II, the need for trained lay workers became more obvious because of a growing shortage of professional workers within the LCMS. The synod began to involve laypeople more. Lutheran Bible institutes sprang up at the circuit level to train these people. These Bible institutes were geared toward part-time attendance. In the 1950s and 1960s, there was a movement within the Synod to support full-time lay education institutions.[4] On June 23, 1959, the LCMS brought into existence a two-year lay training school. The synod's Board for Higher Education asked the Board of Control of Concordia College, Milwaukee, to run a Lutheran Lay Training Institute in conjunction with the college. The board acquired the property of the Milwaukee Bible College. September 19, 1961, twenty-three students entered the new training institute.[5]

When Concordia Milwaukee became a four-year college in 1978, the Lay Training Institute could offer four years of study with a major in theology. By 1986 about half of the students were electing the four-year program. The Lay Training Institute developed workshops, a continuing-education program for Concordia College, and in-service training for teachers, pastors, and laypeople. In 1983 the Lutheran Lay Training Institute moved with the college to Mequon, Wisconsin, a suburb of Milwaukee.[6] It is referred to in the Lutheran Annual as Concordia University at Mequon, Wisconsin (formerly Milwaukee), whereas literature from the institution speaks of Concordia University Wisconsin.[7] The Lay Training Institute is now the Lay Ministry Department within the larger university.

Over the years, the Lutheran Lay Training Institute attracted mature adults who were willing to work in a team ministry when they finished training. The average age of the students in 1986, the twenty-fifth anniversary of the institute, was 35 years old. There were 450 men and women who had been certified as lay ministers in the LCMS at that time.[8] In 2003 the average age of the students was 48.[9] By 2005, 672 men and women had been certified as lay ministers.[10]

The graduates of the Lay Training Institute work especially in adult education, evangelism, visitation, youth, missions, rural ministry, and administration. Occasionally, synodical District presidents authorize certified lay ministers to "serve in a capacity similar to that of a pastor" under the supervision of a pastor in the area, for example, if a congregation is vacant or too small to call a pastor.[11] District presidents have licensed graduates to serve as deacons "in unusual and emergency situations" in a Word and Sacrament ministry.[12] In some situations, congregations that could not or chose not to afford a pastor went beyond synodical regulations and asked male lay ministers to serve as pastors.[13]

Within the last dozen years, the Lutheran Lay Ministry Program has expanded its accessibility and scope considerably. There are two paths toward lay ministry certification presently available. Each is geared to different age levels and personal circumstances. The first option is the on-campus program at Concordia University Wisconsin, which leads toward a baccalaureate degree and can lead to a career path.[14] Students in this Lay Ministry Specialist Degree Program are looking forward to being rostered with the LCMS as certified lay ministers and receiving calls upon graduation. They have the option of taking a double major in theology and lay ministry or of taking a minor in lay ministry and a related major in music, social work, or parish nursing. The lay ministry major and minor is different from the pre-seminary program that requires foreign languages. Students who graduate and are certified as lay ministers are typically called to larger congregations that have multiple staff positions. They are expected to take leadership roles in their areas of expertise. With that in mind, there are five areas of specialization within the lay ministry major from which students pick two in which to take at least three courses: (a) evangelism, (b) mission, (c) parish teaching, (d) social ministry and visitation, and (e) youth ministry. The students who graduate from this program have been successful in getting calls.[15] Salaries are projected to be comparable to that of Lutheran schoolteachers.[16] In addition, the university offers a track designed specifically for women who intend to enter the deaconess program at one of the two LCMS seminaries.

The second option within the Lutheran Lay Ministry Program is a nondegree off-campus program for students who cannot be present physically for the course work. The Theological Education by Extension Program is centered at Concordia University Wisconsin and staffed by Director Albert L. García and Assistant Director John W. Oberdeck.[17] The teaching takes place at fourteen off-campus sites, chiefly churches across the country whose pastors serve as mentors and teachers in the program along with professors from Concordia University Wisconsin.[18] A high school diploma is required in this lay ministry program for admission to the first eleven courses that lead to the Church Worker Certificate (Level I). The courses are taken over a period of three years, usually one Saturday a month, allowing people to continue with a professional life. Students who have a bachelor's or an associate's degree, as most do, can go on to Lay Ministry Certification (Level II), which requires six more courses over another year and a half. The courses are biblical, theological, and practical in focus. The student groups are small, maybe five to ten people. The classes are not free (currently $160 per credit hour or $480 for most courses), so completing the full program of seventeen courses would cost at least $7,520.[19] Full-time beginning salaries for lay ministers average $35,000 to $38,000 with benefits. Some who obtain certification through the extension program do not seek to be rostered or called elsewhere because they want to contribute in their home congregation. Some receive little or no pay. In some districts, female lay ministers deliver children's messages.[20]

In 1965 the LCMS Board for Missions to the Deaf urged that training for full-time lay workers with the deaf be instituted at the Lay Training Institute in Wisconsin. In 1968 Doris Myhre joined the staff to interpret spoken language through sign for deaf students and to teach signing to hearing students.[21] Institute graduates have served in deaf ministry, but it is no longer an integral part of the Lay Ministry Program at Concordia University Wisconsin. Nevertheless, in the LCMS there are sixty-three deaf congregations and about 200 interpreted ministries.[22] The LCMS now has a Deaf Institute of Theology in St. Louis and a summer Church Interpreters Training Institute at Concordia Theological Seminary in Fort Wayne, Indiana. Concordia University, Irvine, California, offers signing as one of its language alternatives.[23]

The Deaf Institute of Theology in St. Louis is a distance-learning program for hearing-impaired students, of whom there were fifty-three enrolled in 2003. It is a nondegree program that makes use of videos, the Internet, and personal mentoring, but students can work toward ordination as pastors or certification in one of the auxiliary offices of the LCMS. For example, one participant in the Deaf Institute of Theology hopes to become a deaconess and worked in the Iowa West District of the LCMS. Another worked in a congregation in Rochester, New York, as a deacon and is seeking ordination. A deacon from Indianapolis, Indiana, is also on the ordination track. The twenty students seeking certification in the Deaf Institute of Theology in May 2005 are training to be Christian caregivers in their congregations, trained for home visits to the sick and elderly, and experienced as Bible study leaders and lay leaders of their congregations.[24] Students must have the approval of a pastor to be admitted to the Deaf Institute of Theology, and if one wants to become an ordained minister, one must be a high school graduate. The Deaf Institute of Theology has not been in existence long. The first class began in February 1999. The institute was founded by Dr. Rodney Rynerson, now retired, and it is currently administered by the Rev. Roger Altenberger.[25]

The Church Interpreters Training Institute is a two- to four-week summer program at Concordia Theological Seminary in Fort Wayne, Indiana, at which students learn to interpret worship services for deaf attendees. Participants in this program who already know how to sign learn religious signing. There were forty-five students enrolled in the 2003 program.[26]

Lay ministers such as those educated at Concordia University Wisconsin and deaconesses are among the auxiliary offices of the LCMS along with teachers, directors of Christian education, directors of Christian outreach, parish assistants, and directors of parish music. The church can establish new auxiliary offices as the need arises. Those who serve in auxiliary offices perform certain functions of the office of public ministry under the supervision of the holders of the pastoral office.[27] In the words of C. F. W. Walther, elaborating on Thesis 8 of his theses on ministry:

The highest office is the ministry of the Word, with which also all other offices are conferred at the same time. Every other public office in the church is part of the same, an auxiliary office which supports the ministry, whether it be that of the elders who do not "labor in preaching and teaching" (1 Tim. 5:17), or that of the rulers (Rom. 12:8 [Luther's translation]) or that of the deacons (the office of service in the narrower sense), or whatever other offices the church may entrust to particular persons for special administration.[28]

Walther, then, makes room for deacons in the auxiliary offices. He equates it with "the office of service."

Like pastors, those who serve in auxiliary offices are called by the church. They "have made a commitment to dedicate their lives to that service unless or until God directs them to other callings."[29] The 1981 report of the LCMS Commission on Theology and Church Relations suggested that lay ministers should be called "lay workers" or "lay assistants."[30] The suggestion has been made that male lay ministers be called "deacons" and female graduates "deaconesses."

The status of both male and female auxiliary workers has been affected by twentieth-century events. During World War II, Lutheran teachers were given deferred draft status as "ministers of the Gospel." In 1965 a request was made to the Synod to ordain male teachers, a request that has been repeated but rejected by the LCMS.[31] The Wisconsin Synod does ordain teachers.[32] In 1969 the possibility of a "male black diaconate" came up at the synodical convention.[33]

The need to clarify the status of auxiliary workers such as lay ministers prompted the LCMS to study and define the biblical view of the pastoral ministry and to clarify the status, role, and function of all other professional church workers and their relation to one another and to the church. A published study that continues to the present dates from 1981: *The Ministry: Offices, Procedures, and Nomenclature, A Report of the Commission on Theology and Church Relations of the Lutheran Church—Missouri Synod*. Samuel Nafzger, executive director of the LCMS Commission on Theology and Church Relations, stated that there is one divinely instituted office of pastor and that the church has freedom to create and abolish auxiliary offices. *Women in the Church: Scriptural Principles and Ecclesial Practice* is one of several reports and studies on a subject that engenders lively discussion within the LCMS. Some in the LCMS fear that women will be ordained as pastors, though the general constituency had seemed more interested in offering women greater opportunity to serve in auxiliary ways.[34] Nafzger clarifies: "Women in the LCMS may hold any professional church work office except that of Pastor (Minister of Religion Ordained)."[35]

A study that has raised questions in certain quarters is *Veiled and Silenced: The Cultural Shape of Sexist Theology* by Alvin J. Schmidt.[36] The book argues that though women had been "veiled and silenced" in classical and Old Testament times, the attitude of Jesus was different. He spoke and worked with women. This view continued briefly through apostolic times and was then reversed until the cultural changes of the present.

In 1983 a Resolution to Classify Ministers of Religion in The Lutheran Church—Missouri Synod (5–09A) recognized three categories. Pastors were in Category I. They were ordained and installed. Teachers and directors of Christian education were in Category II. They were commissioned and installed. Lay ministers and others were in Category III: Certified Professional Church Workers, Lay. They were consecrated and installed. Eligibility involved "graduation from and certification by a synodical college following a synodically prescribed course of study (or equivalent prescribed by the Synod colloquy)." Lay professional church workers were

> consecrated and/or installed upon acceptance of first call issued through the synodical Board of Assignments for one of the following positions: (1) Deaconess, (2) Lay Minister, (3) Parish Worker, (4) Parish Assistant, (5) Director of Evangelism, and (6) persons who otherwise qualify for Minister of Religion classification but who choose not to apply. Classification [was] open to men and women. [One] must be a member of a congregation which is a member of the Synod. . . .[37]

In 1989 the LCMS in convention passed a resolution "To Declare Deaconesses Eligible for Synodical Membership."[38] That same convention instituted the designation "deacon" for a layman temporarily in Word and Sacrament ministry "in emergencies and special circumstances."[39] By 1992 Lutheran female teachers in church schools and also deaconesses were recognized as "Commissioned Ministers of Education."

In 1992 the LCMS in convention passed a resolution "To Study Classification of Professional Church Workers,"

> WHEREAS, There is a concern expressed about the classification of a variety of professional church workers; and

> WHEREAS, The church needs an orderly process of determining such classifications; and

> WHEREAS, The doctrine of the ministry and all areas of service in the church are vital; therefore be it

RESOLVED, That the synodical President appoint a special committee to study roster classification in light of the doctrine of ministry and bring appropriate recommendations to the next synodical convention.[40]

President A. L. Barry appointed members of a Nomenclature Study Committee that met regularly from May 1994 to December 1997 and heard speakers that included Samuel Nafzger, executive director of the LCMS Commission on Theology and Church Relations, and Kristin Wassilak, deaconess director of the Concordia Deaconess Program, both contributors of information to this book.[41] The committee sent a survey to all rostered church workers that included five possible changes in nomenclature. It elicited a response from 3,276 people, the largest response of any survey conducted in the Synod's history.[42] One suggestion was that male nonordained ministers of religion be entitled "deacon" and that female nonordained ministers of religion be entitled "deaconess." LCMS teachers would also then have been entitled "deacon" or "deaconess." Teachers and others objected, and the proposal did not succeed.[43] The overwhelming majority favored a change in nomenclature, and the committee's proposal that there should be two categories, not three. The committee proposed (1) pastors and (2) teachers and associates in ministry. This would eliminate the designation "Minister of Religion," which the committee said was terminology of the U.S. Internal Revenue Service and used also for non-Christian religions. Included in the second category would be teachers, directors of Christian education, deaconesses, certified lay ministers, and directors of Christian outreach.[44] In 1998 the LCMS in convention declined to accept the proposals of the Nomenclature Study Committee on the grounds of insufficient evidence for a need for change and suggested that there was confusion over the understanding of the doctrine of ministry.[45] In February 2003 the LCMS Commission on Theology and Church Relations issued a report titled *The Theology and Practice of "The Divine Call."* This report, however, addressed most specifically the ordained ministry.[46]

In 2001 the LCMS in convention voted to recognize two rosters (rather than three) in the church: (1) Ministers of Religion—Ordained and (2) Ministers of Religion—Commissioned. The latter roster includes teachers, directors of Christian education, deaconesses, directors of Christian outreach, lay ministers, parish assistants, and directors of parish music. LCMS Ministers of Religion—Commissioned are classified as ministers by the U.S. Internal Revenue Service and have the tax exemptions of ordained pastors.[47]

The convention voted to phase out the category of Consecrated Lay Worker as of the 2004 convention because it "creates a potential liability for the Synod by placing non-rostered workers under the supervision of District Presidents."[48] Letters were sent to the individuals presently within that category informing them that the entire category will be removed from the LCMS *Handbook* and from the *Lutheran Annual*. It encourages these individuals to qualify for rostered status with the Synod and to apply.[49] This might mean additional education for many.

The rosters fluctuate in size, of course, but the largest rosters of the LCMS are those of Ordained Minister and Commissioned Teacher. On August 15, 2003, there were 6,025 active ordained ministers and 7,042 active commissioned teachers. This does not include candidates and emeriti, however. The ordained ministers emeriti were many—2,480. The commissioned teachers emeriti were 1,084. In addition to the teachers rostered as teachers alone, there were 242 active teachers who were also rostered as directors of Christian education. This was in addition to the 407 active directors of Christian education rostered for this office alone. There were 92 active commissioned deaconesses, 25 candidates, and 15 emeriti. Looking only at the active rosters: There were 95 commissioned lay ministers; 32 active commissioned directors of Christian outreach; and seven active commissioned parish assistants.[50] The rosters for the directors of parish music were in the process of being formed.[51] By May 2005 the nomenclature had changed and the categories had been simplified. Some categories had been combined, and some were no longer being tracked. Certified Lay Teacher and Lay Teacher classifications had been changed to Non-rostered Teacher. Lay Pastor had been changed to Non-rostered Pastor. In general, most active and emeriti categories had increased in size somewhat.

CLASS NAME	ACTIVE COUNT	CANDIDATE COUNT	EMERITUS COUNT
Ordained Minister	6107	239	2544
Non-rostered Teacher	10108	0	0
Non-rostered Pastor	7	0	0
Commissioned-Teacher	7099	501	1252
Commissioned-Teacher/DCE/DCO	3	0	0
Commissioned-Teacher/DCE	220	24	33
Commissioned-Parish Assistant	9	3	2
Commissioned-Lay Minister	96	7	42
Commissioned-DPM	10	0	0
Commissioned-Deaconess	99	20	19
Commissioned-DCO	30	3	2
Commissioned-DCE/DPM	1	0	0
Commissioned-DCE	445	58	4
TOTAL:	24234	855	3898[52]

There are also people still serving in congregations in these and other roles who are not rostered by the LCMS. These were Certified Church Workers, Lay (Consecrated Lay): lay minister, lay teacher, parish music, parish worker, and Lutheran social worker. Some of these people were eligible for membership in the Synod but opted not to join, namely, the lay ministers and lay teachers.[53] In addition, 18,061 lay teachers were teaching in LCMS schools. These individuals were neither certified church workers nor rostered by the LCMS. There was also a small category of eight lay pastors.[54]

The universities and seminaries of the LCMS offer educational programs for students who aspire to be Ministers of Religion—Commissioned. The director of Christian outreach program is offered at Concordia University, St. Paul, Minnesota. The director of Christian education program is offered at the university in St. Paul, as well as at Concordia University, River Forest, Illinois; Concordia University, Austin, Texas; Concordia University, Irvine, California; and Concordia University, Seward, Nebraska. Parish assistants are educated at Concordia University, Ann Arbor, Michigan. Deaconesses can attend either Concordia Seminary in St. Louis, Concordia Theological Seminary in Fort Wayne, Indiana, or Concordia University, River Forest, Illinois. Teachers are educated throughout the system. Parish nurses who are educated at Concordia University Wisconsin can participate in the university's lay ministry program to be rostered as lay ministers.[55]

The seminaries of the LCMS at St. Louis and at Fort Wayne educate Ministers of Religion—Ordained. For men who are needed in the ministry where they are and because of that cannot physically attend the seminaries, there is a program available through the two seminaries as a distance-learning ordination route called Distance Education Leading toward Ordination (DELTO). The initial ten courses for this program, as prescribed by the LCMS, are available at the district level. Individual districts form their own initial programs for men who are serving or are needed to serve in congregations within the district. For example, the Kansas District has the Kansas lay deacon program. Other districts have such programs or are preparing to establish similar programs, though not necessarily entitled "deacon" programs. What these men are authorized to do in the congregations they are serving before they are ordained depends on the individual district presidents. Some of those who successfully complete the district programs will become pastors through the DELTO program.[56]

Students who successfully complete the entire program, which involves twenty more courses that are coordinated through the seminaries, can be

called, ordained, and rostered by the LCMS as Ministers of Religion—
Ordained.[57] Each student has a mentor, and the students come to the seminary periodically for retreats with other DELTO students. A bachelor's
degree is preferred to enter DELTO.[58] Those who complete the program
are certified that they have completed it, but they do not receive an academic degree.

THE EVANGELICAL LUTHERAN CHURCH IN AMERICA AND ITS PRECURSORS

As in the LCMS, teachers were important in the synods that had
parochial schools and were precursors to the ELCA. Many of these precursor synods of the ELCA had a longer experience than the LCMS with
the diaconate, especially with deaconesses.

Proposals for a form of diaconal ministry for men arose in conventions
of the LCA (1970–1978). The LCA considered including men in the diaconate and perhaps "the professional full-time lay workers of the church
and persons involved in special ministries through congregations and para-
congregational groups."[59] (This idea would resurface again in the
1988–1993 ELCA study of ministry.) Efforts to experiment with deacons
were made in Michigan, New York, Pennsylvania, and New Jersey. Bishop
Perry in the Upstate New York Synod of the LCA started a synod-wide
training program for congregational deacons.[60] Pastor Stephen Boumann
of Trinity Church, Bogota, New Jersey, started Diakonia, an inter-
Lutheran program of training for congregational deacons, both male and
female, in the New York metropolitan area.[61] The Order of St. Stephen,
Deacon, incorporated in Baltimore, Maryland.

In 1975 the Division for Professional Leadership of the LCA created a
Task Force on the Form and Function of the Ministry of Deacons that recommended recognition of the function of deacons and establishment of criteria for deacons. LCA deaconesses favored admitting men to the
diaconate. The recommendation was defeated, however, in 1978. Robert
Marshall, LCA president, ruled that "the defeat of churchwide encouragement did not prevent synods and congregations from proceeding with their
own deacon programs." A study of the matter continued. By 1984 about
two hundred congregations said they had deacons. Some were merely worship assistants, but others preached, taught, carried Communion to shut-
ins, and engaged in community service. The Division for Professional
Leadership recommended, however, that, because of the prospects of
merger with the ALC, the church refer the matter to the Commission for

a New Lutheran Church. Bishop James R. Crumley Jr. remarked: "Now we're able to get rid of things we've never been able to settle before!"[62]

While the LCA was struggling with the issue of deacons, final steps were taken in December 1976 to form the AELC.[63] The AELC would join the LCA and the ALC to form the ELCA on January 1, 1988. The AELC had some strong proponents for the diaconate, one of the most articulate of whom was Stephen Bouman. The East Coast Synod of the AELC recognized the office of deacon in 1982. On May 30, 1983, the bishop of the East Coast Synod consecrated three deacons.[64] The ELCA included former AELC deacons on its roster.[65]

The predecessor churches to the ELCA also had programs to train volunteers to serve rural parishes where there was a shortage of pastors. In the Dakotas, the Rev. Arland Fisk of Minot, North Dakota, started "The Deacon Program" to train lay parish assistants. Lay assistants were permitted to preach and sometimes to administer the sacraments under supervision.[66] In eastern and western North Dakota, the deacon program was large and growing.[67]

The Commission for a New Lutheran Church, charged with the foundational work leading to the first constitution of the ELCA, was unable to resolve all issues concerning the patterns of ministry before the new church began in 1988. These issues had to be resolved to situate the deacons, deaconesses, and lay professional people employed by the merging church bodies. The LCA brought into the new church more than one hundred consecrated deaconesses and almost six hundred lay professional leaders, who were required to have a bachelor's or master's degree. The ALC brought 550 commissioned church staff workers, from parish secretaries to teachers, who had received letters of call. There were some ALC deaconesses as well. The AELC brought 150 commissioned and called teachers and forty-six deacons and deaconesses. The teachers had a long history in the LCMS out of which they came. They were considered ministers of religion, even by the U.S. Internal Revenue Service, which classified them as clergy.[68] The deaconesses were part of the Lutheran Deaconess Association. The deacons were relatively new, but the AELC embraced them and allowed them both liturgical and service functions. They were called by the bishop, consecrated, and nonstipendiary.[69]

The situation was further complicated by the fact that, depending on the church body, some of these church professionals had been consecrated, some had been commissioned, and some had been installed. Some had experienced an imposition of hands when consecrated or commissioned.

Others had not. Some, but not all, had received letters of call.[70] What was to be made of all this in the new church?

The commission recommended that the ELCA carry out a study of ministry and, while the study was going on, the inherited rosters of church workers were to be frozen, with no assurance of a future status in the church.[71] It might have relieved the anxieties of the church workers involved if these matters had been settled before the new church had begun. Procedures were established, however, for new lay professionals to be certified as associates in ministry. They were required to have a bachelor's degree, supervised field experience, and twenty semester credits of theological education.[72] The ELCA turned over issues of ministry, including deacons, to its Division of Ministry. The constitution of the ELCA provided, in continuing resolution 10.11.A87.b (revised in 1991 and renumbered 7.11.A87.b),[73] that

> [d]uring the . . . period of 1988–1994, this Church shall engage in an intensive study of the nature of ministry, leading to decisions regarding appropriate forms of ministry that will enable this church to fulfill its mission. During the course of such study, special attention shall be given to:
>
> 1) the tradition of the Lutheran Church;
>
> 2) the possibility of articulating a Lutheran understanding of the three-fold ministerial office of bishop, pastor, and deacon and its ecumenical implication; and
>
> 3) the appropriate forms of lay ministries to be officially recognized and certified by this church, including criteria for certification, relation to synods, and discipline.[74]

The Board for the Division of Ministry added a fourth plank to this mandate in its "Proposal for the ELCA Study of Ministry, 1988–1993." It added to the study the consideration of the "ministry of all the baptized people of God."[75]

In June 1988 the ELCA Church Council asked the Division for Ministry of the new church to design a study of ministry as laid out above. It was to include forums and hearings with the church at large: "The study shall be participatory and educational, providing opportunities for persons representing various issues and points of view regarding ministry to be heard and to take part in this study."[76] To implement this mandate, the Rev. Dr. Paul R. Nelson, who earned a doctorate from Notre Dame University, became director of a Task Force on the Study of Ministry that was composed of seventeen clergy and lay members. The task force met three times a year and was chaired by Professor John H. P. Reumann of Lutheran Theological Seminary in Philadelphia.[77]

The study process was projected to last from 1988 to 1993, a year less than originally planned because church assemblies of the ELCA meet in odd-numbered years. The first two years of the study, the task force received reports from specially qualified people: seminary professors, pastors, associates in ministry, deacons, deaconesses, rostered teachers, and representatives from other denominations and Lutheran synods, including the LCMS. In 1989 twenty-six open hearings were held across the country.[78] Publications by Lutherans on the office of ministry appeared that included "the office of deacon." A strong argument for an ordained diaconate in the new ELCA came from William Lazareth, bishop of the Metropolitan New York Synod and formerly of the LCA, who argued that

> the restoration of an ordained diaconate (in whatever public roles this church considers helpful) could be of great benefit to the fullness of ministries in the ELCA today. It would also provide the "Lutheran understanding and adaptation of the threefold ministerial office of bishop, pastor and deacon" that is called for consideration in the ELCA constitution (10.11.A87).[79]

The Metropolitan New York Synod continues to have "synodical" deacons.[80] A different point of view came from Michael Rogness, then associate professor of pastoral theology and ministry at Luther Northwestern Theological Seminary, presently professor of homiletics. Both Rogness and the seminary itself were of the former ALC, many of whose members were having difficulty with changes caused by the merger, such as calling the former district presidents "bishops." Without denying the historical reality of the diaconate, Rogness was equivocal about the ordination of deacons in the ELCA. He argued in a short historical essay on "The Office of Deacon in the Christian Church" that "diakonia as service is of course the task of every Christian in every congregation. . . . What is important is that the ministry of diakonia is being carried out, not what titles are used. One difficulty in restoring the diaconate as a distinct order is the diffusion of ministries in a congregation."[81] Rogness had equated the role of a "deacon" with "service" in a general sense with a lack of specificity that some modern scholars of the diaconate would reject. Lazareth had a more immediate experience of deacons and what they do.

Meanwhile, on the ecumenical front, the Faith and Order Commission of the National Council of Churches had sponsored a consultation on diaconal ministry in December 1988 out of which denominational leaders formed a National Diaconal Dialogue Group. The ELCA was represented by Madelyn Busse, director from 1988 to 1997 for rostered lay ministries and candidacy. Eventually she became a diaconal minister herself.[82] The National Diaconal Dialogue Group met for a four- to five-year period and influenced the Task Force for the Study of Ministry and the requirements for diaconal ministers in the ELCA.[83]

In 1989 and 1991 the ELCA Task Force on the Study of Ministry prepared interim reports for the churchwide assemblies. The task force asserted that "no one dogmatic or institutional form of . . . ministry is necessary for salvation or as a guarantee of the Gospel. . . . The justifying ministry of Jesus Christ is the one essential ministry, and all other ministries are derivative and dependent."[84] This allowed for latitude in the task force's proposals.

The 1991 report set forth three models for ordering the ordained ministry in the ELCA and invited response by means of a form returned to the task force by December 31, 1991. It elicited a disappointingly poor response.[85] In the fall and winter of 1991 and 1992, a series of forums were held around the country, focusing on the content of the report.[86] All three proposals retained the ordination of women to the ministry of Word and Sacrament, but the issue of grandparenting in all previously rostered lay ministries was open.[87] The three proposals were a threefold, twofold, and unitary ordering of the office of ordained ministry as follows:

1. The proposal for a threefold ordering was that of "deacons, pastors, and bishops." This proposal included three separate options for ordination: (a) three ordinations, as practiced in the Church of Sweden; (b) one ordination to deacon, pastor, or bishop that would not be repeated if one changed office; or (c) one ordination for pastors only and consecration of bishops or deacons.

2. The proposal for twofold ordering was that of (a) Word and Sacrament and (b) Word and Service. Pastors and bishops were to be ministers of Word and Sacrament, and deacons and other professional church workers were to be in the office of Word and Service. This proposal was without ecumenical precedent.

3. The unitary ordering was to ordain pastors and roster other lay professional church workers. Some advocates of this ordering wanted to use the title of "deacon" for rostered full-time church professionals. Others wanted to consider only some of the rostered groups "deacons." This option allowed for leaving the presently existing deacons and deaconesses much as they were. Although not ordained to the ministry of Word and Sacrament, deacons or deaconesses

were to be consecrated or commissioned. In this unitary ordering, some people envisioned deacons as filling in where there was a shortage of ordained pastors, even preaching and administering the sacraments, just as the ELCA has some nonordained people serving in that capacity (without the title of deacon) today.[88]

To a historian aware of the organic growth of church office over the centuries in response to the needs of each era, the proposals for a threefold, a twofold, and a unitary ordering of ordained ministry offered by the Task Force on the Study of Ministry in 1991 seemed somewhat contrived. One was tempted to ask why everything could not be left as much as possible as it was with regard to church office. The problem with that solution was that in the case of a merger of several church bodies, somewhat different orderings of ministry had evolved. Some resolution was needed. Likewise, ecumenical dialogue necessitates viewing the structures of church office with an eye to what is essential and what can be compromised. Nevertheless, the better part of wisdom would seem to dictate that as much latitude as possible should be allowed. The church bodies that have chosen federalism—allowing individual congregations, districts, or synods to do what they were doing before a merger—may have taken the wisest course.

An issue underlying each of the three proposals of the Task Force on the Study of Ministry was ordination. Some but not all of the merging church bodies had practiced the imposition of hands for consecrated deacons and deaconesses and for some commissioned church staff workers without speaking of the act as ordination. Deaconesses were also spoken of as "set apart." What was ordination? For Martin Luther it was clearly not a sacrament. An interpretive paper prepared by the task force suggested that ordination might be considered "public recognition, affirmation, and confirmation of call from the Church to a public ministry of the Church."[89] This definition could allow more than just pastors to be ordained. There was a minority on the task force who disagreed with such inclusiveness.[90]

At its June 4–6, 1992, meetings, the Task Force on the Study of Ministry voted to recommend "that the ELCA establish a Diaconal Ministry as part of the office of ministry to which persons are called. Approved and called candidates for diaconal ministry shall be ordained as diaconal ministers as part of the office of ministry."[91] A minority dissented.[92] Others made minority comments. The Rev. Teresa Bailey, who has a doctorate in Reformation history from Stanford University, raised the issue of the educational requirements for diaconal ministry excluding minorities:

> To ordain deacons with M.A. plus professional training effectively excludes most minority, poor, and non-English speaking Lutherans. They must petition to be "excused" from white middle class "Standards.". . . Professionalizing deacons furthermore removes them from their traditional role as indigenous congregational leaders who required no extra training prerequisite to recognized calling.[93]

Dr. Bailey could well have been correct. In 2003, 98 percent of diaconal ministers and deaconesses in the ELCA were Caucasian.[94]

"Diaconal ministry," as envisioned by the task force, drew from all three models for the ordering of ordained ministry that it had proposed in its 1991 report to the Churchwide Assembly, according to Paul Nelson, director of the task force.[95] The task force purposefully avoided terms such as "diaconate" or "ministry of Word and Service." In recommending a diaconal ministry, the task force affirmed one office of ministry, a position crucial to many Lutherans, but acknowledged distinct forms within that office. The task force admitted, however, that "the particular form of diaconal ministry proposed . . . would be new to the ELCA."[96] The task force also voted to open rosters for ministers of Word and Sacrament and diaconal ministry to nonstipendiary ministers (those not paid for ministerial duties but on ELCA rosters), both in diaconal ministry and ministry of Word and Sacrament. In the past, rostered ministers generally had to receive financial compensation and serve at least twenty hours each week.[97] The reasoning of the task force for nonstipendiary ministers was:

- Like most institutions in society, the ELCA is facing dwindling revenues to train and support ordained ministers

- and associates in ministry. Yet the need for more such leaders, especially in urban centers with new populations and in many rural areas with shrinking populations, is constantly growing.[98]

The Task Force on the Study of Ministry referred the profile and educational requirements for diaconal ministry to a working group that was to report to its October 1992 meeting, but "diaconal ministry" appeared to have been broadly conceived for those who were willing to complete required theological education, a master's degree, from a seminary.[99] To be specific, the task force listed at least five areas of diaconal ministry: (1) education, (2) mission and evangelism, (3) care, (4) administration, and (5) music and the arts. By "care" the task force meant parish nurses; hospital ministries; ministering to the poor, addicted, prisoners, or immigrants; and advocacy and justice ministries.[100] This variety of tasks appeared to be in conformity with suggestions that diaconal ministries encompass many offices and functions, but they apparently would not encompass all such functions, for the working group was charged with formulating a recommendation on lay ministries in the ELCA.[101]

The task force also had to deal with a common roster of individuals that had been created in 1988, as the ELCA was forming, to encompass lay rostered individuals from the merging church bodies (the LCA, the ALC, and the AELC).[102] Something had to be decided concerning the individuals on this list. It was thought that existing deacons and deaconesses who fulfilled the requirements probably would be able to choose to be diaconal ministers.[103] Task force "working groups" would also report in October 1992 on "standards of Discipline for Grandparented Rosters" and on ordination. "Individuals in a number of synods" had asked for "more clarity on the meaning of ordination for the ELCA."[104]

The recommendations of the task force were to "be submitted to the board of the Division for Ministry in March of 1993 for action, to the Church Council for its recommendations in April of 1993, and ultimately to the Churchwide Assembly of the ELCA meeting in Kansas City in August and September of 1993 for action."[105] Concerns about the role of bishops in the ELCA could overshadow the issue of diaconal ministry. Concerning bishops, the task force recommended that the "title of 'bishop' be retained in the ELCA," that "the term of office for bishops" should "be six years, and [should] be renewable," and that "a service of installation be used for those called to serve as bishops in the church." The task force envisioned the "office of bishop" as "a distinct form within the one office of ministry."[106] The task force was acting "in line with its commitment to cooperate with the Evangelical Lutheran Church in Canada in its study of ministry. . . . The Canadian study [appeared to be] moving in the direction of three ordinations to the offices of pastor, bishop, and diaconal minister. . . . The ELCIC and ELCA have reciprocity of ministers, that is, ordained ministers of one church may serve in that capacity in the other church."[107] The statement about ordination was not to be realized in the Evangelical Lutheran Church in Canada. The "ELCIC does not ordain bishops or diaconal ministers."[108]

By the time the report and recommendations of the Task Force on the Study of Ministry passed the 1993 Churchwide Assembly of the ELCA, there had been some amendments. The Board of the Division for Ministry had voted to delete the recommendation to ordain diaconal ministers, and the Conference of Bishops had concurred with the board.[109] Diaconal ministers were to be consecrated, whereas associates in ministry, the term used for lay-rostered individuals, were to be commissioned. Deaconesses were left as they were on a separate roster.[110] The Division of Ministry of the ELCA was charged with recommending a rite of entry for diaconal ministers to the 1995 Churchwide Assembly in Minneapolis. By 1995 the division had prepared "standards, requirements, and procedures" for diaconal ministry.[111]

Educational requirements for the diaconal ministers include a Master's in Arts from a seminary plus whatever training their specialty requires, but there is some latitude.[112] The activities of diaconal ministers overlap considerably with those of the associates in ministry to encompass a variety of callings, such as directing church music programs, teaching, social work, and counseling. In addition, diaconal ministers are required, at least once, to attend a two-week formation event, which has been held since July 1995 at Gettysburg Seminary, which hosts the ELCA Center for Diaconal Ministry Preparation.[113] There were thirty-four candidates for diaconal ministry at the first formation event in 1995. By July 1999, 135 people had participated,[114] and by 2003 approximately 300.[115] About forty attend each summer.[116] The formation event is cosponsored by the ELCA Division for Ministry and the Eastern Cluster of Lutheran Seminaries (Philadelphia, Southern, and Gettysburg Seminaries).[117] Diaconal ministers must undergo forty hours of spiritual direction, and they are asked to have seven hundred hours of supervised field experience.[118]

Diaconal ministers are not necessarily congregationally based. Some are chaplains in hospitals, and with the approval of the bishop, these individuals can lead eucharistic services, especially if there is no other Lutheran chaplain in that hospital. There is a diaconal minister in the Rocky Mountain Synod who is a grief counselor employed by a "for-profit" chain of funeral homes. This secular organization pays her salary, but she also consults for the synod on death and dying issues.[119] Nonstipendiary posts, though allowed by the constitution of the ELCA, must be approved by the Conference of Bishops.[120] The need to obtain such approval potentially leaves out of diaconal ministry some people of sufficient means or with retirement pensions who would like to serve in areas where there is no budget for them to do so. It also potentially leaves some candidates who have completed their education for the diaconal ministry waiting for a call that brings with it a salary within the ELCA.

One can wish for more salaried positions within the church because many of those seeking to become diaconal ministers need to make a living from the post to which they are called, but that expectation does differ from the situation of most vocational deacons in the Episcopal Church and from most permanent deacons in the Catholic Church, the minority of whom

receive any salary from the church.[121] Privileging the consecration of diaconal ministers who are receiving a salary from the church in the ELCA
might contribute to the relatively modest number of diaconal ministers. In
June 1996 the first ELCA consecrations of diaconal ministers occurred.[122]
As of August 12, 2003, the director for Candidacy of the Division for Ministry reported that there were 66 consecrated diaconal ministers on the rolls
and more than 160 candidates.[123] By 2005 there were more than one hundred consecrated diaconal ministers and about the same number of candidates.[124] Some prospective diaconal ministers in the ELCA have had
difficulty in finding placement, and there are people ready to be consecrated as diaconal ministers who cannot find a call. From the point of view
of many, congregations need a pastor; they can do without a diaconal minister. There needs to be education and further awareness within the congregations of the potential uses and benefits of calling a diaconal minister.
Diaconal ministers hold periodic gatherings,[125] and they publish a newsletter.[126]

With the approval of the bishop and a synodical board or committee,
laypeople in the ELCA can preach and preside over the worship service,
usually in "geographically isolated or economically challenged areas" where
there is no ordained pastor.[127] Laypeople who preach and preside are not
typically diaconal ministers, however, at least for the present.[128] Allowing
nonordained people to preside over the Eucharist is disturbing to many
Episcopalians,[129] with whom the ELCA entered into full communion,
which arrangement included an agreement for the orderly exchange of
pastors and priests.[130]

In addition to dealing with diaconal ministers and with deaconesses, the
Task Force on the Study of Ministry had been charged with studying the
"appropriate forms of lay ministries to be officially recognized and certified
by this church, including criteria for certification, relation to synods, and
discipline."[131] Three rosters were created. We already have considered the
separate rosters for diaconal ministers and for deaconesses. The third "lay"
roster that the ELCA compiled was a roster for associates in ministry. This
roster includes laypeople who were rostered with the Lutheran bodies that
merged to become the ELCA. The associates in ministry roster is by far the
largest of the lay rosters in the ELCA, and the denomination has added
more than half of its present roster since 1988.[132] In 2000 there were 783
associates in ministry serving in all synods of the ELCA, of whom 77 percent were serving in congregations as a result of a call as compared to 43
percent of deaconesses and diaconal ministers.[133] In 2003 there were 1,061
associates in ministry, but about 300 were retired, leaving 703 active asso-

ciates. There were almost the same number of associates in ministry serving in congregations (75 percent), whereas in 2003 there were more deaconesses serving in congregations by virtue of a call (50 percent) and not as many diaconal ministers (33 percent). Associates in ministry are educators, musicians, administrators, youth and music directors, church staffpersons, etc. Associates in ministry are required to have twenty semester credits of theological education and a bachelor's degree, but they can request a waiver if they can demonstrate equivalency. The denomination waives the bachelor's degree requirement for only a few people each year.[134] Associates in ministry are commissioned, not consecrated or ordained. The associates in ministry roster is also the roster on which those from other diaconal associations are rostered in the ELCA, such as deaconesses from the Lutheran Deaconess Association, which has an inter-Lutheran membership. Louise Williams, for example, of the Lutheran Deaconess Association and president of Foundation Diakonia World Federation of Diaconal Associations and Diaconal Communities, is on the ELCA associates in ministry roster.[135]

Besides the churchwide diaconal ministers, deaconesses, and associates in ministry, the ELCA also has synodically authorized ministries, a degree of federalism in the church. The "Guidelines Related to Synodically Authorized or Licensed Ministries" adopted in April 1995 by the ELCA Church Council as policy listed Lay Minister of the Word, Lay Minister of Word and Sacrament, Worship Leader, Catechist, Evangelist, Synodical Missionary, and the Synodical Deacon of the Metropolitan New York Synod.[136] The ELCA is concerned that people in these synodically authorized ministries be trained and supervised, though they are not on the central rosters of the ELCA. Thus the ELCA Division for Ministry funded pilot projects in nine of its synods to "provide examples that may help other synods as they plan a program for synodically authorized ministries."[137] One of these programs was the synodical diaconate of the Metropolitan New York Synod.[138] These synodically authorized ministries fill needs for "pastoral or diaconal leadership for a congregation or other ministry of the church when needs exist which exceed those which can be met by rostered persons."[139]

Studies of church ministry, such as the one in the ELCA, tend to concentrate on full-time professional church workers and to leave out lay congregational deacons who are unpaid. Lutheranism historically has had a considerable degree of flexibility in its conception of deacons. If one seeks historical precedent within North American Lutheranism for two kinds of deacons in the same church, one can look to the Muhlenberg churches that in the eighteenth and nineteenth centuries had both transitional deacons who were on their way to becoming pastors and lay deacons who were elected within individual congregations.

Comparing Diaconal Ministers and Deacons

How do deacons and diaconal ministers compare? Both the United Methodist Church and the ELCA chose to use the term "diaconal minister," though Methodists have switched their terminology to "deacon" since 1993. Catholics and Episcopalians use the term "deacon." "Diaconal minister" allows for the possibility of congregational deacons and for synodically approved deacons in the same denomination without confusion, as in the ELCA. The world organization for deacons and diaconal ministers is as broadly defined as possible: Foundation Diakonia, World Federation of Diaconal Associations and Diaconal Communities.

There are differences between deacons and diaconal ministers besides the terms themselves. There are many more deacons than diaconal ministers. There are more than two thousand vocational deacons in the Episcopal Church, to be precise, 2,584 living deacons in March 2005, of whom 1,272 were males and 1,312 females. There also were 398 people in formation: 185 males and 213 females.[140] There are approximately fifteen thousand deacons in the Catholic Church in the United States.[141] The United Methodist Church has approximately 450 diaconal ministers and is consecrating no more. In 1993 it voted to ordain deacons, and as of June 2003 the United Methodist Church had more than a thousand deacons.[142] By March 2005, the United Methodist Church had 1,234 ordained deacons and 1,362 in candidacy.[143]

In contrast to churches that speak in terms of thousands of deacons, the director for Candidacy of the Division for Ministry of the ELCA reported that there were 66 consecrated diaconal ministers on the rolls and more than 160 candidates as of August 12, 2003.[144] By March 2005, there were more than one hundred consecrated diaconal ministers and about the same number of candidates.[145] Of course, Catholics and Episcopalians began much earlier with permanent and perpetual deacons. The Catholic Church has had permanent deacons since 1968, and the Episcopal Church had perpetual deacons in 1952. The United Methodists began with diaconal ministers in 1976.[146] The ELCA has had diaconal ministers only since 1996, but there are other possible reasons for the fact there are more deacons than diaconal ministers.

The level of education required could contribute to fewer diaconal ministers being recruited than deacons. Diaconal ministers in the ELCA need a theological master's degree. Catholic and Episcopal deacons do not need a master's degree, though some have one. Currently, deacons in the United Methodist Church need either a master's degree or certification. Between 20 and 25 percent were choosing the certification route. Requiring a master's degree of diaconal ministers might be contributing to the relative lack of minorities in the diaconal ministry of the ELCA.

An additional difference among the denominations is that the diaconal ministers and deacons of the United Methodist Church and the diaconal ministers of the ELCA typically are paid for their ministry whereas deacons in the Catholic and Episcopal churches typically are not. On the face of it, one would assume that it is better to be paid, but for many who feel called to be deacons or diaconal ministers, pay is not the issue. They have other sources of income, are willing to serve without pay, or are willing to look for a diaconal role outside of a church institution. Given the constraints of denominational budgets, there are those who would rather be ordained or consecrated to a nonstipendiary position than wait for funds to be found to employ them, especially if they have completed their education. The ELCA has the recommendation of its own Task Force for the Study of Ministry that the church "make greater use of non-stipendiary ministers (not paid for ministerial duties but on ELCA rosters)."[147]

ORTHODOX AND EASTERN CHURCHES

Orthodox churches are sometimes held up as an example of the "continuing presence of deacons," but even in these church bodies, as in the Latin West, deacons lost their charitable responsibilities over time.[148] A great deal is made of their continuing role in the liturgy. Since John Chrysostom, their coming and going in the church has been compared to the flight of angels, but most Orthodox communities cannot afford a deacon.[149] Bishops have deacons and even archdeacons.[150] Permanent deacons fit well into monastic life, but for students in theological study, the diaconate is a preparation for the priesthood.[151] Historically in the Russian Orthodox Church, there were two groups of permanent deacons: (1) Those selected for their musical abilities by large city churches and cathedrals especially, and (2) a larger group who remained deacons because "they were not qualified for promotion." The latter were inadequately educated and poor.[152] In the 1990s, however, some Russian Orthodox deacons were doing social outreach in Moscow.[153]

In the Eastern churches, deaconesses flourished in centuries past. Female deacons are canonically possible, but few of the churches ordain them. There is a movement to revive the "apostolic order of deaconesses."[154] There is at least one female deacon in the Armenian Church.[155]

PRESBYTERIANS

Presbyterians in the United States have lived for a long time with a polity that includes ministers, elders, and deacons, though at times using the terms "teaching elders" and "ruling elders" to distinguish between ministers (of Word and Sacrament) and elders who are members of local sessions (a Presbyterian term for what in other denominations is called a church council or a vestry). Besides ordaining ministers, Presbyterians ordain elders and deacons from the local congregation to what, for most, has been part-time nonstipendiary service in the church. Deacons are rarely paid for what they do in the Presbyterian Church. Being a deacon in a Presbyterian congregation can be time consuming, but it is not a career path. Deacons are not rostered by the national church. Not all Presbyterian congregations have deacons. Some have trustees instead of deacons or in addition to elders and deacons.[156] Some congregations, especially in the southern stream of the Presbyterian Church, use boards of deacons as trustees in charge of buildings and grounds and investments.[157] Using deacons for such material responsibilities is in the tradition of John Calvin's Geneva. One role of the Genevan deacons of the sixteenth and seventeenth centuries was to take the financial load off the pastors, and this continues to be true in the Reformed tradition in some times and places.

Presbyterians have reviewed their theology of church office. A Task Force on the Theology and Practice of Ordination to the Presbyterian Church (U.S.A.) presented a proposal to the 204th General Assembly of that Church in Milwaukee in June 1992 as a first step to acceptance by the denomination.[158] This proposal did not suggest radical changes in current Presbyterian practice, but it did state that "[l]ack of flexibility in the forms and manifestations appropriate for the office of deacon burdens the whole system of the church's ordered ministry, particularly the office of minister of the Gospel."[159]

The proposal suggested that in addition to ordination at the level of the local congregation, deacons could be trained and ordained at the level of the presbytery (composed of a number of congregations in a contiguous geographic area), the synod, (composed of a number of contiguous presbyteries), or the General Assembly, the national body.[160] The deacon, in turn, could serve at any one of these levels.[161]

The General Assembly accepted the report and sent it on to the church for study. If presbyteries like the suggestions made in such a report, they can make overtures to a future General Assembly to make changes in Presbyterian practice. Thus sending the report on to the presbyteries across the country is a step toward possible change. It does not guarantee change, and the change that the task force had suggested did not come about. In 1997 a change that did occur was that the Presbyterian Church (U.S.A.) allowed individual congregations without boards of deacons to ordain an individual as a deacon and commission him or her to a particular function or task. Because some Presbyterian congregations had dropped their boards of deacons or had never had one, this made it possible for individuals to become deacons. This typically happens when the congregation develops some particular task that a deacon could perform, such as running a food pantry. In turn, ordaining one deacon sometimes has provoked congregations to think in terms of instituting or reinstating a full board of deacons. If a congregation has no board of deacons, the tasks that deacons would ordinarily fulfill fall to the elders. These tasks include hospital visitation, fellowship, and some of the charitable tasks of a congregation. Deacons have diverse tasks because they perform those tasks assigned to them by the session, and, of course, those who are not deacons can perform diaconal tasks. For example, some Presbyterian churches have instituted parish nurses. Both elders and deacons can help with Communion and take the Eucharist to shut-ins.[162]

Some Presbyterian congregations have eliminated their boards of deacons and instituted what some call a "unicameral" system, that is, a congregation with only a session of elders and no board of deacons and no trustees. Responses to an inquiry among Presbyterians in 1994–1995 revealed the following reasons for a congregation to eliminate a board of deacons: (1) "it is organizationally simpler"; (2) there "was a mentality that officers began as deacons as a 'training ground' and were 'promoted' to elder as they grew older"; (3) "in a few more conservative churches women were deacons but not elders";[163] (4) a unicameral system "alleviates the conflict between session and deacons"; and (5) it "alleviates the difficulty of coming up with a full slate [of officers] out of scarce human resources (especially in smaller congregations)."[164] On the other hand, remarks against a unicameral system included this pungent comment from Lewis Wilkins, once interim executive presbyter of the Boulder Presbytery, Fort Collins, Colorado (executive presbyter is a position from which one can view many congregations at close hand):

> My very consistent observation is that the deacons' responsibilities that [devolve] upon a unicameral session always are neglected, mostly I

think because the kind of people who enjoy and are good at "govern-ing" rarely are equally good at "hands-on" service of people in need. And I've also watched the "natural deacons" who exist in every con-gregation make themselves scarce at election time if the session is all there is: they are folks who think sitting in meetings is a waste of their volunteer time, 'cause they like to do things that matter to people.[165]

Sadly absent from comments on eliminating the boards of deacons in Pres-byterian churches was any evidence of knowledge of the strong heritage of deacons in Reformed churches emanating from Switzerland in the Refor-mation era, of which the Presbyterian Church (U.S.A.) is one.[166]

As the diaconate spread into different geographic and cultural regions, it did not remain exactly as it had been in Calvin's Geneva. For example, deacons and elders in the Reformed "stranger church" of the French in London sometimes met together as they do today in the Reformed Church in America. Deacons remained a prominent feature in many Reformed churches.[167]

Besides deacons, the issue of church educators remained unresolved in the Presbyterian Church (U.S.A.). The Task Force on Ordination did not necessarily propose ordination for church educators, a lively option in the Presbyterian Church in the United States before its reunion with the United Presbyterian Church in the United States of America in 1984. In 1987 in the reunited church, an overture calling for ordination of church educators failed. The task force did allow that a congregation could elect the church educator as an "elder not in service on the session" and request the presbytery to examine that individual to determine the "sense of call" and "fitness for exercising the office of elder." The task force also suggested that "church educators and other church professionals engaged in full-time forms of ministry . . . may see their ministries corresponding more appropriately to the office of deacon rather than to the office of elder or of minister of the Gospel."[168] Not all church educators, then, would be ordained, but some would be ordained as deacon or elder or as minister, depending on education and the sense of call.[169]

Again at the 2002 General Assembly, a related amendment to the con-stitution of the Presbyterian Church (U.S.A.) was proposed that would have given church educators a more prominent role. This amendment rec-ognized, in effect, a twofold ministry in the Presbyterian Church, one con-centrating on the traditional role of the pastor and preacher and the other on educational ministry.[170] To qualify to be ordained to this educational ministry, the traditional church educator would have needed more educa-tion. The amendments failed to pass.[171] The task force that made this recommendation did not consider recommending the ordination of educators to a fourth office of "Doctor (Professor)" or educator, which was not within the Task Force's mandate:

> The matter of ordaining educators has been before our denomination and its predecessors for decades. Our charge as a task force was to develop a design for the preparation, employment, ordination, and support of Christian educators as ministers of Word and Sacrament with a specialization in educational ministry. We did not reconsider the ordination of educators to a fourth office . . .[172]

In the Reformed Church of Calvin's era, there is no evidence that elders, deacons, or doctors (teachers) were "ordained" to those offices nor is there evidence that John Calvin and the other pastors of Geneva of his era were ever ordained, if ordination entails an imposition of hands. Although Calvin personally favored ordination, the city council of Geneva did not approve of such ceremonies, which could be considered papist and potentially idolatrous. However, alongside pastor, elder, and deacon, there was a fourth office in Calvin's Geneva, that of doctor in the sense of professor. Proposals to recognize church educators in the Presbyterian Church could be justified on the basis of John Calvin's fourfold conception of church office as (1) pastor, (2) elder, (3) deacon, and (4) doctor or teacher. The office of doctor in the sixteenth century, however, was usually thought of as that of a theological professor, many of whom also had been pastors. Ordaining educators to a fourth office rather than including them in the office of pastor might have been more in keeping with historical precedent.

Although conscious of the need for educated ministers, the Presbyterian Church has shortages in rural and economically disadvantaged areas as do other denominations. The Presbyterian Church (U.S.A.) has a provision for lay pastors. After specialized training, lay pastors function on every level as pastors, even sacramentally. For example, they work among immigrant groups or Native Americans, for whom it is important to have someone who shares the culture and can speak the language. These lay pastors are controlled by the presbyteries.[173]

DEACONS ELECTED IN CONGREGATIONS: BAPTISTS, REFORMED, LUTHERAN, AND OTHERS

Like Presbyterians, many denominations continue to elect deacons within individual congregations to serve as part-time volunteers without salary. This is true, for example, of the Baptists, Mennonites, Unitarians, Seventh Day Adventists, the Reformed Church in America, other churches in the

Reformed tradition, and some Lutherans.[174] The roles and functions of these deacons depend, to some extent, on the presence or absence of other officers with whom they can share the work of the congregation. If, in addition to pastors, there are trustees or elders to share financial and administrative responsibilities, the deacons can, in theory at least, concentrate on benevolent concerns.

The Reformed Church in America has both elders and deacons. The deacons are part of the consistory (church council) along with the elders, as is the case in the Netherlands.[175] Deacons are charged with financial administration of the church, care of the sick, visiting the distressed, and benevolent concerns in general. They are ordained by an imposition of hands by the minister.[176] Deacons in the Christian Reformed Church are similar.[177] Even with both elders and deacons on the consistory or church council, Reformed churches originating in the Netherlands have been able to maintain both offices, unlike other denominations that dropped either the elder or the deacon over time. Many of these deacons have an active role in well-coordinated ministries. For example, the deacons of the Deacons' Conference of the Holland [Michigan] (Classis) of the Christian Reformed Church coordinate their efforts but have unique programs within each congregation.[178] At Calvary Reformed Church, deacons have been assigned both to a "fellowship family" within their congregation and to outreach beyond members of their congregations.[179] Deacons have been encouraged to find church members to work with them and have been asked to submit a detailed monthly report evaluating their work.[180] The result in one seven-month period was that 69 families were helped, of whom 34 were nonmember families.[181] In addition to diaconal work within individual congregations, deacons coordinate their efforts with their Christian Reformed classis of churches and with the national program of the Christian Reformed Church.[182] Christian Reformed deacons also cooperate ecumenically, especially with Reformed Church in America deacons.[183]

Baptist deacons encompass both the role of deacons and of what would be the role of elders in other denominations.[184] Baptist deacons have responsibility for finances and governance in many congregations, though some Baptist churches have other financial officers: trustees, stewards, treasurers, and financial secretaries, for example.[185] Baptists in the South have tended to continue to ordain deacons. American Baptist churches have female deacons, but this was true of only some Southern Baptist congregations.[186] Since the 1970s, women have more often been ordained as deacons rather than as deaconesses, though as a title, the term is still current.[187] In this century, Baptist deacons have grappled with the needs of society and problems of poverty at least since Walter Rauschenbusch (1861–1918) and the "social gospel."[188] Much of the literature directed at Baptist deacons has emphasized their service role.[189] As one article on Southern Baptists put it: Deacons have shifted "from management to ministry."[190] Many congregations have used the Deacon Family Ministry Plan whereby a congregation is divided into groups of families, and each group is assigned to a deacon who is responsible for visiting and watching over a specific number of families.[191] Other denominations have used this plan, or variations of it, for example, Menlo Park Presbyterian Church in California.

In the former United Lutheran Church, some congregations called their church council members deacons.[192] Historically, Lutheran churches in North America have had both elders and deacons, but for Lutherans, the title of elder is sometimes used as a synonym for deacon or for a member of a discipleship committee.[193]

Denominations and churches that have organized in the nineteenth or twentieth centuries have incorporated the deacon into their structures, for example, the Seventh Day Adventists and the Boston Church of Christ. Besides deacons, the Boston Church of Christ listed elders, evangelists, women's counselors, and missionaries but no pastors. The evangelists appeared to act as pastors and the elders as senior evangelists.[194]

FRENCH-SPEAKING PARTS OF SWITZERLAND AND FRANCE

Deacons in Switzerland in French-speaking Reformed churches date from as early as the era of John Calvin. In 1541 he labeled the trustees and administrator of the city hospital "deacons" in the ecclesiastical ordinances of Geneva, and beginning in 1549, there were deacons who ran welfare funds for refugees in Geneva. After the dissolution of these welfare funds in the nineteenth century, Geneva had other deacons at work in its churches who were charged with charity and relief.[195] Today in the Suisse Romande, the French-speaking parts of Switzerland (southwest Switzerland around Geneva, Lausanne, Neuchâtel, and Fribourg), both men and women can become deacons. Both men and women also can become pastors.[196]

The modern Genevan church provides for deacons named by each parish council. They must be 20 years old.[197] The nomination of a deacon is announced from the pulpit in the parish church.[198] The deacons in each parish are to organize themselves and determine where they will focus their attention.[199] As for revenues, deacons cannot make fund appeals without the consent of their parish council and the Council of the Protestant Church of Geneva (l'Église protestante de Genève).[200] The money placed in the alms boxes located in the individual churches is handed over to a Commission for the Common Funds of the Protestant Church of Geneva, which is composed of two delegates from each diaconate and two from the Consistory.[201] The commission determines how these funds, and also the gifts and legacies, will be spent.[202]

For a long time, deacons in French-speaking Reformed churches appear to have received no formal training except for what they acquired on the job. Then the Reformed Church initiated a formal diaconal training program specifically for deacons who intended to make it all or part of their career. The Protestant Church of Geneva had 16 trained deacons on July 5, 2001, and 87 pastors. The deacons and pastors receive the same salaries based on their age and the length of time they have served in the church.[203] Not all pastors, or at least not all pastors' wives, are happy that deacons and pastors are paid the same.

The statutes for the Department of Diaconal Ministries of the Suisse Romande date from at least 1967.[204] The diaconal education was modified in 1996. People aspiring to become deacons must have professional training and two years of experience before beginning diaconal training. They cannot be more than 50 years old when they begin diaconal training.[205] The diaconal training itself takes three years, attendance is required, but it is a part-time commitment that allows people to work at another job.[206] There is an oral examination and written work.[207]

Some of the literature surrounding this salaried diaconate in the French-speaking part of Switzerland shows a naiveté as to the rich history of deacons in the area. For example, a piece called "The Nature of the Ministry of the Deacon" states that "in reintroducing the diaconal ministry, our churches of the French-Speaking part of Switzerland are giving a new possibility of a ministry oriented toward the world."[208] The salary might be new, but diaconal ministry oriented toward the world is not new to this part of Switzerland.

Once trained, a deacon in French-speaking Switzerland is consecrated in a service that includes the imposition of hands. Deacons can work full or part time for the church in a congregation or an institution. They can receive a salary from the church, or they can retain their former professions and income. At times when there has been a shortage of pastors, deacons have served in that role.[209] They can teach and preach freely.[210]

Swiss deacons from the Suisse Romande have met with French Catholic deacons.[211] They were invited for the first time to the assembly of deacons of the Catholic Church in France, held February 27–28, 1982, at Nîmes. This annual gathering also included attendees from Portugal, Spain, Germany, and Belgium.[212] *Communion et Diaconie*, a diaconal periodical, recorded the impressions of the attendees. The editorial board of this ecumenical journal consisted of eight Catholics and five Protestants.[213] In some ways it is easier for deacons than for pastors or priests of different denominations to work together. This is reflected in the expansion of diaconal organizations, meetings, newsletters, and publications that cut across denominational boundaries.

ECUMENICAL INTEREST IN THE DIACONATE

Ecumenical interest in the diaconate comes from the deacons themselves but also from church mergers and unions, interdenominational dialogues, and the Faith and Order Commission of the World Council of Churches. The roots of ecumenical discussion about the ordering of ministry go back at least to the world conference of Faith and Order that met at Lausanne, Switzerland, in 1927. This movement evolved into the Faith and Order Commission that, after World War II, became part of the World Council of Churches. The Roman Catholic Church participated fully in the commission after Vatican II (1962–1965).[214]

The Faith and Order Commission began a study on ministry in 1964. That same year, the Faith and Order Commission held a consultation on "The Ministry of Deacons in the Church" and the following year a consultation on "The Deaconess."[215] These consultations resulted in publication of The Ministry of Deacons (1965) and The Deaconess (1966). Faith and Order Commission studies on Baptism and the Eucharist began in 1967. The 1971 commission meeting at Louvain, Belgium, received reports from the studies on Baptism, Eucharist, and ministry. Further study of those documents by member churches led to the text of *One Baptism, One Eucharist and a Mutually Recognized Ministry*, which was received at the 1974 commission meeting in Accra, Ghana. That led to further study and the convergence document, *Baptism, Eucharist and Ministry*, which was received at the 1982 commission meeting in Lima, Peru. The World Council of Churches Central Committee authorized the transmittal of *Baptism, Eucharist and Ministry* (or the Lima text, as it is also known) to the churches.[216]

Baptism, Eucharist and Ministry became an ecumenical best seller, the most successful publication the World Council of Churches had ever produced. By 1990 it had gone through 24 printings with a total of 85,000 copies in circulation. It had been translated into at least 31 languages. *Baptism, Eucharist and Ministry* itself is only 33 pages in its English version, but from 1986 to 1988 the Faith and Order Commission published six volumes of responses to this document from churches and some ecumenical bodies, including that of the LCMS.[217] Sven-Erik Brodd, a priest in the Church of Sweden who is professor of ecclesiology at the University of Uppsala, points out that the diaconate was not a major issue in these responses.[218] It was not left out, however.

Baptism, Eucharist and Ministry considers deacons alongside bishops and presbyters in "Forms of the Ordained Ministry" in the section on ministry. After acknowledging that "the New Testament does not describe a single pattern of ministry," it argues from history that "during the second and third centuries, a threefold pattern of bishop, presbyter and deacon became established as the pattern of ordained ministry throughout the Church." It further asserts that "the threefold ministry . . . may serve today as an expression of the unity we seek" and that "churches not having the threefold pattern . . . need to ask themselves whether the threefold pattern as developed does not have a powerful claim to be accepted by them."[219] *Baptism, Eucharist and Ministry* thus advocates a threefold ministry of bishop, presbyter, and deacon. It further states that

> [t]oday, there is a strong tendency in many churches to restore the diaconate as an ordained ministry with its own dignity and meant to be exercised for life. As the churches move closer together there may be united in this office ministries now existing in a variety of forms and under a variety of names.[220]

Baptism, Eucharist and Ministry states that "[t]he church may also ordain people who remain in other occupations or employment," allowing for nonstipendiary deacons, pastors, and other ministries.[221]

Churches, for example, some Lutherans, with a unitary vision of ministry (one centered on the pastor) took exception to the threefold pattern of ministry. Many Reformation and Free churches felt that *Baptism, Eucharist and Ministry* was attempting to make definitive a historically developed pattern of bishops, presbyters, and deacons. Some respondents objected to the diaconate as a separate order of ministry or to the ordination of deacons. Other respondents, for example, those from the Congregationalist and Baptist traditions, felt they had a more clearly defined role for deacons than *Baptism, Eucharist and Ministry*. Some churches felt that the document was not appreciative of the "rich variety of other institutional forms of ministry in the church." The report neglected, for example, the office of the elder, which is not the pastor, in the Reformed/Presbyterian tradition. The 1990 Faith and Order Commission report on the responses to *Baptism, Eucharist and Ministry* acknowledges that "[a]ttention . . . should have been given in BEM to the ministerial functions of, e.g., elders in the Reformed/Presbyterian tradition." Likewise, churches from the Reformed tradition, whose deacons are elected within congregations and are non-stipendiary, objected to the document's diaconate, which seemed to resemble the model of deacons in churches that, after the Reformation, retained a medieval hierarchy of church office, such as Catholics and Anglicans.[222]

Baptism, Eucharist and Ministry, in the commentaries printed in the right-hand column of the text, had already foreseen some of these problems. For example, on the matter of ordination of deacons, commentary number 31 stated:

In many churches there is today considerable uncertainty about the need, the rationale, the status and the functions of deacons. In what sense can the diaconate be considered part of the ordained ministry? What is it that distinguishes it from other ministries in the Church (catechists, musicians, etc.)? Why should deacons be ordained while these other ministries do not receive ordination? If they are ordained, do they receive ordination in the full sense of the word or is their ordination only the first step towards ordination as presbyters?[223]

A number of respondents to *Baptism, Eucharist and Ministry* welcomed its call for reform of the threefold pattern of ministry:

The function of deacons has been reduced to an assistant role in the celebration of the liturgy: they have ceased to fulfill any function with regard to the diaconal witness of the Church. . . . The traditional threefold pattern thus raises questions for all the churches. Churches maintaining the threefold pattern will need to ask how its potential can be fully developed for the most effective witness of the Church in this world.[224]

Respondents applauded the document's broad description of deacons as representing "to the Church its calling as servant in the world."[225]

By struggling in Christ's name with the myriad needs of societies and persons, deacons exemplify the interdependence of worship and service in the Church's life. They exercise responsibility in the worship of the congregation: for example by reading the scriptures, preaching and leading the people in prayer. They help in the teaching of the congregation. They exercise a ministry of love within the community. They fulfil certain administrative tasks and may be elected to responsibilities for governance.[226]

Baptism, Eucharist and Ministry has influenced ecumenical dialogue and the position of various denominations on deacons. For example, the description of the diaconate in the 1984 Consensus of the American-based Consultation on Church Union (COCU) self-consciously resembled that of *Baptism, Eucharist and Ministry*. Some of the language was identical. The Consensus accepted the threefold pattern of ordained ministry: bishop, presbyter, and deacon. It described the diaconate as a ministry in its own right, not as a stepping-stone to other office, and it emphasized the social service and teaching aspects of the deacon's role.[227] The Consensus admitted, however, that it was impossible to reconcile the various forms of diaconal ministries at that time.[228]

The ultimate goal of the Consultation on Church Union was unity in one church. Since 1962, the churches involved in the consultation had engaged in efforts to find agreement. In 1970 the consultation submitted *A Plan of Union* to the participating churches. It turned out to be premature, but the consultation continued to attempt to work out whatever agreement was possible. The 1984 Consensus was part of that process.[229]

Orders of ministry and polity were key problems in generating enthusiasm for The COCU Consensus among members of denominations participating in the consultation. For Presbyterians, for example, the office of bishop is non-Presbyterian, and the office of elder is dear. Many Presbyterians are ordained elders, though typically all the elders in a congregation do not serve concurrently on the congregation's session (church council). For some, giving up the office of elder would mean to quit being Presbyterian. The office of deacon is less of a problem because it is recognized in many denominations.[230]

The Consultation on Church Union, at the time of the 1984 Consensus, consisted of nine member churches: the United Methodist Church, the Presbyterian Church (U.S.A), the Episcopal Church, the United Church of Christ, the Christian Church (Disciples of Christ), the African Methodist Episcopal Church, the African Methodist Episcopal Zion Church, the Christian Methodist Episcopal Church, and the International Council of Community Churches. The Lutheran Council in the USA, the Catholic Church, and the Reformed Church in America were not official members of the consultation but were represented on the Theology Commission.[231] Today, the ELCA is associated with the Churches Uniting in Christ (CUIC), the renamed Consultation on Church Union, as a Partner in Mission and Dialogue, not as a member communion.[232]

In addition to its influence on the Consultation on Church Union, *Baptism, Eucharist and Ministry* has influenced bilateral ecumenical dialogues: the conversations of the Lutheran World Federation with the Baptist World Alliance, for example, and, in the United States, the Lutheran-Episcopal Dialogue and the Lutheran-Reformed Dialogue.[233] *Baptism, Eucharist and Ministry* appeared a decade too late to influence the Agreement between Reformation Churches in Europe negotiated at Leuenberg, Switzerland, in 1973. This Leuenberg Agreement among Lutheran, Reformed, and related pre-Reformation churches included the Waldensian Church and the Church of the Czech Brethren.[234] By 1989 eighty churches had signed the Leuenberg Agreement—76 European and four Latin American church bodies.[235] They acknowledged differences over ministry and ordination while according altar and pulpit fellowship that "includes the mutual recognition of ordination and the freedom to provide for intercelebration."[236] The Leuenberg Agreement is the only one of the above-mentioned ecumenical dialogues not to mention deacons, but there were others that did not do so as well, for example, the Pullach Report from the 1973 international Anglican-Lutheran dialogue and the 1987 Niagara Report, another Anglican-Lutheran ecumenical text.[237]

As for the Lutheran-Reformed Dialogue, its 1984 report "An Invitation to Action" argued that "no substantive matters concerning ministry . . . should divide" Lutheran and Reformed churches.[238] Churches participating in this dialogue were the ALC, the LCA, the LCMS, the AELC, the Reformed Church in America, the Presbyterian Church (U.S.A.), and the Cumberland Presbyterian Church. "A Statement of Lutherans to Lutherans Reflecting on This Dialogue" stated:

> We did hear language and terminology which is strange to Lutheran ears, for example, teaching elder, ruling elder, doctors, and deacons. But we agreed that the ministry functioning under these terms is congruent with the ministry as we have known it in our own churches in North America. . . . While the language may be different, Lutherans should recognize that they have lived in the United States for over two centuries under a modified presbyterial polity.[239]

Perhaps the strongest argument for openness toward the pattern of ordained ministry in the Reformed tradition came from Warren Quanbeck, an ALC theologian:

> By contrast to the diverse ministries of the early church, the ministry of word and sacrament of the Lutheran church in history seems monolithic and narrow. The long shadow of the medieval concept of priesthood has in fact made Lutheran practice with respect to the ordained ministry less flexible and adaptable than it could have been. But if we understand the ministry of word and sacrament in terms of the New

Testament understanding of revelation or of Luther's understanding of the way God works in coming to his people, a great deal of flexibility becomes apparent. The ordained minister then appears as one who serves the media which God has chosen to effect his gracious presence among humankind, and whatever serves the grace of God in this way is a legitimate, ordained ministry. The most common form of ordained ministry will no doubt continue to be that of servant of the word and sacraments in a local congregation, but any ministry which the church needs in its situation to effect God's gracious presence is possible: missionaries, chaplaincies, counselors, teachers, administrators, and so on.[240]

Quanbeck's statement says nothing of the educational requirements for ordination, however. Does ordination of a teacher, an administrator, or, for that matter, of a deacon presuppose a theological education? If so, how much theological education? Do the preparatory sessions that Presbyterians give to deacons and elders before ordination constitute sufficient theological education to satisfy Lutherans?

The LCMS participants attached a minority report to the 1984 report of the Lutheran-Reformed Dialogue that stated:

> The LCMS participants cannot at this time concur in the opinion that "... Lutheran churches should, at the earliest appropriate time and at the highest level, officially recognize the Eucharists (Lord's Suppers) of those churches which affirm the Reformed Confessions and have them as a living part of their present witness and proclamation."[241]

The start of the ELCA in 1988 spelled the end of old agreements. Not all the churches that merged agreed to fellowship with the Presbyterian Church (U.S.A.). Thus Reformed-Lutheran dialogue began again. The United Church of Christ entered as a new party to negotiations alongside the Presbyterian Church (U.S.A.), the Reformed Church in America, and the ELCA. Three years of conversations concluded at a meeting in Chicago on March 7–8, 1992, that resulted in a recommendation for full communion, sharing of the Lord's Supper, provision for joint services, recognition of one another's ministries, and provision for exchange of ordained ministers of Word and Sacrament. The report "A Common Calling: The Witness of Our Reformation Churches in North America Today" called for continuing dialogue.[242] The report was submitted to the four churches for action and studied in Lutheran and Reformed congregations.[243] This led to A Formula of Agreement among the four church bodies, full communion, the recognition of one another's ministries, and exchange of ordained ministers, even for extended periods of time. A Formula of Agreement was accepted by the General Synod of the Reformed Church of America in 1997,[244] by the 1997 ELCA Churchwide Assembly,[245] by the United Church of Christ, and by the Presbyterian Church (U.S.A.).[246] The LCMS had continued with the Reformed-Lutheran dialogue but did not enter into A Formula of Agreement.[247]

The Lutheran-Episcopal Dialogue presented thornier problems concerning issues of ministry than those of the Lutheran-Reformed Dialogue. Most of the controversy revolved around the bishop and related issues, such as apostolic succession and the historic episcopate in the Episcopal Church. "Apostolic succession" is the succession in church office from the apostles through the imposition of hands by a bishop who, in turn, had experienced an imposition of hands by a bishop in the line of bishops that was thought to go back to the apostles. For years this issue had blocked agreement between Lutherans participating in the dialogue and Episcopalians. The ELCA has bishops, but they are not considered to be in an unbroken line of succession from the apostles. Also, they are not elected for life but rather for six-year terms and can lose an election. (Lutheran bishops of the Church of Sweden are considered to be in that line of succession because of political exigencies at the time of the Reformation.) The LCMS also has district presidents, as did the ALC before it joined in the ELCA in 1998.

Despite differences, accord was reached by a majority of the members of the Lutheran-Episcopal Dialogue of the ELCA and of the Episcopal Church, U.S.A. Again, the LCMS sent participants to the dialogue but was not part of the Concordat of Agreement. The Concordat reads as follows:

> In light of the agreement that the threefold ministry of bishops, presbyters, and deacons in historic succession will be the future pattern of the one ordained ministry of Word and Sacrament in both churches as they begin to live in full communion . . . the Episcopal Church hereby pledges . . . to begin the process for enacting a temporary suspension, in this case only, of the 17th century restriction that "no persons are allowed to exercise the offices of bishop, priest, or deacon in this Church unless they are so ordained, or have already received such ordination with the laying on of hands by bishops who are themselves duly qualified to confer Holy Orders." . . . to permit the full interchangeability and reciprocity of all Evangelical Lutheran Church in America pastors as priests or presbyters and all Evangelical Lutheran Church in America deacons as deacons in the Episcopal Church without any further ordination or re-ordination . . . . Both churches acknowledge that the diaconate, including its place within the threefold ministerial office, is in need of continued study and reform, which they pledge to undertake in consultation with one another . . . The Evangelical Lutheran

Church in America also pledges . . . to begin the process for enacting a dispensation for ordinands of the Episcopal Church from its ordination requirement of subscription to the unaltered Augsburg Confession. . . . The creation of a common, and therefore fully interchangeable, ministry will occur with the full incorporation of all active bishops in the historic episcopate by common joint ordinations.[248]

Representatives of the LCMS were full participants in three rounds of Lutheran-Episcopal Dialogue (1969–1972, 1976–1980, 1983–1991) and, in fact, would stay with the dialogue to the end.[249] However, the LCMS was not part of a 1982 Lutheran/Episcopal Interim Sharing of the Eucharist Agreement, and they abstained from voting on the Concordat of Agreement.[250]

Two members of the dialogue from the ELCA dissented from the Concordat, objecting to the introduction of the historic episcopate into the ELCA as a matter of necessity for church unity. This, they said, was in conflict with the teachings of Scripture and the Augsburg Confession.[251] The Lutheran-Episcopal Concordat was defeated at the ELCA churchwide assembly of 1997.[252]

After the Lutheran-Episcopal Concordat failed to be accepted at the 1997 ELCA Churchwide Assembly, a Lutheran-Episcopal drafting team was called upon to prepare a revised proposal.[253] Todd Nichol registered opposition to the positions of two of the Lutheran members of the drafting team, Martin Marty and Michael Root, in a minority report published in *Lutheran Quarterly*, a scholarly historical journal.[254] The Lutheran-Episcopal Dialogue had difficulties in bringing along all members of both church bodies.[255]

Ultimately both the ELCA (1999)[256] and the Episcopal Church adopted Called to Common Mission and entered a relationship of full communion, recognizing each other as distinct but catholic and apostolic churches "holding the essentials of the Christian faith." As for bishops, the churches agreed over time "to share in the ministry of bishops in an evangelical, historic succession," but the issue of the historic episcopate still rankles today.[257] The LCMS neither adopted Called to Common Mission nor entered into full communion with the Episcopal Church.[258]

As of January 1, 2001, the ministry of pastors of the ELCA and of priests of the Episcopal Church was fully interchangeable, and, when invited, a pastor of the ELCA can serve in an Episcopal church and a priest of the Episcopal church can serve in the ELCA, with the limitation that a pastor of the ELCA cannot serve as the rector of an Episcopal congregation.[259] (A rector, the ultimate person in charge of an Episcopal congregation, still must be a priest of the Episcopal Church.)[260] Priests or pastors can serve for short or extended periods of time with the other church body and still remain on the clergy rosters and pension plans of their respective home church bodies, but if they intend to serve indefinitely, they can apply to be transferred to the clergy roster of the other church body.[261] Lutheran pastors who become Episcopal priests are not required to be ordained again by an Episcopal bishop, though they may originally not have been ordained by a bishop.[262] When serving in the other church body, a pastor or priest will observe the traditions and liturgy of the other church body, to say nothing of mastering the vocabulary. The document governing the exchange of pastors and priests of the two church bodies contains glossaries of selected terms from the Episcopal Church and from the ELCA useful to anyone who has ever been lost in the maze of curates and vicars; vestries and wardens; synods and dioceses; diaconal ministers, deacons, deaconesses, and associates in ministry.[263]

Full communion, of course, also means that members of the two church bodies can take the Eucharist in each other's churches, though, as Lutherans, they might object to the common cup used in many Episcopal churches and, as Episcopalians, they might object to the individual communion cups used in many Lutheran churches.

The issue of the diaconate was unresolved by those who agreed to Called to Common Mission. This was the case with many ecumenical agreements prior to it, commencing with a dialogue between the Church of Sweden and the Church of England that began in the 1920s. That dialogue led to intercommunion between the two churches, though both churches recognized that no conformity existed between them concerning the diaconate.[264]

Likewise, Lutherans and Episcopalians in the dialogue that produced Called to Common Mission agreed to recognize and accept each other's deacons and diaconal ministers. This was despite the fact that the ELCA continues to consecrate diaconal ministers and the Episcopal Church to ordain deacons. The two churches agreed, in paragraph 8, to begin consultation to explore how "some functions of ordained deacons in the EC [Episcopal Church], and consecrated diaconal ministers and deaconesses in the ELCA, can be shared insofar as they are called to be agents of the church in meeting needs, hopes, and concerns within church and society."[265]

According to Carol Schickel, director for Candidacy of the Division for Ministry of the ELCA, "consultations about ordained deacons in the Episcopal Church and diaconal ministers in the ELCA have begun in the past year or two,"[266] but they apparently are not widely known because Ormonde Plater, an Episcopal archdeacon and specialist on the diaconate, commented that nothing had happened at the official level between the two church bodies as of July 2003 with regard to these consultations concerning the diaconate.[267]

There has been strong discontent with the Lutheran-Episcopal agreement expressed by some members of the ELCA, particularly by some who were formerly of the ALC. On the other hand, there also have been attempts to emphasize the commonalities shared by the two church bodies, not least of which is a rich liturgical and musical tradition that renders many Lutherans and Episcopalians comfortable in each others' services.[268]

The Lutheran-Episcopal Dialogue was helped by the Hanover Report of the Anglican-Lutheran International Commission entitled The Diaconate as Ecumenical Opportunity.[269] The Hanover Report was the product of two meetings in 1995 and 1996 in West Wickham of the United Kingdom and in Hanover, Germany, the first in the history of ecumenical dialogues at which the diaconate was the exclusive object of the dialogue.[270] The Hanover Report was published under the auspices of the Lutheran World Federation and the Anglican Consultative Council.

There had also been the renowned philological work of John Collins, but no matter how skillfully done, studies of the meaning of the *diakon-*words in the early church are insufficient to produce universal concord.[271] Many Lutherans today are uncomfortable with ordination of deacons when their equivalent in the ELCA are called diaconal ministers and are consecrated. Lutherans and Anglicans have had different experiences of the diaconate since the sixteenth century, and universal consensus is lacking. Historically, the Church of England, over the objections of the Puritan contingent in the sixteenth and seventeenth centuries, retained the medieval transitional deacons, which Episcopalians have recently called into question.

For dialogue concerning the diaconate, Lutherans could benefit from a deeper understanding of the rich diversity within Lutheranism historically. Besides the Reformation deacons of Johannes Bugenhagen and the example of the Pietist August Hermann Francke, this book has described eighteenth- and nineteenth-century Lutheran deacons in the United States who were transitional to becoming pastors and, for a time, were ordained, coexisting with congregational deacons and with the deacons and deaconesses who came into being with the Inner Mission movement in Europe.

The deeper issue is not differences among denominations in the understanding of the diaconate but whether or not differences can be tolerated. Do the differences in Called to Common Mission fall within the realm of adiaphora? As so often happens in ecumenical agreements in which the issue of the diaconate is not resolved, the signatory churches pledged to work on the issue. This was the case also with The Porvoo Common Statement (1992), adopted in 1996 by the Anglican churches in Great Britain and Ireland and by Lutheran churches in Scandinavia and the Baltic states with the exception of Latvia and Denmark.[272] (The Church of Denmark has since appointed a group to reconsider diaconal ministry in their church.)[273] The Porvoo signatory churches agreed to full mutual recognition and interchange of priests, deacons, and bishops, though the issue of the diaconate had not been resolved. The churches pledged to "work towards a common understanding of diaconal ministry."[274]

In conjunction with the Porvoo Common Statement, a series of conferences on ministry were held in the Scandinavian countries. A conference on deacons was held in 1995 at Lärkkulla, Finland. Out of this conference grew collaboration among some of the participants. This collaboration began as a research project by academic institutions in Sweden, Finland, Norway, and England and evolved into the Anglo-Nordic Diaconal Research Project. The Nordic Ecumenical Council (established in 1940) became involved early on in the project and agreed to coordinate it. The first meeting of the Anglo-Nordic Diaconal Research Project participants was in January 1997. A five-year project plan to run from 1997 to 2002 was agreed upon.[275] The Anglo-Nordic Diaconal Research Project has produced several sophisticated and informative volumes on the ministry of the deacon in Scandinavia and the British Isles.[276]

The issue of bishops comes up also in Lutheran-Methodist dialogues. The final report of the dialogue between the Lutheran World Federation and the World Methodist Council (1984) stated: "Since the New Testament presents diverse forms of ministry, we hold that no particular form of ordained ministry or church order is prescribed by the New Testament as necessary for the church."[277]

Members of the dialogue concluded that "a ministry of oversight like that of bishops is a practical necessity," but apostolic succession was not at issue.[278] Some Methodists acknowledged the influence of *Baptism, Eucharist and Ministry* on continued support within the denomination for diaconal ministers (now deacons). Geoffrey Wainwright, an ordained minister within the British Methodist Church, "which has a single rank of ordained ministry, namely presbyter, and which makes no claim to episcopal succession," advocated adaptation of the structure of bishop, presbyter, and deacon "for the sake of church unity."[279]

The Faith and Order Commission of the National Council of Churches in the United States held consultations on the diaconate in 1987 and 1989. Out of the second meeting a National Diaconate Dialogue Group from eighteen denominations formed: the African Methodist Episcopal, the American Baptist Churches, the Christian Church (Disciples), the Christian Reformed Church, the Church of the Brethren, the Church of the Nazarene, the Episcopal Church, the ELCA, the Greek Orthodox, the LCMS, the Moravian Church in America, the Orthodox Church in America, the Presbyterian Church (U.S.A.), the Reformed Church in America, the Roman Catholic Church, the Southern Baptist Church, the United Church of Canada, and the United Methodist Church. In addition there were representatives from the World Council of Churches and the National Council of Churches. There was liaison with the Consultation on Church Union; with Diakonia, the World Federation of Diaconal Associations and Diaconal Communities; and with Diakonia of the Americas.[280]

With all the attention to church office, the question has been asked, "What became of the laity?" This question was addressed at the First World Convention of Christian Lay Centres and Movements held at the Montreat Conference Center, Montreat, North Carolina, September 5–10, 1993, but there is obviously no definitive answer. However, it appears "the 'laity' have almost disappeared from ecumenical discussion nowadays."[281] Of course, in many denominations, deacons and diaconal ministers are considered lay, even when working full time for the church.

SUMMARY

Within the last two centuries, the scope of service identified with diakonia has expanded greatly, especially within Protestantism. In July 1984 the Central Committee of the World Council of Churches approved a statement on "The Diaconal Task of the Churches Today," describing "[d]iakonia as the church's ministry of sharing, healing and reconciliation . . . the very nature of the church."[282] Because of the nature of the German language, the German-speaking churches make great use of the word *diakonie*. Germans have written prolifically on the subject in both theoretical and practical terms.[283] One author complains of the inflation of *diakonia* into a veritable myth: "Each one speaks so much of serving, baptizing his administrative, partisan, or philanthropic enterprise with this word that has become banal."[284]

Another scholar, John Collins, prefers a narrower use of the word *diakonia*, more in line with its use in Scripture and in the early church when deacons were agents of the bishop, go-betweens and couriers who attended him and spoke for him.[285] This narrower interpretation is upsetting to some modern deacons whose self-understanding is centered in a servant image, but one cannot expect an institution that has lasted twenty centuries to have remained static. The cultures and societies in which the diaconate existed shaped it over time. The office of deacon over twenty centuries has experienced many changes, as one would expect of an institution that has endured so long.

In the first century, deacons, along with the office of widow, seemed to have emerged out of the needs of the church. Many would say the first-century deacons included women. Deacons may have preached and evangelized, if one allows that Stephen and the six others chosen in Acts 6 were deacons or at least acting in a diaconal role. As bishops emerged (separate from elders), deacons became their special helpers and sometimes succeeded them, even to the bishopric of Rome, the seat of the papacy. Deacons participated in the liturgy and led the candidates for Baptism into the water.

By the third century, the office of women as deaconesses solidified in the eastern Roman Empire, apparently in part because of a need in that society for women to perform for other women parallel functions in Baptism and home visitation to what male deacons performed for men. In the western Roman Empire, the widows served the women.

In the third century, it was unclear whether presbyters (priests) or deacons would become paramount in the church because both were in charge of congregations and both seemed to have presided over the Eucharist, at least occasionally. When the hierarchy of church office began to solidify after Christianity was tolerated in the fourth century and then made the official religion of the Roman Empire, presbyters (priests) emerged over deacons, and in the succeeding centuries the diaconate became a stepping-stone to the priesthood. By the thirteenth and fourteenth centuries, even archdeacons, who had once been the chief deacons in their dioceses, were priests. Deacons had acquired prominence in the liturgy, but they had lost their social welfare roles. With the emergence of the parish system and the decline of the large urban churches after the fall of the western Roman Empire in the fifth century, the administration of welfare had fallen increasingly to the individual parish and less to the bishop. Female deaconesses had become members of religious orders, to the extent that they existed at all, and they survived longer in the Eastern Orthodox churches than in the west. Male deacons in the east were allowed a wife if they were married when they were ordained.

The Protestant Reformation of the sixteenth century sidestepped developments of the Middle Ages in church hierarchy and attempted to recover deacons who were in direct contact with the poor, as in the early church described in Scripture. Martin Luther seemed to feel more strongly about social welfare than about the title of "deacon," but Johannes Bugenhagen wrote deacons into the church orders that he prepared for the Danes and the North Germans. Huldrych Zwingli and Zurich administered poor relief without deacons, but John Calvin insisted upon that title for the social welfare workers of Geneva. The example of Geneva created a precedent for Reformed churches as they spread. Plurality of church office became the norm in France, the Netherlands, Scotland, and the parts of Germany that became Reformed. It was favored by Puritans and Separatists in England.

Anabaptists and Mennonites used deacons extensively, and the Baptist churches that emerged out of seventeenth-century England did as well. As these various confessional groups spread to the New World, they tended to take their patterns of church office with them, including deacons.

In the seventeenth and eighteenth centuries, the office of deacon declined among Scottish Presbyterians and in the French Reformed Church. Elders remained, however. Among Congregationalists and Baptists, the deacon emerged paramount as a lay office in the church. Pastors were sometimes called elders. Lutherans who came to the New World had lay deacons elected within congregations on what some would call a Reformed model. They also called assistant ministers "deacons" as was done in Germany, and in the nineteenth century, they ordained some transitional deacons who became pastors.

The nineteenth century saw the emergence of the Inner Mission movement in Germany and Scandinavia with lay brotherhoods of deacons and sisterhoods of deaconesses. This movement spread throughout Protestant Europe into the rest of the world. It was less strong in the United States than in Europe. Deaconesses in the Anglican Communion tended to be parish-based rather than centered in religious communities. The deaconess movement in England arose at the time of the professionalization of nursing under Florence Nightingale and the growth of religious sisterhoods of nuns. In the New World, the deaconess movement caught on, especially among Methodists serving in inner cities. Schools for deaconesses and schools for lay ministry sometimes overlapped. In the nineteenth and early twentieth centuries, Lutherans tended to maintain the "motherhouse" pattern of nurse-deaconesses living together in community.

The turn into the twentieth century witnessed the continued growth of the deaconess movement and the foundation of new motherhouses, but two world wars and the concomitant societal changes took its toll on that pattern of deaconess organization. In the decades after World War II, groups of deaconesses made the garb elective, became salaried, entered into pension plans, and allowed deaconesses to marry. Parish work and social work became lively options for deaconesses in denominations such as the LCMS. Some deaconess groups in Europe and the United States died out. International organizations of deaconesses began to emerge in the post-World War II era, many of which came to include deacons. Today, organizations such as Diakonia, the World Federation of Diaconal Associations and Diaconal Communities serve as a contact point for deacons, deaconesses, and diaconal ministers worldwide. National and regional organizations of deacons have emerged as well.

The diaconate experienced a revival after World War II within the Roman Catholic Church and the Anglican Communion. After the Second Vatican Council, the Catholic Church revived the permanent diaconate and opened it to married men, 35 years of age or older, who are not intended for the priesthood. The Episcopal Church in the United States already had established a "perpetual" deacon. These developments influenced other denominations, including Lutherans, who had elected deacons at the congregational level if they had any at all.

In 1982 the Faith and Order Commission of the World Council of Churches produced *Baptism, Eucharist and Ministry*, a document that accepted and promoted the threefold order of ministry: bishops, pastors, and deacons. This document influenced other ecumenical conversations, such as bilateral dialogues and the Council on Church Union in the United States. This, in turn, influenced the shape of the diaconate in denominations participating in these conversations.

At present, the role of deacons in many denominations is under consideration. There are at least four models alive and coexisting in some denominations. (1) There are deacons elected within individual congregations to serve at the local level, (2) deacons transitional to the priesthood, (3) "permanent" deacons of the sort that emerged from the Second Vatican Council, and (4) communities of deacons or deaconesses that came out of the Inner Mission movement. There is historical precedent for these and other possible forms of the diaconate to inform and enrich discussion on the shape of the diaconate today.

NOTES

1. For more on education in the LCMS, see Suelflow, *Heart of Missouri*, 113–19.
2. *Ministry: Offices, Procedures, and Nomenclature*, 16, 37.
3. C.F.W. Walther, in his elaboration on Thesis 8 of his theses on ministry, "Concerning the Holy Ministry or the Pastoral Office," Part 2 of *The Voice of Our Church on the Question of Church and Ministry: A Collection of Testimonies about This Question from the Confessions of the Evangelical Lutheran Church and the Private Writings of Its Orthodox Teachers Published by the German Evangelical Lutheran Synod of Missouri, Ohio, and Other States as a Witness of Its Faith in Defense against the Attacks of Pastor Grabau of Buffalo, New York*, 3rd ed., in August Suelflow, ed., *Selected Writings of C. F. W. Walther: Walther on the Church*, trans. John Drickamer (St. Louis: Concordia, 1981), 105–6.
4. Jahnke, "Lutheran Lay Ministry" (Spring 1986): 2–3.
5. Jahnke, "Lutheran Lay Ministry" (Spring 1986): 4–6.
6. Jahnke, "Lutheran Lay Ministry" (Spring 1986): 9; Jahnke, "Lutheran Lay Ministry" (Summer 1986): 55.
7. The Lutheran Church—Missouri Synod, *Lutheran Annual 2003* (St. Louis: Concordia, 2002), 25, 747.
8. Schoenbaum, "Lay Ministry Program," 9, 22.
9. Dr. Albert L. García, professor of theology and director of the Lay Ministry Program and of the Theological Education by Extension Program, Concordia University Wisconsin, telephone conversation with author, 15 August 2003.
10. García, telephone conversation, 31 March 2005.
11. [Office of Higher Education, The Lutheran Church—Missouri Synod], *Ten Minutes with a Lay Minister* (n.p.: n.d.), [1].
12. *Lutheran Lay Ministry: A Theological Education by Extension Program* (Mequon, Wisc.: n.p.), [4].
13. Jahnke, "Lutheran Lay Ministry" (Spring 1986): 9–10; Jahnke, "Lutheran Lay Ministry" (Summer 1986): 56.
14. Concordia University Wisconsin, *Lutheran Lay Ministry: Lay Ministry Specialist Degree Program* (Mequon, Wisc.: Concordia University Wisconsin, n.d.).
15. Dr. John W. Oberdeck, assistant director, Lay Ministry Program, Concordia University Wisconsin, telephone conversation with author, 7 August 2003.
16. [Office of Higher Education, Lutheran Church—Missouri Synod], *Ten Minutes with a Lay Minister*, [3].
17. The Lay Ministry Department, Concordia University Wisconsin, 12800 North Drive, Mequon, WI 53097-2402, 262/243-4343.
18. In 2003 the following fourteen sites were used: Miami, Florida; Dundee and Carol Stream, Illinois; Evansville and Indianapolis, Indiana; Slidell, Louisiana; Catonsville, Maryland; Neosho, Kansas City and St. Louis, Missouri; and Eau Claire, Milwaukee, Neenah, and Wausau, Wisconsin. The sites change as programs are completed and new needs arise. By 2005 some of these cities no longer had sites, but others had been added, for example, in Florida and Oklahoma.
19. Dobberfuhl, administrative assistant for the Lay Ministry Department, Concordia University Wisconsin, telephone conversation with author, 7 August 2003; Oberdeck, telephone conversation, 30 March 2005.
20. Albert García, telephone conversation, 15 August 2003.
21. Jahnke, "Lutheran Lay Ministry" (Spring 1986): 9.
22. "Deaf Missions History," http://www.lcmsdeaf.org/history.html (accessed 20 May 2005).

23. Roger Altenberger, director of the Deaf Institute of Theology, St. Louis, Mo., telephone conversation with author, 11 August 2003.

24. Sandi Green, electronic mail to author, 4 April 2005.

25. Altenberger, telephone conversation, 11 August 2003. The Rev. Roger Altenberger, Deaf Missions, The Lutheran Church– Missouri Synod, 1333 S. Kirkwood Rd., St. Louis, MO 63122.

26. Roger Altenberger, director of the Deaf Institute of Theology, telephone conversation with author, 15 August 2003.

27. *Ministry: Offices, Procedures, and Nomenclature*, 12, 34.

28. Walther, "Concerning the Holy Ministry," in Suelflow, *Selected Writings: Walther and the Church*, 73.

29. *Ministry: Offices, Procedures, and Nomenclature*, 29–30.

30. *Ministry: Offices, Procedures, and Nomenclature*, 36.

31. Jahnke, "Lutheran Lay Ministry" (Spring 1986): 9–10.

32. Samuel H. Nafzger, executive director, Commission on Theology and Church Relations, LCMS, telephone conversation with author, 1 August 2003.

33. Jahnke, "Lutheran Lay Ministry" (Spring 1986): 10–11.

34. *Christian News* (17 February 1992): 11.

35. Samuel Nafzger, executive director, Commission on Theology and Church Relations, LCMS, letter to author, 20 August 2003.

36. Schmidt, *Veiled and Silenced*.

37. *1983 Convention Workbook*, 221–22; *Procedures*, LCMS (1983), 178–81, in Jahnke, "Lutheran Lay Ministry" (Spring 1986): 54.

38. Resolution 3-11A, as cited in Wassilak, "Developing Theology for the Female Diaconate," 9.

39. "To Adopt Recommendations of Lay Worker Study Committee Report as Amended," Resolution 3-05B, as cited in Wassilak, "Developing Theology of the Female Diaconate," 9.

40. Resolution 5-21, Overture 5-70, *Convention Workbook*, p. 262, in *1992 Convention Proceedings*, 157.

41. LCMS, "Nomenclature Study Committee," *1998 Convention Workbook*, 8–9.

42. LCMS, "Nomenclature Study Committee," *1998 Convention Workbook*, 8–9.

43. Ostermann, telephone conversation, 13 August 2003.

44. LCMS, "Nomenclature Study Committee," *1998 Convention Workbook*, 8–9.

45. LCMS, "To Address Nomenclature of Church Workers," Resolution 7-14A, Overtures 7-118-31, *Convention Workbook*, pp. 275–78, in *1998 Convention Proceedings*, 151–52.

46. LCMS Commission on Theology and Church Relations, *Theology and Practice of "The Divine Call": A Report of the Commission on Theology and Church Relations of The Lutheran Church—Missouri Synod* (St. Louis: The Lutheran Church—Missouri Synod, 2003).

47. García, telephone conversation, 15 August 2003.

48. LCMS, "To Phase Out Consecrated Lay Workers Category," Resolution 7-13A, Overture 7–12, *2001 Convention Workbook*.

49. Raymond L. Hartwig, secretary of the LCMS, letter to "All Non-Rostered Lay Ministers serving Congregations and other Entities of the LCMS," October 2001.

50. John O'Hara, Research Services, LCMS, electronic mail, 15 August 2003.

51. Mary Diederichs, supervisor for Roster and Statistics, The Lutheran Church—Missouri Synod, telephone conversation with author, 27 August 2003.

52. Tonia Burcham, electronic mail, 19 May 2005.

53. LCMS, *Lutheran Annual 2003*, 634.

54. O'Hara, electronic mail, 15 August 2003.

55. García, telephone conversation, 3 March 2005.

56. García, telephone conversation, 15 August 2003.

57. Hannah Machado, administrative assistant to Dave Wollenburg, Distance Learning, Concordia Seminary, St. Louis, telephone conversation with author, 22 August 2003.

58. Kim Hosier, DELTO secretary, Concordia Theological Seminary, Fort Wayne, telephone conversation with author, 25 August 2003.

59. Gilbert, *Commitment to Unity*, 238.

60. Paul Nelson, director of the Study of Ministry of the ELCA, letter to the author, 30 December 1991.

61. Bouman, "Diaconate," 12–13; Nelson, letter to author, 30 December 1991.

62. Gilbert, *Commitment to Unity*, 337, 517–18.

63. Nichol, *All These Lutherans*, 111.

64. "The Establishment of the Office of Deacon: East Coast Synod, Association of Evangelical Lutheran Churches," in "The Office of Deacon in the East Coast Synod, Association of Evangelical Lutheran Churches" (East Coast Synod Office, 360 Park Avenue South, New York, 1983, photocopy), [1].

65. Dorris, "Reflections on the Diaconate in the ELCA," 281–84.

66. Kerr, *Shape of Ministry*, 39.

67. Nelson, letter to author, 21 December 1991.

68. Nafzger, telephone conversation, 1 August 2003.

69. Busse, "Development of Diaconal Ministry in the ELCA," 92–95.

70. Busse, "Development of Diaconal Ministry in the ELCA," 93–94.

71. Busse, "Development of Diaconal Ministry in the ELCA," 90–91, 95.

72. Busse, "Development of Diaconal Ministry in the ELCA," 95.

73. Nelson, letter to author, 29 June 1992.

74. *Constitutions, Bylaws, and Continuing Resolutions of the Evangelical Lutheran Church in America* (Chicago: ELCA, revised 1989), chapter 10.11.A87.b, in ELCA, *Study of Ministry Study Edition*, 5.

75. (Chicago: Evangelical Lutheran Church in America, 1988), 3, communicated by Nelson, letter to the author, 30 December 1991.

76. Board of the Division of Ministry, "Proposal for the ELCA Study of Ministry, 1988–1993" (Chicago: Evangelical Lutheran Church in America, 1988), 2–4, in ELCA, *Study of Ministry*, 5.

77. The members of the task force were the Rev. Dr. John H. P. Reumann, Philadelphia; Dr. Teresa Bailey, Palo Alto, California; the Rev. Dr. Carl Braaten, Chicago; the Rev. Dr. Norma Cook Everist, East Dubuque, Illinois; Mr. John Graff, Annandale, Virginia; Ms. Gracia Grindal, St. Paul, Minnesota; the Rev. LaVern Grosc, Lincoln, Nebraska; the Rev. Will Herzfeld, Oakland, California; the Rev. April Ulring Larson, Rochester, Minnesota; Ms. Marjorie Leegard, secretary, Detroit Lakes, Minnesota; the Rev. Dr. Fred Meuser, Columbus, Ohio; the Rev. Dr. José Rodríguez, Chicago; the Rev. Dr. Paul J. Seastrand, Missoula, Montana; Ms. Sue Setzer, Charlotte, North Carolina; Sr. Elizabeth Steele, Columbus, Ohio; Dr. Nelvin Vos, Maxatawny, Pennsylvania; and the Rev. Dr. Wayne Weissenbuehler, Denver, Colorado. Liaison members included the Rev. Connie Miller, Iowa City, Iowa (Board for the Division for Ministry); the Rev. Dr. James Cobb, Norfolk, Virginia (the ELCA Church Council), and

the Rev. Dr. Joseph Wagner, executive director for the Division for Ministry. See ELCA, *Study of Ministry*, 6n.

78. "Hearings on Ministry 1989: The Study of Ministry" (Division for Ministry, Evangelical Lutheran Church in America, Chicago, n.d.).

79. Lazareth, *Two Forms of Ordained Ministry*, 84.

80. Richard Bruesehoff, director for Leadership Support, ELCA, telephone conversation with author, 10 June 2003.

81. Michael Rogness, "The Office of Deacon in the Christian Church," in Nichol and Kolden, *Called and Ordained*, 151–60 (quote is on p. 157).

82. Busse, "Development of Diaconal Ministry in the ELCA," 90, 97.

83. Busse, "Development of Diaconal Ministry in the ELCA," 97.

84. ELCA, "Study of Ministry, Report to the Churchwide Assembly, 1991" (photocopy), 17.

85. Appendix B, in ELCA, *Study of Ministry*, 6, 44–60; "Evangelical Lutheran Church in America Division for Ministry Task Force on the study of Ministry, January 23–25, 1992, Synopsis XI" (Chicago: Evangelical Lutheran Church in America, 1992), 1.

86. "Evangelical Lutheran Church in America Division for Ministry Task Force on the Study of Ministry, June 6–8, 1991 and 1991 Churchwide Assembly: Synopsis IX" (Chicago: Evangelical Lutheran Church in America, 1991), 3–4.

87. Nelson, letter to author, 30 December 1991.

88. ELCA, *Study of Ministry*, 30–41.

89. Unidentified and undated interpretative paper prepared by the Task Force for the Study of Ministry, quoted in Busse, "Development of Diaconal Ministry in the ELCA," 102.

90. Busse, "Development of Diaconal Ministry in the ELCA," 102.

91. Division for Ministry Task Force on the Study of Ministry, "Summary of Official Task Force Recommendations, June 1992" (n.p., photocopy); [Evangelical Lutheran Church in America], "Together for Ministry: Final Report and Actions on the Study of Ministry, 1988–1993, Incorporating the Task Force Final Report and Actions of the Board of the Division for Ministry and the 1993 Churchwide Assembly of the Evangelical Lutheran Church in America" (Evangelical Lutheran Church in America, 2000), 11.

92. Busse, "Development of Diaconal Ministry in the ELCA," 102.

93. [Evangelical Lutheran Church in America], "Together for Ministry," 20.

94. Schickel, electronic mail, 12 August 2003.

95. Nelson, telephone conversation, 10 June 1992.

96. [Evangelical Lutheran Church in America], "Together for Ministry (2000)," 10.

97. Division for Ministry Task Force on the Study of Ministry, "Summary of Official Task Force Recommendations, June 1992"; ELCA, Division for Ministry Task Force on the Study of Ministry, "Synopsis XII, June 4, 5, and 6, 1992" (n.p.: photocopy), 2–3.

98. [Evangelical Lutheran Church in America], "Together for Ministry," 8.

99. Bruesehoff, telephone conversation, 10 June 2003.

100. [Evangelical Lutheran Church in America], "Together for Ministry," 10–11.

101. Kerr, *Shape of Ministry*, 39; Nelson, telephone conversation, 10 June 1992.

102. Bruesehoff, telephone conversation, 10 June 2003.

103. Nelson, telephone conversation, 10 June 1992.

104. ELCA Division for Ministry Task Force on the Study of Ministry, "Synopsis XII," 3.

105. ELCA Division for Ministry Task Force on the Study of Ministry, "Synopsis XII," 1.

106. ELCA Division for Ministry Task Force on the Study of Ministry, "Synopsis XII," 2.

107. ELCA Division for Ministry Task Force on the Study of Ministry, "Synopsis XII," 2–4.

108. Carol Schickel, director for Candidacy, Division for Ministry, ELCA, electronic mail to author, 12 August 2003.

109. Busse, "Development of Diaconal Ministry in the ELCA," 102.

110. Bruesehoff, telephone conversation, 10 June 2003.

111. Busse, "Development of Diaconal Ministry in the ELCA," 102–3.

112. Schickel, electronic mail, 12 August 2003.

113. Center for Diaconal Ministry Preparation, 61 N.W. Confederate Ave., Gettysburg, PA 17325-1795.

114. Busse, "Development of Diaconal Ministry in the ELCA," 103.

115. Schickel, electronic mail, 12 August 2003.

116. Schickel, electronic mail, 8 March 2005.

117. [Evangelical Lutheran Church in America Division for Ministry], "Diaconal Ministry Development Timeline" (n.d.).

118. [Evangelical Lutheran Church in America], "Candidacy for Diaconal Ministry," E–5.

119. Carol Schickel, director for Candidacy, Division for Ministry, ELCA , telephone conversation, 16 June 2003.

120. Bruesehoff, telephone conversation, 10 June 2003; Schickel, telephone conversation, 16 June 2003.

121. Edwin Hallenbeck, telephone conversation, 28 July 2003.

122. [Evangelical Lutheran Church in America Division of Ministry], "Diaconal Ministry Development Timeline."

123. Schickel, electronic mail, 8 March 2005.

124. Schickel, electronic mail, 12 August 2003.

125. Bruesehoff, telephone conversation, 10 June 2003.

126. *DiacoNews: Newsletter for Diaconal Ministers*, Division for Ministry, ELCA.

127. Institute for Mission in the U.S.A., "Synodically Authorized Ministries Pilot Project Findings Submitted to Division for Ministry, ELCA" (Trinity Lutheran Seminary, 2199 East Main Street, Columbus, Ohio, April 1998), 2; available from http://www.elca.org; internet; accessed 16 June 2003.

128. Schickel, telephone conversation, 16 June 2003.

129. Ormonde Plater, Episcopal archdeacon, interview, 30 July 2003.

130. Episcopal Church and Evangelical Lutheran Church in America, "The Orderly Exchange of Pastors and Priests under Called to Common Mission: Principles and Guidelines," 1 January 2002.

131. *Constitutions, Bylaws, and Continuing Resolutions*, chapter 10.11.A87.b, in ELCA, *Study of Ministry Study Edition*, 5.

132. Schickel, electronic mail, 12 August 2003 and 8 March 2005.

133. Schickel, "ELCA Rostered Lay Ministries," 1.

134. Schickel, electronic mail, 12 August 2003.

135. Schickel, telephone conversation, 16 June 2003.

136. "Guidelines Related to Synodically Authorized or Licensed Ministries" (ELCA, April 1995), [2]; available from http://www.elca.org; internet; accessed 16 June 2003.

137. Institute for Mission in the U.S.A., "Synodically Authorized Ministries Pilot Project Findings," 2.

138. Institute for Mission in the U.S.A., "Synodically Authorized Ministries Pilot Project Findings," 12.

139. Institute for Mission in the U.S.A., "Synodically Authorized Ministries Pilot Project Findings," 2.

140. Hallenbeck, electronic message, 24 March 2005.

141. Ditewig, telephone conversations, 10 June 2003 and 7 March 2005.

142. Joaquín García, telephone conversation, 17 June 2003.

143. Rubey, electronic mail, 31 March 2005.

144. Schickel, electronic mail, 12 August 2003.

145. Schickel, electronic mail, 8 March 2005.

146. Yocom, "Ministry Studies," 104.

147. [Evangelical Lutheran Church in America], "Together for Ministry," 8.

148. Bouman, "Diaconate," 11. On orthodox and Eastern churches, see Irenaeus Doens, "Der Diakonat in den griechischen und slawischen Kirchen," and Robert Clément, "Der Diakon in den orthodoxen und unierten Kirchen des Ostens in der Gegenwart," in Rahner and Vorgrimler, *Diaconia in Christo*, 136–89.

149. Salaville and Nowack, *Le rôle du diacre*, 48.

150. Stéphanos Charalambidis, "Le service des tables," in Charalambidis, Lagny, Granger, and Schaller, *Le diaconat*, 32–37, 48.

151. Gillet, "Deacons in the Orthodox East," 417–21.

152. Georges Florovsky, "The Problem of Diaconate in the Orthodox Church," in Nolan, *Diaconate Now*, 95–96.

153. Sister Teresa [Joan White], electronic mail, 16 August 2003.

154. Plater, *Many Servants*, 36, 105–6.

155. Sister Teresa [Joan White], electronic mail, 13 August 2003.

156. MacInnis, *Deacon in the Church Today*.

157. Mark Tammen, director of Constitutional Services for the Presbyterian Church, Louisville, Kentucky, telephone conversation with author, 17 June 2003.

158. Theology and Worship Ministry Unit, Presbyterian Church (U.S.A), *Theology and Ministry Unit Proposal of the Task Force on Theology and Practice of Ordination to Office in the Presbyterian Church (U.S.A.)* ([Louisville]: Theology and Worship Mission Unit, Presbyterian Church [U.S.A.], 1992).

159. Theology and Worship Ministry Unit, Presbyterian Church (U.S.A), *Theology and Ministry Unit Proposal*, 102.

160. The Office of Presbytery Deacon is described in Lewis Wilkins, "Renewing the Office of Deacon: Sign of Hope or Waste of Time?" in Rogers and Mullen, *Ordination Past, Present, Future*, 28–30.

161. Task Force on the Theology and Practice of Ordination to Office in the Presbyterian Church (U.S.A.), "A Proposal for Considering the Theology and Practice of Ordination to Office in the Presbyterian Church (U.S.A.)," ([Louisville, 1991], photocopy).

162. Tammen, telephone conversation, 17 June 2003.

163. Alan Elmore, electronic mail to Mark Tammen, director of Constitutional Services for the Presbyterian Church, Louisville, Kentucky, 20 April 1995.

164. Presbyterian Church (U.S.A.), "Note 143," *PCUSA Weekly* (25 May 1995): n.p.

165. Lewis Wilkins, electronic mail to Mark Tammen, 24 April 1995.

166. Olson, "Protestant Deacons in Geneva and Europe," 156–65.

167. Olson, "Des Gallars and the Genevan Connection of the Stranger Churches," 38–47.

168. Theology and Worship Ministry Unit, "Theology and Ministry Unit Proposal of the Task Force on Theology and Practice of Ordination to Office in the Presbyterian Church (U.S.A.)" ([Louisville]: n.p., n.d.), 38.452, 38.453, 38.514.

169. Aurelia Fule, letter to author, 17 July 1992.

170. Presbyterian Church (U.S.A.), "Minister of the Word and Sacrament: Concentration in Educational Ministry, 02-A: . . . 02-A.1. Add 'Teacher' to Pastoral Office—On Amending G-6.0202a."

171. Ken Ross, reference librarian, Presbyterian Historical Society, 425 Lombard Street, Philadelphia PA 19147, 215/627-1852, telephone conversation with author, 11 August 2003.

172. Presbyterian Church (U.S.A.), "Minister of the Word and Sacrament: Concentration in Educational Ministry . . . General Background."

173. Tammen, telephone conversation, 17 June 2003.

174. "Keeping Posted," *Wonder and Wild Honey* (newsletter of the First Unitarian Church of Providence, Rhode Island) (May 1990): 7.

175. van Klinken, *Diakonia, Mutual Helping*, 131.

176. Paul Fries, "Office and Ordination in the Reformed Tradition," in Andrews and Burgess, *Invitation to Action*, 95.

177. For a study of deacons by members of the Christian Reformed Church, see Berghoef and De Koster, *Deacons Handbook*.

178. Louwerse and van Groningen, "Office of Deacon," 226.

179. Louwerse and van Groningen, "Office of Deacon," 229–30.

180. Louwerse and van Groningen, "Office of Deacon," 229–30, 238.

181. The last seven months of 1992 (Louwerse and van Groningen, "Office of Deacon," 231).

182. Louwerse and van Groningen, "Office of Deacon," 233, 236.

183. Louwerse and van Groningen, "Office of Deacon," 235.

184. Thomas, *Deacon in a Changing Church*.

185. Asquith, *Church Officers at Work*, 55–65.

186. Stancil, "Recent Patterns and Contemporary Trends," 24–25.

187. Stancil, "Recent Patterns and Contemporary Trends," 25; Obituary, "Deaconess Mary M. L. Watson, a Longtime Community Activist," *Providence Sunday Journal* (7 September 2003): Local News.

188. Deweese, *Emerging Role of Deacons*, 52, 58–59; Smith, *Deacons' Upholding the Pastor's Arms*.

189. For example, Naylor, *Baptist Deacon*.

190. Stancil, "Recent Patterns and Contemporary Trends," 22.

191. Foshee, *Now that You're a Deacon*.

192. For Lutheran council members called deacons, see Traver, *Deacon and Worship*; and Etan, *Diary of a Deacon*, 7.

193. For Lutheran elders, see Beiderwieden and Fortkamp, *Pastor—Elder Handbook*, 1.

194. "Let Them Serve," *Boston Church of Christ* 13, no. 5 (29 March 1992): 4–7, 12.

195. "Des Diaconies sont instituées dans les paroisses de Saint-Pierre-Fusterie, Saint-Gervais, Pâquis-Prieuré-Sécheron et dans la paroisse suisse-allemande pour exercer la bienfaisance et s'occuper des oeuvres d'assistance et de prévoyance de la paroisse, de concert avec les pasteurs et le Conseil de paroisse." ("The diaconates are instituted in the parishes of Saint Pierre-Fusterie, Saint Gervais, Pâquis-Prieuré-Sécheron and in the Swiss-German parish in order to exercise charity and to be occupied with works of

assistance and prevenance.") (Article 304 of chapter 10, "Diaconies et Comités de Bienfaisance" [n.p.: n.d.]).

196. Albert-Luc de Haller, responsable des ministères et des stages, Église Protestante de Genève, letter to author, 5 July 2001.

197. "Les diacres (hommes et femmes), dont le nombre n'est pas limité, sont nommés par les Conseils de paroisse . . . . Ils doivent être âgés d'au moins 20 ans." ("The deacons [men and women], of whom the number is not limited, are named by the parish councils . . . . They must be at least twenty years old.") (Article 305, chapter 10, "Diaconies et Comités de Bienfaisance").

198. "La nomination d'un diacre est annoncée du haut de la chaire, dans le temple de la paroisse." ("The nomination of a deacon is announced from the pulpit, in the church of the parish.") (Article 306, chapter 10, "Diaconies et Comités de Bienfaisance").

199. "Chaque Diaconie pourvoit à son organisation interne. Elle détermine l'ordre de ses séances, son mode de procédure, et, sous réserve d'entente avec le Conseil de paroisse, les oeuvres auxquelles elle veut s'intéresser." ("Each diaconate tends to its own internal organization. It determines the order of the meetings, the mode of procedure, and, with the reservation of agreement with the parish council, the works in which it will interest itself.") (Article 307, chapter 10, "Diaconies et Comités de Bienfaisance").

200. "Les Diaconies ne peuvent faire ni appel au public, ni collecte sans l'autorisation de leur Conseil de paroisse et du Conseil de l'Eglise." ("The diaconates cannot make an appeal to the public nor a collection without the authorization of their parish council and of the Council of the Church.") (Article 310, chapter 10, "Diaconies et Comités de Bienfaisance").

201. "Le produit des troncs placés dans les temples de Saint-Pierre, de la Fusterie, de Saint-Gervais, des Pâquis et de la paroisse suisse-allemande pour recueillir les dons destinés aux pauvres est versé à un Fonds commun, placé sous le contrôle d'une commission composée de deux délégués de chaque Diaconie et de deux délégués du Consistoire." ("The product of the trunks placed in the churches of Saint Pierre, of the Fusterie, of Saint Gervais, of the Pâquis and of the Swiss-German parish, in order to collect the gifts destined for the poor, is handed over to a common fund, placed under the control of a commission composed of two delegates from each diaconate and of two delegates from the Consistory.") (Article 308, chapter 10, "Diaconies et Comités de Bienfaisance").

202. "La Commission du Fonds commun des Diaconies répartit le produit des troncs, ainsi que tout ou partie des sommes recueillies d'autre part, ou des dons et legs faits aux Diaconies sans autre indication . . ." ("The Commission of the Common Funds of the Diaconates divides the product of the trunks, and thus also all or part of the sums gathered elsewhere, or of the gifts and legacies made to the diaconates without other designation.") (Article 309, chapter 10, "Diaconies et Comités de Bienfaisance").

203. de Haller, letter to author, 5 July 2001.

204. Département Romand des Ministères Diaconaux, *Diacre, signe du Christ-serviteur aujourd'hui* (n.p.: Atelier Grand, n.d.), parts 1–6; *Le ministère des diacres envoyés en milieu professionnel ou diacres en mission*, a report adopted by the council of the *Département romand des ministères diaconaux*, May 26, 1982, and by the assembly of the *Département romand des ministères diaconaux*, June 26, 1982 (n.p.: n.d.), 1–4; "Programme de formation au ministère diaconal sur 3 ans" (Département romand des ministères diaconaux, 1984, photocopy), 1–2.

205. [Département Romand des Ministères Diaconaux], "Cursus de la formation diaconale" (n.p.: photocopy, 1996), p. 3/12.

206. [Département Romand des Ministères Diaconaux], "Cursus de la formation diaconale," p. 4/8.

207. [Département Romand des Ministères Diaconaux], "Cursus de la formation diaconale," p. 7/8.

208. "En réintroduisant le ministère diaconal, nos Églises romandes se dont donné une possibilité nouvelle d'un ministère orienté vers le monde" (Section four of Département Romand des Ministères Diaconaux, "La nature du ministère du diacre," a page subordinate to the page, "Département Romand des Ministères Diaconaux," available from www.protestant.ch/direct/diacre/histoire).

209. "Que fait un diacre?" Département romand des ministères diaconaux, *Diacre*, parts 2–4, 6; Le ministère des diacres, 1–4.

210. "Révision de la Constitution—Titre VI, textes adoptés en 3éme débat le 11 mars 1999."

211. For France, see Ziegert, *Der neue Diakonat.*

212. Dermaux, "Impression," 33.

213. Bridel, "La rencontre des lecteurs," 3.

214. *Baptism, Eucharist and Ministry, 1982–1990*, 7–8.

215. Brodd, "Escalating Phenomenon," 17.

216. *Baptism, Eucharist and Ministry, 1982–1990*, 5.

217. *Baptism, Eucharist and Ministry, 1982–1990*, 8–10, 34; Thurian, *Churches Respond to BEM.*

218. Brodd, "Escalating Phenomenon," 18.

219. *Baptism, Eucharist and Ministry*, 24–25.

220. *Baptism, Eucharist and Ministry*, 27.

221. *Baptism, Eucharist and Ministry*, 31.

222. *Baptism, Eucharist and Ministry, 1982–1990*, 83, 125–26; McKee, *Diakonia.* 99.

223. *Baptism, Eucharist and Ministry*, 27.

224. *Baptism, Eucharist and Ministry*, 25.

225. *Baptism, Eucharist and Ministry*, 27; *Baptism, Eucharist and Ministry, 1982–1990*, 83.

226. *Baptism, Eucharist and Ministry*, 27.

227. Moede, *COCU Consensus*, 47–48, 52–54.

228. Brodd, "Escalating Phenomenon," 30.

229. Moede, *COCU Consensus*, v, vii, 1–2.

230. On the issue of ministry and *The COCU Consensus*, see "Mutual Recognition and Reconciliation of Ordained Ministry," in *Churches in Covenant Communion, the Church of Christ Uniting.* Approved and recommended to the churches by the Seventeenth Plenary of the Consultation on Church Union, December 9, 1988 (n.p.: Consultation on Church Union, 1989), 20–25.

231. Moede, *COCU Consensus*, v, 55.

232. Schickel, electronic mail, 8 March 2005.

233. Norgren and Rusch, "Toward Full Communion" and "Concordat of Agreement," 22; Andrews and Burgess, *Invitation to Action*, 2, 27; *Baptists and Lutherans in Conversation*, 6; for a discussion of the features of bilateral ecumenical dialogues, see Meyer and Vischer, *Growth in Agreement*, 3–4.

234. "Leuenberg Agreement," in Joint Commission of the Lutheran World Federation and World Alliance of Reformed Churches, *Toward Church Fellowship.*

235. Joint Commission of the Lutheran World Federation and World Alliance of Reformed Churches, *Toward Church Fellowship*, 14.

236. "Leuenberg Agreement," in Joint Commission of the Lutheran World Federation and World Alliance of Reformed Churches, *Toward Church Fellowship*, 41, 47–48.

237. Brodd, "Escalating Phenomenon," 21–22.

238. "Joint Statement on Ministry," in Andrews and Burgess, *Invitation to Action*, 29, 31.

239. Andrews and Burgess, *Invitation to Action*, 111–12.

240. Warren Quanbeck, "Church and Ministry," in Andrews and Burgess, *Invitation to Action*, 104–5. Quanbeck prepared his essay for a consultation held September 20–21, 1971, in Chicago by the Division of Theological Studies of the Lutheran Council in the U.S.A.

241. Andrews and Burgess, *Invitation to Action*, 8.

242. Lutheran-Reformed Committee for Theological Conversations, "A Common Calling."

243. " 'Full Communion' Proposed for 4 Denominations," *The News of the Presbyterian Church (U.S.A.)* (April 1992): 5; Lewis, "Full Communion Proposed for Four Denominations," 3–4.

244. "The Orderly Exchange of Ministers of Word and Sacrament Policy Paper of the Reformed Church in America, November 4, 1999," in "The Orderly Exchange of Ordained Ministers of Word and Sacrament: Principles, Policies, and Procedures," (January 2000), 17; available from http://www.elca.org/ea/Relationships/reformed/OrderlyExchange.html; accessed 16 June 2003.

245. "Policy and Procedures Related to the Availability of Ordained Ministers between the Evangelical Lutheran Church in America and Church Bodies with which a Relationship of Full Communion Has Been Established," in "The Orderly Exchange of Ordained Ministers of Word and Sacrament," 4.

246. "Orderly Exchange of Ordained Ministers of Word and Sacrament," 1.

247. Nafzger, telephone conversation, 1 August 2003.

248. "Concordat of Agreement between the Episcopal Church and the Evangelical Lutheran Church in America," in Norgren and Rusch, *Toward Full Communion*, 99–102, 104.

249. Nafzger, telephone conversation, 1 August 2003.

250. "Statement of Lutheran Church—Missouri Synod Participants," in Norgren and Rusch, *Toward Full Communion*, 115–16, 118.

251. Robert Goeser and Paul Berge, "The Dissenting Report of the Lutheran-Episcopal Dialogue, Series III," in Norgren and Rusch, *Toward Full Communion*, 111–12.

252. Nichol, "Minority Report," 91.

253. Nichol, "Minority Report," 91–92.

254. Nichol, "Minority Report," 91–97.

255. Kittelson, "Enough Is Enough!" 249–70; Madson, "Lutheran-Episcopal Concordat and Porvoo," 21–33.

256. Schickel, electronic mail, 12 August 2003.

257. Episcopal Church and ELCA, "The Orderly Exchange of Pastors and Priests under Called to Common Mission: Principles and Guidelines" (January 1, 2001), 2.

258. Nafzger, telephone conversation, 1 August 2003.

259. Episcopal Church and ELCA, "Orderly Exchange of Pastors and Priests," 2, 14.

260. Episcopal Church and ELCA, "Orderly Exchange of Pastors and Priests," 14.

261. Episcopal Church and ELCA, "Orderly Exchange of Pastors and Priests," 5–6.

262. Plater, interview, 30 July 2003.

263. Episcopal Church and ELCA, "Orderly Exchange of Pastors and Priests," 8–11, 17–21.

264. Brodd, "Escalating Phenomenon," 19.

265. Episcopal Church and ELCA, "Orderly Exchange of Pastors and Priests," 8.

266. Schickel, electronic mail, 12 August 2003.
267. Plater, interview, 30 July 2003.
268. Cady and Webber, *Lutherans and Episcopalians Together*.
269. *The Diaconate as Ecumenical Opportunity: The Hanover Report of the Anglican-Lutheran International Commission* (London: Anglican Communion Publications, published for the Anglican Consultative Council and the Lutheran World Federation, 1996).
270. Brodd, "Escalating Phenomenon," 25.
271. Collins, *Diakonia*, 13–14.
272. The signatory churches were the Church of England, Church of Ireland, Scottish Episcopal Church, Church of Wales, Evangelical-Lutheran Church of Finland, Evangelical-Lutheran Church of Iceland, Church of Norway, Church of Sweden, Estonian Evangelical-Lutheran Church, and the Evangelical-Lutheran Church of Lithuania. See Borgegård and Hall, *Ministry of the Deacon*, 1:5.
273. Brodd, "Escalating Phenomenon." 45.
274. *Together in Mission and Ministry. The Porvoo Common Statement with Essays on Church and Ministry in Northern Europe.* Conversations between the British and Irish Anglican Churches and the Nordic and Baltic Lutheran Churches (London: Church House Publications, 1993), as quoted in Brodd, "Escalating Phenomenon," 26.
275. Gunnel Borgegård, preface to *Ministry of the Deacon*, 1:6–7.
276. Borgegård and Hall, *Ministry of the Deacon*, vol. 1; and Borgegård, Fanuelsen, and Hall, *Ministry of the Deacon*, vol. 2.
277. *The Church Community of Grace.* Final Report of the Joint Commission between the Lutheran World Federation and the World Methodist Council 1979–1984, General Lake Junaluska, NC, 1984, quoted in Brodd, "Escalating Phenomenon," 34.
278. Norgren and Rusch, *"Toward Full Communion,"* 23.
279. Geoffrey Wainwright, "Reconciliation in Ministry," in Thurian, *Ecumenical Perspectives on Baptism, Eucharist and Ministry*, 129–30.
280. "National Diaconate Dialogue Group" (n.p., n.d., photocopy); Plater, *Many Servants*, 107.
281. Raiser, "Towards a New Definition of the Profile of the Laity," 1.
282. K. Slack, *Hope in the Desert: The Churches' United Response to Human Need, 1944–1984* (Geneva: 1986), 134, quoted in Collins, *Diakonia*, 254.
283. Csipai, *Diakonie als Ausdruck christlichen Glaubens in der modernen Welt*; Ulrich et al., *Diakonie in den Spannungsfeldern der Gegenwart*; Diakonisches Werk Freiburg, *Diakonie*; and Evangelische Sozialstation, Freiburg i. Br., *Pflege ist Vertrauenssache*.
284. "Chacun parle tellement de servir, baptisant son entreprise administrative, partisane ou philanthropique du mot devenu banal . . ." (Bridel, *Aux seuils de l'espérance*, 62).
285. Collins, *Diakonia*, 335–37.

BIBLIOGRAPHY

Abbott, Walter, ed. *The Documents of Vatican II in a New and Definitive Translation with Commentaries and Notes by Catholic, Protestant and Orthodox Authorities.* 1966. Reprint, New York: Crossroad, 1989.

"About the International Diaconate Centre." Available at http://www.kirchen.de/drs/idz/en/idz/ (accessed June 11, 2003).

Aland, Kurt. *A History of Christianity.* Translated by James L. Schaaf. 2 vols. Philadelphia: Fortress, 1985–86. Originally published as *Geschichte der Christenheit.* 2 vols. Gütersloh: Gütersloher Gerd Mohn, 1982.

Alexander, Gross, James Scouller, R. V. Foster, and T. C. Johnson. *A History of the Methodist Church, South, the United Presbyterian Church, the Cumberland Presbyterian Church, and the Presbyterian Church, South, in the United States.* Pages 143–255. The American Church History Series 11. New York: Christian Literature Co., 1894.

Alves, Abel Athouguia. "The Christian Social Organism and Social Welfare: The Case of Vives, Calvin and Loyola." *Sixteenth Century Journal* 20, no. 1 (1989): 3–21.

Anderson, Margaret. "The Distaff Side of Pastoral Care: The Deaconess as Chaplain." *Issues in Christian Education* 39, no. 1 (Spring 2005): 4.

Andrews, James, and Joseph Burgess. *An Invitation to Action, a Study of Ministry, Sacraments, and Recognition.* The Lutheran Reformed Dialogue Series III, 1981–1983. Philadelphia: Fortress, 1984.

"The Anglican Communion: Statistics." *Distinctive Diaconate* 44 (April 1999): 3–4.

The Ante-Nicene Fathers. Vols. 4–5, 7. Edinburgh: Christian Literature Publishing, 1885–86. Reprint, Grand Rapids: Eerdmans; New York: Charles Scribner's Sons, 1903, 1905.

Aquinas, Thomas. *Summa Theologiae.* Vol. 57, *Baptism and Confirmation* (3a.66–72). Edited and translated by James Cunningham. New York: Blackfriars with McGraw-Hill, 1975.

Archives d'État de Genève. *Archives hospitalières.* Ka 6, "Livre de Memoire commencé le premier mars 1680 et finy le 30e decembre 1691."

———. *Archives hospitalières.* Kg 15, July 1554–July 1555.

———. *Registres du Conseil.* Vols 39–40, 1515–1546.

Armstrong, Regis, and Ignatius Brady, trans. *Francis and Clare: The Complete Works.* New York: Paulist Press, 1982.

Arndt, William F., and F. Wilbur Gingrich. *A Greek-English Lexicon of the New Testament and Other Early Christian Literature: A Translation and Adaptation of Walter Bauer's "Griechisch-Deutsches Wörterbuch zu den Schriften des Neuen Testaments und der übrigen urchristlichen Literatur."* 4th rev. ed. Chicago: University of Chicago Press, 1957.

"Articles of Incorporation of the Lutheran Deaconess Association, Inc., as Amended May, 1975 and November, 1979." Mimeograph.

Asquith, Glenn. *Church Officers at Work.* Rev. ed. Valley Forge: Judson, 1977.

Aubert, Marie-Josèphe. *Des femmes diacres: Un nouveau chemin pour l'Église.* Le point théologique 47. Paris: Beauchesne, 1986.

Bachmann, E. Theodore. *The Story of the Philadelphia Deaconess Motherhouse, 1884–1959.* Gladwyne, Penn.: n.p., 1960.

———, and Mercia Bachmann. *Lutheran Churches in the World: A Handbook.* Minneapolis: Augsburg, 1989.

Baker, J. Wayne. *Heinrich Bullinger and the Covenant: The Other Reformed Tradition.* Athens: Ohio University Press, 1980.

Baldovin, John. *The Urban Character of Christian Worship: The Origins, Development, and Meaning of Stational Liturgy.* Orientalia Christiana Analecta 228. Rome: Pontificium Institutum Studiorum Orientalium, 1987.

Baldwin, Joanna. "The Deaconess Community of St. Andrew." *Journal of Ecclesiastical History* 12, no. 2 (October 1961): 215–30.

Bancroft, Jane. *Deaconesses in Europe and Their Lessons for America.* New York: Hunt & Eaton, 1890.

Bangerter, Otto. *Frauen im Aufbruch: Die Geschichte einer Frauenbewegung in der Alten Kirche, ein Beitrag zur Frauenfrage.* Neukirchen-Vluyn: Neukirchener, 1971.

Baptism, Eucharist and Ministry. Faith and Order Paper, no. 111. Geneva: World Council of Churches, 1982.

Baptism, Eucharist and Ministry, 1982–1990: Report on the Process and Responses. Faith and Order Paper, no. 149. Geneva: WCC Publications, 1990.

Baptists and Lutherans in Conversation, a Message to Our Churches, Report of the Joint Commission of the Baptist World Alliance and the Lutheran World Federation. Gingins, Switzerland: Imprimerie La Colombière, 1990.

Barnett, James M. *The Diaconate: A Full and Equal Order; A Comprehensive and Critical Study of the Origin, Development, and Decline of the Diaconate in the Context of the Church's Total Ministry and a Proposal for Renewal.* New York: Seabury, 1981.

———. *The Diaconate: A Full and Equal Order; A Comprehensive and Critical Study of the Origin, Development, and Decline of the Diaconate in the Context of the Church's Total Ministry and the Renewal of the Diaconate Today with Reflections for the Twenty-First Century.* Rev. ed. Valley Forge: Trinity Press International, 1995.

Bash, Anthony. "Deacons and Diaconal Minstry." *Theology* 102, no. 805 (January/February 1999): 36–41.

Bassler, Jouette M. "The Widows' Tale: A Fresh Look at 1 Tim 5:3–16." *Journal of Biblical Literature* 103 (1984): 36–40.

Beiderwieden, George, and Gary Fortkamp. *Pastor—Elder Handbook*. Springfield, Ill.: The Lutheran Church—Missouri Synod Central Illinois District, 1985.

Bellamy, V. Nelle. "Participation of Women in the Public Life of the Church from Lambeth Conference 1867–1978." *Historical Magazine of the Protestant Episcopal Church* 51, no. 1 (1982): 81–98.

Bergendoff, Conrad. *The Church of the Lutheran Reformation: A Historical Survey of Lutheranism*. St. Louis: Concordia, 1967.

Berghoef, Gerard, and Lester De Koster. *The Deacons Handbook, a Manual of Stewardship*. Grand Rapids: Christian's Library Press, 1980.

Bernoulli, W. *Das Diakonenamt bei Calvin*. Greisensee: Verlag des Schwiz. Ref. Diakonenhauses, 1949.

Beyreuther, Erich. *Geschichte der Diakonie und Inneren Mission in der Neuzeit*. Berlin: Christlicher Zeitschriftenverlag, 1983.

Bielby, Sara, and Arthur Just Jr. "Serving Christ by Serving Our Neighbor: Theological and Historical Perspectives on Lutheran Deaconesses." *Issues in Christian Education* 39, no. 1 (Spring 2005): 7–13.

Biéler, André. *Gottes Gebot und der Hunger der Welt—Calvin, Prophet des industriellen Zeitalters: Grundlage und Methode der Sozialethik Calvins*. Translated by A. Döbeli. Zürich: EVA-Verlag, 1966.

Bingham, Joseph. *The Antiquities of the Ancient Church*. Vol. 1. London: Reeves & Turner, 1878.

Bishops' Committee on the Permanent Diaconate. *Diaconal Reader: Selected Articles from the* Diaconal Quarterly. Washington, D.C.: National Conference of Catholic Bishops, 1985.

———. *Permanent Deacons in the United States: Guidelines on Their Formation and Ministry, 1984 Revision*. Washington, D.C.: National Conference of Catholic Bishops, 1985.

Bligh, John. "Deacons in the Latin West since the Fourth Century." *Theology* 53 (November 1958): 421–29.

Bloch, Herbert. *The Atina Dossier of Peter the Deacon of Monte Cassino: A Hagiographical Romance of the Twelfth Century*. Studi e Testi 346. The Vatican: Vatican Press, 1998.

Bodensieck, Julius, ed. *The Encyclopedia of the Lutheran Church*. 3 vols. Minneapolis: Augsburg, 1965.

The Book of Discipline of the United Methodist Church 2000. Nashville: United Methodist Publishing House, 2000.

Borgegård, Gunnel, and Christine Hall, eds. *The Ministry of the Deacon*. Vol. 1: *Anglican-Lutheran Perspectives*. Uppsala: Fyris Tryck, 1999.

———, Olav Fanuelsen, and Christine Hall, eds. *The Ministry of the Deacon*. Vol. 2: *Ecclesiological Explorations*. Uppsala: Fyris Tryck, 2000.

Bouman, Stephen. "The Diaconate: Consecrated Displaced Persons." *Lutheran Forum* 18, no. 1 (Lent 1984): 10–13.

Bovon, François, Ann Brock, and Christopher Matthews, eds. *The Apocryphal Acts of the Apostles*. Cambridge: Harvard University Press, 1999.

Bouwsma, William. *John Calvin: A Sixteenth Century Portrait*. New York: Oxford University Press, 1988.

Boyer, Marjorie. "The Bridgebuilding Brotherhoods." *Speculum* 39 (1964): 635–50.

Bradshaw, Paul. *Liturgical Presidency in the Early Church*. Bramcote: Grove Books, 1983.

Brandt, Wilfried. *Für eine bekennende Diakonie: Beiträge zu einem evangelischen Verständnis des Diakonats*. Neukirchen-Vluyn: Aussaat/Neukirchener, 2001.

Bridel, Claude. *Aux seuils de l'espérance: Le diaconat en notre temps*. Paris: Delachaux et Niestlé Éditeurs, 1971.

———. "La rencontre des lecteurs." *Communion et Diaconie*, no. 13 (June 1982): 3.

Brodd, Sven-Erik. "The Deacon in the Church of Sweden." In *The Ministry of the Deacon*. Vol. 1: *Anglican-Lutheran Perspectives*. Edited by Gunnel Borgegård and Christine Hall. Uppsala, Sweden: Nordic Ecumenical Council, 1999.

———. "An Escalating Phenomenon: The Diaconate from an Ecumenical Perspective." In *The Ministry of the Deacon*. Vol. 1: *Anglican-Lutheran Perspectives*. Edited by Gunnel Borgegård and Christine Hall. Uppsala, Sweden: Nordic Ecumenical Council, 1999.

Brown, Peter. *The Body and Society: Men, Women, and Sexual Renunciation in Early Christianity*. New York: Columbia University Press, 1988.

Brown, Raymond E. *Priest and Bishop: Biblical Reflections*. New York: Paulist Press, 1970.

Brucker, Gene. "Bureaucracy and Social Welfare in the Renaissance: A Florentine Case Study." *Journal of Modern History* 55 (March 1983): 1–21.

Burgess-Cassler, Karen, ed. *Celebrating Servants: God's People at Work; A Devotional Guide for Congregation Committees and Groups*. Valparaiso, Ind.: Lutheran Deaconess Association, 1999.

Burn, John. *Livre des anglois à Genève*. London: n. p., 1831.

Burtchaell, James Tunstead. *From Synagogue to Church: Public Services and Offices in the Earliest Christian Communities*. Cambridge: Cambridge University Press, 1992.

Busse, Madelyn Herman. "The Development of Diaconal Ministry in the ELCA." Pages 89–108 in *From Word and Sacrament: Renewed Vision for Diaconal Ministry*. Edited by Duane H. Larson. Chicago: Evangelical Lutheran Church in America, 1999.

Cady, G. Scott, and Christopher L. Webber. *Lutherans and Episcopalians Together: A Guide to Understanding*. Boston: Cowley Publications, 2001.

Calvin, John. *Institutes of the Christian Religion*. Edited by John T. McNeill. Translated by Ford Lewis Battles. 2 vols. Philadelphia: Westminster, 1960.

———. *Institution of the Christian Religion Embracing Almost the Whole Sum of Piety, and Whatever Is Necessary to Know the Doctrine of Salvation: A Work Most Worthy to Be Read by All Persons Zealous for Piety, and Recently Published*. Translated by Ford Lewis Battles. Atlanta: John Knox, 1975.

Canon Law Society of Great Britain and Ireland, trans. *The Code of Canon Law in English Translation*. London: Collins Liturgical Publications, 1983.

The Catalogue 2002–2003: The Episcopal School for Deacons. Rev. ed. Berkeley: n.p., 2002.

Center for Diaconal Ministry. *Lutheran Deaconess Association Connections*. Vol. 8. Valparaiso, Ind.: n.d.

Chadwick, Henry. *The Early Church*. New York: Penguin, 1967.

Chandler, Mary. *The Pastoral Associate and the Lay Pastor*. Collegeville, Minn.: Liturgical Press, 1986.

Charalambidis, Stéphanos, Gustave Lagny, Émile Granger, and René Schaller. *Le diaconat*. Églises en dialogue 11. France: Maison Mame, 1969.

Chastel, Stephen. *The Charity of the Primitive Churches: Historical Studies upon the Influence of Christian Charity during the First Centuries of Our Era, with Some Considerations Touching Its Bearings upon Modern Society*. Translated by G. A. Matile. Philadelphia: J. B. Lippincott, 1857.

Chrisman, Miriam. *Strasbourg and the Reform: A Study in the Process of Change*. New Haven: Yale University Press, 1967.

Church Army USA. *The Heart of God for the Broken*. N.p., n.d.

"Church of England. July General Synod. The Women in the Episcopate-Working Party." *Distinctive News of Women in Ministry*, no. 18 (September 2002): 1–2.

"Church of England. July General Synod. The Working Party on Women in the Episcopate." *Distinctive Diaconate News*, no. 51 (September 2002): 1.

Churches in Covenant Communion, the Church of Christ Uniting. Approved and recommended to the churches by the Seventeenth Plenary of the Consultation on Church Union, December 9, 1988. Princeton, N.J.: Consultation on Church Union, 1989.

Clark, Elizabeth. *Ascetic Piety and Women's Faith: Essays in Late Ancient Christianity*. Studies in Women and Religion 20. Lewiston: Edwin Mellen Press, 1986.

———. *Jerome, Chrysostom, and Friends: Essays and Translations*. New York: Edwin Mellen Press, 1979.

———. *Women in the Early Church*. Message of the Fathers of the Church 13. Wilmington, Del.: Michael Glazier, 1983.

Clasen, Claus-Peter. *Anabaptism: A Social History, 1525–1618, Switzerland, Austria, Moravia, South and Central Germany*. Ithaca: Cornell University Press, 1972.

Coleman, K. Virginia, of Diakonia of the Americas and the Caribbean. Letter to Sister Frieda Gatzke, directing deaconess, Deaconess Community, Evangelical Lutheran Church in America. 11 September 1989. Photocopy.

Collins, John N. *Deacons and the Church: Making Connections between Old and New*. Harrisburg, Penn.: Morehouse, 2002.

———. *Diakonia: Re-interpreting the Ancient Sources*. New York: Oxford University Press, 1990.

Collinson, Patrick. *The Elizabethan Puritan Movement*. Berkeley: University of California Press, 1967.

Commission for the Study of Ministry. "Report of the Commission for the Study of Ministry, 1992 General Conference: The United Methodist Church." N.p., n.d. Photocopy.

Commission on Theology and Church Relations of The Lutheran Church—Missouri Synod. *Theology and Practice of "The Divine Call": A Report of the Commission on Theology and Church Relations of The Lutheran Church—Missouri Synod.* St. Louis: The Lutheran Church—Missouri Synod, 2003.

Concordia College, River Forest, Ill. "Concordia Deaconesses Program." Chicago: Concordia College, n.d.

Concordia Deaconess Conference. "Constitution." N.p. [prior to March 15, 1989]. Mimeograph.

Concordia Deaconess Conference and Concordia Deaconess Program, The Lutheran Church—Missouri Synod. "Our Clara . . . ." In "3D: A Decade of Deaconess Dedication, 1980–1990, Our History . . . ." N.p., n.d. Photocopy

Concordia Deaconess Program, Concordia College, River Forest, Ill. "Curriculum." Chicago: Concordia College, n.d. Photocopy.

Concordia Seminary, St. Louis. *Academic Catalog 2002–2003, Concordia Seminary, St. Louis, Missouri.* St. Louis: Concordia Seminary, n.d.

———. "Deaconess Addendum to the 2002–2003 Academic Catalog." St. Louis: Concordia Seminary, n.d.

———. *Graduate School, Concordia Seminary, St. Louis: Addressing Contemporary Issues with the Historic Christian Faith.* St. Louis: Concordia Seminary, n.d.

Concordia University, River Forest, Ill. "Deaconess Field Work Manual [1991–1992]." Chicago: Concordia University, 1991. Photocopy.

Concordia University Wisconsin. *Lutheran Lay Ministry: A Theological Education by Extension Program.* Mequon, Wisc.: Concordia University Wisconsin, n.d.

———. *Lutheran Lay Ministry: Lay Ministry Specialist Degree Program.* Mequon, Wisc.: Concordia University Wisconsin, n.d.

Congar, Yves. *Lay People in the Church: A Study for a Theology of the Laity.* Translated by Donald Attwater. Westminster, Md.: Newman Press, 1957.

Connelly, R. Hugh. *Didascalia Apostolorum: The Syriac Version Translated and Accompanied by the Verona Latin Fragments.* Oxford: Clarendon, 1929.

Consejo Episcopal Latinoamericano (CELAM). *El Diaconado Permanente en America Latina.* Documentos CELAM 8. Bogotá, Columbia: Departamento de Vocaciones, 1968.

Cooke, Bernard. *Ministry to Word and Sacraments: History and Theology.* Philadelphia: Fortress, 1976.

———, and Gary Macy, eds. *A History of Women and Ordination.* Vol. 1: *The Ordination of Women in a Medieval Context.* Lanham, Md.: Scarecrow Press, 2002.

Cooper, James, and Arthur Maclean, trans. *The Testament of Our Lord: Translated into English from the Syriac with Introduction and Notes.* Edinburgh: T&T Clark, 1902.

Corwin, E. T., J. H. Dubbs, and J. T. Hamilton. *A History of the Reformed Church, Dutch, the Reformed Church, German, and the Moravian Church in the United*

States. The American Church History Series 8. New York: Christian Literature Co., 1895.

Coudal, Mary Beth. "Deaconesses Bring Healing." *Response* (February 2003): 30–32.

Cragg, Gerald R. *The Church in the Age of Reason, 1648–1789*. Rev. ed. 1970. Reprint, New York: Penguin Books, 1981.

Craighill, Peyton G., ed. *Diaconal Ministry, Past, Present, and Future: Essays from the Philadelphia Symposium, 1992*. Providence: North American Association for the Diaconate, 1994.

Crain, Margaret Ann, and Jack L. Seymour. *A Deacon's Heart: The New Methodist Diaconate*. Nashville: Abingdon, 2001.

Csipai, Arno. *Diakonie als Ausdruck christlichen Glaubens in der modernen Welt*. Handbücherei für Gemeindearbeit 49. Gütersloh: Gütersloher Gerd Mohn, 1971.

Daily Christian Advocate: The General Conference of the United Methodist Church 4, no. 12 (May 16, 1992).

Dautzenberg, Gerhard, Helmut Merklein, and Karlheinz Müller, eds. *Die Frau im Urchristentum*. Basel: Editiones Herder, 1983.

Davies, J. G. "Deacons, Deaconesses and the Minor Orders in the Patristic Period." *Journal of Ecclesiastical History* 14 (April 1963): 1–15.

Davies, Steven L. *The Revolt of the Widows: The Social World of the Apocryphal Acts*. Carbondale, Ill.: Southern Illinois University Press, 1980.

Davis, Natalie. "Poor Relief, Humanism, and Heresy." Pages 17–64 in *Society and Culture in Early Modern France: Eight Essays by Natalie Zemon Davis*. Stanford: Stanford University Press, 1975.

Davis, Stephen J. *The Cult of Saint Thecla: A Tradition of Women's Piety in Late Antiquity*. Oxford: Oxford University Press, 2001.

Day, E. Hermitage. *The Subdiaconate: A Historical Note*. "Theology" Occasional Papers 2. London: SPCK, 1935.

De Celano, Thomas. *Vita Prima S. Francisci Assisiensis et Eiusdem Legenda ad Usum Chori*. Florence: Collegii S. Bonaventurae Ad Claras Aquas (Quaracchi), 1926.

The Deaconess: A Service of Women in the World Today. World Council of Churches Studies 4. Geneva: World Council of Churches, 1966.

Deaconess Beacon. [Newsletter of the Concordia Deaconess Program, Concordia University, River Forest, Illinois].

"The Deaconess Community of the Evangelical Lutheran Church in America." Available at http://www.deaconess-elca.org/ministries.html (accessed 9 June 2003).

———. "Auxiliary of the Deaconess Community." Deaconess Community of the Evangelical Lutheran Church in America, 1988.

———. "Bylaws of the Deaconess Community of the Evangelical Lutheran Church in America." N.d. Photocopy.

———. "Candidacy for the Deaconess Community of the ELCA." January 2003.

———. *The Deaconess*. Vols. 19–20. 1990–1991.

———. *The Deaconess Community of the Evangelical Lutheran Church in America*. [Chicago]: Deaconess Community of the Evangelical Lutheran Church in America, 1989.

————. "Invest One Year . . . Be a Diaconal Associate." [Chicago]: Deaconess Community of the Evangelical Lutheran Church in America, 1988.

————. Materials presented by the Deaconess Community to the Task Force on Ministry of the Evangelical Lutheran Church in America, cover letter, Sister Frieda Gatzke. 3 October 1989. Photocopy.

————. "Place Apart for Personal Retreat." Deaconess Community of the Evangelical Lutheran Church in America, 1989.

"The Deaconess Community of the Evangelical Lutheran Church in America, News: Deaconess Community Heaps Blessings on LSS Programs." Available at http://www.deaconess-elca.org/news.asp (accessed 9 June 2003).

"The Deaconess Community of the Evangelical Lutheran Church in America, Welcome." Available at http://www.deaconess-elca.org/welcome.html (accessed 9 June 2003).

"Deaconess Internship." Booklet. Chicago: Concordia College, n.d. Photocopy.

"Deaconess, M.D." *The LDA Today: A Newsletter of the Lutheran Deaconess Association* 8, no. 2 (Fall 2002): 1.

"Deaconess Mary M. L. Watson, a Longtime Community Activist." Obituaries. *Providence Sunday Journal* (7 September 2003).

The Deaconess Program, Concordia College. *The Deaconess Clara Strehlow Endowment Fund.* Chicago: Concordia College. N.d.

————. "Deaconess . . . Serving the Lord and His People." N.d. Photocopy.

The Deaconess Program, Concordia University. "Deaconess Program Fact Sheet." N.d. Photocopy.

————. "Non-Traditional Programs Fact Sheet." N.d. Photocopy.

————. "Undergraduate Program Fact Sheet Curriculum." N.d. Photocopy.

Deaconesses: A Movement for Laywomen Who Feel Called to Serve God Full-Time through the United Methodist Church. [New York]: General Board of Global Ministries, the United Methodist Church, n.d.

Deanesly, M. "The Archdeacons of Canterbury under Archbishop Ceolnoth (833–870)." *English Historical Review* 165 (January 1927): 1–11.

Delitzsch, Franz. *Vier Bücher von der Kirche: Seitenstück zu Löhes drei Büchern von der Kirche.* Dresden: Justus Naumann, 1847.

[Département Romand des Ministères Diaconaux]. "Cursus de la formation diaconale." 1996. Photocopy.

Département Romand des Ministères Diaconaux. *Diacre, signe du Christ-serviteur aujourd'hui.* Atelier Grand, n.d.

————. "La nature du ministère du diacre." A page subordinate to the page, "Département Romand des Ministères Diaconaux." Available at www.protestant.ch/direct/diacre/histoire.

Der Direction der Diakonissenanstalt, ed. *Was, wann, wie, wer, wo, warum: Fragen und Antworten und noch zu beantwortende Frage der Diakonissenanstalt Kaiserswerth.* Essen: Essener Druckerei Gemeinwohl, n.d.

Der Leitung der Diakonissenanstalt, eds. *Jahresbericht über die Diakonissenanstalt Kaiserswerth.* Düsseldorf: Joh. Brendow & Sohn, 1958.

"Der Prophet ohne Gemeinde." In *Gesegnetes Werk*. Berlin: Wichern-Verlag Herbert Renner, 1948.

Dermaux, Francis. "Impression—autour et alentour." *Communion et Diaconie: Revue d'information et de recherche sur le service Chrétien* 13 (June 1982): 33.

Deweese, Charles. "Deaconesses in Baptist History: A Preliminary Study." *Baptist History and Heritage* 12 (January 1977): 52–55.

———. *The Emerging Role of Deacons*. Nashville: Broadmann, 1979.

DiacoNews: Newsletter for Diaconal Ministers. Division for Ministry, Evangelical Lutheran Church in America.

The Diaconate as Ecumenical Opportunity: The Hanover Report of the Anglican-Lutheran International Commission. London: Anglican Communion Publications, published for the Anglican Consultative Council and the Lutheran World Federation, 1996.

Diaconato no Brasil: Teologia e orientações pastorais. São Paulo: Edições Paulinas, 1988.

"Diak-Aid." *Diakonia News* 58 (July 1990): 314.

Diakoneo: Serving Deacons and All Servant Ministers in North America. Published by the North American Association for the Diaconate, Inc., an Anglican Organization Serving Deacons and Diaconal Ministers in North America.

"*Diakoneo* Wins Polly Bond Award." *Diakoneo* 24, no. 2 (Eastertide 2002): 17.

"Diakonia and the World Council of Churches: 1948–1973." *Diakonia News* 78 (July 1990): 21–22.

"The Diakonia Calendar, 2002." *Diakonia News* 88 (November 2001): [46].

"Diakonia of the Americas and the Caribbean." *Diakonia News* 88 (November 2001): 30–33.

Diakonia News: Newsletter of Foundation Diakonia World Federation of Diaconal Associations and Diaconal Communities.

Diakonia News: Newsletter of the World Federation of Diaconal Associations and Sisterhoods.

"Diakonia's New President." *Diakonia News* 88 (November 2001): 3–5.

Diakonisches Werk Freiburg. *Diakonie, Wir sind für Sie da! Allgemeine Sozialberatung, Bezirkssozialarbeit*. Freiburg: Diakonisches Werk Freiburg, n.d.

Dickens, A. G. *The Counter Reformation*. Norwich: Harcourt, Brace, & World, 1969.

Directory of Deacons, Episcopal Church, Anglican Church of Canada, Evangelical Lutheran Church in America. Providence: North American Association for the Diaconate, 1991.

Division for Ministry Task Force on the Study of Ministry, [Evangelical Lutheran Church in America]. "Summary of Official Task Force Recommendations, June 1992." N.p. Photocopy.

Division of Ordained Ministry, General Board of Higher Education, United Methodist Church. "Theological Education for the Ordained Deacon." N.p., n.d.

Dix, Gregory, ed. *The Treatise on the Apostolic Tradition of St. Hippolytus of Rome, Bishop and Martyr*. Revised by Henry Chadwick. London: SPCK, 1968.

Documentary History of the Evangelical Lutheran Ministerium of Pennsylvania and Adjacent States, Proceedings of the Annual Conventions from 1748 to 1821, Com-

piled and Translated from Records in the Archives and from the Written Protocols. Philadelphia: Board of Publication of the General Council of the Evangelical Lutheran Church in North America, 1898.

Donnelly, John Patrick, and Michael W. Maher, eds. *Confraternities and Catholic Reform in Italy, France, and Spain.* Sixteenth Century Essays and Studies 44. Kirksville, Mo.: Thomas Jefferson University Press, 1998.

Doran, Robert, trans. *The Lives of Simeon Stylites.* Cistercian Studies Series 112. Kalamazoo, Mich.: Cistercian Publications, 1992.

Dorris, Tom. "Reflections on the Diaconate in the ELCA." *Currents in Theology and Mission* 18, no. 4 (August 1991): 281–84.

Dosker, Henry. *The Dutch Anabaptists: The Stone Lectures Delivered at the Princeton Theological Seminary, 1918–19.* Philadelphia: Judson, 1921.

Dougherty, Mary Agnes. *My Calling to Fulfill: Deaconesses in the United Methodist Tradition.* New York: Women's Division, General Board of Global Ministries, The United Methodist Church, 1997.

Douglass, E. Jane Dempsey. *Women, Freedom, and Calvin: The 1983 Annie Kinkead Warfield Lectures.* Philadelphia: Westminster, 1985.

Doumergue, Émile. *Jean Calvin.* Vol. 5: *La pensée ecclésiastique et la pensée politique de Calvin.* Lausanne: Georges Bridel, 1917.

Downey, Glanville. *A History of Antioch in Syria from Seleucus to the Arab Conquest.* Princeton: Princeton University Press, 1961.

Dunn, James D. G. *Unity and Diversity in the New Testament: An Inquiry into the Character of Earliest Christianity.* Philadelphia: Westminster, 1977.

Durnbaugh, Donald, ed. *Every Need Supplied: Mutual Aid and Christian Community in the Free Churches, 1525–1675.* Philadelphia: Temple University Press, 1974.

Echlin, Edward P. *The Deacon in the Church, Past and Future.* Staten Island, N. Y.: Alba House, Society of St. Paul, 1971.

Egli, Emil, Georg Finsler, Walther Köhler, Oskar Farner, eds. *Huldreich Zwinglis sämtliche Werke 4.* Vol. 91 of Corpus Reformatorum. Leipzig: M. Heinsius Nachfolger, 1927.

Église Nationale Protestante de Genève. *Les Diaconies de la ville de Genève: Leur origine et leur activité de 1850 à 1900 avec le tableau des membres; Rapports présentés à la séance annuelle du Consistoire et des Diaconie, le 27 novembre 1900, par MM. Henri Heyer, ancien pasteur, et Louis Johannot, Diacres de la Fusterie.* Geneva: Librairie Henry Kündig, 1901.

Eichner, Karl. *Wilhelm Löhe: Ein Lebensbild.* Chicago: Wartburg, 1908.

Eisen, Ute E. *Women Officeholders in Early Christianity: Epigraphical and Literary Studies.* Collegeville, Minn.: Liturgical Press, 2000.

Elm, Susanna. *"Virgins of God": The Making of Asceticism in Late Antiquity.* Oxford: Clarendon, 1994.

Elmund, Gunnel. *Den kvinnliga diakonin i Sverige 1849–1861, Uppgift och utformning.* Bibliotheca Theologiae Practicae. Lund: Gleerups, 1973.

"England in 2005." *Diakonia News* 88 (November 2001): 14.

English, John C. "John Wesley and the Principle of Ministerial Succession." *Methodist History* 2, no. 2 (1964): 31–36.

Episcopal Church and Evangelical Lutheran Church in America. "The Orderly Exchange of Pastors and Priests under Called to Common Mission: Principles and Guidelines." January 1, 2002.

Esser, Caietanus, ed. *Opuscula Sancti Patris Francisci Assisiensis.* Bibliotheca Franciscana Ascetica Medii Aevi 12. Rome: Collegii S. Bonaventurae ad Claras Aquas, 1978.

Etan, Raymond. *The Diary of a Deacon.* Philadelphia: Castle Press, 1925.

[Evangelical Lutheran Church in America]. "Candidacy for Diaconal Ministry." N.p., n. d.

———. "Guidelines Related to Synodically Authorized or Licensed Ministries." The Evangelical Lutheran Church in America, April 1995. Available at http://www.elca.org (accessed June 16, 2003).

———. "The Study of Ministry, Report to the Churchwide Assembly, 1991." Photocopy.

———. *The Study of Ministry Study Edition, Report to the 1991 Churchwide Assembly.* Chicago: Evangelical Lutheran Church in America, 1991.

———. "Synopses IX–XII." June 1991–June 1992. Chicago: Evangelical Lutheran Church in America, 1991–92.

———. "Together for Ministry: Final Report and Actions on the Study of Ministry, 1988–1993, Incorporating the Task Force Final Report and Actions of the Board of the Division for Ministry and the 1993 Churchwide Assembly of the Evangelical Lutheran Church in America." [Chicago]: Evangelical Lutheran Church in America, 2000.

[Evangelical Lutheran Church in America, Division for Ministry]. "Diaconal Ministry Development Timeline." N.d.

———. "Hearings on Ministry 1989: The Study of Ministry." N.d.

Evangelische Sozialstation, Freiburg i. Br. *Pflege ist Vertrauenssache: Wir pflegen Menschen zu Hause.* Freiburg i. Br.: Evangelische Sozialstation, n.d.

Everson, Susan Corey. "The Demise of a Movement: A Study of Norwegian Lutheran Deaconesses in America." Paper, University of Minnesota, May 1979.

Faith and Order Secretariat. *The Deaconess: A Service of Women in the World Today.* World Council of Churches Studies 4. Geneva: World Council of Churches, 1966.

Fanuelsen, Olav. "The Education and Formation of Deacons in the Nordic Churches and the Church of England." In *The Ministry of the Deacon.* Vol. 2: *Ecclesiological Explorations,* edited by Gunnel Borgegård, Olav Fanuelsen, and Christine Hall. Uppsala: Nordic Ecumenical Council, 2000.

Fazy, Henri, ed. *Les Chroniques de Genève.* Geneva: Georg & Co, Libraires de l'Institut, 1894.

Fehler, Timothy G. *Poor Relief and Protestantism: The Evolution of Social Welfare in Sixteenth-Century Emden.* Aldershot, England: Ashgate, 1999.

Fenler, Timothy G. *Poor Relief and Protestantism: The Evolution of Social Welfare in Sixteenth-Century Emden.* Aldershot, England: Ashgate, 1999.

Ferguson, Thomas. *Lifting Up the Servants of God: The Deacon, Servant Ministry, and the Future of the Church.* North American Association for the Diaconate Monograph Series 12. Providence: North American Association for the Diaconate, 2002.

———. *The School for Deacons: Lifting up the Servants of God: The Deacon, Servant Ministry, and the Future of the Church.* N.p., n.d.

Ferrari, Guy. *Early Roman Monasteries: Notes for the History of the Monasteries and Convents at Rome from the Fifth through the Tenth Century.* Rome: Pontificio Istituto di Archeologia Cristiana, 1957.

Fiensy, David. *Prayers Alleged to Be Jewish: An Examination of the "Constitutiones Apostolorum."* Brown Judaic Studies 65. Chico: Scholars Press, 1985.

"Finding Inner Life in an Outside Tent." *One World* 75 (April 1982): 17–18.

Finn, Thomas M. *Early Christian Baptism and the Catechumenate: Italy, North Africa, and Egypt.* Collegeville, Minn.: Liturgical Press, 1992.

———. *From Death to Rebirth: Ritual and Conversion in Antiquity.* New York: Paulist Press, 1997.

———. *The Liturgy of Baptism in the Baptismal Instructions of St. John Chrysostom.* The Catholic University of America Studies in Christian Antiquity 15. Washington, D. C.: Catholic University of America Press, 1967.

Fiorenza, Elisabeth Schüssler. *In Memory of Her: A Feminist Theological Reconstruction of Christian Origins.* 10th ed. New York: Crossroad, 1994.

Flannery, Austin, ed. *Vatican Council II: The Conciliar and Post Conciliar Documents.* Wilmington, Del.: Scholarly Resources, 1975.

Fliedner, Heinrich. *Der Diakonissenvater D. Theodor Fliedner: Der deutsch-evangelischen Christenheit.* Kaiserswerth a. Rhein: Verlag der Buchhandlung der Diakonissen-Anstalt, 1930.

Fliedner, Theodor. "Journey to North America." Translated by Bertha Mueller. *Concordia Historical Institute Quarterly* 44, no. 4 (November 1971): 147–56 and *Concordia Historical Institute* 45, no. 1 (February 1972): 31–41.

Flynn, Maureen. *Sacred Charity, Confraternities and Social Welfare in Spain, 1400–1700.* Ithaca: Cornell University Press, 1989.

Foshee, Howard. *Now that You're a Deacon.* Nashville: Broadman, 1975.

Fout, John, ed. *German Women in the Nineteenth Century, a Social History.* New York: Holmes & Meier, 1984.

Framo, Chita R. "The Retiring President's Report." *Diakonia News* 88 (November 2001): 1–3.

Frasier, Richard. "Office of Deacon." *Presbyterian: A Journal for the Eldership, Covenant Seminary Review* 11 (Spring/Fall 1985): 13–19.

Frend, W. H. C. *The Early Church.* Philadelphia: Fortress, 1982.

Gaintner, J. Richard. *New England Deaconess Hospital: Building toward a Second Century of Compassionate Care.* Newcomen Society of the United States Publication 1443. New York: Princeton University Press, 1995.

Gavitt, Philip. *Charity and Children in Renaissance Florence: The Ospedalia degli Innocenti, 1410–1536.* Studies in Medieval and Early Modern Civilization. Ann Arbor: University of Michigan Press, 1990.

Geaney, Dennis. *Emerging Lay Ministries.* Kansas City: Andrews & McMeel, 1979.

Genequand, Jean-Étienne. "La prison de Saint-Antoine, ancienne maison de discipline." *Revue du Vieux Genève* (1981): 52–54.

The General Board of Higher Education and Ministry, Division of Ordained Ministry, [the United Methodist Church]. *Deacons: Connecting the Church and World*. Nashville: [The United Methodist Church], n.d.

Gerhardt, Martin. *Johann Hinrich Wichern und sein Werk*. 2d ed. Hamburg: Agentur des Rauhen Hauses, 1948.

Gerhardt, Martin von. *Johann Hinrich Wichern: Ein Lebensbild*. 3 vols. Hamburg: n.p., 1927–1931.

Gibaut, John St. H. *Sequential or Direct Ordination? A Return to the Sources*. Joint Liturgical Studies 55. Cambridge, England: Grove Books, 2003.

Gifford, Carolyn, ed. *The American Deaconess Movement in the Early Twentieth Century, by Isabelle Horton*. Women in American Protestant Religion, 1800–1930. New York: Garland, 1987.

Gilbert, W. Kent. *Commitment to Unity: A History of the Lutheran Church in America*. Philadelphia: Fortress, 1988.

Gillet, Lev. "Deacons in the Orthodox East." *Theology* 58 (November 1955): 415–21.

Giordani, Igino. *The Social Message of the Early Church Fathers* (in Italian). Translated by Alba I. Zizzamia. Paterson, N.J.: St. Anthony Guild Press, 1944.

Glimm, Francis X., Joseph M. F. Marique, and Gerald G. Walsh, trans. *The Fathers of the Church, a New Translation*. Vol. 1: *The Apostolic Fathers*. New York: CIMA, 1947.

Gohde, Jürgen, and Hanns-Stephan Haas, eds. *Wichern erinnern—Diakonie provozieren*. Hannover: Lutherisches Verlagshaus, 1998.

Golder, Christian. *The Deaconess Motherhouse in Its Relation to the Deaconess Work*. Pittsburgh: Pittsburgh Printing, 1907.

———. *Die Geschichte der weiblichen Diakonie*. Cincinnati: Jennings & Pye, 1901.

———. *History of the Deaconess Movement in the Christian Church*. Cincinnati: Jennings & Pye, 1903.

González, Justo. *The Story of Christianity*. Vol. 1: *The Early Church to the Dawn of the Reformation*. New York: Harper & Row, 1984.

Goodspeed, Edgar J., and Robert M. Grant. *A History of Early Christian Literature*. Chicago: University of Chicago Press, 1966.

Götz, Justus. *Wilhelm Löhe: Im Dienst der Kirche; Quellen und Urkunden zum Verständnis Neuendettelsauer Art und Geschichte*. 2d ed. Neuendettelsau: Buchhandlung der Diakonissenanstalt, 1933.

Grandjean, Henri. "La Bourse Française de Genève (1550–1849)." Étrennes Genevoises 1927. Geneva: Édition Atar, 1927.

Greenslade, S. L., trans. and ed. *Early Latin Theology: Selections from Tertullian, Cyprian, Ambrose, and Jerome*. The Library of Christian Classics 5. Philadelphia: Westminster, 1956.

Gregory, Bishop of Nyssa. *The Life of Saint Macrina*. Translated by Kevin Corrigan. 1987. Reprint, Toronto: Peregrina, 1989.

Gregory, Bishop of Tours. *A History of the Franks: Selections, Translated with Notes*. Translated by Ernest Brehaut. Records of Civilization, Sources and Studies. New York: W. W. Norton, 1969.

Grein, Richard. *Baptism and the Ministry of Deacons*. North American Association for the Diaconate Monograph Series 1. Providence: North American Association for the Diaconate, 1987.

———. *The Renewal of the Diaconate and the Ministry of the Laos*. North American Association for the Diaconate Monograph Series 3. Providence: North American Association for the Diaconate, 1991.

Grell, Ole Peter, and Andrew Cunningham, eds. *Health Care and Poor Relief in Protestant Europe 1500–1700*. Studies in the Social History of Medicine. London: Routledge, 1997.

Greve, Diane. "Statistics on Ministry of Deaconesses." Memo to Karl Lutze: Lutheran Deaconess Association, Valparaiso, Ind., 19 October 1990. Photocopy.

Grierson, Janet. *The Deaconess*. London: CIO, 1981.

Grimm, Harold. "Luther's Contributions to Sixteenth-Century Organization of Poor Relief." *Archiv für Reformationsgeschichte* 61 (1970): 222–33.

Grinager, Dorothy. "Report to National Program Division Plenary, October 21, 1991." Committee on Deaconess Service. Photocopy.

Gryson, Roger. *Le ministère des femmes dans l'Église ancienne*. Gembloux, Belgium: Éditions Duculot, 1972.

———. "L'ordination des diaconesses d'après les 'Constitution Apostoliques.' " Response to A. G. Martimort. *Mélanges de science religieuse* 31 (March 1974): 41–45.

Gutton, Jean-Pierre. *La société et les pauvres: l'exemple de la généralité de Lyon, 1534–1789*. Paris: Société d'Édition "Les Belles Lettres." 1970.

Hackel, Sergei. "Mother Maria Skobtsova: Deaconess Manquée?" *Eastern Churches Review* 1 (Spring 1967): 264–66.

Hagemann, Elisabeth. *Diakonissen: Fra Kirkens Første Dager til Vår Tid*. Oslo: Lutherstiftelsens, 1928.

Hall, Basil. *Humanists and Protestants, 1500–1900*. Edinburgh: T&T Clark, 1990.

Hallenbeck, Edwin F. *A Working Paper of Trial Liturgy for Celebration of Deacon's Ministry*. Providence: North American Association for the Diaconate, 1996.

———, ed. *Diakonia Prophetic Praxis Agir: The Dotac Conference Brasil 1999*. Providence: North American Association for the Diaconate, 2002.

———, ed. *The Orders of Ministry: Reflections on Direct Ordination, 1996*. Providence: North American Association for the Diaconate, 1996.

———, ed. *A Working Paper of Guidelines for Deacon Programs*. 2d ed. Providence: North American Association for the Diaconate, 2002.

———, ed. *A Working Paper Report of NAAD Visioning Workshop: New Orleans, LA, March 18–20, 2002*. Providence: North American Association for the Diaconate, 2002.

Halton, Thomas, and Joseph P. Williman, eds. *Diakonia: Studies in Honor of Robert T. Meyer*. Washington, D.C.: Catholic University of America Press, 1986.

Hammann, Gottfried. *L'amour retrouvé: La diaconie chrétienne et le ministère de diacre du christianisme primitif aux réformateurs protestants du XVIe siècle*. Paris: Les Éditions du Cerf, 1994.

Hanawalt, Emily Albu, and Carter Lindberg, eds. *Through the Eye of a Needle: Judeo-Christian Roots of Social Welfare*. Kirksville, Mo.: Thomas Jefferson University Press, 1994.

Harnish, John E. *The Orders of Ministry in the United Methodist Church*. Nashville: Abingdon, 2000.

Hartley, Ben L. and Paul E. Van Buren. *The Deacon: Ministry through Words of Faith and Acts of Love*. Nashville: Section of Deacons and Diaconal Ministries, General Board of Higher Education and Ministry of the United Methodist Church, 2000.

Hartwig, Raymond L., secretary of The Lutheran Church—Missouri Synod. *Letter to All Non-Rostered Lay Ministers Serving Congregations and other Entities of the LCMS, October 2001*.

Hatch, Edwin. *The Organization of the Early Christian Churches: Eight Lectures Delivered before the University of Oxford, in the Year 1880*. London: Longmans, Green, & Co., 1901.

Hattstaedt, Otto. "History of the Southern Wisconsin District of the Evangelical Lutheran Synod of Missouri, Ohio and Other States: Submitted to the Synod of Southern Wisconsin in Conventions Assembled in Watertown, June 22–28, 1927, and in Janesville, June 25–29, 1928." Translated by the Wisconsin Historical Records Survey Division of Community Service, Programs Work Projects Administration. University of Wisconsin and State Historical Society of Wisconsin, 1941. Typescript.

Heeney, Brian. *The Women's Movement in the Church of England 1850–1930*. Oxford: Oxford University Press, 1988.

———. "Women's Struggle for Professional Work and Status in the Church of England, 1900–1930." *The Historical Journal* 26, no. 2 (June 1983): 329–47.

Hefele, Charles Joseph. *A History of the Councils of the Church from the Original Documents*. Vol. 2: A.D. *326 to* A.D. *429*. Edinburgh: T&T Clark, 1896.

Hein, David, and Gardiner H. Shattuck Jr. *The Episcopalians*. Westport, Conn.: Praeger, 2004.

Heintzen, Erich. *Love Leaves Home: Wilhelm Loehe and the Missouri Synod*. St. Louis, Concordia, 1973.

Hendel, Kurt. "The Care of the Poor: An Evangelical Perspective." *Currents in Theology and Mission* 15 (December 1988): 527.

Henderson, G. D. *Presbyterianism*. Aberdeen: University Press, 1954.

Herbermann, Charles, Edward Pace, Condé Pallen, Thomas Shahan, and John Wynne, eds. *The Catholic Encyclopedia: An International Work of Reference on the Constitution, Doctrine, Discipline, and History of the Catholic Church*. 15 vols. New York: Appleton, 1907–1912.

Herzel, Catherine. *One Call: Deaconesses across the World*. New York: Holt, Rinehart & Winston, 1961.

Heyer, Henri. *L'Église de Genève 1555–1909, esquisse historique de son organisation suivie de ses diverses constitutions, de la liste de ses pasteurs et professeurs et d'une table biographique*. Geneva: Librairie A. Jullien, 1909. Reprint, Nieuwkoop: B. De Graaf, 1974.

Hildemann, Klaus D., Uwe Kaminsky, and Ferdinand Magen. *Pastoralgehilfen-anstalt—Diakonenanstalt—Theodor Fliedner Werk: 150 Jahre Diakoniegeschichte.* Cologne: Rheinland-Verlag, 1994.

Hill, Joyce. *Bede and the Benedictine Reform: Jarrow Lecture, 1998.* N.p., n.d.

"History of the Lutheran Deaconess Motherhouse at Milwaukee." Paper presented to the Task Force on the Study of Ministry, Evangelical Lutheran Church in America, Chicago, Ill. October 1989.

Höfer, Josef, and Karl Rahner, eds. *Lexikon für Theologie und Kirche.* 11 vols. Freiburg: Herder, 1957–67.

Hofmann, Beate, and Michael Schibilsky, eds. *Spiritualität in der Diakonie: Anstösse zur Erneuerung christlicher Kernkompetenz.* Stuttgart: W. Kohlhammer, 2001.

Holman, Susan R. *The Hungry Are Dying: Beggars and Bishops in Roman Cappadocia.* Oxford Studies in Historical Theology. Oxford: Oxford University Press, 2001.

Holmes, Michael W., ed. *The Apostolic Fathers: Greek Texts and English Translations.* Updated ed. Grand Rapids: Baker, 1999.

Holum, Kenneth G. *Theodosian Empresses: Women and Imperial Dominion in Late Antiquity.* Berkeley: University of California Press, 1982.

Hopko, Thomas, ed. *Women and the Priesthood.* Crestwood, N.Y.: St. Vladimir's Seminary Press, 1983.

Hornef, Josef. *Kommt der Diakon der frühen Kirche wieder?* Vienna: Seelsorgerverlag Herder, 1959.

Hornef, Joseph, and Paul Winninger. "Chronique de la restauration du diaconat (1945–1965)." In *Le diacre dans l'Église et le monde d'aujourd'hui.* Unam Sanctam 59. Paris: Les Éditions du Cerf, 1966.

Horton, Isabelle. *The American Deaconess Movement in the Early Twentieth Century.* Edited by Carolyn Gifford. Women in American Protestant Religion, 1800–1930. New York: Garland, 1987.

———. *The Burden of the City.* New York: Fleming H. Revell, 1904. Reprinted in *The American Deaconess Movement in the Early Twentieth Century,* edited by Carolyn Gifford. Women in American Protestant Religion, 1800–1930. New York: Garland, 1987.

———. *High Adventure: Life of Lucy Rider Meyer.* Women in American Protestant Religion 1800–1930. 1928. Reprint, New York: Garland, 1987.

Howson, J. S. *Deaconesses or the Official Help of Women in Parochial Work and in Charitable Institutions: An Essay Reprinted, with Large Editions, from the* Quarterly Review, *Sept. 1860.* London: Longman, Green, Longman, & Roberts, 1862.

Hübner, Ingolf, and Jochen-Christoph Kaiser, eds. *Diakonie im geteilten Deutschland: Zur diakonischen Arbeit unter den Bedingungen der DDR und der Teilung Deutschlands.* Stuttgart: W. Kohlhammer, 1999.

Hünermann, Peter. "Conclusions Regarding the Female Diaconate." *Theological Studies* 36 (June 1975): 325–33.

———, Albert Biesinger, Marianne Heimbach-Steins, and Anne Jensen, eds. *Diakonat: Ein Amt für Frauen in der Kirche—Ein frauengerechtes Amt?* Ostfildern, Germany: Schwabenverlag, 1997.

Ide, Arthur. *Woman as Priest, Bishop and Laity in the Early Catholic Church to 440 A.D. with a Translation and Critical Commentary on Romans 16 and Other Relevant Scripture and Patrological Writings on Women in the Early Christian Church.* Women in History 9b. Mesquite: Ide House, 1984.

Ignatius the Deacon. *The Correspondence of Ignatius the Deacon: Text, Translation, and Commentary.* Translated by Cyril Mango. Corpus fontium historiae Byzantinae 39 and Dumbarton Oaks Texts 11. Washington, D.C.: Dumbarton Oaks, 1997.

Innes, William. *Social Concern in Calvin's Geneva.* Allison Park, Penn.: Pickwick, 1983.

Institute for Mission in the U.S.A. "Synodically Authorized Ministries Pilot Project Findings Submitted to Division for Ministry, ELCA." Trinity Lutheran Seminary, 2199 E. Main Street, Columbus, Ohio, April 1998; available from http://www.elca.org (accessed 16 June 2003).

International Center for the Diaconate, Freiburg, Federal Republic of Germany. "The Diaconate Worldwide." Secretariat for the Permanent Diaconate of the National Conference of Catholic Bishops, Washington, D.C., 1992. Photocopy.

Jacobs, Henry. *A History of the Evangelical Lutheran Church in the United States.* The American Church History Series 4. New York: Christian Literature Co., 1898.

Jäger, Alfred. *Diakonie als christliches Unternehmen, Theologische Wirtschaftsethik im Kontext diakonischer Unternehmenspolitik.* 2d ed. Gütersloh: Gütersloher Verlagshaus Gerd Mohn, 1987.

Jahnke, Ronald. "Lutheran Lay Ministry: 25 Years [Parts 1–3]." *Concordia Historical Institute Quarterly* 59 (Spring and Summer 1986): 2–6, 9–10, 55–56.

Jahresbericht über die Diakononissen-Anstalt Kaiserswerth 121 (October 13, 1956–1957).

Jahresgruss 1988 aus dem Evang. Diakonissenmutterhaus "Frankenstein" in Wertheim/Main 178 (December 1988).

Jeske, Richard L. *The Role of the Diaconate and the Unity of the Church.* North American Association for the Diaconate Monograph Series 13. Providence: North American Association for the Diaconate, 2002.

Jesus lebt! Jesus siegt! Überblick über die Entwicklung des Deutschen Gemeinschafts-Diakonieverbandes (Bandsburger Werk) in des ersten 25 Jahren, 1899–1924. Bad Blantenburg: Buchbruderei n. Verlag "Harfe." n.d.

The Joint Commission of the Lutheran World Federation and the World Alliance of Reformed Churches. *Toward Church Fellowship, Report of the Joint Commission of the Lutheran World Federation and the World Alliance of Reformed Churches.* Rolle, Switzerland: Imprimerie La Colombière, 1989.

Joly, Robert. *Le Dossier d'Ignace d'Antioche. Université Libre de Bruxelles, Faculté de Philosophie et Lettres, Travaux, 69.* Brussels: Éditions de l'Université de Bruxelles, 1979.

Jordan, W. K. *Philanthropy in England 1480–1660.* New York: Russell Sage Foundation, 1959.

"Kaire!" *Diakonia News* 78 (July 1990): 27.

Kaiser, Jochen-Christoph, and Martin Greschat, eds. *Sozialer Protestantismus und Sozialstaat: Diakonie und Wohlfahrtsflege in Deutschland 1890 bis 1938.* Stuttgart: W. Kohlhammer, 1996.

"Kaiserswerth and London." *Diakonia News* 87 (November 2000): [5].

Kantzenbach, Friedrich. *Wilhelm Löhe—Anstösse für die Zeit.* Neuendettelsau: Freimund-Verlag, 1972.

———. *Wilhelm Löhe die Kirche in ihrer Bewegung Mission Diakonie.* Neuendettelsau: Freimund-Verlag, 1962.

Katscher, Liselotte. *Krankenpflege und das Jahr 1945: Der Zusammenbruch und seine Folgen am Beispiel der Schwesternschaft des Evangelischen Diakonievereins.* Reutlingen: Diakonie-Verlag, 1993.

Keller, Rosemary, Gerald Moede, and Mary Moore. *Called to Serve: The United Methodist Diaconate. Edited by Rosalie Bentzinger.* Nashville: Division of Diaconal Ministry of the United Methodist General Board of Higher Education and Ministry, 1987.

Kerr, John. *The Shape of Ministry: A Study of Ministry in the ELCA.* Minneapolis: Augsburg Fortress, 1990.

Kidd, B. J. *Documents Illustrative of the Continental Reformation.* Oxford: Clarendon, 1911.

Kingdon, Robert M. *Geneva and the Consolidation of the French Protestant Movement, 1564–72: A Contribution to the History of Congregationalism, Presbyterianism, and Calvinist Resistance Theory.* Madison: University of Wisconsin Press, 1967.

———. "Social Welfare in Calvin's Geneva." *American Historical Review* 76 (February 1971): 50–69.

———, ed. *Registres de la Compagnie des Pasteurs de Genève.* Vol. 2: *1553–1564.* Geneva: Librairie Droz, 1962.

"Kingston." *Diakonia News* 78 (July 1990): 4–5.

Kirsch, Paul. "Deaconesses in the United States Since 1918: A Study of the Deaconess Work of the United Lutheran Church in America in Comparison with the Corresponding Programs of the Other Lutheran Churches and of the Evangelical and Reformed, Mennonite, Episcopal, and Methodist Churches." Ph.D. diss., New York University, 1961.

———. "Recent Trends in Deaconess Work." *Lutheran Quarterly* 15 (Fall 1963): 29–47.

Kittelson, James M. "Enough Is Enough! The Confusion over the Augsburg Confession and Its *Satis Est.*" *Lutheran Quarterly* 12, no. 3 (Autumn 1998): 249–70.

Klaassen, Walter, ed. *Anabaptism in Outline: Selected Primary Sources.* Scottdale, Penn.: Herald Press, 1981.

Klapisch-Zuber, Christiane. *A History of Women in the West.* Vol. 2: *Silences of the Middle Ages.* Cambridge: Harvard University Press, Belknap Press, 1992.

Klassen, Peter. *The Economics of Anabaptism, 1525–1560.* London: Mouton, 1964.

Kopecek, Thomas A. *A History of Neo-Arianism.* 2 vols. Patristic Monograph Series 8. Cambridge: Philadelphia Foundation, 1979.

Kraemer, Ross S. ed. *Maenads, Martyrs, Matrons, Monastics: A Sourcebook on Women's Religions in the Greco-Roman World.* Philadelphia: Fortress, 1988.

———, and Mary Rose D'Angelo, eds. *Women and Christian Origins.* Oxford: Oxford University Press, 1999.

Krause, Gerhard, and Gerhard Müller, eds. *Theologische Realenzyklopädie*. Berlin: de Gruyter, 1981.

Kressel, Hans. *Wilhelm Löhe als Prediger*. Gütersloh: C. Bertelsmann, 1929.

———. *Wilhelm Löhe: Der lutherische Christenmensch; Ein Charakterbild*. Berlin: Lutherisches Verlagshaus, 1960.

———. *Wilhelm Löhe der lutherische Missionär*. Neuendettelsau: Freimund, 1949.

———. *Wilhelm Löhe: Ein Lebensbild*. 2d ed. Erlangen: Martin Luther-Verlag, 1954.

Krimm, Herbert, ed. *Das diakonische Amt der Kirche*. 2d ed. Stuttgart: Evangelisches Verlagswerk, 1965.

———, ed. *Quellen zur Geschichte der Diakonie*. 3 vols. Stuttgart: Evangelisches Verlagswerk, n.d.

Kunnacherry, Kuriakose. *Deaconesses in the Church: A Pastoral Need of the Day? A Study Text*. The Syrian Book Series. Kottayam, Kerala, India: St. Joseph's Press, 1987.

Kwatera, Michael. *The Liturgical Ministry of Deacons*. Collegeville, Minn.: Liturgical Press, 1985.

Lagerquist, L. Deane. *From Our Mother's Arms: A History of Women in the American Lutheran Church*. Minneapolis: Augsburg, 1987.

Lambin, Rosine. "Le costume des diaconesses, plus d'un siècle d'évolution spirituelle: Les tâtonnement (1840–1960)." *Bulletin de la Société de l'Histoire du Protestantisme Français* 145 (April, May, June 1999): 359–73.

———. "Le costume des diaconesses protestantes: un inventaire après des années de rupture (1960–1980)." *Bulletin de la Société de l'Histoire du Protestantisme Français 145* (July, August, September 1999): 597–619.

Lane, Peter. "Poverty and Poor Relief in the German Church Orders of Johann Bugenhagen, 1485–1558." Ph.D. diss., Ohio State University, 1973.

Lassen-Willems, James. *Are Deacons the Enemy?* North American Association for the Diaconate Monograph Series 2. Providence: North American Association for the Diaconate, 1989.

Latourette, Kenneth Scott. *Christianity in a Revolutionary Age: A History of Christianity in the Nineteenth and Twentieth Centuries*. Vol. 1: *The Nineteenth Century in Europe: Background and the Roman Catholic Phase*. New York, Harper & Brothers, 1958.

Lauterer, Heide-Marie. *Liebestätigkeit für die Volksgemeinschaft: Der Kaiserswerther Verband deutscher Diakonissenmutterhäuser in den ersten Jahren des NS-Regimes*. Göttingen: Vandenhoeck & Ruprecht, 1994.

Lazareth, William H. *Two Forms of Ordained Ministry: A Proposal for Mission in Light of the Augsburg Confession*. Minneapolis: Augsburg, 1991.

Le ministère des diacres envoyés en milieu professionnel ou diacres en mission. A report adopted by the council of the Département romand des ministères diaconaux, May 26, 1982, and by the assembly of the Département romand des ministères diaconaux. June 26, 1982. N.p.: n.d.

Lee, Elizabeth. *As among the Methodists: Deaconesses Yesterday, Today, and Tomorrow*. New York: Woman's Division of Christian Service, Board of Missions, The Methodist Church, 1963.

Leith, John. *Assembly at Westminster: Reformed Theology in the Making*. Atlanta: John Knox, 1973.

Lembke, Helga. *Wicherns Bedeutung für die Bekämpfung der Jugendverwahrlosung*. Hamburg: Friedrich Wittig, 1964.

Lemons, J. Stanley. *The First Baptist Church in America*. East Greenwich, R.I.: Meridian Printing for the Charitable Baptist Society, 1988.

Lenker, John. *Lutherans in All Lands, the Wonderful Works of God*. 4th ed. Milwaukee, Wisc.: Lutherans in all Lands, 1894.

Léonard, Émile. *A History of Protestantism*. Vol. 2: *The Establishment*. Edited by H. H. Rowley. Translated by R. M. Bethell. London: Nelson, 1967.

Less, Jeffrey D. *A View from the Omnivorous Presbyterate*. North American Association for the Diaconate Monograph Series 6. Providence: North American Association for the Diaconate, 1991.

"Let Them Serve." *Boston Church of Christ* 13, no. 5 (March 29, 1992): 1–7, 12.

Letzig, Betty. "Deaconesses Past and Present." *New World Outlook* (May-June 1992): 29–31.

Lewis, Carol. "Full Communion Proposed for Four Denominations." *News, Presbyterian Church (U.S.A.)*. News Briefs—9211. 20 March 1992.

Libersat, Henry. *Permanent Deacons: Who They Are and What They Do*. Liguori, Mo.: Liguori Publications, 1989.

Lindberg, Carter. *Beyond Charity: Reformation Initiatives for the Poor*. Minneapolis: Fortress, 1993.

———. "Luther on Poverty." *Lutheran Quarterly* 15, no. 1 (Spring 2001): 85–101.

———. "Luther on the Use of Money." *Christian History* 6, no. 2 (1987): 17–19, 34.

———. "Luther's Concept of Offering." *Dialog* 25 (Fall 1996): 251–57.

———. "The Ministry and Vocation of the Baptized." *Lutheran Quarterly* 6, no. 4 (Winter 1992): 385–401.

———. " 'There Should Be No Beggars among Christians': Karlstadt, Luther, and the Origins of Protestant Poor Relief." *Church History* 46 (September 1977): 313–34.

———. "Through a Glass Darkly: A History of the Church's Vision of the Poor and Poverty." *The Ecumenical Review* 33, no. 1 (January 1981): 37–52.

———, ed. *Piety, Politics, and Ethics: Reformation Studies in Honor of George Wolfgang Forell*. Sixteenth Century Essays and Studies 3. Kirksville, Mo.: Sixteenth Century Journal Publishers, 1984.

Liptak, David, and Philip Sheridan. *The New Code: Laity and Deacons; A Pastoral Guide to the New Code of Canon Law on the Laity and Deacons in Question and Answer Form*. Vol. 2. Lake Worth, Florida: Sunday Publications, 1985.

List, Theresa. "LCMS Deaconesses: Who We Are, How to Become One, and How We Can Enrich Your Congregation or Institution." *Issues in Christian Education* 39, no. 1 (Spring 2005): 23–29.

Loach, Jennifer. *Edward VI*. Edited by George Bernard and Penry Williams. New Haven: Yale University Press, 1999.

Loetscher, Lefferts. *A Brief History of the Presbyterians*. 4th ed. Philadelphia: Westminster, 1983.

Lohbeck, Elsbeth. *Andreas Bräm (1797–1882): Ein Wegbereiter der Diakonie im Rheinland und Gründer des Neukirchener Erziehungsvereins*. Cologne: Rheinland-Verlag, 1989.

Löhe, Wilhelm. *Etwas aus der Geschichte des Diakonissenhauses Neuendettelsau*. Nürnberg: Gottfr. Löhe, 1870.

Louwerse, Anthony L., and Jay Van Groningen. "The Office of Deacon." *Reformed Review: A Theological Journal of Western Theological Seminary, Holland, Michigan* 46, no. 3 (Spring 1993): 226–43.

Lumpkin, William. *Baptist Confessions of Faith*. Philadelphia: Judson, 1959.

Luther, Martin. *D. Martin Luthers Werke: Kritische Gesamtausgabe*. Vol. 6. Weimar: Hermann Böhlaus Nachfolger, 1966.

———. *Three Treatises: Martin Luther*. Philadelphia: Fortress, 1970.

The Lutheran Church—Missouri Synod. *Convention Workbook: Proceedings (1992)*.

———. *Lutheran Annual 2003*. St. Louis: Concordia, 2002.

———. "Nomenclature Study Committee." *Convention Workbook (1998)*, 8–9.

———. "To Address Nomenclature of Church Workers." Resolution 7-14A, Overtures 7-118-31, *Convention Workbook*, pp. 275–78. Cf. *1998 Convention Proceedings*, 151–52.

———. "To Phase Out Consecrated Lay Workers Category." Resolution 7-13A, Overture 7-12, *Convention Workbook (2001)*, 241–42.

———. "To Study Classification of Professional Church Workers." Resolution 5-21, Overture 5-70, *Convention Workbook*, 262. Cf. *1992 Convention Proceedings*, 157.

Lutheran Deaconess Association. *A Deaconess! What's That? Deaconesses Serve . . . To Make a Difference Today!* Grade 3 and Up. N.p., n.d.

———. *A Deaconess! What's That? Deaconesses Serve . . . To Make a Difference Today!* Kindergarten and Up. N.p., n.d.

———. *A Deaconess! What's That? Deaconesses Serve . . . To Make a Difference Today!* Middle School and Up. N.p., n.d.

———. "Among You as One Who Serves." n.d.

———. "Could a Deaconess Serve with Us?" N.p., n.d.

———. "Excerpts from 'A Proposal for the Future of the Lutheran Deaconess Association.' " N.p., November/December, 1980. Mimeographed.

———. "How Can I Become a Deaconess? Educational Plans Offered by the Lutheran Deaconess Association, Valparaiso, Indiana, Including Information on Educational Options, Practical Ministry Opportunities, Finances, Consecration, Application Procedure." N.p., n.d.

———. "Presentation to Task Force on the Study of Ministry, Evangelical Lutheran Church in America, Chicago, Ill., October 7, 1989." Mimeographed.

The Lutheran Deaconess Association Center for Diaconal Ministry. "Becoming a Deaconess Isn't for Everyone." N.p., n.d.

———. "Deaconess Education Catalogue." N.p., n.d. Mimeographed.

Lutheran-Reformed Committee for Theological Conversations. "A Common Calling: The Witness of Our Reformation Churches in North America Today." March 1992. Photocopy.

Maag, Karin. *Seminary or University? The Genevan Academy and Reformed Higher Education, 1560–1620*. St. Andrews Studies in Reformation History. Aldershot, England: Scolar Press, 1995.

MacCulloch, Diarmaid. *Thomas Cranmer: A Life*. New Haven: Yale University Press, 1996.

MacDonald, Margaret Y. *Early Christian Women and Pagan Opinion: The Power of the Hysterical Woman*. Cambridge: Cambridge University Press, 1996.

MacInnis, John. *The Deacon in the Church Today*. Philadelphia: Presbyterian Board of Christian Education, 1940.

Mackay, T. *The English Poor: A Sketch of Their Social and Economic History*. London: J. Murray, 1889.

Madson, Meg H. "The Lutheran-Episcopal Concordat and Porvoo." *Lutheran Quarterly* 13, no. 1 (Spring 1999): 21–33.

Makris, Georgios, ed. *Ignatius Diakonos und die Vita des Hl. Gregorios Dekapolites*. Translated by Michael Chronz. Stuttgart: B. G. Teubner, 1997.

"Marilyn J. Clark Memorial." *Deaconess and Home Missionary News and Views* (December 1991): [2].

Martimort, Aimé George. *Deaconesses: An Historical Study*. Translated by K. D. Whitehead. San Francisco: Ignatius Press, 1986.

Martin, John Hilary. "The Ordination of Women and the Theologians in the Middle Ages." *Escritos del Vedat* 16 (1986): 115–77 and *Escritos del Vedat* 18 (1988): 87–143.

Martineau, Robert. *The Office and Work of a Reader*. Rev. ed. London: Mowbrays, 1980.

Mary J. Drexel Home and Philadelphia Motherhouse of Deaconesses, Fiftieth Anniversary, 1884–1934. Philadelphia: n.p., n.d.

Matthies, Helene. *Wilhelm Löhe: Leben und Werk*. Hamburg: Agentur des Rauhen Hauses, 1951.

Maurer, Wilhelm. *Historical Commentary on the Augsburg Confession*. Translated by H. George Anderson. Philadelphia: Fortress, 1986.

McCloy, Shelby. *Government Assistance in Eighteenth-Century France*. Durham, N. C.: Duke University Press, 1946.

McComb, Louise. *Presbyterian School of Christian Education: The First Seventy Years (1914–1984), An Informal History*. N.p.: Presbyterian School of Christian Education, 1985.

McCord, James I. and T. H. L. Parker. *Service in Christ: Essays Presented to Karl Barth on His 80th Birthday*. Grand Rapids: Eerdmans, 1966.

McCoy, W. Keith. *The Deacon as Para-Cleric*. North American Association for the Diaconate Monograph Series 9. Providence: North American Association for the Diaconate, 1998.

McKee, Elsie. *Diakonia in the Classical Reformed Tradition and Today*. Grand Rapids: Eerdmans, 1989.

———. *John Calvin on the Diaconate and Liturgical Almsgiving*. Geneva: Librairie Droz, 1984.

McKenna, Mary. *Women of the Church: Role and Renewal*. New York: P. J. Kenedy & Sons, 1967.

McNeill, John T. *The History and Character of Calvinism*. London: Oxford University Press, 1954.

Meeker, Ruth. *Six Decades of Service, 1880–1940: A History of The Woman's Home Missionary Society of the Methodist Episcopal Church*. N.p.: Continuing Corporation of The Woman's Home Missionary Society, 1969.

Meland, Roar. "The Deacon in the Church of Norway." In *The Ministry of the Deacon*. Vol. 1: *Anglican-Lutheran Perspectives*. Edited by Gunnel Borgegård and Christine Hall. Uppsala: Nordic Ecumenical Council, 1999.

The Mennonite Encyclopedia: A Comprehensive Reference Work on the Anabaptist-Mennonite Movement. 4 vols. Scottdale, Penn.: Mennonite Publishing House, 1956–1959.

Merz, Georg. "Wilhelm Löhe und die Innere Mission." In *Um Glaube und Leben nach Luthers Lehre: Ausgewählte Aufsätze*. Edited by F. W. Kantzenbach. Munich: Christian Kaiser, 1961.

Meyer, Carl, ed. *Moving Frontiers: Readings in the History of The Lutheran Church—Missouri Synod*. St. Louis: Concordia, 1964.

Meyer, Harding, and Lukas Vischer, eds. *Growth in Agreement: Reports and Agreed Statements of Ecumenical Conversations on a World Level*. Faith and Order Paper, no. 108. New York: Paulist Press, 1984.

Meyer, Lucy Rider. *Deaconesses, Biblical, Early Church, European, American: The Story of the Chicago Training School for City, Home, and Foreign Missions*. 2d ed. Chicago: Message Publishing Company, 1889.

———. *Deaconesses, Biblical, Early Church, European, American with an Account of the Origin of the Deaconess Movement in the Methodist Episcopal Church of America*. 4th ed., abridged and rev. Oak Park, Ill.: The Deaconess Advocate, 1897.

———. "The Mother in the Church." *Methodist Review* (September–October 1901): 1–16.

Meylan, Henri. *La haute école de Lausanne*. Lausanne: F. Rouge & Cie, Librairie de l'Université Lausanne, 1937.

Miles, James. "The Pastor-Deacon Relationship." *The Priest* (October 1989): 13.

Miller, Timothy S. *The Birth of the Hospital in the Byzantine Empire*. Baltimore: Johns Hopkins University Press, 1985.

The Ministry: Offices, Procedures, and Nomenclature; A Report of the Commission on Theology and Church Relations of The Lutheran Church—Missouri Synod. St. Louis: Concordia, 1981.

The Ministry of Deacons. World Council Studies 2. Geneva: World Council of Churches, 1965.

The Ministry of Women: A Report by a Committee Appointed by His Grace the Lord Archbishop of Canterbury with Appendices and Fifteen Collotype Illustrations. New York: MacMillan, 1919.

Mission Education and Cultivation Program Department, General Board of Global Ministries, The United Methodist Church. *The Office of Deaconess: Servants in*

Your Midst, the United Methodist Church. Cincinnati: General Board of Global Ministries Service Center, n.d.

"The Mission of NAAD." *Diakoneo* 24, no. 4 (Pentecost 2002): 1.

Mitchell, Nathan. *Mission and Ministry: History and Theology in the Sacrament of Order.* Vol. 6, *Message of the Sacraments.* Wilmington, Del.: Michael Glazier, 1982.

Mitchison, Rosalind. "The Making of the Old Scottish Poor Law." *Past and Present* 63 (May 1974): 58–93.

Moede, Gerald, ed. *The COCU Consensus: In Quest of a Church of Christ Uniting.* Princeton: Consultation on Church Union, 1985.

Moens, W. J. C. "The Relief of the Poor Members of the French Churches in England as Exemplified by the Practice of the Walloon or French Church at Sandwich (1568–72)." *Proceedings of the Huguenot Society of London* (January 10 and March 14, 1894): 321–38.

Mollat, Michel. *The Poor of the Middle Ages: An Essay in Social History.* Translated by Arthur Goldhammer. New Haven: Yale University Press, 1986.

Mottu-Weber, Liliane. "Des vers à soie à l'Hôpital en 1610: Un bref épisode de l'histoire de la soierie à Genève." *Revue du Vieux Genève* 12 (1982): 44–49.

Muhlenberg, W. A. *Two Letters on Protestant Sisterhoods.* New York: Phair & Co., 1853.

Müller, Christine-Ruth, and Hans-Ludwig Siemen. *Warum sie sterben müssten: Leidensweg und Vernichtung von Behinderten aus den Neuendettelsauer Pflegeanstalten im "Dritten Reich."* Neustadt a.d. Aisch: Degener, 1991.

Musurillo, Herbert, trans. *The Acts of the Christian Martyrs.* Oxford: Clarendon, 1972.

"National Diaconate Dialogue Group." N.p., n.d. Photocopy.

National Directory for the Formation, Ministry, and Life for Permanent Deacons in the United States. Washington, D.C.: United States Council of Catholic Bishops, 2005.

A National Study of the Permanent Diaconate of the Catholic Church in the United States. Washington, D.C.: Publication Office United States Catholic Conference, 1981.

A National Study of the Permanent Diaconate of the Catholic Church in the United States, 1994–1995. Washington, D.C.: United States Catholic Conference, 1996.

Naylor, Robert. *The Baptist Deacon.* Nashville: Broadman, 1955.

Neill, Stephen. *A History of Christian Missions.* New York: Penguin Books, 1964.

Nelson, E. Clifford, ed. *The Lutherans in North America.* Philadelphia: Fortress, 1975.

Neusner, Jacob, Peder Borgen, Ernest S. Frerichs, and Richard Horsley, eds. *The Social World of Formative Christianity and Judaism: In Tribute to Howard Clark Kee.* Philadelphia: Fortress, 1988.

New Catholic Encyclopedia. 15 vols. New York: McGraw-Hill, 1967–79.

New Catholic Encyclopedia. 2d ed. 15 vols. New York: Thomson, Gale, 2003.

The News of the Presbyterian Church (U.S.A.). (April 1992).

Nichol, Todd. *All These Lutherans: Three Paths toward a New Lutheran Church*. Minneapolis: Augsburg, 1986.

———. "Minority Report: Called to Common Mission: A Lutheran Proposal for a Revision of the Concordat of Agreement." *Lutheran Quarterly* 13, no. 1 (Spring 1999): 91–97.

———, and Marc Kolden, eds. *Called and Ordained: Lutheran Perspectives on the Office of Ministry*. Minneapolis: Fortress, 1990.

Nightingale, Florence. *The Institution of Kaiserswerth on the Rhine for the Practical Training of Deaconesses, under the Direction of the Rev. Pastor Fliedner, Embracing the Support and Care of a Hospital, Infant and Industrial Schools, and a Female Penitentiary*. London: London Ragged Colonial Training School, 1851.

The 1986 Sindicators Meeting. *Laos and the Diaconate*. North American Association for the Diaconate Monograph Series 4. Providence: North American Association for the Diaconate, 1999.

Nolan, Richard T., ed. *The Diaconate Now*. Washington, D.C.: Corpus Books, 1968.

Nolf, J. *La réforme de la bienfaisance publique à Ypres au seizième siècle*. Ghent: Librairie Scientifique E. Van Goethem, 1915.

Norgren, William, and William Rusch. *"Toward Full Communion" and "Concordat of Agreement."* Lutheran-Episcopal Dialogue, Series III. Minneapolis: Augsburg, 1991.

North American Association for the Diaconate. "Recognition of Diaconal Ministry in the Tradition of St. Stephen." 14 June 2003.

Nowell, Robert. *The Ministry of Service: Deacons in the Contemporary Church*. New York: Herder & Herder, 1968.

O'Connell, Marvin R. *The Counter Reformation, 1559–1610*. New York: Harper & Row, 1974.

"Office of Deacon in the East Coast Synod, Association of Evangelical Lutheran Churches." East Coast Synod Office, 360 Park Avenue South, New York, 1983. Photocopy.

[Office of Higher Education, The Lutheran Church—Missouri Synod]. *Ten Minutes with a Lay Minister*. N.p., n.d.

Ohl, J. F. *Deaconesses and Their Work*. Milwaukee: King-Fowle-McGee, 1894.

Olesen, Edith. *Diakonien i kirkens historie*. Kobenhavn: J. Frimodts, 1969.

Olson, Jeannine. *Calvin and Social Welfare: Deacons and the Bourse française*. Cranbury, N.J.: Susquehanna University Press, 1989.

———. "The Family, Second Marriage, and the Death of Nicolas Des Gallars within the Context of His Life and Work: Evidence from the Notarial Records in Paris and in Pau." *Bibliothèque d'Humanisme et Renaissance* 63, no. 1 (2001): 73–79.

———. "The Friends of Jean Calvin: The Budé Family." Pages 159–68 in *Calvin Studies Society Papers, 1995, 1997: Calvin and Spirituality; Calvin and His Contemporaries*. Edited by David Foxgrover. Grand Rapids: CRC Product Services, 1998.

———. "Les amis de Jean Calvin: La famille Budé." Pages 97–105 in *Calvin et ses contemporains*. Edited by Olivier Millet. Geneva: Librairie Droz, 1998.

————. "Nicolas Des Gallars and the Genevan Connection of the Stranger Churches." Pages 38–47 in *From Strangers to Citizens: The Integration of Immigrant Communities in Britain, Ireland, and Colonial America 1550–1750*. Edited by Randolph Vigne and Charles Littleton. Brighton, England: Sussex Academic Press, 2001.

————. "Protestant Deacons in Geneva and Europe after John Calvin." Pages 155–65 in *Caritas et Reformatio: Essays on Church and Society in Honor of Carter Lindberg*. Edited by David M. Whitford. St. Louis: Concordia Academic Press, 2002.

————. "Social Welfare and the Transformation of Polity in Geneva." Pages 155–68 in *The Identity of Geneva: The Christian Commonwealth, 1564–1864*. Edited by John B. Roney and Martin I. Klauber. Contributions to the Study of World History, no. 59. Westport, Connecticut: Greenwood Press, 1998.

O'Malley, John W. *The First Jesuits*. Cambridge: Harvard University Press, 1993.

————. *Trent and All That: Renaming Catholicism in the Early Modern Era*. Cambridge: Harvard University Press, 2000.

————. *Tradition and Transition: Historical Perspectives on Vatican II*. Wilmington, Del.: Michael Glazier, 1989.

"Ontario Approves Deacons for Seven Dioceses." *Diakoneo* 13, no. 5 (November 1991): 1.

O'Meara, Thomas Franklin. *Theology of Ministry*. New York: Paulist Press, 1983.

"The Orderly Exchange of Ordained Ministers of Word and Sacrament: Principles, Policies, and Procedures." January 2000. Available at http://www.elca.org/ea/Relationships/reformed/OrderlyExchange.html (accessed 16 June 2003).

Orme, Nicholas, and Margaret Webster. *The English Hospital 1070–1570*. New Haven: Yale University Press, 1995.

Otterbein, Adam J. *The Diaconate According to the Apostolic Tradition of Hippolytus and Derived Documents*. The Catholic University of America Studies in Sacred Theology 95. Washington, D.C.: Catholic University of America Press, 1945.

Packull, Werner. "The Beginnings of Tyrolian Anabaptism." *Sixteenth Century Journal* 12 (Winter 1991): 717–26.

Painter, Franklin. *Luther on Education*. St. Louis, 1964.

Palladius. *Palladius: The Lausiac History*. Translated by Robert T. Meyer. Ancient Christian Writers: The Works of the Fathers in Translation 34. London: Longmans, Green & Co., 1965.

Parker, Charles H. "Public Church and Household of Faith: Competing Visions of the Church in Post-Reformation Delft, 1572–1617." *Journal of Religious History* 17, no. 4 (December 1993): 418–38.

————. *The Reformation of Community: Social Welfare and Calvinist Charity in Holland, 1572–1620*. Cambridge: Cambridge University Press, 1998.

Paton, David. "Chinese Deaconess." *Theology* 81 (July 1978): 263–71.

Pauck, Wilhelm, ed. *Melanchthon and Bucer*. Library of Christian Classics 19. London: SCM, 1969.

Paul VI. *Sacrum Diaconatus Ordinem (General Norms for Restoring the Permanent Dia-conate in the Latin Church, June 18, 1967)*. Translated by United States Catholic Conference. N.p, n.d.

Pearson, A. F. Scott. *Thomas Cartwright and Elizabethan Puritanism 1535–1603*. Cambridge: Cambridge University Press, 1925.

Pelikan, Jaroslav, and Helmut Lehmann, eds. *Luther's Works*. 55 vols. St. Louis: Concordia; Philadelphia: Muhlenberg and Fortress, 1955–76.

"The Permanent Diaconate Today: A Research Report by the Bishops' Committee on the Diaconate of the NCCB and by the Center for Applied Research in the Apostolate" (June 2000): 1–8. Available at http://www.nccbuscc.org/deacon (accessed 9 June 2003).

Pettegree, Andrew. *Foreign Protestant Communities in Sixteenth-Century London*. Oxford Historical Monographs. Oxford: Clarendon, 1986.

———. "The Stranger Community in Marian London." In *Marian Protestantism, Six Studies*. St. Andrews Studies in Reformation History. Aldershot: Scolar Press, 1996.

———, Alastair Duke, and Gillian Lewis, eds. *Calvinism in Europe, 1540–1620*. Cambridge: Cambridge University Press, 1994.

Philippi, Paul. "Le ministère du diacre dans l'Église Protestante Allemande en tant que problème théologique et oecuménique." *Étude théologique et religieuse* 40, no. 4 (1965): 277–88.

Piepkorn, Arthur. "The Sacred Ministry and Holy Ordination in the Symbolical Books of the Lutheran Church." *Concordia Theological Monthly* 40 (September 1969): 552–73.

Pierard, Richard. "The Bedfellows of Revival and Social Concern." *Christianity Today* 24 (4 April 1980): 23–25.

Plater, Ormonde. *The Deacon in the Liturgy*. Rev. ed. Harrisburg: Morehouse, 1992.

———. *Historic Documents on the Diaconate*. North American Association for the Diaconate Monograph Series 7. Providence: North American Association for the Diaconate, 1991.

———. *Many Servants: An Introduction to Deacons*. Cambridge: Cowley, 1991.

———. *Music and Deacons*. North American Association for the Diaconate Mono-graph Series 8. Providence: North American Association for the Diaconate, 1995.

———, comp. *Calendar of Deacon Saints*. North American Association for the Diaconate Monograph Series 5. Providence: North American Association for the Diaconate, 1998.

———, ed. *Deacons in the Episcopal Church: Guidelines on Their Selection, Training, and Ministry*. North American Association for the Diaconate. Providence: North American Association for the Diaconate, 1991.

Pohjolainen, Terttu. "The Deacon in the Evangelical-Lutheran Church of Fin-land." In *The Ministry of the Deacon*. Vol. 1: *Anglican-Lutheran Perspectives*. Edited by Gunnel Borgegård and Christine Hall. Uppsala, Sweden: Nordic Ecumenical Council, 1999.

Poplin, Irene Schuessler. "A Study of the Kaiserswerth Deaconess Institute's Nurse Training School in 1850–1851: Purposes and Curriculum." Ph.D. diss., University of Texas, Austin, 1988.

Pound, John. *Poverty and Vagrancy in Tudor England.* 2d ed. Seminar Studies in History. New York: Longman, 1986.

Powell, Douglas. "Ordo Presbyterii." *Journal of Theological Studies,* n.s. 26 (October 1975): 290–328.

Prelinger, Catherine. *Charity, Challenge, and Change: Religious Dimensions of the Mid-Nineteenth-Century Women's Movement in Germany.* Contributions in Women's Studies 75. New York: Greenwood, 1984.

———, and Rosemary Keller. "The Function of Female Bonding: The Restored Diaconessate of the Nineteenth Century." In *Historical Perspectives on the Wesleyan Tradition: Women in New Worlds.* Vol. 2. Edited by Rosemary Keller, Louise Queen, and Hilah Thomas. Nashville: Abingdon, 1982.

Presbyterian Church (U.S.A). "Note 143." *PCUSA Weekly* (25 May 1995): n.p.

Proceedings and Papers of the Conferences of the Lutheran Deaconesses in America, 1st–30th, 1896–1951. Philadelphia, Edward Stern, n.d.

"Programme de formation au ministère diaconal sur 3 ans." *Département romand des ministères diaconaux, 1984.* Photocopy.

Pugh, Wilma. "Social Welfare and the Edict of Nantes: Lyon and Nîmes." *French Historical Studies* 8 (Spring 1974): 349–76.

Pullan, Brian. "Catholics and the Poor in Early Modern Europe." Pages 15–34 in *Transactions of the Royal Historical Society,* 5th ser., vol. 26. London: Butler & Tanner, 1976.

———. *Orphans and Foundlings in Early Modern Europe: The Stenton Lecture 1988.* Reading, England: University of Reading, 1989.

———. *Rich and Poor in Renaissance Venice: The Social Institutions of a Catholic State to 1620.* Cambridge: Harvard University Press, 1971.

Rahner, Karl, and Herbert Vorgrimler, eds. *Diaconia in Christo über die Erneuerung des Diakonates.* Freiburg im Breisgau: Herder, 1962.

Raiser, Konrad. "Towards a New Definition of the Profile of the Laity in the Ecumenical Movement." In *The World Convention of Christian Lay Centres and Movements: Weaving Communities of Hope.* Montreat, N.C.: n.p., 1993.

Rasche, Ruth. "The Deaconess Sisters: Pioneer Professional Women." In *Hidden Histories in the United Church of Christ.* Edited by Barbara Zikmund. New York: United Church Press, 1984.

Ratigan, Virginia Kaib, and Arlene Anderson Swidler, eds. *A New Phoebe: Perspectives on Roman Catholic Women and the Permanent Diaconate.* Kansas City, Mo.: Sheed & Ward, 1990.

Reid, J. K. S., trans. and ed. *Calvin: Theological Treatises.* Library of Christian Classics 22. Philadelphia: Westminster, 1954.

Reiner, Hannelore. *Das Amt der Gemeindeschwester am Beispiel der Diözese Oberösterreich: Entstehung, Funktion und Wandel eines Frauenberufes in der Kirche.* Vienna: Evangelischer Presseverband in Österreich, 1992.

Reitz-Dinse, Annegret. *Theologie in der Diakonie: Exemplarische Kontroversen zum Selbstverständnis der Diakonie in den Jahren 1957–1975*. Neukirchen-Vluyn: Neukirchener, 1998.

Reports to the 74th General Convention, Otherwise Known as the Blue Book: Reports of the Committees, Commissions, Boards and Agencies of the General Convention of the Episcopal Church, Seventy-Fourth General Convention, Minneapolis, Minnesota, July 30–August 8, 2003. New York: Church Publishing, 2003.

Reverdin, Olivier, J. Sautier, Olivier Fatio, Louise Martin, Liliane Mottu-Weber, Michel Grandjean, and Cécile Holtz. *Genève au temps de la Révocation de l'Édit de Nantes 1680–1705*. Mémoires et documents publiées par la Société d'histoire et d'archéologie de Genève 50. Geneva: Librairie Droz, 1985.

Reynolds, Roger. "A Florilegium on the Ecclesiastical Grades in CLM 19414: Testimony to Ninth-Century Clerical Instruction." *Harvard Theological Review* 63 (1970): 235–59.

Richardson, Cyril, ed. *Early Christian Fathers*. Library of Christian Classics 1. New York: Macmillan, 1970.

Rius-Camps, J. *The Four Authentic Letters of Ignatius, the Martyr: A Critical Study Based on the Anomalies Contained in the Textus Receptus*. Rome: Pontificium Institutum Orientalium Studiorum, 1979.

Robinson, Cecilia. *The Ministry of Deaconesses*. London: Methuen, 1898.

Rodgers, Margaret. "Attitudes to the Ministry of Women in the Diocese of Sydney: An Historical Study, 1884–1839 [sic]." *Reformed Theological Review* 39 (September–December 1980): 73–82.

———. "Deaconnesses [sic] and the Diaconate: An Anglican Debate." *St. Mark's Review* (December 1980): 38–47.

Roelker, Nancy. *The French Huguenots: An Embattled Minority*. The Forum Series. St. Louis: Forum Press, 1977.

Rogan, Helmut. *Paulus Diaconus—Laudator Temporis Acti: Königsdarstellung und Aufbauprinzip der Buchschlüsse als Antwort auf die Frage nach dem von Paulus intendierten Ende der Historia Langobardorum*. Graz: Verlag für die Technisse Universität Graz, 1993.

Rogers, Jack, and Deborah Mullen, eds. *Ordination Past, Present, Future: An Invitation to Dialogue*. Louisville: Presbyterian Publishing House, 1990.

Röper, Ursula. *Mariane von Rantzau und die Kunst der Demut: Frömmigkeitsbewegung und Frauenpolitik in Preussen unter Friedrich Wilhelm IV*. Stuttgart: J. B. Metzler, 1997.

Roset, Michel. *Les Chroniques de Genève*. Edited by Henri Fazy. Geneva: Georg & Co, Libraires de l'Institut, 1894.

Ross, J. M. "Deacons in Protestantism." *Theology* 58 (November 1955): 425–36.

Rossi, Mary Ann. "Priesthood, Precedent, and Prejudice: On Recovering the Women Priests of Early Christianity." *Journal of Feminist Studies in Religion* 7 (1991): 73–93.

Roth, Deborah. "The Female Diaconate: A Ministry from the Past, for the Future." Master's thesis, Concordia Seminary, St. Louis, 1986.

Rotzetter, A., W. C. Van Dijk, and T. Matura. *Un chemin d'évangile: l'esprit francis-can hier et aujourd'hui*. Paris: Mediaspaul, 1982.

Rousseau, Philip. *Basil of Caesarea*. Berkeley: University of California Press, 1994.

Rünger, Helmut. *Die männliche Diakonie, Gestalt und Auftrag im Wandel der Zeit*. Witten: Luther-Verlag, 1965.

Sabatier, Paul. *Life of St. Francis of Assisi*. Translated by Louise Houghton. London: Hodder & Stoughton, 1920.

Sachs, Leslie. "Thomas Cranmer's Reformatio Legum Ecclesiasticarum of 1553 in the Context of English Church Law from the Later Middle Ages to the Canons of 1603." Doctor of Canon Law diss., Catholic University of America, 1982.

Salaville, S. and G. Nowack. *Le rôle du diacre dans la liturgie orientale: Étude d'histoire et de liturgie*. Paris: Institut Français d'Études Byzantines, 1962.

Sattler, Michael. "The Schleitheim Confession of Faith." Pages 89–96 in *The Protestant Reformation*. Edited by Lewis W. Spitz. Englewood Cliffs, N.J.: Prentice-Hall, 1966.

Schaaf, James. "Wilhelm Löhe's Relation to the American Church: A Study in the History of Lutheran Mission." Doctoral diss., Ruprecht-Karl University of Heidelberg, 1961.

Schafer, Karl. "Hundert Jahre Adelberdt-Diakonissen-Mutterhaus Kraschnitz zu Stendal." *Die Innere Mission* 52 (August 1962): 225–33.

Schäfer, Theodor. *Die Geschichte der weiblichen Diakonie: Vorträge*. Hamburg: Wolf Lothar Oemler, 1879.

———. *Wilhelm Löhe: Vier Vorträge über ihn nebst Lichtstrahlen aus seinen Werken*. Gütersloh: C. Bertelsmann, 1909.

Schaff, Philip, ed. *A Select Library of the Nicene and Post-Nicene Fathers of the Christian Church*. Vols. 11, 13; and 2d ser. vols. 3, 6, 12, 14. New York: Christian Literature Co., 1892–93, 1895, and Charles Scribner's Sons, 1899, 1900, 1905.

Schamoni, Wilhelm. *Familienväter als geweihte Diakone*. Paderborn: Ferdinand Schöningh, 1953. Translated by Otto Eisner under the title *Married Men as Ordained Deacons*. Margate, England: Thanet Press, 1955.

Schering, Ernst. *Erneuerung der Diakonie in einer veränderten Welt*. Bielefeld: n. p., 1958.

Schickel, Carol, director for Candidacy, Division for Ministry, ELCA. "ELCA Rostered Lay Ministries: Who We Are." *Lutheran Partners* (November–December, 2000): 1–8.

Schillebeeckx, E. *Celibacy*. Translated by C. A. L. Jarrott. New York: Sheed & Ward, 1968.

Schlegel, Ronald. " 'Daddy' Herzberger's Legacy." *Concordia Historical Institute Quarterly* 47 (Fall 1974): 139–43.

Schmidt, Alvin J. *Veiled and Silenced: The Cultural Shape of Sexist Theology*. Macon, Ga.: Mercer University Press, 1989.

Schneider, Joanne. "Das Schülerlebnis der bayerischen Mädchen." In *Frauen in der Geschichte IV*. Düsseldorf: Pädagogischer Verlag Schwann-Bagel, 1983.

Schoedel, William R. *Ignatius of Antioch: A Commentary on the Letters of Ignatius of Antioch*. Edited by Helmut Koester. Philadelphia: Fortress, 1985.

Schoenbaum, Barbara. "The Lay Ministry Program, a Quarter-Century of Service." *Lutheran Witness* (November 1986): 9, 22.

Schuster, Kurt. *Spezialistentum und Diakonie in der Kirche*. Theologische Existenz Heute. Munich: Chr. Kaiser, 1964.

Schweizer, Eduard. *Church Order in the New Testament*. Translated from the German by Frank Clarke. Naperville, Ill.: Alec R. Allenson, l961.

Schwesternverzeichnis des Evangelischen Diakonissenmutterhauses Frankenstein in Wertheim/Main, 1985. N.p., 1984.

Secretariat for the Permanent Diaconate of the National Conference of Catholic Bishops. "Annual Report on the Permanent Diaconate in the United States, 1991." Photocopy.

Section of Deacons and Diaconal Ministries, Division of Ordained Ministry, General Board of Higher Education and Ministry, the United Methodist Church. *The Ordained Deacon: Stories Connecting Word and Service*. Nashville: n.p., n.d.

Sehling, Emil, ed. *Die evangelischen Kirchenordnungen des XVI. Jahrhunderts*. 15 vols. Leipzig: O. R. Reisland; Tübingen: J. C. B. Mohr, 1902–1980.

Shaw, Russell. *Permanent Deacons, 1986 Revision*. Washington D.C.: United States Catholic Conference, 1986.

Sherman, Lynn. *The Deacon in the Church*. New York: Alba House, 1991.

Shober, Theodor. *Treasure Houses of the Church: The Formation of the Diaconate through the Lutherans William Loehe, Hermann Bezzel, and Hans Lauerer*. Edited by Frederick Weiser. Translated by Bertha Mueller. Neuendettelsau: Neuendettelsau Deaconess Institution Press, 1961.

———. *Wilhelm Löhe: Ein Zeuge lebendiger lutherischer Kirche*. Giessen: Brunnen, 1959.

———. "Wilhelm Loehe: Witness of the Living Lutheran Church; A Translation of Wilhelm Löhe, Ein Zeuge lebendiger lutherischer Kirche." Translated by Bertha Mueller. N.p., n.d. Photocopied paper.

Slesinski, Robert. *Essays in Diakonia: Eastern Catholic Theological Reflections*. American University Studies 7, Theology and Religion 199. New York: Peter Lang, 1998.

Smiar, Nicholas. "Poor Law and Outdoor Poor Relief in Zurich, 1520–1529: A Case Study in Social Welfare History and Social Welfare Policy Implementation." Ph.D. diss., University of Chicago, 1986.

Smith, J. Alfred. *Deacons' Upholding the Pastor's Arms*. Elgin, Ill.: Progressive National Baptist Publishing House, [1983].

Souvenir Booklet Commemorating the Fortieth Anniversary of the Lutheran Deaconess Motherhouse and Training School, 1895–1935, 2500-2600 West North Avenue, Baltimore, Maryland. United Lutheran Church in America, [1935].

Spaeth, Adolph. *The Deaconess and Her Work*. Translated by Julie Mergner. Philadelphia: United Lutheran Publication House, 1911.

Spitz, Lewis W. *The Protestant Reformation, 1517–1559*. New York: Harper & Row, 1985.

———, ed. *The Protestant Reformation*. Englewood Cliffs, N.J.: Prentice-Hall, 1966.

St. H. Gibaut, John. *Sequential or Direct Ordination? A Return to the Sources.* Joint Liturgical Studies 55. Cambridge, England: Grove Books, 2003.

Stancil, Bill. "Recent Patterns and Contemporary Trends in Deacon Life." *Baptist History and Heritage* 25 (April 1990): 22–30.

Stark, Rodney. *The Rise of Christianity: A Sociologist Reconsiders History.* Princeton: Princeton University Press, 1996.

Steininger, Russell. "History of the Female Diaconate in the Lutheran Church in America." Ph.D. diss., University of Pittsburgh, 1934.

Stephen the Deacon. *La Vie d'Étienne le Jeune par Étienne le Diacre.* Translated by Marie-France Auzépy. Birmingham Byzantine and Ottoman Monographs 3. Aldershot: Ashgate, 1997.

Stevenson, J., ed. *A New Eusebius: Documents Illustrative of the History of the Church to A.D. 337.* London: SPCK, 1957.

Sticker, Anna. *Friederike Fliedner und die Anfänge der Frauendiakonie: Eine Quellenbuch.* 2d rev. ed. Neukirchen: Neukirchener Verlag der Buchhandlung des Erziehungsvereins, 1963.

———. *Friederike und Karoline Fliedner: Die Diakonissenmütter.* Essen: Verlag der Diakonissenanstalt Kaiserswerth, 1951.

———. *Theodor Fliedner: Der Diakonissenvater.* Essen: Verlag der Diakonissenanstalt Kaiserswerth, 1951.

———. "Theodor Fliedner: Of the Beginnings of the Female Diaconate." Translated by Bertha Mueller. N.d.

Stiefel, Jennifer H. "Women Deacons in 1 Timothy: A Linguistic and Literary Look at 'Women Likewise . . .' (1 Tim 3.11)." *New Testament Studies* 41, no. 3 (July 1995): 442–57.

Strohm, Theodor, and Jörg Thierfelder, eds. *Diakonie im "Dritten Reich": Neuere Ergebnisse zeitgeschichtlicher Forschung.* Heidelberg: Heidelberger Verlagsanstalt, 1990.

Strohn, Christoph. *Johannes a Lasco (1499–1560): Polnischer Baron, Humanist und europäischer Reformator.* Tübingen: Mohr Siebeck, 2000.

Suelflow, August. *The Heart of Missouri.* St. Louis: Concordia, 1954.

———, ed. *Selected Writings of C. F. W. Walther.* St. Louis: Concordia, 1981.

Sunshine, Glenn S. "Geneva Meets Rome: The Development of the French Reformed Diaconate." *Sixteenth Century Journal* 26, no. 2 (Summer 1995): 329–46.

Taft, Robert. *Beyond East and West: Problems in Liturgical Understanding.* Washington, D.C.: Pastoral Press, 1984.

Tappert, Theodore G. "The Church's Infancy, 1650–1790." In *The Lutherans in North America.* Edited by E. Clifford Nelson. Philadelphia: Fortress, 1975.

Task Force on the Theology and Practice of Ordination to Office in the Presbyterian Church (U.S.A.). "A Proposal for Considering the Theology and Practice of Ordination to Office in the Presbyterian Church (U.S.A.)." [Louisville, 1991]. Photocopy.

Taub, Samuel. *The Permanent Deacon in the Church Today.* N.p.: Order of St. Benedict, 1989.

The Theology and Worship Ministry Unit, Presbyterian Church (U.S.A). *A Proposal for Considering the Theology and Practice of Ordination to Office in the Presbyterian Church (U.S.A.).* [Louisville]: Theology and Worship Mission Unit, Presbyterian Church (U.S.A.), 1992.

Thiele, Friedrich. *Diakonissenhäuser im Umbruch der Zeit: Strukturprobleme im Kaiserswerther Verband deutscher Diakonissenmutterhäuser als Beitrag zur institutionellen Diakonie.* Stuttgart: Evangelisches Verlagswerk, 1963.

Thiersch, Heinrich W. J. *Über das Diakonenamt.* Lüdenscheid: Oekumenischer Verlag Dr. R.-F. Edel, 1990.

Thomas, Donald F. *The Deacon in a Changing Church.* Valley Forge: Judson, 1969.

Thompson, Bard, ed. *Liturgies of the Western Church.* Philadelphia: Fortress, 1961.

Thompson, Ernest. *Presbyterians in the South.* 3 vols. 1894–. Reprint, Richmond: John Knox, 1963, 1973.

Thompson, Robert. *A History of the Presbyterian Churches in the United States.* 3d ed. American Church History Series 6. New York: Charles Scribner's Sons, 1902.

Thurian, Max, ed. *Churches Respond to BEM.* Faith and Order Papers, nos. 129, 132, 135, 137, 143, 144. Geneva: World Council of Churches, 1986–88.

Thurston, Bonnie. *The Widows: A Women's Ministry in the Early Church.* Minneapolis: Fortress, 1989.

———. *Women in the New Testament: Questions and Commentary.* Companions to the New Testament. New York: Crossroad, 1998.

Tierney, Brian. *Medieval Poor Law: A Sketch of Canonical Theory and Its Application in England.* Berkeley: University of California Press, 1959.

Tobriner, Alice, ed. *A Sixteenth-Century Urban Report.* Social Service Monographs, 2d ser. Chicago: School of Social Service Administration, University of Chicago, 1971.

Traver, Amos. *The Deacon and Worship, a Study Book for Church Councilmen.* Philadelphia: United Lutheran Publication House, 1941.

Treasure, Catherine. *Walking on Glass: Women Deacons Speak Out.* Bristol: Longdunn Press, 1991.

Trinterud, Leonard. *The Forming of an American Tradition: A Re-examination of Colonial Presbyterianism.* Philadelphia: Westminster, 1949.

"U.S. Catholic Bishops—Secretariat for the Diaconat." Available at http://www.usccb.org/deacon/worldstats.htm (accessed 11 June 2003).

Uhlhorn, Gerhard. *Christian Charity in the Ancient Church.* New York: Charles Scribner's Sons, 1883.

Ulrich, Heinrich-Hermann et al., eds. *Diakonie in den Spannungsfeldern der Gegenwart.* Stuttgart: Quell, 1978.

"United Kingdom Liaison Group." *Diakonia News* 78 (July 1990): 20.

United Methodist Church Deaconess and Home Missionary News and Views (December 1991).

Van Braght, Thieleman J. *The Bloody Theater or Martyrs Mirror of the Defenseless Christians Who Baptized Only Upon Confession of Faith, and Who Suffered and Died for the Testimony of Jesus, Their Saviour, from the Time of Christ to the Year A.D. 1660.* Scottdale, Penn.: Mennonite Publishing House, 1951.

Van Klinken, Jaap. *Diakonia, Mutual Helping with Justice and Compassion.* Grand Rapids: Eerdmans, 1989.

Vedder, Henry. *Balthasar Hübmaier: The Leader of the Anabaptists.* 1905. Reprint, New York: AMS, 1971.

Viller, Marcel, F. Cavallera, and J. de Guibert. *Dictionnaire de Spiritualité ascétique et mystique, doctrine et histoire.* Paris: Gabriel Beauchesne et Fils, Éditeurs, 1932–.

Vööbus, Arthur, trans. *The Didascalia Apostolorum in Syriac.* Vol. 1: *Chapters I–X.* Corpus Scriptorum Christianorum Orientalium, Editum Consilio Universitatis Catholicae Americae et Universitatis Catholicae Lovaniensis 402. Scriptores Syri 176. Louvain: Secrétariat du CorpusSCO, 1979.

Vossen, Carl. *Florence Nightingale, Geliebtes Kaiserswerth.* Düsseldorf: Hub. Hoch, 1986.

Wacker, Emil. *The Deaconess Calling, Its Past and Its Present.* Translated by E. A. Endlich. Philadelphia: The Mary J. Drexel Home, 1893.

Walker, Williston. *A History of Congregational Churches in the United States.* American Church History Series 3. New York: Christian Literature Co., 1894.

———. *The Creeds and Platforms of Congregationalism.* New York: Charles Scribner's Sons, 1893.

———, Richard Norris, David Lotz, and Robert Handy. *A History of the Christian Church.* 4th ed. New York: Charles Scribner's Sons, 1985.

Wanegffelen, Thierry. *L'Édit de Nantes: Une histoire européenne de la tolérance du XVIe au XXe siècle.* Paris: Librairie Générale Française, 1998.

Warner, Laceye. "Wesley Deaconess-Evangelists: Exploring Remnants of Revivalism in Late 19th Century British Methodism." *Methodist History* 38, no. 3 (April 2000): 176–90.

Wassilak, Kristin. "Deaconesses: Engaging the Church in Diakonia." *Issues in Christian Education* 39, no. 1 (Spring 2005): 15–21.

Watson, Susanne K. *Formation of Ministering Christians.* North American Association for the Diaconate Monograph Series 11. Providence: North American Association for the Diaconate, 1999.

Weiser, Frederick. *Love's Response: A Story of Lutheran Deaconesses in America.* Philadelphia: Board of Publication of the United Lutheran Church in America, 1962.

———. "Serving Love: Chapters in the Early History of the Diaconate in American Lutheranism." Bachelor's thesis, Lutheran Theological Seminary, Gettysburg, 1960.

———. *To Serve the Lord and His People, 1884–1984: Celebrating the Heritage of a Century of Lutheran Deaconesses in America.* Gladwyne, Penn.: Fortress for the Deaconess Community of the Lutheran Church in America, 1984.

Wenger, John. *Glimpses of Mennonite History and Doctrine.* Scottdale, Penn.: Herald Press, 1949.

Wentz, Abdel. *A Basic History of Lutheranism in America.* Rev. ed. Philadelphia: Fortress, 1964.

———. *Fliedner the Faithful.* Philadelphia: Board of Publication of the United Lutheran Church in America, 1936.

Wesley, John. *The Journal of John Wesley with an Introduction by Bishop Gerald Kennedy.* Abridged by Nehemiah Curnock. New York: G. P. Putnam's Sons Capricorn Books, 1963.

White, Joan (Sister Teresa, CSA). "The Development and Eclipse of the Deacon Abbess." Pages 111–16 in *Studia Patristica*, vol. 19, *Papers Presented to the Tenth International Conference on Patristic Studies Held in Oxford, 1987: Historica, Theologica, Gnostica, Biblica et Apocrypha*. Edited by Elizabeth A. Livingstone. Leuven: Peeters, 1989.

White, Woodie W. "From the Bishop: Deaconesses Touching 'Forever.' " *Hoosier United Methodist News* (May 2000).

Wilkinson, John, trans. *Egeria's Travels: Newly Translated with Supporting Documents and Notes.* 3d ed. Warminster, England: Arts & Phillips, 1999.

Williams, George Huntston. *The Radical Reformation.* Philadelphia: Westminster, 1962; Sixteenth Century Essays and Studies 15. 3d ed. Kirksville, Mo.: Sixteenth Century Journal Publishers, 1992.

_____, ed. *Spiritual and Anabaptist Writers: Documents Illustrative of the Radical Reformation.* Library of Christian Classics 15. Philadelphia: Westminster, 1957.

Williams, Louise. "From My Perspective . . ." *The LDA Today: A Newsletter of the Lutheran Deaconess Association* 3, no. 2 (Fall 2002): 2.

———. *Growing in Ministry: Formation for Diaconal Service.* North American Association for the Diaconate Monograph Series 10. Providence: North American Association for the Diaconate, 1999.

Wilson, Stephen G., and Michael Desjardins, eds. *Text and Artifact in the Religions of Mediterranean Antiquity: Essays in Honour of Peter Richardson.* Studies in Christianity and Judaism/Études sur le Christianisme et le judaïsme 9. Waterloo, Ontario: Wilfrid Laurier University Press, 2000.

Winninger, Paul. *Vers un renouveau du diaconat: Présence Chrétienne.* Bruges: Desclée de Brouwer, 1958.

Winninger, Paul, and Yves Congar. *Le diacre dans l'Église et le monde d'aujourd'hui.* Unam Sanctam 59. Paris: Les Éditions du Cerf, 1966.

Witherington, Ben, III. *Women in the Earliest Churches.* Society for New Testament Monograph Series 59. Cambridge: Cambridge University Press, 1988.

Wolf, Edmund. *The Lutherans in America: A Story of Struggle, Progress, and Marvelous Growth.* New York: J. A. Hill, 1889.

Woman's Home Missionary Society. *The Early History of Deaconess Work and Training Schools for Women in American Methodism, 1883–1885.* Detroit: Hines Press for the Woman's Home Missionary Society, Methodist Episcopal Church, [c.1912]. Reprinted in Carolyn Gifford, ed. *The American Deaconess Movement in the Early Twentieth Century.* Women in American Protestant Religion, 1800–1930. New York: Garland, 1987.

"Working Draft: ELCA Division for Ministry—Lutheran Deaconess Association Understanding of Relationship." April 1992. Photocopy.

"Worldwide Statistics on the Diaconate as of 2001." 1–3. Available at http://www.usccb.org/deacon/worldstats.htm (accessed 11 June 2003).

Wright, David F., trans. and ed. *Common Places of Martin Bucer*. The Courtenay Library of Reformation Classics 4. Berkshire, England: Sutton Courtenay Press, 1972.

Yocom, Rena. "Ministry Studies: A United Methodist Perspective." Commission on Faith and Order, National Council on Churches of Christ, USA. March 16, 1990. Photocopy.

Zagano, Phyllis. *Holy Saturday: An Argument for the Restoration of the Female Diaconate in the Catholic Church*. New York: Crossroad, 2000.

Ziegert, Richard. *Der neue Diakonat: Das freie Amt für eine missionarische Kirche—Bilanz einer französischen Bewegung 1959–1977*. Göttingen: Vandenhoeck & Ruprecht, 1980.

INDEX

Deaconesses
  Calvin's doctrine of, 127
  communities of, 75–76 (*See also* Communities, ascetic; Communities, monastic)
  medieval decline of, 89, 105*n290*
  nineteenth-century (*See* Deaconess movement)
  NT understanding of, 25–26
  ordination of (*See* Ordination)
  post-Reformation Protestant, 166–67
  recent nomenclature changes for, 352
  twentieth-century (*See* Lutherans, twentieth-century American deaconesses among)
Deaconesses, ancient, 29, 39–43, 49*n140*, 54–62. *See also* Olympias; Pulcheria
  geographic distribution of, 28–29, 32, 35, 41–43, 54
  roles of in light of NT, 25–26, 29, 39–42, 44*n29*, 49*n137* (*See also* Baptism; Charity; Discipline, ecclesiastical; Teaching)
Deaconries, 77–78
Deacons. *See also* Baptism; Charity; Diaconate; Discipline, ecclesiastical; Liturgy
  ancient, 28–39, 43, 46*n72*, 47*n89*, 52–53, 56–58, 62, 67–69, 95*nn55–56*
  congregationally elected, 459–61
  French-speaking Swiss, 461–63, 484*n195*–485*n204*
  marriage of, 26, 72, 102*n181*
  medieval, 89–92, 109
  medieval decline of, 68–69
  nineteenth-century Catholic, 207–8
  nineteenth-century Protestant, 209–10, 232–33, 239–41 (*See also* Bruder; Das Rauhe Haus)
  ordained Lutheran, 182–84
  ordination of (*See* Orders, sequential; Ordination)
  permanent (*See* Anglican Communion, twentieth-century diaconate among; Diaconate, twentieth-century Catholic; Methodists, twentieth-century diaconate among)

post-Reformation Catholic, 184–85, 195
post-Reformation Protestant, 154–60, 170–71, 176, 194–95 (*See also* Baptists, role of deacons among; Congregationalists, role of deacons among; Dutch Reformed, role of deacons among; Low Countries, deacons in; Presbyterians, role of deacons among)
post-Reformation Reformed, 164–66 (*See also* Low Countries, deacons in)
Reformation-era Catholic, 136 (*See also* Confraternities; Orders)
Reformation-era Protestant, 108–10, 115–17, 119, 121–29, 131–35, 142–43
roles of in light of NT, 17–19, 22–26, 44*n22*
secular roles of (*See* Charity; Charity, secular structures for; Christianity, legalization of)
Decius, 37
Decretum, 84
Defensors, 64
Diaconate, 474–77. *See also* Deacons; Ministry, office of
  ancient (*See* Deaconesses, ancient; Deacons, ancient)
  as affected by legalization of Christianity (*See* Christianity, legalization of)
  comparison of current terms for, 454–55
  current trends in (*See* Baptism Eucharist and Ministry; Called to Common Mission; Deacons, congregationally elected; Deacons, French-speaking Swiss; ELCA, development of current diaconate in; Formula of Agreement; LCMS, auxiliary offices in; Orthodox churches, current status of diaconate in; Presbyterians, current diaconal trends in)
  evolution of, 19–20 (*See also* Deaconesses, ancient; Ministry, office of)
  focus in scholarship concerning, 10
  functions of, 17–20 (*See also* Deaconesses; Deacons)